Practicing Archaeology

A Training Manual for Cultural Resources Archaeology

Thomas W. Neumann
Pocket Park - Wentworth Analytical Facility

Robert M. Sanford
University of Southern Maine

ALTAMIRA
PRESS

A Division of Rowman & Littlefield Publishers, Inc.
Walnut Creek ■ *Lanham* ■ *New York* ■ *Oxford*

AltaMira Press
A Division of Rowman & Littlefield Publishers, Inc.
1630 North Main Street, #367
Walnut Creek, CA 94596
www.altamirapress.com

Rowman & Littlefield Publishers, Inc.
4720 Boston Way
Lanham, MD 20706

12 Hid's Copse Road
Cumnor Hill, Oxford OX2 9JJ, England

British Library Cataloguing in Publication Information Available

Library of Congress Cataloging-in-Publication Data

Neumann, Thomas William.
    Practicing archaeology : a training manual for cultural resources archaeology / Thomas
W. Neumann, Robert M. Sanford.
        p.   cm.
    Includes bibliographical references and index.
    ISBN 0-7591-0094-2 (cloth : alk. paper)
    1. Archaeology—Vocational guidance—United States. 2. Archaeology—Methodology. 3.
Historic sites—Conservation and restoration—United States—Handbooks, manuals, etc. 4.
Historic preservation—United States—Handbooks, manuals, etc. 5. United States—Antiquities
—Collection and preservation—Handbooks, manuals, etc. I. Sanford, Robert M. II. Title.

CC107 .N49 2001
930.1'023—dc21   2001033295

Printed in the United States of America

♾™ The paper used in this publication meets the minimum requirements of American National Standard for
Information Sciences—Permanence of Paper for Printed Library Materials, ANSI/NISO Z39.48–1992.

Contents

6: The Phase II Process: Testing and Evaluation   159

7: The Phase III Process: Mitigation through Data Recovery   201

8: Laboratory Structure, Processing, Analysis   245

9: Report Preparation and Production   273

Appendix A: Core Federal Regulations and Standards   A-1

Appendix B: Basic Training   B-1

References Cited

Index

About the Authors

Preface

Each of us has been doing Section 106-mandated archaeology for a living for over a quarter-century. That work has been done in every culture area east of the Rockies, which gives us the dubious distinction of being among the very few who have not worked in the American Southwest.

We have taught in private and state universities, ranging from AAUP Category I (doctoral) to AAUP Category III (two-year) institutions. We have established research departments and archaeology programs. We have set up then run our own cultural resources firm, and have worked in firms owned by others. We have reviewed and implemented state and Federal cultural resources policy. We have worked as government regulators administering such policy. In all of those settings, we have hired graduates of university archaeology programs.

This text is a response to those experiences, especially the needs we have had in the public and private sector.

We have spent most of our working lives in the private sector or in government, and one recurring theme we have heard from our colleagues has been how much they would like to have their prospective employees know how extra-academic, professional archaeology works. There are ever so many things that full-time archaeologists need to be aware of -- if not know -- to work in the day-to-day compliance world. There are many wonderful method-and-theory texts, and many field and laboratory methods texts that explain how to do archaeology *qua* archaeology. Lost against the need to explain the larger concepts is the need to explain the day-to-day tasks and procedures that are just as important. One result that many of us have noticed is that recent graduates who we hire can, indeed, excavate and recognize how to apply processed archaeological data with the latest theoretical concepts to research problems. But ... they are in a fog about how to set up a survey, how to respond to a bid request and structure a budget, how to allocate resources in the context of time and budget, or even how to work within the Section 106 Process (which perhaps is a bit unfair; given the latest avatar, that probably makes them no more befuddled than many of the rest of us).

The text here is an abridged rendering of what a person needs to know -- in addition to the standard classroom, field, and laboratory courses -- to do professional archaeology in the United States after he or she gets out of college. It was conceived of more as an introduction than a training manual, although we are told it works quite well as the latter. It reflects what we have found to be useful to know in professional practice. A lot of that was never explained to us in college, and still seems to be left out of textbooks.

It is because a lot of things still seem to be left out that we have provided information on the workplace normally not given in college texts; this is very much in response to remarks and questions from students who are about to receive or who have just received their degrees. They have said countless times how much they wanted to know where jobs are, what the workplace numbers are, and what they would need to know after getting out of school to be able to do work in anthropological archaeology. That might help in appreciating the attention given here to workplace and disciplinary demographics: Neither of us is aware of any text that treats these topics, even though students really want to -- and need to -- know. It seems like the right thing to do to outline all of that, both for them and for those who have the awesome and humbling task of advising them.

The text also reviews our frequent mistakes and problems in private practice. The central way in which archaeologists learn archaeology is by sitting around sharing stories. That probably is the real function of an archaeology laboratory: a venue for an ongoing, transgenerational, informal seminar. We have certainly made our share of mistakes. It only seems right that others learn from them.

If one sets aside, for a moment, the classical archaeology people, there are two main populations in the United States who do archaeology for a living. One set is in the university setting. That group makes up around a fifth of the total number.

Everyone else works in the private sector or in government.

Thomas W. Neumann
Robert M. Sanford

30 May 2000

Acknowledgments

We greatly appreciate the extensive work done by our editor and publisher at AltaMira Press, Dr. Mitch Allen. It was his vision and energy that brought this text to completion.

Any text requires input and comment from a lot of people. We have had the good fortune of working with reviewers who corrected errors, freely gave of their advice, recommended better wording of critical passages, and often gleefully scribbled with wanton abandon all over the early drafts. We are grateful for the efforts made by:

* Mr. Chad Braley (Vice-President, Southeastern Archeological Services, Inc., Georgia),
* Dr. Paul Brockington (President, Brockington and Associates, Inc., Georgia),
* Dr. Dave D. Davis (University of Southern Maine),
* Ms. Hester A. Davis (State Archaeologist, Arkansas Archaeological Survey),
* Mr. Thomas Gresham (President, Southeastern Archeological Services, Inc., Georgia),
* Ms. Connie Huddleson (Laboratory Director, Brockington and Associates, Inc., Georgia),
* Dr. Joseph W. Joseph III (President, New South Associates, Inc., Georgia),
* Dr. Thomas F. King (Senior Advisor and Training Consultant, National Preservation Institute, Silver Spring, Maryland),
* Mr. David M. Lacy (Forest Archaeologist, Green Mountain and Finger Lakes National Forests, U.S. Department of Interior),
* Dr. Francis P. McManamon (Chief, Archeology and Ethnography Program, and Departmental Consulting Archeologist, Archeology and Ethnography Program, National Center for Cultural Resource Stewardship and Partnerships, National Park Service),
* Dr. Mary Spink Neumann (Behavioral Scientist, Centers for Disease Control and Prevention, Atlanta),
* Mr. Paul Nordman (State Auto Insurance Companies, Columbus, Ohio),
* Ms. Peggy Nordman (Breen, Winkle, and Company, Inc., Columbus, Ohio),
* Dr. Jim Peterson (University of Vermont),
* Dr. Adrian Praetzellis (Director, Anthropological Studies Center, Sonoma State University),
* Dr. Richard S. Sanford (Professor Emeritus, Clarkson University), and
* Mr. Thomas Wheaton (New South Associates, Inc., Georgia).

We appreciate Brockington and Associates, Inc., New South Associates, Inc., and Southeastern Archeological Services, Inc., and Mail Boxes Etc. (Five Forks Trickum, Lawrenceville, Georgia) for letting us disrupt daily business flow while taking photographs or discussing aspects of private-sector practice. We are especially thankful to Mr. Jerald Ledbetter (Southeastern Archeological Services, Inc.) for making personal project photographs available to us, and for letting us examine his Phase III project in east-central Georgia.

Dr. Benjamin Z. Freed (Research Associate, Zoo Atlanta, and Adjunct Faculty, Department of Anthropology, Emory University) provided much needed advice on and help with graphics memory management.

Dr. Nathan Hamilton (University of Southern Maine) used the second, much revised, draft of the text for his archaeology class. We are grateful for the suggestions and observations provided by Hamilton and his students. Chapters 1 through 3 were used in Neumann's Emory University archaeology classes from 1998 through the spring of 2000. Again, student comments were invaluable.

Insightful and constructive comments on the first two drafts of the text were made by undergraduates at Emory University and Agnes Scott College: Ms. Jennifer Carden (Anthropology, Emory), Ms. Angela Cronan (History, Emory), Ms. Amy Judd (Anthropology, Emory), Ms. Rachel Miller (Business, Emory), and Ms. Virginia Wallace (Anthropology, Agnes Scott).

The staff at the Five Forks Trickum Branch and the Peachtree Corners Branch of the Gwinnett County, Georgia, Public Library provided extensive research and technical assistance.

We appreciate the technical assistance provided by Ms. Lori McArthur, Mr. Joe Thomas, and Ms. Sherri Thomas of Mail Boxes Etc. (Five Forks Trickum, Lawrenceville, Georgia).

We are particularly thankful to St. John Neumann Parish, especially Msgr. James Fennessy, Rev. Mr. Gary Womack, and Ms. Joanne Walding, for allowing us to make use of computer facilities in production of earlier drafts.

Neumann thanks Rob Sanford particularly for all that he did to make this text a reality. His continuing insistence that such a text was realistic and marketable, his patience throughout all aspects of the production, and his simple good humor reflect the continued maturation of an 18-year friendship.

Sanford appreciates the indulgence and support of his wife, Robin, and his children (Corey, Dan, and Morgan), all of whom helped him look up information. His father, Richard Sanford, carefully reviewed and commented on multiple manuscript drafts, helpfully presenting the perspectives of an engineer and an avocational archaeologist. Many archaeologists answered questions, provided comments, and did all kinds of helpful things. Several anonymous reviewers made numerous important comments and suggestions.

For Neumann, his wife Mary Spink Neumann is the basic reason for the existence of the text. Her belief that this was a text that should be written, her unceasing encouragement, and her habitual positive spin on all aspects of the endeavor are more than anything responsible for the text becoming a reality. It is Neumann's great good fortune to have as his best friend and partner an internationally renowned anthropological archaeologist with common sense, business acumen, vast Federal experience, and arguably one of the most extensive mental collections of ethnographic anecdotes available. And -- with no argument -- the most extensive mental collection of humorous stories, jokes, and related anecdotes.

Textual Analysis

Early in the development of this text, reviewers were rightly concerned about length and reading level. The reading level of the text here averages at that expected for a second-year college student; the length, in words, is now about the same as introductory archaeology texts such as Fagan's *In the Beginning* (roughly 194,000 words) but a fair bit shorter than more advanced texts such as Renfrew and Bahn's *Archaeology* (roughly 292,000 words).

The following provide some sense of the structure of the text. This should help instructors in explaining to students the accessibility of the document, as well as planning for existing or proposing new courses.

* Average Reading Level[a] *Practicing Archaeology*: Grade 14.3 (sophomore)

* Average Reading Level[a] *In the Beginning* (Ninth edition): Grade 15 (junior)

* Average Reading Level[a] *Archaeology*: Grade 16 (senior)

* Average Reading Level[a] Wauchope quotes in Chapter 1: Grade 16 (senior)

* Our Choice for Most Annoyingly Over-Used Word or Phrase (main text and footnotes):

"important," "importantly"	142 times
"remember," "remembered"	40 times
"by the way"	31 times
"of course"	29 times
"critical," "critically"	25 times

* Reviewers' Choice for Most Annoyingly Over-Used Word (main text and footnotes):

"very"   91 times

Chapter	main text # words	footnotes #fn	# words	text boxes # boxes	# words	total words	reading level[a]
1	13,710	29	4,356	4	3,256	21,322	grade 15 (junior)
2	13,935	6	758	9	5,497	20,190	grade 16 (senior)
3	13,403	10	1,786	16	9,741	24,930	grade 14 (sophomore)
4	7,011	5	696	10	9,660	17,367	grade 15 (junior)
5	20,424	9	1,040	17	9,801	31,265	grade 13 (first-year)
6	20,151	7	1,108	18	11,617	32,876	grade 14 (sophomore)
7	18,826	9	1,415	16	17,580	37,821	grade 14 (sophomore)
8	11,419	10	638	9	5,542	17,599	grade 16 (senior)
9	8,558	6	552	9	4,867	13,977	grade 13 (first-year)
Appdx B	3,450	2	371	2	618	4,439	grade 15 (junior)
Total	130,887	93	12,720	110	78,179	221,786	grade 14.3

a. Neumann, Mary Spink. 1994. *Developing Effective Educational Print Materials.* Centers for Disease Control and Prevention, Division of STD/HIV Prevention, Training and Education Branch, Atlanta, p.23.

The type-face for the text was chosen to maximize readability (see also pp. 290-291). The main body of the text is set in 11-point AGaramond. The text boxes are set in 9-point CG-Omega.

Credits

Unless otherwise noted, all photographs are property of T.W. Neumann. Copyright for logo used for "*We learned about archaeology from that ...*" text boxes held by T.W. Neumann, and used here with permission.

Sanborn Map image p. 103 reproduced with the permission of The Sanborn Library, LLC.

Photographs pp. 190, 192-193 provided courtesy of R. Jerald Ledbetter and Southeastern Archeological Services, Inc., Athens, Georgia.

Photographs pp. 247, 254, and 258 provided courtesy of Paul Brockington and Brockington and Associates, Inc., Norcross, Georgia.

Photographs pp. 292-293 provided courtesy of Sherri and Joe Thomas, and Lori McArthur of Mail Boxes Etc., Lawrenceville, Georgia.

White-board caricature in Neumann's image in "About the Authors" created by Marshall Seese, who still got an A in the class.

Photograph of Sanford in "About the Authors" taken by Robin Sanford (Rob is the one on the right).

Image of Neumann and Sanford was taken by Mrs. Styles in the early 1980s. A widow, she must have been in her 80s when we interviewed her. There are so many images of our afternoon with her. One was her remark, as we sat in the old part of the house where the brace-beams of the timber-frame structure were exposed in the corners, about her college days at Elmira College. "And who is that writer who lives there?" she asked us. "Oh darn, what's his name?" she continued. "Mark Twain?" we suggested. "Oh yes, that gentleman," she acknowledged as the conversation went on to other things.

It was not a lapse in memory, nor a failing memory; we have seldom met a more alert and vibrant person than Mrs. Styles. We honestly think that Twain remained a vivid and alive image for her. But the enforced use of the present tense was memorable.

We handed off the camera to Mrs. Styles, and she took the photograph here. We got back into the car after Mrs. Styles went back inside. The wonderfully poignant memory, fresh and keen, remains of our leaving. As we sat in the car, windows down as we worked up our interview notes, there came from inside the sound of Tchaikovsky, rendered impeccably on the small Steinway we had noted in the parlor. The music had been open on the piano when she had had us come in and chat; she had been playing when we had driven up.

Archaeologists who do cultural resources work become a part of the landscape and the local culture. It is participant observation in the most fundamental sense, and carries with it the emotions and sense of place that ethnographers have for "their" people, be they in Sicily or New Guinea. The airs of Mrs. Styles' rendering of Tchaikovsky, or the furrowed face of Mr. L_____ as he recounted his experiences in the South Pacific, or the wonder of mapping the Confederate winter camps above Manassas Junction during the period when PBS first broadcast Ken Burn's "The Civil War," form intensely strong feelings of our nation's past, be it prehistoric, historic, or living in the presence of people like Mrs. Styles. We work to save those memories, those images, those anecdotes of Twain as he, a man in his 70s, dealt with that new women's college. Who otherwise will record this? Will remember this? Will know this?

No one reads the small print of photo credits. That is what lawyers do. And it is perhaps for the best. But it is sad that Mrs. Styles and Mr. L_____ and the others will fade in memory.

Addendum

Please note that, after this text was finalized, there was a phrasing change in the Section 106 regulations. "Phase III data recovery," meaning in the context here that full-scale excavation used to mitigate or resolve the adverse effect that would be caused by an undertaking, is also considered to be an *adverse effect*. However, such full-scale excavation to recover archaeological data is considered to be an *acceptable* adverse effect, the new phrasing results in the labeling of data recovery as a compensatory mitigation, compensatory action, or compensatory adverse effect. That is, excavation becomes an adverse effect that offsets other adverse effects.

(The logic and implications are that it would be better to leave a Register-eligible site undisturbed by any means, including excavation, if at all possible. However, if the site or a portion of it will be destroyed regardless, then the lesser evil is to excavate and record the portion that will be destroyed. This also underscores archaeological excavation as controlled destruction.)

While that new phrasing is germane here to the discussions treating the Section 106 regulations and Phase III data recovery, it does not result in any real changes in how the Section 106 Process works, at least as far as the practicing archaeologist is concerned. The practical effects, except for those who have to compose MOAs, are essentially nil.

More details for particular phrasing as they pertain to Memoranda of Agreement (MOAs) are given at the National Preservation Institute's Web site, www.npi.org, by going first to "Tools for Cultural Resource Managers," then to "Stipulations for Memoranda of Agreement." At that point, the Web site presents in total the text from Chapter 15 of King's (2000a) *Federal Projects and Historic Places: The Section 106 Process* (AltaMira Press, Walnut Creek).

From a broader perspective, a text requires anywhere from six to 10 months between completion -- when the writing is finished and layout and type-setting begin -- and publication. Because of other factors, this timetable was extended here. The text was finalized in the fall, 1999; the camera-ready proofs were set in the spring, 2000. Incidental revisions allowed by the layout have been made into June, 2001, but all substantive writing ended early in 2000.

Often there are changes in application procedures or government regulations during the period when writing has ended and the book is released. This happens all of the time with the textbooks of practiced, professional fields, be it medicine, law, engineering, or aviation: The how and why of what is done often is very time-sensitive, especially when it involves Federal regulations. This really has not been an issue for archaeology, since archaeology has only recently -- comparatively speaking -- become a partially regulated profession mainly practiced outside of universities and museums. Such procedural and regulatory changes are things that all of us in private practice get used to. Thus, even during the writing of this text, the regulations (36 CFR Part 800) were changed, requiring substantial rewriting of some sections.

1:   Introduction and Overview of Professional Archaeology

1.1.   Introduction: Purpose, Audience, and Overview of Contents

Archaeology in the United States is now a practiced profession. About 80 percent of all archaeologists who are employed as such work either in private industry, or as government regulators often overseeing the archaeological work of that private industry (Table 1.1.).

Archaeology also has been a growth industry: Between 1977 and 1993 alone, Federal positions for archaeologists increased at a compound rate of 8.2 percent per year (Figure 1.1.). Although there are only around 8,400 people who work full-time in the United States as archaeologists or other kinds of anthropologists, well over half of them work outside of an academic setting (see Table 1.1.; an estimated 200 non-archaeology anthropologists do Anthropology in the private sector [Laabs 1999:142]). By comparison, only 25 percent of the nation's 19,000 sociologists and 20,000 historians work outside of an academic setting (Hopke 1993:v3:135; v4:380). The vast majority of those extra-academic anthropologists -- nearly 94 percent -- are archaeologists.

These figures, and where it is that archaeologists now are found, startle most people. They certainly startled us. What caused this shift from an academic-based field to a government-regulated private-sector industry? Whatever should an archaeologist be doing working outside of a university or museum setting?

The answers rest in a series of historic preservation laws and mandates, beginning with the National Historic Preservation Act (NHPA) of 1966, that often require archaeology to be done as part of the construction and development process. The culmination of nearly a century of legislation and court rulings, the NHPA and subsequent laws require that archaeological work be done whenever Federal moneys, lands, or permits are involved in a land-alteration project. That is, before a road can be widened using Department of Transportation funds, or before a water treatment plant can be built in a floodplain where a 404 Wetlands permit is needed from the Corps of Engineers, the Federal agency enabling that work has to check to see if archaeological sites or other cultural resources important to the nation, be it in terms of history or basic research potential, will be lost. In short, the skills of archaeologists often are needed before any construction project involving the Federal government can be done, a requirement that continues to catch engineers, planners, developers, and bank loan officers off-guard if their training has overlooked this.

Many states have counterpart NHPA legislation. Many counties and municipalities also have statutes and regulations requiring that a given area be checked for surface and subsurface cultural remains before construction can proceed. As a result of all of this, archaeology currently is an integral discipline in the maintenance and expansion of the physical infrastructure of the United States.

Table 1.1. Where Anthropologists/Archaeologists Work in the United States (Sources: American Anthropological Association *Guide to Departments* for years 1977-1998; 1998 *Federal Civilian Workforce Statistics. Occupations of Federal White-Collar and Blue-Collar Workers as of September 30, 1997*, U.S. Office of Personnel Management, Washington, D.C.; Brentlinger 1992 *Guide to Federal Jobs*; Society for American Archaeology *1995 Membership Directory*, cf. Melinda A. Zeder. 1997. *The American Archaeologist: A Profile.* AltaMira Press, Walnut Creek).

Full-time Anthropologists Employed as Anthropologists in Academic/Museum Settings, 1998[a]:	3,791
Number of Above Who are Archaeologists:	1,111
Percent:	29.3%
Number of Anthropology PhDs/Yr, United States only (since 1977)[b]:	372 ± 33.7
Number of Above in Archaeology/Yr:	87 ± 11.5
Percent:	23.5%
Number of Federal Anthropologists (GS-190) and Archaeologists (GS-193), as of September 1997[c]:	1,140
Number of Above Who are Archaeologists (GS-193):	1,050
Percent:	92.1%
Estimated Number of Archaeologists in State/Local Government[d]:	≥ 500
[Required by Federal law; several counties also require positions]	
Estimated Number of Archaeologists in Private Sector[e]:	≥ 2,778
Estimated Total Number Archaeologists Employed as Archaeologists:	≥ 5,439
Percent Employed in Private Sector:	51.1%
Percent Employed in Public Sector:	28.5%
Percent Employed in Academic Sector:	20.4%

a   Figures based on simple random sample of 312 individuals from the 5,974 holding non-government academic and museum positions in the United States listed in the index in the American Anthropological Association *Guide to Departments*, 1998-1999. Error rate approximately ± 5.5 percent at a 95 percent confidence level. Full-time employment in the "academic" sector (higher education and non-government museums) did not include individuals listed as part-time, adjunct, emeritus/emerita, or associate. Those listed "in other schools or institutions" were included only if position held could only have been held by an anthropologist.

b   Figures taken from American Anthropological Association *Guide to Departments*, 1977-1978 through 1998-1999 issues. Number of awards is listed by institution, allowing for a count of those from institutions in the United States. Total number of doctorates awarded based on tabulation totals provided in each *Guide*, corrected for obvious listing errors, such as inclusion of the University of Alabama undergraduate majors as doctoral awards in 1991 and 1992. Total number of archaeology-specific doctoral degrees based on counts of Anthropology dissertation topics listed in the back of each *Guide*, corrected for late entries.

c   1998 *Federal Civilian Workforce Statistics. Occupations of Federal White-Collar and Blue-Collar Workers as of September 30, 1997*, U.S. Office of Personnel Management, Washington, D.C., Table W-B2, pp.28-29. GS-190 General Anthropologist can be held only by individuals with degrees in Anthropology, which would include both synchronic and diachronic Anthropology. GS-193 Archeologist can be held only by individuals with degrees focusing on anthropological archaeology. By way of comparison, and referring back to notation in footnote (a) about anthropologists in other schools and institutions: GS-101 Social Scientist can be held by anthropologists as well as by sociologists and psychologists. Many anthropologists, including archaeologists, are employed in Federal positions as social and behavioral scientists, but those positions are not reserved for those with Anthropology degrees.

d   Assumes an average of 10 state and local government archaeologists per state, not counting protectorates and territories. Archaeologists are required for most state Departments of Transportation, and also are required for archaeology staffing within the State Historic Preservation Office.

e   The Society for American Archaeology *1995 Membership Directory* (pp.141-154) listed 408 archaeology firms, offices, or divisions, as well as 348 independent consulting archaeologists not double-listed in the American Anthropological Association's 1995 *Guide to Departments*. Of those 408, 33 firms/offices/divisions employed 393 full-time archaeologists, based on figures either from American Anthropological Association *Guide to Department* listings, or from personal knowledge. The average number of full-time employees for those 33 would be 11.91 individuals. Assuming that only the largest firms/divisions would list themselves in the American Anthropological Association's *Guide to Departments* (it is hardly cost-effective for a firm to do so, which is why most do not), and that other firms generally would be far smaller, that 11.91 average was divided in half (= 5.955) then applied to all 408 firms. This is a rule-of-thumb accounting trick that is used for projecting non-profit organization fund-raising sources: Take the average of the top 10 percent or so donations, divide that average in half, then use it for the entire population involved. It is sloppy but usually comes out close enough. In any case, using the 11.91 figure would suggest a total private-sector employment of 4,859, which, while probably closer than 2,777 to the truth (given the large number of migrant archaeologists serving as project-hires), would be very hard to accept, even by us. By the way, there are no better numbers than these for how many archaeologists work in the private sector. Zeder (1997), whose summary profiled Society for American Archaeology membership only (p.3), lamented the absence of information and accounting of "crew members, crew chiefs, and field directors"(p.11). In our experience talking with extra-academic archaeologists, most working in the private-sector and state government do not belong to the Society for American Archaeology, and therefore are missed in professional censuses.

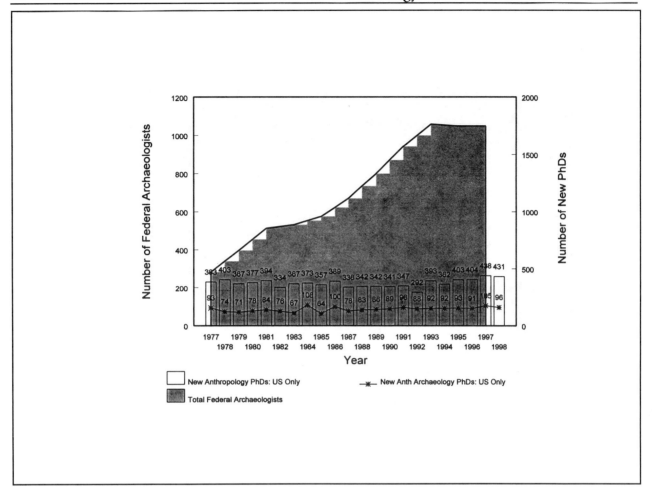

Figure 1.1. Comparison of the Total Number of Federal Archaeologists with Annual Number of New Anthropology and Anthropological Archaeology PhDs in the United States: 1977-1998 (Sources: 1998 *Federal Civilian Workforce Statistics. Occupations of Federal White-Collar and Blue-Collar Workers as of September 30, 1997*, U.S. Office of Personnel Management, Washington, D.C.; Ms. May Ing, U.S. Office of Personnel Management 10 June 1999; American Anthropological Association *Guide to Departments*, 1977-1978 issue through 1998-1999 issue; American Anthropological Association doctoral award and dissertation data corrected for duplicate entries, late listings, and clerical errors, especially in the 1991 and 1992 PhD totals). This figure illustrates well the kind of dramatic and sustained growth experienced by the Federal archaeological work force because of research mandated by Federal statutes. Private-sector positions expanded even more rapidly.

In this and the following chapters, we want to go through what this profession of archaeology involves. We have found that faculty in most colleges and universities are not fully aware that archaeology in the United States now is mainly an extra-academic field this fundamental change in the field;[1] fewer know how this affects the empirical and theoretical bases of their institutions or the Anthropology departments there.

We are concerned with explaining how professional archaeology is now done in the United States. There are four basic audiences:

* The academic sector, consisting of students and faculty, who are trained or do the training in archaeology that is then used outside of that university setting;

* the private sector, especially the myriad of stand-alone archaeology firms and the divisions within engineering/architecture firms that do most of the day-to-day archaeology of the nation, and which provide employment for the vast majority of those students trained within the academic setting;

* the government/public sector, especially the archaeological regulatory segment; and finally

---

1. The Society for American Archaeology's Consulting Archaeology Task Force report pinpointed the lack of cultural resource curricula in universities as a key problem in the discipline (Dr. J.W. Joseph III, President, New South Associates, Inc., personal communication, March 1999) Aspects of that report were incorporated in the volume edited by Bender and Smith 2000, especially in Schuldenrein and Altschul 2000 (see also Sassaman 2001). All stress the need for increased emphasis on cultural resources training within the academic sector.

*   the broader historic preservation/environmental compliance industry (along with general engineering and development firms) concerned about their statutory obligations for having archaeological work done.

The text means to inform the reader about what is involved in doing professional archaeology, with particular attention given to those things that normally are *not* taught in a university setting but that *are* expected to be known by the student when entering private or government practice.

This first chapter sets out the history of how a primarily university- and museum-based field came, in the United States, to be an extra-academic profession. A central reason for why things are now done the way they are had to do with events that took place in the 1930s as part of the Works Progress Administration (WPA) archaeology. Attention is given to those experiences because their effects are still felt, and felt not only in how things are done, but in the relationship among the three archaeology worlds -- academic sector, private sector, and government/public sector.

The university environment prepares the student to practice. It also provides the profession with the theoretical advances and research discoveries that enable those who do this work on a daily basis better conceptual tools for the understanding of the nation's past. It is the same kind of alliance that exists in engineering, medicine, law, chemistry, biology, and architecture, and for exactly the same reasons: The academic sector provides research and development while preparing students to work outside of the university, the private sector uses that research while employing those students, and the government sector monitors on behalf of society the work that is done.

Chapter 2 covers the historic preservation laws and how they work on an everyday basis in terms of practiced archaeology. For the professionals -- the private- and government-sector archaeologists -- this is a low-level review that can serve as a reference source.[2] Most of that population will have a reasonably thorough understanding of the statutes and

regulations. For students, project-hires, faculty, and non-archaeological professionals involved in the historic preservation process, this can serve as a primer for how and why archaeology is done in the way that it is outside of a university setting. For those who have need of archaeological compliance, especially firms that frequently subcontract such work, this chapter should help the corporation's historic preservation officer or environmental compliance officer make sound business decisions when setting out requests for proposals.

Chapter 3, which treats basic business and contract issues, is aimed at all involved audiences. Anthropology faculty and their students probably will not be familiar with much of this (except, of course, for those universities that maintain operational "teaching-hospital-like" programs in cultural resource management). The third chapter also should help engineering and developing firms get a sense of how archaeological subcontractors approach bids. For the novice entering into private practice, Chapter 3 will give a sense of what is involved in the day-to-day business aspects of the field.

Chapter 4 treats preparation of historic backgrounds. This is the first "methods" chapter, and in our experience is rarely part of Anthropology curricula. Well-developed historic backgrounds are necessary parts of the Phase I identification process. The chapter should allow the educated lay reader to have a sense of the historic background tasks involved in the cultural resources process.

Chapter 5 treats the Phase I Process. This is a resource identification step that in addition to the historic documentation mentioned in Chapter 4 uses field reconnaissance and intensive survey. It also is not often taught within an academic setting, even though most archaeology in the United States ("most" in the sense of "most field work") involves Phase I work. We assume that there are texts on Phase I, although we have not seen them. It may be that Chapter 5 is the only place in the professional literature where a student can learn what actually is involved, a rather sobering caution for the reader. For students, their faculty, and recent project-hires, Chapter 5 is meant to cover the topics that need to be known to be able to enter as seamlessly as possible into the post-academic world of professional archaeology. For project-hires, the information should also help them coordinate what they need to be doing as part of *their* client's project (for project-hires, the firm using them may be considered their "client"). The university-based archaeologist will quickly notice that Phase I is a powerful yet affordable surveying procedure that need not be restricted to compliance work.

For those more familiar with Phase I procedures, Chapter 5 simply serves as a coordinating and review chapter. For the non-archaeologist, Chapter 5 should

---

2. The use of the term "professional" here and below, in contrast with "academic," follows accepted American Association of University Professors (AAUP) usage, where scientists in higher education will be labeled as "faculty" or "academics," while scientists working in the same field in industry or government will be labeled as "professionals" (e.g., Hamermesh 1996:32). After all, the principal organ of the AAUP is called *Academe*, and refers to the professorate's life within the "academy." Similar usage of "professional" is found throughout Federal code (e.g. 36 CFR 61 Appendix A), and has always been implicit with the old SOPA (Society of Professional Archaeologists) organizational title, the current ROPA (Registry of Professional Archaeologists) title, and even in regional professional organizations (e.g., Georgia Council of Professional Archaeologists).

help in establishing what bidding ranges should be on cultural resources projects, and what should be covered in those bids.

Chapters 6 and 7 -- Phase II (testing and evaluation) and Phase III (full excavation, data recovery, or mitigation) procedures respectively -- are similar in terms of methods to the testing and full excavation covered in university field and methods courses. We do not duplicate coverage of those methods there: Method-and-theory texts, combined with sound academic courses, do a far better job of this than we could do. Rather, we place those procedures into their regulatory and corporate contexts, and discuss some of the methods that have been concocted to deal with the situations faced in private practice (many of which are *not* taught in a university setting). Both Phase II and Phase III are handled a bit differently than the corresponding testing and full excavation are in an academic research setting. Most private-practice and government-sector archaeologists are aware of what is involved in a Phase II or Phase III project, from excavation tricks to OSHA (Occupational Safety and Health Administration) requirements. Students also must be aware of these, as must be their instructors. New project-hires will need this information to help them re-program their academic training in preparation for what their supervisor's instructions will be.

For the client audience, be it the firm's historic preservation/environmental compliance officer or the lay client, Chapters 6 and 7 should help them to know what they should be getting as part of the contracted cultural resources work. That is, those chapters should help them make more effective business decisions as informed consumers.

Chapter 8 treats laboratory analysis. The laboratory aspect is a hidden aspect of professional work, but arguably among the most critical. The laboratory work includes both processing and interpretation of cultural remains. It corresponds, to use a computer analogy, to the step between the machine language (the bits and clicks of the machine) and the analogue program (such as the word processing program). It is the step that allows sense to be made of the archaeological remains recovered. The chapter should also give a sense of what is needed in the professional work place, and why things cost what they do. For the student, project-hire, and faculty member, this should help to give a sense of scale for the work involved.[3]

Chapter 9 covers another topic not always taught: how to set up and produce an archaeological site report. It is not unusual for nascent archaeologists to be expected to figure out on their own how to put a complete site report together. It is part of the rite of passage for a master's degree, and most -- ourselves included -- figured out how to do so by imitating what had already been written. It worked after a fashion, but we see no reason not to explain the mechanics of report preparation, particularly given the importance of the final report within professional life. After all, that report must survive a peer review so stringent that final payment on a contract depends upon a peer-acceptable report being completed. Actually, it is not so hard given a basic outline, and knowing what are the sensible questions to ask and answer.

For the client audience, it is important to know what that report should include. Like Chapter 2, this simply helps in getting a sense of the process, so that when it comes to answering to the Senior Vice-President for Operations or to the CFO why all of this archaeology is being done, something resembling a cogent answer can be given.

There are two appendices. Appendix A gives the core Federal regulations and standards. Used with Chapter 2, those regulations should arm anyone using this text with the basics of what is needed to understand the legal aspects of professional archaeology. Appendix B is a basic outline of what an undergraduate or a graduate archaeology student should have been exposed to by the time they have graduated. It is meant to help students in planning their education.

1.2. Brief History of Extra-Academic and Professional Archaeology, and Cultural Resources Legislation

Archaeology performed in response to statutory mandates is variously referred to as "cultural resource management," "contract archaeology," "private-sector archaeology," or "public archaeology." Cultural Resource Management or CRM (the most common term) is the latest stage in the evolving relationship of archaeology and government.[4] The very term summarizes the overall approach formalized by

---

3. This chapter, by the way, is also meant to help faculty in arguing for then justifying what is needed, professionally, for any archaeology program. We are aware of the questions that can arise from university administrators and from non-archaeology colleagues about why certain seemingly obvious things are needed. This chapter might help in carrying the argument. This is also the intention behind some of the comments in Chapter 1 and in Appendix B. Having such standards consolidated should assist in arguing for the legitimacy of what a sound archaeology curriculum and program need.

4. Easily the best history of Americanist archaeology is Willey and Sabloff's 1993 *History of American Archaeology*. We draw on its cultural-historical framework here. Although their's is more an academic history, pretty much everyone begins their archaeological career in an academic setting. And in any case archaeology until very recently *was* a solely university and museum field. Willey and Sabloff are thorough in presenting the factors that, from the perspective of our discussion here, led to modern, professional archaeology. Patterson's 1995 *Toward a Social History of Archaeology in the United States* focused on the social dynamics of the discipline in a manner similar to, but with considerably more detail than, what is presented here. It is an excellent study of how attitudes found in modern archaeology, especially toward compliance archaeology, developed.

government statutes: Cultural materials represent resources sufficiently important to society that they must be managed. The perception of cultural materials as resources and the protocols for their management developed as archaeology developed.

A strong argument can be made that the archaeology done in any nation really focuses, or at least focuses mostly, on national identity (e.g., Fagan 1997:8 *passim*; even the Southern Song Dynasty [AD 1127 - 1279] did archaeology as a matter of imperial identity, see Paludan 1998:138). Archaeological remains often are seen as the remains of national ancestors as well as evidence for the presence of a people in a particular territory. It is a hagiographic demonstration of territorial rights. Thus, archaeology in Ireland, Israel, Mexico, China, Japan, and many other countries is as much an exercise in historical and national identity as it is in scientific research. The emergence of cultural resources legislation in the United States, and the distribution of funding for archaeological research, is not very different in its original justification, and in the reasoning behind the laws.

Archaeology started in the United States with the idea that the people who produced the prehistoric mounds and associated artifacts found in the eastern half of the nation were culturally related to Euroamericans. Specifically, the prehistoric Mound Builders were seen by some to be the Ten Lost Tribes of Israel, mentioned in Christian and Jewish scriptures, who disappeared with the Babylonian conquest; their remains, then, would be collaterally related to the Western Intellectual Tradition and therefore worthy of documentation.[5] Because of that possibility, there was a strong cultural interest in learning more about those Mound Builders, who many felt had been overrun and displaced by the peoples encountered by Europeans in the fifteenth and sixteenth centuries.

---

5. Of course, there were others, like John Adair, who saw in the aboriginal peoples of the Southeast clear evidence that *they* were descendants of the Ten Lost Tribes. Or again Thomas Jefferson, who with Meriwether Lewis felt it very likely that the Mandan were the descendants of Welsh explorers, and had instructed the Corps of Discovery to be particularly alert for "Welsh Indians" (Ambrose 1996:77, 154). Yet others, following from Isaac de La Peyrère argument concordant with Luther's disdain for allegorical interpretations of the Bible, believed that the people encountered by Europeans in the Western Hemisphere were descendants of a Pre-Adam creation (not surprisingly referred to as Pre-adamites) and therefore were not human in that important, chosen-by-God, stewardship-of-the-world sense. Indeed, Thomas (1983:41-50) argued that the equation among the sixteenth-century British of socially inferior people with animals lent itself not only to the treatment, but also belief that such people were indeed little more than beasts, with the corresponding lack of rights.
    Finally, there was the Church's argument that the peoples of the Western Hemisphere *were* human -- meaning that they were capable of language and reason and thus must have souls -- and being such should be brought back to the Flock. The Church's view of things did not influence Euroamerican cultural values, but was responsible for the massive missionary work launched by Franciscans and Jesuits throughout Spanish and French America.

Public, in the sense of government, involvement in archaeology has taken two courses in the United States. One course has been judicial and legislative: court rulings protecting culturally important structures or landscapes; laws enacted to do the same for something specific or for a culturally sanctioned class. The other course has been direct support of that archaeological research.

Direct aid for archaeological research has happened three times in the United States, and each time it has resulted in a fundamental change in how archaeology was done. Further, each subsequent period of aid has responded strongly -- and has set professional policy in response -- to the perceptions or actualities of the previous intervention, meaning that one had to understand how things were done before to appreciate why they were being done the way they were now.

The first direct government involvement was the Congressional mandate that the Smithsonian solve the Mound Builder question (Willey and Sabloff 1993:41). Beginning in 1878, Congress further required that the Smithsonian dedicate $5,000 of its budget toward answering the Mound Builder question. The research topic of "Mound Builder Origins" had been formally introduced with the publication of Squier and Davis's *Ancient Monuments of the Mississippi Valley* in 1848. The ensuing debate over the next half-century prompted increasingly formal and precise excavation methods in response to a problem-oriented methodology.

The Mound Builder question was answered with the publication in 1894 of Cyrus Thomas's monumental study in the aptly named *Twelfth Annual Report of the Bureau of Ethnology 1890-'91*. The work done to resolve the Mound Builder question was, after 1894, responsible for the emergence of the cultural-historical approach essential to diachronic cultural interpretation. It also is notable that, with the answer came a lifting of the Congressional mandate on spending, with funds redirected by the Smithsonian's director to archaeological and ethnographic work in the Southwest. This should help underscore the earlier remarks on archaeology and its relationship to cultural/national identity.

The second major government involvement in archaeological research was the archaeology performed under the aegis of the Works Progress Administration (WPA) between 1935 and 1943. This generated a vast body of data and, while only a fraction was analyzed, provided the greatest expansion in our understanding of the prehistory of the nation. It also had a lasting impact on the view of excavation without analysis or dissemination: Because of the emphasis on excavation, proportionately few of the sites excavated under the WPA were analyzed and reported. That lack -- failure would be a disservice, since at the time it was believed that getting the stuff out of the ground would be more of a problem than analyzing then writing about it -- would become the driving inspiration for the approach taken by archaeologists for the next 40 years.

The third case of government direct aid came with the National Science Foundation (NSF), which first supported archaeological research in 1954, combined with nearly two decades of graduate student support through the National Defense Appropriations Act. The existence of NSF funding for faculty and doctoral research, combined with an expanding post-World War II economy and population, resulted in an enormous expansion of academic archaeology. That expansion, combined with the socio-political demographics that come from a large, even-aged stand producing intellectual progeny in its own image, resulted in an entirely new vigor for archaeology, including the now-realistic expectation for each new doctoral candidate to excavate a new site. It also resulted in the cultural resources environment; the attitudes toward non-academic, professional archaeology; and a host of other things, many of which were in direct response to the archaeology that came out of the 1930s through the 1950s.

1.2.1. Initial Federal Involvement in Cultural Resources

Federal funding of archaeological research, based upon Congressionally mandated funding, began in the nineteenth century, and was driven by the question of Mound Builder ethnic origins. This work was performed by a Federal "agency" as well, the Smithsonian Institution. However, aside from the Smithsonian, the role of government in archaeology was slight. The concept that archaeological and built-environment materials were some kind of resource of importance to society emerged gradually.

The first major incident involved the Mount Vernon Ladies' Association of the Union, which in 1853 purchased the remaining 550 acres of George Washington's Mount Vernon estate, including the residence, outbuildings, and tomb, for the purpose of preservation. This was socially important in that members of the upper classes had taken it upon themselves to protect what was seen to be an important element in the nation's emergence and identity.[6] The preservation of the Washington estate

set a social precedent and, while not statutory, still was politically powerful (see Hosmer 1981:184-185, 525-527).

A second major incident, following conceptually from the protection of Mount Vernon, was court action that prevented demolition of Independence Hall in 1876. Again, this was prompted by the importance to society of the physical preservation of places where nationally important events took place, preservation that held precedence over the private interests of any one individual or small group of individuals.

The third major incident in the emergence of cultural resources legislation was the Supreme Court ruling in 1896 that prevented the Gettysburg Railroad from cutting through the Gettysburg Battlefield; this suit was brought up by veterans [United States v. Gettysburg Electric Railway Company 160 U.S. 668]. The ruling had been presaged by legislation in the 1880s protecting Revolutionary War battlefields. In its decision, the Supreme Court approved Federal appropriation, with compensation, of the Gettysburg Battlefield. The result was that the taking of privately owned lands of national historic value could be construed as a valid application of the Federal government's powers of eminent domain. An early and important decision in "taking" arguments, this case is still commonly cited (Sanford 1984:20). This also provided legal precedence for preservation of a historic property, and in a way that presented the property as a resource.

These three incidents involved two of the ways in which the past is preserved. Buildings represent physical structures where important persons lived or events transpired. Battlefields represent areas where important events occurred, even though the traces of those events may no longer be visible or even present. There is, though, a third category: situations where only the traces of past activity exist. That is, archaeological sites, especially prehistoric archaeological sites: What the nineteenth- and early twentieth-century literature called "antiquities."

Legislation protecting antiquities, even though emplaced rather early, still took longer to become established. Maybe this was because of the cultural distance demonstrated to exist between pre-Euroamerican and current Euroamerican populations. Legal action began in 1889 with legislation aimed at protecting the late prehistoric Puebloan ruin, Casa Grande, in Arizona. However, given the concern over other threatened prehistoric sites -- especially ruins -- in the Southwest, as well the desire to protect Civil War battlefields, more encompassing legislation in the form of the Antiquities Act was enacted in 1906 (see also Rosenberg 1981, Fowler 1982).

---

6. The country after all was less than 70 years old, while George Washington was venerated in a reverential manner that would frighten people today. It should also be remembered that laws in state-level societies tend to protect the interests of those with power. That is, the upper or elite classes set the culture's agenda for what is to be considered important, and what not. And since those classes also control the resources that would allow their vision to become a reality, it usually *does* become a reality. This is not an issue of whether it is right or wrong; it is just the way stratified societies work and is a well-recognized anthropological phenomenon. Knowing about it, though, has been a practical

---

survival guide for all archaeologists ever since funding became important.

The Antiquities Act of 1906 (34 Stat. 225) provided for the protection of historic or prehistoric remains, "or any object of antiquity," on Federal lands. Further, it established regulations and sanctions regarding disturbance or damage of those remains, while authorizing the President to designate National Monuments on Federal lands. It is no accident that such legislation appeared when it did with the authority it gave to the Executive Branch, since this was consonant with the interests of then-President Theodore Roosevelt.

The designation of places as National Monuments was the first official attempt to achieve a national policy on antiquities as a class. The Antiquities Act pertained to Federal lands only; archaeological materials on private lands were exempt.

The next major package of legislation was the Historic Sites Act of 1935 (49 Stat. 666). This, in essence, was the first attempt to join together under one statute a Federal policy that would encompass the decisions regarding historic structures, battlefields, and antiquities. It went beyond the Antiquities Act of 1906, although it was restricted to historic resources of national importance. In its particulars, this Act foreshadowed the National Historic Preservation Act. Because of this, and because it is still cited as part of statutory authorization, we will provide a little detail.

The Historic Sites Act of 1935 was aimed at preserving objects, buildings, sites, and antiquities of "National significance" by declaring a national policy of preservation "for the public use[,]... inspiration[,] and benefit of the people of the United States [**Section 1**]." This followed from the Chief of the National Park Service having designated "uniqueness" as a determining characteristic of "significance" in 1934. The Act had seven major points:

(1) declared as a national policy the preservation for public use of "historic sites, buildings and objects of national significance for the inspiration and benefit" of the country;

(2) authorized the Secretary of the Interior, through the National Park Service (NPS),

   (a) to gather information on what are now called cultural resources or historic properties;
   (b) to survey those to determine which would have "exceptional value as commemorating or illustrating the history" of the country;
   (c) to conduct the necessary research to gain accurate information about those historic properties;
   (d) to acquire exceptionally important properties (provided the owner approves [although ONLY if the owner is a religious denomination, an educational institution, or what would now be termed a not-for-profit

or a non-profit operation] and Congress allocates moneys specifically for the purchase);

   (e) to make cooperative agreements with state and local governments to do the same, again providing that Treasury funds are not spent without Congressional approval;
   (f) to restore then maintain what are now called cultural resources and, where desirable, establish museums associated with them (that is, provide public education and interpretation);
   (g) to erect historic markers (this is where all of those historic markers along highways came from);
   (h) to operate and manage those cultural resources for the benefit of the public, with permission to charge the public a fee;
   (i) to organize a corporation to do the above should the ability be beyond the fiscal ability of the given state or the District;
   (j) to develop educational programs; and
   (k) to fine anyone not doing the above $500 plus cost of proceedings [$500 in 1935 was equivalent to about $6,200 in 1998 dollars];

(3) established the Advisory Board on National Parks, Historic Sites, Buildings, and Monuments, consisting of 11 citizens competent in history, archaeology, architecture, and human geography [Anthropology, it will be remembered, developed in the United States from cultural geography] appointed by the Secretary of the Interior, expenses paid to be only those related to travel in discharging their duties [has not changed; only a $100 per diem is paid to members of the statutory descendent of the Board; see U.S. Government. 1992. *Policy and Supporting Positions*, p.138];

(4) the Secretary of the Interior can cooperate or seek cooperation from other Federal agencies, establish technical advisory committees, and provide that technical assistance "*without regard to the civil-service laws*" [meaning one could contract those services, important in that it would come to allow private industry to contract to do agency work in the 1960s and 1970s, before the privatization of government was widespread];

(5) restricted the Act to Federal jurisdiction [this is the second place in the Act where state's rights seem especially mentioned; it was, after all, only 70 years after the Civil War];

(6) authorized funding appropriations from Congress, as deemed appropriate and needed; and

(7) established the precedence of the Act over any other acts that might seem to cover the same issues.

The Historic Sites Act of 1935 was the direct precursor of the National Historic Preservation Act (NHPA) of 1966. It dealt with historic properties as the NHPA would; it established the equivalent of the Advisory Council on Historic Preservation, with a composition not all that different from that in existence now [except for Geography, but then universities began dissolving Geography departments in the 1970s]. The only major difference was enforcement: The Historic Sites Act had penalties; the NHPA only allowed for the prosecution of civil suits. It also established the National Landmarks program, the precursor to the National Register of Historic Places, but essentially restricted inclusion to Federal-level (that is, national) properties.

1.2.2. WPA Archaeology and Its Influence on Modern Professional Archaeology

Although there were several New Deal agencies or programs -- such as the Civilian Conservation Corps (CCC) and the Tennessee Valley Authority (TVA) -- involved in archaeology to a greater or lesser extent, the best known involvement of archaeology with government was with the Works Progress Administration. "WPA archaeology" has come to be the phrase more often used to describe the period and the associated work. When modern, professional archaeology is looked at, especially how NHPA is set up, it becomes clear that the experience of archaeology and the WPA was the central contributing factor.[7]

It is revealing to use WPA archaeology as a theme in understanding how earlier perceptions of government-archaeology interactions came to structure current professional practice, as well as to appreciate why the current laws and regulations are set up the way they are. Remember that the people who would lobby and structure the archaeological preservation mandates in the 1960s either worked as part of the WPA archaeology program, or were trained directly under archaeologists who had been involved in and were reacting to it (see Patterson 1995).

The WPA, which existed from 1935 through 1943, was part of Roosevelt's New Deal, which was launched to work the United States out of the Great Depression.[8] The Depression was the first clearly documented instance of the Keynsian Paradox of Thrift: Too much saving, or in this case too little spending, can stop a capitalist economy. It is economic constipation. The laxative was an infusion of capital from the one source with the capacity to help: The Federal government.

The idea behind programs like the WPA was to get as much money as possible back into circulation by using public money to support labor-intensive projects in areas suffering the highest unemployment. There were many WPA- and CCC-sponsored projects. Many of the nation's parks benefitted from new buildings, picnic shelters, and trails, built to such high standards that many remain in use. Highways were built, bridges were built, numerous public buildings were built. Under the WPA, there was a Writers Program, where county histories were written. There was a photography program, where countless thousands of photographs were taken of everyday American life, good and bad. There was a music-recording program. There were education programs.

What all of those projects had in common was that they served a public need (it was, after all, public money) in a way where most of the money spent went for pay to the worker. That is what was sought: an infusion of cash into the hands of as many people as possible so they would go out and spend it. And one of the best, labor-intensive fields that could accommodate a sizeable population of unskilled labor was archaeology.

WPA archaeology represented the first large-scale interaction between the Federal government as a sponsor and regulator, and the academic archaeological community as service provider. It was a learning experience for both. Although it would be a bit extreme to call WPA archaeology a "make-work" program, the purpose of the program was primarily to employ people, albeit doing something that the society would want to have done anyway. Because of that priority, the archaeology was perceived -- from the vantage of the archaeologists involved -- often to be of secondary interest to the government (Wauchope 1966:vii).

WPA archaeology had a lasting impact on archaeology in the United States, especially in the Southeast where the Federally sponsored projects were most common. The intellectual legacy was extensive and profound, including a gigantic advance in overall knowledge about the nation's prehistory, a large sample of large-area village and mound excavations, the building of

---

7. See also Patterson 1995:73, 78. Patterson (p.79) observed that it was "With WPA archaeology still fresh in their minds" that the Committee on the Recovery of Archaeological Remains was formed in 1944 (Johnson, Haury, and Griffin 1945). The Committee was instrumental in how the Missouri Basin Surveys were set up and conducted (see below). Among other issues, the Committee sought to correct the problems experienced in the adequacy and quality of archaeological research as well as in the governmental oversight of the research process when future, Federal-initiated archaeological work was undertaken.

---

8. It is useful to remember that the entire industrial world was caught in the Great Depression, not just the United States. The solutions were roughly the same for all of those countries: massive government involvement, resulting in entirely new ways of approaching problems.

the basic cultural-historical sequences, and the establishment of professional networks and reputations that would last -- in primary or, through students, secondary form -- well into the early twenty-first century. One needs only wander through the Bureau of American Ethnology Bulletins to appreciate the overwhelming impact that the Federally sponsored archaeology had on the data base.

WPA archaeology left another legacy, too. It involves how archaeologists in the academic sector perceive the archaeology done by the private sector at the behest of government mandates. It also involves how archaeology in the United States restructured its expectations for quality research. In this, as with the actual research accomplished, WPA archaeology had a profound impact on how archaeology is done now, and what is considered acceptable or unacceptable work. And those perceptions not only influenced how cultural resources archaeology would be done, they also influenced the perception of the kind of archaeology done as part of the cultural resources process. For these reasons, it is useful to spend a little time talking about WPA archaeology.

There are four aspects of WPA archaeology that seem to stick in the profession's collective mind:

(1) The *perception* of extraordinarily mindless and clearly nonsensical bureaucratic expectations of the unenlightened government regulators;

(2) the occasionally slovenly work that took place under deadline conditions;

(3) the excavation for the sake of excavation and not solution of a research problem; and

(4) the lack of analysis and publication.

Understanding why NHPA specifically, and professional archaeology generally, are set up the way they are is best achieved by understanding the WPA legacy *as perceived by the archaeology community*. Again, remember that it was that community, or its immediate intellectual progeny, that would either help develop the initial cultural resources legislation or would teach its students that work done under such conditions was not really legitimate research. The bifurcation in the archaeology of the United States, mentioned in 1.2.3.3 below, really seems to have started at this point.

The archaeology that emerged in the 1960s and 1970s did so very much in response to those four aspects, especially the last three. The first is simply the way that the academic community often has viewed governments (for descriptions of some modern examples, see Gross and Levitt 1994:30-31; Goodstein 1996:34; Nanda and Warms 1998:32, 352-355),

including those sponsoring their research, a view that can be found off and on back to the late Middle Ages (e.g., Tuckman 1978:22).

1.2.2.1. Government Regulation versus Academic Independence

Not the least of our burdens was the enormous amount of work that the government required. Much of it was meaningless: "How many artifacts excavated during the period? How many linear feet of trenches excavated...?" ...it was criminally time-consuming nonsense, imposed on already harried archaeologists who urgently wanted to devote more attention to the research itself. At frequent intervals I had to submit the following reports: major purchase requisition for sponsor, balance sheet, petty cash account, report of sponsor expenditures other than payroll..., laboratory time sheets, field party's time sheets, mileage records for each vehicle, equipment inventories, equipment transfer sheets...,accident reports, equipment receiving reports, and monthly budget requests for WPA-furnished supplies [Wauchope 1966:viii].[9]

Fussell (1983:128 *passim*) remarked, observing his university colleagues, that university faculty refuse to suffer any kind of subordination to others, much less criticism of their actions, even if it comes from those supporting their work. This of course is very well known, and is something that they share with the medical profession.[10] This attitude also is endemic to

---

9. Wauchope (1966) provided a rare, participant-observer, ethnographic account of WPA archaeology as experienced by a university faculty member. The Preface to the SAA Memoir has often been reprinted, and probably was one of the most frequently read reserved readings for archaeology method-and-theory classes between 1966 and 1986. The accounts are charmingly delightful, full of the raw, vibrant experience of a young college professor caught in the character-filled world not just of the rural South, but of the rural *Georgia Mountains*. "For when you approach a mountain house for the first time, in north Georgia, the man on the front porch is likely to disappear quickly, the womenfolk hide, and the hounds begin to bay. Once they become your friends, however, their concern for you can become downright embarrassing" (p. xiii). That he cherished the famous Georgia hospitality is evident and expressed (p. xvi). That he recognized one of the region's major resources -- characters -- is so clear that most of the Preface is anecdotal. That hospitality continues, by the way. Even at this writing [March 1998] when Hall County has been devastated by tornados, not only are people driving through simply stopping off for a couple hours to lend a hand in cleaning up, but there are stories like those of the hardware store owner who, called by a neighbor about how the water was lost, wandered out on the off-hour, messed about for a half-hour to get the commodes and drinking water re-established, then refused any payment: "Oh, it was simple enough," was his reply. That Wauchope would have delighted in Bailey White should help the reader understand the respect that we have for the work -- and the approach to that work -- that Wauchope had. The quotes here and following are used to illustrate a point; only an addle-pated puzzle-wit would think that personally libelous intentions regarding Wauchope were concealed behind our comments.

10. Which has gone so far as to adopt the title "doctor," as if they did research and actually explained (*docēre*) the results.

the field, and normally is harmless except in cases where public funds -- and therefore public jurisdiction -- are involved. The first major interaction of publicly funded archaeology with academic archaeologists came with WPA archaeology.[11] The friction was not universal: TVA archaeology came out of the experience quite fine, but then it was directed by a physicist-turned-archaeologist, W.S. Webb. However, the image of government expectations being nonsensical in the least and occasionally criminal survived the WPA experience. This would have a bearing on two sets of attitudes in the 1970s and beyond:

(1) The idea that strictly following statutory requirements somehow limited legitimate archaeological research and therefore could in some cases, and in good conscience, be ignored by the archaeologist concerned; and

(2) the literature that was submitted to and eventually passed by government reviewers was somehow of lesser quality than that literature reviewed by academic archaeologists themselves.

There is a second issue here that strikes as curious in a professional environment: the seeming protest over the managerial requirements of a large-scale operation using public funds. Exactly 50 percent (57 of 114 words) of that paragraph complained about basic business accounting issues: payroll, time-sheets, purchases, care for employees. All of these are essential elements in any managerial situation, even more so when one has jurisdiction over the allocation of someone else's funds, as Wauchope did with WPA funding in Georgia. Patterson (1995:73) also identified these kinds of managerial issues as problems, endemic to WPA archaeology, that seem to have come from the lack of experience on the part of the university-based archaeologists in handling these kinds of things. That such business administration was seen to be an unjustifiable demand on the limited time of the research archaeologist should illustrate that, at the time, archaeology still viewed itself more as an academic -- in an Edwardian sense of separate from and better than being a merchant -- field. In today's world that would be nonsense; in the 1930s, it most certainly was not, which is why Wauchope felt it to be such a nuisance that he stormed about it in the opening of his monograph.

There were other contributing factors to the academic-government-sponsor friction, but the experience of WPA archaeology in the 1930s resulted in the perception 40 years later of compliance archaeology as somehow less or lacking, and of government review as being intrusive to research integrity. It is from this

experience that academic archaeologists even now rarely recognize the research reports produced as part of the compliance process as "peer reviewed," even though the government review process frequently is done by doctoral-level archaeologists, often with considerably more field and publication experience than university archaeologists, in a more thorough and stringent manner, and with far greater and more serious penalties for errors, than found in scholarly journals specifically or the academic world in general.[12]

1.2.2.2. Quality of Work under Deadline Conditions

This was not a fair dilemma with which to confront archaeologists. We should not have to choose between two evils: either failing to employ the needy and, incidently, not getting archaeology done at all, or employing too many and getting it done in a slovenly way. The system bred false values. Big efficient operations became the symbols of the successful archaeological director, as some projects employed enormous laboratory staffs to process the hundreds of thousands of artifacts that poured in from several large field parties operating concurrently. Even graduate students in anthropology usually require long field experience and some intellectual maturity before they can produce significant results.... [Wauchope 1966:viii].

WPA archaeology was performed under conditions and on a schedule that was not of the principal investigator's choosing. Other factors resulted in situations beyond the archaeologist's ability to control, most of which came from sometimes weak managerial skills combined with trouble communicating with

---

11. Just as in a previous world the term "arm chair anthropologist" was a supreme phrase of insulting dismissiveness, so too for archaeologists is the phrase "like WPA archaeology."

12. The refusal of the academic community to accept professional reports as a legitimate part of the archaeological literature continues to be a source of resentment among practicing professionals, including very much those working within university-based cultural resources programs. This is a very serious problem, which the not infrequent labeling of that material by academic anthropologists, rather condescendingly, as "grey literature" only exacerbates. A pair of incidents in the mid-1980s helps in appreciating that sense of aggravation. In one, a faculty member at a large Midwestern university was seeking promotion to full professor. Supporting documentation included a number of 100- to 200-page archaeological compliance reports, which had come to serve as the data base for part of the state. The chair of the department, a social anthropologist, looked at the list and said dismissively "This is not *real* research." The *candidacy* for promotion was denied. There was a similar incident at a large private university in the Northeast where such reports were discounted as not really research and therefore not applicable to the promotion process, the remarks from an ethnographer being "this is nothing more than glorified accounting." In that case as well, the research reports were excluded and the promotion was denied. However, in both cases the universities concerned had no trouble in retaining then using the overhead generated through the research funding secured by the archaeologists that produced those reports. (As we were writing this, we learned from a friend of ours who recently received her doctorate from a prestigious university that her advisors pointedly warned her not to list on her vita any reports written in the private sector. To do so, they noted, would result in her automatic exclusion from consideration for any university position for which she might apply.)

those having less education.[13] From the WPA experience came the strongly held belief that work done under government deadlines and mandates would somehow be sloppy. Further, the impression arose that any kind of work done by those outside of the academy was suspect. This became important in terms of how the final legislation for cultural resources archaeology would be written and executed; it also became important in how academic archaeologists would view the quality and legitimacy of professional archaeological work.

The WPA specifically, as well as the National Youth Administration (NYA) that it administered, was funded at the Federal level but administered at the state and county level. This proved a complicating factor for archaeologists, not so much because of the field work performed but because the WPA was meant to employ unemployed people at the local government level. This meant that every change in county location required that the field laborers come from the new county. This produced logistical complications, the most obvious being that one could not train a field crew and drag it along from site to site mindless of county jurisdictions.

---

13. In writing about laboratory processing and the need for trained staff, Wauchope (1966:viii) made a very curious remark: "...most of our field workers had only a grade school education, and few of our laboratory 'technicians' had been to college." Wauchope was in a difficult situation: He was performing surveys in montane, county-balkanized north Georgia, and as such had to start over with raw recruits in each new area/county jurisdiction where he entered. He clearly managed to explain what he needed done quite well; his work is a solid tribute to his skills as a doctor in the strict sense of the title. What is remarkable about his remark, though, is the feeling that lack of education would preclude training people -- or developing a suitable protocol -- to get the tasks done. This would suggest that people lacking college degrees cannot be educated, which falls perilously close to suggesting that learning ability is innate and is reflected by the level of the degree one holds -- and we are sure Wauchope would be aghast that such an interpretation could be made of his remarks. However, it was exactly that kind of attitude, expressed by Leslie White in 1968 at the University of Colorado where he remarked in a visiting lecture that people who had to do Anthropology outside of an academic setting obviously were just not good enough to get university appointments, that remains as one of the primary sticking points in the interactions between academic and professional archaeologists. That is, if one is doing archaeology outside of a university or museum setting, then one obviously was just not good enough to work in a *real* research setting. This attitude is not at all unique to archaeology or even Anthropology, and is creating a great deal of ill-will between those within higher education and those working in industry and government. This issue is examined again in the text boxes "Attitudes, Social Contracts, and Research Funding" in section 1.2.3.3., and "Expectations and Demands of the Contracting World" in section 3.1.

1.2.2.3. Reasons for Excavation: Chosen Research Problem versus Circumstantial Research Problem

The main thing to recall is that although WPA was interested in archaeology, it was more concerned with giving employment to a great many people, and that whenever those two aims clashed it was archaeology that suffered....

Perhaps even worse was the violence we knew our archaeological materials were being subjected to. When several hundred unskilled men, with sparse supervision, dug up artifacts, dropped them into boxes, passed unusual specimens around from hand to hand (and, I might add, from hand to pocket), tied them up and labeled the containers, packed them on trucks and unpacked them at headquarters, washed them, and re-boxed them -- all this in what was often a spirit of light-hearted irresponsibility and incomprehension -- the chances are that proveniences were garbled, if not deliberately falsified. My confidence in the system was not increased by my chief foreman's jocular tales of how, on previous WPA projects, he had often decided that the day's take in cherts at one site was not impressive enough, and he therefore sent his men, when the boss was away, to fill up their pottery bags at some richer site nearby [Wauchope 1966:vii].

Excavation for the sake of excavation and not for the sake of solving a previously identified research problem was the third legacy of WPA archaeology. This has had a profound impact on the cultural resources legislation and on the way professional archaeology now is done.

At one level, archaeology has always been a problem-oriented field in the United States, even though the term in its modern sense came from Binford's (1962, 1964) articles in *American Antiquity*. The purpose may not always have been consciously framed after the 1890s, but almost always there lurked the idea that, in excavating, the materials recovered would somehow address unanswered questions about the country's past. Sites then were selected to resolve problems; after the 1890s and before the 1970s, these rarely were clearly worded, deductive-inspired exercises, but still they were aimed at providing more "information" on the culture history of the region of concern.

Archaeologists selected sites, then, to address their research concerns. Often in the period before the 1930s and after the 1940s, these were sites rich in artifacts; however, the point is that the site was selected to a given end. To some extent that held with WPA archaeology as well: Large, set-piece field operations on specific sites were executed in precisely that way. However, as Wauchope's anecdote underscores, there was a realization that a driving research paradigm was not the cause for sites being excavated, at least not as much as the region's unemployment rate or the well-intended initiatives of the field party.

The idea of excavating for the sake of excavating was evident throughout WPA archaeology, even if it was not always the case. By the 1970s, though, that image had grown and resulted in a determined effort to make sure that sites would not be tampered with unless the archaeologist had a very good reason for doing so. This was reinforced by the recognition on the part of the archaeological community that archaeological sites are nonrenewable resources (see Neumann, Sanford, and Palmer 1992), and that excavation constitutes a destroy-as-read data retrieval system (which existed, by the way, in very early computer systems).

There is a second issue that the remarks made by Wauchope raises: professional training. WPA archaeology employed the local people in the excavation process. They were taught to recognize and retain certain objects (many were familiar already with what those objects were, common for all rural peoples in the 1930s; Wauchope's remarks regarding things passed around from hand to pocket is tacitly based upon the reader already knowing that); they were taught to move site fill and sort through it for artifacts. They were doing exactly what field laborers in Middle America, the Middle East, and many other places have been doing for their archaeological supervisors for well over a century.

The lack of trained personnel -- meaning with a college degree and exposure to archaeology -- was seen as a major problem, as the need that Wauchope felt to mention this as a reason for how data occasionally were compromised argues. That perception became important in the cultural resources legislation that emerged in the 1960s and 1970s. As a result, the lowest level of education and training acceptable for doing archaeology *qua* archaeology on behalf of some Federal agencies not only is a college degree (and only 20.3 percent of adults in the United States have a college degree; *Chronicle for Higher Education Almanac* 28 August 1998, p.6), but also field training then supervised full-time employment doing archaeology.[14] And by "acceptable" is meant that it is set forth either in agency regulations or within their contracting

guidelines, all of which also is part of the legacy of WPA archaeology.

1.2.2.4.   Analysis and Publication

Having published the main factual results of the survey in journal articles, I did not feel under too great a pressure to rush the final report, and it is a good thing, for there were many materials to study, and my duties after leaving Georgia, interrupted still further by World War II, left me little time to devote to them: a few weeks out of every summer vacation, plus evenings during the school year [Wauchope 1966:ix].

One of the lasting complaints about WPA archaeology that continues to influence modern professional archaeology involves dissemination of results. Wauchope's comment quoted above might seem a bit odd if this was not explained: "Why ever should he make a point of saying that he had already published his results? Surely he would have published his results...wouldn't he?"

One outstanding legacy of WPA archaeology was that, after excavation, much of the material recovered was never analyzed, much less reported. There are horror stories, many founded on fact, of university-leased warehouses stuffed with WPA-generated archaeological materials, much of which remains even today unwashed and in the original paper bags from the field. Over the decades, the bags deteriorated and broke, mixing provenience with provenience until entire collections were nothing more than a giant assortment of prehistoric materials lacking any context. It would be interesting to know just how many sites were excavated under WPA-sponsored work, and just what proportion resulted in a completed report.

There are any number of reasons for why the materials were not analyzed and the results, published. Some of the reasons would include a real lack of desire for writing up materials in which the archaeologist had no research interest. These were not necessarily sites with which the archaeologist wanted to deal. Doing so would take time away from work in the archaeologist's own area of concern. Further, where would the funding come from to do that analysis, now that the WPA had ended? Remember, this is well before the era of the National Science Foundation. Equally, passing along the work to students years after could compromise the student's future: In archaeology as in the rest of Anthropology, there has always been the expectation that students will generate their own data from their own field work instead of working on someone else's. Better to excavate a new site, and do so with a better trained crew and a detailed, chosen research problem, than to use possibly flawed data.

---

14. There are 372 academic programs in the country that award an undergraduate degree in Anthropology (The College Blue Book 1997:v.3:448-451). Anthropology majors make up one to two percent of students at an institution (for private universities, majors tend to be around two percent; for public universities, around one percent); about one-fourth of the doctorates awarded in Anthropology are in archaeology. There were around 526,222 faculty in the nation's universities as of 1992 (*The Chronicle of Higher Education Almanac* 29 August 1997, p.26, 28 August 1998 p.29; this figure, drawn from the U.S. Department of Education, keeps getting repeated); currently, 3,791 or so of college faculty are full-time anthropologists (around 3,083 are full-time faculty within Anthropology/Sociology/Geography departments; the remainder are full-time faculty working as anthropologists in other departments/schools [around 460], or are full-time non-government museum personnel [around 248]; see again Table 1.1). That represents 0.7 percent of the nation's college and university faculty.

Part of the reason that material did not get analyzed and published was that time just got away from people, as Wauchope indicated. In any event, one of the legacies of WPA archaeology was that results were not written up anywhere nearly as often as they should have been. That legacy influenced two aspects of subsequent archaeological work: (1) The professional expectation that any excavation had to be followed by analysis and publication (or at least an attempt to publish); and (2) the statutory requirement for analysis of the site and the production of a final research report.

1.2.3.   Post-War and Formulation of Professional Archaeology

After World War II, the pace of academic life in general and archaeological research in particular quickened. The United States had emerged from the War as the largest intact industrialized nation. Personnel returning from military service were given access to the GI Bill, which would underwrite the cost of attending college should they so desire. Many did so desire, and college and university enrollments swelled. Between 1950 and 1960, the national population grew 8.0 percent, but the college population grew 40.0 percent (Westmeyer 1985:142). By 1964, 40 percent of the adults between 18-21 years of age were enrolled in a college or university. With the post-War academic and industrial expansion came the continued massive Federal projects, especially in the western United States. And with those projects came increasing support for preparatory archaeological work.

Since it was the first large-scale involvement of archaeology with Federal sponsorship and requirements, WPA archaeology set the tone for such future relationships, not only in terms of successes and failures, but also in terms of specific provisions placed in future legislation and regulations. There were other, large-scale Federal exercises -- TVA and the Missouri Basin Project/River Basin Survey -- that emerged after the programs of the 1930s ended. The success of these was due in part to the learning that took place during WPA archaeology, both by the academic archaeologists who provided the service, and by government managers.

1.2.3.1.   The Missouri Basin Project

If WPA archaeology set a kind of tone for what to do or not do with large-scale, Federally assisted archaeological work, the Missouri Basin Project established in many respects all of the pieces that would emerge in professional archaeology at the national level. These included National Park Service coordination, the subcontracting with non-government archaeologists to perform the work, the

formation of joint academic-government committees to draft memoranda of agreement and memoranda of understanding, the initial forays into formal legislative lobbying, and formal legislation. In a way, it represented in miniature what would happen 20 years later at the national level. It also established all of the steps that would need to be taken to actually develop an extra-academic cultural resources industry.

The Missouri Basin Project, like WPA archaeology before it, established many professional reputations while greatly expanding knowledge of the area in which the work was done. However, it also continued to encounter the same kinds of problems that were exposed with the WPA projects: budgetary limits forcing decisions between administrative support and actual field work, reporting rates, and the difficulties of having this kind of archaeology accepted as legitimate by the same academic community that actually provided the qualified people needed to direct such work.

The best summary of the Missouri Basin Survey history was given by Lehmer (1971:1-7), from which the following is drawn. The Missouri Basin Project began to emerge in early 1945, when plans became public for the post-War development of the Missouri River into a series of reservoirs for flood control and power generation. These reservoir projects were under the jurisdiction of the U.S. Army Corps of Engineers and the Bureau of Reclamation. Those agencies were contacted by representatives from the Society for American Archaeology, the American Anthropological Association, and the American Council of Learned Societies, with the initial coordination of those societies coming from archaeologists in the Smithsonian. From those three academic societies would come the Committee for the Recovery of Archaeological Remains (Johnson, Haury, and Griffin 1945; see fn. 7), which functioned essentially as an advisory as well as lobbying group, testifying formally before Congressional committees and working informally to provide much-needed information to the public not only paying for all of this, but being claimed -- in absentia -- to be benefitting from that spending.

The National Park Service, which already had responsibility for natural and cultural resources within Federal jurisdiction (Hosmer 1981:926 *passim*), along with the Smithsonian Institution were seen as the natural coordinators of any salvage archaeology that would be necessitated by the proposed reservoir project. A Memorandum of Understanding between the National Park Service and the Smithsonian was finalized in October of 1945. Under that Memorandum, the National Park Service provided planning, funding, and administration, especially in dealing with non-Federal agencies actually performing archaeological work (at this time, private-sector archaeology did not exist; "non-Federal archaeology" essentially meant museums, historical societies, and university Anthropology departments). The Smithsonian served both as an advisor in the planning, as well as another archaeology provider. In the end, most of the actual field work would be done by the Smithsonian.[15]

The Missouri Basin Project began administratively -- for all practical purposes -- in 1945. Field work seems to have started in the summer of 1946, when the first archaeologists were hired (until 1976, the Federal budget year began at the start of July; it now begins at the start of October). The entire project ended in June 1969, when the River Basin Surveys was closed, with material and personnel transferred to the National Park Service Midwest Archeological Center.

The Missouri Basin Project was notable for several things[16]: There were professional archaeologists involved at the outset and at all levels of the organization; there were staff historians and a historical research program; and there was enabling legislation, specifically the Antiquities Act of 1906 (34 Stat. 225), the Historic Sites Act of 1935 (49 Stat. 666), and over the last nine years the Reservoir Salvage Act of 1960 (74 Stat. 220). Funding was hybrid, spread between the Federal agencies and various participating institutions. In 1961 and 1962, this was augmented by National Science Foundation funding to the Smithsonian.

In addition to the Smithsonian, Lehmer (1971:7) listed eight universities, two state historical societies, and one museum as the institutions participating.

---

15. To do the archaeology, the Smithsonian created the Department of River Basin Surveys within the Bureau of American Ethnology. The River Basin Surveys was responsible for all of the Smithsonian's salvage archaeology within the United States; the Missouri Basin Project, then, was an administrative unit within the River Basin Surveys. When in 1964 the Bureau of American Ethnology was combined with the U.S. National Museum's Department of Anthropology into the Smithsonian's Office of Anthropology, the Missouri Basin Project -- by then the only salvage operation managed by the Smithsonian -- was dropped as an administrative unit, and the work along the Missouri became synonymous with the River Basin Surveys. This is one of the reasons why the terms "Missouri Basin Project," "Missouri Basin Survey," and "River Basin Surveys" have come to be used interchangeably by archaeologists, especially those distant in time and space from the actual events.

16. Lehmer (1971:17) also noted that another contribution of the Missouri Basin Project was formalization of the Plains archaeological term "feature," which had first been used by Strong and by Spaulding in 1938. A *feature* refers to some artificial yet nonportable aspect of a site, such as a storage pit, trash pit, hearth, structure foundation, and so on. For the non-archaeologist: Features are considered the ultimate parts of archaeological sites, since they contain artifacts in context, meaning that the things the people used were all dropped together in one place at one time. Features are excellent signatures of site depositional INTEGRITY, one of the basic criteria for a site's eligibility for listing on the National Register. This is considered again in Chapters 2, 5, and 6.

Over 800 sites were identified; 94 were excavated (Lehmer 1971:194-195, 200). Final reports had been prepared on 44 of the sites by 1971 (Lehmer 1971:194-195, 200), a yield of 46.8 percent. The final reports on what would now be termed Phase II and Phase III exercises took an average of 5.6 years, but that is a bit misleading. True, the longest took 16 years to finish; however, six were finished within a year and eight were finished within two years.[17]

One of the major complaints that has stood regarding WPA archaeology was the lack of reporting; the Missouri Basin Project managed to generate a number of final reports, and to do so in a timely fashion. Reporting of results, though, would continue to be a problem until the emergence of non-academic professional archaeology in late 1960s.

1.2.3.2. Legislation, Expansion of Government, and Academic Growth

The Missouri Basin Survey represented a cooperative agreement among the National Park Service, the Smithsonian, the Corps of Engineers, and the Bureau of Reclamation to recover threatened cultural resources before they were damaged as the series of hydroelectric and flood-control reservoirs were built along the Missouri River in North and South Dakota. The

---

17. For comparison: Professional reports of similar detail on sites of similar size are now expected to be finished within six months to a year, while the professional archaeologist continues working on several other compliance projects at the same time.

On the topic of publication rates in general: *The Chronicle of Higher Education Almanac* (28 August 1998, p.32; 25 August 1993, p.35) noted that the average yield for "Professional writings published or performances presented in last two years" for all college and university faculty, regardless of field, was:

Publication Rate for Previous Two Years: Percent of Academic Faculty Producing/Publishing at the Rate Given

Items	1995-1996	1989-1990
none	36.6 percent	45.3 percent
1 - 2	23.1 percent	25.7 percent
3 - 4	18.8 percent	15.8 percent
5 - 10	14.8 percent	10.8 percent
11 - 20	4.3 percent	1.9 percent
21 - 50	1.5 percent	0.4 percent
> 50	0.9 percent	0.1 percent

"Writings published" would include books, monographs, research journal articles, and, for some fields, abstracts. The largest number would be journal articles. Most AAUP I and IIA institutions now expect junior faculty to produce at least two research articles per year to be eligible for tenure. Most professional archaeologists who serve as project managers produce six to 10 peer-reviewed monographs each year; senior personnel also produce around one written conference paper as well as one regional research article every two years. Failure of reports to pass that peer review results in suspension of the last phases of payment on the project until a satisfactory (meaning peer-acceptable) report is produced. This is a bit different than what occurs in a college or university setting.

Inter-Agency Archeological Survey existed from 1946 to 1969; it was administered by the National Park Service.

A direct outcome of the River Basin Survey was the Reservoir Salvage Act of 1960 (74 Stat. 220). This was the second of a pair of acts that refined the Historic Sites Act of 1935, the first being the Federal-Aid Highway Act of 1956, which had required that planning take into account minimizing damage done to what are now called cultural resources. The Reservoir Salvage Act provided for the salvage of archaeological sites threatened by dams and reservoirs. The Act provided funds and agency support for emergency or salvage archaeology, including consultations, surveys, and full-scale excavations. It was the first legislative action prescribing archaeological salvage on a national level, and was the first to prescribe mitigative measures to off-set what now would be called adverse effects of a Federal undertaking (Fish 1980).

Together, the Federal-Aid Highway Act and the Reservoir Salvage Act made provisions to recover data from archaeological sites before certain types of Federally sponsored land-alteration activities destroyed those sites, something now covered by NHPA and eventually expanded by 1974 to include all Federally enabled activities. Equally interesting is that, of these, the Reservoir Salvage Act probably covered the majority of sites that such activities would endanger, simply because prehistoric archaeological sites in the United States frequently are found on relatively level land within 100 m of streams and rivers.

The expansion of the academic community after World War II was accompanied in the late 1950s by an increase in Federal funding to underwrite scientific research. This was a direct response to a perceived threat from the Soviet Union, the idea being to increase the training and production of scientists in the United States to counter that Soviet threat. Two sets of funding became important in archaeology: the National Science Foundation (NSF), active since passage of the National Science Foundation Act in 1950, which underwrote everything from student training and dissertation research to research done by established faculty; and the National Defense Education Act, which until the early 1970s supported graduate students during the academic year.

Archaeology is labor-intensive in the field work stage. Traditionally, academic research would be supported either by grants from foundations (accessible only to faculty and museum archaeologists), or through academic field courses (accessible as a method of underwriting field research to graduate students as well as established faculty). The number of foundations underwriting -- or capable of underwriting -- archaeological research was not great; the number of university field courses was (and really still is) limited.

However, with the establishment of NSF in 1950, a new way to support field work, both at the faculty and the graduate level, was available. Funding was made available to university faculty and museum personnel through whatever administrative division/program managed funding for Anthropology. Funding also was available to graduate students through NSF Dissertation Improvement Grants.

The legacy of NSF and other Federal-level funding initiatives through the 1970s was one of expanded research, exploration of new approaches to archaeological field work and analysis, increased training opportunities, and perhaps most important, a requirement on the part of the person doing the field work to have a well-planned and -scheduled research project in place *before* going into the field. The archaeological research was research chosen by the investigator.

1.2.3.3.   Bifurcation

Beginning in the late 1960s, a second kind of archaeology, one outside of the academic/museum world, began to emerge in the United States.

Shifts in social values along with maturation of the post-War children resulted in a series of changes that would transform archaeology from an academic discipline to an extra-academic profession. Some of this traced directly to attitudes held by those adults -- the parents of those children -- who entered college on the GI Bill after the Second World War: There was an increased demand for relevant, career-oriented, practical courses and degrees (Westmeyer 1985:144). Even by 1940, most professional, managerial, and so-called "white collar" positions required a bachelor's degree. Those surviving the War (who, remember, had already "paid their dues" by doing without during the Depression of the 1930s) wanted from a college education the skills and background that would place them into that increasingly inaccessible white-collar world. Colleges and universities began seeing more and more students drawn from families that had no history of attending college; the equation of an education with general vocational preparation -- actually the original basis of higher education in the United States -- was re-established.

That ex-serviceman cry for educational (meaning occupational) relevance was picked up by his children in the middle 1960s and early 1970s (see also Westmeyer 1985:142 *passim*), and corresponded as well to a renewed legislative-statutory effort to define then protect cultural resources. In little more than a decade, from 1966 through 1979, a flurry of acts, amendments, and executive orders protecting cultural resources -- including archaeological sites -- was implemented. This corresponded as well to a period of increased interest nationally, or at least among the college and university population, in social issues. Many remember this period as one involving the Vietnam War; many forget that it was also the societal world that produced President Johnson's "Great Society" and its emphasis on society's social responsibilities.[18] That interest in social issues resulted in a surge in majors in the social sciences, especially Anthropology, as well as an interest in North American archaeology (helped greatly by it being a subfield of Anthropology), history, the environment, parks, and all of the related topics. And it was from exactly that world, with all of those concerns and interests, that modern professional archaeology came, for the first of those major legislative acts was the National Historic Preservation Act of 1966.

The National Historic Preservation Act (NHPA) is covered in detail in Chapter 2. The NHPA went beyond the Historic Sites Act of 1935 by declaring that any time public moneys or permits results in land alteration of any kind, or the transfer of public property gave land-use control to another party, the affected project area would have to be checked first for cultural resources that might be eligible for listing on the National Register of Historic Places, before the action could be undertaken. While architects and architectural historians might be available to handle above-ground, historic structures, the only group capable of checking to see if archaeological sites might be present would be archaeologists. And in 1966, the only archaeologists available outside of the Federal government were university faculty or museum curators.

From 1966 forward, the NHPA was the single most important piece of legislation in anthropological archaeology.[19] Its passage enabled both a full-time historic preservation industry, as well as one that could be dedicated entirely to dealing with archaeological sites potentially imperiled by Federally enabled activities. The scale of this impact on potential archaeological work, when everyone had time to pause and consider, was staggering. As a consequence of NHPA's Section 106, every bridge improvement or road widening using Federal funds, every construction project undertaken in a floodplain under jurisdiction of the U.S. Army Corps of Engineers, every alteration of wetland perimeters, every sewage treatment plant, every landfill, every runway extension, every interstate

natural gas pipeline or electrical transmission line corridor, every microwave tower complex, every flood control system, every Federally assisted urban renewal project must first have a qualified archaeologist assess the area that would potentially be disturbed to see if archaeological resources would in any way be compromised. And this was just the start. Every conceivable Federally assisted project necessary for the development or repair of the nation's infrastructure required archaeological assessment; every Federal agency was required to inventory the cultural resources within or under its jurisdiction. Every state was required to designate a State Historic Preservation Officer (SHPO; now more of an office than a single person) as well as provide a comprehensive state plan for the research value and relative merit of all potential historic and prehistoric cultural resources within the state's jurisdiction.

And, just as everyone thought that was enough, many states compiled then enacted counterpart NHPA (or NEPA) legislation bearing upon state-level undertakings involving state land, monies, or permits. In addition, a number of counties entered into this, passing counterpart legislation at the local level.

The NHPA was followed in 1969 by passage of the National Environmental Policy Act (NEPA), which required Federal agencies to protect environmental quality that may be adversely affected through actions those agencies make possible. Part of that environment was seen to be cultural resources. Thus, preparation of Environmental Impact Statements (EIS) and Environmental Assessments (EA) required taking into account cultural resources, including archaeological sites.

In 1971, President Richard Nixon issued Executive Order No. 11593 "Protection and Enhancement of the Cultural Environment." This Order directed all Federal agencies to locate, inventory, and, where appropriate, nominate all properties under their jurisdiction eligible for listing on the National Register of Historic Places. Further, Federal agencies were directed to develop procedures and take such actions as needed to protect, preserve, and enhance non-Federal cultural resources eligible for the National Register.

Additional acts between 1966 and 1979 included:

*   the Coastal Zone Management Act of 1972, which required protection and management of cultural resources, potentially threatened by Federally enabled activities, found in coastal areas;

*   the Housing and Community Development Act of 1974, which allowed the Department of Housing and Urban Development to delegate its NHPA Section 106 obligations to block-grant recipients;

---

18. It is interesting to note that the three administrations responsible for most of the social legislation in the United States -- Theodore Roosevelt's, Franklin Roosevelt's (who, it will be remembered, took his inspiration for the New Deal from his cousin's legislative vision a quarter-century earlier), and Lyndon Johnson's -- also were responsible for the vast majority of the core historic preservation legislation.

19. Actually, since over half of all anthropologists are employed as a consequence of the legislation, it simply is the single most important piece of legislation affecting Anthropology in the United States.

*   the Archeological and Historical Preservation Act of 1974 (the Moss-Bennett Act), which required Federal agencies to notify the Secretary of the Interior whenever their actions would do irreparable damage to archaeological resources, then authorizes the Federal agency to use up to one percent of its own project funds (or request the Secretary of the Interior to undertake appropriate measures) to preserve those resources ("preservation" does not mean keeping the original physical site intact, but instead means preserving the data or information of the site);

*   the Tax Reform Act of 1976, which treated rehabilitation of buildings of certain ages, again as an issue of historic preservation; and

*   the Archeological Resources Protection Act of 1979, which prohibited the taking of historic or prehistoric artifacts from public lands without a permit, and further established that any violation constituted a felony punishable by up to five years in prison and payment of $250,000.

These acts did not appear out of nowhere. One of the great forgotten actions in anthropological archaeology has been the concerted effort to have legislation emplaced that would protect archaeological sites. This began informally among the myriad of amateur archaeological societies that sprouted up across the country, some as early as the late 1800s. As long as horse-plowing continued, collecting of prehistoric artifacts from farm fields enjoyed wide popularity, and many amateur societies emerged from those interested in such things. In place, then, was an audience quite interested in archaeological materials.

Also in place was a government-academic alliance, developed in part through the WPA days, in part through the ongoing archaeological work within TVA, and in part through the Smithsonian's River Basin Surveys. Early in the history of the nation, really, had been a concern for and therefore government interest in archaeological materials.

The third factor that emerged out of this background was a growing interest in public education. Anthropological archaeologists have always been interested, at least as a professional body, in making sure that the greater non-archaeological community appreciates what the archaeological community does. This has been driven mostly by a very real concern for teaching others about what the archaeologists love. It also has been driven by a combined recognition that archaeological sites are finite and nonrenewable, and therefore subject to destruction (intentionally or not); and also that the continued exploration of such sites depends in the end on the good will of society writ large in providing the wherewithal to do the necessary research, be it funding or access.

Attitudes, Social Contracts, and Research

The structure of research funding in academic science specifically and the social sciences in general has undergone considerable change since the 1960s. This change reflects the changes in the society overall, and has particular relevance for research done in archaeology.

The National Science Foundation (NSF), established by the National Science Foundation Act of 1950, was founded mainly in response to Vannevar Bush's (1945) argument establishing a social contract between scientists and the broader society. That contract held that, in return for Federal support and relative autonomy, the researcher would produce and share freely knowledge that would be of benefit to the society. Hence, in exchange for its continuing support, the society expects beneficial results. It is from Bush's argument that NSF and similar Federal-level scientific funding programs emerged.

Anthropology was the first of the social sciences to be supported through NSF when Gordon Willey received the first NSF Anthropology funding – for $11,500 to do a settlement pattern study in the Yucatan – in 1954 (Greene 1985:1). From the two Anthropology awards given in 1954 (the other went to Robert Braidwood), well over 120 regular research awards in Anthropology were being supported each year by the late 1980s, with nearly half of the allocated funds going to archaeological projects.

NSF funding proved and continues to prove invaluable for research throughout the sciences. For archaeology specifically, research performed by faculty as well as by doctoral candidates was and to a small degree – relative to those seeking funding – continues to be supported. However, there was an interesting pattern that emerged in the distribution of that funding.

By the late 1970s and early 1980s, around 50 or so grants were being awarded by NSF each year for non-doctoral archaeological research, each averaging around $39,300 (American Anthropological Association 1978:9-11, 1980:5, 1981b:3-4). Although not legally bound to do so, almost all were awarded to museums or to universities/colleges, generally because those were by far the most common applicants. Of those 50 or so awards, only 12-17 were set in the United States (however, see also fn. 27). Keep in mind that in the early 1980s there were around 1,000 or so archaeologists in university and museum settings alone. NSF funding, then, went to 5.0 percent of that population (again, see also fn. 27).

There were two issues at this point: (1) disparity in the geography of the funding, and (2) the kinds of sites that were funded. The first is obvious, and led to a general grumbling among academic archaeologists who worked in parts of the United States lacking prehistoric standing architecture. The second was more subtle: The research funded through NSF tended toward large, set-piece excavations, and not infrequently toward monumental sites outside of the country (Patterson 1995:80; see project listings American Anthropological Association 1978:9-11, 1981:3-4). This selection pattern seemed influenced by and to influence the training approach taken within university settings, as reflected in the standard texts (so-called method-and-theory texts).

Funding

We have at least 18 such texts here (including upgrades), from Hole and Heizer's (1969) second edition through the Renfrew and Bahn (1991) text to Fagan's (1997) latest avatar. Those texts over the years increasingly stressed how to disassemble large, complex occupations such as monumental sites or cave sites, and included discussions on everything ranging from field strategies to how to structure a large staff of specialists (although neither of us can recall much discussion on how one should *manage* such a specialist, professional population). What disappeared from these texts were the non-monumental, open-field sites that would come, in time, to be the core of compliance archaeology. Implicit with this unconscious editorial selection was the assumption that smaller and/or more architecturally challenged sites probably could be handled pretty easily if one could handle the large and architecturally complex sites. (That actually may be true; we certainly know from personal experience that working on non-monumental sites does not help in dealing with large architectural compounds.) That editorial choice also left an image of what constituted proper archaeological research, or the approach toward such research: large, well-staffed, fixed-placed, and sustained. Although the emergence of NSF funding and review procedures for archaeology can be traced historically back to a reaction to WPA archaeology (or could be with a little imagination and teleology), the predilection for such sites is ironic in light of Wauchope's (1966: viii) remarks about "big efficient operations" existing at the expense of smaller research efforts.

Despite Bush's (1945) vision of reciprocal societal obligations between the publicly funded scientist and the work of the scientist toward the betterment of society (or at least the explanation of how eventually that might apply), the contract broke down, as Byerly and Pielke (1995) noted. With that breakdown came a diminution of public funding for scientific research.

The social sciences have been very susceptible to this decline, an issue well beyond the scope of this aside, or even this text. For example, responding to the increasing concern about research support, Smith and Torrey (1996) noted in a policy paper that Federal funding for social science infrastructure had been declining in real terms since 1971, and as a proportion of the Federal research budget over the same time, dropping from 8.5 to 4.0 percent. However, Federal funding continues to be the primary source of research funding for the social sciences.

The academic community had been concerned about the decline of public research funding. Lederman's 1991 report as the president-elect of the American Association for the Advancement of Science (AAAS) entitled *Science: The End of the Frontier?* probably gave the best sense of this and, importantly, underscored the increasing differences between research done within the academic sector versus research done in the private sector. For those who are in an academic setting, and for those who are in a professional setting, it seems to us useful to examine how Lederman understood the scientific world to work.

The gist of Lederman's position-and-policy paper was that Federal support for scientific research had been shrinking since its high point in 1968, and that Congress should be advised that such a decline would eventually threaten the nation. The paper called for increased research funding, and presented its argument in part through a series of colored-text side-bars that consisted of direct quotes from researchers whose research was suffering from lack of funding. Statements were attributed "Professor of Chemistry, Yale" or "Professor of Physics, U. of Texas." Some of the remarks included concern that no one wanted to be a faculty researcher anymore, and that the universities were having a harder and harder time attracting qualified people.

Lederman's 1991 paper shows how environment can affect perceptions and therefore influence language and cultural values (as anthropologists know all too well), and is a useful lesson for academic and extra-academic archaeology.

Stop for a moment. Where does most research in the United States take place? Know the answer? Is there a shortage of scientists?

There are 23 quotes in those colored-text side-bars in Lederman's paper, representing exactly 9.2 percent of the responses received from the AAAS informal survey. ALL of those quotes come from university faculty. There is not a single remark from outside of a university setting. Remember, this is the nation's *largest* general science association, where the majority of the 600,000-plus membership works outside of higher education. While there is a lament about people leaving the academy, in actuality every new *faculty* position advertized in the physical, life, or social sciences was drawing at that time (and, in the spring of 2000, still draws) anywhere from 1,000 (physics and mathematics) to 200 (social sciences) applications. That is, the idea that there is a shortage of scientists is an image perpetuated by the academic community about which unemployed or at least not-academically-employed physicists and chemists (and even some archaeologists) become extremely angry. And for good reason.

Even though NSF funding has been limited for archaeological work done in the United States, and even though social science funding in general has been declining nationally, that decline has been in the form of funding directed toward academic-sector programs. It does not hold for where most of the empirical research is now being done.

For archaeology, there is no shortage of funding for research, provided it is understood that the funding is made available through government-mandated compliance. (This issue of funding availability is true in chemistry, genetics, and other fields with economic bases outside of the academic sector, a logical extrapolation from Bush's vision).

For archaeologists, Bush's frontier is still endless, or at least has not ended. It is not that there has been an increase in NSF or similar program funding. Rather, the structure and research demographics of the field have changed. Most of the funding, most of the research (especially data-based field research), and most of the research articles in regional journals and papers given at regional conferences now are done by private-sector archaeologists (for example, in 1996, 22.1 percent of the papers delivered at the annual meetings of the Society for American Archaeology – the national organization – were given by members of the private sector, while 80 percent of the papers given at the annual meeting of the Middle Atlantic Archaeological Conference were given by members of the private sector).

There is an image – and archaeology is more susceptible to it than most fields – that true research is performed within an academic setting. However, for many fields this is not the case, and the most startling happens to be archaeology. (In terms of Nobel Prizes and similar awards, only a handful of academic institutions can compete with private-sector corporations like Bell Labs or IBM; most true, pure research in the physical, life, and social sciences now is done outside of a university setting, and has been for at least the last 15 - 20 years.) The image is perpetuated in part because occupational demographics changed so very quickly, but it also is perpetuated because the academic community, which trains archaeologists just as it does chemists and geneticists, is unaware that such a change has taken place.

Lederman's concern remains quite real in terms of university research; it is an excellent example of the misunderstanding of overall research and science in the country when considered from a wider perspective. That is, it equates "research" with "academic research." It also is very similar to the difficulties that the professional archaeological community faces when dealing with its academic colleagues, be it as researchers or as part of unified whole where the academic archaeologist is exploring new research questions or procedures, or training new archaeologists, for which the professional lacks the discretionary time.

American Anthropological Association. 1978. NSF Funding for Anthropology October 1, 1976, to September 30, 1977. *Anthropology Newsletter* 19(3):9-11.

_____. 1980. Anthropology funding in FY '79 tops $22 million. *Anthropology Newsletter* 21(7):1, 5.

_____. 1981. NSF Awards: FY 1980. *Anthropology Newsletter* 22(4):3-4.

Bush, Vannevar. 1945. *Science: The Endless Frontier.* U.S. Government Printing Office, Washington D.C.

Byerly, Radford, Jr., and Roger A. Pielke, Jr. 1995. The changing ecology of United States science. *Science* 269:1531-1532.

Fagan, Brian M. 1997. *In the Beginning.* Ninth edition. Longman, New York.

Hole, Frank, and Robert F. Heizer. 1969. *An Introduction to Prehistoric Archeology.* Second edition. Holt, Rinehart, and Winston, New York.

Lederman, Leon M. 1991. *Science: The End of the Frontier?* American Association for the Advancement of Science, Washington, D.C.

Patterson, Thomas C. 1995. *Toward a Social History of Archaeology in the United States.* Harcourt Brace College Publishers, Fort Worth.

Renfrew, Colin, and Paul Bahn. 1991. *Archaeology: Theories, Methods, and Practice.* Thames and Hudson, London.

Smith, Philip M., and Barbara Boyle Torrey. 1996. The future of the behavioral and social sciences. *Science* 271:611-612.

That entire attitude, combined with the social activism of the 1960s and early 1970s, resulted in a concerted, savvy legislative lobbying of state and Federal government, a lobbying effort that began in 1945 and continues to this day. By the early 1980s, archaeologists, through a mixture of political sophistication, intense effort, fundamental love of and belief in what they do, and just good luck of having the right agenda at the right political time, had managed to frame out an entire professional industry based upon archaeological research (and, amusingly, not really be aware that that is what was created). Further, the enabling legislation, which did not just say such things were good but empirically defined that importance by levying fines and prison sentences, was so deeply buried in the overall legal fabric of the country that it could not easily be taken back out.

All of this was fortuitous for another reason: Beginning in the 1980s, social science funding through the Federal government was increasingly cut. Between 1968 ("the peak year" in the "'golden age'" of scientific funding, as Lederman [1991:5] stated) to about 1988, Federal support of scientific research dropped 20 percent, even though the number of scientists doubled nationally (Lederman 1991:5). That is, suddenly there was no money. For a labor-intensive research field like archaeology that had come to define the excavation of new -- and large -- archaeological sites as the only really legitimate way to make a name in the field, this was catastrophic.

It would have been utterly devastating to archaeological research in the United States had the legislation of the late 1960s and the 1970s not been enacted. Without the consequent funding, combined with the simple destruction of archaeological resources that would have occurred due to the Federally enabled activities, archaeology probably would be back to the proportionally small number of people that existed in the 1940s. However, just the opposite happened.

Several other changes were taking place in the immediate professional-social environment. Beginning in the middle 1960s, archaeology underwent a transformation in its approach toward research. This was The Great Methodological Debate, and it took an inductively oriented field reflexively operating with a Boasian paradigm of culture, to a more consciously framed, problem-oriented field. This surge was driven in part by that same cry for research relevance that returning troops had expected of higher education, and that influenced college curricula of the period.

There also was an expansion of higher education: more institutions, more faculty, more Anthropology departments. The near-panic of the late 1950s about a lack of scientists created a sustained (and continuing) effort to create more scientists, resulting by the late 1970s in a tremendous surplus of scientists, at least relative to academic positions.

And the changes occurred swiftly, and in an effective environment that altered so fast that the perceived environment of the academic Anthropology culture failed to notice the change. As a result, by the late 1980s, approximately three of every four archaeologists were working either in government or in the private sector, doing archaeology required of Federal, state, or local statutes. Yet the academic community was so unaware of this transformation that courses and texts rarely mentioned the existence of that extra-academic world or, when they did, often were mistaken in their presentations.

1.3. Current Structure of Archaeology in the United States

Regardless of where it is practiced, anthropological archaeology is concerned with understanding how and why human cultures changed their structure over time. Refinements in field technique, analytical procedures, or even how archaeological research questions are asked all represent means to the end of learning about the why of culture change. Any concept of culture change is necessarily diachronic. Recognition of the importance of the answers to questions about culture change is one of the reasons why archaeological sites in the United States are classified by the Federal government as limited and nonrenewable resources. They are treated in Federal law in much the same way as environmental resources are (Neumann, Sanford, and Palmer 1992).

1.3.1. Archaeology within the Academic World

Archaeology emerged in the United States during the debate over the origins of the myriad burial and temple mounds that were revealed as forests were cleared for farm land. Remember, this debate became so important to the identity of the early nation that, beginning in the 1840s and continuing into the mid-1890s, Congress ear-marked $5,000 a year for the Smithsonian to resolve the question of if the Mound Builders were cultural ancestors of Europeans or not. In addition to raising the quality of research, as any lively debate will, this investigation into the prehistory of North America resulted in placing archaeology within the emerging field of Anthropology.

The Mound Builder Debate ended in 1894 with the demonstration that the mounds were made by ancestors of American Indians; archaeology in the United States -- and later the Western Hemisphere --

Kinds of Archaeology in the United States

There are actually two kinds of archaeology available in the United States. The first is referred to as Classical or "Old World" archaeology. This is found in Art History, Classics, Classical Archaeology, and History departments, and represents a method of historical inquiry. The subject matter generally involves the Classical civilizations that emerged in the Mediterranean basin; archaeology is used as a method to fill in unrecorded details about otherwise known peoples, places, or events.

The second kind of archaeology is referred to as anthropological or "New World" archaeology. This is a subdiscipline of Anthropology, and is a self-contained field that functions more as diachronic ethnography or cultural geography. Traditionally, anthropological archaeology has focused more often on prehistoric sites; it is the prevailing archaeology practiced in the Western Hemisphere.

There is a blurring of lines between the two sets: Historical archaeology in the United States often is part of an Anthropology department, its application a creative melding of the historiography of classical archaeology and the diachronic ethnography of anthropological archaeology. The techniques used in the field generally are similar between classical archaeology and anthropological archaeology, although anthropological archaeologists tend to stress ecological reconstruction, knowledge of soils, and the like.

Primarily because of the relative subtlety of the data, anthropological archaeology is the major theoretical and methodological contributor; every logical and experimental trick imaginable is needed to reconstruct – then irrefragably demonstrate – past human behavior. Anthropological archaeology also is the field specified in and required by Federal and state statutes involving historic preservation and environmental compliance. Mostly because of this, anthropological archaeology is the kind of archaeology discussed here.

was seen to be focused on that same population.[20] At the same time, physical anthropologists ("Anthropology" in Europe is synonymous with physical Anthropology in the Western Hemisphere) dealt extensively with native skeletons recovered by those archaeologists; ethnographers and linguists, under Franz Boas and his students at Columbia, sought to record as much as possible about vanishing

---

20. When Cyrus Thomas demonstrated this in the *Twelfth Annual Report of the Bureau of Ethnology* in 1894, Congress withdrew the funding stipulation for continued archaeological research into the Mound Builder Question. The funds, however, were not lost to the Smithsonian: J.W. Powell, who had lost his arm in the Civil War and came to be director of the Smithsonian, had developed a love for the American Southwest. The funding was redirected to that region, which was blessed with living native tribes and (compared to anything in the eastern United States, at least) spectacular ruins.

native cultures and languages. Thus, it made perfect sense administratively to place archaeologists in the same departmental unit as ethnographers, linguists, and physical anthropologists. By the early 1900s, when Anthropology departments began to form as distinct entities in the nation's universities, the place of archaeology as one of Anthropology's five basic subfields was secure.[21]

The academic archaeology that emerged focused on recovery of prehistoric remains, be they in the United States proper or in the ruins of Mesoamerica, Central America, or South America.[22] It became a field of museums and colleges, of summer field courses that enabled the university professor to get laborers to help with field work in exchange for academic credit (or for adventure, which historically has always sold better among college students anyway). All of that changed in the 1930s, when the Roosevelt administration included archaeology -- because of its low matériel overhead relative to labor costs -- as part of the WPA. That inclusion, combined with an increasing number of Federal historic preservation statutes and, in the 1940s, the River Basin Surveys along the Missouri, inaugurated the link of archaeology as an information-retrieval field with the Federal government.

Archaeology remained, though, part of the university and museum world well into the early 1980s. The

formation of the National Science Foundation in 1950, combined with Bush's post-War statement of the scientific community's moral obligation to the society that supports it,[23] resulted in a massive expansion of higher education in the country.[24]

Through the early 1960s, archaeology was mainly the province of higher education and of museums. Research focused on reconstructing culture histories, that is, setting out a chronicle of what transpired through the past of the Western Hemisphere. In the early and middle 1960s, a young ethnographer-turned-archaeologist, Lewis Binford, redirected anthropological archaeology by noting that (1) archaeology was a form of diachronic ethnography or diachronic Geography; and (2) archaeology could demonstrate the cause-and-effect of culture change.[25] The associated debate, known as The Great Methodological Debate because it focused on the philosophical structuring of research questions, reshaped how archaeology was done. That debate was so encompassing that the idea of problem-oriented research -- a Binfordian derivative first used for archaeological research -- even became the catch-phrase of ethnographers reviewing National Science Foundation Anthropology proposals.

---

21. Anthropology traditionally maintains five subfields: ethnography, social anthropology, archaeology, linguistics, and physical anthropology. The first four are considered cultural anthropology, although ethnographers and social anthropologists for a time declared themselves to be "cultural anthropologists," leaving the poor archaeologists and linguists feeling very left out indeed. For that reason, one hears of a "four-field approach" in Anthropology, by which is meant that combined ethnography-social anthropology focus (known as sociocultural anthropology or synchronic anthropology) along with the other three fields mentioned above. Of the 3,083 full-time *faculty* in colleges and universities, our research for Table 1.1 suggests that 1,646 (53.4 percent) are sociocultural anthropologists, 919 (29.8 percent) are archaeologists, 326 (10.6 percent) are physical/biological anthropologists, and the remaining 192 (6.2 percent) are linguists.

22. It was not until the 1960s that historical archaeology began gaining credence among anthropological archaeologists. Hosmer (1981:888-889) noted tellingly that

> If historians who deserted the universities during the depression were considered second-class citizens in their professional groups, archaeologists who sifted the debris from colonial American historic sites were heretics. Their pioneer efforts did not really achieve any respectability until well after World War II.

Anthropological archaeology has long been synonymous with prehistoric archaeology, which is unfortunate. This corresponds to the tendency among social scientists to see Anthropology as the study of "primitive peoples" (see quote from Minderhout 1986:20, i.e., "Sociology Texts: Anthropology is the Study of Primitive Peoples").

23. Bush, Vannevar. 1945. *The Endless Frontier.* Government Printing Office, Washington, D.C. Bush's document, appearing right at the end of the War, set the tone for the role of academic research in the United States. Bush argued that scientists have a moral obligation not just to do the research, but to show how their research fits into the larger needs of the society. This did *not* mean that research had to be applied; rather, research has a role in society that ultimately has to do with the betterment of that society (see also box "Attitudes, Social Contracts, and Research Funding").

24. The increased emphasis on publication for tenure and the extreme nature of the German university model initiated by Johns Hopkins can be traced directly to this post-War infusion of research capital.

25. Irving Rouse remarked in an interview many years ago that:

> no archeologist deserves to be called an anthropologist unless and until he or she uses archeological data to solve anthropological problems, including problems of cultural, linguistic, and physical anthropology. To put this another way, I think archeologists ought to be studying prehistoric ethnology as well as prehistoric social anthropology [American Anthropological Association 1983:8].

We concurred. There is tremendous potential in the alliance of professional archaeology with academic archaeology, particularly since professional research of necessity is couched in the kind of diachronic ethnographic terms that so captivated Rouse. Any number of Phase II or III compliance reports do this, Ledbetter's 1992 *Archeological Investigations of the Vulcan Tract, Bartow County, Georgia* being as serviceable an example as any. A good sense of how Rouse systematized this diachronic anthropological approach can be found in his 1972 *Introduction to Prehistory: A Systematic Approach*, a text notable for its expectation of people being able to read, having no photographic illustrations and only 14 minimalist line-drawing diagrams.

In essence, the goals of anthropological archaeology shifted from questions like "when did agriculture first appear" or "where were ceramics first made" to questions like "why on Earth did agriculture emerge at all, considering it is nutritionally less viable than hunting-and-gathering" or "how did the appearance of ceramics alter the structure of past societies." The questions asked were questions about how a human culture works as a behavioral adaptation, and how functions or processes within a given culture in the past allowed people to survive and reproduce. The approach came to be known as "Cultural Processual," and really does underlie how academic archaeology operates, although the surface models have changed.

A cultural processual approach, at least the cultural ecological portion, remains the basis of how extra-academic archaeology does archaeological research (and how extra-academic Anthropology does Anthropology). The answering of processual questions required a change in research designs, shifting from strategies that would produce a large number of varied artifacts to strategies that would identify then seek to recover past remains capable of addressing those specific, processual questions.

Academic archaeology currently is immersed in a transition from concerns about the logical rigor for the structuring of research questions -- methodology in the philosophical sense -- along with questions about culture process and culture change, to issues regarding cultural idiosyncracies such as sexual differences in culturally sanctioned behavior, class structure and contamination of cultural-historical interpretations, social dominance hierarchies, and the like (see Patterson 1995, Fagan 1997; cf. Gross and Levitt 1994, Fox 1996).

Knowing the demographic structure of the academic field is useful, whether a person is a student or is advising students (Table 1.1.). Unlike Sociology, where 75 percent of the 19,000 sociologists work in an academic setting,[26] less than half of the 8,400 or so

practicing anthropologists and archaeologists are found in higher education. Of the 3,781 anthropologists working full time as anthropologists in the nation's universities and museums, around 3,083 hold full-time faculty appointments in one of 372 academic departments. Around 919 of these faculty members are archaeologists. Entry into the faculty world requires a doctorate.

Ninety of the 372 departments offer a doctorate; another 68 award a terminal master's degree. There are 201 departments that provide only a BA or BS (or, in 20 cases, both). The balance offer Anthropology concentrations as part of a Sociology major. Together, in 1998 around 7,600 BA or BS degrees, 1,100 masters, and over 400 doctorates in Anthropology were awarded in the United States, based on figures from the American Anthropological Association *Guide to Departments 98-99*. The number of doctorates has held around 372 ± 33.7 for the last 20 years, the number of master's degrees has doubled, and the number of bachelor's degrees has grown by about 20 percent, again based on a review of *Guides to Departments* from 1977-1998. Although the American Anthropological Association *Guide to Departments 96-97* (p.310) stated that 308 ("nearly all academic") positions were advertised in the AAA *Anthropology News-letter* during the 1995-1996 academic year, the actual number was 260, based upon a count of the actual number of different announcements printed in the *Anthropology Newsletter*. Around 52 of those either required or at least could have been filled by an archaeologist.

The structure of academic Anthropology and archaeology stands like this in the early twenty-first century: Research has ranged beyond culture process and culture change to include a growing postprocessual interest in looking at individual behavior, postmodernism in the sense of relativistic epistemology, critical archaeology, cognitive archaeology in the sense of cosmological/ideological reconstruction, and the like, all logical outgrowths of culture processual questions (and arguably a by-product of the academic community's decreasing generation of or access to primary field data). Access to research funding requires a faculty appointment or association with an institution that will allow adjunct faculty to run sponsored programs through the school (uncommon). The National Science Foundation funds 15-20 archaeology-specific projects in the United States. Of the 7,600 or so who receive a bachelor's in Anthropology, about 4.9 percent receive a doctorate. Of the 400 or so who receive a doctorate, less than 50 percent will be employed in higher education. That is, less than 2.5 percent of individuals receiving an undergraduate degree in Anthropology will enter and remain within the academic sector.

---

26. Hopke, William E. 1993. *The Encyclopedia of Careers and Vocational Guidance. Volume 3 Fis- Para*, p.130; *Volume 4. Park - Z*, p. 380. Ninth Edition. Fergussion Publishing, Chicago. A sense of extra-academic disciplinary relevance can be had by looking at the Federal work place demographics. Three positions are of interest here: GS-184 Sociologist, which can only be filled by a person with a graduate Sociology degree; GS-190 Anthropologist, which can only be filled by people with degrees in Anthropology or Archaeology; and GS-193 Archeologist, which can only be filled by a person with a degree in anthropological archaeology.

The 1997 OPM statistics used in Table 1.1. noted that there were 44 Federal Sociology jobs, down from 70 in 1989; 90 Federal Anthropology jobs, up from 53 in 1989; and 1050 Federal Archaeology jobs, up from 800 in 1989 (the 1997 data from OPM 1998:28-29; the 1989 data from Brentlinger 1992:80, 84, 85).

It might be noted as an aside that, of Historians, Hopke (1993, vol. 3:135) stated that "approximately 20,000 historians are employed full time in the 1990s, most of whom work in colleges and universities." The figure excluded high school history teachers, who are enumerated simply as "teachers" for Department

of Labor purposes. OPM (1998:29) listed 662 Federal Historian positions. We did not locate figures on what proportion of historians work within higher education.

Over 90 of those new doctorates each year specialized in archaeology.[27]

---

27. The numbers for employment within the academic sector actually are more sobering. Of those 260 or so new faculty hires, on average only 75 percent will receive tenure. Further, in Anthropology, 50 percent of faculty hires select people who have received their doctorates within the previous year; another 30 percent, within two to three years. Ninety-five percent of the hires documented from AAA *Newsletter* and *Guide to Department* sources over the last 10 years have been restricted to individuals receiving their doctorates within five years of the announcement date. The irony of this -- Anthropology long ago declared itself to be a cumulative discipline, where it takes time to develop the skills, expertise, and subtlety needed for research and teaching -- is that older Anthropology doctorates are excluded from consideration for faculty positions. It could be worse: Physicists have a maximum one-year shelf-life.

There also is an interesting pattern in selection for faculty. Although there are 90 doctoral programs in Anthropology in the United States, graduates from five (5.6 percent) of those programs -- Michigan, Chicago, UC-Berkeley, Columbia, and Harvard -- account for about 30.4 percent of full-time Anthropology faculty. Nine other programs -- Arizona, UCLA, Cornell, Illinois, Indiana, Pennsylvania, Stanford, Wisconsin, and Yale -- account for another 25.8 percent.

Thus, over half of Anthropology faculty come from 15.5 percent of the doctoral granting institutions. It is noteworthy that only four of those programs -- UCLA, Illinois, Indiana, and Wisconsin -- maintain to our knowledge anything resembling active training in professional archaeology; the majority of private-sector and government archaeologists are drawn from other graduate programs in Anthropology. This creates a very real danger for a kind of intellectual in-breeding or provincialism: Many members of the academic community have remained their entire careers, including as students, within an environment that itself has no full-time extra-academic experience, yet nearly 80 percent of all positions requiring graduate-level archaeologists are outside of that world. This also heightens a growing bifurcation within American archaeology between the academic and professional communities, the latter arguing that the former's lack of first-hand experience with compliance archaeology is resulting in students unprepared to enter professional practice.

But perhaps the most revealing set of figures we discovered working up the demographics for Table 1.1. has to do with geographic research interests. These figures really helped us get a sense of why, if most of the archaeological work done in the United States is outside of the university, that kind of work is not discussed very often within the university setting. And it may also go a long way in explaining how the current bifurcation of professional and academic archaeology has come about.

We found in examining the geographic areas of archaeological interest/expertise among our faculty and museum sample for Table 1.1. that 43.2 percent of university archaeologists focused on work outside of the United States (16.9 percent of faculty archaeologists have research interests in Mesoamerica). Around 29.5 percent of our sample faculty had geographic specializations within the United States; another 15.9 percent had specializations that included the United States as well as other parts of the world (the balance either did not list an area, or were overly general about their area). That is, nearly half of all full-time faculty archaeologists do not deal with the archaeology in the United States on a regular basis. Therefore, it should not be surprising that the major issue for the archaeology within the United States -- the Section 106 Process and the emergence of a professional archaeology -- would escape their notice.

This pattern is even more marked among recent PhDs. Over the two years 1997 and 1998, the AAA *Guide to Departments* listed 204 doctorates awarded in anthropological archaeology. Of those, 72 (35.3 percent) were set in the United States (29 or 14.2 percent were set in the American Southwest). The locations of another 19 (9.3 percent) were not clear to us from the dissertation titles, or were not geographically specific in their topics. The

Fortunately for archaeology, not only is an academic life rewarding, extra-academic positions are even more numerous while also being very rewarding indeed.

1.3.2. Archaeology outside of the University

Archaeology remained an university or museum field into the late 1960s. This was true even with the WPA archaeology and the River Basin Surveys. All of those programs were run using university or museum -- usually university -- archaeologists. University and museum archaeologists were the only people around, and there were probably no more than 200 of them to begin with (see also Patterson 1995:73-83). An esoteric, romantic, and engaging field, in the days when only 10-13 percent of the country even attended college (today, 38 percent do, with around 20.3 percent of the country's adults holding at least an undergraduate degree; *The Chronicle of Higher Education Almanac* 28 August 1998, p.6).

Recognition of anthropological archaeology's capacity for "mining" the information potential of such sites was the central reason why Federal law designated anthropological archaeology as the preferred discipline for research on Federal sites, or on sites adversely affected by Federally sponsored/permitted activities.[28]

States and local governments with historic preservation statutes generally follow that protocol. Technically, archaeological sites -- prehistoric or historic -- represent information repositories, the information being related to how human cultures survive, adapt, and reproduce over time. Because of this, archaeology now is largely an environmental compliance, extra-academic field.

In the United States, about 30 percent of archaeologists with graduate degrees work in government regulatory positions at the Federal or state level, 50 percent work in engineering or historic preservation firms, and the remaining 20 percent work in higher education or museums.[29] Based upon where

---

remaining 113 dissertations (55.4 percent) were set outside of the United States (30 or 14.7 percent were in Mesoamerica, another 19 or 9.3 percent in the Near East or Mediterranean basin). Thus, for people working on their doctorates, the nuances of United States professional archaeology would not be matters of great interest, and again it would not be surprising at all that they would be unaware of, say, the Section 106 Process. And for those eventually hired as faculty, it would not be unusual for them to not talk about this as part of archaeology -- or even general anthropological -- instruction. All of this may help explain why cultural resources curricula are generally absent in universities.

28. 36CFR 61 Appendix A "Professional Qualifications Standards."

29. Ironically, archaeology in the United States is the only other social science field besides Political Science in which a person with a bachelor's can obtain reasonably compensated employment in

Tip: Where and How Positions in Archaeology Are Announced

For firms seeking to fill managerial archaeology positions, or for students seeking employment, there are five basic locations where positions are publicly announced. The first and most focused are bulletin boards in Anthropology departments. On the positive side, both national and local/regional searches tend to be posted. Often, regional firms will send around notices that there are positions available, and these will be posted. Occasionally, such a notice will be a phone call made to faculty, who then will mention this to students in class or in the archaeology laboratory. On the negative side, it is very difficult to get access to these announcements unless one has a reason to regularly be on the given campus. Further, such points of dissemination are limited: There are not all that many Anthropology departments in any one given area.

The second location for advertising available positions is in the American Anthropological Association (AAA) *Newsletter*. These involve national as well as regional searches. The *Newsletter* appears (usually) during the second week of each month, September through May; most position notices are academic in nature. The Society for American Archaeology (SAA) publishes a *Bulletin* every two months that has a few position announcements; private-sector positions not mentioned in the AAA *Newsletter* will be here, but the academic announcements usually are duplicated. Announcements in the SAA *Bulletin* for private-sector positions tend to be dated. Both the AAA *Newsletter* and the SAA *Bulletin* maintain Web pages that will carry these notices.

A third location is the employment section of a major newspaper. Most major newspapers, such as the *Washington Post*, regularly carry regional position announcements under "archaeology," "cultural resources," "engineering," and/or "environmental." Announcements can be regional or national, and are almost entirely private sector in nature. Again, these can be accessed over the

Internet, and unlike the professional societies, such access is readily had through the local public library.

The fourth and, according to corporate principals, currently the best place to find managerial position announcements is the Internet. Notable sites are ACRA-L, ARCH-L, and HistArch (Mr. Thomas Wheaton, Vice-President, New South Associates, Inc., personal communication, March 1999).

The fifth location involves government-sector positions. Although Federal hiring has been cut back considerably, announcements for Federal positions are given in the non-government publication *Federal Jobs Digest* (*FJD*). The *FJD* is available through most public libraries, either as a hard copy or as an Internet subscription. The National Park Service (NPS) maintains a listing of archaeology field work opportunities on the Internet as well (http://www.cr.nps.gov/aad/fieldwk.htm).

State and local governments each have their own advertising patterns; check with the local government, state Department of Labor, or the local public library to get a sense about these. Many states make notices available through the Internet as well.

As with most job searches, it is most important to make contact with the firms and agencies that may be hiring, and to check with them constantly. For academic positions this, of course, is pointless: The academic market has been a buyer's market of staggering proportions since the early 1980s.

Finally, for those interested in working in private-sector archaeology, do not forget to look in the phone book: Many archaeology firms or divisions are listed in the Yellow Pages. It often does not hurt to call ahead, arrange an interview, then go in to chat with the principals of a given firm.

---

the bulk of archaeologists work and where most of the field work is performed and articles written, archaeology in the United States can be said to be an environmental compliance, extra-academic,

government-regulated field. Knowing the demographic structure of the field, and knowing as well how it is set up, what it seeks to do, and what Federal law requires of it, helps immeasurably in planning career choices.

their major. Essentially anyone with proper field and laboratory training, and holding a college degree, is eligible to serve as a field technician on projects involving Federal contracts.

Field technicians exist in two forms in the country. The first are the unaligned, migrant laborers, the so-called motel archaeologists. This population moves from project to project around the country; life time in this state is around two years. Less than a quarter of work force is unionized (although no firm to our knowledge currently has a union contract).

The second population is made up of those who obtained sufficient laboratory or field experience in addition to that provided in the basic college courses, either through internships or the migrant archaeology pool. The people work as staff archaeologists in firms, state government (especially as part of DOT archaeology staffs), and local government throughout the country. In either case, starting compensation packages approximate a Federal GS-5 for a bachelor's and GS-7 for a master's.

Currently, most training that an archaeologist receives will be within a college or university setting; often, it will be provided by archaeologists who themselves have spent nearly all of their post-graduate lives within an academic setting and therefore lack much in the way of a native's first-hand experience of the extra-academic world. Further, roughly half of those faculty archaeologists do not have research foci in the United States. It is not surprising, then, that academic training in archaeology generally functions with the expectation that the student eventually will teach in a university setting, and probably deal with the kind of archaeological research projects with which they are familiar. It is also not surprising that there is little exposure, be it in the class room or in the texts, to the

We learned about archaeology from that ... "So, you would like to work as an archaeologist..."

Every year we receive a flurry of phone calls from undergraduates interested in positions in archaeology. Most of these come from people who have just received their bachelor's degrees, who have called the Anthropology departments of the local college or university, who in turn direct the calls to us.

Usually, the students have a BA or a BS in Anthropology and would like to do archaeology. What, they ask, is available? The first question we ask is what their background is in archaeology: Have they had a field archaeology course? A method-and-theory course? A lab course? We remind them – or probably tell them for the first time – that a field course in North American archaeology is required for employment, and in the absence of that, one can at least start in at an entry level in a laboratory setting if one has had a method-and-theory course along with a North American archaeology course. We remind them, as we remind the

reader, that private-sector firms are *not* in the business of training students to do archaeology: That is the responsibility of colleges and universities, and is one of the reasons why this text was written to begin with.

We will then go on to note that most archaeology positions are to be found in the private sector, with some available in Federal or state government. These are accessible to people with bachelor's degrees and some field training, although people with master's degrees are VERY marketable.

That, by the way, is true in nearly all of the sciences: Given a choice between a doctorate and a master's, and with a life-plan that includes eating, generally a master's degree has a greater probability for employment in the degree field than the doctorate. It may or may not be right -- we could go on and on about this -- but it is the way the extra-academic employment world works, and has been exhaustively documented each year since

September 1990, and May 1991, in those "Career" segments in *Science*.

We have learned several things in speaking with those recent Anthropology graduates. The first is that they all remark: "No one told us about *that!!*" We have found that their academic advisers have not told them about the structure of the job market, have not told them about the requirements for employment in the private or public sector, and rarely have even mentioned the existence of the Section 106 Process. The students have no idea of where to look for position announcements, of what to have a background in when thinking about doing archaeology, and of what courses they should have taken if they wanted to do archaeology. Very few are aware of how degree relates to employability.

Actually, it is rather sad, but it need not be this way. Hopefully, the information in this chapter particularly, as well as in Appendix B, will help a bit.

Federal statutes governing the practice of archaeology in the country. The emphasis as well as the experience involves other things: formulating research capable of examining theoretical constructs, interpreting within the confines of those constructs, and working outside of the country. The assumption is that the student will face archaeological projects that are pre-conceived, large, well-funded, long running, and staffed with specialists.

Actually, most of the work that the student will do as an archaeologist will be outside of an academic setting, either as a government regulator or as a private-sector archaeologist working because a client is required to satisfy preservation statutes. Although a wide assortment of sites will be faced, including industrial-scale, monumental architecture sites in urban settings, the vast majority of sites encountered will be small, partially disturbed prehistoric or rural historic sites found as part of the Section 106 Process. The nascent archaeologist will find the emphasis to be less on choosing a research topic then addressing it with field work than it will be having the site chosen by circumstances then being able to wrap the data around existing theoretical issues while designing a state-of-the-art research program that will address those issues.

The practicing archaeologist is very much a general practitioner, needing to have the field, analytical, and

theoretical skills required by the full range of possible archaeological sites.

Appendix B provides a detailed outline of the basic archaeological curriculum. The capacity of the institution to deliver training -- either directly or through cooperative agreements with other institutions -- should be the deciding criterion for continued enrollment if the goal is to work within professional archaeology. Just because a college or university has an Anthropology department or program does not mean that it can provide professional-level training; the costs in terms of field, laboratory, library, and classroom support often are beyond the budgets set out by the institution (this is a serious problem with new programs in regional state universities, since higher education budgets are limited at the state level). The ability to provide that training is not automatic; it is not a right but a privilege of institutional foresight to provide field instruction in archaeology.

The extent to which an employee-applicant fulfills professional training should be the criterion by which hiring decisions are made by the private-sector firm.

Four out of every five archaeologists in the United States who work as archaeologists do so outside of a university or museum setting.

2: Laws, Regulations, and Protocols

2.1.   Purposes and Objectives

The purposes of the laws, regulations, and guidelines[1] surrounding cultural remains are to define what is or is not important, and to establish a procedure for accessing the information that those remains can provide. The objectives, then, are to

* set forth the criteria for assessing relative importance of cultural remains (that is, defining *significance*);

* outline the procedures through which that assessment must go;

* delineate the responsible parties involved in making such assessments;

* identify and then define the extent of jurisdiction and responsibility that each party has in the evaluation process;

* set forth the criteria for making *determinations of significance*, as well as indicating which party can or cannot make such determinations;

* set forth the criteria for the archaeological and historic preservation work performed; and

* set forth the criteria for who can perform the archaeological and historic preservation work.

The reason that field work is done the way it is done in professional archaeology is due entirely to operationalizing those objectives. To understand the field procedures discussed later, it is necessary first to understand what those field procedures are meant to accomplish. And what they are meant to accomplish involves satisfaction of the governing cultural resources regulations.

It should also be emphasized here that one of the central intents of such regulations, like the Section 106 Process, is to allow government agencies as well as private-sector concerns whose projects are enabled

---

1. In law, legislation provides authority, regulations set required procedure, and guidelines give advice and guidance needed to accomplish the intent of the legislation on a day-to-day basis.

    For a thorough and comprehensive discussion of cultural resources legislation, see King 1998. For discussion of the Section 106 Process, see King 2000a. Both the National Park Service (NPS; see http://www.cr.nps. gov/history/train.htm) and General Services Administration (GSA) offer excellent short courses on the Section 106 Process and its particulars, which we recommend highly.

through Federal actions to plan ahead for the delays that may occur. The process lets Federal agencies, and the engineering and construction firms that work with or require permits from Federal agencies to anticipate then take into account the historic preservation needs of the greater society.

There are several inter-related Federal statutes, along with an assortment of counterpart legislation at the state and local levels, that regulate different aspects of archaeology and its performance in the United States. However, the most important of these is the National Historic Preservation Act of 1966, as amended. What the National Historic Preservation Act (NHPA) asked and required, especially its Section 106, made it possible for archaeology to become a compliance industry and, as a result, for government at different levels to serve as a regulator of the archaeological resource and its investigation.

The NHPA and related legislation in effect give the society the right of first refusal for handling the physical remains of the past. Section 106 in essence requires that any change in a physical property, be it ownership or outright construction, using Federal money, requiring Federal permits, or occurring on/in Federal property, first have the property checked to see if elements important to the history or prehistory of the United States will be threatened. All of this is done to make sure that cultural remains that the society would like to preserve -- or at least document -- are not inadvertently lost.

Inherent in this process are assessments: assessments about what should be saved or not saved, about where the responsibilities of the government agencies begin and end, about where the responsibilities of the private corporation receiving the funds or permits begin and end, and about what should be expected as minimal documentation. These kinds of judgments would seem, at first glance, to be fraught with peril, and it is exactly at this point that archaeologists in university settings have been uneasy, and quite rightly so. For example, what should be saved of an archaeological site imperiled by construction? Just how is such a decision made? Who makes it? What criteria are used?

For the entire process to work, those questions as well as all of the others that can be imagined from that litany of assessments had to be worked out. The trick, of course, is not to provide an answer for every situation, but instead to set up a procedure that guarantees the best-balanced answer for every situation. This is what the laws, regulations, and guidelines do: They describe a process and the rules for its execution.

The associated regulations establish the procedures needed to make all of this work. They answer questions about how to know what is important and worth saving, and therefore what is not. They outline

the responsibilities that all of the parties have in the process; they also specify who is or is not a participating party in that process. It is a surprisingly simple and therefore elegant system treating rather objectively what at first glance would be judged a series of value judgments about worth and importance of cultural remains. It also serves to avoid conflict of interests by providing a clever series of checks and balances based upon strongly held self-interests.

The regulations do some other things as well. For example, they specify who has the authority to say if a cultural resource really is important, that is, *to make a determination of significance*. It is *not done by* the practicing archaeologist, by the way. Federal guidelines also outline what needs to be taken into account as archaeological work is done, analyses are performed, and results are presented. Who is allowed to do all of this? The regulations address that, too, listing the kinds of people permitted to do the work, and spelling out what backgrounds those people have to have.

The key legislation is the National Historic Preservation Act of 1966 (as amended). NHPA essentially linked all of the previous statutes and historic preservation legislation, and is responsible for the emergence of archaeology as an extra-academic profession in the United States. The NHPA did several things:

*   It authorized the Secretary of the Interior to expand the National Register of Historic Places to include state and local "historic properties," in addition to national properties, while also establishing procedures for nominating such properties for listing on the Register.

*   It required that each governor appoint a State Historic Preservation Officer (SHPO) who would develop state preservation plans and coordinate historic preservation activities in the particular state or territory.

*   It provided for local historic preservation pro-grams, referred to as certified local government (CLG) programs, that would assist in carrying out the state's historic preservation programs.

*   It made provisions for grants-in-aid for historic preservation.

*   It established the Advisory Council for Historic Preservation (the ACHP or the Council), which would advise the President and Congress while also revising Federal and Federally assisted programs.

*   It required Federal agencies to establish procedures for identifying, inventorying, and evaluating the Register eligibility of historic

properties that could be adversely impacted by an agency enabled undertaking.

* It established the National Historic Preservation Fund.

Three NHPA sections are especially important for archaeology: Sections 101, 110, and 106. Section 101 established the State Historic Preservation Officer and required formulation of state historic preservation plans. Section 110 required all Federal agencies to survey and inventory their properties for cultural resources, both standing structures and archaeological sites.

However, it was Section 106 that proved central. Section 106 required each Federal agency to take into account how their undertaking would affect cultural resources listed or eligible for listing on the National Register of Historic Places, and to allow the Advisory Council to comment before the undertaking occurred.

NHPA has proven so robust, and what has come to be called the Section 106 Process has worked so well, that many states have followed with similar legislation, as have some county and municipal governments.

2.2. Federal Laws and Regulations: Section 106 Process

The NHPA of 1966 was concerned with providing an orderly process to handle "properties" -- what came to be called "cultural resources" -- that might be imperiled by Federal undertakings. The NHPA consisted of several broadly worded sections that set out the pieces needed to achieve the goal of evaluating historic properties prior to their destruction or alteration by a Federal undertaking. Of those, three NHPA sections are important here: Sections 101, 110, and 106.

Section 101 [101(b)(1)(A)] required that each state have a State Historic Preservation Officer (SHPO) appointed by the governor. The SHPO would be the person responsible for the state's cultural resources. In effect, the SHPO would be an apologist for the state's cultural resources. As originally envisioned, that role of apologist was in contrast to the Federal agency whose action was potentially imperiling the cultural resource; the role has come to be such an apologist in any dyadic relationship where a public agency has enabled action that could potentially alter or destroy cultural resources that might be eligible for listing on the National Register of Historic Places, or an equivalent listing at the state or local level.

On American Indian tribal lands, the equivalent authority to the SHPO is the Tribal Historic Preservation Officer (THPO). The THPO's responsibilities are the same as those of a SHPO, as are its roles in the Section 106 Process. For this reason, one often sees "SHPO/THPO" written when procedures are discussed.

Section 101 also required that each state develop a STATE HISTORIC PRESERVATION PLAN [101(b)(3)(C)]. The STATE PLAN would summarize the status of the state's prehistoric and historic research. It would also identify research themes, historic contexts, and the basic questions that would need answering. The State Plan presents the overall agenda for what might be considered important or not important. After all, what might be a threatened cultural resource eligible for listing on the National Register for one party may not be a cultural resource of any consequence for another. The State Plan serves as a place to start.

Tip: State Historic Preservation Plans

Every state, commonwealth, territory, and protectorate is required to have a State Historic Preservation Plan. The State Plan outlines the basic cultural historical sequence for the given area, while also identifying the critical questions that remain in understanding the past and why it occurred in the way it did. Such documents are available from the jurisdiction's historic preservation officer. Practicing archaeologists working in those jurisdictions are expected to be conversant with, if not already have copies of, the State Historic Preservation Plan.

Section 110 set out the historic preservation responsibilities of the Federal agencies to manage resources. Section 110 required that *each* Federal agency establish the procedures to then begin inventorying its property holdings to see if those holdings included any structure or archaeological site that *could* possibly be listed on the National Register of Historic Places. Further, once identified, the agency was required to move toward nomination of eligible properties for listing on the National Register of Historic Places. Section 110 (b) also required each Federal agency to initiate recordation procedures in situations where action by the agency would substantially alter or destroy entirely a historic property. The costs of this and related historic preservation activities were designated "eligible project costs," and could be included in the budget for the undertaking (**Section 110 [g]**; the Archaeological and Historic Preservation Act of 1974 would clarify what proportion of the budget might be involved in historic preservation activities).

Section 106 required that Federal agencies take into account any damage a project they authorize might do to any cultural resources that could be or are listed on the National Register. It further required that the Advisory Council on Historic Preservation be given a chance to comment on that Federally enabled action. A little reflection suggests that any "taking into account" will mean that the area affected by that project be checked first to see if Register-eligible properties are present. While this would be made explicit in the subsequent regulations, implicit was the requirement that prior to any Federal undertaking, the affected property or area would have to be examined to see if anything was present that could be listed on the National Register.

2.2.1. Section 106

Section 106 (16 U.S.C. 470f) reads as follows:

The head of any Federal agency having direct or indirect jurisdiction over a proposed Federal or federally assisted undertaking in any State and the head of any Federal department or independent agency having authority to license any undertaking shall, prior to the approval of the expenditure of any Federal funds on the undertaking or prior to the issuance of any license, as the case may be, take into account the effect of the undertaking on any district, site, building, structure, or object that is included in or eligible for inclusion in the National Register. The head of any such Federal agency shall afford the Advisory Council on Historic Preservation established under Title II of this Act a reasonable opportunity to comment with regard to such undertaking.

2.2.2.   Implementing Section 106: 36 CFR Part 800 "Protection of Historic Properties"

Section 106 is a paragraph long. It just sets out one of the intentions of NHPA. The protocol for doing what Section 106 asks is contained in 36 CFR Part 800 and is referred to as "The Section 106 Process" [**36 CFR 800 Subpart B: 800.3 - 800.13**]. The following is based upon those regulations published in 64 FR 27071 on 18 May 1999, and printed in 36 CFR Part 800 on 1 July 1999 (see also Appendix A).

2.2.2.1.   Some Concepts: Historic Property, Undertaking, Effect, Lead Agency, Determination

It is useful to start by clarifying terms [see also **36 CFR 800.16**], some of which are misleading if not counter-intuitive. The terms are used in specific ways within the regulations; substitute terms often are used among the professional archaeological community.

A PROPERTY refers to any historic or prehistoric district, site, building, structure, or object. Archaeologists, ourselves included, frequently use the term CULTURAL RESOURCE in roughly the same way. HISTORIC PROPERTY in the statutes refers to any historic or prehistoric district, site, building,

Category of Property: How Cultural Resources

There are five categories of properties or cultural resources (*National Register Bulletin #16: Guidelines for Completing National Register of Historic Places Forms*, pp. 41-42): Object, Site, Building, Structure, and District. These carry implications for Register-eligibility.

OBJECTS are things like monuments, mileposts, statues, fountains, and similar location-specific items whose significance is related both to where they were placed and the purpose they served. Objects are portable, within a commonsense reason that probably would withstand discussion around a kitchen table on a Saturday but not within a court. Generally, relocated objects, because they have been moved, lose any Register-eligibility.

SITES are locations of significant events, prehistoric or historic occupations or activities, buildings, or structures. The buildings or structures can still be in place, or in ruins, or can survive only as archaeological traces. "Site," then, is somewhat equivalent to the term "place." For the practicing archaeologist, trained in dealing with archaeological SITES, this concept is used a little differently for National Register purposes. What clearly IS a site is rather obvious: Pretty much anything. But the threshold for when a site becomes a site is not defined. This issue is considered a little more in Chapter 5.

Sites can range from the standard archaeological site, inclusive of burial mounds and structure ruins, through battlefields, to rock carvings, petroglyphs, and even locations at which historically significant events occurred. Archaeologists, with the exception perhaps of those who work in the Southwest, think more in terms of a SITE usually being subsurface remains. The procedural definition for Section 106 purposes is broader.

BUILDINGS refer to structures that shelter human activities. Houses, barns, outhouses, businesses, churches, and similar things that English speakers would classify as "buildings" are considered to be BUILDINGS. What is colloquially referred to as a "compound" (like a farm compound or a parish compound) is considered to be a BUILDING as well, provided all structures (colloquial sense) are essentially unchanged and part of the original group that functioned as a unit. Otherwise, the complex of structures, some of which are intact and some of which are absent or substantially altered, is considered a "district," with CONTRIBUTING (that is, essential parts of the overall district) or NONCONTRIBUTING (that is, extraneous elements physically present but one would wish they were not) ELEMENTS. An eighteenth-century farmstead, with its house, barn, chicken coop, and outhouse, would conceptually be a BUILDING. However, if the barn had been replaced by a microwave tower, then it would be better to consider the compound a DISTRICT, and the microwave tower a noncontributing element.

STRUCTURES refer to elements of the built environment that do not include BUILDINGS. For anthropologists, this represents a linguistic classification issue, separating BUILDINGS (which house or enclose human activities) from STRUCTURES (which represent pretty much everything else essentially non-portable that people might build larger than themselves but *not* meant to enclose human activities).

Are Grouped

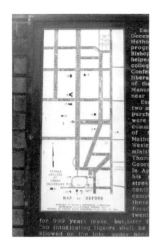 

Figure 2.1. Monument Plaque Describing Oxford, Georgia, Historic District. Left unmentioned is the bell in the clock tower of Seney Hall on the Oxford College campus. Purchased from a monastery by a late-nineteenth-century professor summering in Spain, the bell bears a Latin inscription identifying its dedication to the Virgin Mary and proclaiming that "all will be bless'd within the Voice of this bell," rather droll for a Methodist college. The inscription is the source of Polly Stone Buck's (1986) title The Blessed Town, a gentle and charming description of Oxford at the turn of the century. Because of the character of the Historic District, the community and College have served as the setting in recent years for movies and television series.

A bridge would be a structure, as would a highway, a railroad tunnel, a hydroelectric dam (maybe; it could also be a building, since there are rooms for generators, power regulation, and so on), a Civil War breastwork, an aqueduct or a subway, or even a canal.

DISTRICT refers to a collection of BUILDINGS, SITES, STRUCTURES, or even OBJECTS that all have a unifying theme. These all are concentrated in space, and have a continuity in terms of time, aesthetics/style, historical association, or other unifying theme. A DISTRICT is a set and presents interesting problems.

Districts may be *CONTIGUOUS* or *DISCONTIGUOUS*. Contiguous historic districts are districts where everything within the geographic boundaries of the proposed district falls into the unifying principle, be it historic association, architectural style, or whatever. Discontiguous districts refer to situations where many of the buildings and structures that made up a unified whole still remain, but interspersed are elements that do not belong with that set, such as buildings or structures built later or in a style inconsistent with the unifying theme, and other elements that are intrusive to the unifying theme.

For example, the Oxford Historic District in Oxford, Georgia, is a discontiguous historic district (Figure 2.1). It consists of eight buildings, one monument, and a cemetery located on the campus of Emory University's Oxford College, along with eight residences, the Old Church, a cemetery (part of the original town plan), and the Yarbrough Oak (a tree that owns itself, the Commissioners of Oxford having deeded the tree to itself in 1929; the obvious issue of whether the tree signed off on participation in the Section 106 Process is not addressed; Figure 2.2), all spread over an area about a mile and a half north to south and a half mile east to west.

The buildings are associated with the founding of the Emory College community in the 1830s and 1840s. The church is allowed because of its architecture and because it was a contributing element in the overall community. The cemetery was part of the original town plan, and also a contributing element.

However, there are several buildings and objects that are not part of that district that are located within that 0.75 square mile area: The "new" dormitories on the college campus, along with the library, the science building, and the gymnasium; several of the residences built after World War II; and, for the sake of completeness, all of the other trees that do not yet own themselves. The campus also has a Civil War cemetery, left from when the campus buildings were used for hospitals by both Union and Confederate forces during and immediately after the Siege of Atlanta in 1864. The cemetery is considered to be part of the district as well, again as a contributing element.

(Oxford survived the Savannah Campaign reportedly because either [1] Sherman's roommate at West Point had graduated from what is now Oxford College or [2] Sherman was a close friend of Judge Floyd, a resident in the nearby county seat of Covington. Accounts differ, and every little community in Georgia that was not burned has a similar story. What is known is that when passing through Covington, Sherman received an invitation to dine with the sister of Sam Anderson, who was a cadet with Sherman at West Point. He received the invitation too late to accept [Ms. Mellie Davis, Oxford College, March 1998, personal communication]. By the time one finishes figuring out how many friends Sherman evidently had in Georgia – considering that Oxford, Covington, Madison, Milledgeville [the capitol, no less], and Macon were *not* burned – it is a wonder that the state seceded at all. Dyer's [1999] recent study documenting the extent of Union sympathizers

Figure 2.2. *The Yarbrough Oak. The Yarbrough Oak would be an fascinating example of an OBJECT in the historic preservation sense. There was a short period, in Georgia at least, when trees were deeded to themselves. The Yarbrough Oak has owned itself since 1929. It also has the equivalent of a pension fund, maintaining a chequing account, in its name, that is literally handled by Newton County, Georgia (all of Joyce Kilmer's remarks to the contrary, the Yarbrough Oak does need someone else to write out its cheques). The account allows the tree to pay for its own upkeep. It is not known if the Yarbrough Oak votes in town elections; it is, after all, a tax paying member of the community. Until a few years ago, the tree would have been required to pay state income tax, as part of an intangible tax, on its bank account. And given the way Georgia income tax filing is done, the tree would also have had to file a Federal income tax form with the Internal Revenue Service.*

throughout the South would support the argument that the numbers of Union sympathizers – who also assisted the Union throughout the Civil War – in the towns that survived may have been the reason *why* those towns survived.)

It should be noted that SITES, especially subsurface remains, within the bounds of a DISTRICT are considered to be a part of the district and considered legally to be listed on the National Register, unless specially *excluded*. This holds even if the sites are currently unknown. This automatic inclusion of subsurface remains as part of the district is rarely remembered, even at the Federal or state regulatory level. For example, when Oxford College was considering building a new fine arts center in an open area that is within the bounds of the historic district (just north of the campus, behind Allen Memorial Church), the College would have been required to do Section 106 testing over that open area for archaeological SITES had Federal funds been involved.

When the practicing archaeologist encounters a situation involving work in a historic district, especially a discontiguous district, it is well to speak with the SHPO and the ACHP to make sure everyone understands what is included and what is required.

Buck, Polly Stone. 1986. *The Blessed Town: Oxford, Georgia, at the Turn of the Century.* Algonquin Books of Chapel Hill, Chapel Hill.

Dyer, Thomas G. 1999. *Secret Yankees: The Union Circle in Confederate Atlanta.* Johns Hopkins University Press, Baltimore.

structure, or object *included in or eligible for listing on the National Register* [**36 CFR 800.16 (l)**]. Historic properties may also include "properties of traditional religious and cultural importance to an Indian tribe or Native Hawai'ian organization" provided they meet criteria for listing on the National Register. (Despite its common usage, by the way, the term "cultural resource" is not in the Section 106 code.)

An UNDERTAKING [**36 CFR 800.16 (y)**] is any activity using Federal funds, requiring Federal permits, or involving Federal properties. The *determination* of if there is an undertaking is made by the Federal agency. Synonyms used by archaeologists would be PROJECT or FEDERAL PROJECT, terms not found in the regulations.

Undertakings, if they involve land alteration or a change of property jurisdiction, may have an EFFECT. An EFFECT means a change in character or use of a *historic property*. Thus, there will be an effect *only* if historic properties -- that is, cultural resources eligible for listing on the National Register -- are present. Effects may or may not be deleterious. An ADVERSE EFFECT [**36 CFR 800.5 (1)** and **(2)**] changes or potentially changes the character of cultural resources present ["Criteria of Adverse Effect" are given in 36 CFR 800.5 (1)].

The area within which the undertaking may cause direct or indirect changes to the character of any historic properties is the AREA OF POTENTIAL EFFECT [**36 CFR 800.16(d)**]. An AREA OF POTENTIAL EFFECT can extend beyond the actual area where construction is planned.

The LEAD FEDERAL AGENCY or AGENCY is the Federal agency issuing the funds or the permit, or responsible for the property that will be worked on/in or will be transferred [**36 CFR 800.2 (2)**]. The Lead agency is responsible for complying with Section 106, *regardless* of who actually does the work. The only time when the agency is exempt involves the Community Development Block Grant Program, in which the local government and not the Department of Housing and Urban Development, takes on that role.

Even if the agency only issues a permit, it is still the party responsible for compliance, not the permit recipient. Thus, when a sewage treatment plant is set in a floodplain, the Corps of Engineers (COE) first must issue a permit (termed a "404 Wetlands Permit," from Section 404 of the Federal Water Pollution Control Act of 1972). The COE becomes the Lead agency responsible for Section 106 compliance, not the local government or private contractor that actually got the permit. This does not necessarily mean that the COE will actually do the work; it may be a condition of the permit that the recipient has the archaeology done. However, the COE is held responsible for seeing to it that the work has been done.

2.2.2.2. Significance and 36 CFR 60

Section 106 requires that a Federal agency take into account the potential of an undertaking, which it has enabled, to harm cultural resources -- those districts, sites, buildings, structures, objects -- that could be listed, or already are listed on the National Register. To do that often means that the entirety of the area of potential effects be somehow examined to see if such properties are present, a methods issue that will be considered in Chapters 4 through 6. But it also means assessing whether or not any identified cultural resource *could* be so listed on the National Register. A cultural resource that is eligible for listing on the National Register is said to "possess the quality of significance" [**36 CFR 60.4**].

What is "SIGNIFICANCE"? The term "significance" appears in 36 CFR Part 60 "National Register of Historic Places," under section 60.4 "criteria for evaluation." 36 CFR Part 60, produced in response to NHPA, sets out the rules for what can and cannot be listed on the National Register (see Appendix A). The term "significance" is raised more often in professional archaeology than perhaps any other policy-ladened term, and does cause confusion for people who have not had the concept explained. This is an instance of taking a word in common use with a generally understood meaning -- "significance" -- and redefining it more narrowly.

"Significance" in the Section 106 Process -- and normally in professional practice -- connotes being eligible for listing on the National Register of Historic Places. Thus, a cultural resource is significant *if* it is *eligible* for such listing. And the criteria for such listing? The criteria for listing of a structure or an archaeological site on the National Register of Historic Places are given in 36 CFR 60.4 *criteria for evaluation* [a-d] and *criteria considerations* [a-g].

36 CFR 60.4 *criteria for evaluation* [a-d] states that "the quality of significance ... is present" if a property HAS INTEGRITY and satisfies one of the following:

[a] is associated with a nationally, regionally, or locally important event;
[b] is associated with a nationally, regionally, or locally important person;
[c] is a good example of a product of a master craftsman or a good example of a period or style [this is usually for architecture]["embody the distinctive characteristics of a type, period, or method of construction..."]; or
[d] has potential to provide data important for addressing major research questions [prehistoric archaeological sites that qualify almost always do so for this reason].

Criterion [d] as it applies to a given area would have been adumbrated in the State Historic Preservation

Integrity

"Integrity" is a concept that is at once very easy to understand and very misleading. Searching the National Park Service Web site for "integrity" in the spring of 1999 resulted in 981 items being listed. For a property to be eligible for listing on the National Register, it must have integrity as well as satisfy the criteria of significance listed in 36 CFR 60.4 [a] - [d]. We have often used catch-all phrases like "intact relative to other examples" to quickly capture the essence of integrity as it applies to archaeological sites. This may not have been a wise decision in all cases, but actually it does capture the core of what integrity relative to archaeological sites involves. A little elaboration on this would not be out of place.

Aspects of Integrity

36 CFR 60.4 lists seven aspects of integrity: Location, design, setting, materials, workmanship, feeling, and association. The best definitions for these are given in the National Park Service's (1995) *How to Apply the National Register Criteria*, which are paraphrased below.

Integrity of LOCATION refers to the particular place where an event happened, a building was built, or an object was placed. Archaeologists would think of the term "context" here, and their term would not be too different from how the LOCATION as an aspect of integrity works. When we discussed OBJECTS as a type of historic property, and what rendered them potentially eligible for listing on the National Register, it was integrity of LOCATION that was most important.

Integrity of DESIGN has to do with how true the building, structure, or whatever is to the original way in which it was conceived then produced. Thus, it is not an issue of aesthetics as much as it is an issue of how much the original plan, as actually produced, has survived or survives subsequent modification.

Integrity of SETTING has to do with how close things are now to the original *character* of the place where the event occurred, the building was built, and so on. Thus, topography, vegetation, and relationships among other features natural or artificial all have to do with SETTING. Setting is considered particularly important for historic districts; for the historic preservation firm, setting becomes an issue when structures like flood walls or levees are built.

Integrity of MATERIALS refers to how close to the original building materials, or the original deposit materials, those making up the property are now. A recent structure built to resemble one from the past lacks integrity of MATERIALS. Take for example the seventeenth-century Governor's Mansion in Williamsburg, reconstructed in the 1930s: It may be listed on the Register, but one thing it lacks is integrity in terms of MATERIALS. The building is less than a century old.

Integrity of FEELING has to do with how well the property continues to capture the sense of period or aesthetics with which it belonged when the criteria of evaluation (those important people, events, craftsmen, or even potential data) rendered the property possibly eligible for listing on the

Register. Eisenhower's house in south-central Pennsylvania may be extensively remodeled from the eighteenth-century farmhouse, but it retains its sense of FEELING for the 1950s and the 1960s, which was the period during which the President was associated with it.

Integrity of ASSOCIATION holds if "the place where the event or activity occurred ... is sufficiently intact to convey that relationship to the observer." "Sufficiently intact" becomes subject to documentation, since the verb "convey" implies a lack of objective criteria.

Neither FEELING nor ASSOCIATION are sufficient by themselves to support eligibility for listing on the National Register.

Integrity and Archaeological Sites

While all four 36 CFR 60.4 *criteria for evaluation* could hold for an archaeological site, very often it is criterion [d], potential of the site to yield information important in history or prehistory, that is cited. This means that the archaeological deposits must be conducive for yielding such information.

The archaeologist faces two issues, then. The first has to do with whether or not the site could yield information that is important in resolving research questions. That importance can be documented through the literature, exploration of where research questions stand relative to the nature of the archaeological site encountered, and so on. The State Plan further helps out, but usually that will be greatly augmented by whatever the background literature review has revealed about the status or historic or prehistoric research relative to the period or type of archaeological site being treated.

The second issue faced by the archaeologist also has to do with the potential for the archaeological site to yield information, but this has to do with how intact the deposit is relative to its information potential. Thus, the National Park Service (1995) stated:

The assessment of integrity for properties considered for information potential depends on the data requirements of the applicable research design.... It is important that the significant data contained in the property remain sufficiently intact.

Here, the word "intact" means "physically undisturbed relative to the way it has been in the past," or "physically undisturbed *ceteris paribus*." For archaeological sites, it is the *context* in which things are found combined with the *associations* among those things that enable questions about the past to be answered. Context for the archaeologist is where things were last deposited or left relative to the behavior that caused their leaving; association has to do with whether things are found with the other things they were dropped with. That is, does the stuff belong together or not.

Archaeologists are worried about *patterns* in physical remains and less in the remains themselves. Artifacts that are "out of context" normally are so compromised in their ability to yield information that the archaeologist will consider them worthless scientifically. This is one of the reasons why archaeologists become furious with those who loot archaeological sites: The looting not only destroys the context and association so vital to information retrieval from a site, it renders the artifacts recovered virtually worthless scientifically. The artifacts lack context and association.

For archaeological sites, especially those being considered under 36 CFR 60.4 [d], evaluation of integrity will involve LOCATION (e.g., stratigraphic context), ASSOCIATION (e.g., being able to be dated to, that is associated with, a particular period or culture), MATERIAL (e.g., preservation of organic artifacts), and DESIGN (e.g., a tool kit that remains essentially intact). When giving illustrative examples of how integrity would work with archaeological sites, the National Park Service (1995) invoked ASSOCIATION four times, MATERIALS three times, and DESIGN and LOCATION twice each. Even though it cannot be the sole reason, ASSOCIATION becomes the most frequently cited reason.

Information potential is reflected also in part by what the status of information already is for the subject or period of concern. This has to do in part with research questions, and in part with whether the information itself is rare or not. We have phrased our discussions of integrity relative to archaeological sites, both here and elsewhere, as meaning "intact relative to known examples." This phrasing generally captures the essence of data potential relative to questions of current research importance. It also follows from the National Register Bulletin 15 (1995):

Comparative information is particularly important to consider when evaluating the integrity of a property that is a rare surviving example of its type. The property must have the essential physical features that enable it to convey its historic character or information. The rarity and poor condition, however, of other extant examples of the type may justify accepting a greater degree of alteration or fewer features, provided that enough of the property survives for it to be a significant resource.

How would this apply to archaeological sites? Although National Register Bulletin 15 is not specific about archaeological sites in this respect, it uses the hypothetical example of a severely disturbed mill site to illustrate how the idea of comparative information might work. We have removed the word "mill" from the following:

A...site contains information how site pattering reflects historic functional requirements, but parts of the site have been destroyed. The site is not eligible for its information potential if a comparison of other...sites reveals more intact properties with complete information.

This comparative information potential has long been part of how Register eligibility has been evaluated for archaeological sites. For example, the Advisory Council for Historic Preservation's (1991) *Treatment of Archeological Properties* noted (p.30):

The importance of information which a property may yield must be evaluated within an appropriate comparative context – i.e., what is already known from similar properties

or other pertinent information sources. The information likely to be obtained from a particular property may be important if, for a given area, the information is unavailable elsewhere; or because it would confirm or supplement in an important way information obtained from other sources. In some cases, however, the existence of other information sources ... may render the information contained within the property less important, with the result that the property will not be eligible under Criterion D.

Advisory Council on Historic Preservation. 1991. *Treatment of Archeological Properties: A Handbook.* National Park Service, U.S. Department of the Interior, Washington, D.C.

National Park Service. 1995. *How to Apply the National Register Criteria.* National Register Bulletin 15. National Park Service, Washington, D.C. (http://www.cr.nps.gov/nr/bulletins/nr15_8.html)

Parker, Patricia L., and Thomas F. King. 1995. *Guidelines for Evaluating and Documenting Traditional Cultural Properties.* National Register Bulletin. National Park Service, Washington, D.C. (http://www.cr.nps.gov/nr/bulletin.html)

Plan mandated by Section 101, although arguments additional to the state plan also serve. The practicing archaeologist will most often be thinking in terms of criterion [d].

INTEGRITY is a complex topic. Broadly, it means remaining as physically true as possible to the reasons why the property is eligible for the National Register. Often, this means that the site, structure, or whatever is undisturbed or unaltered relative to currently known examples (see box "Integrity"). For archaeological sites, this is not only an issue of being physically intact, but also an issue of the data potential being comparatively undisturbed. For example, a plowed Mississippian site probably would not be seen as having sufficient integrity for listing on the National Register, since there are a large number of less disturbed Mississippian sites known and excavated, *ceteris paribus*. However, a plowed Paleoindian site in the eastern United States may well be seen as having sufficient integrity to be considered significant, since examples of such sites, plowed or not, are not common (see also National Park Service 1995).

36 CFR 60.4 *criteria considerations* set forth criteria for what can and cannot be listed. For example, a church as a religious property cannot be listed, nor a cemetery as a cemetery (although, if the cemetery somehow has unique and representative structures within it, or if the church is an excellent and unique example of architecture or design, then they might be eligible based upon *those* reasons of "distinctive characteristics of a type"). This is also true for buildings that have been moved from their original locations or structures that have been substantially refurbished, both cases obviously violating basic integrity. Properties "that have achieved significance within the past 50 years" generally also are excluded.

There are exceptions. For example, a relocated building, or even a building completely rebuilt, may be considered eligible if it is unique to its type and the considerations are based upon architectural merit and/or the absence of anything else. The Governor's Mansion in Colonial Williamsburg is a good example: Only the foundation of the structure remained when excavations were done in the 1930s. The structure standing today was built on site in the 1930s and is a reconstruction based upon period drawings and written descriptions.

Structures less than 50 years old can be included "if...of exceptional importance" (see 36 CFR Part 65, NHPA Section 110 (f), and 36 CFR 800.10; see also section 2.3.2.2. below).

By the way, ships and aircraft can be considered eligible, although we ourselves are never sure if it is for being historic objects or for being historic structures. [36CFR 60.3 (j) treats ships as "objects."] The B-29 *Enola Gay*, during its residence and restoration in

Maryland, was listed by the State of Maryland as a historic structure, not object, and was considered eligible for listing on the National Register. And this was in the late 1980s, well before its 50th anniversary.[2]

It must be remembered that the Section 106 Process, and procedures similar to it, are not meant to stop construction or development. Rather, they are meant to provide enough of a pause where cultural resources can be assessed and, if found to be of interest to society writ large, either avoided entirely or recorded in sufficient detail *before* being compromised. The National Register is only a list meant to alert agencies. Just because something is eligible for listing or actually is listed on the National Register, does not mean that it cannot be destroyed; it just means that sufficient information must be collected about the structure or site, such that its continued existence is redundant, before it is destroyed.[3] This often confuses the non-professional historic preservation community as well as the engineering/development community.

2.2.2.3. The Parties in the Section 106 Process

The Section 106 Process is a consulting process in the sense of "seeking, discussing, and considering the views" of those immediately involved in what is going on [36 CFR 800.16 (f)]. The regulations identify six sets of CONSULTING PARTIES who must be included by the Federal agency in the Process if affected by it [36 CFR 800.2 (c)].

The first consulting party will be the State Historic Preservation Office[r] or SHPO. As mentioned above, the SHPO is the apologist for cultural resources within the particular state, commonwealth, territory, or protectorate.

The second consulting party is the Tribal Historic Preservation Office[r] or THPO. The THPO is the official representative of affected Indian tribes for the

---

2. The first B-29 was not produced until late in 1942; the *Enola Gay* was assembled in 1944. Its listing on the Register is due entirely to its use in dropping the first atomic bomb. Still, its Register-eligibility is interesting: The aircraft itself, donated by the Air Force to the Smithsonian, was not all in one piece. Rather, it consisted of several pieces that were re-assembled into a whole for purposes of display. A question of integrity would be here, we would think: If the *Enola Gay* cannot fly, does it still have integrity? By the way, as a B-29, it has very little integrity: All of the defensive gun emplacements except for the tail position were removed before its flight to Japan. Those who flew B-29s might also argue that the failure of the engines -- especially the number three engine -- to burst into flames for absolutely no reason at all also would raise questions about the *Enola Gay*'s integrity as a real B-29.

3. We use the term "redundant" in the sense of physical existence or information content. We recognize that such a term leaves out certain values of a site, such as importance to descendent cultural communities, especially aboriginal communities.

purposes of Section 106. The THPO is involved as a consulting party in the Section 106 Process only when tribal lands are somehow affected [36 CFR 800.3 (c)]. The THPO may, on tribal lands, also function in a role of SHPO [36 CFR 800.2 (c) (2) (i)].

The third consulting part will be any Indian tribe or Native Hawai'ian organization that attaches religious or ceremonial importance to a Register-eligible property affected by the proposed undertaking [36 CFR 800.2 (c) (3), especially 36 CFR 800.2 (c) (3) (iv)]].

Federal agencies are specifically instructed [36 CFR 800.2 (c) (3) (i)] to make sure that Indian tribes and Native Hawai'ian organizations have a chance to comment on the effects of a proposed undertaking when it could potentially affect culturally sensitive or important properties.

The fourth consulting party is the local government within whose jurisdiction the undertaking will occur. There are situations in which the local government may assume the Section 106 role of the Federal agency, in lieu of that agency (e.g., Community Development Block Grant Program), but that is a detail beyond the scope of the discussion here (see instead King 1998, 2000a).

The fifth consulting party is the applicant for Federal funding or permit (phrased in 36 CFR 800.2 (c) (5) as "applicant for Federal assistance") whose project may be caught up in all of this. Note that while that individual or organization may be a consulting party by virtue of a Federal enabling action, the agency enabling that action -- that undertaking -- still assumes responsibility for the Section 106 Process. Phrased another way: Regardless of who actually does the work, and who actually will be altering the landscape, the Federal agency has sole and total responsibility for compliance with Section 106.

The last set of consulting parties are any others that may have a demonstrated legal or economic interest in the undertaking or the affected cultural resources that are eligible for listing -- or already are listed -- on the National Register.

The regulations make considerable allowance for the input of consulting parties. The Federal agency is charged with involving those parties in the Section 106 Process. However, as with the pre-1999 Section 106 Process, only two parties -- the Federal agency along with one consulting party: The SHPO and/or the THPO -- have any real authority in deciding whether or not something is going to be done. This is reflected in later stages in the Process, where it is clear that historic properties will be adversely affected. We will come back to this in a bit, but at that point there are only two entities that can sign-off on the plans to offset those adverse effects: The Federal agency and the SHPO/THPO. While the views of other consulting parties may be solicited and, in the case of a disagreement between the agency and SHPO/THPO, be taken into account by the ACHP as it casts its third and deciding vote, generally no consulting party beyond the SHPO/THPO has much statutory power to directly alter events. But we will come back to that.

In most situations, though, the practicing archaeologist will be dealing with two principal parties, the Federal agency and the SHPO/THPO.

The Advisory Council on Historic Preservation

The Advisory Council on Historic Preservation (the ACHP or the Council) serves as an independent, policy-advising agency to the Federal government, specifically the President and Congress. The 19-member Council consists of

* the Secretary of the Interior
* the Secretary of Agriculture
* four heads of Federal agencies appointed by the President
* the Architect of the Capitol
* one governor
* one mayor
* Chair of the National Trust for Historic Preservation
* President of the National Conference of State Historic Preservation Officers
* four experts in historic preservation, appointed by the President
* four general members of the public, also appointed by the President

Members drawn from the public serve four-year terms; other presidential appointees serve for as long as the President wants them.

Originally, the ACHP met four times a year. Those 10 members who are not government employees receive a $50 per diem when they gather in Washington, D.C. (United States Government 1992:138; Federal contracting requirements required at that time per diem reimbursements of $80 for employees working on the East Coast); they must cover their transportation to and from the meetings. The frequency of meetings came under Congressional review in the early 1990s, with the suggestion that the number be reduced to once a year to reduce government expenses.

The ACHP has a permanent staff with offices in Washington, D.C., and in Colorado. The ACHP provides a publication series on historic preservation procedures, excellent training programs (in conjunction with the General Services Administration), along with Section 106 project reviews.

2.2.2.4.   Steps along the Way: The Process

The Section 106 Process is described in 36 CFR 800 Subpart B [**36 CFR 800.3 - 800.13**; see Appendix A]. The intent here is to set the role of the practicing archaeologist into the larger context of that process. It is best to start with an annotated outline of the Section 106 Process. After that we want to describe what the practicing archaeologist will be doing relative to the steps in that process.

36 CFR 800.3 - 800.5 set out the following steps for the Section 106 Process (see Figure 2.3.):

1. The agency first needs to determine if there is an undertaking and, if so, if there is any chance that it could have an effect on historic properties. If there is no such chance, the Section 106 Process ends at this point.

2. If the undertaking has the potential to cause effects, then the agency needs to:

    2.1.   identify the appropriate SHPO/THPO;
    2.2.   identify other consulting parties;
    2.3.   develop a plan to involve the public;
    2.4.   review existing information on historic properties potentially affected by the undertaking, as well as the likelihood for as-yet unknown or unidentified historic properties being present within the area of potential effects; and
    2.5.   consult with the SHPO/THPO on what else might be needed to be known or done.

3. Next, the agency determines the scope of identification efforts needed, including the area of potential effects as well as what information is available about historic properties or potential historic properties within that area. This will include soliciting information from the consulting parties. It is also to include contact with Indian tribes and Native Hawai'ian organizations on properties "of religious or cultural significance," even if those may be located off of tribal or native lands.

4. If, after the process so far, it seems like a good idea to physically check the area of the undertaking for historic properties, then the Federal agency in consultation with the SHPO/THPO will "make a reasonable and good faith effort to carry out appropriate identification efforts" [**36CFR 800.4 (b)(1)**]. For the practicing archaeologist, this would be part of the Phase I identification process (see Chapter 5).[4]

5. The cultural resources identified in Steps 3 and 4 are to be evaluated, by the Federal agency and in consultation with the SHPO/THPO "and any Indian tribe or Native Hawai'ian organization that attaches religious and cultural significance" to that resource [**36 CFR 800.4 (c)(1)**], to see if they are eligible for listing on the National Register (assess the resource in terms of its eligibility for listing, 36 CFR 60.4). For the practicing archaeologist, this may be part of a Phase II testing investigation, although it also is possible that the Phase I survey investigation failed to locate any archaeological materials that could be considered eligible for listing on the National Register.

    Note, though, that it will be the Federal agency alone that will determine Register eligibility. The SHPO/THPO and, if involved, the Indian tribe or Native Hawai'ian organizations will either agree or disagree.

    5.1.   If the agency, the SHPO/THPO, and, if involved, the Indian tribe or Native Hawai'ian organization agree that the properties are eligible, then the properties will be treated, for the purposes of the Section 106 Process, if they actually are listed on the National Register.

    5.2.   If the agency and either the SHPO/THPO or the Indian tribe/Native Hawai'ian organization disagree about the eligibility of the properties, then the ACHP will be consulted. When the disagreement is between the agency and the SHPO/THPO, it is the agency that asks for ACHP determination. When it involves a native group -- and this can only be in situations where the involved property has "religious or cultural significance" -- it is that group that must ask the ACHP [**36 CFR 800.4 (c)(2)**].

    5.3.   If the SHPO/THPO does not respond to the agency's conclusions, then the SHPO/THPO is presumed to agree with the agency ("Agree without Comment").

---

4.   There are three levels of field investigations: Phase I identification, a good-faith effort to see if Register-eligible cultural resources might be present; Phase II testing, evaluation of Register-eligibility of resources not excluded during the first step; and Phase III data recovery, mitigation of adverse effects usually by full-scale excavation.

The terms for these levels or steps vary between the eastern and western parts of the country. For the eastern and most of the midwestern United States, terms like "Phase I" or "Phase II" will be used. In the western United States and in some parts of the Midwest, descriptive terms like "identification," "reconnaissance and intensive survey," "testing," or "evaluation," drawn from the Secretary of the Interior's Guidelines, will be used. We think it preferable for the profession to use the Phase-designations, both because they are more commonly used and widely recognized, and because they imply a sequential series of evaluative steps. However, we try to use both sets of terms through the text here.

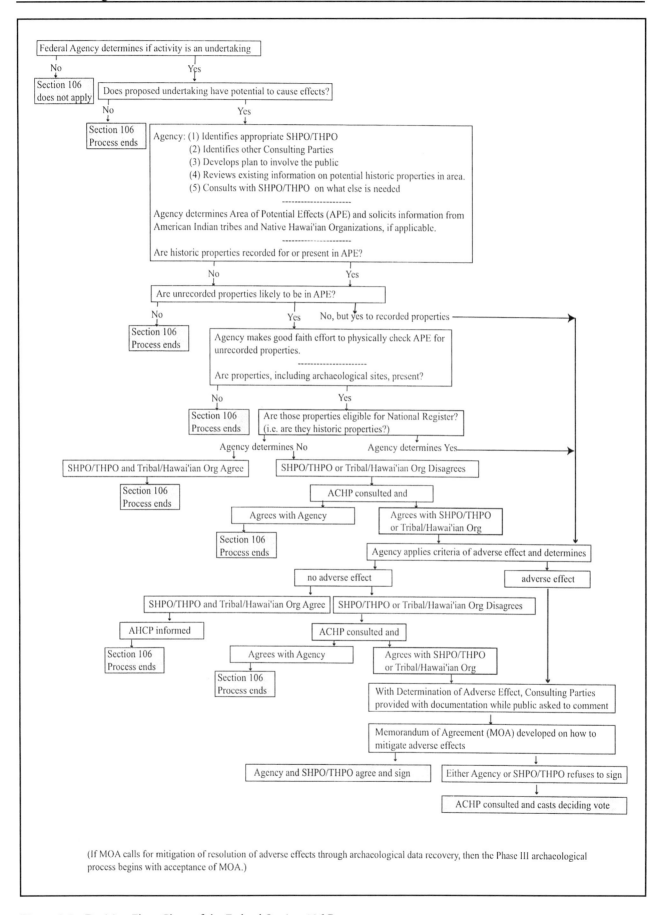

Figure 2.3. Decision Flow-Chart of the Federal Section 106 Process.

6. If no cultural resources were identified during Step 4, or if the cultural resources identified were not considered eligible for listing on the National Register, documentation of those results are given to the SHPO/THPO. Since those results would have come from the procedures agreed to in Step 5, the SHPO/THPO will have to agree that nothing eligible for listing on the National Register was present. The results are supposed to be made available to the public writ large but in any case the agency's responsibilities for Section 106 are considered fulfilled and the process ends.

7. If historic properties -- that is, cultural resources eligible for listing on the National Register -- were identified or assessed as such during Step 5, then the effects of the undertaking on the properties will be determined (that is, the Criteria of Adverse Effect will be applied [**36 CFR 800.5 (a)**]). It is at this point that the possible differences in interpretation between the agency, the SHPO/THPO, and the other consulting parties come to the fore, with a series of procedural steps outlined for each contingency.

   7.1 If the agency concludes that there will be no adverse effect, and if the SHPO/THPO agrees, then the ACHP must receive documentation summarizing that conclusion as well as the concurrence of the SHPO/THPO. The agency's Section 106 responsibilities end at this point. If the SHPO/THPO or one of the other consulting parties does not concur, the ACHP must receive the documentation for a 30-day review period while the agency notifies the SHPO/THPO.

   7.2 If the agency concludes that there will be an adverse effect, then the agency must notify the ACHP and work with the SHPO/THPO as well as the involved consulting parties to find a way to avoid or reduce those effects. The agency, the SHPO/THPO, or another consulting party can ask the ACHP to participate, although its participation does not need the invitation of any party.

An adverse effect means that there is a Register-eligible cultural resource whose character will be substantially changed as a byproduct of the Federally enabled undertaking. It is for this contingency that the Section 106 Process was designed: There is something out there that society probably would want to know more about before it is destroyed or greatly altered. Now, given that, come, let us reason together to find a way to satisfy society's desires while at the same time allowing the undertaking to proceed.

With a finding of adverse effect, all interested parties are invited to participate as consulting parties *should they so request* [**36 CFR 800.5 (e) (1)**]. All consulting parties are provided, by the agency, with the documentation so far compiled. The public is invited to comment as well at this stage.

The decision process is a somewhat convoluted two-sided arrangement. One side involves the Federal agency. The other side most often only involves the SHPO/THPO. The SHPO/THPO has the capacity to act, to induce action within the process. However, on that same side are the other consulting parties in addition to the SHPO/THPO: the Indian tribes and Native Hawai'ian organizations, the local governments, and the parties directly involved with the undertaking. They have power within the Process at this point only if they choose to speak out. Otherwise, it is a two-party interaction between the Federal agency and the SHPO/THPO, with the ACHP available to break any difference of opinion.

In reality, the agency controls the fate of the Register-eligible cultural resource -- the historic property -- while the SHPO/THPO, on the other side, is concerned about the fate of that resource, which they are charged to protect on behalf of the citizens of the state or the members of the tribe/native people. In the vast, vast majority of cases, the agency and SHPO/THPO work out a solution that takes the adverse effects into account -- project redesign, data recovery, whatever. In some situations, the ACHP may be invited to participate in that agreement.

With a determination of adverse effect, the agency and the SHPO/THPO work out then sign a MEMORANDUM OF AGREEMENT or MOA (if the ACHP is not a signatory, it must be sent a copy of the MOA; it has 30 days in which to respond). The agency, the SHPO/THPO, and the ACHP acting on behalf of the SHPO/THPO are the only signatories with the authority to execute, amend, or end the agreement [**36 CFR 800.6 (c)(1)**]. Other of the consulting parties may be -- and often should be -- invited to sign the MOA ("invited signatories"). However, their concurrence with or signing of the MOA is not needed, and refusal to sign does not invalidate the MOA.

There are cases where one of the two parties -- the SHPO/THPO or the agency -- refuses to sign an MOA. In these situations, the agency can request comment from the ACHP, which must respond in 60 days. The ACHP gathers in the existing documentation, as well as any additional documentation that the agency can provide (including arranging on-site inspections/visits). The ACHP, having considered the information in the absence of an MOA, then provides its comments to the agency, with copies going to the SHPO.

What if there is further challenge to this? Say, for example, the SHPO/THPO refused comment out of whatever concern it had or whatever friction it experienced over the years with the agency. Further, say there was equal distrust by the public in the agency's conclusions, but the ACHP, after careful evaluation, found that the agency had correctly assessed the situation. What then?

If the ACHP concurs, the agency is advised to reconsider its findings. However, the ACHP's inquiry does not suspend the undertaking. Instead, it may refer the matter to the Secretary of the Interior.

For the practicing archaeologist, one outcome from Step 7 may be the agreement that the only way to avoid the adverse effect on the archaeological site is to recover sufficient data from the threatened part such that its physical existence is redundant. In the context of the Process, full-scale archaeological excavation of a Register-eligible site is seen to be a way to avoid or mitigate an adverse effect. This, then, would be Phase III data recovery or mitigation (see Chapter 7).

Enforcement and Penalties

What happens if the Section 106 Process is not followed? Neither NHPA nor its procedural regulations 36 CFR Part 800 provides statutory penalties. Rather, enforcement is based upon civil suits for failure to comply. Suits for non-compliance may be brought by any group. For example, when the Transco Incident occurred, the Alabama SHPO filed suit, as did the FERC since the failure of Transco's archaeology vendor placed FERC in a state of non-compliance with Section 106. The subcontracting archaeologist in effect is part of the hiring firm from the perspective of the Agency and the SHPO. One assumes Transco filed suit against the archaeology firm, or against its bond.

Information on enforcement and penalties is available in:

Kanefield, Adina W. 1996. *Federal Historic Preservation Case Law, 1966-1996: Thirty Years of the National Historic Preservation Act*. A Special Report Funded in Part by the United States Army Environmental Center/Advisory Council on Historic Preservation, U.S. Government Printing Office, Washington, D.C.

2.2.2.5.   Re-examination and Comment in Detail on the Section 106 Process

The elegant balance and simplicity of the Process should be evident at this point. Contrary to the fears -- and sometimes the continued lack of understanding and suspicion -- about the research integrity of private-sector archaeology, there is in fact a check and balance built into the process. The archaeologist may

indeed be tempted to cut slack for the client, but the agency review archaeologists quite likely will catch any irregularity in the report, or in the immediate step afterwards when materials from the project are turned over to the agency. Again, the agency may be tempted to ignore or undervalue the importance of the cultural resources in a project area. The SHPO or THPO, though, with its intimate knowledge of cultural-historical patterns within the state or on tribal lands, normally will catch such an irregularity. Indeed, in some states, the SHPO intentionally maintains an adversarial relationship with Federal agencies in order to better execute its role as an apologist for the state's cultural resources.

The following presents the Section 106 Process from the vantage of the practicing archaeologist.

First Part: What Already Is Known

The first step in the Section 106 Process for the practicing archaeologist is to learn what cultural resources are already known to be present. This is part of the identification process. If Federal properties are involved, this information should have been compiled by the agency, as directed in Section 110. In reality, the scale of the exercise, combined with the cut-back since 1975 in the Federal work force and budgets, has delayed this. It is not unusual for Federal agencies to subcontract private archaeology/architecture firms to conduct an inventory of their properties. One of the largest such projects, the Legacy Project, has involved the HABS/HAER documentation of all standing structures on Federal military installations. This was in response to Section 110.

In day-to-day situations, where the undertaking is enabled through Federal funding or permits, this step of the Section 106 Process will involve checks of the state's site files as well as basic historic background research (see Chapter 4). The end product may be included in a preliminary situation study, or just as often in the Phase I report.

At this point in the Process, the agency or the client should have provided a map showing the area that will be affected by the anticipated undertaking. (The area of potential effect will have been set by the Lead agency, not by the archaeologists or the property owner.) This enables the practicing archaeologist to assess the geophysical conditions that might have a bearing on archaeological site preservation and/or integrity.

Part of the Section 106 Process involves developing predictive models for locations of archaeological sites and sometimes for all potential cultural resources. Historic or comparatively recent resources may have left signatures on the landscape that can be handled with standard field procedures (see Chapter 5).

Everyone learned about archaeology from that ... The Transco Incident

The Transco Incident, which refers to the $35.5 million settlement reached between the Federal Energy Regulatory Commission (FERC) and the Transco Energy Company (Transco) for cultural resources and pricing violations, best illustrates the implications of proper professional practice in the United States. Failure to execute the procedures in proper order, regardless of good faith, results in enormous penalties. The penalties for professional mistakes are on a scale normally not found in a university setting, but held as perennial threats for malpractice by engineers, architects, lawyers, and physicians.

The following is drawn from reports in *Public Utilities Fortnightly* and the *New York Times*.

In the late 1980s, Transco, a gas pipeline firm based in Houston, sought permits from the Federal Energy Regulatory Commission (FERC) to build a natural gas pipe line from Tampa to Texas. As a Federal undertaking, the corridor project was subject to Section 106 requirements. The Lead agency was FERC. As a condition of the permit, FERC required

Transco to see that the actual Section 106 work was done. This was, after all, a Federally enabled undertaking: FERC was issuing a permit allowing Transco to put in the natural gas pipe line. FERC was required to comply with Section 106 of NHPA before allowing the project to proceed.

Transco contracted an archaeology firm, which we will call NW Associates, Inc., to perform the necessary work to meet Section 106 compliance demands. (The name of the firm has been changed here since, while it soon went out of business after the incidents described below, there are a couple more recent but unrelated firms that have chosen nearly identical names to that of that now-defunct concern.)

The planned corridor went through five states: Florida, Alabama, Mississippi, Louisiana, and Texas. As the reader would quickly guess, each state's SHPO would have authority to review the cultural resources investigation of the proposed pipe line corridor (area of potential effects) through their jurisdiction.

NW Associates undertook the work with the same energy and intensity one would expect of any archaeology firm. The contract was awarded by competitive bid; the bid submitted

addressed specifically the Scope of Work (SOW) as developed by Transco in consultation with FERC and the different state SHPOs. SOWs are work orders, and are reasonably precise in their expectations and requests.

Testing of the pipe line corridor through the 150 miles of Alabama followed the standard procedure. NW Associates performed the expected state site file background check, developed a historic background, examined the overall prehistory, and ran a Phase I reconnaissance and survey program over that 150 miles of south Alabama countryside. The Phase I work encountered cultural resources, including archaeological sites. Some sites, NW Associates concluded, were essentially write-offs, sites not eligible for listing on the National Register. Others, though, seemed to hold promise for Register eligibility. These NW Associates came back to as part of a Phase II testing program.

The Phase II testing program identified a series of sites that, NW Associates informed Transco, appeared eligible for listing on the National Register. Identified, NW Associates proceeded to perform the necessary Phase III data recovery exercises.

However, in situations where the cultural resource is not visible or expected, predicative models are of use.

A predictive model is the first foray of professional archaeology into actuarial archaeology, the logical next step from the predictive modeling alluded to in the Secretary of the Interior's *Guidelines* when discussing Phase I survey procedures. Various physical geographic conditions are taken into account to produce a statement of probability that cultural resources -- most often prehistoric -- will be found within the area delimited. For example, studies in West Virginia, Pennsylvania, and Maryland each indicated that around 85 percent of prehistoric archaeological sites are located within 100 m, and 95 percent within 200 m of a stream with a flow rate over 12 cubic feet per second, and on land with slopes of less than 10 percent. This identifies areas with a high potential for prehistoric archaeological sites. The Federal agency or the client may request development and application of such a model to the situation at hand, should such a model not already exist.

Sometimes as part of this planning process, DISTURBANCE STUDIES are done. Disturbance studies examine the project area and vicinity not only in terms of what physical remains -- archaeological as well as structural -- might be directly affected, but also what previous disturbance has taken place in and immediately adjacent to the project area. Disturbance studies are planning tools that can show what portions of the project area may be disturbed to the point where cultural resources could no longer exist, or exist with any integrity. Disturbance studies are more often needed or used for urban areas, where there has been a history of extensive filling, excavation, and overall land alteration.

Second Part: Phase I (Reconnaissance and Intensive Survey) Investigations

If it is concluded that cultural resources *could be* present, then the next step is to see *if any* cultural resources *are* present. Most Federal agencies as well as

By 1989, NW Associates had assembled its reports, the Phase I survey of the corridor through Alabama, the Phase II reports treating the sites it determined required further investigation, and of course the Phase III reports on those sites that NW Associates determined were eligible for listing on the National Register. The collection of reports was then passed to Transco for submission to FERC.

Stop here. If the entire discussion of the Section 106 Process in the preceding sections has been looked at and understood, then there should be a whole bunch of procedural and statutory authority issues apparent at this point. Found them?

NW Associates completed the cultural resources reports and sent them on to Transco. Transco then sent them on to FERC. FERC passed them on, as a consulting party in the Section 106 Process, to the Alabama SHPO. And the Alabama SHPO hit the ceiling.

NW Associates had failed to follow basic regulatory procedures. Instead of completing a Phase I report and sending it through the chain of command to be reviewed by the Alabama SHPO, then developing a Phase II program in response to the

SHPO's comments, and eventually a Phase III data recovery investigation in response to the SHPO's concurrence with FERC's determination of Register-eligible resources being present within the bounds of the proposed undertaking, it had done all of that itself.

NW Associates had made the determinations of eligibility without consulting with the Alabama SHPO (or with FERC archaeologists). Having made its own determinations, it structured a Phase II program, and again made its decisions. *Then*, it made a decision to take some of the sites to Phase III, all without consulting with the Alabama SHPO.

NW Associates had exceeded its authority. The Alabama SHPO, as defender of the state's cultural resources, was outraged. It filed suit against FERC for failure to comply with NHPA Section 106. FERC, suddenly hammered, turned around and charged Transco with non-compliance with the NHPA.

On 29 May 1991, FERC approved a $35.5 million settlement between Transco and the FERC enforcement section of its Office of General Council. The settlement found, among other things, that Transco

began construction of the pipe line before properly completing National Register eligibility surveys, and that 48 of the 77 Register-eligible sites were lost as a result (Rogers 1991:37).

Of the final settlement, $10 million represented fines associated with marketing and pricing violations unrelated to the historic preservation issues. Another $12 million represented civil penalties ($11 million) and investigation fees associated with the NHPA violations ($ 1 million). The remaining $13.5 million was paid to Alabama for "remediation and future environmental and cultural resource research and protection" (Rogers 1991:37).

There are several lessons here, but the basic one is: Professional, Section 106 archaeology is a no-nonsense world. Mistakes, even procedural errors, carry serious consequences. This is one of the reasons why so much detail is provided in this chapter.

Rogers, Lori M. 1991. FERC hears gas industry concerns, announces Transco settlement. *Public Utilities Fortnightly* 1 July 1991:36-37.

Transco settles claims in Alabama. *New York Times* 31 May 1991:D4.

---

states and firms in the eastern and midwestern United States call this first examination a "Phase I" survey; in some parts of the Midwest as well as over most of the western United States, the terms "reconnaissance survey" or "intensive survey" are used. Those terms come from the Secretary of Interior's Standards and Guidelines (48 FR 44716-44742; see Appendix A). This is a field-evidence identification step, which also will be called "identification."

In archaeology, a Phase I examination involves a surface-subsurface field reconnaissance as well as a historic and prehistoric background check to see if any sites or structures are known for the project area, and if any such sites or structures are listed on the National Register, or even up for nomination. This is the good-faith effort required of 36 CFR 800 to see if properties eligible for listing on the National Register are present within the project area. Historic architectural reconnaissance also is done as part of Phase I. The Phase I survey is capable of EXCLUDING the possibility that a property is Register eligible, usually

because of disturbance or lack of evidence. Phase I work rarely is sufficient to suggest that the property satisfies criteria needed for listing on the National Register. In any case, the Phase I survey results are reviewed by the SHPO/THPO, which receives them in a report submitted by the Lead agency.

This is very important for the practicing archaeologist: The Phase I archaeological report must be sufficient for both the agency and the SHPO/THPO to judge for themselves the merits of the conclusions reached by the practicing archaeologist on behalf of the Lead agency. "Sufficient" means structured in the way that the agency and the SHPO/THPO need the cultural resources information at this particular stage of the Section 106 Process, nothing more or less. The archaeologist is serving really as someone else's eyes; the information presented not only needs to be clear, it needs to answer all of Section 106 questions the Lead agency and especially the SHPO/THPO need answered to make their determinations. Anything more is really superfluous at this point.

The SHPO has the final say, in a sense; in any case, they must be able to respond before any further work, much less construction or property transfer, is done. That is, both the SHPO and the Lead agency must be in agreement about the results of the work before any of the activities prompting the Section 106 Process continue beyond this step.

Chapter 5 covers how the archaeological Phase I survey investigation is done and level of detail needed.

It is possible that the Phase I investigations either did not find anything, or what was found clearly would not satisfy the criteria for being listed on the National Register. In that situation, if the SHPO concurs, the Section 106 Process ends.

Third Part: Phase II (Testing) Investigations

Further work will be needed if the Phase I reconnaissance/intensive survey results found or identified cultural resources, but it was not clear if those resources failed to satisfy criteria for listing on the National Register. This next stage will be called by most Federal agencies as well as states in the eastern and midwestern United States Phase II testing or evaluation. In the western United States as well as some parts of the Midwest, the term "testing" or "evaluation" will be used instead of Phase II.

The purpose of Phase II testing is to assess whether the site or structure could be listed on the National Register. For the practicing archaeologist, the purpose usually is to see if the deposit has integrity, and to get some sense of its data potential. That is, if the Phase I survey results could not exclude a property from being eligible for listing on the National Register, the Phase II testing results must be sufficient to decide one way or another. Phase II field work provides a feel for the nature of the deposit, should the issue involve subsurface remains. This is important should work need to continue beyond Phase II to full data recovery.

Again, the Phase II testing results are reviewed by the SHPO/THPO, which receives them in a report submitted by the Lead agency. The report must be sufficiently detailed to enable the SHPO/THPO to judge for itself the merits of the conclusions reached by the archaeologist on behalf of the Lead agency. The SHPO/THPO has the final say, in a sense; in any case, they must be able to respond before any further work, much less construction or property transfer, is done.

As with Phase I, both the SHPO/THPO and the Lead agency must agree about the results of the work before any of the activities prompting the Section 106 Process continue beyond this step. For all practical purposes, the Phase II testing stage is still one seeking to establish if cultural resources eligible for listing on the National Register exist within the bounds of the project area.

Chapter 6 covers how the archaeological Phase II testing investigations are set up and executed.

It is possible that the Phase II investigation will conclude that the cultural materials would not be eligible for listing on the National Register. If the SHPO/THPO and other consulting parties concur, then the Section 106 Process ends at this point for the agency, which only needs to submit the final report on the Phase II testing investigation.

However, if the Phase II investigation found that the cultural materials would indeed be eligible for listing on the National Register, then the procedures become more formal and deliberate. This is what the Section 106 Process, and really all of the NHPA, exists to handle: Balancing the needs of society with respect to cultural resources that it considers very important -- historic properties -- against the equally legitimate needs of society to have the proposed undertaking completed.

Fourth Part: Determination of Adverse Effect

The fourth part of the Section 106 Process as it is experienced by the practicing archaeologist is the agency's determination of if there will be an adverse effect from the undertaking. If the effect will be adverse, this part of the process will result in the composing and signing of a MEMORANDUM OF AGREEMENT or MOA, ideally between the agency and the SHPO/THPO, agreeing on the measures appropriate for dealing with -- that is, for resolving -- the pending adverse effect. Determination of adverse effect is done by the Lead agency in consultation with the SHPO/THPO and other parties.

A Memorandum of Agreement (MOA) will be executed in situations where there are Register-eligible properties present within the area of potential effects, and those properties will be adversely affected by the undertaking as currently envisioned. The MOA will outline how the agency plans to resolve those adverse effects. Ideally, those plans are formulated in consultation with the SHPO/THPO and any other consulting parties. Normally, only the agency and the SHPO/THPO are signatories on the MOA.

The MOA outlines what both parties agree to about the next step in the process, and what will be needed to complete the next step in the process. This also protects both the agency and the SHPO/THPO, not so much because current personnel are duplicitous, but because the personnel within the offices and agencies may change. We experienced one situation where the MOA was worked out between the state and the agency, then the state's archaeological regulator left, as did the agency's historic preservation officer, and new people had to deal with the undertaking, one that we had contracted into under the previous persons. The new SHPO personnel initially wanted to revamp the entire exercise agreed to in the MOA; the MOA protected our client's interests. Actually, it also protected the society's, since it avoided the down-time of having to go back and re-negotiate (and re-educate).

The practicing archaeologist probably will be a direct contributor to the details of the MOA, since the agency will be using the professional archaeologist's expertise to formulate a plan that best satisfies the SHPO's/THPO's desire to off-set the adverse effect of the undertaking while preserving the goals of the undertaking. In a professional setting, the SHPO/THPO and practicing archaeologist also will be in communication -- as they should have been throughout the process -- in the developing process of designing a solution that is best for the cultural resource.

At the end of the Phase II testing report, or at least before the MOA is finalized, a TREATMENT or DATA RECOVERY PLAN for Phase III (full, formal archaeological excavation) will be developed for the archaeological site. For some Federal agencies, the Data Recovery Plan will be let under such a heading as a separate contract, with its own Scope of Work and its own Request for Proposals (see Chapter 3). For other agencies, or under other circumstances, the Scope of Work for the Phase II testing may well include a request to develop a Phase III Treatment or Data Recovery Plan; one can conclude from such a request either that the Phase I survey results were unequivocal in their indications that the archaeological deposit probably would satisfy the quality of significance as set for by 36 CFR 60.4, or that properties already known to be eligible if not already listed on the Register are within the area of potential effects, and Phase I only served to confirm presence and site boundaries.

The Data Recovery Plan will review the nature of the undertaking and its anticipated effects, the previous work done on the site, and the reason why the site is significant (*sensu stricti*). It will then set out the basic research issues involved, then outline the research design that will be followed to achieve those research goals. The Data Recovery Plan will be formulated in consultation with the SHPO/THPO and with agency archaeologists; at times, it is politically wise to involve regional academic archaeologists in the design process as well.

At this stage of the undertaking -- the project, from the archaeologist's perspective -- the options to reduce or avoid the adverse effects are, conceptually, several, but practically, very few. Those options would include:

*   abandoning the undertaking;
*   redesigning the undertaking (many different sub-options); or

*   recording the historic property -- that imperiled, Register-eligible cultural resource -- in such a way that its continued existence, or at least the continued existence of the portion that is about to be lost, is redundant.

Ideally, all of the options have been considered by the agency, the SHPO/THPO, and the other consulting parties, and should have been presented for comment at public hearings. The most that any recordation exercise will cost the agency will be one percent of the overall project budget; that limit was set by the Archaeological and Historic Preservation Act. Thus, it may be cost-effective to underwrite the third option, which archaeologically represents what is called Phase III data recovery or mitigation (because it mitigates the adverse effects of the undertaking).

Fifth Part: Phase III (Data Recovery/Mitigation) Investigations

Phase III, also called "mitigation" and "data recovery," is the ultimate, final step in the Section 106 Process as far as the practicing archaeologist is concerned. Phase III data recovery occurs when the cultural resources are listed or considered eligible for listing on the National Register, and there is no way for the undertaking to avoid compromising the integrity of the resource. It is the responsibility of the Federal agency at this point to "mitigate the adverse effects" of the undertaking. (Sometimes the best choice is to do nothing and sacrifice the site. At times the needs of society that will be satisfied by the undertaking take precedence over data recovery from a Register-eligible site.)

The Section 106 Process requires that a Federal agency take into account any adverse effects caused by the proposed undertaking. The implication is that the agency is to make a good faith effort to avoid adverse effects. If those effects cannot be avoided, then they are at least to be minimized. This is really a language, grammatical issue. It is seen to be that because such effects can be avoided either by redesigning the project to avoid the impacts on the cultural resources, or by actually excavating or otherwise thoroughly recording the cultural resources. With the archaeological site or historic structure adequately recorded, the adverse effect of its physical destruction is to some extent off-set because it has been preserved, albeit in recorded form. The adverse effects of the undertaking on historic properties would have been mitigated.

Phase III often is called "mitigation." MITIGATION can be done in two basic ways: The cultural resource is somehow avoided, either through redesign or abandonment of the undertaking; or the information content of the resource is recorded to the point where the existence of the resource, or the portion that will be damaged, is redundant. Once more, it must always be remembered that the Section 106 Process is not meant to halt construction or impede any kind of undertaking. Rather, the Section 106 Process serves to make sure significant resources are recorded before being destroyed or severely altered.

For architectural features, Phase III mitigation will include the HABS/HAER Process (HABS: Historic American Buildings Survey; HAER: Historic Architecture and Engineering Recordation; see 48 FR 44730 in Appendix A).[5] In essence, the HABS/HAER Process produces enough detailed information that anyone, any time in the future, could reconstruct an exact replica of the structure. This, by the way, underscores the importance of how the object appears, versus any physical association -- accumulated *mana*, in anthropological terms -- that would be concordant with the quintessentially American hagiolatry of venerating relics simply because they are old.

For archaeology, Phase III mitigation usually is full-scale archaeological excavation. In many respects, this is identical to the set-piece full-scale excavations taught in colleges and universities. However, it differs somewhat in its intent, which is to make the continued existence of the about-to-be-compromised cultural resource redundant. It also differs in the limits of its execution, limits that are physical (only within the physical boundaries of the area of potential effects and no more) and to some extent analytical (there is a finite budget and a very real schedule that MUST be met; the purpose is to deal directly with questions that make the site significant, and not pursue exciting although tangential issues; this can be done by someone else in the future using the field notes, artifacts, and prepared report). The entire research plan would have been set out once as part of the Data Recovery Plan, and again within the Scope of Work produced by the agency or the client, so there should be no confusion over when the expected research has been completed. The Phase III stage also is formalized

for the practicing archaeologist, and has limits for the agency, which we will deal with in a moment.

Chapter 7 covers the essentials of the Phase III data recovery process from the needs of the professional.

2.2.3. Additional Factors and Agency Regulations

There are a series of controls on the Section 106 Process, meant to handle the vagaries of life, that can be mentioned at this point (see also ACHP 1991 *Treatment of Archeological Properties: A Handbook*).

Funding Limitations

How much does the Lead agency have to spend on all of this? Where does the money come from?

The Archeological and Historic Preservation Act of 1974 (Moss-Bennett Act; P.L. 93-291) stipulated that the Lead agency was obligated to pay only up to one percent of the Federal funds provided for the project for the entire Section 106 process. Thus, for the Lock Haven Local Flood Control Project, which was done in the late 1980s and early 1990s, with a total project cost of $134 million, the Corps of Engineers had only to pay up to $1.34 million on cultural resources work. That becomes a finite pie; in the Lock Haven case the SHPO, by requiring extensive Phase I and Phase II work, caused the Corps to "use" the entirety of that "budget" before all of the Register-eligible properties that would suffer adverse effects from the undertaking could be handled. The funding limit provides the moneys to actualize the Section 106 Process, but protects the agency and the public from situations where the SHPO wishes to explore research issues beyond the intent of the Process.

Review Time

After the Lead agency has submitted its report at each stage to the SHPO/THPO, the SHPO/THPO has 30 days to respond. The clock starts when the SHPO/THPO feels that the information provided to it is adequate. Failure to respond at the end of that time defaults to an "Agreement without Comment." This avoids ploys that would delay or cancel undertakings without cultural resource justification. Without a deadline, the SHPO/THPO would have too much veto power; the "individual," in this case the state, being able to dictate its interests at the expense of the greater society, represented by the Federal agency.

Professional Qualifications

Section 106 and state/local counterpart legislation require that all undertakings involving public monies,

---

5. HABS/HAER in effect involves developing the blueprints and design drawings for existing structures so that they could be rebuilt. With an existing building, this is essentially taking an architect, a tape measure, and a notebook and doing all of the design drawings in reverse. More to it, of course, but you should get the idea. With the HABS/HAER process, the structure could disappear, but there would be sufficient documentation to rebuild it pretty much as it was before being lost.

One immediately thinks of the Governor's Mansion in Williamsburg, and how the HABS/HAER process would have been influenced by the experience they faced having only a structure's foundation and a set of rather minimalist renderings of a structure from which to reconstruct an entire residence. That probably entered into the arguments, but the core reasons for HABS/HAER were World War II and Philadelphia.

Awareness of what had happened to London during the Nazi Blitz prompted civic leaders in Philadelphia in 1942 to prepare for devastation of the eastern seaboard. That concern in turn led to an effort to record nationally important structures, like Liberty Hall, in detail sufficient such that its destruction during war-time bombing would be off-set by having plans sufficiently detailed for the demolished building to be accurately rebuilt (Hosmer 1981:767-771). It is from this that HABS/HAER recording emerged.

lands, or permits, have to be evaluated for their impact to Register-eligible properties before the undertaking can begin. NHPA required the governor of each state to appoint a State Historic Preservation Officer (SHPO) and devise a state plan. "Significance" in effect connotes eligibility for listing on the National Register; the criteria are in 36 CFR 60.4: Integrity + a-d. So, who is going to do all of this anyway?

Who could do the work was stipulated in 36 CFR 61 Appendix A as well as in The Secretary of the Interior's Guidelines [48 FR 44738-44739]. Under some Federal contracts, field workers must have a BA or BS in anthropological archaeology or a closely related field. This seems to vary by agency. However, for all Section 106 projects the principal investigator ("professional archaeologists" in the phrasing of 36 CFR 61) must have

* at least an MA or MS in anthropological archaeology or closely related field;
* one year of full-time professional experience or equivalent in training in archaeological research, administration, or management;
* at least four months full-time supervised experience in North American archaeology; and
* demonstrated ability, such as a completed graduate thesis or published reports, to carry research on to completion.

Further, a professional in prehistoric archaeology must have at least one year of full-time supervisory experience in the study of prehistoric archaeological resources. A professional in historical archaeology must have the same amount and kind of experience in the study of historical archaeological resources.

Field Work Requirements and Professional Standards

The expectations, guidelines, and requirements for archaeological field work and reporting are contained in three documents:

* "Archeology and Historic Preservation; Secretary of the Interior's Standards and Guidelines" [48 FR 44716-44742; see Appendix A];

* Proposed 36 CFR 66: "Recovery of Scientific, Prehistoric, Historic and Archeological Data: Methods, Standards and Reporting Requirements (Proposed Guidelines)" [42 FR 5374-5479]; and

* Advisory Council on Historic Preservation *Manual of Mitigation Measures (MOMM).*

These documents outline expectations for data collection, analysis, and report preparation. The guidelines include archaeological and architectural investigations. It is beyond the scope of this text to

detail these. Generally, the guidelines are synonymous with the expectations of ethical research as set forth by the governing professional associations in North American archaeology (Society for American Archaeology) and architectural history.

Professional Certification

Archaeology is at an interesting point in its development as a field in the United States. Historically an academic and museum field, it has become over the last 20 years an extra-academic, practiced profession. This is starting to raise questions of credentialing and certification.

Most fields that involve a commitment of public resources or public well-being to an individual's professional judgment are licensed. Thus, engineers, architects, geologists, nurses, physicians, accountants, land surveyors, beauticians, lawyers, and so on are required by different states to obtain a license. Getting the license requires the candidate to pass a specific test or series of tests, and for many fields, also serve a period of apprenticeship or internship prior to taking those tests. Some fields require a course of training as well, engineering and in some states medicine being examples. Even with a medical degree or a law degree, most states will not allow the person to practice until a series of board or certification exams have been passed.

Archaeology is not a credentialed, certified field. At least not yet. However, proto-certification programs have emerged in different states to accomplish this same end, requiring that to practice archaeology within the state the archaeologist demonstrate past experience practicing archaeology in the state. (True.) The intent is to make sure that the professional archaeologist is familiar with the state's archaeology and therefore is responsive to the needs of the resource. That it also gives a competitive business advantage to local firms has been entirely overlooked by most professional archaeology associations.

Curatorial Requirements

Curatorial standards are set out in 36 CFR Part 79. This, too, was a byproduct of the WPA experience, although in immediate terms it came about more from the inability of many colleges and universities to provide continuing professional-quality curation of materials recovered during Federal-sponsored projects (see especially Trimble and Meyers 1991). Curatorial requirements and overall issues of laboratory processing are treated in Chapter 8.

Reporting Standards

The guidelines for report preparation are part of the legacy from the experience with government-sponsored archaeology during the WPA. The profession has come to recognize that the most important issue is not so much curation of artifacts as it is preparation of field notes and compilation of a summary report sufficient in its analysis and detail to allow anyone, at any point in the future, armed only with the report, the field notes, and the artifacts, to work with the data base as if the site was still available. The statutes and guidelines for reporting of archaeological data (see The Secretary of the Interior's Guidelines [48 FR 44738-44739]) probably can be summarized best by saying that they are intended to produce a document that would allow someone entirely unfamiliar with the culture history and environment of the project area to make sense of the work that was done and, given the material recovered and the field records (including both notes and photographs), be able to pick up where the original investigator left off, even two centuries later.

2.3. Additional Regulations and Requirements

2.3.1. The Section 106 Process and the National Environmental Policy Act

The National Environmental Policy Act of 1969 (NEPA) declares a national policy to protect the environment through evaluating proposed Federally enabled actions. The environment is defined to include both natural and cultural resources, giving a valid role for aesthetic considerations in evaluating the quality of the environment (e.g., visual resources, settings). The NEPA is administered by the Council on Environmental Quality (CEQ), which the Act established. The implementing regulations for NEPA were issued in response to Executive Order 11991 by the CEQ in 1978 as 40 CFR parts 1500 - 1508, and were binding as of 30 July 1979. Those regulations also included guidelines for conducting Environmental Assessments (EA) and preparation of Environmental Impact Statements (EIS) (U.S. Council on Environmental Quality 1978).

The NEPA [Section 101 (b) (4)] states that to carry out the policy of NEPA, it is the "responsibility of the Federal Government to use all practicable means" to "preserve important historical, cultural, and natural aspects of our national heritage." Thus, NEPA "expanded the scope of Federal protection to include sites having local or regional importance but lacking a national significance" for projects that required Federal EISs (Rosenberg 1981:768). Section 102 mandates an interdisciplinary approach towards the preparation of each EIS, and directs such statements to include a discussion of "any irreversible and irretrievable commitments of resources."

As a result, a number of items in the NEPA regulations deal with or relate to archaeological resources. For example, 40 CFR 1500.2 (f) directs

Federal agencies to work towards an enhancement of the "quality of the human environment." Section 1502.16 (g) directs an EIS to discuss historic and cultural resources, "including the reuse and conservation potential of various alternatives and mitigation measures." In order to "allow for a calculation of the scope, intensity, and nature" of a proposed action on archaeological resources, an evaluation must be based on "real data about the location, characteristics, and potential of the archaeological resources" (Scovill, Gordon, and Anderson 1977:51). In order to deal with broad or programmatic EIS planning, an inventory based on sampling is required.

Since both NEPA and NHPA deal with cultural resources, how do they relate? The procedures for implementing NEPA relative to NHPA are found in two places: 36 CFR 800.8 and 36 CFR 805. 36 CFR 800.8 (a)(1) recommends, whenever possible, integrating the work required by NHPA with that required by NEPA. This is best done by beginning early in the undertaking to coordinate the requirements of both. However, 36 CFR 800.8 (a) (1) makes a point of cautioning that "a finding of adverse effect on a historic property does not necessarily require an EIS under NEPA," underscoring that satisfaction of historic preservation requirements under NEPA *does not automatically satisfy* an agency's obligations for compliance with Section 106. For the cultural resources section of an EA or EIS done under NEPA to satisfy an agency's requirements under Section 106, that cultural resources section has to have been done in the same way that it would have been done through the Section 106 Process [**36 CFR 800.8 (c)(1) and (2)**; see King 2000a:80-82].

Many corporate environmental officers assume that satisfaction of NEPA also satisfies whatever obligations they have relative to Section 106. That is not a safe assumption.

The NEPA does extend some aspects of cultural resources in a direction not originally anticipated by the NHPA, particularly in the realm of setting and visual impact, although 36 CFR 800.5 (a)(2)(v) included alteration of setting, including visual setting, as types of adverse effect. However, it is here that issues involving cultural landscapes begin to overlap with issues of aesthetics as considered by NEPA: The NEPA included aesthetic and economic considerations as well as natural environment considerations in evaluations of actions affecting the environment. Thus, when issues of "area of potential effects" under NHPA come into play, such as alteration of the setting of historic structures or a historic district, the NEPA regulations become collateral governing principles.

There seems to be a lot of confusion about compliance with NEPA relative to NHPA Section 106, both within the environmental science field as well as within

United States archaeology. There is a tendency for the archaeology done as part of the Section 106 Process to be thought of as environmental compliance work like environmental assessments and environmental impact statements, which is not quite correct. This is further muddled by cultural resources being considered when complying with NEPA. Our experience has been that the cultural resources section of many Environmental Impact Statements (EIS) would not satisfy Section 106 requirements, leaving the Lead agency, the private-sector firm whose work has been enabled by the agency, and the practicing archaeologist or environmental consulting firm all exposed to civil law suits. Part of the confusion comes about because NEPA protocols and NHPA protocols seldom are presented to or worked with by the same professional audience. The predictable result is confusion about requirements where the two mandates overlap: cultural resources.

This confusion between NEPA and the NHPA Section 106 often is increased because the counterpart Section 106 legislation at the state or local level often is embedded in counterpart NEPA legislation, New York's State Environmental Quality Review Act (SEQR) being an excellent example. Thus, early EISs often assumed that the requirements of NEPA could be met by "enumerating the known sites that would be destroyed or damaged and by proposing an undefined and professional unsubstantiated level of salvage as a means of lessening the effects of destruction" (Scovill, Gordon, and Anderson 1977:43).[6]

NEPA also uses the term "significance," but in a way different than the Section 106 Process (42 CF 15028.27 discusses the meaning of "significantly" as used in NEPA; see also box "NEPA and 'Scientific Significance'"). This can be misleading as well.

"Significance" under NEPA is a function of "context" and "intensity." "Context" includes short-term and long-term effects, and varies with the setting of the proposed action. "Intensity" refers to "unique

NEPA and "Scientific Significance"

There are differences between NEPA significance and NHPA significance. The criteria for NHPA significance – the guiding framework for the Section 106 Process and for compliance archaeology generally – are given above and were set out in 36 CFR 60.4. Scientific significance, as part of a NEPA EIS, is assessed for a proposed action by examining the following criteria:

1. How plentiful is the resource?
2. What percentage of the resource is within the area?
3. What is the resource's relation to other, surrounding resources?
4. What is the variety of archaeological evidence?
5. What range of research questions could the resource answer?
6. What specific questions could a study of the resource answer?

Thematically, cultural resources under NEPA are conceptualized as a variant of natural resources; it is almost as if cultural resources were added into a framework designed to treat other issues. Historic properties – that is, cultural resource eligible for listing on the National Register – under NHPA were considered unto themselves in legislation and regulations aimed at cultural resources alone.

characteristics of the geographic area, such as proximity to historic or cultural resources" [42 CF 15028.27 (b) (3)]. A consideration of "intensity" includes the degree to which the action may adversely effect districts, sites, highways, structures, or objects listed in or eligible for listing in the National Register of Historic Places or may cause loss or destruction of significant scientific, cultural, or historical resources [42 CF 15028. 27(b) (8)].

NEPA provides an integrated approach to environmental resources. However, NEPA is a process and, like the Section 106 Process, cannot be used to halt a proposed action if the EIS complies with the process. NEPA allows for destruction of significant archaeological resources, provided the impact of its loss is documented and evaluated first, and alternative (and mitigative) actions, evaluated. However, our understanding is that Section 106 supersedes this. NEPA actions are initiated through Federal agencies, which brings the Section 106 Process into force first as far as cultural resources are concerned. It is our understanding that the Section 106 Process has statutory precedence over NEPA in the area of cultural resources (see 36 CFR 800.8 (b): Just because NEPA is not required does not automatically mean that Section 106 is not); see also 36 CFR 805.3 (c)]. In any event, agencies are encouraged to coordinate their actions so that the requirements under Section 106 and those under NEPA are satisfied at the same time, so that effort is not duplicated [36 CFR 800.8].

---

6. This is quite different from the Section 106 requirements that a good-faith effort be made by the Federal agency to identify properties that could be listed on the National Register within the area of potential effects. NEPA cultural resource sections continue often to be completed simply by checking the state site files to see if a given project area contains any known archaeological sites or historic structures; if none are listed, the EIS will state that no archaeological sites will be affected. In contrast, the Section 106 Process requires that the project area be physically checked *in addition to* site file examination; just because the state site files do not report the presence of cultural resources does not mean that none are present. For the Section 106 Process, checking to see if sites already are known for an area is only a preliminary, background step that is a *part* of the Phase I survey process. It is often for this reason that NEPA EISs fail to satisfy minimal NHPA Section 106 compliance.

2.3.2. Other Legislation, Regulations, and Guidelines

2.3.2.1. Additional Legislation

In addition to NHPA and NEPA, there are nine other pieces of Federal legislation immediately germane to cultural resource management:

* The Department of Transportation Act of 1966

* Federal-Aid Highway Act of 1968

* Coastal Zone Management Act of 1972

* Housing and Community Development Act of 1974

* Archeological and Historic Preservation Act of 1974

* American Indian Religious Freedom Act of 1978

* Archeological Resources Protection Act of 1979

* Abandoned Shipwreck Act of 1987

* Native American Graves Protection and Repatriation Act of 1990

It is useful to briefly review these acts as they bear upon the management of archaeological resources. With the exception of the legislation aimed directly at American Indian concerns, the legislation deals with specific cases that would be covered in any event under NHPA. This is recognized in several places within 36 CFR Part 800, where agencies are urged to coordinate their activities so that the requirements of Section 106 and those of the other statutes are not needlessly duplicated.

Section 138 of the Federal Highway Act of 1966 and Section 4 (f) of the Department of Transportation Act were amended by the Federal-Aid Highway Act of 1968. The Act required the Secretary of Transportation to take into account the historic significance of sites on public lands that would be affected by a particular project, before that project was approved. This accounting, detailed in Section 4(f), was to include exploring all feasible and prudent alternatives to the highway design that would adversely effect those cultural resources. As with NEPA, 36 CFR 800.3 (b) encourages agencies to coordinate their actions so that the requirements under Section 106 and those under the Department of Transportation Act and related legislation are not needlessly duplicated. Section 4(f) analyses, often carried out in conjunction with NEPA, "are a major preoccupation of DOT agencies" (King 2000b:11).

The Coastal Zone Management Act of 1972 (CZMA) recognized the importance of protecting and managing coastal resources. In addition to biological, hydrological, and economic resources, aesthetic qualities such as scenic, cultural, and historic values were described by the law as important components of coastal resources. Archaeological sites are required to be considered in evaluating impacts in coastal zones. The CZMA was also intended to facilitate compliance with the principles established under NEPA, and is one of several such laws intended to coincide with the primary historic preservation laws (Fish 1980:694).

The Housing and Community Development Act of 1974 treated community development grants. Under this Act, the Department of Housing and Urban Development may delegate its Section 106 responsibilities to the local government receiving the Community Development Block Grant, in which case that local authority takes on the role of the Federal agency for the purposes of the Section 106 Process [36 CFR 800.12 (c)]. Of equal importance, programs under the Act may be exempted entirely from Section 106 compliance in emergency situations, such as natural disasters, threats to public health, and so on. This is treated specifically in 36 CFR 800.12 "Emergency Situations." The essence of this is that, in situations where there is a public emergency, solutions should not be held up by worrying first about satisfying historic preservation statutes; immediate public welfare has primacy.

The Archaeological and Historic Preservation Act of 1974 (AHPA), also known as the Moss-Bennett Act, amended the Reservoir Salvage Act of 1960, which provided for the salvage of archaeological material threatened by dams and reservoirs. The AHPA was intended to avoid the loss of archaeological data by requiring proper planning and surveying. This was done by providing procedures for the types and timings of required archaeological investigations (Fish 1980:693). The AHPA authorized Federal expenditure to recover data from sites facing destruction and to conduct surveys in threatened areas. "The main thrust of the law is that timely and thoughtful scientific investigation should occur when there is no alternative to destruction" (Fish 1980:693). However, the law permits agencies, confronted with discovery situations -- situations where, after a project has been started, archaeological materials are discovered -- to follow the AHPA and its regulations instead of the Section 106 Process. Recognition of this alternative is given in 36 CFR 800.13 (b) (2); the issue of discovery situations is covered in 36 CFR 800.13.

The most important aspect of the AHPA, though, was the limit it placed on the Federal obligation to underwrite evaluation and mitigation of cultural resources that may be potentially compromised by a Federally enabled undertaking. That limit was set at one percent of the total budget for the undertaking. It should be noted, though, that the 1980 amendment to the NHPA [Section 208 (3) 16 U.S.C. 469c-2] allowed Federal agencies, in consultation with the

Secretary of the Interior and notification of the House of Representative's Committee on Interior and Insular Affairs and the Senate's Committee on Energy and Natural Resources, to waive that limit. Further, this limit does not affect the total amount that the agency may spend, which could go beyond one percent.

The American Indian Religious Freedom Act of 1978 set a Federal policy to preserve the religious rights of American Indians through access to sites and possession of sacred objects. Federal agencies are directed to ensure that Federal policies and programs consider these rights. Tribal leaders are to be consulted in the administration of these duties. This act, although intended for Federal agencies, provided structure for the involvement of American Indians in cultural resources matters -- a key issue in complying with the subsequent Native American Graves Protection and Repatriation Act of 1990.

A considerable amount of attention is devoted in 36 CFR 800 to these and other issues involving American Indian concerns relative to archaeological materials. The code goes to great length in recognizing the need for ongoing communication with American Indian tribes, and sensitivity to their concerns during the Section 106 Process. It is for this reason that Indian tribes, as well as Native Hawai'ian organizations, are listed as consulting parties for the Section 106 Process. Further, it is for these and related reasons that those cultural populations can call upon the ACHP if it is felt their concerns have not been addressed, including undertakings that may potentially affect religious or culturally important properties outside of tribal or native lands.

The Archeological Resources Protection Act of 1979 required that the Tennessee Valley Authority (TVA) along with the Department of Interior, Department of Agriculture, and Department of Defense issue uniform regulations regarding treatment of archaeological resources on Federal and Indian lands, primarily in terms of permitting, ownership, and penalties. The regulations, which are identical, appear under four different titles in the *Code of Federal Regulations*, and are cited accordingly depending upon the agency involved (see also [36 CFR 800.3 (b)]:

* Tennessee Valley Authority: 18 CFR Part 1312: Protection of Archaeological Resources: Uniform Regulations

* Department of the Interior: 43 CFR Part 7: Protection of Archaeological Resources: Uniform Regulations

* Department of Agriculture: 36 CFR Part 296:Protection of Archaeological Resources: Uniform Regulations

* Department of Defense: 32 CFR Part 229: Protection of Archaeological Resources: Uniform Regulations

(By the way, those are not typographic errors. "Archaeology" is spelled in two ways within the Federal statutes.)

The Abandoned Shipwreck Act of 1987, passed in acknowledgment of the role of shipwrecks and underwater sites as part of the cultural heritage of the United States, sought to:

* protect natural resources and habitat areas;

* guarantee recreational exploration of shipwreck sites; and

* allow for appropriate pubic- and private-sector recovery of shipwrecks consistent with the protection of the historical values and environmental integrity of the shipwrecks and the sites.

The Abandoned Shipwreck Act encourages states to create underwater historic districts and parks, and to otherwise inventory and manage underwater resources.

The Native American Graves Protection and Repatriation Act (NAGPRA) of 1990 (Public Law 101-601) greatly improved the protection of American Indian graves and sacred sites on Federal and tribal land. NAGPRA defined key terms such as "burial sites," "cultural affiliation," "cultural items," "Native American," and "right of possession." The act led to the return of funerary and other sacred items from Federal and Federally-funded institutions to American Indian groups culturally affiliated with the human remains or artifacts. This also affects the treatment and disposition of burials and funerary objects encountered through cultural resource assessments in compliance with NHPA Section 106. NAGPRA directs Federal agencies undertaking cultural resources work to consult more closely with American Indian groups (see box "NAGPRA and Cultural Perspectives").

Section 3 of NAGPRA deals with possession of claimed and unclaimed American Indian human remains and objects, and intentional or inadvertent excavation of these remains or objects from Federal and tribal lands. Section 7, dealing with repatriation of American Indian remains and artifacts from Federal agencies and museums may also affect the archaeological practitioner, especially in the case of additions or new construction on Federal property where curation or storage is already an issue.

NAGPRA and Cultural Perspectives

When NAGPRA first came under serious consideration, there was a great deal of concern among archaeologists and other anthropologists about the loss of scientific information. NAGPRA in effect allows affiliated Indian tribes to take back not only skeletal remains but also any funerary or ritual objects, whether associated with a burial or not, then to dispose of those items in a manner consistent with the particular culture's current values. While there still is a lot of concern among that archaeological, anthropological community, it is important to place NAGPRA in a comparative cultural context. Burials and human remains can serve to illustrate this.

Americans use what is called an Eskimo kinship system for reckoning relationships. This refers to a terminological system that classifies relations in the way with which Americans are familiar: Mother, Father, Aunt, Uncle, Cousin, Sister, Brother, Niece, Nephew. Generational distance is recognized by adding the term "great" or, for parent terms "grand" in front of each generation: great-aunt, great-uncle, grandson, great-great-grandmother.

The language used, English, is also based upon time. Time is a measurable thing; it has connotations in the language of distance and proximity, of nearness and familiarity. Old things are far away in time, distant. People tend to think in their languages, and to define reality around them based upon how that language organizes and implies relationships within the world. And of course the speaker thinks that *that* world is the world as the language describes it.

As a result, for an English speaker a person who has been dead for a long has been dead for a long time. Both the language's handling of time, and the kinship terms handling relationship, result in a feeling of distance and lack of immediate relationship in a practical, day-to-day sense.

American Indian cultures do not necessarily figure kinship in the same way. Other ways of figuring relationships among kin, such as those called the Crow kinship system or the Iroquois kinship system (the second-most common system on the planet after Hawai'ian), do not recognize great generational distances while at the same time classifying some cousins as well as some aunts and uncles as siblings and parents respectively. Further, for many Indian languages, time is not an organizing element. Time is not something that is measured, or can be measured. Rather, it is like beauty: It is a quality, not a quantity; it is flowing, all around, and experienced. The concept of distance in time is, well, inconceivable. Combined with the kinship system, this can result in a feeling of immediacy of relationship not only with a member of the parent's generation dead for a year, but a person several generations back who has been dead for centuries. That individual is thought of, and very emotionally felt, to be as closely related as someone who has recently died.

Appreciating this helps in understanding why American Indians, arguing with archaeologists or English speakers in general, will quickly go to the example of "how would you feel about having *your* grandfather exhumed then put into a warehouse for storage or a museum case for display?" For the speaker of that Indian language, not only is that how the matter is felt, there is no other way that the matter can be expressed, experienced, or conceived. For the native English speaker, the example sounds bizarre, since human remains that are really, really old cannot possibly be very closely related to any living person. For the English speaker, the example – especially since it is being expressed by the other person in English who is therefore assumed to be using those cultural ground rules – represents a misuse of the language in describing the issue. And, as a result, the English-speaking archaeologist or anthropologist is more inclined to be outraged at the loss of what his or her culture considers important information.

2.3.2.2. Regulations

There are eight sets of Federal regulations governing implementation of cultural resources work (see King 1998 for details). These spell out in detail -- and in language much clearer and readily understood than used in this text -- the obligations of historic preservation practitioners in general and practicing archaeologists in specific. These codes are:

* 36 CFR Part 60 "National Register of Historic Places" (see Appendix A; all professional archaeologists are intimately familiar with this, especially 36 CFR 60.4)

* 36 CFR Part 61 "Procedures for Approved State and Local Government Historic Preservation Programs" (this governs certification of local governments; see also 36 CFR 800.3 (c) (4) and NHPA Section 101 (c) (1))

* 36 CFR Part 63 "Determinations of Eligibility for Inclusion in the National Register of Historic Places" (see also 36 CFR 800.4 (c))

* 36 CFR Part 65 "National Historic Landmarks Program" National Historic Landmarks (NHL) are seen to be extraordinarily significant to the nation, and command like consideration and treatment. NHPA Section 110 (f) sets out the policy for this. The additional requirements as they pertain to Section 106 are given in 36 CFR 800.10.

* 36 CFR Part 78 "Waiver of Federal Agency Responsibilities under Section 110 of the National Historic Preservation Act" This reinforces yet again the suspension of the Section 106 process in situations of immediate emergencies involving human life and health [36 CFR 800.12].

* 36 CFR Part 79 "Curation of Federally-Owned and Administered Archaeological Collections" This sets out the expectations for long-term curation of archaeological collections and associated records.

* 36 CFR Part 800 "Protection of Historic Properties" These are the basic regulations for the Section 106 Process (see Appendix A).

* 36 CFR Part 801 "Historic Preservation Requirements of the Urban Development Grant Action Program"

* 43 CFR Part 7 "Protection of Archaeological Resources: Uniform Regulations" These regulations applied to the Department of the Interior; identical regulations exist for Agriculture, Defense, and the TVA. These regulations were discussed above, and essentially treat permitting and penalties.

2.3.2.3. Guidelines

The legislation provides the authority; the regulations provide the required procedures. Guidelines give the day-to-day advice and guidance needed to accomplish the intent of the legislation. Guidelines are protocols; they do not have the force of law. However, the regulatory agency is bound by the guidelines to the extent needed to avoid being "arbitrary and capricious," and the guidelines themselves usually address the circumstances by which they may be exceeded or modified. For the Section 106 Process and comparable legislation, there are three sets of formal guidelines:

* 47 FR 46374 "Guidelines for Exemptions under Section 214 of the National Historic Preservation Act" NHPA Section 214 (16 U.S.C. 470v) authorizes the ACHP, in consultation and concurrence with the Secretary of the Interior, to set out exceptions to the Section 106 Process. Section 214 is one sentence of 67 words; 47 FR 46374 provides a little more detail.

* 48 FR 44716 "Archeology and Historic Preservation: Secretary of the Interior's Standards and Guidelines" See Appendix A and 36 CFR 800.2 (a)(1), 36 CFR 800.4 (b)(1). After NHPA and 36 CFR 800, this is probably the most important document for the practicing archaeologist to understand.

* 36 CFR 68.3 (e) "Secretary of the Interior's Standards for Rehabilitation and Guidelines for Rehabilitating Historic Buildings" See also 36 CFR 800.5 (a)(2)(ii).

2.4. State Laws, Regulations, and Protocols

State laws, and the regulations drawn from them, fall into three broad sets: (1) counterpart Section 106 statutes; (2) counterpart NEPA statutes ("little NEPAs"); and (3) other, hybrid statutes such as focused burial legislation. Most require that any state-enabled land-alteration/jurisdiction project be examined first for cultural resources. States also maintain the state's equivalent of the National Register.

In many states, the SHPO also has jurisdiction over actions enabled by state funding or permits, or involving state property. Undertakings then trigger a process that may be similar to Section 106 at the Federal level, or a roughly equivalent process similar to NEPA EIS reviews. This authority and where it is vested varies by state; in some situations, the SHPO does have such authority both for archaeological and architectural resources. In other states, the authority may be spread among the state archaeologist and an agency like the Department of Natural Resources or the Department of Environmental Resources.

Sixteen states along with the District of Columbia and Puerto Rico have so-called "little NEPAs" that handle the cultural resources issues at the state level (Table 2.1.). How these actually work varies by state, and the practicing archaeologist needs to be familiar with the procedures of the state within which work is done.

Table 2.1. List of States and Commonwealths with Comprehensive Environmental Policy Acts ("Little NEPAs").

Arkansas	Minnesota
California	Montana
Connecticut	New York
District of	North Carolina
Columbia	Puerto Rico
Florida	South Dakota
Hawai'i	Virginia
Indiana	Washington
Maryland	Wisconsin
Massachusetts	

All states and territories have an environmental assessment (EA) requirement of some kind or another, depending on where a project is located and the nature of the project. Some states, such as Vermont and Oregon, have a comprehensive environmental assessment requirement built into a permit process for all actions of a certain magnitude. Other states rely on state-level EA/EIS that is not as comprehensive as NEPA: Arizona, Delaware, Georgia, Louisiana, Michigan, New Jersey, North Dakota, Pennsylvania, Rhode Island, and Utah. Not all of those last mentioned have equal consideration over cultural resources; Georgia, for example, does not, instead depending in part upon a pair of burial-and-graves statutes that require survey of an area whenever the historic land-use changes (e.g., change from farm land to housing development).

While procedures may vary by state or commonwealth, the regulations are quite accessible. Most have the regulations and even permit applications set out on the internet. Many states also have state-wide archaeological societies with internet home pages that include links to state archaeological laws and assessment procedures. Federal agencies such as the NPS, and professional societies like SAA and ROPA, also have internet sites that provide links. While the internet provides a great deal of information, the practicing archaeologist still should contact the SHPOs of the given state for copies and clarification of regulations and procedures.

2.5. Municipal and County Regulations

Approximately 10 percent of the nation's 3,066 counties have counterpart Section 106 legislation, at least in a very broad sense of the term "counterpart." Most of this legislation, and its statutory regulations, are set within development licensing regulations. That is, the issuance of a license for a housing development depends in part on a developer's compliance with the county's equivalent of Section 106.

As at the state level, some of these regulations resemble Section 106, some resemble NEPA. It depends entirely on the legislative history of the local area. Those that follow a Section 106 procedure will have a local archaeologist whose role will be similar to that of a SHPO, while the entity that will be involved in the land-alteration activity will be in the role of the Lead agency, regardless of if it is a private-sector firm or a public agency.

The ability to monitor and enforce the process varies by locale. Some areas have municipal or county archaeologists who work with the planning commissions. The necessary permits for construction are not released until the archaeologist or equivalent historic preservation officer is satisfied that cultural resource compliance has occurred. In other areas, there may be a historic preservation commission that recommends zoning or permitting actions to the local planning board, but which lack statutory authority beyond social censure. These are usually found in situations lacking any counterpart historic preservation regulation, or having a counterpart to NEPA.

It becomes the practicing archaeologist's responsibility to find out what kinds of statuary regulations exist within the business domain of his or her firm. The best place to start is with the SHPO, which should know what exists at the local level in the given state.

3: Proposals and Contracts

3.1. Purpose and Objectives

For the professional practitioner, archaeology done as part of the compliance process begins with a response to a request for such work to be done. This response may be a statement of qualifications, or it may be a bid that has with it both a summary of what the professional archaeologist proposes to do and how much that effort would cost. All of this is part of the proposal process, the purposes of which are to

* identify clients or potential clients who have need of cultural resource services;

* provide a statement of how or in what areas the archaeology firm/division qualifies to provide the needed services;

* state what the firm would do to satisfy the needs of the client (or, often, identify what services the client will need to satisfy their legal obligations);

* propose and eventually settle on the cost to do the work in a way that best serves the needs of the client;

and, most important for the private-sector archaeologist,

* secure the immediate and future business of the client.

The cultural resources process is a consulting process in the same way that engineering, medicine, and law are. Archaeologically, its purposes are to identify and, if need be, recover data from Register-eligible archaeological deposits before those deposits are compromised. Professionally, its purposes are to secure then perform that consulting work not just in a way that is best for the cultural resource, but also at a cost that is fair to the client *and is fair to the firm.*

The cultural resources consulting process differs from the way in which archaeological research is identified and supported in a university setting. For the university archaeologist, the research problem is self-selected, often being identified by the investigator as an unresolved scholarly issue. Once identified, the academic archaeologist attempts to convince funding sources that the identified research problem is among the most important research problems currently under

Expectations and Demands of the Contracting World

The division of perspective between academic and practitioner is rather different and has a longer tradition. Even today in virtually every profession there have been complaints that professional education is too academic, theoretical, or unrealistic, and that it fails to prepare novices for practice....The practical contingencies of day-to-day work so vary from the ideal or hypothetical circumstances assumed or demanded by academics in professional schools that novices are said to suffer reality shock or burnout on entering practice. Those who survive adapt their expectations and actions to the practical exigencies of work by using compromised situational judgments informed but not always dominated by the standards they were taught in school [Freidson 1986:212].

The change in archaeology from an university and museum field to an extra-academic profession has been accompanied by changes in how research and people are supported, by the nature and structure of the work place, and by the kind of attitude or personality best suited for that world. This difference is greatest in the area of funding, a difference that is compounded by the current training regime.

The first experience that most archaeologists will have with archaeology comes within an academic environment. Many will remain in that environment through their master's and even their doctorates. Training will be provided by faculty who, almost always, went from undergraduate to graduate school to a faculty appointment, without ever spending full time in the extra-academic world. This can create a few problems. The first problem is that of accepting business practices as professionally legitimate and not of a second-class or morally inferior nature.

The academic world is the first world experienced. As a result, the people in that world become significant others, in Jules Henry's sense of the term. That is, during the course of training, the student comes to assess personal/professional worth by the approval – or its lack – received from the more senior academic community. Entering into the extra-academic world becomes traumatic for many because of the common remark that "If you were really good, you would have a tenured position in a university," as physicist Richard Helms of Applied Research Corporation in Maryland remarked (quoted in Travis 1994:1915). This is true of all traditionally academic fields, not just anthropological archaeology. For anthropologists, this is further compounded by vestiges of the Edwardian, upper-class attitude that selling one's services is demeaning. That is, marketing Anthropology to help a client is tainted and a kind of betrayal of the field.

The differences between the academic and extra-academic world on mercantile legitimacy – or its suspect nature – increase in how funding is obtained, and the kind of approach one needs to take to get it. Professional archaeology is driven entirely by the contracting process. More to the point, the practicing archaeologist is marketing services in competition with other archaeologists, in a partially regulated marketplace. Failure to obtain contracts with sufficient frequency in most cases will exclude the individual from full-time participation. This means that, to be successful as an archaeologist also requires being successful in business. This calls for an approach or attitude toward a field quite different than that found in an academic setting.

The differences also exist in how work is structured and managed. The private-sector work place requires managing multiple projects simultaneously, while also writing proposals and bids to keep business coming in. All of that work also has deadlines, so the comparative luxury in an academic setting of being able to set things aside for a while – a luxury enjoyed even more by tenured faculty – does not exist. Work on a project is comparatively short and intense, and is filled with interruptions. Remarking on her transition to the private sector after 25 years in university settings, archaeologist J. Cynthia Weber observed that "nine to five

review by that source. The funding source may have a review board of university and museum archaeologists who will assess the merits of the proposed research relative not only to the state of the discipline, but also relative to other research proposals. Once accepted, the funds in a sense are immediately available for the investigator starting at the time that the research effort is scheduled to begin. There is no delay, and staff (and the grantee) can continue to draw wages without interruption.

For the private-sector archaeologist, the need for cultural resources work will be "announced" and the professional then offers the needed services for a given cost relative to a given schedule. Sometimes the need for such work is widely and formally publicized, as with the announcements of Federal-level Section 106 projects in the *Commerce and Business Daily*. At other times, the need for such work is made known by word-of-mouth among the development community, who will call the SHPO to get a list of certified archaeologists, then call names on that list and ask for a price quote. Very often members of the development community will, when made aware that archaeological compliance work is needed, call other members of that community and ask who it is they have used in the past. Those outside of the communications network may never be aware that such a need existed.

Further, winning the award does not result in a transfer of funds. Often, the entirety of the field work will have to be finished first before *some* of the funds will be released by the government to the contracting archaeologist. This means that support for the archaeological research must be made by the firm; payment by the government agency is, in reality, a reimbursement of expenses already incurred. This will happen again when the draft report is submitted, and when the final report is submitted and accepted.

meant nine to five, 5 days a week, 50 weeks a year. Gone were the luxury of working at my pace, working when I wanted ..." (American Anthropological Association 1981:10).

An analogy presented by a friend who teaches at a large research university captures well the difference between academic and private-sector archaeology. He compares the difference to that between a quiet drive between two cross-roads on an under-used rural highway, and driving in the Monte Carlo Gran Prix. The first can be conducted at one's own pace and permits studying the countryside. The second is much faster paced, throws more curves, and involves a lot of shifting of gears. Both trips are equally valid; they just do different things.

Private-sector archaeology requires broad knowledge and tremendous professional flexibility. Project and research problems are constantly changing, and since compliance archaeology requires wrapping a data set chosen by circumstances around pre-existing research questions, private practice also requires knowing what those research problems are and how data – hypothetically – may address them. In effect, the practicing archaeologist works as a researcher on behalf of the greater society, which has designated the research questions and archaeological resources to be things of central concern. Private practice is practice on a publicly set agenda.

The private-sector world, much more than the academic and the public-sector world, also is insecure. Cash flow and one's wages depend upon winning contracts and awards from public- and private-sector clients. There is absolutely no certainty. In this, then, it is precisely like nearly every other professional field in the country.

Travis (1994: 1915-1916) listed a few of the traits needed for the world of contracting science. "Best suited," he wrote, "are aggressive types who combine an entrepreneurial streak

with the desire to tackle a variety of technical problems with relevance to the real world.... contract research is a fast-paced, rapidly changing, and intellectually challenging career." Travis continued, quoting one firm's CEO, that the people who do best in such a world enjoy collaborative, interdisciplinary research, and tend as well to be gregarious and outgoing. The idea is to work together enthusiastically with people toward a common goal in which all will benefit.

As a result of how the realities of the private-sector world are structured, individuals – especially those with doctorates – need to develop a new outlook and attitude, and acquire new skills, to survive. This includes writing proposals and developing bids that are responsive and competitive. It requires seeking out clients, developing contracts in the private and public sector, then keeping up those contacts by asking what their current and future needs are. It requires knowing which firms, agencies, divisions, and so on are likely to need the kind of service provided, and it requires knowing as well where and how those needs are made known. It requires marketing. And it requires knowing what it is that the client needs to have done, then doing that work on behalf of the client and the archaeological resource. As Travis (1994:1916) wrote: "Know the customer."

American Anthropological Association. 1981. Profile of an anthropologist: Mastering the business of archeology. *Anthropology Newsletter* 22 (9):10.

Freidson, Eliot. 1986. *Professional Powers: A Study of the Institutionalization of Formal Knowled*ge. University of Chicago Press, Chicago.

Travis, John. 1994. Science's "Fourth Estate": Signing up for contract research and development. *Science* 265:1915-1916.

As with the academic archaeologist seeking funding, the professional process requires that a proposal of some kind be prepared, submitted, and accepted before work begins. However, the similarity ends there. For the professional, the proposal generally is submitted in response to a formal Request for Proposals (RFP), which also will contain a Scope of Work (SOW or Scope; within Federal government this is called a Statement of Work) stipulating the kinds of work requested.

The SOW is a work order in the sense that it outlines what kind of work is desired; that is, it is a request by the client for particular things to be done. The client is interested only in completing the work in such a way that the main project may proceed. It is always useful to keep in mind that the archaeological work is going to be done on behalf of a client who, often, views the cultural resources process as another regulatory step that must be completed before his or her project can continue. Even if captivated and fascinated with the

archaeology, the client still will consider the cultural resources mandate to be a development expense that is not of his or her choosing.

The RFP will have a deadline for submission of the proposal and bid; the submitted proposal demonstrates familiarity with and capacity to perform the kind of cultural resources work requested. The bid -- which if accepted will essentially be the project budget -- is structured to permit the work to be completed within the time frame set out in the RFP. "Completed" means doing what is requested in the SOW: Anything more will be a cost absorbed by the professional and, unless there is an objection initially to the SOW, secondary to the client's needs.

The development of a SOW is at times informal. Players include various potential bidders, each of whom may contact the client and suggest better or more acceptable procedures to complete the work. The SHPO or THPO may have helped the client frame the SOW, since satisfaction of the process requires approval by the SHPO/THPO. The client, if a large firm or a Federal/state agency, may have a staff archaeologist who has worked out the SOW but may be asking for too much relative to the needs for compliance with statutes or to the amount the firm is willing to pay.

For government contracts, the SOW will be carefully compiled, often first by staff archaeologists then revised in consultation with the SHPO/THPO. Archaeologists in the public sector as often as not have doctorates, and usually have greater familiarity with and active field experience in the regional archaeology than their academic-sector colleagues. The SOW pretty much sets out what it is they would do or want to have done if they themselves were doing the work. One of the tasks of the professional archaeologist, then, is to make the intent of the SOW a reality.

3.2.   Government Contracts

Government contracts and awards represent situations where it is the governmental body itself that serves as the client. These situations generally involve compliance with Section 106 or similar counterpart legislation associated with construction, development,

permitting, or similar changes in jurisdiction over land. The RFP will be issued by and the proposal/bid evaluated by contracting or project officers in that agency. The Federal government has a highly organized and formal proposal and bidding process, accompanied by specific codes and guidelines. Further, most agency personnel involved with contracts and awards will have received basic Project Officer Training. State and local government agencies vary in how well organized and how formal their contracting and awards procedures are. Unless otherwise noted, Federal procedures will serve as the model throughout most of the following discussion.

3.2.1.   Levels of Government and Needs

Federal, state, and local government agencies often are required themselves to satisfy historic preservation mandates requiring archaeological work. While Federal agencies will only be involved with Federal code, state and local governments may be required to respond either to Federal Section 106 or to local statutes.

Although it is possible that any Federal agency would be required to go through the Section 106 Process (for example, because of construction, or building/grounds

Jargon

There are a number of phrases and terms used in private- and public-sector archaeology that are unfamiliar to those in the academic sector. Most of these have been used in this chapter.

Best-and-Final or *BAFO*: A best-and-final offer is the final agreed cost set for services, negotiated after an initial bid has been submitted. "Best-and-Final" connotes a revisiting of an initial offer that results in a lowering of cost to the point where it is the best that the agency can hope to get, and is at the final financial limit that the bidder can afford. See also sections 3.2.4. and 3.3.4.

Billable: Being "billable" means doing work for which funds from an awarded contract have been released.

Boilerplate: "Boilerplate" refers to written material that is used over and over again, with only slight modification. Most corporate qualifications statements as well as much of the methods and historic/prehistoric background sections of compliance reports are boilerplate. It connotes something that, now worked out, is stamped out in a mass-produced way, with little thought.

CEO or *Chief Executive Officer*: The CEO is the head of the firm or incorporated organization, subject only to the board of directors or board of trustees, depending on how the corporation is organized. The CEO is THE senior decision-making individual, and generally is a major if not majority stock-holder. Usually, the CEO also enjoys the title of "President."

CFO or *Chief Financial Officer*: The CFO is the individual responsible for all corporate finances. In organizational structure, the CFO usually is positioned in the tier immediately below the CEO, and may enjoy as well the title of "Senior Vice-President of Finance" or something similar. Most CFOs are major corporate stock-holders. Like the CEO, the CFO is a corporate officer who generally can sign-off on contracts and agreements on his or her own authority.

Deliverable: A deliverable is a physical product, almost always a written document, expected in the RFP. A report or a management summary is a deliverable. So would be a brochure, museum or public education display, or even a video production.

Go-Ahead or *Notice-to-Proceed*: "Go-Ahead" or "Notice-to-Proceed" means that the contracting agency has approved the contract, has arranged for access to the project area, and has released the funds for the archaeology firm to do the work. Work on the project should not start until the agency has given the go-ahead.

Hanging Fire: "Hanging fire" means "seriously pending." It is a common business expression, and derives etymologically from the failure of a cannon or match-lock to fire after having been touched by a flame. "Hang fire" came to mean, in the British Navy of the late eighteenth and early nineteenth centuries, something that had been set into motion and was about to explode with devastating effect, but for unknown reasons had not yet done so.

renovation), the following are by far the most common agencies soliciting Section 106 work:

*   Department of Defense (DoD), specifically the Departments of the Army, Navy, and Air Force, and the U.S. Army Corps of Engineers (COE);

*   Department of the Interior, primarily the National Park Service (NPS);

*   Department of Agriculture (USDA), primarily the National Forest Service (NFS);

*   Department of Transportation (Federal DOT), including Federal Aviation Administration (FAA), Federal Highway Administration (FHWA), and Federal Transit Administration (FTA);

*   Department of Energy (DOE); and

*   The Bureau of Land Management (BLM).

Occasionally, other agencies will issue RFPs for Section 106 work: The NRCS (Natural Resources Conservation Service, also part of the USDA) is one example; the Fish and Wildlife Service is another; the Tennessee Valley Authority (TVA) is a third.

With the exception of the Corps of Engineers, most DoD work will involve military installations. In some cases, DoD will attempt to issue the RFP itself; more often, it will call upon the National Park Service to develop the RFP and SOW, and in effect to manage the project on its behalf.

DoD, and most National Forest Service and BLM situations involve Federal property. The client, then, is the landowner. Corps of Engineers, Federal DOT, and FERC work often involves non-Federal property that will be acquired or at least require easements. The COE, Federal DOT, and FERC compliance projects will have those agencies as clients, but may well involve non-government properties.

The organizational level at which the project is managed by the Federal government depends upon the agency. For example, COE projects will be handled at the District level (each District has jurisdiction over the navigable waterways of a certain region of the country). Regional NPS offices may well be the location of project and contracting officers for work on military installations in their particular region. The individual National Forest often handles its own solicitation and contracting process, rendering individual forest parks -- or at times sets of National Forests -- the contracting agency.

Indefinite-Quantities Contracts: An indefinite-quantities contract is an award to provide services across a pre-determined range for a given period. That is, the number of contracts or the amount of work is undefined or indefinite. Such contracts, very common among Federal agencies for archaeological services, are somewhat similar to being on retainer, with the advantage that any work will be directed to the firm, but without the advantage of receiving a monthly retainer fee. *All Federal indefinite-quantities contracts are fixed-price contracts.* Other terms for this are *open-end contract* and *programmatic service.*

IFB (Invitation for Bid): Essentially the same as an RFP (see below), this is a solicitation by the Federal government expressing its needs to potential vendors.

Low-Ball Bid or *Low-Balling*: Low-balling is proposing a bid or budget that is substantially below market cost, and in all likelihood cannot be done without the bidder dipping deeply into cash reserves or asking for addition funds from the client later (very unwise; see also text box "*We learned about archaeology from that ..,* Back Billing for Proposal Preparation").

Qualifications Statement: This is discussed below. A Qualifications Statement summarizes the qualifications and resources of the archaeology firm/division.

RFB or *Request for Bids*: The RFB is a Request for Bid, which usually requires only a price quote and no technical proposal.

RFP or *Request for Proposals*: An RFP is a Request for Proposals. This is a public announcement soliciting proposals and bids on work. The RFP is the document that is received after one answers the announcement. It tells what to do to offer a bid, and it contains the Scope of Work (SOW).

RFQ or *Request for Quotation*: The RFQ is a Request for Quotation. This is a request for a price quote and, often, the firm's capabilities. We have also heard it referred to as a *Request for Qualifications.*

SOW or *Scope*: The SOW is the Scope of Work (Federal agencies often call this the *Statement of Work*). It will just as often be called the Scope; even if written as "SOW," it will still be read as "scope." The SOW is a task or work order from the client outlining in detail the kind of cultural resources work needed. An essential part of the SOW for the archaeological bid is the large-scale (e.g., one inch to 50 feet) project area map. Such maps often are topographic and have included not only existing landscape features, but also notations on what kinds of land disturbance or construction is planned for what parts of the project area.

Being Billable

In professional practice, there is a term: "being billable" or "to be billable." Being billable means that one is working on a project where the contract has been awarded and funds have been released (and funds still remain in the project budget). Thus, field work, laboratory analyses, report preparation, and similar project-specific activities are all billable tasks, while proposal preparation normally is not. Most firms require employees to keep time sheets – usually in quarter-hour increments – with the name of the project, nature of work done on that project, and the amount of time spent recorded. At the end of a given period, the time is added up by project, and management will work out how much time at a given pay rate has been devoted to each project currently being done by the firm. All of this not only helps track cash flow relative to labor, but allows those labor hours to be billed against the correct project budget (this is known in accounting as "job cost accounting"). Keeping everyone billable means that the entries on everyone's time sheets can be assigned to a specific – and existing – project budget.

The most common state agencies requiring archaeological compliance work are the state Departments of Transportation (DOTs). This is because requirements for archaeological work can be triggered either by the involvement of Federal highway funds, by permitting needs (for example, bridge footings in floodplains), or by the involvement of state funds or state land. Several states maintain an archaeology staff at the DOT. That staff will perform much of the needed Phase I reconnaissance and intensive survey work, as well as much of the background work, but they usually subcontract more substantial archaeological work to private-sector firms. Other agencies, such as the given state's version of a Department of Natural Resources or Division of Parks and Recreation, may have staff archaeologists and may issue their own proposal solicitation packages.

Contract needs and associated processes for state and local governments can become complicated for four reasons. The first reason relates to what series of statutes the archaeological work is required. The state or local government may be required to comply with Section 106 because Federal monies or permits are involved, or that same government may be required to comply with state or local counterpart legislation.

The second compounding factor is how well-organized and -developed the archaeological contracting process -- or the contracting process in general -- is at the state or local level. Some states and local governments have a highly formal procedure for soliciting and awarding contracts; Maryland and New York are good examples. Knowing how the Federal system works helps with these cases, more because of the organization involved.

Other states and local governments may be more informal in the structuring of the RFP and SOW, and may be equally informal in how funds are released. We found this to be the case with county and with village governments in parts of New York, where the RFP and SOW often were little more than a brief letter with a photocopy reduction of project map.

The third compounding factor is how contracting is overseen. Some states have each department or agency handle all its own contracting; others run the administrative portion of this through a central office. If the agency requiring services has an in-house archaeologist, then that person will likely run the RFP process. If the agency does not have in-house expertise, then the SHPO office (in conjunction with the administrative offices) may handle the RFP.

Finally, it is useful to know that the Federal government as well as some state agencies try to make the contract process more efficient by using cost-based categories. Government service requirements fall into one of two categories in terms of the bid amounts: Large costs where it is sensible to get multiple bids, and small amounts where it is cost effective to go with a single vendor (to use an extreme example, it makes no sense to put out to bid the purchase of a single pad of paper). In simple terms, a *small purchase* in Federal contracting currently is the acquisition of supplies or services less than $100,000 (a number of restrictions do apply). The authority for a small purchase agreement rests with the agency contracting officer, with required input from the concerned project officer. Federal acquisitions policies include a "Small Purchases" aspect. State and local governments often have similar simplified and streamlined process for selecting service providers. This threshold must be known if it is a borderline project.

3.2.2.   Where Government Needs are Published

Because they are part of the public sector, and because they disburse public funds, government contracting opportunities tend to be widely publicized. After all, it is everyone's tax money being made available; it is only fair that anyone qualified to do the work be made aware of the opportunity.

Government contract needs (announcements of solicitations) are distributed in two forms: As hard-copy, printed documents; and as electronic documents. Because of the legal requirement to make government contracting needs known to the widest range of people, most printed versions are duplicated electronically.

The two most common and widely examined documents for Federal contract opportunities are the *Federal Register* (*FR*) and the *Commerce and Business*

Orientation to the Federal Contracting Process

The Federal government subcontracts a myriad of services in response to the current political climate of governmental privatization and private-sector structure. Because of that and the consequent reduction of the Federal work force, services once performed in-house by agencies now are performed by outside vendors whose services are sought, proposals reviewed, and actions managed by government officials. Included here are private-sector archaeologists.

The following, which applies to Federal contracting regardless of agency, is abridged from the Federal Project Officer's training course given to employees of the Centers for Disease Control and Prevention (DAP/OAGM/OMA/OS/ DHHS 1991; Management Concepts Incorporated 1991).

The Roles of Contracting Officers and Project Officers

Federal contract administration has two sets of officials: The *Contracting Officer*, who advises during the project formulation phase but administers the award; and the *Project Officer*, who helps formulate the award (that is, the Statement of Work or SOW), but who serves as an administrating advisor. This is confusing for private-sector vendors since the project officer will be the person with whom they have constant and immediate contact. The project officer will in effect serve as a supervisor in that he or she is making sure that the tasks requested in the SOW are being performed to professional satisfaction. (As often as not, the project officer was the person who *wrote* that SOW and therefore knows exactly what is desired.) However, the funds will move and the deadlines will be enforced by the contracting officer, who has the responsibility and authority to do that. Further, with few exceptions only the contracting officer has the authority to enter into or modify contracts. Project officers cannot change the terms or conditions of a contract, although they may be delegated limited authority to act on behalf of the contracting officer in matters of technical direction.

The Regulations

The regulations governing Federal contracts and acquisitions are contained in 40 CFR parts 1500 - 1508. These are more commonly known as the "Federal Acquisitions Regulations" and abbreviated "FAR."

Different agencies also have special or more focused regulations. The business office of most firms will be aware of these, but the professional archaeologist should be generally familiar with these as well.

Acquisition Processes

The Federal government has two broad categories of funding mechanism: Assistance and acquisition. *Assistance* is where services, money, or property are transferred to accomplish public support or stimulation. The instruments used are grants and cooperative agreements. *Acquisition* refers to the government's need to obtain goods or services. The instrument for acquisition almost always is a contract. The Section 106 Process in which the Federal government is the client is a contracting process since the government needs the services of the archaeologist.

There are three acquisition processes within Federal government: Sealed bidding, contracting by negotiation, and small purchases.

Sealed Bidding

Sealed bidding begins with a published Invitation for Bid (IFB), which specifies the government's needs. The bids will be publicly opened at a predetermined place and time, with each bid received announced. Only price and price-related factors are considered. Related factors include whether the bidder is "responsible," that is, has the financial capacity, organization, record, and so forth to do the requested work.

Sealed bids are firm fixed-price contracts, or are fixed-price contracts with economic price adjustment clauses. Such bids are used where the requested services are clear-cut. DoD indefinite quantities contracts for archaeological services on particular military installations may be of this type, where the service is priced based upon cost per unit area.

Sealed bids are preferred for Federal contracts and must be used if

(1)   there is time for bids to be submitted and reviewed,
(2)   price and price-related factors will determine award,
(3)   discussion is not needed, and
(4)   a number of sealed bids can be expected.

If any of those conditions cannot be met, then the agency has the option of contracting by negotiation.

Contracting by Negotiation

Sealed bidding cannot be used in situations where discussion is needed after the government has offered the award to a bidder. In those situations, contracting by negotiation is done. There are six discrete steps involved in this acquisition process.

(1)   An advanced notice of a forthcoming solicitation is published in the *Commerce and Business Daily* (*CBD*).

(2)   A Request for Proposal (RFP) is transmitted to a number of sources, including those who may be on an established list of vendors as well as those who responded to the *CBD* announcement. The RFP will contain a Statement of Work (SOW, also called a Scope of Work) specifying the kind of work needed by the government. Those responding to the RFP will submit a *technical proposal*, which explains how the services needed by the government will be done, and a *cost proposal*, which will set out the costs for doing the work outlined in the technical proposal.

(3)   Technical proposals will be evaluated against technical criteria, and normally will be done so independent of

the cost proposal. The contracting officer will then determine which proposals are in the *competitive range* for doing the work, based upon cost and technical factors. Those within that range have a reasonable chance of being selected for the award. A debriefing will be made available to unsuccessful offerors as soon as they are determined.

(4)   Oral or written discussions may be held with those whose offers were within competitive range. Those discussions, if needed, are meant to clarify technical aspects of the proposal as well as to give offerors a chance to revise cost and technical aspects of their proposals.

(5)   After discussions with the different offerors, the contracting officer will request a best-and-final offer from the remaining firms.

(6)   The government will then select a vendor whose best-and-final offer is the one most advantageous to the government. That selection can take into account factors other than cost.

Small Purchases

Because sealed bidding and contracting by negotiation are time-consuming, they are expensive. For needs costing below $100,000, that kind of award process may not be cost effective. In such situations, the contracting officer, with input from the project officer, may follow small purchase procedures. A range of quotes will be solicited, but the process is simplified. Small purchase acquisitions normally are set aside exclusively for small businesses.

There are three kinds of small purchase procedures: Purchase orders, imprest funds, and blanket purchase agreements (BPA). Purchase orders are one-time offers by the government to buy supplies or services, and may follow from a Request for Quotation (RFQ). Imprest funds is a source for making small purchases by the agency and is not an issue for practicing archaeologists. Blanket purchase agreements (BPAs) represent situations where the same kind of services is repeatedly needed, although each instance is less than $100,000. There is an overall cost limit that cannot be exceeded when the costs for all of those repeated services are added up.

Types of Contracts

There are two sets of contract types in the FAR: Fixed-price and cost-reimbursement. The contracting officer chooses the type.

Fixed-Price Contracts

Fixed-price contracts obligate the contractor to provide the government with a service or supply at a pre-set cost. There are a variety of these, among which *firm fixed-price* and *indefinite-delivery type* contracts are likely to be encountered by professional archaeologists.

A firm fixed-price contract places a great deal of risk on the firm, with a minimum amount of risk or need for oversight by the government. In essence, the contractor agrees to deliver a service for a pre-set fee. If things go wrong and costs go above that originally projected, the contractor pays for the cost overruns. If things go better than planned, the contractor pockets the difference as profit.

Indefinite-delivery type contracts are entered if the delivery date for the service or supply is unknown. There are three types:

(1)   *definite-quantity contracts*, where specific quantities of supplies or renderings of service are requested within a given period by the government;

(2)   *requirements contracts*, where the contractor agrees to fill all acquisition requirements of the particular contract during the contract period; and

(3)   *indefinite-quantities contracts*, where instead of a specified quantity being stated, the contract sets a limit on the least and most number that can be ordered or acquired at any one time, and a limit as well on the total quantity.

For indefinite-quantities contracts, the archaeology firm may have submitted a basic rate schedule for services over the duration of the contract. The Federal agency may not know how much in the way of those archaeological services will be needed, nor how much any one of those services may cost.

Cost-Reimbursement

The second type of contract is a cost-reimbursement contract, of which there also are a number of variations. The cost-reimbursement contract is used when the cost of the contract cannot be reasonably estimated while the scale of the project is very large. In these situations, the contractor agrees to provide the "best effort" in fulfilling the what the contract requests; in return, the costs incurred combined with a reasonable profit will be charged. That combined cost-profit is the contractor's fee. That fee is set and cannot be changed unless the SOW in the contract is changed by both contracting parties.

The government and the contractor negotiate an *estimated total cost*. This is the best estimate by both parties of what it should cost, given the fee structure, to accomplish the task specified in the SOW. This also becomes the limit that the contractor cannot exceed without risking any additional reimbursement. Cost-Reimbursement contracts also contain a Limitation of Cost clause that limits government liability if the contract runs over budget.

Government takes a risk with cost-reimbursement contracts, since there is no guarantee that the worked specified in the SOW will be finished as desired. The contractor only promises to "use its best effort"; failure to finish is not a breach of contract. If the work is not finished, the government is left with either cutting off additional funds or with funding the additional costs (called "funding the cost overrun"). Neither is a desirable option, which is why this is the less preferred type of contract from a government perspective.

Unlike fixed-price contracts, cost-reimbursement contracts require much more monitoring by the project officer. The project officer is expected to make sure that the contractor is indeed doing its best while controlling costs.

DAP/OAGM/OMA/OS/DHHS (Division of Acquisition Policy/Office of Acquisition and Grants Management/Office of Management and Acquisition/Office of the Secretary/Department of Health and Human Services. 1991. *DHHS Project Officers' Contracting Handbook*. Department of Health and Human Services, Washington, D.C.

Management Concepts Incorporated. 1991. *Basic Project Officer*. Prepared by Management Concepts Incorporated, Vienna VA, on behalf of the Department of Health and Human Services.

Additional information on the Federal contracting process and archaeology is given in:

Jameson, John H., Jr., John E. Ehrenhard, and Wilfred Husted. 1992. *Federal Archeological Contracting: Utilizing the Competitive Procurement Process*. Archeology and Ethnology Program Technical Brief 7. [www.cr.nps.gov/aad/pubs/tch7.htm]

Daily (*CBD*). The *FR* is a public document announcing all code and regulation changes as well as funding allocations and needs. The electronic version is located at http://law.house.gov/7.htm; print versions are available at the local Federal document repository.

The *CBD* is a compilation of bid notices for Federal contract services of $25,000 or more. Where the Federal government is contracting by negotiation, the agency is directed to publish an advanced notice or synopsis of the planned acquisition so that the contracting community is informed of the pending solicitation. The *CBD* is available by subscription for around $250 annually; most firms, many universities, and some public libraries maintain subscriptions.

The *CBD* is also available electronically through the National Electronic Procurement Assistance Center (NEPAC) at http://www.cbgd-net.com for around $250 annually. The NEPAC specializes in providing indexing, searching, and electronic distribution of the *CBD*. However, free trial searches can be conducted. The NEPAC provides an efficient means to navigate the *CBD* data, and includes query support.

For no fee, electronic *CBD* searches can be conducted through the U.S. Department of Commerce, as well as through GovCon™. As electronic data bases continue to accumulate and expand, the ability to index and search them will increase in importance.

Many Federal agencies are now placing RFPs on the Internet, BLM, NPS, and DOE being good examples. DOE, for instance, posts and regularly updates notice of RFPs on its Web pages. A particular project will have all SOW components accessible as well. Qualified contractors can receive an access to more detailed information.

Some government agencies maintain a list of pre-qualified vendors; this is not unusual for those needing archaeological services. The opportunity to get on such a list will be announced in the *FR* or a similar state-level publication as a Request for Qualifications (RFQ). Firm qualifications can be submitted at any time to the agency, which will then keep them on file while placing the name of the firm on a mailing list. When a solicitation announcement comes up, the firm will automatically receive a copy of the RFP.

Several states maintain the equivalent of the *FR*, such as the *Maryland Register*, in which pending contracts are announced. There also is a rapidly developing trend among state agencies to imitate the Federal initiative to post electronic notices of contracting opportunities.

Last, the Contractor's Corner Information Center (http://www.infmart.com/cc/) contains a guide to procurement of contracts at the state, Federal, and global levels, in addition to a link to the *CBD*. This

Proposal and Bid Management

The life blood of an archaeology firm or division is securing compliance contracts. This means that the compliance needs of firms and government agencies need to be identified or known, RFPs obtained, and proposals written then submitted. Submission deadlines are fixed, certainly for Federal bids and often for most private-sector bids, to the minute. Turn-around time varies, but can range from 10 - 40 business days. To support the firm and its employees, several of these need to be under preparation at once. Continued cash flow is critical to meet payroll and overhead obligations, and continued cash flow requires a continuous stream of proposals/bids being written and submitted. It is useful to remember that most project awards will not result in all funds paid over at once to the firm. Rather, a portion of the funding award will be released at pre-determined stages, called *milestones*, after given tasks have been completed to the satisfaction of the contracting firm or agency. In some cases where the project is large or of a long duration, the funding allocated for a particular portion of the project may be accessed by the firm submitting monthly bills to the agency. Regardless, usually some percentage – 10 percent is common – will be held back until the absolute last bit of work on the project is completed.

Identifying, preparing, then submitting bids are together a series of movements in the complex, choreographed pavane of daily business operations. How it is done varies by the firm.

Identifying contract opportunities may be restricted to corporate officers (almost always true of entrepreneurial

firms), or to a Sales/Marketing branch, or not restricted at all and instead open to everyone. Preparing bids usually is a division of labor, with senior project managers proposing cost and technical specifics, junior technical personnel providing support and specifics as needed, secretarial personnel assembling forms and corporate documentation, and the designated contracting officer coordinating the entire exercise.

Remember that all involved already will have project commitments. That is, the senior project managers will be involved with ongoing projects, junior technical personnel will be assigned to work on aspects of those projects, secretarial staff will be handling the day-to-day affairs, and the corporation managers will be coordinating the firm's or the division's activities while looking for additional business.

(In smaller firms, corporate managers also are senior project managers; in larger firms, managers tend to coordinate and assign personnel, and may be called upon to market, write proposals, and so on. In firms where archaeology is one of many services provided, the senior management personnel, including the individual supervising the archaeology division, may not even be archaeologists.)

Proposal preparation is NOT billable time. The funding of that time comes from the corporation, specifically from corporate overhead. The actual funds hopefully are located in the firms cash reserve and are not part of a short-term (read: high-interest) loan. In the absence of continuous cash flow, a short-term business loan may be needed to bridge

Web site contains a wealth of information about doing business with the Federal government, including links to the various agencies. The state links include access to departments of general services, state contracts registers, purchasing departments, and miscellaneous business links.[1]

3.2.3. Responding to a Request for Proposals (RFP)

There is a wide array of cultural resource services that may be sought. The services can be single project and limited: Historic backgrounds, Phase I reconnaissance and intensive survey, Phase II testing, Data Recovery Plan, Phase III data recovery. Or the sought-for services may be to provide the full array of services for a Federal installation or agency over a set period (called *indefinite quantities contracts* since it is unknown how much work actually will be needed). Or some mix.

Federal RFPs for archaeological services tend to have four basic parts:

1. **The Schedule,** including contract forms, pricing/cost relative to requested services, a list of what the contractor is to deliver (called *deliverables*) and when those are to be provided, designation of Federal project officers (the individuals responsible from the Federal side for making sure the work is done correctly and on time);

2. **Contract Clauses,** drawn from Federal Acquisition Regulations (FAR) (48 CFR Chapter 1) and including requirements and restrictions specific to the requested work, as well as general Federal requirements ranging from prohibitions on gratuities through illegal pricing to small-business set-asides and drug-free work place mandates;

3. **Representations and Instructions,** containing pages to be completed by the archaeological contractor, documenting things like the TIN (Taxpayer Identification Number), corporate status, type of business organization, and other specifics the rules for which were set forth under

---

1. It is worthwhile to keep up on computer technology and Internet capabilities. An electronic format may soon become the only allowable means of bidding and responding to proposals for some government agencies.

the period when income resumes in order to meet payroll and other obligations. NO FIRM WANTS TO BE PUT IN THAT SITUATION IF AT ALL POSSIBLE. The best analogy is that proposal preparation drawing on overhead is like having the car's headlights on: There is a limited amount of time in which to act before the battery is dead.

Because the proposal and bid process is needed to get work, and because it is not billable, bid or proposal management is required. Although firms manage the process in different ways (and this would include *all* professional and scientific firms: Engineering, architecture, geology, as well as archaeology), they generally will include the following tasks and duty assignments:

1. Monitoring public notification announcements for RFPs;

2. Monitoring appropriate news media to identify emerging situations where services likely will be needed, then contacting the affected parties;

3. Identifying the specific project RFP (this may include the government solicitation number and agency);

4. Determining the deadline for when the bid and proposal must be delivered to the client or agency;

5. Setting the in-house deadline for completing the bid and proposal;

6. Assigning personnel and their roles in preparing the proposal, including who is going to do the overall coordination;

7. Itemizing and preparing the documentation needed;

8. Identifying client or agency contacts to whom questions can be directed; and

9. Developing a schedule for completing then submitting the proposal.

Supporting documentation may include vitae, short two-page biographical sketches of key personnel, various qualifications statements, and SF-254 and 255 forms indicating staff qualifications as well as current and anticipated staff commitments for the period of the proposed award. Much of that documentation will be "boilerplate," that is, previously written material that, with minor changes, can be included in any proposal.

The schedule is the big thing. There are what are called "drop dead" dates. This means, simply, that if the deadline is not met, even to the minute, the proposal will not be considered by the client or agency.

Contract Clauses and which are now being attested to by the corporation's contracting officer, along with specific instructions for how the proposal and bid are to be prepared and the number of copies to be submitted; and

4. **Attachments**, including the SOW as well as supporting documentation such as reports previously completed on the work requested, institutional requirements, field work requirements, reporting standards, and curation standards.

A Federal RFP can easily run 50 single-spaced pages in hard-copy form, with the SOW being about 10 pages. This of course depends upon the situation, but should give some sense of scale. RFPs normally are very well organized and clearly written. They must be, not just to get the job done, but to cut down on any potential ambiguity that could legally compromise the process.

Usually, the Federal RFP will arrive as the larger document, along with a second document that has a "Solicitation, Offer and Award" form (SF [Standard Form]33) attached to the myriad of Representation-and-Instructions forms. That second, considerably smaller document is meant to be filled-in by the bidder and returned as part of the submitted bid.

Some bids are open; others are sealed. Sealed bids will have costs/pricing and related schedule submitted under one cover, and a technical proposal addressing the SOW under another. At the Federal agency, each will be examined and ranked by separate sets of people.

Evaluation and award are based on a two step-process. The first is a technical review in which the firm's technical expertise and qualifications, as well as the technical merit of what it proposes to do are all considered. The idea is to evaluate what the firm would do and how it would do it, without being distracted by cost considerations. The second step in the process treats contractual and award issues, specifically if the firm satisfies any contracting restrictions (e.g., small-business or minority-owned small-business set-asides) and what cost is being proposed.

If the proposals are equivalent in terms of technical merit and if the firms otherwise qualify under any contracting restrictions, then the firm with the lowest bid will be offered the contract to do the requested work. Most Federal RFPs reserve the right to make awards to the next lowest bidder if, in their judgment, the lowest bid is too low to actually perform the work.

Generally, the Agency will negotiate with the lowest first-round bidders -- usually a maximum of three -- to see if an even lower cost can be arranged. This is the "best-and-final" offer made by the firm.

3.2.3.1.   Contents of a Bid Package

Responses to government RFPs consist of three parts:

*   A qualifications statement, which outlines corporate capabilities in terms of facilities, matériel, and personnel;

*   A technical proposal, in which details regarding professional accomplishment of tasks sought in the SOW are addressed; and

*   A bid or offer, in which cost specifics as well as representations, certifications, and related agreements are attested.

Each of these is discussed in detail below. The qualifications statement serves both to address questions about the structure and expertise of the firm raised in the RFP, and to market or advertise that expertise. The technical proposal is essentially a creation of the firm specific to the RFP and its SOW. The bid materials generally consist of costs and pricing schedules unique to the firm along with completed forms sent along by the government agency with the RFP.

3.2.3.2.   Completing the Forms

There can be up to four sets of forms requiring completion on a Federal bid:

*   Form SF-33, which is primarily a cover sheet but does address payments and discounts;

*   A services and price or cost schedule;

*   A series of check-lists in which the bidder certifies and represents certain aspects of the firm; and

*   Forms SF-254 and SF-255, which list the qualifications of primary project personnel as well as anticipated/current proportional distribution of their already-committed time.

The SF-33 form will contain the solicitation number; the type of solicitation; a time-frame in which the offered prices/costs will still be honored; a percent discount schedule given to the Federal agency for prompt payment; and name, title, address, and phone number of the person authorized to sign for the offer. Most firms will have a discount schedule of some sort, which is meant to encourage prompt payment.

The services and price/cost schedule varies by the requested task. For single-project exercises, such as a Phase I survey or Phase III data recovery, this may well be a lump sum bid. For indefinite quantities contracts, where the solicitation is for a firm to provide a range of services over a fixed period, the services and price/cost schedule will be more of a unit price list. For example, the Federal agency may request rates -- projected and adjusted for up to four years -- for Phase I reconnaissance and intensive surveys be given in terms of cost per acre relative to various parcel size ranges and to low, medium, or high probability of cultural resources being present.

Federal solicitation packages also have a series of pages on which the bidder attests to satisfaction of given Federal requirements, or represents the firm as of a certain type with certain practices. Some of these are statements that basic ethics have indeed been followed (e.g., that the costs have been determined independent and in ignorance of the pricing structure of other firms, or that the firm has not been declared ineligible for the award of Federal contracts). Some statements are descriptive of the type of business the bidder actually is, such as a corporation, partnership, joint venture, nonprofit, or individual person. This includes statements relating to whether or not the concern is a small business (and criteria are again provided, as they were in the Contract Clauses section of the RFP), or if it is a small disadvantaged business or a women-owned small business. And some statements are specific in detail, such as providing the firm's TIN or DUN number, corporate status, and names and titles of those authorized to negotiate on behalf of the business concern. (A DUN number is an index reference number that classifies a firm's primary and secondary lines of business. The index is compiled and maintained by Dun and Bradstreet as *Dun's® Census of American Business*.)

The SF-254 and SF-255 forms are, together, statements of qualifications as well as of personnel/corporate commitments (when speaking about these forms, it is usual to speak of them as a set, that is, to say "a 254/255 form is needed"). It is one thing to bid on a project; it is quite another to actually be able to fit it in given existing commitments. (One of the representations that will have been made is whether or not people have been hired to prepare the proposal, or have been retained to obtain the award.) The form requests proportional allocation of time, and in effect requests that the firm note how much of each person's time is going to be spent on *this* Federal project.

3.2.3.3.   Qualifications Statement

Qualifications statements contain specific information on the capabilities and past performance of a firm. They are meant to summarize what the firm is capable of doing, as well as how it is structured. Most qualifications statements will contain the following kinds of information:

*   Corporate organization and incorporation information, including nature and accomplishments of key professional personnel and support staff;

*   specifics of various corporate subdivisions, such as historians, geologists, laboratory staff, graphics, and publications;

*   structure of the physical plant, especially its analytical, curatorial, graphics, and publishing capabilities;

*   in-house and field capabilities and matériel, such as total station surveying equipment, CAD/CAM, GPS, GIS, and computer capabilities;

*   a clear and concise discussion of corporate capabilities, illustrated by a series of abstracted projects that show the firm's capacity to do specific kinds of work;

*   a clear statement about bonding and liability insurance (always required for government contracts); and

*   a list of corporate clients serving as references.

Qualifications statements are documents -- almost always previously prepared -- that outline the qualifications of the given firm or division relative to the kinds of work sought. These will more often be a part of the technical proposal than a part of the bid. However, there are at times Requests for Quotation (RFQ), in which the Federal agency requests firms to provide a quote on how much a given project would cost. Included in the response to the RFQ will be the firm's statement of qualifications.

Qualifications statements also are marketing tools. This means that they both provide information about the firm, and they promote or advertise the qualifications of that firm. All qualifications statements are exercises in rhetoric. This does not mean that they lack substance: Everything claimed in most firm's qualification's statements is true. However, the choice of words and nature of presentation are meant to further sway the reader.

Qualifications statements are made-to-order from two sets of previously assembled information: information on different aspects of corporate capabilities; and information on personnel. The information on corporate capabilities will cover things like physical plant and facilities, equipment, communications, laboratory and curatorial capabilities, graphics department, past accomplishments, and so on. That is, any aspect of the firm or division that accentuates its

Federal Acquisition Regulations: Contractor Qualifications

Federal contracting protocols are presented in the Federal Acquisition Regulations FAR (48 CFR 1500-1508). These cover everything from Submission Offers in English (48 CFR Chapter 1 Section 52.214-34) through the various contract clauses mentioned above to how protests on awards are filed (48 CFR Chapter 1 Section 33.101).

The FAR also outlines minimum standards that must be met by a contractor to receive an award:

1. adequate financial resources;

2. ability to meet required delivery or performance deadlines;

3. record of satisfactory performance under similar situations;

4. either (4.1.) has in-house organization, personnel with technical expertise required, past experience doing similar kinds of work, accounting system, and overall operational controls; or

    (4.2.) has the capacity to put the items in (4.1.) into place for the duration of the award (in effect, assemble a virtual firm or virtual research team);

5. either (5.1.) has the needed technical/production equipment and facilities required to do the work; or

    (5.2.) has the ability to put those resources into place for the duration of the award;

6. satisfactory record of integrity and business ethics; and

7. is otherwise qualified and eligible to receive a Federal award under governing laws, statutes, and regulations.

The Federal Contracting Officer will be the person making the determination of if the firm submitting the bid, or under consideration for the award, meets those criteria. Information on past performance will be solicited, not from the bidding firm, but from sources other than the bidder who are familiar with or aware of that past performance. Thus, topics that also will be addressed in a qualifications statement will be those that deal directly with the above list on "Contractor Qualifications," and include a list of "Client References" and history of project performance that the Federal Contracting Officer can use to verify the bidder's claims.

Employee Safety Training

Some Federal clients like the COE require that all field personnel have current CPR and first-aid certification. CPR certification is current for one year; first-aid certification is current for three years. The currency is a condition of award. Some contracts require that personnel have the OSHA 40-Hour training as well, and there may be other training requirements particular to the needs of the project.

CPR and first-aid instruction often can be done at the office. Many firms schedule Red Cross instructors to come in, and everyone in the firm spends the day or a goodly part of the day receiving the training. The Red Cross is more than willing to make the arrangements for group training. Red Cross training is not free; rates vary. However, the Red Cross does have its "Challenge Program" that allows individuals to take a hands-on test that, if passed, may reduce some of the training costs for the firm.

ability to provide top-of-the-line, cutting-edge professional services in a timely manner will be mentioned.[2]

Those sections on the firm's capabilities will exist as semi-independent entities that can be mixed and matched as the situation requires. That is, the information is "boilerplate," and will be cobbled together for the needs of the given proposal.

The second part of the qualifications statement will consist of specifics on personnel. This information will be provided at least as a curriculum vitae, the form of which varies by individual. This will be very similar to vitae used by academic archaeologists, but with funding, courses taught, and service items usually left out.   A second item that may be provided for personnel will be a short biographical sketch. This will generally focus on the *professional* biography of the person.

---

2. Qualifications statements are marketing tools, and need to be assembled with an eye -- and ear -- toward marketing needs. The writing is upbeat, active, and positive. There are catch phrases -- "an industry leader," "one of the major providers," "highest quality," "prompt and responsive" -- that are meant to create an air of quality. Qualifications statements follow the philosophy of telling people what you want them to think of you: Eventually, if there are no counter-arguments, the image given will be the image accepted. This, by the way, is the basic rule of propaganda.

To those of us who, as we did, come out of non-business school settings, the first exposure to this kind of phrasing on behalf of archeological services is a bit jarring to say the least, and really does seem to be in bad taste. And that reaction comes even though our universities often used similar phrases in their catalogues and on their Web sites. By the way, this is one of the reasons why we recommend that students take a rhetoric or a logic course (see Appendix B). For an instructive discussion of rhetoric from an anthropological perspective, see Weiss, Gerald. 1977. Rhetoric in Campa narrative. *Journal of Latin American Lore* 3:169-182.

In a professional firm, vitae generally are straight boiler-plate requiring little amendment (some firms will have personnel update vitae every quarter to keep abreast of the publication rate; others just use proposal requirements as the opportunity to have people update vitae). Biographical sketches tend to be modified relative to proposals: That is, personnel will take previously written documents and change them with an eye toward the specific needs of the proposal.

Although it depends upon the RFP and the needs of the project, it is not unusual for the curriculum vitae of all professionals, including intended subcontractors and technical consultants, to be included. This certainly holds for Phase III data recovery projects and for all indefinite quantities contract proposals. If it is expected that special analyses, required of the SOW, are to be done, and if that work will be done by a subcontracting laboratory, then an equivalent qualifications statement for that subcontracting facility will be needed.

3.2.3.4.   Technical Proposal

Technical proposals are specific responses to the SOW in the RFP. They directly address the nature of the research problem, and outline in detail what the firm intends to do to satisfy the SOW.

Most SOWs will actually have five sets of information:

* how the problem came to be;

* what has been done so far;

* what they would generally like to have done;

* what special things they want to have done; and

* a series of project maps.

The nature of the problem and a summary of previous work will vary by project. The general work that is requested normally will fall into the Phase I - Phase II - Phase III possibilities discussed in Chapters 5-7, or will be of a research design or historic background nature, the latter discussed in Chapter 4. That is, the general services requested will not be unusual, and it will only be a matter of addressing questions like surface reconnaissance, shovel test spacing, or excavation unit depth and coverage. These are technical, field- or analysis-related questions, and can be handled with the specifics appropriate to the nature of data in the part of the country concerned.

The technical proposal is a direct response to the SOW, and rather straightforward. Most will consist of the following, or some variant:

Evaluation of Proposals and Bids

Most Federal RFPs will contain a section, titled "Evaluation Factors for Award," that outlines in detail what will be considered in determining who will receive the award. It is not unusual for the weights given to those factors to be set out as well. State and sometimes local government evaluation procedures will do the same thing. The purpose is to make sure that the selection process is as fair and objective as possible, meaning that, given a different review panel but the same set of proposals and bids, the results would still be the same. The process is designed to be reasonably impartial, and depends upon procedures and not reviewer's personal opinions to achieve this.

Evaluation factors fall into two sets: General business factors, which will include all business-related variables including cost; and technical factors, which will include the technical proposal itself as well as factors directly related to its potential success.

Most Federal RFPs will include phrasing that reserves the agency's right to select a proposal that is not necessarily the lowest bid. This helps the agency to ensure that minimum project standards will be met. It also will remind the reader that the agency can select a bid based upon the initial proposal, and not enter into discussions with the bidders of the best set of offers (called "best-and-final" [see below], see also **48 CFR Chapter 1 clause 52.215-16**). Proposals and their bid amounts are evaluated based upon realism, completeness, and credibility.

Technical proposals tend to be scored on a rating system, regardless of if that system is specified in the RFP.

*   Introduction and summary of the proposed compliance activity, including what brought the needed action about as well as anticipation of any special compliance concerns or issues;

*   Description of the project area and nature of the project itself, often best done as a verbatim repetition of this part of the SOW;

*   Overall research design, including:

    *   general historic and prehistoric background relative to the project area and standing research questions;

    *   previous research conducted in the area; and

    *   previous research done in the project area, if any.

*   Research methods, including:

    *   proposed specifics of field methods (e.g., for Phase I survey: How many shovel tests at what spacing across what kind of terrain of what slope, with fill screened through what size mesh);

Generally, there will be one or more technical reviewers in the agency who will go through the proposal, with a rating sheet set to one side. After being evaluated, there will be a gathering of technical evaluators and a meeting to rate or rank the submitted proposals.

Technical evaluation criteria can include some or all of the following:

*   Understanding of the project, its purpose and its needs;

*   knowledge of potential and actually research problems as they apply to the project area and region;

*   adequacy of research design and methods, including the design itself as well as field methods and laboratory analyses (including here the capacity of the existing or virtual laboratory);

*   qualifications of the lead project personnel;

*   the firm's record for doing the kind of work requested, or its capability to do the requested work;

*   the feasibility of the proposed schedule, especially relative to the needs of the agency ("timeliness"); and

*   current obligations of the bidder that may or may not interfere with completing the project.

*   laboratory analyses and methods (including cleaning, cataloguing, labeling); and

*   recommended curation and turn-over of any recovered material.

*   Discussion of any specific analyses or services provided by research specialists; and

*   Scheduling, including specific delivery dates.

For Phase II testing through Phase III data recovery projects, the technical proposal needs to return frequently to the overall concern driving the compliance project, which will often be outstanding research questions identified in the state historic preservation plan. For Phase I survey projects, a general discussion of the historic and prehistoric background, along with consideration of what already is known about the project area and vicinity, usually will be sufficient.

Most of the general prehistoric and historic background will be modified from boilerplate, or at least previously written material will be culled for useful parts. Research methods may be boilerplate or may be entirely new, depending on the nature of the project: For example, Phase I surveys usually will involve the same kinds of laboratory processing, and ignoring the size and topography of the project area, the same basic field methods that are seen as appropriate for the region of the country where the work is to be done. Phase II and Phase III exercises, though, will need to be tailored to the specific needs of the identified site.

It should be noted that some provision needs to be made for the final location of any recovered material. Government clients may require data to become the property of the applicable Federal, state, or municipal entity. Who is the designated ultimate repository and how will the artifactual, botanical, faunal, pedological, and other data forms be curated until ultimate disposition? Who will have access and under what conditions? This category also relates to the respondent's proposal of facilities.

The real core of most technical proposals is less the proposed specifics about field work, and more the demonstrated understanding of the status of archaeology in the region to date, and how the research -- and any creative application of laboratory analyses -- can help resolve outstanding research questions. This makes the technical proposal both a research proposal and a qualifications/certification document.

Almost all compliance work requires wrapping a pre-selected research opportunity around an existing research problem. To do this requires knowing what the existing array of regional or national research problems are, and how the data potentially present might be used to resolve those problems. Given that, the technical proposal in its core becomes an exercise in taking what may be present or recovered and showing how it can be tied into questions and issues central to the region's history and prehistory.

It is not unusual for SOWs, especially Phase II testing and Phase III data recovery, to contain specific research questions. These reflect issues of which the agency or SHPO/THPO archaeologists are aware, and which they strongly suspect the potential data can address. It is the responsibility of the review agency archaeologist to know what questions need answering relative to the regional data base, and then to recognize how the non-renewable resource -- archaeological sites -- can best be used to address those questions.

The practicing archaeologist, then, becomes part of that greater societal process by helping to refine then executing the overall work set forth by society writ large -- the state's historic preservation plan -- as well as by that society's expert representative, the public-sector archaeologist. Although by no means entirely so, the practicing archaeologist still is only someone brought in to perform the work that others -- society,

or the public-sector experts -- have neither the time nor skills to do themselves.

3.2.3.5. Competitive Budget Estimates

The final determination of a budget being competitive is if the proposal is awarded *and* the firm remains profitable after doing the work. "Profitable" here is in a very strict sense: Making a profit while compensating employees fairly for their labor.

Competitive bids require a fine understanding of just how much effort will be required by what sorts of personnel at what pay levels. Federal agencies set minimum pay standards for labor of various levels of technical expertise. Archaeological contracts are for professional services and thus do not have minimum pay standards, but pay rates submitted by a contractor during contract negotiations must be adhered to and are subject to audit. The pay scale used in computing overall project costs must be in line with those requirements in order to be competitive in attracting skilled labor.

The bid can consist of up to four sets of cost figures:

*   estimated cost of labor for specific, project-related tasks;

*   costs or anticipated costs for specialists, such as lithic analysts or palynologists;

*   costs for special analyses, such as radiocarbon dates; and

*   logistical and related field costs, such as mileage, crop damages, and per diem.

The per diem rate is usually estimated based on prevailing Federal government rate for the area of the country in which the contract work is to be done. "Related field costs" may well include site security, landscape restoration, crop damages, and the like. Many Federal projects will require restoration of an area after archaeological research has been done. Expendable items, such as film, bags, and other field or laboratory supplies, will be covered by the overhead rate and usually are not itemized in the budget.

Requests for special analyses often are given in the SOW; for example, the Federal agency may request that a given number of radiocarbon dates be obtained, or that obsidian hydration analyses be done on a certain number of artifacts. In a similar way, the SOW may all but require that specialists be written in, as when requests are made for detailed soils or sediment analyses. Some firms have in-house capabilities in this regard; others have working

We learned about archaeology from that ... The State DOT Proposal

There are times when an RFP and its SOW will be confusing or inexact. As of this writing, Federal government personnel each are now performing the work of 2.6 people 10 years ago, a frightening figure when it is recalled that the Federal work force was frozen during the Carter administration. Federal government personnel specifically, and most of the state government people we have known, are bright, resourceful, insanely dedicated, and harried beyond belief. As a result, things can get garbled. One such case was an RFP from a state for a highway bridge replacement.

The firm we were involved with at the time had just opened its regional office, and was trying to break into the state government market. The State Department of Transportation (State DOT) RFP appeared to be an ideal opportunity.

Most of the RFP was clear. However, the requested contents for the technical proposal were not at all clear. The instructions said not to belabor issues of prehistoric background and the status of research – these were ancillary – just show that the work could be done and how much it would cost. One reading suggested that a standard discussion of the region's prehistoric and historic archaeology might be given, albeit it in abbreviated form (but what is meant by "abbreviated?"), along with all of the other bits of information one normally will supply for a technical proposal. Another reading, though, suggested that State DOT *only* wanted a statement of how the work would be done, and absolutely did NOT want any kind of historic or prehistoric background. What to do?

RFPs will have a contact person listed, along with a phone number and (now) e-mail address. The project appeared ours for the writing, but we were stymied about how to handle the ambiguity for the technical proposal. We asked the main office about this, suggesting that we call State DOT, and were ordered not, under any circumstances, to contact the State DOT project representative. The reasoning was that such a question would expose the firm as being wet-behind-the-ears and not a *real* player in the regional market; in effect, the firm would *lose face*. Well, which of these should we do, we asked. The answer was to do the second: Provide specifics on how field work would be done. So we deleted a beautifully developed prehistoric and historic background that drew upon the State Historic Preservation Plan and recently published research.

DOT awards of this sort are made publicly in this state. There is an auditorium, and the DOT representative will read out the opinions about each submitted proposal before announcing the award. All bidding firms will send representatives. It is very high profile indeed. We fortunately were not there; another person who had worked on the proposal was. The criticism – mentioning time and again the name of the firm – was scathing. Actually, it was worse: It was stated that our proposal was the absolute worst that had ever been submitted to State DOT. Somehow not surprisingly, the project was awarded to a competitor.

The lesson is to take advantage of contacts and opportunities to ask for clarification.

---

agreements with suitable professionals. Very often, though, the firm may take on a specialist for the specific project, with that specialist in effect becoming a subcontractor for the firm. This process results in the creation of a virtual laboratory or virtual analytical research team, one that is put together for the duration of the project.

It should also be remembered that there are curation costs. At some point, any recovered cultural materials will be turned over, with the field records, to an appropriate curatorial facility. In some cases, the materials will go to the SHPO/THPO or to a facility working with the SHPO/THPO. In other cases, it will go to the Federal agency: Some Corps of Engineers Districts maintain their own facilities. And yet *other* cases will result in deposition of the materials with a private-sector curatorial firm. In most of these cases, there will be a one-time, unit-based curation cost [ranging on the order of $150/cubic foot of storage, the 1997 cost at one university curatorial facility in Georgia, for example; to $300 - 1,000 per archive box in California]. For small projects, this is incidental; for large, Phase III data recovery exercises, which can easily produce 15 cubic feet of material, the curatorial costs can be substantial.

Assembling a bid involves drawing on three and sometimes four sets of figures: A kind of rule-of-thumb bit of information for common tasks, a known estimate of how much effort actually had been needed to do the work in the past, a sense of what the competition will be bidding, and (if known) the cost ceiling for the contract.

There will be two broad sets of variables in setting up a budget, given all that has been said so far: the tasks that are to be done, and the personnel -- meaning pay-grade -- that will be used to perform those tasks. Most projects consist of five basic task sets:

1. start-up, involving all that is done to prepare to execute the project, be it field work or background research;

2. field work, involving the actual data collection;

3. analysis, involving analysis and cataloguing any data obtained;

4. report preparation and delivery, involving not just writing, but preparation of illustrations, assembly of the report, then delivery of that report to the client; and

5. final report delivery along with turn-over of any materials recovered and any field records generated.

This is as good a place as any to mention that, in some situations on larger or long-duration projects, the client will be billed for work at the following stages:

*   after field work is completed;

*   after the draft report is submitted; and

*   after delivery of the final report.

Payment at each stage will be a percentage of the total agreed bid, say 50 percent after completion of field work, 35 percent after completion of the draft report, and the balance at the end of the project. For larger or long-running projects, it is possible that some funds will be released by the Federal agency during the field work phase. That release may come after a certain amount of field work has been completed (*milestones*); in other cases, a pre-set portion of the award has been allocated for each stage of the project, and the firm will bill the Federal agency on a monthly basis. In both cases, some form of written report (called a "management update" or "monthly management report," usually equivalent to a letter of several pages) will be presented to the agency, be it monthly or at the end of the particular milestone. That report, by the way, will constitute one of the deliverables specified in the contract award.

All of this means that funding of the start-up and the field work will come out of corporate cash reserves or a business loan. Start-up, report preparation, and delivery of the final report with turn-over tend to have rule-of-thumb estimates on costs and personnel involved. Most firms have a series of basic estimates for these task sets. These vary by the nature of the compliance project, and are addressed in Chapters 5, 6, and 7.

"Rule-of-thumb" suggests perhaps an exactitude that is misleading: Firms have a basic sense of how much effort will be needed by what people to do the work required of a given project for the particular task set, very much like most people have a sense of roughly how much a common grocery or general goods item will cost. In fact, those labor estimates are manipulated much like one mentally adjusts cost estimates when thinking of the cost for groceries or for a stack of lumber.

Profit and Overhead

Keep in mind that profit margin and overhead all are incorporated into the cost estimates for the project. Unless the Federal agency requests otherwise, the overhead and profit margin are incorporated into the hourly labor estimates. Federal law restricts profit margins on Federal cost-reimbursement contracts, often to seven - 10 percent. Corporate overhead for field-type firms is, on average, 100 percent (which is a fair figure, by the way), although this varies by part of the country. (By comparison, social science and behavioral science firms charge around 60 percent overhead.) Thus, with 10 percent profit and 100 percent overhead, it means that around 45 percent of the *billed* hourly labor rate is for payroll; 45 percent, overhead; and the rest, profit.

Field work -- including here library and historic research -- and laboratory analyses generally can be estimated with some precision. Field work estimates are based upon how much effort has been needed in the past to do the work. A few firms will keep time-motion studies for Phase I, Phase II, and Phase III projects, relative to field and soils conditions. This is something that we have always done, and it requires little more than keeping tack in the general field notes of how much work was accomplished by each person each day. Related figures are given in Chapters 5, 6, and 7. Figures based upon such records tend to be extremely accurate, and allow the firm to bid on a project with the kind of competitive precision that, if the project is awarded, it is known it can be done in the time and cost proposed. One certainly wants to win every project bid upon, but not in a way that results in a loss, either in terms of cash flow or in terms of personnel.

One variable for field and laboratory cost, then, is how much time it will take to do the work. The second variable is the pay grade of the personnel doing the work.

Most firms have several basic personnel categories that resolve into at least seven basic pay grades. Examples are given in Table 3.1.

In setting out a bid for a proposal, labor estimates will be made. In the back of everyone's minds will be an awareness of the skills needed to do the tasks. That will translate first to the person in the firm who would be doing the work, then to that person's pay grade. It will be *that* figure that will end up in the budget estimates.

For each task set, then, there will be an array of person-hours relative to pay grade and task. It is from that information that a final budget estimate will be made.

Table 3.1. Basic Personnel Categories and Pay Grades

Personnel Category	General Role	Average Corporate Pay Scale (PI = 1.0)	Approximate Equivalent: Federal General Schedule (GS) Series
1. Principal Investigator	Responsible for project and will sign off on the submitted report; in most firms, the same as the project manager	1.00	GS - 14/15
2. Project Manager Project Director	In firms that segregate project supervision from corporate management, the project manager is separated from the principal investigator. The project manager accepts all responsibility for the project, but has no authority and does not sign off on the project supervised or written; at times authorship is ascribed to the Principal Investigator instead. If the PM is the PI, let 1.0 = 0.5 and recompute pay scale	0.50	GS - 11-13
3. Historian	Responsible for historic background research and for site files research; reports to the project manager for the particular project only	0.31	GS - 10/11
4. Field Supervisor Archaeologist II	This is the crew chief or foreman; may be reassigned to tasks of equal skill level; usually this is a person with an MA	0.31	GS - 9
5. Field Archaeologist Archaeologist I	These may be staff personnel or project hires and perform the skilled archaeological work required; for Federal projects, all personnel have a BA and a couple years of field experience	0.25	GS - 7
6. Laborer	Laborers are general (unskilled-in-archaeology) workers who may be hired to provide basis labor assistance	0.19	GS - 1
7. Laboratory Supervisor	The laboratory supervisor governs the laboratory; usually has an MA	0.38	GS - 10/11
8. Laboratory Technician	Laboratory technicians do basic laboratory tasks and low-level analytical work; may be filled by Field Supervisors and Field Archaeologists should the work be available and field work lacking	0.23	GS - 7
9. Graphics Supervisor	The Graphics Supervisor governs work flow into the Graphics Department or Division	0.31	GS - 10/11
10. Graphics Technician or Illustrator	Executes the graphics needed by the Project Manager/Principal Investigator; the Graphics people often will photograph the artifacts	0.23	GS - 7
11. Editor	Many firms have an in-house editor, whose responsibilites include wiring, consistency, and sometimes report production	0.31	GS - 10
12. Secretary	The secretarial staff represent administrative aid d'camps; they are responsible for office mechanics, ranging from assembling reports to recording payroll	0.19	GS - 2-4

Wages and Employee Descriptors

The Department of Labor/Employment Standards Administration Wage Hour Division (DoL/ESAWHD) identifies types of work and pay scales based upon duties and responsibilities. Federal agencies often use the job titles in describing the kinds of worker expected to be performing given tasks. Further, some Federal agencies use the associated hourly pay scale as a guideline for how much each level of expertise should be paid by the bidder. For example, the ESAWHD recognizes Archeologist I, II, and III, identified in terms of responsibilities and associated with a pay rate. Thus, an Archeologist I should be receiving at least $12.75 per hour, a reasonably fair entry-level wage for a person with a bachelor's degree. (The national average by 1999 for entry-level liberal-arts college majors in non-technical jobs was around $31,800, and a bit more if the person had majored in Anthropology, English, or Philosophy.)

It is wise, by the way, to identify occupational positions in the project budget and bid using the terms and descriptors found in the DoL/ESAWHD. One reviewer of this text noted that this cannot be over-emphasized: Use *all* of the DoL/ESAWHD jargon and – especially – their formats. These usually will be familiar to the Federal agency, and their use will be taken not only as an indication of competence, but also as an indication of good-faith labor law compliance.

There are two remaining factors that need to be considered. The first is the rate schedule that is used. Most firms have two scales, one for government clients and another, higher price range for private-sector clients. Generally, the rate schedule for government contracts runs 30 - 50 percent below the rate schedule for private-sector clients, depending upon the pay grade. (Some firms maintain their desired profit margin by off-setting the larger but lower yielding government contracts with the somewhat smaller but higher yielding private-sector contracts.)

The second factor is part of the country in which the work is to be done. The following example, which occurred when we were contacted recently by a developer shopping around for a Phase I reconnaissance survey price quote on a five-acre development, can give some sense of this: For a Phase I survey in the Southeast, the cost can range from $40 (firm) to $80 (opening bid) per acre, inclusive of field work, analyses, and report; in the Middle Atlantic, the cost will be around $1,000 per acre. There can be quite a range in pricing from region to region, and from project to project. Our experience in government has shown that the range of bids for a particular project can also be quite large. For any firm entering into a new market, it is very wise to figure out the competition's pricing.

One last series of items to note here. It is sometimes proper to set out an explanation of cost details in an overall budget, especially for complex projects. It is fair to be creative *within the context and pre-approved structure* of the proposal and bid as it pertains to the RFP. Creativity by itself and for its own sake is never rewarded in the market place; however, creative and imaginative solutions that solve *other people's problems* is rewarded.

3.2.4. Structuring and Negotiating the "Best-and-Final"

The proposal or bid budget, if awarded, becomes the project budget. It is vitally important that the numbers submitted during the bid process are realistic for profitable completion of the project. If the numbers do not show profitability in the immediate sense, then the project must, if accepted, be seen as a short-term investment that can lead to profitable work. Remember also that if one starts to demand too much from one's personnel, they not only will bolt to another firm, they will also leave with a detailed knowledge of the firm's pricing and bidding protocols. Further, expecting -- demanding -- that people constantly work for less than their market value is theft. There are firms that actually *do* operate on the assumption that, when one person leaves, others will fill in, and develop an indentured, gulag-like work place based upon exploiting the labor of others for the profit of corporate owners. They fortunately are limited and are to be avoided.

It is just as possible, as all who have gone through business ethics know, to structure out a fair compensation package that also is competitive.

The submitted bid proposal, if competitive, may -- at the discretion of the Federal Contracting Officer for the agency -- result in the firm being asked to negotiate a "best-and-final" offer. This really asks that the firm level with the Federal agency and say what their final, least-cost bid would be. This is a negotiating exercise, anticipated in the RFP request for a list of names and titles of corporate individuals authorized to negotiate (FAR [48 CFR] Chapter 1 clause 52-215.11). At the state or local level, the best-and-final process is used less often and straight bids are more common. In such cases, it may be useful to imagine the proposal as a best-and-final offer, then see if that would change it. This helps ensure a competitive sealed bid.

Three things occur simultaneously during the best-and-final process. The first is a lowering or adjustment of cost in a way that will provide the firm with the award. The second is a refining of the work that the Federal agency needs to have done. And the third is an attempt to guess what others may be willing to do. For the Federal agency, that last point is the only one that has meaning, since it presumably will drive the potential vendor to offer the very best cost for services. The potential vendor may be one of three, or actually may be one of one. A skilled Federal negotiator -- and believe us, the vast majority are -- will not reveal this. The Federal agency has a carrot; how far will the ... donkey lunge to get it?

Negotiating best-and-final provides the same thrill as playing poker. Many approach it in that fashion. We offer some strategic and tactical advice.

Always remember that the final bid agreed to verbally will be the project budget. That is, keep in mind that winning is wonderful, but winning is NOT always getting the award; rather, it is enhancing the future of the firm. This may be equivalent to getting the award and being able to accomplish the work using only the funds drawn from the contract. Or it may be a risk investment situation where it is possible that completion of the project will require drawing on corporate cash reserves, and minimizing that draw-down will require extra effort on the part of all involved personnel. (Most employees are more than willing to go to the front and sacrifice for the good of everyone, provided they get something back in return, and provided that they do not feel that they are being exploited. For some, "something back" will be association; for others, it will be wages. It is a managerial responsibility to know who requires what kind of reward to stay involved. People will work like idiots if they feel that everyone is in the situation together, which is why firms that start up in garages so often succeed. See also the boxes "Comments on Management" and "Managing Professionals" in Chapter 7.)

It is not necessarily bad to offer a bid that potentially could create a loss; some cash flow may be better than no cash flow, and the in-road that the project may make into the agency and the market place may be an investment worth the cost of the overhead needed to make up for the loss. That is, a tactical set-back may still be a useful strategic step. *But such a course of action needs to be considered with great care, and rarely is a sound decision.* Instead, it may point to fundamental business problem.

It is almost always preferable that the best-and-final offer is one that can be accomplished in the time frame and budget proposed. That is, any reduction in costs means a reduction in available labor, which must be accompanied by a change in the work order expected by the Federal agency. The Federal agency is charged with complying with Section 106, which means complying with the anticipated needs of the particular SHPO or THPO. The agency negotiators must remain true to the needs of the cultural resource, as it were. Indeed, Federal Contracting Officers are instructed to evaluate proposals in part upon their budgetary realism.

Sources on Negotiating

There is a staggeringly large literature on negotiation within the marketplace. A trip to the local bookstore gives some sense of this, of course. A trip to the local used-book store often provides a better and more sobering perspective on the viability of those business-related negotiating books: One of the largest sections in three of our local used-book stores is of now-abandoned marketing and sales books. If any of these things really worked, you wonder, then why are new ones constantly written and old ones, sold off?

There are, though, a series of guides produced by Roger Fisher and William Ury that may be worth looking over. Fisher and Ury set up and ran the Harvard Negotiation Project; Ury later directed the Program on Negotiation at Harvard Law School before working at Emory University's Carter Center for Policy Studies in international conflict resolution. Theirs is a negotiating approach focused on win-win situations; on separating people from the issue; on understanding the other party's concerns; on avoiding fix-position/stare-down-the-opponent adversarial interactions; and on making sure that, when negotiating, a person has a BATNA: *Best Alternative to a Negotiated Agreement.*

We think the texts are well worth looking through, and may be of benefit to those archaeologists who have not taken business classes.

Fisher, Roger, and Danny Ertel. 1995. *Getting Ready to Negotiate: The Getting to Yes Workbook. A Step-by-Step Guide to Preparing for Any Negotiation.* Penguin Books, New York.

Fisher, Roger, William Ury, and Bruce Patton. 1991. *Getting to Yes: Negotiating Agreement without Giving In.* Second edition. Penguin Books, New York.

Ury, William. 1993. *Getting Past No: Negotiating Your Way from Confrontation to Cooperation.* Penguin Books, New York.

We learned about archaeology from that ... Vignettes on Site Closure and Restoration Relative to Budget Planning

Many Federal awards require that the contractor restore tested areas to initial conditions. Such restorations represent material and labor costs, and it is wise to have included these as budget items. There are two cautionary tales that illustrate the need to keep these things in mind.

We were engaged by a firm to do a Phase I survey/Phase II testing of a series of archaeological sites in the Great Lakes Region on behalf of the Corps of Engineers. For one site, field methods consisted of plowing the site then doing a transit-based, piece-plotted surface collection. That is, two crew members were sent out with leveling rods and plastic bags, another stayed behind to take dictated notes, and one of us read off distance and bearing for each of the artifacts flagged earlier during a walk-over of the field.

After finishing with the site, we were told that the contract also required that the now-plowed field be seeded then covered with (wheat) straw. The project budget had no provision for this. Still, we were told to seed the plowed land to protect it from the winter rains (keep in mind that this was October in the north land; curious kind of grass that would take root and grow, one would think).

Do you have any idea what grass seed costs? How much grass seed is needed to cover how much land? How even to effectively broadcast it? We spent a productive day learning the basics (all unbudgeted). Grass seed, it turns out, is not inexpensive, especially given the rate at which it should be dispersed. Several hundred dollars were spent simply getting the stuff. And, how is it dispersed?

There are grass-seed broadcasters, things that consist of an open-bottom canvas bag that rests over a whirligig that spins horizontally – in a plane parallel with the ground – in response to a side hand-crank. The whole device hangs in front from a strap around the neck. One pours the seed into the bag, then begins to crank while walking.

It does not take very long to seed a field. The next exercise was trickier: Straw.

Yes, the agreement with the agency stipulated placing straw down over the grass seed. How much straw is needed to cover a hectare? How much does a bale of straw – or even a bale of hay – cost?

This was dairy country. Farmers had straw, of course. For that matter, they had hay, too. But all of it was dedicated to livestock use.

The rule-of-thumb among landscapers is that a bale of straw, be it wheat or pine, will cover an area of about 36 square feet (say, 3.3 m²) for seeding, and about half that for mulching. Thus, only around 3,030 bales of straw would be needed. Normally, a bale of straw in the late-1980s cost around $3 at a home-gardening center, depending on a number of factors. The cheapest we could find any straw in that area at the onset of winter was at $10 a bale.

Consider the budget implications for the moment. The project budget itself was about $12,500 for the site. This was meant to cover field work, analyses, and report production. No one, it turned out, had given any thought to landscape restoration costs.

We managed to find straw for less than the market value, and very little straw at that. So, we did what we could (the SOW only said to put down straw, we were told; it did not say how much straw to put down), and spent another four unbudgeted person-days spreading it about. The cost for the straw stayed below $1,000, but with labor and seed we already had used the equivalent of about a quarter of the budget for the site. The people who had written the proposal and prepared the budget were furious with the field crew for the cost over-run. The over-run came from failure to understand the realities of the field and of SOW requirements in the RFP.

A second example gives another perspective on budgets and budget management. While sometimes it is best to have employees do the landscaping, it may be politically as well as quality wise to hire a local landscaping firm to do the work. Involving members of the community is good public relations, and of course a local firm will be able to respond to problems, such as when the 1 x 2 m test unit in Mrs. Stevenson's backyard begins to settle and leave a noticeable depression.

Most people are surprisingly willing to let archaeologists blast out holes in their front yards – we are talking here of archaeology done in the urban/suburban worlds of flood levees and highway corridors. They become restive when the backfill does not settle, but things generally sort themselves out in a year: If the work has been subcontracted to a landscaper, then the landscaper gets most of the complaints until the land falls back to normal.

However, one of the more harrowing budget problems we faced was when we backfilled Phase II test units that had been opened in the middle of a northern winter and taken to several meters below grade.

Temperatures that year fell to -10°F. We managed to keep working during those times by building small structures over the test units. However, at the end of the field work, the contract required that we backfill and seed.

The project budget did not provide for contracting a landscaper, so the work was to be done by the firm when conditions permitted. However, the firm's CFO took it upon himself – without telling the project manager – to hire then direct a landscaper to backfill units. In February. After three months of sub-zero weather. Those costs were then billed to the project's budget. The work was done using an endloader. And, yes, the piles of backdirt *did* end up in the excavation units ... as frozen, solid lumps.

It was said that the field in which the testing had been done looked like a Mandan earth lodge community or, to the less fanciful, like those curious sugar-loaf limestone mountain spires in the Kweilin area of Kwangsi Chuang in south China.[a]

In many cases, the piles were two meters high. And they remained that way for nine months, since the pushing in of frozen earth in effect insulated it and prevented it from thawing.

The landscaping firm was local, but the local people, outraged at the landscape devastation, complained often and loudly, creating an enormous public relations nightmare. Oh yes, and the budget: The project, bid with no margins for problems much less any for landscape restoration, ended up devoting 10 percent of its revenues to landscaping. As we understood later, the project recorded a loss, a loss that turned out to be ... equal to 10 percent of the original project budget.

It is always best to plan ahead, and to provide budget lines for all expected project costs.

_____

a. For anyone worried about these things, this was the last place that Chennault parked the Flying Tigers before their contracts expired and they were re-formed as the China Air Task Force under the 10th Air Force. See also Chapter 4: *"We learned about archaeology from that ... Interviews."*

3.3.   Private-Sector Contracts

Private-sector contracts are a bit different than Federal government contracts. Although a government agency may require that the work be done, the arrangement for that work will be between the private-sector firm and the archaeology corporation or division. In some cases, there may be a formal RFP and SOW; in other cases, the arrangements may be made over the phone. One of the great advantages of private-sector work is that the work can be done quickly, with an immediate and sensitive response to the needs of the client. Private-sector contracts tend to go through people who have the authority to say yes or no to an offer and to a schedule. Schedules and turn-around on project proposals can be within a week.[3]

The private sector is not really interested in doing archaeology; rather, archaeology is a regulatory step that may or may not have been anticipated, but still is one that needs to be cleared. The sooner cleared, the sooner their project can start and the sooner the cash flow needed to re-pay development loans can begin.[4]

---

3. The private sector differs from the academic sector in many ways, but perhaps one of the most striking is the speed and responsiveness with which it can and does act. For example, the time between when a position opens and when the new employee begins working often is on the order of two weeks to a month in the private-sector, but generally is nine to 15 months in the academic sector. Some of this is due to differences in operational schedules: Colleges and universities are partially locked into the pace of the academic-year calendar and a pre-structured year-long budget; private-sector firms providing professional services have a multiplicity of overlapping schedules reflecting different projects at different stages. Such firms also usually have a more stream-lined decision-making process, with lower-level managers having greater authority for hiring and taking on new projects, than have academic institutions.

    Some of the lack of responsiveness, though, is due to habits of occupied environment, which in the university setting is extremely unharried and secure compared with other settings. Perhaps unfairly, the private and public sectors perceive the academic sector as dawdling; for people who have been natives of both worlds, which is true for almost the entirety of both public- and private-sector communities, the slowness of response to most things by the academic sector is legend.

4. This attitude will vary by the part of the country and background of the client. In some areas, developers, engineers, and architects are well aware of cultural resource compliance requirements, and schedule their permitting and loan application activities to take those needs into account. Some banks will even make sure that such environmental regulations have been met before approving a loan, which if nothing else apprises the developer that cultural resources needs must be met.

    In other parts of the country, the development and design community may be unaware of cultural resource requirements. The loan for construction may already have been approved and disbursed, and general and subcontractors hired, when the developer, contractor, or engineer first learns that some kind of cultural resources work will be needed, and that the project cannot start until the archaeological work is completed.

    Business people caught in this latter situation almost always will blame the government and the archaeologist for their own lack of awareness of basic requirements. That is really a non-issue as far as the archaeologist is concerned, or it should be treated that way.

3.3.1.   Types of Private-Sector Clients and Needs

There are a wide assortment of private-sector clients, and really no easy way to classify them. One way that has some marketplace use sorts potential clients as follows:

* private-sector clients with local or regional markets, and subject to local or state compliance laws;

* private-sector clients with local or regional markets, and subject to Federal requirements and thus Section 106;

* interstate private-sector clients subject to local or regional compliance laws; and

* interstate private-sector clients subject to Federal requirements and thus Section 106.

Examples of local or regional firms include housing developers, contractors, utilities, and local engineering firms. With the exception of utilities (including here telecommunications and cable television), most of these clients' project needs involve *areas* or *tracts* of land. Governing statutes may be Federal, as in the case of a golf course emplaced in a flood plain (making it subject to Corps of Engineers issuance of a 404 Wetlands permit), and thus trigger the Section 106 Process. Or governing statutes may be local, as is the case for Anne Arundal County in Maryland, which has archaeological compliance as a condition for issuance of a development permit for subdivisions.

Firms with local or regional markets are comparatively small, operate with comparatively little margin and cash reserves, and may not be aware of the archaeological regulatory environment. For the practicing archaeologist, the advantage is that working with a comparatively small firm allows speedy response to project needs, something that is in the interest of the client. The disadvantage is that the client is much more anxious *because* of that limited reserve and, possibly, because the regulatory stipulations came *after* the development loan was awarded and *after* subcontractors were hired.

It is all well and good to argue, as we have been doing throughout this text, for the societal importance of cultural resources. And perhaps under other

---

    What *is* an issue is knowing that the aggravation felt by the client is prompted by a loan that requires scheduled interest payments -- and sometimes a construction crew that is inactive but is also drawing funds from that same loan. For the client, the required archaeology represents a costly delay. It does not hurt at this point to consider one's skill in negotiation, and to remember that the archaeologist is the only person who can resolve the factors responsible for that delay.

circumstances, the small-business client would agree. But usually when it is the small business itself that is involved, the client is viewing the compliance requirements with a mixture of trepidation, confusion, tremendous anxiety, and therefore irritation if not fear. The practicing archaeologist's responsibilities will include allaying those fears, usually by getting the work done properly but expeditiously, and relieving the client of those regulatory concerns. One archaeological entrepreneur has been in the habit of saying the following to assuage the concerns of clients: "Don't worry, we will get you into compliance."

Firms with interstate markets tend to be larger, with several levels of jurisdiction and organization, and with needs that may involve Federal or local statutes. The organizations are sophisticated; the negotiating and contracting, subtle. Such firms have in-house legal staffs, portions of which are assigned to environmental regulation.[5] The archaeologist becomes one more subcontractor in a very large process.

Whereas the CEO of an archaeology firm may work as a "social" equal with the CEO of a local business, it is less likely that that will happen when dealing with a major oil exploratory firm. There, the corporate contact will be a project officer or, perhaps, branch or division manager. The practicing archaeologist becomes just another vendor, in a world of vendors.

3.3.2. Locating Private-Sector Clients

Most states have a list of consulting archaeologists practicing within the state; the list will be at the SHPO, the Office of Historic Preservation, the State Archaeologist, the Department of Natural Resources, or the Secretary of State. Often, the first point of contact for the private-sector client will be the local or state government; just as often, the first indication for that same client that archaeological consultants even exist will be that same list of archaeologists. The SHPO or equivalent body will distribute that list to the private-sector firm at the same time that it learns that archaeological compliance is expected. The list, then, becomes a contact list, and many private-sector firms will begin simply by calling the names on that

list. Thus, if the practicing archaeologist is not on that list, no notice will be received of potential projects.

The list is typically sent out by the SHPO or equivalent agency, along with an information packet to the potential client. It is then up to the recipient to contact one of the archaeological consultants on the list.

The list may be divided into specialty areas or levels of experience, and this is now varying by state (see Chapter 2 text box "Certification"). A number of states now maintain lists of firms and individuals who, in the view of the SHPO, are qualified to practice within their jurisdictions. Further, many states, such as New York and Maine, will indicate if the professional archaeologist is qualified in historic or prehistoric archaeology, or is qualified to perform Phase I survey versus Phase III data recovery, or a similar limitation.

While there may be plenty of professional archaeologists not on the list who are qualified to work in the state, most SHPOs (and on tribal lands, THPOs) and state archaeologists are simply unwilling to take the chance on an unknown, with the attendant risk of substandard work. As stewards of the resource base, they find the list a powerful management and regulatory tool.

Additional action marketing or publicizing archaeological services will vary by region of the country, and can be taken under advisement. For example, archaeology firms historically are listed in the Atlanta "Yellow Pages," but we rarely have seen similar listings in other metropolitan areas. Being on a historic preservation board often is useful, since it brings the archaeologist into contact with the greater development community, as well as the local or state political community. Towns contemplating Certified Local Government status require an archaeologist and may appreciate a volunteer, making this too a chance for establishing contacts.

Participation in local archaeology societies or "archaeology weeks" generally announces one's interests to the *archaeological* community, but much less to the private-sector community that needs or may need archaeological services. It does, though, inform the SHPO/THPO and other regulators of the practitioner's existence and interest in the local archaeology. It becomes, then, more a kind of informal professional certification than a marketing tool (although public talks to community service groups -- Lion's Club, Kiwanis -- on compliance archaeology can combine the two). Participation in local archaeological societies sometimes helps archaeological specialists who serve as subcontractors on larger compliance projects. And in that vein, journal articles and conference papers work even better as advertising copy.

---

5. It has been our experience that the professional archaeologist's understanding of cultural resource requirements specifically and environmental requirements generally is more extensive than many interstate and international firms. Several such firms in our experience -- telecommunications, engineering-and-architecture, and petroleum/natural gas -- have tended to confuse NEPA with Section 106 and NHPA, and actually put themselves in a situation of non-compliance. The point here is that a lawyer employed by the legal affairs division of a large, multinational corporation does not automatically know more, or even anywhere near, what a practicing archaeologist knows about the legal aspects of his or her profession. Thus, there is an opportunity for diplomatic enlightenment. It is the professional practitioner's responsibility is to make sure that *everyone* comes out of the process a winner: the client, the society, and especially the archaeologist's own firm.

"Cold calling" also is useful, but requires tactical insight. "Cold calling" refers to contacting firms that the archaeologist recognizes as needing -- or about to need -- professional services. The contact will be verbal, and *must* be with someone in the firm who has the capacity to make decisions about taking on a consultant to solve a pending or imminent problem. Doing *that* requires getting past the individual's "gate keeper," who will be the secretary, receptionist, or administrative assistant. All of this falls into the area of "outside sales," for which there are enormous numbers of how-to books as well as business school courses. Once a contact is made, a presentation will need to be packaged then delivered. This takes advantage of all of that public-speaking and teaching skill developed in an academic setting.

A variant on "cold calling" is to mail out a qualifications statement or similar piece of catalogue advertising. This, though, is becoming increasing less productive: for small recipient firms, because everyone is overwhelmed already; for large recipient firms, because the document will never make it past the gate keeper. (Copies of stand-alone qualifications statements are useful to have on-hand, though, since they can serve as expanded business cards.)

Finally, a rather clever way of maximizing exposure is to make sure that area college and university Anthropology or Sociology departments know of the firm and its availability to do archaeology. People often phone the local college's or university's Anthropology department whenever they have need of archaeological services. In some situations, there are no archaeologists on staff (around 10 percent of doctoral-granting Anthropology departments in the United States do not have archaeologists). In other situations, the staff archaeologist has other concerns, and usually does not have the time or logistical capacity to respond to a potential client's needs. In both cases, knowing that the firm exists allows those departments to pass along the name of the firm to a caller clearly interested in doing business.

3.3.3. Assembling a Bid Package

RFPs from private-sector clients differ from those of government agencies. Instead of the formal packet of solicitation forms; representations; certifications; and contract clauses outlining proper, ethical, and legal protocols; the RFP issued by the private-sector client generally will consist of a cover letter and the equivalent of a SOW. The letter will request a proposal and bid, and may provide deadline particulars. The SOW, frankly, can be anything from a professional-quality document prepared under the guidance of the SHPO or the enabling agency's archaeologist, to a hastily assembled request with unclear specifications. Most often, the SOW is a workable document, mainly because most often the

private-sector client's first contact with a firm is for Phase I reconnaissance services, and such work usually is more forgiving of a poorly worded SOW. Anything more complicated -- Phase II testing or Phase III data recovery -- as often as not will be done through the same firm, and by that point the archaeology firm or division has a pretty good idea of what the client needs to have done. [6]

Responses to private-sector clients/RFPs vary. Initially, this will include the full qualifications statement, particularly the sections documenting insurance, bonding, and especially previous corporate clients. Reputation is very important. Business concerns are parts of a business community, and often follow the lead of other members of that community: If one member of that community has been satisfied with the work provided by a given archaeological contractor, then most others will turn to the same contractor when such work is needed.[7]

The technical aspect of the proposal can be written either for a professional audience or for a lay audience; it is possible to do one document that covers both. The private-sector client wants to understand how the money given to the archaeologist is being spent and, to a lesser extent, why (meaning why the statutes are in place, rarely anything more). It is their money, after all. Keep in mind that small development firms are entrepreneurial firms, which means that the firm is mentally viewed as an extension of the person of the

---

6. The continued use of the archaeology firm will be driven by several factors, including the personality of the client's owner, the quality and reaction to of the work performed initially, and the cost. Business relationships often are personal relationships, at least "personal" in a Machiavellian sense. Until they are sure of their vendor, private-sector firms will keep shopping around for the best price. If it turns out that the price -- and the turn-around time -- are good, the shopping normally becomes cursory or stops entirely.

Knowing that you have a dependable plumber who can be called at any hour is a tremendous relief, and archaeology firms/divisions represent the same kind of time- and anguish-saving service within the greater environmental compliance world. This reinforces the importance of high quality and quick turn-around time: If a firm is known to be sensitive to the special needs of the client, responsive, fast, and of a quality that clears the required archaeological work quickly, then that firm will hold the business of a client indefinitely.

7. An excellent examination of the development community can be found in Joel Garreau's 1991 *Edge City: Life on the New Frontier.* Doubleday, New York. Using different parts of the country as he went through the nature of edge-city development, Garreau presented a wealth of information on how the development community works. This ranged from demographic and fiscal requirements for projects, through the temperament of the people involved, to the specifics of various laws as they pertain to commercial ventures. For anthropological archaeologists living among the business community, Garreau's book gives valuable insights into how the natives of that world live and work, allowing then the private-sector archaeologist to interact profitably with that community.

entrepreneur.[8]

What to an outsider is petty is (unconsciously) to the

---

8. There is a considerable literature in business and management on personality types, business organization, and organizational growth and development (for sources, e.g., Keirsey and Bates 1984; Miner 1985; Hirsh and Kummerow 1990; Kroeger and Thuesen 1992; Tieger and Barron-Tieger 1992; Narramore 1994; Kummerow, Barger, and Kirby 1997). Most assessments work with the Myers-Briggs Type Indicator® (see Myers and McCaulley 1985; Myers 1993), which appears to be the most accurate and certainly is the most widely used assessment instrument among human resources departments, churches, and career counselors and psychologists (Narramore 1994:239; Kummerow, Barger, and Kirby 1997:4; see also Miner 1985 for international use). The Myers-Briggs system is based on four dichotomous personality trait sets, each indicated by one of two letters: E (e.g., extroverted, team player) or I (e.g., introverted, prefers to work on own); S (e.g., sensing, focused on present) or N (e.g., intuitive, focused on future, never have enough time); T (e.g., thinking, analytical) or F (e.g., feeling, great sense of group feeling); and J (e.g., judging, highly organized) or P (e.g., perceiving, adaptable, procrastinates).

Highly regarded and well known, we have made use of it for corporate and volunteer organizations; it is an excellent way to get a handle on the personnel resources you have. Despite its long history of widespread use and dependable results, it is relatively unknown to anthropologists. Of interest here are entrepreneurs and managers.

Entrepreneurs found companies. They tend to be brilliant at envisioning a business enterprise (Zaleznik 1983:162; Kroeger and Thuesen 1992:347), at understanding market dynamics and possibilities (Kroeger and Thuesen 1992:366), in setting up the enterprise so that it works (Miles et al. 1983:383-385), and in willingness to take risks based upon their vision (Keirsey and Bates 1984:31-32, 36-37; Kroeger and Thuesen 1992:347). However, entrepreneurs as a class are also notorious for having weak managerial skills; poor social skills with personnel (Miner 1985:352-353; Tieger and Barron-Tieger 1992:192-193); and poor time management skills (Tieger and Barron-Tieger 1992:275). Since the firm is an extension of the person of the entrepreneur, there also is a need to dominate and control (Miner 1985:351; see Holder 1972:52). The mix can range from endearingly benign to vindictively despotic; the Myers-Briggs system does not deal with expression of type in that way.

Entrepreneurs found companies, and the companies will take on the personality of their founders and owners (Narramore 1994:198, 206; see also Hirsh and Kummerow 1990). As firms mature and develop, the needs shift from those of the risk-taking developer to the common-sense consolidator. These are the managers, and they have personalities very different from entrepreneurs.

Entrepreneurs found, even invent businesses; managers sustain and nurture those businesses (Mintzberg 1971:B97; Beer 1980:5-6; Zaleznik 1983:162; Keirsey and Bates 1984:46; Miner 1985:31-32, 355-356; Freidson 1986:149, 151, 211-212; Kroeger and Thuesen 1992:393-397; Tieger and Barron-Tieger 1992:220, 232). Managers tend to coordinate actions relative to an overall agenda, in part of their corporations and in part of their own within the context of their corporations. Unlike entrepreneurs, who tend to be visionary, managers tend to be grounded in the here-and-now, and tend to prefer objective external -- and adhered to -- measurements and criteria. In essence, they are much more practical (Miner 1985:32). Managers tend to react rather than act; they also tend to be more internal in their reasoning and need for approval: Managers have a great capacity, well beyond what is found in the United States generally, to keep their own counsel and plan accordingly (Kroeger and Thuesen 1992:393-397). It is the managerial population -- which in the Myers-Briggs Type system tend to be SJs -- that keep things running smoothly once the entrepreneurs -- the SPs -- have set things into motion.

By the way, for those willing to run all of this down, you might be interested to know that archaeologists -- along with historians, researchers, and college faculty who want to teach advanced students -- tend to be a Myers-Briggs Type INTP (Tieger and Barron-Tieger 1992:205-206). Their sample, though, probably was restricted to university archaeologists.

---

entrepreneur a serious issue because it is a personal issue. Do not underestimate this: We still have an outstanding bill from 1985 from a developer in central New York for $35; he felt he could get away without paying. And so far has.

3.3.3.1.   Contents of a Bid Package

Bid packages for private-sector clients vary. However, the following should be included:

*   cover letter that provides an abstract of how what is proposed will satisfy the needs of the client;

*   specific outline of what is proposed to be done; this can be part of the letter or it can be a separate document;

*   qualifications statement that is structured for a private sector audience; and

*   detailed budget that is set up to justify *each* expense.

The cover letter usually is a *pro forma* confirmation of a telephone conversation. Still, it carries legal (and litigious) weight, and should summarize the firm's understanding of the client's needs and the firm's ideas for satisfying those needs.

(Notes should be made summarizing any discussion of a proposed project, as well as a hard-copy compilation of any discussion with a client or possible client. Every person on staff should maintain a "Record of Communication" log, which documents phone calls, face-to-face conversations, and any other communication-interaction with a client, government official, or supervisor/manager in the firm. The "Record of Communication" will include the person's name and title/occupation, date and time of the conversation, phone number or e-mail address, and specifics about what was discussed. E-mail messages should be printed out and filed with the other "records of communication.")

Either contained within the letter, or as an attachment, the firm will provide the private-sector client with what amounts to a technical proposal. (If contained all in a letter, it will be referred to as a "letter proposal.") This will clearly outline a research strategy that satisfies the cultural resource compliance needs of the project. The research strategy must be structured in a way that is readable to the educated layman while also being professionally solid.

The qualifications statement will present not only the technical qualifications of the firm, but will do so in the language and tone of a business concern, while at the same time providing -- concisely -- substantive details about previous work, financial stability,

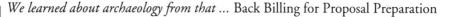

We learned about archaeology from that ... Back Billing for Proposal Preparation

Preparation of proposals and bids are understood to be normal business expenses, and therefore are to be funded out of corporate overhead. Proposal and bid preparation can be time-consuming and therefore expensive, at least on paper: Most proposal work is done by salaried personnel, so while the number of hours devoted to the effort may be high, it is also quite possible that most of the actual salary already is covered through existing contracts. This is an accounting matter that, at the moment, is tangential to the issue here.

Because of the time devoted to and expense involved in proposal preparation, firms on occasion attempt to back-bill the client for the work in preparing that accepted proposal and bid. This makes clients very angry. For example ...

We were involved a number of years ago with a firm bidding on a state-mandated compliance project. Set in an urban area, the project involved historic and prehistoric archaeological work, urban archaeology, as well as extensive historic research. The scale of the project along with the high-profile nature of the work not only was exciting, it also would result in wonderful publicity for whatever firm won the award. (In the end, network film crews would do a story on the project, broadcast during the Super Bowl. Reasonably good definition of "high profile.") Because of the potential, a large number of the firm's upper-level personnel put in upwards of 80 hours each over a two-week period researching and structuring a technical and bid package. That time was in addition to day-to-day project and office management chores, which resulted in a seriously exhausted bunch of people by the time the document left the office. (One person even put in back-to-back 80-hour weeks.)

The product was a sound and good proposal, excellent technically and certainly competitive financially. However, a week or so after submission, the architecture-and-engineering firm, along with the state, told us that the award was going to another firm. Like all of these things, the proposal was mentally set to one side and life went on. Frankly, everyone was so tired, and had so much else to do anyway, that any disappointment was muted at best.

About a month after the award, the architecture-and-engineering firm retained by the state to do the construction contacted our firm and offered the project. There was, of course, jubilation at the news, but there arose the question of why we were now awarded the contract.

It turned out that the firm originally chosen had, indeed, submitted a lower bid. Considerably lower, in fact. Then, with the start-up of the project, that firm submitted a bill to the architecture-and-engineering firm to cover the cost of their proposal and bid preparation. The firm was immediately dismissed, the contract canceled, and our firm was hired instead.

insurance, bonding, and similar issues of concern to any group investing a great deal of money in the purchase of a service.

The budget needs to be detailed and clear about why the costs are needed. Private-sector clients are aware that services cost, and are willing to pay for those services (although treating with entrepreneurial developers is an experience, believe us). However, they expect to have some sense of why it is that the costs are what they are. The phrasing of the qualifications statement, combined with how it is the firm has interacted with the client, will determine just how much detail is needed to assuage the uneasiness of the client in this regard.

There are several variables involved here: part of the country, class accent, client background and position within the firm, previous interaction, and nature of the work to be performed. The client will feel comfortable with the professional practitioner if those variables are within the range of what he or she is use to treating -- or, in some cases, expects to treat. We have found that courtesy, honesty, and a quiet assurance will work just as well as all of the joke-telling glad-handing one associates with professional sales and marketing people.

3.3.3.2. Qualifications Statement

Qualifications statements have been discussed in Section 3.2.3.3 Qualifications Statements. These provide a description of the firm while also giving details about financial structure, technical expertise, previous project successes, insurance and bonding, and client references. More than with Federal qualifications statements, qualifications statements assembled for a private-sector audience are couched in the phrasing and terms that capture the interest business community. At this point, they *are* exercises in mercantile rhetoric. However, they *must* contain substance at important points -- insurance, previous work, sometimes financial strength -- to be evaluated by the client.

Most qualifications statements prepared for potential private-sector clients contain the same sorts of things mentioned in Section 3.2.3.3. Qualifications Statements:

* corporate organization and incorporation information, including nature and accomplishments of key professional personnel and support staff;

*   specifics of various corporate subdivisions, such as historians, geologists, laboratory staff, graphics, and publications;

*   structure of the physical plant, especially its analytical, curatorial, graphics, and publishing capabilities;

*   in-house and field capabilities and material, such as total station surveying equipment, CAD/CAM, GPS, GIS, and computer capabilities;

*   a clear and concise discussion of corporate capabilities, illustrated by a series of abstracted projects that show the firm's capacity to do specific kinds of work;

*   a clear statement about bonding and liability insurance (always required for government contracts); and

*   a list of corporate clients serving as references.

A qualifications statement is more or less like a catalogue. It presents what it is that the firm can do, the resources it has, and what it has done (successfully) in the past. It is substantive; it is completely true. It is also outright advertising.

Perhaps more important than with qualifications statements, or their equivalents, filed as part of Federal RFQs and RFPs, is the inclusion of a list of clients familiar with and willing to vouch for the work performed by the firm. People in most cultures trust those who appear to have met with approval by others of whom the evaluator approves. That is, acceptance by people that one accepts usually results in a person passing muster. That is the purpose of a references list in the qualifications statement, and also is part of the function of a list of previous projects (since a listing of those projects tells for whom the work was done).

Private-sector clients read at two levels (see also text box below: "Contact, Appearance, and Social Acceptance"). The first is the rhetoric, the tone and phrasing and structure of the document. Fluency in the language of a profession indicates ability and capacity. This holds as much for fields like Chemistry and Archaeology as it does for how one treats the neighbors from another culture who might be struggling with English: The ability to adroitly handle the language is unconsciously taken as an indication of ability.[9] The qualifications statement will be read by private-sector clients like that: It is the primary communicator of competency, professionalism, and respectability.

No one is fooled by the cosmetics and appearance, by the way; rather, the capacity to structure the document fluently in the phraseology of the business community is evidence that the firm is a serious, private-sector entity that *will* be sensitive and responsive to the needs of the business concern seeking help. For Anthropology people, this is very much a rite of passage, a demonstration that the firm/division understands the needs of the client at a fundamental level, so fundamental in fact that the firm/division can assemble a qualifications statement of this type.

The second level at which the document is read is that of its substance. Business concerns exist because they *do* understand the ins-and-outs of day-to-day market needs. The qualifications statement will be read, first, for its phrasing and structure, more or less to see if this is a document from a firm that acts like and is responsive to a business. It will then be read at a level for detail and facts: Can the work be done in the time frame needed? Has this firm done this kind of work before? Who says so? Do we know those people? What about finances: Is this firm solvent? Is this firm bonded? If they bolt, is there someone we can file a claim against? Who insures these people, and for how much? Look, just how long have these people been in business?

Qualifications statements are assembled out of the same boilerplate used for all clients, public sector or private sector. Many firms have a pre-packaged document that is sent out on an as-needed basis, and this often is sufficient. However, like any marketing document, it makes sense to have such a document tailored to the needs of the given audience.

3.3.3.3.   Project Design and Working with the Regulatory Agencies

The private-sector client usually will have been informed of the need for archaeological work by a public-sector regulator. The client may or may not have experienced this before, but in any event will be eager to have the work done quickly and expertly.

There generally are two ways in which the client will have been asked to fulfill archaeological or historic preservation requirements. The first will be through the Federal Section 106 Process. This will mean that the SHPO/THPO and possibly a Federal agency archaeologist will have been helping the client put together an SOW. The SOW often will be sound, certainly will meet with the approval of the SHPO/THPO, and in all becomes a coordinated effort by the public-sector archaeologist and the private practitioner in assembling a sensible and responsive solution to the compliance needs. The public-sector archaeologists, both in the SHPO/THPO and the agency, are functioning here in much the same way that the CDC (Centers for Disease Control and

---

9. This is why archaeologists, for example, constantly drop terms about local ceramic and projectile point types: It is an informal testing to see if the person is legitimate, since command of the field's jargon is taken to reflect professional qualifications.

Time Sheets

Firms maintain two sets of employees: Those who are paid at an hourly rate, and those who are salaried. Hourly employees working on Federal awards are protected by Federal labor guidelines and are entitled to over-time and holiday double-time rates; salaried employees are working at a fixed rate and receive neither compensation. Hourly employees will be working around 2,080 hours per year, and will receive compensation for those and any additional hours. Salaried employees tend to be paid substantially more, but also to work around 2,600 - 3,100 hours per year, based upon our experience with different firms and on Department of Labor figures. Indeed, in one firm we dealt with, it turned out that, given the number of hours worked, salaried employees made considerably less, per hour, than hourly employees.

Time sheets serve to keep track of fund allocation relative to project budgets and cash flow. For hourly employees, these are real numbers; that is, the hourly employee really is receiving wages for the time set forth on the time sheet, and it is fair – if one has a reasonably responsible accounting or finance office – to say that the money is being drawn down from the budgets concerned.

For salaried employees, this becomes a problem; for many, it actually is a moral and religious problem. A salaried employee's labor already has been bought, technically at a rate equivalent to that for the first 2,080 hours, which is the billable rate. Anything more is being done *gratis* for the firm, which often is expected of the employee, so much so that failure to do so will result in dismissal. Only that first 2,080 hours will be drawn down from the project budget, at least in real money terms.

For an hourly employee, this is not an issue; for a salaried employee, especially if the person is managing a project and its budget, it is. Entry in of the actual time needed to do the work very often results in an on-paper show of a project running over budget. On paper, that is true; in terms of actual cash flow, of course, it is not.

This raises the question of what a person should be doing in keeping track of time on the time sheet. There are two tacts that are taken for the salaried employee: Stop tracking hours on a project after a certain point, or keep track of all hours. In our experience, the first option is the one chosen in most cases. And it is that option that raises serious moral and ethical problems.

Providing the labor in effect for free but under threat of dismissal is providing labor under duress, which is theft. Technically, it also makes the provider an accessory to the theft. It also results in a misleading sense of what a project actually requires to be done. For small firms, where everyone is in the thing together, it is not a problem: Everyone views the salary as a yearly lump-sum portioned out on a bi-weekly or monthly basis, and the goal instead is to keep the cash coming in. In a way, it is profit-sharing. Small family run businesses have worked like that for centuries. For larger firms, this is problematic, since such behavior on the part of the salaried employee can become enabling behavior for the taking of labor without fair compensation. We are aware of situations where upper management of firms expect such a donation of labor by employees, and where the evident profit generated by the uncompensated time in effect goes back into a profit margin disbursed to that managerial tier.

Prevention) or the USDA County Extension Service does: Public resources present to help the greater citizenry. For the professional archaeologist, it is important to speak with the public-sector archaeologists, but remember always to keep the client informed that this *is going to be done*, as well as what has been said *when it is done*. No one in the United States likes to be talked about behind their backs, and the image of archaeologists gathering together in some kind of coven for purposes of consultation raises the justifiable ire of the client in just the same way that having a collection of physicians speak in one's presence -- as if the patient was not there -- does.

The second way in which the client will have been asked to satisfy compliance obligations will be at the state or local level, where there is much less direct help available for the client. In this situation, the professional archaeologist becomes not only the one who will do the work, but also the one who will put together an SOW that meets the needs of the resource but is just as fair to the client.

In that second situation, the professional archaeologist is in the same position as any professional -- physician, advocate, architect. The professional archaeologist has an ethical obligation both to the client and to the archaeological resource (which really is the greater society's non-renewable information resource). The same possible conflicts-of-interest that exist with a physician or advocate potentially exist with the archaeologist. Simply put: One acts in the best interests of those in whom they have put their trust.[10]

---

10. Reviewing this chapter, it is interesting to find that nearly all discussion of ethics is in the part that treats business issues.

Archaeology is like tennis or golf in the 1930s. For tennis, it was a player's obligation to call whether a shot was in or out, regardless of any official's call. And there is the story of Bobby Jones, who had hit into the tangled undergrowth adjacent to a fairway. In he went. Pause. Silence. Then out he came, held up a finger, then went back in. The ball soon emerged. Jones, away from all eyes, had swung and missed, and made that known.

Archaeologists, especially during the semi-isolated Phase I process, are their own moral authority. The sort of person who usually ends up doing archaeology has that same kind of 1930s tennis - golf sense of self-policing, of honesty. This carries over in situations where clients turn to the archaeological firm/division for help. One is placed in a dual role of SHPO/THPO representative

Contact, Appearance, and Social Acceptance

Before ending a general discussion on archaeological business practices, it probably would not hurt to address the issue of dress and parasemantics.

Archaeology is an extra-academic profession dominated by private-sector practitioners. Most of the people with whom the professional archaeologist will interact are themselves in the private sector, or they are in government. Both sets expect certain things of their professional consultants.

The first is appropriate dress. This is *NOT* mentioned in an academic setting. Dress is a statement of membership; it also is a statement by the individual of how they view, and how much they respect, the people with whom they interact. It is parasemantics and display, as those who have had introductory Anthropology courses quickly recognize. And the business and government communities are sensitive to this kind of expression (as would be any member of any culture). For those coming out of a college or university setting, this is very important to understand since it rarely is an issue within the academy, at least among faculty and students (it is an issue for those in administration).

There is appropriate business dress; this especially needs to be adopted whenever interacting with clients, and done so relative to their expectations. We will not go through all the details here – the best discussions available for how to dress appropriately are Molloy's (1988) *New Dress for Success* and (1996) *New Women's Dress for Success*, and the apposite sections of Fussell's (1983) *Class*. "Appropriate" varies by the nature of the firm, the area of the country, and kind of interaction. Office wear in stand-alone archaeology firms tends to be casual; office wear within engineering-architecture firms – particularly older established firms – tends to be more formal. Anyone working in a professional environment needs to be aware of things like this. How people are treated and the respect that they command – both within and outside of an organization – depend greatly on what physical image they display within the context of the particular firm.

The second item we offer with a certain amount of caution. Most professionals – and many businessmen and politicians – maintain what one of us calls a "Wall of Respect." That is, a wall upon which are the framed diplomas, the *Who's Who* certificates, the photographs of the office resident shaking hands with ... well, you get the idea. At one level, this is

expected and it works quite well. Physicians do this all of the time, and it is meant to reassure the patient that the person examining them has been declared competent by others ... who, it turns out, have similar displays on *their* walls.

Academics, especially anthropologists, are aghast at such things, which demonstrates rare good taste on their parts. As Fussell (1983:119, 125) observed, such displays generally are an indication of class insecurity, and are associated with The Middles. And that, of course, is the point. Such displays in a business or professional consulting setting are meant to be viewed by members of the middle class, merchants and similar miscreants. The displays reassure them that the individual so identified has received general societal accolades, and if approved by social betters, must needs be sufficient for the task at hand. Be assured that the heads of large established firms, who tend to be upper-middle or upper class in background, will *not* be found trotting along to sit in the office of a practicing archaeologist.

A similar atmosphere of quiet, upper-middle class confidence can be achieved by structuring the corporate offices in a way to express such competence. One local firm has done this brilliantly, with dark, hardwood floors covered with stray Q'asqai carpets and an elegant, understated tone. There are a couple diplomas on the off-white, hand plastered walls, but rare, and generally lost amidst prints and illustrations appropriate to the concern and work of the firm. One does not need to see the awards to know, when stepping into the office, that they are in the presence of a competent, successful, and highly professional firm. Well, at least until they see that all of the computers are Macintoshes. Even then, such a selection tells more of an upper-class quirkiness, combined with an ability to afford to be different ... and afford to have those things anyway. (It is an excellent firm, by the way.)

Fussell, Paul. 1983. *Class: A Guide through the American Status System*. Summit Books, New York.

Molloy, John T. 1988. *New Dress For Success*. Warner Books, New York.

Molloy, John T. 1996. *New Women's Dress for Success*. Warner Books, New York.

3.3.3.4. Competitive Budget Estimates

As mentioned in Section 3.2.3.5. Competitive Budget Estimates, the bid can consist of up to four sets of cost figures: Estimated cost of labor for specific, project-related tasks; costs or anticipated costs for specialists, such as lithic analysts or palynologists; costs for special analyses, such as radiocarbon dates; and logistical costs,

such as transportation and per diem.

Assembling a bid involves drawing on three sets of figures: A kind of rule-of-thumb bit of information for common tasks, a known estimate of how much effort actually had been needed to do the work in the past, and a sense of what the competition will be bidding.

There will be two broad sets of variables in setting up a budget, given all that has been said so far: The tasks that are to be done, and the personnel -- meaning pay

---

(unofficial and not deputized) and service provider. One is a *consultant* in the strict sense; one is there to deliberate then to counsel the client.

grade -- that will be used to perform those tasks. As mentioned in Section 3.2.3.5, most projects consist of five basic task sets:

1. start-up;

2. field work;

3. analysis;

4. report preparation and delivery; and

5. final report delivery and turn-over of any materials recovered and any field records generated.

Labor estimates are treated in Chapters 5 - 7, and need not be repeated here. Most firms have at least two pricing sets, a lower set for Federal clients, and a second higher set for private-sector clients. The rate schedule for private-sector clients obviously will be used here. Otherwise, budget structuring will be the same as outlined in Section 3.2.3.5. for Federal clients.

There is a caveat, though. Federal and, to some extent, state-government bids tend to be sufficiently regulated that the range of bid options is relatively narrow. This is NOT true for private-sector clients. Those clients fall into two broad sets: Large interstate firms with time-sensitive agendas, and smaller locally based firms.

The larger firms, such as natural gas pipe line firms or telecommunications firms, tend to be caught in several time-sensitive schedules that require quick turn-around on the archaeological compliance. Their solicitations are national in scope, and the bidding can be at a level higher than that used for public-sector clients. Large firms recognize that professional quality has a commensurate cost, and are -- within common sense -- willing to pay for that. (It does not hurt to remember that top managers in large firms are mostly ESTJ in the Myers-Briggs Type system [see again sources in fn. 8], which means that the Fisher, Ury and Patton [1991] and Ury [1993] negotiating strategy of objective criteria will work quite well here.) Their goal is to finish the project and to do so with the least amount of difficulty from the Federal and state governments. The professional archaeologist is one of many concerns that will help that large firm achieve its corporate goals.

Small local firms, such as developers, present a different problem, and this becomes a local or regional market/competition issue. Local firms tend to be very sensitive to even the smallest of cost outlays, and we are talking of figures in the tens of dollars. Once an archaeology firm meets with development/bank/real estate community approval, though, there are no problems *provided there are no major rate schedule changes.* Thus, while time is important, cost is an even

bigger issue. (Many of these will be entrepreneurial or family businesses; see fn. 8.)

Treating local private-sector clients requires a native-like understanding of local values. Some archaeology firms will under-price their labor in the local market, thus cornering that market. After all, once one is viewed as the dependable vendor for that community, that community rarely will seek someone else.

Other firms use a strategy that quality costs, people know this, and going with the standard (and a bit higher) private-sector client rate will result in being selected. Americans equate quality with cost, at least within reason. It is not just that a car that costs $36,000 is seen to be a better car -- in the sense of more dependable and longer-lasting -- than one that costs $11,200; a gallon of paint that costs $36 is seen -- expected, really -- to be of better quality than something that costs $15. Thus, pricing out a real-cost for services can be seen as a statement of quality.

The ability to structure a competitive budget estimate for a private-sector client is one that requires a knowledge of the market in the given area. This is a business and marketing issue, for which there are large numbers of books and people who can help, not to mention undergraduate and graduate-level curricula that can be taken. It is best to begin with a standard market analysis, then consult with one's banker, before going further.

The American Cultural Resources Association (ACRA) lists on its Web site information on wages and other information useful in preparing competitive bids (http://www.acra-crm.org). ACRA also sponsors workshops on bidding and budgets.

3.3.4. Structuring and Negotiating the "Best-and-Final"

There are two levels of private-sector project. The first involve firms involved in large, interstate projects. these have the potential to involve Phase I through Phase III work, and are subject to Section 106 protocols. Such firms are soliciting bids on a national scale, and these firms will often be involved in a negotiating process not unlike the Federal "best-and-final" process described in section 3.2.4.

The second level of private-sector contract involves local firms, often developers. These firms tend to be run by entrepreneurs, and tend to open by squabbling over costs. There is no best-and-final process as such; rather, the contractor or developer will have spoken with a range of available (meaning here local) firms, gotten some sense not only of price range but also of compatibility (from verbal, over-the-phone communication), then bargained for the best price. Once the vendor is chosen, that vendor will remain the go-to vendor for that developer or contractor, at least until the rate schedule changes. Further, given that developers and contractors are all of a community, like horse people and archaeologists, breaking into a development community -- if achieved -- opens up a large market.

In situations involving local firms dealing with local compliance projects, the best-and-final process really happens at the outset. There is no arranged, choreographed minuet of submissions then selection of three firms then discussions with each. Time is of the essence, as is a belief in being able to sense quickly what a firm really is like. The best-and-final often occurs during the same conversation, or with the same letter proposal, as the opening bid.

Finally, it does not hurt to keep in mind a business tactic we learned years ago: Call the potential client and say "I want your business; tell me what it is I need to do to get your business."

4: Preparing the Project Background

4.1.   Purpose and Objectives

The first formal step in doing the compliance project is the background research. This is an identification step, a gathering together of what already is known about the project and about the project area, both in terms of potential or known cultural resources as well as in terms of the nature of the land itself. This is normally a part of the Phase I identification process. For Section 106 projects, this preparatory or background research is the first identification step required of the Federal agency [36 CFR 800.4 (a)] after there is a determination of an undertaking with potential effects. The Secretary of Interior's Standards and Guidelines [48 FR 44716-44742] sets forth the standards expected for documentation, in effect using that background to establish clearly the criteria that will be needed for any evaluation of significance.

The purposes of the background research are to

*   review the nature of the project or undertaking itself;

*   review existing information of cultural resources that may be potentially affected by the planned project;

*   assess the likelihood that cultural resources would be located within the project area;

*   summarize the history and the prehistory of the region so that the overall context of cultural resources potentially present can be appreciated;

*   state what already is known about the archaeology and ethnography/ethnohistory of the region so that any cultural resources -- particularly sites -- present can be evaluated for Register-eligibility in terms of 36 CFR 60.4 *criteria for evaluation*;

*   summarize what is known of the current physical characteristics of the project area that may influence the condition of the archaeological deposit; and

*   summarize what is known of the past physical characteristics of the project area that may influence both the types of archaeological sites that might be present as well as any potential impact there may have been on the integrity of the deposit.

The background research puts the project and associated archaeological research into the broader context of what is known and why the work is being done. It also is a credentialing step: The nature and thoroughness of the project background informs the review agencies of the practicing archaeologist's preparation for the work that was undertaken. It is uncommon, although not unknown, for the background research to be a stand-alone document (for example, preservation plans and disturbance studies for Federal agencies both would qualify; see below). In many western states, the background research is particularly critical when Phase I reconnaissance and intensive surveys do not require subsurface testing. Usually, the background research is part of the larger compliance report, be it Phase I survey, Phase II testing, or Phase III data recovery.

Normally, the background research will be part of the draft report -- often as the second (environmental background) and third (cultural background) chapters -- submitted to the Federal agency or to the SHPO/THPO on behalf of the client. Thus, often some field work already will have been done before the review agency has had a chance to see if the practicing archaeologist really is competent in the archaeology of the review agency's jurisdiction.[1] The quality of the research background enables the SHPO/THPO or similar review agency to judge if the archaeological work and the recommendations by the practicing archaeologist are dependable.

Although regulations in most states urge that the historic and prehistoric background research for a project area be finished prior to the field work, this does not always happen. It is not unusual that the two tasks are done concurrently or in reverse order. For Phase II and Phase III projects, knowing what specific sites have been excavated in the region may or may not have much of a bearing on how the particular site being examined actually *gets* examined. Often all that is needed for the field work is a sound understanding of the nature of the sites and the archaeology of the region.

However, for Phase I reconnaissance and survey projects, since their responsibility is identification, it is important to have advance knowledge of what archaeological sites have been recorded for the project area or corridor (for Section 106 projects, the area of potential effects which may extend well beyond the immediate construction zone), since failure to locate these during field work will result in reviewers requesting additional testing to see if the boundaries of the site were improperly recorded. Such a request would require a return to the field, not only representing additional (and unbudgeted) project costs but also creating with the review agency and possibly the client a (legitimate) sense of professional ineptitude. Knowing beforehand that a project area is listed as having archaeological remains within it allows the practicing archaeologist to adjust field work to make sure that that site really is present or absent.

---

1. This pertains more to firms or principal investigators new to the awareness of the review agency and its jurisdiction; this is not an issue for long-standing firms, sometimes to the point where the background reviews submitted are cursory in detail, often at the behest of the review agency, which is getting tired of reading the same thing over and over again. By the way, such a diminution of background information is extremely misguided: EACH report must be able to stand alone in the presumed absence of any other source for the history or prehistory of the region. The reports submitted as part of the compliance process will, in two centuries, be an archival gold mine of primary documentation, and may in fact be some of the only secondary information on the prehistory or history of a given area. Always err on the side of redundancy in this; if people in the distant future are annoyed by it, then they can complain about it to you then.

4.2.   Project History

There are two aspects to the project history:

(1) the history of the undertaking itself, including what is intended to be done and what other options may have existed; and

(2) the history of the project area, both in general and in terms of past research efforts.

4.2.1.   History of the Undertaking

The history of the undertaking covers the nature of the proposed project, the reasons why it is going to be done, and what other options have been explored along with the reasons those options were not chosen. Summarizing the history of the undertaking in this fashion, with attention given to what has been considered, helps both the client and the review agency -- usually the SHPO/THPO -- to have a sense of how feasible it would be to re-design the project to lessen the impact on any Register-eligible cultural resources that may be affected. Remember that the report submitted by the archaeologist not only is a research report in the sense of primary research, it is also a planning document that is part of the larger planning process.

Where is the information for the history of the undertaking going to come from? In most cases, the Scope of Work (SOW or Scope) as well as the original RFP (Request for Proposals) will contain a summary of how the undertaking came to be in the form it now exists. Both the RFP and most certainly the SOW will have a clear indication of what it is that the undertaking will involve; almost always, this will include detailed design and project maps showing just how the land will be altered, where buildings and roads will be sited, and similar specific indications of intended actions such as placement of buried utilities or septic fields. In fact, in almost all cases the practicing archaeologist needs to have a detailed project map before the project can be planned and bid, if only to have a sense of scale and of terrain (and, for built-up areas, where to have the utilities check for buried pipes and cables).

Additional information usually will be supplied by the client after the project has been awarded to the archaeologist's firm. This can include earlier project design maps, previous studies conducted on the area (including even percolation [perc] test data and similar engineering analyses), and even some historic background material. Any other information on the project and its history is obtained generally by asking the client. (Or if the information is lacking entirely, then the client needs to be contacted and that information obtained.) If the project has in any way been controversial, then local newspapers will have

We learned about archaeology from that ... The Lock Haven Flood Protection Project

In the late 1980s, we directed the Phase II evaluation of the Lock Haven Flood Protection Project, located along the West Branch of the Susquehanna River in the central Pennsylvania town of Lock Haven.

This was a large, albeit not overly complex project, involving historic and prehistoric sites (some already listed on the National Register) as well as historic districts. In essence, after having been flooded out innumerable times, the community had requested and received funding (directed by a House of Representatives appropriations bill to the U.S. Army Corps of Engineers) to have a combination levee-floodwall built around the city of 10,000. The project would protect the city from future floods, but would cut through sites eligible for listing as well as those already listed on the National Register. Further, the floodwaters displaced by the flood protection structure would increase the frequency with which one of the historic districts outside of the city would be flooded, obviously an adverse effect (and also a good example of how the Area of Potential Effects can go well beyond the area of construction activity). Part of the Phase II exercise, and the associated Phase III data-recovery plan for one of the prehistoric sites listed on the National Register, required a summary of what the project would involve, and what other options had been considered in the past.

There was nothing especially unusual about the Lock Haven Project, which is why it is a good example to use in pointing out what such histories of undertakings can or might include.

The history of the undertaking began with a general discussion of how the city and adjacent communities are situated. This would allow a clear understanding of the problems involved and what limits there would be on solutions. The West Branch of the Susquehanna rises in the Allegheny Plateau; after leaving the Plateau it flows east for about 35 miles, then south through a water gap another 30 miles to join the Susquehanna River at Sunbury. The Susquehanna is the main river that drains central Pennsylvania and south-central New York, and is under the jurisdiction of the U.S. Army Corps of Engineers, Baltimore District. When it drops down off of the Plateau, it enters the two-mile wide, relatively level land between the Allegheny Plateau on the north side of the river and Bald Eagle Mountain on the south. This is part of the central Pennsylvania Ridge-and-Valley physiographic province, which consists of long ridges around 1,500 to 2,000 feet high that arch southwest to northeast, with comparatively narrow but level valleys between. Rivers flow through those valleys. About two miles from where the West Branch drops down from the Plateau, and immediately upstream from the confluence with Bald Eagle Creek, is the flood plain community of Lock Haven.

The community, then, is overlooked by upland areas on both sides of the bottom land. On the south, 1,820-foot high Bald Eagle Mountain is around two miles away; on the north, the

1,500-foot high edge of the Plateau looms just above the river. ("Mountain" in central Pennsylvania is not an isolated peak or elevation, as it is in parts of the Northeast or the West; rather, "mountain" refers to the entire *length* of a ridge, and Bald Eagle Mountain is a more or less continuous ridge over 75 miles long.)

Because it is placed on that flood plain, with high land all around, Lock Haven is particularly prone to flooding. This began the second step in the history of the undertaking: What the current problem is and why it needs to be solved. As near as we could figure out, using early explorer's accounts, histories, and Corps of Engineers records, large and often devastating floods have been recorded in the Lock Haven area since at least 1668. The West Branch really is a shallow stream, at least compared to its width. Water can and does come up quickly and to a good depth. The city-scape is essentially level over most of the business and some of the residential areas. When the water comes up, the town is badly damaged.

This constant history of flooding, combined with the importance of the city (it is the county seat, was for many years the location of Piper Aircraft, and currently operates an airfield – Piper Airfield – on the east end of town on the old Piper property) resulted in Federal attempts made to deal with the flooding beginning in the 1920s. That history of flood protection designs and efforts then formed the third part of the history of the undertaking: Knowing the problem, what has been tried to solve it?

One of the earlier attempts to solve the flooding was to control the headwater

carried stories. That information is available from the associated public library or from the newspaper's files.

A history of the undertaking needs to cover some specific details:

*   What is it that is planned and why is it going to be done?

*   When was the project conceived and what is the rough time table?

*   Who is doing the design work?

*   Who will be doing the construction (that is, who is the general contractor)?

*   What will be the extent of land alteration, both in terms of area and depth?

*   Will the land alteration be construction only, road grading, tree removal, and grading and other topographic changes?

discharge that contributed to the West Branch flooding at Lock Haven. In the 1920s and the 1930s, the Corps of Engineers suggested building a series of small dams in the upper portions of the West Branch drainage. These would then capture the water from the different upstream tributaries, and help regulate the flow downstream. (Beaver dams, by the way, work on the same principle, representing scaled check-dams that slow run-off; the Southeast is filled with a myriad of small earthen dams, put in during the early days of soil conservation to help save the land and now lost amidst the woodlots of the region.) The only other option that the Corps of Engineers had was to build a levee-floodwall system around the town, thus protecting it from the occasional flooding. This would require running a levee-floodwall system in an arc around the town and along the river front, starting and ending with the raised berm of US 220, a four-lane controlled access highway built intentionally on an artificial embankment along the south edge of the community. Floods then would be conceded, and the idea would be to just keep the floodwaters out.

Both options had good and bad points, and that became the fourth step in the history of the undertaking. Building dams upstream was much more expensive than building a levee around the town; such dams also would take more land out of production while creating historic preservation problems proportional to the land that would be in the dam catchments. Expense, though, was the primary issue.

Building a levee-floodwall also had problems. Leaving aside the historic preservation issues (which, while considerable from an archaeologist's perspective, must needs be thought secondary to the immediate, real-life concerns of the residents), the building of such a flood-protection structure would necessarily displace that volume of water that normally would have covered and filled the town. That water would have to go some place. The concern was that the displaced water would end up inundating two areas: The immediately upstream portion of the West Branch valley, since placing a levee along the south edge of the river would narrow the available flood channel and cause water to pool above the city until it could drain out; and downstream. Further, the water would have dropped any sediment above the city and, combined with the increased volume due to the constricted flood channel, increase downstream topsoil loss from fields due to the increase capacity of the flood waters to carry sediment.

There were, of course, two other options (excluding the one where nothing at all would be done). The first would be to move the town. This is a not uncommon solution nationally, where the frequently flooded community is moved to higher ground. That was not a viable option because there is no higher ground to move the community to: The floodplain is pretty flat until one reaches the toe slope of the mountain (the term "toe slope" and the meeting of the Allegheny Plateau with the north side of the West Branch are two entirely different situations: The word "precipitous" comes to mind, but still seems like a euphemism). Further, the cost of moving a 10,000-resident county seat, business district and all, would far exceed any costs of levee-floodwall construction.

The other option would be to move the river. That, by the way, is feasible in engineering terms, but would be unrealistically expensive.

The only practical options, then, for providing flood protection to the city of Lock Haven consisted of upstream dams or of a levee-floodwall system. Of the two, the second was considered more sensible in terms of cost, guarantee of protection, and number of people adversely affected.

That concluded the history of the undertaking, stripped of its supporting details and specifics of chronology. It explained why the project was being done, what other options had been considered, and why those options had been dismissed. Arguments about details – placement of the floodwall or the levee, heights as well as depth-of-footings for those, and related matters were considered as well, since placement and depth of disturbance have a bearing on archaeological sites. Since footing and height arguments are issues of engineering and mechanics relative to floodwaters and associated pressures, and are not things that can be changed, the only remaining issue was where the overall flood protection structure would go. And that decision was based upon what the community needed to protect combined with where, in soils engineering terms, the best location would be. That resulted in a very narrow corridor, and along that corridor were prehistoric and historic archaeological sites, including one with 4-meters of prehistoric deposit. What happened with that, though, is the subject of another story.

See

Neumann, Thomas W. 1989. *Phase II - Intensive Survey, Historic and Prehistoric Archeological Investigations at Lock Haven, Clinton County, Pennsylvania.* Three volumes. U.S. Army Corps of Engineers, Baltimore District.

For Phase III data recovery projects, and for Phase II testing projects that look as if Register-eligible archaeological sites will be threatened, it also is important to detail what other design options have been considered for the project, and why those options were unacceptable. The reason for this kind of information is to set out why the project was not re-designed to avoid damaging the cultural resources. The SHPO or the THPO may or may not be aware of this, but it is important to put all of the issues down on paper so that all of the players -- especially the Consulting Parties if this is a Section 106 exercise -- know what has been covered. It is always possible, although highly unlikely, that the Advisory Council for Historic Preservation (ACHP) will be called in to referee a disagreement between the Federal agency and the SHPO/THPO. Having the design options set out in the document reviewed by the ACHP will make life a lot easier for everyone and speed the process along to a sensible and just conclusion.

We learned about archaeology from that ... The Glenfield to Lowville Project

A history of a project area helps the practicing archaeologist to set bounds on testing, and expectations for testing results. A good example of this is a New York State Department of Transportation (NYS-DOT) project we did in upstate New York.

The project consisted of road corridor modifications of State Route 12, mostly easing of curves, correction of intersections, and limited bridge repair. The section of road was around seven miles long, and ran along the eastern base of the Tug Hill Plateau as it sloped toward the Black River valley.

This part of New York was settled in the late 1700s, and property arrangements were influenced by French custom: The original fields were long and narrow, at right-angles to the general south-north flow of the river. The road itself, as it existed when we were dealing with it, had been put in in the 1930s. Prior to that time, travel between Lowville and Glenfield required zig-zagging back and forth since the roads followed the perimeters of the farm fields, and since those farm fields continued to follow their original layout. That is, a person would travel north for a while, then west, then north again, then perhaps east (or west), then north ... until thankfully reaching the intended destination.

In the 1930s, the state simply ran a new road more or less directly from Lowville to Glenfield. The road ran with complete disregard to where the farm field boundaries were, instead following the toe slope of the Plateau.

Knowing that the road went in in the 1930s, and that much of it was built on fill (it ran mostly on a berm raised just out from the slope proper), allowed us to judge areas of fill, disturbance, and likelihood for the kinds of cultural resources that might be present. For example, there was only a small possibility of early historic sites being directly associated with road, simply because the road was comparatively new; the only places where such would be the case would be where the older roads were integrated into that 1930s design.

The Lowville-Glenfield Project was interesting for a number of other reasons. For example, this was the first time that we came up against the

For Phase I survey projects, most of the questions that need answering involve what it is that is going to be done.[2] This will allow the review agency -- be it the SHPO/THPO or the county archaeologist -- to have a sense of what is going on. It is contextual, background information just as much as it is immediately important, cultural-resource-planning information.

In nearly all cases, the history of the undertaking will be presented in the first chapter of the report. In some Phase II testing and Phase III mitigation reports, the first chapter will contain an abbreviated summary of the undertaking's history, and the third chapter (treating the history and prehistory of the region) will contain a detailed synopsis of the undertaking.

4.2.2. History of the Project Area

The first part of a project history involves what the undertaking itself is; the second part involves the history of the project area. This includes what has happened directly within the project area, along with what, if any, archaeological research has been done. This background segment may include interviews of landowners, local historians, and area residents. It also includes research done at the state site files, contacting the SHPO/THPO to see if any properties within the project area have been nominated for the National Register, historic research at the local libraries, and map research. The history of the project area will be presented as parts of the second and/or third chapter of the final report.

The history of the project area needs to answer some basic questions:

* What has been the history of land use of the project area?

* Are archaeological sites recorded for the project area?

* Has anyone ever examined the project area for the presence of archaeological remains?

* Are Register-eligible properties present within the bounds of the project area?

This is accomplished usually by asking local people, especially the landowners or adjacent residents, by reviewing histories contained in the local library, by going through the state archaeological site files, and by contacting the SHPO/THPO.

---

2. As an aside, it is worth noting that "failure to adequately describe the project" is one of the most commonly cited flaws of NEPA environmental impact statements (EISs). This should point up the susceptibility of professionals to gloss over this vital aspect of the project documentation.

importance of sorting out what was a structure and what was not for a project area. NYS-DOT surveys required that all structures and buildings be photographed, preferably in three-quarters view. This allowed architectural historians in Albany the chance to see if our first-hand exterior assessment of the structure's architectural/design characteristics would in any way qualify the structure for the National Register, or at least warrant a closer look.

State Route 12, though, ran along the east toe slope of the Tug Hill Plateau as it drained down to the Black River (beautiful country, by the way). As mentioned above, it was built out a bit from that slope in most places, pretty much as a berm, which of course would also work like a small dike for run-off from the slope above. Further, by cutting diagonally across that

French-influenced field patterning, it had split a number of pastures into two parts.

So, what is a structure? A bridge is a structure, right? Fine. So, define "bridge," please.

That stretch of highway had any number of crossings over streams, 67 we think the number was. Most were crossed with a six-foot diameter corrugated steel pipe. There also were a number of small tunnels about the same size that allowed cattle to move from one pasture under the road to another pasture.

We began dutifully photographing each of the 67 culvert-like bridgings of streams. After a day of this nonsense, we decided to wander back over to the Region 7 DOT office in Watertown and ask just what *their* definition was

for a bridge. The official definition for a bridge, we learned (and we now reveal to the wider world hungry for this knowledge) is 20 feet, 1/8 inch, or at least was so in New York. Anything shorter is a "culvert," which for cultural resources purposes for NYS-DOT was not considered at the time a structure, building, or anything else (everyone thankfully having forgotten the category "object").

Figure 4.1. Virtually all county seats as well as many other small communities have public libraries, a legacy of Jefferson's vision for the country. These house not only local histories and special collections, but also reference librarians who are very aware of who is doing what historically in the community. The holdings in public libraries, especially those specific to the history, economics, and ecological particulars of the community, rarely are duplicated in university research libraries, which is why it is important to have the staff historian or someone with equivalent project responsibilities examine the local library collections.

4.2.2.1. Interviews

Two sets of individuals are interviewed: Community historians and similar people who know about the area; and local residents and property owners. If there is a local Indian tribe, it may need to be contacted as well regarding culturally-sensitive or religious sites.

In our experience, every county and just about every community no matter how small, has at least a community historian, and sometimes a local historical society. While the role of the historian may be an official position, in most cases it is a role that has been taken on or assigned by the community to a person tremendously interested in the community and its history. That is, the community historian is a volunteer in most cases; it is an avocation, not a vocation. These people are the community's equivalent of an elder in the anthropological sense, and should be located if at all possible.

How does the practicing archaeologist locate the community's historian or historical society? The easiest way is to either go to the information/reference desk of the public library and ask, or to go to the court house or town hall and ask. (For Section 106 projects involving local communities as Consulting Parties, the representative of that community will know who to contact.) The people who do the community's history have been around for a while, are known by just *everyone*, and are almost always more than willing to assist with both oral accounts and with the location of additional information.

One of the most important sources of primary and secondary research information, both personal contacts and printed sources, for the history of an area is the local public library. Research- and information-desk librarians particularly are focal nodes of information about communities, and should be among the first people contacted in the search for leads on the history of the community and the project area (Figure 4.1).

Once located, the questions asked of the community's historian need to be specific at least in overall intent. These should focus on the general history of the project area as well as sources available on that history.

Asking more specific questions about the undertaking for which archaeological compliance is required may become tricky in some cases. Some Federal and state contracts will prohibit speaking about the undertaking with unauthorized non-project personnel. This is particularly true in situations where the undertaking is controversial or sensitive. If the contract allows, always ask if the historian is aware, personally or through hear-say, of any archaeological sites, historic roadways or other features, or historic structures located in or near the project area. At these times, it is very useful to have a map of the project area relative to the greater community, available. But again, *showing such maps -- especially planning maps -- to non-project personnel should be done only if the contract so allows and one is authorized to do so.*

The second population to be contacted are the local residents. It is a basic field courtesy to speak with the property owner and with the property resident (see also Chapter 5, Section 5.2.2. "Contacts, Public Relations," as well as *"We learned about archaeology from that... The Catfish Creek Project"*). Often these may be the same, although obviously not always, as in tenant situations. Such contact is extremely important if there is any intention of crossing the individual's property, and even more important if any subsurface testing is anticipated for that property.

The need for interviews of local residents in the vicinity of a project area varies by the situation, although interviews may be required by state or local mandates. In Maryland or Georgia, for example, there is no requirement that formal interviews be conducted; we really have not felt that Phase I survey projects were in any way compromised by not conducting interviews with owners of adjacent properties when development was planned on a given parcel of land. In New York though, surveys done on behalf of the Department of Transportation require interviews of each resident adjacent to the project corridor, and we have benefitted from the information obtained during the interview process.

The main purpose for interviewing the property owner or resident as well as nearby residents is more

We learned about archaeology...
Interviews

One of the most interesting– and instructive – interview exercises we did involved the Limestone Creek Project in Manlius, New York. As NYS-DOT projects went, this was surprisingly straight-forward: a slight easing of a curve entering a small stream crossing (Limestone Creek) along with replacement of the bridge. Although most of the residents would not have their land more than incidentally affected, NYS-DOT protocol required interviewing all residents along the right-of-way.

Fascinating exercise, really. The project involved interviewing – for a couple hours – a person who had been dead for 44 years, a charming chat with an octogenarian whose feet could not reach the floor, discovery of a minor military munitions factory in the basement of a putatively abandoned mill, and ... oh, phooey, it was a fun project, and let's leave it there. Oh yes, and the exploding car, can't forget that. If a person wants to have a sense of what project interviews might involve, this seems as good an example as any.

When one does interviews for a highway corridor project, one begins at one end on one side of the road, then works his or her way down to the end of the project, crosses through traffic, and comes up the other side. This avoids excessive crossing of busy highways. The start of the Limestone Creek Project was non-descript: a health club. Then there were a couple residences where people politely said that their houses were thus-and-so years old (as near as they could remember, the age corresponding roughly to our initial estimates) and that, no, they were not aware of any other cultural resources. Then we came to a light-blue frame house, a two-storey side-gabled affair with a one-and-a-half storey side-gabled garage in back, which had an exterior stairway to the upper half-storey.

The door of the house opened, and the woman who met us remarked, in response to our initial questions, that she only rented the house. "And the owner?" we asked. "Oh him," she answered, motioning with her hand toward the garage, "he lives back there."

Back there we wandered, clambering up the wooden stairs, and knocked on the door. The door was answered by age: a man with sunken yet lively eyes, olive skin, and more wrinkles than a linen suit in a Savannah August. We introduced ourselves, mentioning who we were and our reason for being there, and he invited us in for one of the most interesting experiences in our archaeological lives. Mr. L____, it turned out, was dead, mainly because he was color-blind.

The story was fascinating. When World War II broke out in December 1941, Mr. L____ had enlisted in the U.S. Army Air Corps (AAC), as did many young men brought up hearing of the horrors of foot soldiers and the trenches of the Great War. He went through the testing and physicals, and was found to be color-blind. Ah, said the Army, just the person for us. He was signed up and shipped off – as anyone would expect – to Panama.

Okay, okay, why Panama? The AAC (which in a year would become the U.S. Army Air Force) maintained two training programs. One was focused on training officers. These were young men who had the wits and physical health, including eyesight, to qualify them as pilot material. They would be trained to fly, and would eventually be commissioned as second lieutenants. These people were trained at a series of airfields in the United States, at a cost in 1941 dollars of around $2,000 a cadet (around $19,500 in 1998 dollars).

There was a second set of young men, men who were mentally and physically capable of flying, except that they were color-blind. The AAC wanted such men, because at the time all of the tricks of camouflage still would not deceive a color-blind person. Color-blind men (and 10 percent of men are color-blind) were ideal for spotter and reconnaissance flights, since they could locate targets for bombing missions. Mr. L___ was color-blind and was potentially ideal.

There was a second advantage. Since color-blind pilots could not be commissioned as officers (as we understood from Mr. L___), they would be trained to be commissioned as sergeants. Flight training was done in Panama, and only for $500 a person ($4,875 in 1998 dollars, about the cost of a single-engine VFR license now). He trained, for those who are interested in these things, in P-40B Tomahawks, the aircraft used by the Flying Tigers in south China.

Mr. L___ was shipped to the Pacific Theater, first flying P-40E Kittyhawks then eventually P-38s. A P-38 was a twin-engine aircraft with enormous range, extraordinary speed, and incredible operational flexibility, used variously as a medium bomber, interceptor, ground-support aircraft, and reconnaissance aircraft. Mr. L___ was one of Kenney's Kids in the Fifth Air Force, flying P-38s to protect bombers and to identify camouflaged Japanese positions, so that the B-24s could then come in and neutralize the target.

Mr. L___ was flying out of New Guinea; he did not say, but presumably he was working out of either Dobodura or Marilinan near the

northeast coast, and was involved in action in the Solomons and the Bismarck Sea. During one flight, Mr. L___ was jumped by a Japanese fighter and shot down. He managed to bail out over the north side of that extreme eastern end of New Guinea. And he drifted down into the jungle and oblivion.

World War II involved a huge number of people. If a young man disappeared and there were no witnesses, there was a period during which he was considered missing with the possibility that he might turn up. The time, we think, was 30 days. Thirty days passed, and there was no word on Mr. L___. He was declared "missing in action and presumed dead," and his personal effects were shipped Stateside along with notification of next-of-kin. The next day, he walked into the AAF base accompanied by an Australian reconnaissance patrol. And that was 1943.

Here it was, 1987. Since 1943, Mr. L___ had been trying to convince the American government that he was alive. He returned to Manlius, his home town, where everyone knew him. He moved back in with his mother in his childhood house, eventually inheriting it. However, he kept trying to clear his social security number ("Dead," the Federal government said) and obtain veteran benefits ("You were killed in action," the VA patiently reminded the putative cadaver as it pleaded its case). His friends in the community were absolutely no help, as anyone might expect in a situation where everyone knows everyone else and the problem is mind-bogglingly absurd. Mr. L___ remarked, exasperated, that whenever he went down to the Manlius post office to have his actual physical existence confirmed, the people would just laugh at the nonsense of it all. And NOT confirm that he was alive. Oh well.

The story does not end there. Naturally, given this situation, we asked if the ignorance of the Federal government extended to taxes. "Surely," we said, "if the government was unaware of your existence, then you were exempt from income taxes." "No," he answered. He had been informed in no uncertain terms that,

while the Federal government generally and the Social Security Administration and VA specifically did not consider him alive and therefore eligible for benefits, the IRS did, and he was taxed accordingly. Thus, the old saying about the only certain things in life being death and taxes remains true.

Down the road we wandered again. Most of the houses had been put in in the early nineteenth century, although a few dated from the late 1700s. We crossed a small side road and went on to an isolated house, a small off-grey storey-and-a-half affair, side-gabled and covered with asbestos tile. The lot sat low and alone, adjacent to Limestone Creek. We could tell, walking up the side road, that a mill-race channel had once run behind the house. Across the creek, against one of the mill-structure avatars, were other indications of how the creek had been used for water power.

We went up to the front door. In central New York, front porches tend to be enclosed. Even the old Dutch stoops, those three-steps-up-to-a-concrete-pad that are just large enough to allow the standard aluminum frame storm door to open out and knock the visitor off into the snow, even those are enclosed in a closet-like structure to keep out the winter. We knocked on the door, peering inside toward the second, original front door. That was a half-glazed, floating-panel affair, the old porch now a collection of miscellaneous items including an abandoned dining room chair.

As we gazed through the storm door, almost ready to leave, there was a movement of the curtains against the window of that interior, half-glazed wood door. All that we noticed were two EYES, eyes behind incredibly thick lenses. And those eyes watched. Remember, the house and lot were partially isolated on a lot bounded by large, looming trees, and we already had interviewed The Dead. This was, frankly, eerie. And The Cat did not help.

The door opened, and out came Mrs. S___, one of the most charming, pleasant people we have had the fortune to meet, in a world that is full of engaging people. "Diminutive" exaggerates her height: She was

Figure 4.2. *"The mill complex was shown on all of the early historic maps…. It was an industrial accretion, beginning as a red-brick affair on the east edge of the creek, then having more and more parts added, of brick and stone and wood, taken apart and re-built and in all clearly employing the construction workers of the area profitably for 175 years before closing down, presumably from sheer exhaustion of the local nail and mortar supply."*

barely four feet high (we had just exposed a burial at another project area during a Phase I monitoring situation, two adult females actually, and our estimate of stature based upon skeletal evidence for one was around 4.08 feet, which shocked us; here suddenly was an adult of the same height). Mrs. S____ welcomed us into the little porch-stoop area, and while we sat on the floor, she perched herself on the chair, her feet eight inches above the ground. And we chatted.

A native of Quebec and mother of 10, with sons and daughters living all around, Mrs. S____ had married a Manlius native around the time of the War. She was in her early 80s – a vibrant, enchanting woman with grey-blue eyes that danced in merriment. Yes, she knew about the project, and hoped that it would solve the flooding that she experienced each year in her basement, where water came up to the fifth step. Oh, and yes, please feel free to take pictures of and look at that mill race in the back.

"Yes, don't you know, it used to power the mill that once was across the street," she said. "Go ahead and move the cat, he won't mind," she added as this orange THING wandered out and marked territory with its chin on some of the most impermanent territorial features available: our shins.

"Oh, you mean where that little shopping center is now?" we asked, scratching the cat behind the

ears, as its back arched and its tail rose.

"Oh yes, that one," she confirmed, eyes gleaming with pleasure, "although you know, it hasn't always been there. Oh no, was a mill when we first moved here." News to us, and we noted it accordingly.

We crossed the creek from Mrs. S____'s house. All along the project, we were taking the requisite photographs of features and general corridor appearance, again a requirement of NYS-DOT Phase I projects. Now we came to the mill complex.

The mill complex was shown on all of the early historic maps, and on the Sanborn maps for as long as Sanborn had mapped Manlius (Manlius is the home of Stickley furniture, the person and group that gave the world that remarkable quarter-sawn oak Mission-style furniture; the factory was just beyond the project area). It was an industrial accretion, beginning as a red-brick affair on the east edge of the creek, then having more and more parts added, of brick and stone and wood, taken apart and re-built and in all clearly employing the construction workers of the area profitably for 175 years before closing down, presumably from sheer exhaustion of the local nail and mortar supply.

The mill appeared abandoned, and we did our pictures and wandered around

the back of the place. One learns a lot looking at the backs of buildings, since these tend to preserve the sequence of construction – which Sanford calls "building stratigraphy" and promises someday to actually work up a system for the rest of us to understand. There was a loading dock and a door that did not look like it really wanted to remain closed, so in the interests of science we grabbed a flashlight from the car and set out to explore the inside.

And in we went. NYS-DOT had indicated that the building was unoccupied with no owner known, so our entry did not really concern us. One learns much from buildings by looking at parts, probably in this order: The basement, and the attic. One learns more about buildings by looking in their basements, and we meandered through a literal maze of corridors in search of stairs that would go down. The Sanborn maps also had shown that, in the 1870s, the mill was connected by a tunnel to a steel foundry across the road (long gone, the property now occupied by a supermarket), and it seemed a good idea as well to check and see if that tunnel remained intact.

Down the stairs we went, but we already were puzzled. We had gone around the back of the building; there were no cars there. NYS-DOT had indicated that the building was unused, to the point where they had no indication of property ownership. But we could hear people doing things

Figure 4.3. *"There was, though, a gap between two of the buildings in which 50-cm diameter trees...partially shaded a concrete pad.... We asked, innocently enough, what had happened in the late 1930s to the building that had been present...."*

down those old, worn wooden stairs, the edges of their pine treads polished and rounded. And lights were on, which in our experience suggested that the electricity had not yet been turned off and that the building was still in use. Not always, but *that* is, believe us, the topic of another story we will NOT tell.

Down the stairs, and tentatively quizzical faces looking up. Hello, we say, we are archaeologists with NYS-DOT. There is a road project planned for this area, and we are looking for the building owners, or at least people who might tell us something about this building.

Quiet. And upturned, non-committal faces.

One person comes forward, mid-30s, salt-and-pepper goatee-like beard, dark, almost black hair. Not a smile, but not a frown.

To make a long story interesting: It turned out that the "abandoned" mill was now the site for a missile assembly contractor. In the basement of this seemingly abandoned building was the hand-assembly of the fin segments for air-to-surface missiles. Lots of missiles. Lots and LOTS of missiles. The answers we got were unspecific, and we sort of wandered out in a fashion a lot more directly than we did entering, thankful always of the extreme care and security that goes into American munitions manufacture.

We wandered up the street, now getting busy as the afternoon

lengthened (and our hopes of knocking down the corridor interviews in a day diminishing). This stretch, beyond the mill complex, consisted of buildings built in the 1880s to 1910s, again asbestos-tile-sided affairs, two to three storeys, three times as long as wide. There was, though, a gap between two of the buildings in which 50-cm diameter trees (boxelder [*Acer negundo*], if memory serves), leaned out as volunteer plants that now partially shaded a concrete pad that, from the oil stains, was used for parking.

We found a resident – knocking on doors seems to cause this – a woman in her late 30s or early 40s, round face and short, greying hair. Friendly, as all of the people we have had the pleasure to meet are. Then there was the startler.

After asking the standard questions about the corridor we asked, innocently enough, what had happened in the late 1930s to the building that had been present. Clearly, a building *had* been present, given the concrete slab over a foundation. The size of the trees strongly suggested they had started growing around 50 years earlier (see Chapter 5, Section 5.3.1.1. "Land-Use History Based on Vegetation Succession").

Our informant was taken aback, and looked at us with a mix of awe and very real suspicion. The absence of a building: It was due to an accident in the late 1930s. Apparently there had been a garage in that slot of property, and there had been a car up on a rack,

and the welder had been working around the gas tank ...

It turned out that she was a distant relation of the person killed in the blast. It explained the open area, of course, and the trees more or less were consistent with the event, since they would have started growing around a half-century earlier. It also taught us to be more circumspect in how we asked our questions about corridor history, while confirming in our own minds the importance of knowing about tree diameters relative to tree ages.

The Limestone Creek Project is useful here not because the interviews revealed anything unusual about the project corridor. The tunnel, it turns out, had long ago been filled in (the assistant manager of the supermarket, when informed that there once was a tunnel between his building and the "abandoned" mill complex across the road, actually blanched; amazing how aware people are of allegedly secret activities in their neighborhoods). It is useful to give some sense of the nature of what such interviews involve, and the nature of people who live in the areas where archaeologists work. Archaeology is Anthropology, as Willey and Phillips pointed out both in 1956 and again in that 1958 monograph. The practicing archaeologist needs to delight in the panoply of human experience.

Oh yes, and to write all of these things down.

to learn if any cultural resources are known for the project area that may not have been caught by the more formal records of local history or of state site files. People resident on their land have a wealth of knowledge that comes from messing about with that land. Many will have information about cultural resources and area history that has never been solicited.[3] Specific questions in addition to those found in structured interviews like those used by NYS-DOT (see also box "Interviews") include time tables for when and how the land was used. The landscape history that will be formulated during Phase I work (see Chapter 5, Section 5.3.1.) should make a very good estimate of this; informant confirmation helps secure the interpretation and bolsters any argument presented to the review agency about the veracity of the practicing archaeologist's interpretation of past land-use, especially depositional integrity.

There is a second element in this: courtesy and community relations. It is a simple matter of courtesy to speak with the people resident on the land that will be tested or examined. Never mind if they will have a knowledge of the landscape history or previous land-use: They live there, and to enter in to work is to enter into their homes, their territory, their personal space. It is incredibly rude not to speak with them and take the measure of the world in conversation with them. That one behaves in such a proper and civil way also gains the respect of the wider community, with whom the practicing archaeologist and associated crew must interact, sometimes rather intimately, on a daily basis for the duration of the project.

4.2.2.2. State Site Files Search

The history of the project area includes previous archaeological investigations. This information is available from at least one of two sources: The state site files, and the State or Tribal Historic Preservation

Office[r] (SHPO or THPO). Sometimes these are in the same overall office; sometimes not. This varies greatly by the state, commonwealth, territory, or protectorate in which the archaeologist is working.

It is best to begin at the state's site files. All states and political equivalents maintain a file of previously identified archaeological sites. Those sites normally are given a trinomial site number, consisting of an initial number representing the alphabetic order of the state for the 48 continental states (Alaska is 49 and Hawai'i, 50; the result of a coin toss that happily was alphabetical), followed by a two-letter alphabetic abbreviation for the county where the site is or was, then a site number based upon the order in which the site was recorded by the state site files. So, for example, the Paleoindian - Late Archaic site of 44FX1517 is (or was; there are houses on it now) located in Virginia (the 44th state alphabetically), specifically in Fairfax County (that FX), and was the 1,517th site recorded in the county.

Not infrequently, sites will also have a colloquial name. For example, site 44FX1517 is also called the Hobo Hill Site. It is usually better to be in the habit of referring to the site by its site number rather than name. This reduces possible ambiguity in the distant future, and makes keeping field notes much easier.

State site file searches are relatively easy. They are easy because the project is located in a county (a consequence of the way American physical reality works), and the site files will be arranged by county. Most site file offices have a master state map showing where sites have been identified, or a series of USGS topographic maps upon which the bounds of the site have been penciled in. All that the practicing archaeologist needs to know is where -- in map terms -- the project area is, then go to the site files and find out if any sites are recorded for that tract of land.

A number of states, such as Maryland and Georgia, have converted their site files to a computer-based GIS (geographic information system). Some states also are making access to that computerized site file available through the Internet, provided specific security protocols are observed (see box "Access to State Site Files"). (It might be noted that some states now charge up to a $250 access fee each time the site files are used; Mr. Thomas Wheaton, New South Associates, Inc., personal communication, March 1999.)

The background work done at the state site files should come away with the following information on every site within about two kilometers of the project area:

*   site number and, if present, name;

*   location of site;

---

3. In addition to structured interview formats like those used by NYS-DOT, open-ended questions might also be used. How people respond to questions varies by part of the country and by social class relative to the interviewer. For example, in New England and to some extent in southern Appalachia, it is common not to volunteer information unless asked. In rural areas of the upper Midwest, especially in Iowa and Minnesota, as well as in similar settings in Wisconsin and Michigan, a general statement of what is of concern and why you need to know it will have people not only volunteering information, but suggesting a number of other people who might be contacted (and, in Minnesota, inviting you to stay for lunch). But in those areas as well as in the South, while people will be generous with their knowledge and time (you will be asked to sit a spell), it may be considered proper to spend time chatting about things in general before getting around to the reason you are there. For a sense of regional differences as well as dominant values, we recommend reading through Joel Garreau's 1981 *The Nine Nations of North America*. Houghton Mifflin, Boston. It is a bit dated in some ways, but the central issues of what is considered important in the given region, and how people view things, remain sound.

Access to State Site Files

Archaeology in the United States is not only a private-sector endeavor, it also is a commercial endeavor. There is a considerable economic substratum dealing in prehistoric and historic artifacts. The individual values for artifacts vary greatly: We have seen Savannah River points listed for $2-4 (Overstreet 1996:507); exquisitely knapped Scottsbluff projectile points, for $1,500 (Overstreet 1996:837); and Clovis points, for $7,000 (Hothem 1999b:14). Except for Paleoindian points, which often list around $500-1,500 (Overstreet 1996; Hothem 1983, 1999a, b), most prehistoric projectile points run for between $10-60. Grooved stone axes from the eastern and midwestern United States list for around $500-600 (Hothem 1996). However, pottery from the Southwest – and presumably entire pots or figurines from the eastern United States, if ever these were found intact – go for mid-range four-figure sums. Bottle collectors and Civil War curio collectors, who will pillage historic sites with a ruthless, Borg-like efficiency and sense of care about the needs of others, also can claim from a ready market two-to three-figure sums for things like entire bottles or excellent-condition belt buckles.

Archaeologists – academic as well as professional – are aware that there is a "black market" in prehistoric and historic antiquities. This often is mentioned in textbooks, and receives a generic notice along with a general condemnation. It probably would not hurt to explain what is going on, and to help clarify why the state site files are essentially professional privileged information.

As far back as human history allows, and probably even earlier, the remains of preceding cultures have been removed and used by succeeding generations. Included in this kind of activity is "grave robbing," and it seems to have taken place around the world and in all cultures. Basically, if there is a stratified society, then there is defined wealth as well as social groups/classes denied access to that wealth. Given the chance, other people either of the same or of later cultures will relocate and recover those material items temporarily placed away in tombs or (less often) everyday habitations.

In the United States, things like Indian artifacts (arrowheads and, in the Southwest, decorated pottery) have always commanded a certain market presence among a proportionally small population of people. "Proportionally," but not necessarily numerically: Even a few thousand people can create a tidy marketplace, as the economics of scholarly archaeology books testifies. For example, in the hills of Kentucky, Tennessee, and West Virginia, there long has been a thriving trade in artifacts (and skeletal remains) taken from prehistoric rock shelters. The areas are impoverished, and the rock shelter remains represent cash flow that immediately benefits the family. This is critical especially during coal-mine strikes, and with hunting helped put food on the table. In fact, the cash economy from Indian artifacts helped feed people and support families who had no other access to cash income and who were weathering economic pressure from the mining companies.

---

* horizontal bounds of site;

* depth at which materials were found;

* presence or absence of features;

* cultural historical affiliation;

*. when recorded;

* when, if ever, investigated;

* nature of investigation;

* where and in what form research results were published (that is, full citations); and

* National Register status if appropriate.

It is useful to have a photocopy of the USGS map or maps for the vicinity of the project area, and to note where previously recorded sites are located; in some areas of the country, the final compliance report will include a copy of the portions of the USGS map where the project is located. (Inclusion of such a map depends greatly on how restricted public access is to site location information in the state; many states quite rightly do not want that kind of information

placed in a document to which the general public may have access. See box "Access to State Site Files") On that map segment will be shown the locations and bounds of known archaeological sites. Check first, though, with the particular office's protocol: Some site file offices and states do not allow transferring map information.

If sites are located within the project area, it is important to obtain copies of any previous reports and journal articles on the site or sites. Full reports may be filed with the site files, with the SHPO/THPO or equivalent historic preservation office, or with the state archaeologist's office (which may or may not be an administrative unit separate from the SHPO within the given state).

It is even more important to note from those reports the depth at which cultural materials were found, and exactly what it was that *was* found. This includes whether or not features were present, since these are excellent signs of site integrity as well as sources of information.

Site file information will be presented in two ways in the third chapter of the compliance report. The first way will be as a table and accompanying figure that summarize the known archaeological sites in the two-

Even now, 10 complete projectile points can have a market value equal to a week's pay for the average wage earner in the United States; one good Paleoindian point or a grooved-stone axe from a prehistoric burial, nearly two weeks' wages.

It is, of course, much larger and more complex than that. Anthropologically, it is normal, or at least not unusual, human behavior to recycle human artifacts. Archaeologically, it is devastating to the data base. Culturally, it is illegal in many cases, particularly on public lands. Whether or not such activity is legitimate depends very much on social class and, to a lesser degree, household income, such collecting normally being viewed with disapproval if not disdain by the upper social classes, but with tolerance and often approval by the lower social classes.

Most individuals who engage in this activity, labeled variously as "pot hunters" or "looters," have a very good idea of where archaeological sites are located. They tend as well to ignore Federal and state legal statutes, following instead a curious American theological turn of conscience in arguing that each person is the final judge of the morality of his or her actions, and therefore if judged proper by his or her own immediate sense of the situation, then it *is* legitimate (in theology and ethics, this is called "situational ethics"). This is derived from the Reformation and its focus on individual interpretation of Christian Scripture, through the Enlightenment with its concern for the individual, and

also is at the base of most extreme right-wing militia movements. In practical terms, though, it means that legal penalties are just business costs, and that anything that can help in locating profitable artifact deposits will be used.

This is why state site files have restricted access, and why site locations are generally exempt from state "right-to-know" and "open records" laws.

(We came across the following identification and pricing guides in a large, national-franchise bookstore recently. The stocking of these, one of which is now in its fifth edition, should underscore the extent and profitability of that market in prehistoric artifacts.

Hothem, Lar. 1983. *Arrowheads and Projectile Points: Identification and Values*. Collectors Books, Paducah.

_____. 1996. *Indian Axes and Related Stone Artifacts*. Collectors Books, Paducah.

_____. 1999a. *Indian Artifacts of the Midwest. Volume II*. Collectors Books, Paducah.

_____. 1999b. *Indian Artifacts of the Midwest. Volume III*. Collectors Books, Paducah.

Overstreet, Robert M. 1996. *The Overstreet Indian Arrowheads Identification and Price Guide*. Fifth edition. Avon Books, New York.)

kilometer vicinity of the project area (see Chapter 5, Section 5.2.1. Site and Region Documentation; see also Figure 5.2.) The second will be in brief narrative form for those better researched sites in cases where they are examples of regional history or prehistory.

4.2.2.3. SHPO/THPO (State/Tribal Historic Preservation Office[r])

In most states, the SHPO/THPO or equivalent historic preservation office will have copies of every compliance report done for the state. The reason for going to the site files first when the files are separate from the SHPO/THPO is to know just *what* reports need to be examined for the project area. It is usually wise to have budgeted funds for copying reports already filed with the SHPO/THPO. In time, this may not be an issue as states, such as Missouri and Georgia, make more and more of the original compliance reports available through the Internet. However, at this point, it is wise to send someone over to the SHPO/THPO office and make copies of the reports germane to the project. Some of those reports may also be available for sale.

Since the SHPO/THPO is charged with protecting and enhancing the state's or tribe's cultural resources,

it will also be aware of any properties that are under consideration for nomination to the National Register. Such contact with the SHPO/THPO will also assure that they are aware of the project.

4.2.2.4. Local History

Assembly of the local history is a focused exercise in historiography. The local history does two things:

(1)   places any historic cultural resources in their general historic/cultural context, especially relative to the State Plan; and

(2)   identifies potential resources in the project area.

That historic/cultural context is the evaluative element of 36 CFR 60.4 *criteria for evaluation* in assessing if the site has the quality of significance in National Register terms (see Chapter 2, Section 2.2.3.2.; see also Secretary of Interior's Standards for Historical Documentation [48 FR 44728-44729]). This is especially true for criteria [a] - [c] (those dealing with associations with persons, events, or master craftsmanship). All of this must be considered in the context of the State Historic Preservation Plan.

Chain of Title

Although it normally can be done for a lot less by a title-search company, under some circumstances it is useful or important to the project for the practicing archaeologist to run the equivalent of a "chain of title." A CHAIN OF TITLE refers to a documented chronicle of ownership for the property or parcels within the project area.

How is this done? Chains of title normally are more tedious than complex, although it does depend upon the quality of the records involved. For many states, running a chain of title requires first going to the court house for the county in which the project area is located. In the court house will be an area dedicated to property records. This may be a real estate area, a deeds and titles area, a tax records area, a property area; the title really will vary by the county and the part of the country where the work is being done. (If in doubt, ask someone where records for property ownership and title transfers are.)

The information that generally is needed is the tax map designation or similar bit of locational information for the property. The current owner (who clearly is involved in the cultural resources process or the project would not be happening) will have that information as a title abstract (which itself cuts down on the time involved), although it is not too difficult to go in knowing where in the county the property is and working out matters accordingly.

Armed with the location of the parcel, it is only a matter of working back through the previous owners until the records run out. They may run until the mid-1600s in some places in the Middle Atlantic; they may end with the deeding of the land over from the indigenous population to some Euroamerican settler in the 1790s (as a case we know in Tennessee, where the land was granted directly to the farmer's ancestor by the resident Cherokee population, and is a clear and above-board title). Or, it may run out flat in 1910 (another situation we experienced, this time in western New York, where all of the county's property information was lost in a fire in 1910).

Chain of title is useful for historic purposes in connecting a piece of land with a family or a known individual, thus helping establish association of the property with important people (criterion [a] of 36 CFR 60.4 *criteria for evaluation*). It is not unusual for information on the property to include a summary of the buildings and structures present, and their assessed value, always a useful bit of information if the buildings and structures no longer are present. A chain of title can also help in creating genealogies of residents in the project area. This kind of background research is great fun as well, as we have found most historic background research to be.

Most local histories begin either with the local historical society or with the local public library. Each will have numerous source materials that may or may not mention the project vicinity. In the eastern and midwestern United States, many counties compiled at least one county history in the late 1800s (sometime around the nation's centennial). Often there is a second history written around the 1860s and a third, written around the time of the bicentennial in the late 1970s.

There often are local, specialized histories, as well as special collections in the local library. It is common on the East Coast for the local public library to have a special historic collections room, or a similar place containing special primary sources on the history of the county and its communities. Another library might have some of the same books in their general circulation collection, making it advisable to check more than one place if a desired document has restricted access.

4.2.2.5. Map Research and Area Reconstruction

Maps are a major source of historic information. These are important for locating previous historic occupations as well as for working out potential disturbance in a project area. There are four basic categories of map that show the locations of structures at specified times: USGS topographic maps, county maps/county history maps, Sanborn Fire Insurance maps, and USDA NRCS (formerly Soil Conservation Service) soil maps.

The entire country has been mapped by the U.S. Geological Survey, and most of the country has that map information now presented in what are called 7.5' topographic quadrangles ("7.5'" means "7.5 minutes of a degree"; each map covers 7.5' of latitude and 7.5' of longitude). Those maps include cultural features, such as residences, non-residential out buildings, bridges, paths, old rail lines, and countless other features. All maps have a date for when they were compiled. The USGS topographic maps are periodically updated, and thus become powerful sources for the history of an area.

Mapping of the country began in the late 1880s around Annapolis, and has continued non-stop. The initial mapping was done as 15' quadrangles (maps that were 15' latitude and 15' longitude on a side, representing then the area of four 7.5' quadrangles). Those maps were periodically updated through the 1930s before the system began focusing on 7.5' maps, although it should be cautioned when using these 15' maps that often no changes were made in the presence or absence of structures shown when the maps were updated.

Tip: Setting Up a Map Matrix

In the mid- and late 1980s, we performed a number of Phase I cultural resource surveys on behalf of the New York State Department of Transportation (NYS-DOT). The requirements for the Phase I surveys were a little different than those for strictly archaeological Phase I surveys, since we were charged with initial documentation of architectural features along corridor right-of-ways. The widening or redirecting of a road not only could remove a house or structure, it could also change the visual setting in which such a structure existed. If that structure was eligible for listing on the National Register, then that change could materially affect its eligibility and would constitute an adverse effect.

People also locate along or near roads (or, more exactly, roads are placed in a way to connect where people live and congregate), so highway corridor surveys have a higher than normal likelihood for historic archaeological sites. The requirements for NYS-DOT Phase I surveys, then, included two features not commonly encountered in other Phase I projects: Photo documentation of the corridor and of the buildings and structures along it; and map documentation/historic documentation of all known structures to have existed in the project area.

The photo documentation included both general views of the highway as well as of proposed corridors: General project photographs, in a phrase. The photographs also included one or two three-quarter views of all buildings and structures along the corridor. In doing this, and in thinking

back on our work and the work of many others, it is apparent that that photographic documentation of the New York cultural landscape in the 1980s probably will become a wonderful resource for researchers in the centuries to come, being a focused and thorough – and precisely mapped – exercise in recording a cultural landscape.

The map information we learned to summarize in a matrix. This proved a valuable tool because it summarized quickly the important information of where structures exist or existed, as well as when they were known to have been present. All of the historic maps of the project area or corridor were copied over in the report as color photographs (as were photographs of the corridor and structures/buildings, a contract specification for decision-making; color photographs are not archivally stable; black-and-white photographs are). Also present was a line-drawing of the project area, on which was shown where previous structures or buildings had been, each with a alphanumeric label.

The matrix would have a left-hand column listing the structure or building, then vertical columns headed with the date and name of the map examined. The cells then were filled in with the presence or absence (or rebuilding) of the feature in question. This gave precise information on presence or absence of structures and building along the project corridor.

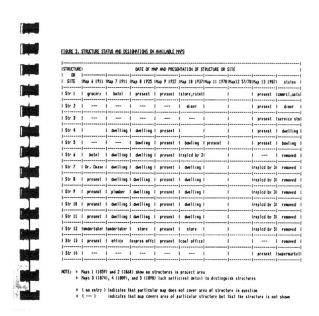

Figure 4.4. Example of part of a summary map figure used in a New York State Department of Transportation cultural resources survey in the 1980s. The structure numbers correspond to those on the project map, a portion of which is shown in Figure 4.5 on the right.

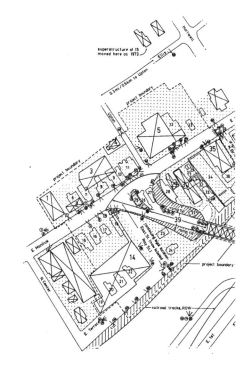

Figure 4.5. Example of a project map showing locations of structures tabulated in Figure 4.4. Note locations of structures 25 -27 (see also Figure 4.6). These are the buildings mentioned in box "We learned about archaeology from that ... The East Syracuse Project."

Preservation Plans and Disturbance Studies

"Preservation Plans" refer to historic preservation plans prepared at the behest of a Federal agency or installation. These tend to be miniature equivalents of state historic preservation plans, and are tied to the specific situation of the installation or agency property for which they are prepared.

Preservation plans will contain a set series of information: The physical geography of the Federal property, a cultural history/cultural geography of that property, a summation of work done to-date, then a relation of the cultural history to the larger State Historic Preservation Plan. Keep in mind that the jurisdiction for cultural resources on Federal land still rests in the Section 106 Process with the SHPO, and therefore needs to be placed in the context of the state.

Preservation plans are planning documents that have two major components: (1) the core research questions/historic issues that appear to bear on cultural resources potentially within the project, and (2) sensitivity determinations for the property. Sensitivity determinations refer to the likelihood that historic or prehistoric cultural remains will be located on/in various landscape types of the property.

Preservation plans will include a synopsis of what already is known about historic and prehistoric sites/structures within the agency's jurisdiction, and normally will place those in a larger context of Register eligibility. Keep in mind, too, that potential resources, based upon historic documents, will be mentioned as well. For example, early Spanish forts at Parris Island just up from Port Royal Sound in South Carolina (on the golf course, no less) were sort of anticipated from very early historic records.

"Disturbance studies" also are planning documents, and summarize the past land use of a project area. They differ from preservation plans in that they focus on a given project area, and look more at the probability of the project area still containing historic or prehistoric cultural remains with some semblance of integrity.

Most of the disturbance studies we have seen or been involved with have been in urban or semi-urban environments. Presumably, this kind of work could be done over any landscape.

A sequence of USGS maps documents with some precision when buildings appeared or disappeared from the cultural landscape. A series of such maps becomes an extraordinarily powerful chronicle of historic development in an area (see box "Setting Up a Map Matrix"). However, it should be noted that areas of urban expansion no longer show individual structures, but rather a magenta-purple shading indicating a built environment.

A second major source of information about structures and ownership are various historic county maps. Detailed county maps were made in many parts of the country around the same time that many of the county histories were produced in the nineteenth century. These maps are scaled, show the locations of residences, and usually give the name of the occupant of the residence. Such maps may be bound in with county histories, but more often exist as large, rolled painted-canvas maps meant to be hung. The combination of a map date and names associated with structures make these documents particularly powerful tools in reconstructing the historic landscape. It is not unusual for small-town city offices to have one or more such maps framed and hanging on the wall, or to have nineteenth-century "bird's-eye views" of the community similarly framed and hanging. It is fairly easy to photograph such maps *in situ*.

A third and, for urban environments, one of the best sources of information are the Sanborn Fire Insurance maps, compiled, published, and updated for a number of municipalities between the 1880s and the 1930s. These maps are available on microfilm or microfiche,

and are delightful sources of information. The only drawback is that they were made only for urban areas.

The Sanborn Fire Insurance maps were color-coded maps of city-scapes, meant to give assessors a sense of fire risk for given areas. The maps were done at 1-inch to 50-foot scale, and are remarkably detailed in most cases. The color coding served to point up material from which the buildings and structure were made, and therefore their fire risk. The notations on the maps indicate the number of stories, if business or residence, and very often the name of the family or the business occupying the building at the time the map was made or updated. In addition, adjacent structures -- strict sense of the term -- will be shown on occasion, so one can work out presence and nature of bridges, railroad corridors, roadways, mill races, and so forth.

Any field work done in an urban setting, especially in a part of a city that has been a city of note since the late nineteenth or early twentieth centuries, will need to make use of the Sanborn Fire Insurance maps. The information from the maps can be digitized then scaled, allowing the maps to be overlaid and, when used in conjunction with a map matrix, becomes a powerful cultural resources planning tool for a project area.

A fourth source of map information are county soil survey books. These are sources of information that can easily be overlooked. Around half of the 3,066 counties in the United States have had a soil survey done by the old USDA Soil Conservation Service

Generally, disturbance studies use historic documents – written histories combined with historic maps – to plot out the areas of a proposed undertaking that may or may not be severally disturbed. The threshold for this, by the way, is not as apparent as it may seem.

For example, when the work was done for the Camden Yards ball field, we were involved in structuring the general probability that the landscape would be disturbed. It was found that portions of the urban environment had been built over, and part of that built-over environment included Babe Ruth's father's tavern, the 1915 or 1916 one in which Babe Ruth is pictured behind the bar with his brother and his father (see Ward and Burns 1994:160-161). That tavern – built into a row house brownstone – had been torn down in the 1950s, the remains of which were located under the loading dock of a warehouse. Disturbance had not extended deeper than the second above-surface course of bricks of the building (the basement had been filled with rubble, while the two-seat brick-lined privy remained as chocked-full of debris as it had the day that that portion of Baltimore had gone to a public sewer system). The firm performing the work also digitized the 120-odd extant

historic maps, scaled them, then used that information to pinpoint cultural resources germane to overall state historic preservation plan questions, that tavern being one.

Disturbance studies are first-pass (to use the computer coding term) exercises in actuarial archaeology (see box "Actuarial Archaeology, Sensitivity, Probability Areas, and Predictive Models" below). They do not give more than a qualitative statement on the likelihood of cultural resources remaining intact within the bounds of the project area. They do, though, include detailed histories and prehistories of that project area that allow for a sense of what *may* still survive, given that qualitative probability statement, within the project bounds.

Ward, Geoffrey C., and Ken Burns. 1994. *Baseball: An Illustrated History*. Knopf, New York.

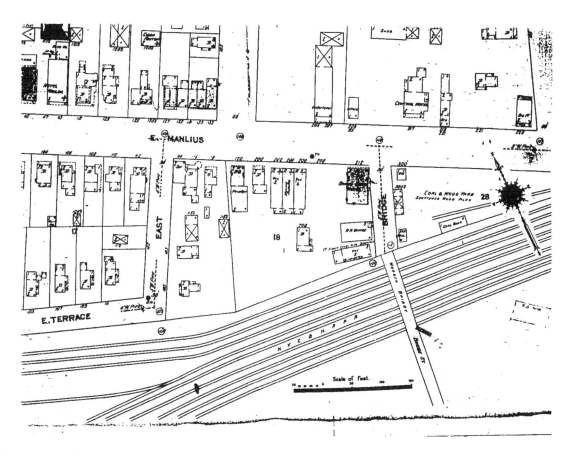

Figure 4.6. Portion of a Sanborn Fire Insurance Map, showing East Syracuse, New York (1911). The three houses on the south corner of East and E. Manlius were the ones removed when the new road bridge went in in 1927 (see "*We learned about archaeology from that ... The East Syracuse Project*"). (Map: Copyright 1911 The Sanborn Map Company, The Sanborn Library, LLC All Rights Reserved. Further reproductions are prohibited without written permission from The Sanborn Library, LLC.)

We learned about archaeology from that ... The East Syracuse Project

An area that has been mapped frequently and in detail over the years provides not just a chronicle of who lived where or what buildings were around, but sometimes also insight into the values and needs of the local community. One such instance was a bridge-replacement project we did for the New York State Department of Transportation (NYS-DOT) in the Village of East Syracuse.

The project needs were simple enough. East Syracuse grew up adjacent to a rail yard, expanding from a main street area that first formed along the north side of the tracks. On the south side of those tracks a community also emerged. Communication between the north and south sides of the rail lines for years consisted of grade crossings. By 1911, the railroad had built a raised pedestrian bridge over the rail lines,

presumably to allow people – primarily railroad workers – from the south side of the tracks to get over to the north side. That bridge was removed and replaced by 1927 by a steel-truss structure, which had large earthen ramps raised at either end to allow the bridge to clear the rail lines by about 22 feet. By 1987, the bridge had seriously deteriorated, and it was to be replaced. Our responsibility was to perform a Phase I archaeological and architectural reconnaissance of the project area.

The project was well-documented by 13 maps, beginning in 1859 and continuing to 1987. Detailed map resources included NYS-DOT design maps from 1911, 1927, and 1970, as well as Sanborn maps from 1911, 1925, and 1937. Counting the now long-gone 1911-ish pedestrian bridge as well as the current structure and its approaches, the project area contained 49 past or present structures or buildings.

The map research served to document the changing streetscape of the areas

north and south of the rail lines. The temporal and spatial resolution of the mapping made working on this project very satisfying, since changes could be tracked in near-decade increments over the core period of the original bridge construction. It also helped us greatly by showing what portions of the landscape had been filled in, dug out, or otherwise disturbed on an industrial scale. It also revealed something telling about the period when the steel-truss bridge was put in.

The street systems north and south of the tracks were on a grid, with streets running either parallel with or normal to the track lines. A few of those streets extended over the tracks as grade crossings into the 1920s, and were interesting in that they had comparatively few houses along them, and the houses – to judge from the evaluations implied by the Sanborn maps – were small and comparatively inexpensive. Thus, as one might expect with an established right-of-way, existing traffic flow, the entire new 1927 bridge, around 300 feet of bridge and fill-ramps, was placed

---

(now part of USDA NCRS), with the soils classified and the extent of those classified soil bodies mapped (see Chapter 5, Section 5.3.1.2.). This information is presented in a standard soft-bound booklet, at the back of which will be a series of aerial photographs with the bounds of the soil bodies lined in. The aerial photographs are dated; the aerial photographs are sufficiently clear to see structures, buildings, roads, and often to make an educated guess at how the land was being used at the time the photograph was taken. This information, by the way, becomes useful in re-constructing landscape history (see Chapter 5, section 5.3.1.1.)

4.3. Environmental Background and Soil Survey

All cultural resource assessments provide a summary of the physical geography and ecology of the project area and its immediate vicinity. This will constitute the second chapter of the compliance report. The purpose of the environmental background is three-fold:

(1) to recount how the ecological system has changed over time so that the prehistoric background and any prehistoric sites may be put into their proper environmental-resource context;

(2) to document how conditions exist now; set out what the base line ecological systems in which the project area is located are, so that variations from these may be appreciated when the field work and landscape conditions are discussed in the submitted report; and

(3) to set out what the expected soil/geological conditions are.

In our experience, this section in most compliance reports usually is inadequate, and can be quite easily expanded and improved.

The environmental background provides both a temporal-environmental setting for any cultural remains encountered for the project area, as well as a current-situation account of the condition of the physical deposit. The first involves what the people in the past had to deal with: If there was a snow pack over 60 cm deep during the winter before 2000 B.C., then the people could not move around the countryside since the snowshoes that made travel across the snow pack surface possible probably were not yet present in the Western Hemisphere.

The second has to do with the ideal versus the actual as it might exist today. Many archaeological reports, especially compliance reports, portray the ecological

diagonally across the tracks and street-grid in such a way that three of the more expensive residences (including a two-storey, turreted building, probably Queen Anne in style) had to be removed. The grade crossings of course were closed off, and the bridge became the only way to get across the tracks.

This was, to say the least, very intriguing. Sanborn maps often tell what the buildings were used for, and we were interested to note that the three structures taken out by the north ramp of the bridge consisted of that likely Queen Anne building, a semi-detached building that had served in 1911 as a saloon but was, by 1925, listed as a dwelling, and an adjacent building listed in 1911 and 1925 as a store.

We have always wondered about the decision that was made, during 1927 at the height of Prohibition, about the placement of that bridge in a way that did not fit traffic flow, did not fit

existing streets, but that did take out more and more expensive buildings than would seem, from our reading of the maps and the soils, warranted.

(Prohibition began with ratification of the 18th Amendment in 1919; the Volstead Act of 1920 gave policing authority to the Federal government. Prohibition legally ended with ratification of the 21st Amendment in 1933, although it tended to be ignored anyway. The German ethnic community felt particularly betrayed by it, since it removed the various beer gardens and seemed to be legislation aimed specifically at them and their ethnic heritage.)

Our interest in what had happened was increased by the condition of the 1927 NYS-DOT design map: An attempt had been made to erase a good deal of the design part of the drawing. Equally interesting was the major map error on the south side: A building shown directly in the way of the ramp, suggesting that residents

both north and south of the proposed bridge location would be equally compromised, actually was shown about 100 feet farther east than it really was (actually, when care was taken to enhance the map, it was clear that the building had been drawn in the middle of a pre-existing and active four-way street intersection, an almost impossible mapping error to draw).

One wonders now, over 70 years after the event, if those structures had represented a "speak easy," or if they were in any way related to illicit trade in liquor. Or if so, if authorities had long turned the other way, but something went awry and the bridge was used to settle matters. Would make an interesting historical research project in any event.

Fascinating stuff, maps and histories.

---

system as it *might* develop in the absence of human interference. Nonsense, obviously, since people must be present for this entire exercise to have any meaning, and the presence of people will alter ecological systems in fundamental ways. The information that needs to be presented consists of the kind of vegetation and animal community that might be expected in the absence of a resident industrial-agricultural population, along with the nature of the plant-animal community that really is there, or at least has been present in recent history. The first is rather easy, and actually will be a summary page or two in most county soil survey books. The second requires thought, and generally has to be constructed from a variety of sources involving landscape ecology. That is, the first is easy; the second is not, which is why the second tends to be ignored.

(It probably would be thematically more proper to put any paleoenvironmental/paleoecological studies at this point. However, we have always placed such synopses in with the prehistoric or historic background narratives. This is because the paleoecological conditions represent the setting within which and to which the past cultures adapted, and it has always seemed to us a better idea to place the discussion of any past physical world side-by-side with a discussion of the culture and especially the technology that was a response to that world. It may only rarely be taught

now in the academic world, but the driving theoretical basis of extra-academic archaeology -- and extra-academic Anthropology -- still is cultural ecology.)

Equal here is the nature of the soils. Archaeology is an information-retrieval field. Computer science plays with retrieval of information (strict sense as set out by Claude Shannon) from a configured environment, usually magnetic. Archaeology retrieves information from sediments or, much more often, active or once-active soils. Just as there are firms that will recover information from damaged hard drives, archaeologists really are trying to retrieve information on how people lived from complex, three-dimensional overwritten media dominated by soils, that themselves change in character over time. Soils, and a summary of soils is so important to archaeologists that failure to understand the basics will seriously jeopardize the work being done.

The county soil survey generally will provide the basics of what to expect in the project area as far as the soil is concerned. A review of the soil survey maps presented in the back of the soil survey book will suggest the extent to which the ground cover may have changed. This, of course, results in a change in the nature of the soil, although not necessarily in the physical distribution of the physical remains that are the concern of the archaeologist.

Tips: Civil War Battlefields

Immediately after the Civil War, the U.S. Army Corps of Engineers published a massive compilation of all of the battlefield maps used or made during the conflict. A facsimile of the map portion of the publication has been re-published, and is a treasure trove for cultural resources purposes. In many cases, the detail is surprising, and more to the point, the maps are scaled. Used in the field in conjunction with various summaries of ordinance (e.g., Thomas 1985; Coates and Thomas 1990), it is possible to plot troop movements over the battlefield for the duration of the engagement with great resolution. The battlefield maps are useful both for documenting historic structures and other features of the landscape, just as they are for later working out the dynamics of battlefield engagements, one of the most challenging and rewarding exercises in cultural resources work.

Original Document:

Davis, George B., Leslie J. Perry, and Joseph W. Kirkley. Compiled by Calvin D. Cowles. 1891-1895. *Atlas to Accompany the Official Records of the Union and Confederate Armies.* Government Printing Office, Washington, D.C.

Republished as:

Davis, George B., Leslie J. Perry, and Joseph W. Kirkley. Compiled by Calvin D. Cowles. Introduction by Richard Sommers. 1983 [1891-1895] *The Official Military Atlas of the Civil War.* Gramercy Books, New York.

See Also:

Thomas, Dean S. 1985. *Cannons: An Introduction to Civil War Artillery.* Thomas Publications, Gettysburg.

Coates, Earl J., and Dean S. Thomas. 1990. *An Introduction to Civil War Small Arms.* Thomas Publications, Gettysburg.

These and similar publications are specific in the ordinance and munitions issued to various detachments, Union and Confederate, as well as the ordinance and, by reason of operation, munitions captured then deployed by those detachments.

It is important for the practicing archaeologist to have a sense of what soils will be present where in the project area, and what their general physical properties are. Keep in mind here that farming communities, especially tobacco farmers, were very careful in their selection of soils, both in terms of slope and texture. In fact, it would be interesting to develop a historic ethnoscientific exercise in the historic-agricultural classification of the land based upon soils.

4.4.   Historic Background Narrative

The historic background narrative is a miniature, somewhat detailed history of the region and vicinity of the project area. It serves not only to summarize the major events and personages of the area, but also to relate those personages and events to the State Historic Preservation Plan (see Chapter 2, Section 2.2 Federal Laws and Regulations: Section 106 Process). Details on both are important, since 36 CFR 60.4 *criteria for evaluation* [a] and [b] are concerned with nationally, regionally, or locally important persons or events. The State Plan gives a sense of what is or is not important in this regard. Thus, the historic background narrative provides information on these and is constructed toward those ends.

This historic background narrative should be conscious always of the relationship to the State Plan just as it should of the location of the project area relative to the overall history. When the background research is done, effort is needed to make sure that references to the project area, or even areas near the project area, are brought out. Considering nearby past events or nearby past residents helps to confirm in the review agency's mind that, were any such events or people located any closer, then the practicing archaeologist no doubt would have come across them.

The historic background makes use of the following sources:

*   local and county histories, both primary and secondary sources;

*   map research;

*   site file information; and

*   oral histories from the local community.

Many firms actually have in-house historians who do this work. It is incredibly fascinating and satisfying research, since it allows a person to become intimately familiar with the history of a particular community.

The historic background narrative is put together with an eye toward two primary issues:

*   the research themes identified in the State Historic Preservation Plan; and

*   what already has been identified in terms of historic archaeological sites AND historic standing buildings/structures in or near the project area.

Actuarial Archaeology, Sensitivity, Probability Areas, and Predictive Models

Combining state site file research with disturbance studies results in a series of exercises that borders on what we are calling "actuarial archaeology" (see Neumann, Sanford, and Palmer 1992:122-123). That is, professional archaeology as a resource management discipline has worked its way into a situation where it is needed for planning, and what the planning people need is some sense of whether or not archaeological sites will be located in a given area.

We are aware of work done for prehistoric sites in this regard: Portions of Maryland (Kavanagh 1982), Pennsylvania (Hay, Hatch, and Sutton 1987), and West Virginia (Neumann 1992) have used extant site file information to develop quantitative probability models of differing levels of resolution that help identify landscapes likely to contain prehistoric archaeological sites.

This work grew out of the need by planners and state agencies to have some sense of just how likely it would be for archaeological sites to survive in a given area. Early attempts were qualitative, and consisted of statements in the range of "level land near rivers on the inside of meanders have a good chance of having prehistoric archaeological sites." Later work in effect quantified those physiographic variables, so that in eastern West Virginia it is known that 94.8 percent of all prehistoric archaeological sites will be located on land with a slope under 10 percent within 200 m of a stream with a flow rate of at least 12 cubic feet per second.

We think that a good way in which to develop a risk-based probability statement for cultural resources on the landscape is to first record physiographic mensuration variables, such as distance of the site from water, stream flow rate, current slope of the land, elevation above sea level, and cultural-historical affiliation. The next step is to do a cluster analysis using numerical classification based upon single-linkage Euclidian distances for each cultural-historical set. It is likely that the sites will sort themselves into subsets. The third step is to work out the averages and other descriptive statistics for sites contained within each cluster.

The last step depends upon the goal of the exercise. Results can be presented as a table or as a map for a particular area.

It is important that the site file data for a particular geographic area be used only for that area, at least if the information is available. It is also important NOT to rely on soil survey analyses, such as crop suitability or soil type, in working up probability statements for prehistoric sites, since the soil types currently found in most places are not the soils that people were facing half-a-millennia ago (since soil-type depends on covering vegetation, sediment accumulation on fields, and the like; the type of soil in a given place can and does change over time in response to those factors).

Exercises like this are becoming increasingly easy with the conversion of site files to GISs (geographic information systems). Currently, the results are given either as qualitative visual maps showing known presence of archaeological sites, along with descriptive statistics. It will be comparatively easy soon (or really now) to go the next two steps in working out a hierarchy of site locations then providing a probability statement for areas on the landscape where sites of given cultural-historic affiliation may be found.

Hay, Conran, James W. Hatch, and J. Sutton. 1987. *A Management Plan for Clemson Island Archaeological Resources in the Commonwealth of Pennsylvania.* Pennsylvania Historical and Museum Commission, Bureau of Historic Preservation, Harrisburg.

Kavanagh, Maureen. 1982. *Archeological Resources of the Monocacy River Region.* Maryland Geological Survey Division of Archaeology File Report No. 164.

Neumann, Thomas W. 1992. The physiographic variables associated with prehistoric site location in the upper Potomac River Basin, West Virginia. *Archaeology of Eastern North America* 20:81-124.

Neumann, Thomas W., Robert M. Sanford, and James F. Palmer. 1992. Managing archaeological cultural resources as environmental resources: An aid for local governments. *The Environmental Professional* 14:117-125.

All information on sites, buildings, or structures within the project area needs to be included.

There is a danger for the practicing archaeologist of overlooking built-environment resources. If an architectural historian is not normally part of the background research work, it is wise to remain aware of the need to ask the SHPO/THPO about the likely presence of such cultural resources.

It is also well to keep in mind how the land was used by historic peoples. Some of this is the obvious use of land in large, clearly important ways, such as timbering, mining, or farming. But a lot of this is not obvious: backyard gardens, wells, outbuildings, paths, and the like. There is a field of *landscape archaeology,*

which examines not just great formal gardens with known designers and histories, but also the daily domestic gardens and yard use so common for most of the history of the country (see especially Kelso and Most 1990, a series of illustrative essays on landscape archaeology and its research potential; excellent examples of method through interpretation and reconstruction are found in A. Noël Hume 1974 and I. Noël Hume 1974; for bibliography, see Firth 1985).[4]

---

4. It is all too easy for archaeologists to undervalue this recent history. Interestingly, much of the fairly immediate past seems to drop from the cultural memory, leaving seemingly mysterious structures such as root cellars to be misinterpreted as ancient Viking houses, bore holes for splitting boulders as ancient Viking

4.5.   Prehistoric Background Narrative

Like the historic background narrative, the prehistoric background narrative does two things at once: It addresses the local prehistory as it relates to the overall trends in the prehistory of the region, and it does so with reference to the State Historic Preservation Plan. Assembling the prehistoric background proceeds differently from that of the historic background narrative.   The prehistoric background requires familiarity with the often disparate sources on prehistoric archaeology for the area. That information is located in a variety of sources:

*   national summaries of prehistory that also mention the region where the project area is;

*   regional summaries that include where the project area is;

*   local summaries of prehistory that include where the project is;

*   individual site reports filed with the SHPO/ THPO or equivalent agency;

*   individual reports published in a seemingly infinite number of possibilities;

*   national, regional, or local journal series containing articles treating different facets of the prehistory; and

*   whatever information the staff historian managed to pry out of the state site files.

It is interesting, in a way, thinking about the differences between sources for the historic background versus those for the prehistoric background. Our experience with area histories has always captured our wonder in the vibrancy of the past. Such histories contain enormous, very specific detail on times and events. One would think that preparation required research comparable in extent. And it did, but usually by people who prepared local histories that are then used by the archaeologist or staff historian to prepare those backgrounds.

The prehistoric background, by comparison, has somewhat less detail in terms of specifics, but covers a much greater time range and involves substantially more extensive background reading and research. This is why many firms, if they can afford it, have both prehistorians and historians/historical archaeologists on staff. Both can and are more than capable of doing work in either area, but it makes life

so much simpler and the product so much more pleasant if the chores can be divided (keep in mind that in all of the firms with which we have worked, historic and prehistoric people have had a very sophisticated understanding of what the other's area of expertise and interest involves).

The preparatory work for the prehistoric background narrative involves reading the pertinent monographs and journal articles. A great deal of the information relevant to the practicing archaeologist is located in four places:

*   the state site files,

*   the compliance reports filed with the SHPO/ THPO,

*   the conference papers delivered at the regional conferences, and

*   the research articles published in the regional journals.

Those local and regional studies become the primary sources of information.[5]

The prehistoric background narrative is put together with an eye toward three things:

(1) the overall chronology or prehistoric sequence (for example, Paleoindian-Archaic-Woodland);

(2) the State Historic Preservation Plan; and

(3) what is known and has been excavated within the immediate region/vicinity of the project area.

If any of this includes a site or sites within or partially within the project area, then of course that information must be included.

---

ship-docking sites, tobacco cleavers as ancient Viking battle axes, and neatly stacked field stones by immigrant farmers from southwest Ireland as ancient aboriginal burial cairns.

---

5. This is why professional archaeologists, given a choice between spending well over $2,000 to attend a national archaeology conference or spending $300-800 to attend a regional archaeology conference, generally chose the latter: It provides more information that is of immediate need. "Immediate need" involves the needs of the client and the state populations, which also tend to go to the more locally focused conferences.

National conferences are expensive, and attendance requires some cost-benefit justification. The academic population often will have some if not all of that cost subsidized by their institutions; firms must underwrite those expenses and they must be overall investments that will recoup the costs. This cost-benefit issue is one of the two main reasons why private-sector attendance at the annual SAA meetings is proportionately low compared to that of the academic sector. The second reason is that few businesses can justify having a large number of employees absent for the amount of time that the conference takes. Usually only senior personnel will attend a national conference and will do so with a specific purpose in mind.

The intention behind the prehistoric background narrative is a bit different than that for the historic background narrative. With the historic background narrative, the idea is to have some sense of what had happened in or near the project area; the issue is less on the deposit or what the deposit might contain (not always, but often enough). With the prehistoric background narrative, there is also the issue of what objects are likely to be found in deposits, the conditions under which the deposits exist (including depth just as much as nature of contents), and how those relate to the overall prehistory of the region.

Historic background narratives are more a matter of knowing what transpired and how deposits may fill in gaps in knowledge, while prehistoric background narratives are as concerned about the structure of the deposits and their likely contents as they are with what all of that stuff might mean.

5:   The Phase I Process: Identification of Possible Historic Properties

5.1.   Intent and Goals

Phase I refers to the identification of archaeological resources through reconnaissance and intensive survey mentioned in the Secretary of Interior's Standards for Identification [48 FR 44720-44721].[1] The Phase I survey represents "a reasonable and good faith effort to carry out appropriate identification efforts"[**36 CFR 800.4(b)(1)**] to locate potential historic properties. In practical terms, this means that the purpose of the Phase I survey is to see if archaeological resources are present within the surveyed area. If archaeological resources are present, the Phase I survey also seeks to get some sense of the horizontal extent of those resources and, to a far lesser degree, the vertical extent as well as the cultural affiliation and integrity of the deposit. This helps review agencies decide if there might be a *chance* that the sites are "historic properties," that is, eligible for listing on the National Register. If that seems possible, the Phase II testing and evaluation process will be started.

The Phase I process seeks answers to the following:

*   Are there artifacts or some kind of cultural materials present within the project area?

*   If there are artifacts present, are they contained in an archaeological deposit that should be called a site, if it has not been so labeled already?

*   What is the horizontal and, to a much lesser degree, vertical extent of the archaeological deposit?

---

1. "Phase I" is the term used in most parts of the eastern and midwestern United States; "reconnaissance survey" and/or "intensive survey" (or, in Colorado and Wyoming, "Class III Cultural Resources Inventory") are the terms often used instead of "Phase I" in parts of the western United States. We find "Phase I" preferable not only because it is a bit more widely used and understood, but because it implies a conditional step in an *sequential* evaluation process.

* What is the general cultural affiliation of the archaeological materials?

* What is the likelihood of depositional integrity?

Phase I identification in the field is a reconnaissance; during that reconnaissance archaeological and landscape questions are answered. That is, is there anything present and, if so, does it have depositional integrity? The question of depositional integrity is the most important concern; while Phase II testing is used to *establish* site depositional integrity, often Phase I provides sufficient data to *exclude* site depositional integrity. It is the issue of depositional integrity that is muddled or misinterpreted by most Phase I surveys (see Chapter 2: "Integrity"). This is due to an inability to read landscape features and to employ soil development criteria.

The Phase I identification process is arguably the most important of the archaeological cultural resources steps. This is for two reasons. First, Phase I is a diagnostic step; that is, the results from Phase I work dictate what actions will be taken regarding archaeological resources. Second, unlike all of the other methods used in the professional practice of archaeology, those associated with the Phase I process rarely are taught in an university environment. It is the importance of the Phase I process combined with the lack of attention to this during professional training that results in the detail given below.

It is hard to over-emphasize the importance of the work done for a Phase I survey. The results of the Phase I survey will serve as the starting point for all subsequent archaeological resource management decisions. It is at the Phase I level that a decision will be made whether there is any chance at all that the project area contains archaeological remains that satisfy criteria for listing on the National Register of Historic Places (**36CFR 60.4 [a-d]**). Although the Phase I work is meant to be identification or survey work, it often serves as a kind of site evaluation step, if only in an exclusionary sense. In situations where subsurface investigations are done, the Phase I survey often can give enough information to tell if the integrity of the deposit has been compromised. This means that the proper data must be collected.

The Phase I survey also provides estimates of site limits and of site contents, at least to a limited depth. If further examination (Phase II testing) is recommended and is done, the testing program will be based upon the Phase I results.

Related to questions about site depositional integrity is the question about what constitutes an archaeological site. If one artifact is found in one shovel test within the project area, does that artifact represent an archaeological site? Some firms and states use the term "spot find" for isolated sets of small numbers of artifacts. This will be considered a little more when site forms are discussed (see section 5.4.4.); the point is that if the archaeological practitioner calls some assortment of artifacts an "archaeological site," then the site will have to be recorded in the state site files, a step that could be misleading in the review process and, in some states, automatically set off Phase II testing.

5.2.   Project Structure and Pre-field Preparation

The largest number of projects undertaken by a firm will be Phase I projects. Although most are small, Phase I projects often provide most of the income for a firm, and do so in a way that evens out the sways in cash flow that accompany larger, but temporally more widely spaced Phase II testing and Phase III data recovery projects. However, there is a lot of competition for Phase I projects. To be competitive, such projects need to be budgeted tightly with very little margin for error. Success depends upon good pre-field planning and preparation.

Most firms have a standard procedure for assembling then executing Phase I investigations. While some of the steps are done as part of the bid process, most need to be completed before actual work begins if the project is to remain profitable. Pre-field preparation includes:

* knowing what sites, especially National Register eligible sites and properties, have been recorded within or near the project area;

* contacting landowners to ensure that permission and proper legal clearance have been received to conduct the field work;

* contacting local utilities to ensure that subsurface cables, gas lines, water mains, and similar items are marked or are absent from the project area if subsurface testing will be done;

* knowing at the start how much labor has been allocated;

* planning and scheduling personnel tasks, both those that will commit office personnel as well as those that will require field personnel;

* arranging logistics, including billeting, provisioning, and transport where circumstances require;

* making sure that equipment is available for the needs of the project; and

* planning the actual testing or surface survey pattern.

The Phase I process requires that the client supply a detailed project map, one that has project boundaries or corridor clearly marked. Pre-field planning, and sometimes even the basic bid, are virtually impossible without such information.

5.2.1. Site and Region Documentation

The Phase I process is aimed at learning if archaeological sites *that might be* eligible for listing on the National Register are present within the project area. This requires checking the state site files to see if any archaeological sites already have been recorded for the project area, or if there are any sites within the general vicinity of the project. Knowing that archaeological sites have been previously identified within the project area will alter reconnaissance and testing protocols over the domain of where those sites are supposed to be.

All states maintain a site file, which is a list of known archaeological sites within the state. In most states, that list usually is arranged by county, with the sites within the county labeled numerically in the order in which they were found. Depending on the state, those site files will be housed at and under the jurisdiction of the SHPO, the Office of Historic Preservation, the Office of the State Archeologist, the state's archaeology laboratory, or a similar facility or agency.

The site files contain a synopsis of each recorded archaeological site including where it is or was; when it was recorded; what it contained (cultural-historical affiliation); condition/integrity; when collected, tested, or excavated; and where results of those investigations were reported. This information is stored basically in two ways. The first, older way consists of hard-copy paper records. These will include a standardized form, attached to which will be a copy of the USGS 7.5' map section where the site is or was located, along with the boundaries of the site drawn on that map. (Some states maintain a file of USGS 7.5' maps, with the sites all recorded on the map sheets instead of each site individually on its site form.) The second and increasingly common way is for site information to be stored in a GIS (geographic information system) file.

Regardless of how the information is stored, the person organizing the Phase I project will need to convert project boundaries to the USGS 7.5' map or maps involved, then gain access to the site files. Access requires either sending someone over to the site files, or accessing those site files through the Internet. Internet access generally has protection protocols to prevent looters from gaining too much knowledge about site locations. Those protocols vary by state.

The site information required for a Phase I project includes not only those touched on or crossed by the project (or within the area of potential effects for Section 106 undertakings), but also those within a given distance of that project area. This informs both the project manager as well as the agency reviewer of what might normally be expected in the general region, and how frequently such sites occur. A common practice is to list all known sites within 2.0 km of the project boundaries. Some Federal agencies and states only expect a listing of sites within 1.6 km (1.0 mile) of the project area. In states where acceptable, this information will be presented later in the final report, first as a map showing the location of the project area or corridor relative to known sites, then as a tabulated list of sites that gives (see also Figure 5.1):

* The site number (and name, if any),

* cultural historical affiliation,

* associated reports/publications, and

* National Register eligibility if known.

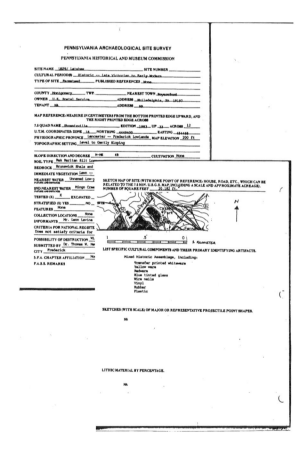

Figure 5.1. Site File Form with Map Information. All site forms in the state site files will provide information on where the site is located, and will include a map of some kind as well. The site recorded here -- a nineteenth-century farmstead-- no longer exists, having been replaced by a post office.

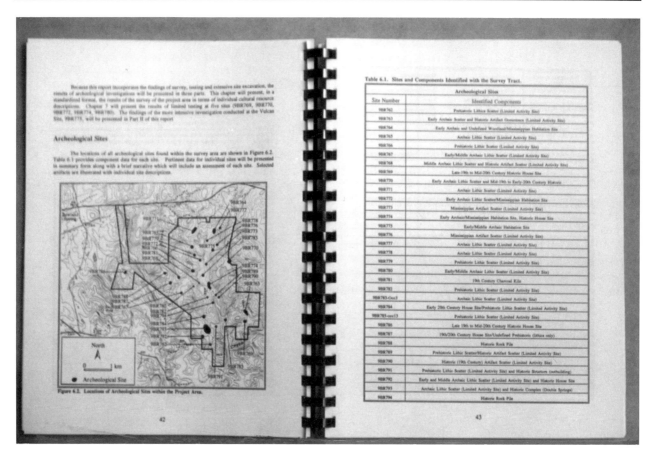

Figure 5.2. Example of figure from a Phase I report showing locations of archaeological sites within the vicinity of project area, along with the table describing those sites. Archaeologists work with regional patterns, and compliance archaeology treats regional-scale impacts. An effective way to present information on the regional status of archaeological sites is to provide a map of the project vicinity, along with a table briefly summarizing the sites and their investigative status. (The image is intentionally blurred to keep site locations confidential.)

This information not only helps in preparing the Phase I project, it also anticipates questions from reviewers about what sites already are known and their National Register status or eligibility potential. Anything that anticipates then answers questions from reviewers expedites the project's completion, which is good for the client and doubly good for the firm (reduces additional work, thus making the bid package more competitive, and enhances the reputation of the firm, thus attracting future business).

5.2.2. Contacts, Public Relations

Prior to starting field work, two types of local contact may be needed: Landowners and utilities. First, contact must be made with property owners whose land will be examined, especially if Phase I investigations involve some kind of subsurface testing (see "*We learned about archaeology from that ... The Catfish Creek Project*"). In situations where the project involves some sort of development and it is the developer-landowner requesting Phase I services, obviously such permission has been given. In other

situations, where a highway or pipe line corridor is involved, such permission often is needed for individual property holders, since the project is crossing privately held land. Further, in some states, such as Georgia, state law requires that written permission be obtained from the landowner then submitted to the SHPO or equivalent agency before field work starts, even if it is the landowner actually requesting the Phase I survey. There also may be some issue of title in dispute or negotiation, particularly in the case of a large project or one in which there is a possibility of involving additional lands for mitigation or to accommodate alternative designs.

It is the client's responsibility to obtain entry permission from landowners, and to give those people some idea of when archaeologists, among others, will show up. The practicing archaeologist needs to make sure that such permission has been given before sending crews out to the field.

At the Phase I level, the issue is one of courtesy and informing. For construction projects where private land will be crossed, the Lead agency -- Federal or state

We learned about archaeology from that... The Catfish Creek Project

Contacting landowners in the field prior to testing is not as self-evident as it might seem. This comes from our experience with a highway corridor project in a major dairy state, which for purposes here we can call the Catfish Creek Project.

The Catfish Creek Project was in response to a set of four alternate route designs by the state's DOT (Department of Transportation), the intent being to modify a rather nasty, banked curve, so sharp that it actually made a right-angle turn. Design options included reworking the curve, or building one of three possible new stretches of road that in effect would bypass that curve and present drivers with something close to a straight stretch of highway, sort of like running a hypotenuse opposite that right-angle curve. The road length would be about a mile regardless of the option chosen, although given the different paths possible, the new stretch of road could cut across any place in a half-mile band.

We became involved through follow-up Phase I subsurface testing. The original testing had been done a year earlier, and now DOT had come up with a couple new options and needed to have those new corridors checked.

Prior to going into the field and conducting interviews, we were warned by DOT to make sure that we spoke to people *before* we started testing. Okay, we said, fine, we do that anyway, and left matters at that. Another silly DOT superfluous comment, we thought, instructing us in the obvious, grumble, grumble, mutter, grumble.

When we started contacting the landowners, though, and doing our corridor interviews, we learned that the DOT comments were far from redundant or self-evident. Apparently when the first round of Phase I testing had been done, the field crew – from out-of-the-region – just pulled up to the edge of a pasture, piled out of the truck, climbed over (or through) the fence, and began shovel testing. This was the stretch of proposed corridor that was the straightest and most direct, actually cutting across two pastures that were separated by the creek. This route option would interfere with the fewest number of existing residences, and probably would require the least amount of land preparation prior to construction.

The two pastures were owned by the two most prominent individuals in the immediate area, individuals who were none too keen about the new project anyway. It also turned out that neither was aware that a testing crew had come into the area and had started testing; instead, they learned from observant neighbors that there were

people out in the pasture digging, those neighbors of course asking the owners what all of the activity in their pastures was about. Justifiably irate, the owners drove out to the pasture and ... well, it does not take much imagination to reconstruct the conversation that followed.

The locals had colored the tale a bit over the following year, so we discounted the part about the shotguns. But the point was that the initial Phase I testing had created problems through failure to observe one of the most basic field courtesies: informing the landowners about what was going on and making sure it was okay to do the testing first.

In a pasture setting this is especially important to do, since even properly backfilled shovel tests will still present possible treacherous footing for livestock. The last thing any firm needs to face is liability for a damaged dairy cow, which in year 2000 would cost $1,300 and above, depending on commercial productivity, registration, and part of the country. In horse country, the damages could be easily one to two orders of magnitude higher.

So, at the risk of stating the obvious: Not only make sure that landowners are aware that Phase I testing is planned and have given permission, but also make sure to contact them face-to-face *before* testing begins.

-- usually will send a notice to each property owner stating that archaeological testing is planned and asking for permission to do that testing. Alternatively, the agency may require that the client or applicant submit proof that this notice has been provided. A form, called a *right-of-entry form*, will be completed by the landowner and returned to the Lead agency, with a copy given to the archaeological subcontractor.

Publicity sometimes is augmented by public notice, such as the local newspaper, announcing that such work is starting. However, for small, private projects there usually is no requirement of, nor client interest in, any kind of public notice or publicity.

(If there is a public hearing process for the overall project, it is a good idea to fit the Phase I archaeological survey within the framework of the

hearing scheduling. This may be a regulatory requirement since in some states and localities the archaeological Phase I is supposed to be part of the overall environmental planning process. Normally, there are public hearings well in advance of projects, both in terms of the undertaking itself as well as in terms of the historic preservation process. The latter is required of the Federal agency in the Section 106 Process, instructing it to solicit the public's views, to involve the public in the Process, and to keep the public informed [36 CFR 800.2 (d); 36 CFR 800.6 (a) (4); some agencies also have specific regulations and guidelines regarding NHPA Section 106 implementation]. At such hearings, the planned project corridor or area will be shown, allowing individual land holders to get a sense of what portion of their property may be involved. At such a time, alternatives to the proposed project also will be presented, as well as the reasons why those alternatives did not seem to be as good as the one now proposed. It is not unusual for the Phase I work to play a role in the evaluation and selection of alternative designs.)

Prior to going into the field, the Lead agency should have supplied a list of names of affected landowners as well as copies of the right-of-entry forms. Project maps should also indicate where local property boundaries are. On first arriving in the area of the project, it becomes the project manager's responsibility to contact those landowners who have given permission: This is a matter of courtesy just as much as a matter of safety. Under no circumstances should property be entered, much less tested, without first receiving at least oral permission from the landowner or renter. Where applicable, the appropriate forms should also be secured prior to wandering over someone's land. Further, if there is a tenant or on-site land manager, that person should be informed directly about what is going on.

In situations where a landowner has not given permission to enter the property, the responsibility goes back to the client. Technically speaking, this is not within the purview of the archaeology firm, which has only subcontracted to provide archaeological services.

The second category of contact is an issue only if subsurface work is anticipated; this involves checking with local utilities for the presence of buried cables, water lines, and gas lines. Sometimes it is obvious that this is not an issue: remote, rural settings; recently or actively plowed fields; and the like. However, in urban, old suburban or resident settings, and similar places, the utility companies need to be checked with beforehand before digging is done. In some states, the law requires checking first before digging of any kind is done. (It is risky at best to rely on the landowner's knowledge to verify existence and location of buried utility easements and infrastructure.) A number of states and communities have a centralized clearinghouse that sends crews out to mark, with spray paint or pin flags, the paths of buried utility lines and mains.[2]

Not every underground utility is public infrastructure. For example, there may be buried private utilities -- water pipes, power cords, intercom lines -- between

We learned about archaeology from that ... The Scared Mom

Every field worker should carry personal identification. The field supervisor should have a copy of the contract, right-of-entry letter, or the Phase I (or Phase II or III) archaeological permit if in a state that requires such. For example ...

In a small village near the Canadian border, we headed up the road after an unsuccessful attempt to interview a landowner adjacent to a state DOT project set not too many miles from a prison. Our knocks went unanswered, but we did see a small shadow flitting about behind the curtains. We decided that the person must be overly shy about strangers and, not wishing to cause alarm, we left and went back to the field vehicle. Not long after starting to drive off, we suddenly found we were being followed, and then practically forced off of the road by a stranger ... male, at least six-foot-three and about 300 pounds.

We were glad we were observing our rule about working in pairs, but we were, to say the least, a little concerned. The man came over to our car door and demanded some identification. Apparently, the hamlet lacked an official police force and had simply delegated such tasks to the largest person in town. It was just our luck that the person who would not answer the door – that small flitting shadow behind the curtains – was this guy's mother. It took some convincing to get him to believe that we were not burglars casing his mother's house. We had personal identification, but nothing official from the DOT. Finally though, he accepted our story after we unfurled the 12-foot long highway realignment project map and showed that we could explain it.

Always be prepared to explain and verify the reasons for your presence.

houses, garages, well-head water-pumps, tool sheds, and yard lights. Power cables might not meet electrical code and, in addition to being unknown to public utility and regulatory authorities, may be hazardous. Some older houses in areas east of the Mississippi have antiquated storm-water or grey-water buried drainage systems that are still operational but bring water in from a different direction than, say, the more obvious septic system. Recent housing developments should have base maps that show the locations of private and quasi-private utilities, such as the lay-out of the septic field drain system, on file with the permitting agency at the county courthouse.[3]

---

2. Most people are unaware that such requirements exist, much less how searches for buried utilities are done. If such a search is going to be done at the behest of the archaeologist or client, the people whose land is going to be checked need to know that (1) a buried-utility crew carrying remote sensors is going to be coming onto their land and (2) they will be marking the location of buried utilities either by spray-painting different colored lines across their (often times lovingly tended) lawns and gardens, or by placing different colored pin flags into their lawns and gardens. Make sure that people understand what is going to happen, especially if it will involve any kind of physical alteration to their property.

---

3. Whether or not a residence or facility is on septic or public sewer may not be known to the owners. We know of cases where people had switched from septic to public sewer, even showing the papers granting public easement, but the sanitation authority refused to believe them (or, in an instance with a church, bill them, despite the church's insistence that they do so). We know of at least two opposite cases as well, where the house owners thought

5.2.3. Labor Estimates

Labor estimates for the entire Phase I project will be made at the time the bid is submitted to the client. This is necessary to establish a realistic bid, one that is at the same time competitive but capable of being done, and was discussed in Chapter 3. The bid, when accepted, becomes the project budget, and it is the project manager's responsibility to adhere to that budget.

For budgetary purposes, a Phase I project will have five categories:

1. start-up;

2. field work;

3. analysis;

4. draft report preparation and delivery; and

5. final report delivery and turn-over.

Details of the bid package were given in Chapter 3. The issue here is to give some sense of the labor that will be required at each step of the Phase I process.

Each of those five categories will have three variables: The level or pay grade of the assigned personnel, the number of hours needed by an individual to complete a given task, and the hourly pay rate for the individual or individuals assigned to each task. The differences between companies among those three variables is what makes the bid process so variable; it is astute juggling of those variables that allows firms to be competitive.

"Start-up" refers to the labor estimates needed to prepare for field work. This will include securing and loading a field vehicle with needed equipment; arranging for any necessary accommodations; working out locations of surface reconnaissance or shovel-test transects, backhoe placement (as well as lining up equipment and operators), as well as securing regional information like USGS topographic maps, county soil surveys, and municipal maps; and doing basic background research at the local library, courthouse, historical society, and state site files, a task done by the staff historian in larger firms.

Labor estimates will vary by the scale of the project as well as the expectations that the SHPO/THPO may

have for the exercise. There are few rules of thumb for allocating labor time at this stage of a project. For example, for a small 20 ha project requiring shovel testing in a mixed pasture-woodlot, eight person-hours allowed for equipping and for working out the details of the testing program will be adequate. This will include requesting apposite soil survey documents and USGS maps. Background historic research may range from eight to 40 or more person-hours, depending on the distance from the main office and each other the sources are, the presence or absence of previously known sites, prior project area background preparation, and the extent of associated background history.

By the time the start-up phase of the project is completed, the project director should have:

(1) a loaded vehicle equipped to do the work needed;

(2) specific knowledge of where personnel will be deployed as soon as the field crew arrives in the field, as well as what each individual will need to do; and

(3) preliminary knowledge of any archaeological sites or historic structures known for the project area, along with a detailed knowledge of soils, geology, and topography.

The "Field Work" estimates are comparatively easy, varying only by the SHPO/THPO or local agency testing protocols and the nature of the terrain; most firms, in fact, have a "fixed" per-acre Phase I rate, at least relative to expected field conditions. Most field data collection for Phase I projects fall into three categories: shovel testing, done in most states east of the Rockies; ground-surface reconnaissance, which is done in areas with good surface visibility and is common in western and southwestern states; and heavy equipment work, used both in urban settings and in areas with substantial overburden.

The majority of Phase I *subsurface* exercises involve shovel testing (shovel testing is explained in section 5.3.2.1. below) or, less often, some form of controlled surface collection in plowed or previously plowed fields (which may be thought of here as a variant on subsurface testing). Shovel testing or other subsurface examination rarely is done as part of Phase I in most western states (see section 5.2.7.2. below). Instead, a ground-surface reconnaissance is done.

When shovel testing is involved, Phase I labor estimates are computed in two steps. The first step involves knowing how many shovel tests are needed to test a given unit area (usually an acre since most construction and real estate maps are figured in acres) then computing how many shovel tests would be needed for the project area. For example, shovel tests

---

they were on public sewer, were being billed accordingly (billing for public sewer often is done by applying a multiplier to the volume of water used by the house or facility; there are no "sewage meters"), only to learn -- when their septic fields failed for lack of maintenance -- that they had never been connected to the sewer system.

spaced at 20-m intervals on parallel transects 20 m apart result in around 10.1 shovel tests per acre; a five-acre parcel will require around 51 shovel tests, assuming no subsequent testing will be needed.

The second step takes the number of shovel tests that can be completed by a person in an hour ("completed" meaning located, excavated, recorded, and backfilled), and divides that figure into the total number of shovel tests required to test the project area. The final number usually is rounded into half person-day increments. Thus, while 51 shovel tests probably will be completed in 11.3 - 12.8 person-hours (see Table 5.1), figuring either 12 or 16 person-hours for the labor estimate is probably best, with 16 hours allowing 16 extra shovel tests should they be needed for additional testing.

Phase I controlled surface-collecting, which as often as not will be done in the same regions where shovel testing is common, is somewhat easier to figure, requiring only knowing the area to be collected (again, usually in acres although not as often), then the area that can be collected by a person in an hour ("collected" including setting out surface collection grids, collecting, then bagging the collected material). These figures generally take into account the additional testing that is done around shovel tests that contained archaeological materials (Table 5.1).

"Open-ground" surface reconnaissance, as in western states or in more exposed areas of Plains states, depends upon coordination of available maps with GPS positioning of survey crews then recordation of their positions relative to landscape features or cultural materials concentrations. There is no easy way to figure labor, since part of the labor costs involve getting personnel to the area demarcated in the initial Phase I sample design (very much "reconnaissance" in these cases), and part of the labor costs involve examination of the area initially sought by that Phase I sampling design. Labor estimates are situational, figured on a project-by-project basis. Firms in those markets have standardized labor figures for the kinds of terrain, relative to state protocols and type of project (Federal- or state-mandated).

Urban Phase I subsurface field work also is a case-by-case matter. There are no overall guidelines, except to note that heavy equipment will be billed to the firm -- meaning against the archaeologist's project budget -- on an hourly basis, usually in half-day or full-day increments. Arrangements generally can be made through the client or its contractor to have pavement, rubble, or similar obstructions removed or at least rendered unobstructive. In other situations -- such as Phase I "subsurface" work done in the foundation floor of an urban structure -- labor costs will correspond to those associated with installation of new plumbing or drains, and need to include either rental of necessary equipment or hiring of necessary labor.

Table 5.1. Labor Estimates for Some Different Phase I Testing Methods. Figures are based on time-motion studies, and generally hold for all weather and field conditions. Screen sizes 1/4-inch (0.635 cm) in all cases.

Method	Number Per Hour
30-cm diameter, 40 cm deep, with fill screened	4.0 - 4.5
30-cm diameter, 40 cm deep, shovel-sorted	6.0 - 6.5
50 x 50 cm, 50 cm deep, with fill screened	1.0 - 1.2
Controlled surface collection, 10-m grid square	3.0 - 5.0

(Rate depends on density of artifact spread; time includes setting out pin flags or similar markers to set off the locations of the squares. Labor increases as the size of grid units decreases.)

By the time the field work has been completed, there should be a project map showing where artifacts/features were or were not located; a compiled project binder with the original shovel test, surface survey, or similar forms included; and a general sense of the archaeology of the project area along with the history of the landscape as indicated by the vegetation and the soil (except for projects involving basements of urban buildings, which tend to have less in the way of recognizable vegetation).

"Analysis" labor estimates vary by region. Compared to computing most field testing estimates, there are even fewer rules of thumb for estimating labor needs for analysis, since the amount of laboratory processing labor will vary by SHPO/THPO or equivalent regulatory office protocols (including labeling and records requirements), by the normal artifact yield for sites in the region, and by in-house laboratory procedures. Our experience in the eastern and midwestern United States can give some sense of scale: Most Phase I projects will require about one hour of analysis time for a laboratory technician for every four to five hours of total field time, plus one hour of laboratory supervisor time for every 16 hours of field time. However, most firms have worked out by trial-and-error a realistic labor estimate for Phase I analysis, and those are the figures that should be used.

By the time the analysis step is completed, the artifacts will have been cleaned or otherwise processed, labeled, and placed in labeled archival bags that have archival-grade paper labels enclosed. The bags will be placed in archival-grade storage boxes as specified in the SOW, or in SHPO/THPO or curatorial facility protocols. A hard-copy inventory of the artifacts will have been produced, a copy of which will stay with the artifacts while another will be handed to the project director for use in writing the report. Any special analyses -- measurements, weights, classifications -- that a particular project may need also will have been done, although Phase I analyses rarely require more than a basic count and general classification-description of recovered materials. Such additional levels of analyses will need to be budgeted for at the outset.

Labor estimates for "Report Preparation and Delivery" take into account the following tasks:

* Report writing;

* site form completion and assignment of site numbers;

* figure/illustration preparation;

* report production (assembly and copying/printing); and

* physical delivery.

While an archaeologist may consider that the archaeology is the "product" of the Phase I exercise, such a notion is very misleading. The "product" or, technically, the "deliverable" is the report that will be reviewed by the government lead agency and by the SHPO/THPO or equivalent review agency. That report is the physical object that the client wants and needs so that the client's own project may continue to completion. From the perspective of the client, the Phase I exercise is merely a regulatory step that must be completed so that the important things about life may go on. The Phase I report is what is needed for that regulatory step to be taken.

Phase I reports usually are very simple to do. The specifics are given in Chapter 9; the issue here is to round out a sense of labor allocation within the Phase I project. Usually, most of the Phase I will have been written out earlier; the opening chapter, the general cultural and environmental background, and the laboratory methods all will be similar to chapters in other Phase I reports prepared for the same general area. The industry term here is "boilerplate," by which is meant previously written material that can be transferred to a new report with a minimal -- but conscientious -- amount of change. For any project manager dealing with a Phase I report, this takes an hour. Labor, then, is negligible.

The new and made-for-the-project effort will involve the chapters and chapter sections dealing with specifics of the cultural and environmental background important to the project area, historic background as it pertained to the vicinity of the project area, field work and results, site forms if they had to have been submitted, and any figures and tables involved.

The rule of thumb for report production, used by the firms we are familiar with, is 40 person-hours for the first site (or an area with no sites), then eight hours

added for each additional site. That labor estimate takes into account any graphics that the project manager needs to have prepared in draft form for the graphics staff.

There should be a separate line item in the budget for graphics production, although this will depend upon how the particular firm is organized. Labor estimates vary by staff, complexity of figure, and sophistication of facilities: Anywhere between 1.0-4.0 hours per figure as an average will cover most situations and facilities.

Labor required for report production, including assembly then printing, varies by the size of the report and the number of copies of the draft requested in the SOW. This also varies greatly by the way in which the firm is organized: In some firms, virtually all of the report, from text through graphics, will be assembled on computer by the project manager, and the only remaining task will be making copies then binding the documents; in other firms, the project manager approves the text and graphics, the field supervisor will coordinate assembling of graphics and chapters, while secretarial staff will compile, print, then assemble and bind the draft report.

(Some draft reports are already being composed entirely on computer then submitted for review as e-mail attachments, bypassing the need for production of a physical draft report. This is now occurring in the review process for other environmental fields, and is likely to become a regular practice for archaeological reports as well.)

Regardless of *how* the report is delivered, be it physical hard copy or an electronic copy, *what* is being delivered is a *draft* report, not a final report. The draft report is submitted for review to the SHPO/THPO and to the government lead agency. This is why it is a "draft" and not a "final" report. In some instances, the report may be approved as it stands, and no further work or revisions will be needed. In other cases, corrections or additions to the report will be requested. If all of the steps in the Phase I process have been followed conscientiously and according to the SOW, there will be no need for additional analysis or field work, which at this stage would be done at the firm's own expense since it would not have been budgeted for.

It should be noted that the "final" report will be a physical hard copy, even if the draft report was approved without need for revision and was submitted electronically. The issue is curation: Physical documents are durable and accessible regardless of technology available; electronic documents are neither.

Budgets and labor estimates for the Phase I project -- like Phase II testing and Phase III data recovery projects -- include allowances for revising and reproducing the draft report. The amount of time and costs associated with this last part of the Phase I project usually will be about the same as the labor time and costs for the initial, start-up phase of the project. Personnel involved, though, will be different: Start-up will make use of field supervisors/crew chiefs, while the last part of the project usually will require additional secretarial help instead, again mainly for document assembly tasks and project-related bookkeeping.

5.2.4. Staffing Needs

Phase I projects have two staffing requirements, those involving non-field support and those involving field work. In larger firms, different people may be used for those staffing needs; in smaller firms, the same set of people may provide both field and non-field support. Since being competitive is the final criterion for private-sector survival, having a wide assortment of skills in addition to those associated with basic archaeology is important both to the employee and to the firm. This also applies to the state and Federal government work place, where over 20 years of work force reduction has resulted in the need for agency personnel to wear many different hats, and do so with considerable professional panache.

Staffing needs and tasks include:

*   *secretarial*, specifically preparation of correspondence; coordination and recordation of project communications; maintenance of office records including travel vouchers, work orders, and payroll; and scheduling;

*   *project management*, specifically coordination and assignment of project personnel, preparation then monitoring of the project budget, execution of the research design, personnel management, logistical management, writing of the report, client and agency relations;

*   *field labor*, specifically all aspects of standard field work as well as equipment assembly and maintenance;

*   *laboratory labor*, specifically all tasks from the cleaning of artifacts through their identification and tabulation to coding into a master data base, conservation tasks as needed, preparation for turn-over to a permanent curatorial facility;

*   *graphics*; and

*   *cultural backgrounds*, specifically background research into the history and prehistory of the project vicinity, which includes site file searches, maps, research on the history of the project vicinity (on rare occasions even including courthouse title searches).

5.2.4.1. Non-Field Support Personnel

Non-field staffing includes pre-field, field, and post-field parts of the project. The pre-field portions of the project involve the bid process, research design, and project set-up. The seeming oxymoron of non-field staffing for the field portion of a project involves office management (pay roll, project management) and lab activity. Post-field activity includes everything from laboratory analysis to report preparation, production, and assembly. (Some firms will treat these non-field tasks as overhead expenses; other firms will place these in as budget lines to keep track of cash flow and time allocation of office personnel.)

Meeting project needs, be it Phase I or any other kind of project, is done either by assigning in-house personnel, or by hiring outside personnel to assist in-house personnel. That second set, referred to as *project-hires*, is drawn from a professional migrant population that shifts from one project to the next in a manner very similar to that found in the construction industry. Project-hires usually are only needed for the field work portion of a project, and then only because the scale of the project is such that it cannot be completed using permanent employees of the firm.

Pre-field and post-field parts of projects usually are staffed by people drawn from the permanent employees of the firm.

5.2.4.2. Hiring or Assigning Field Personnel

Having sufficient personnel to accomplish the needs of a project is rather important. This should be self-evident; experience with many firms over the years suggests that it is not. Rather, the number of projects and their labor demands often exceed the capacity of the personnel to satisfy those demands. There are three solutions:

(1) turn down additional work, which may not be wise since in the long term it can create the impression among that general client population that, while the firm may be quite good (it is, after all, in demand), to get work done expeditiously it makes better sense to just call someone else;

(2) overwork the salaried personnel, which results in in-house resentment, a decrease in morale and quality of work, and a correspondingly high turn-over rate, such that time is spent either looking for new employees in a rapidly shrinking labor pool (everyone having learned to avoid the given firm) or in further abusing the remaining employees; or

(3) hire people (*project-hires*) in from the outside for the duration of the project that needs the extra labor.

Most firms choose the third option. The advantage of project-hires, as with any firm that makes use of temp services, is that it provides for coverage of wild swings in the market. After all, this is why temp services exist for many fields, clerical through professional: There are lean times and fat times, and firms can hire-on temporary personnel without much effort in searching or interviewing. That such a population has in effect advertised itself willing to work for less than a permanent employee (by voluntarily being a part of that temporary labor pool), while the existence of the industry suggests that there is a surfeit of such willing labor, the firm making use of such labor does enjoy a buyer's market.

To some extent, this holds for professional archaeology. There is a project-hire population; that is, there are migrant, temporarily employed archaeologists who move from project to project. There is no centralized clearinghouse for that labor pool. Instead, firms call each other, requesting that those firms make known to the project-hires currently with them that a new archaeological project of such-and-such dimensions and duration will be available at such-and-such a time.

The advantage is that a firm generally can cover its immediate labor needs in this way. The disadvantage for the firm is that the employees not only are temporary with no permanent loyalty to the firm, often they have college degrees in Anthropology. And, to use the famous phrase that our colleague Dr. Ron Cochran at Rocky Mountain College coined: "Anthropologists are professional gossips."

Much of the information about the day-to-day activities in archaeology in the United States is communicated through the project-hire community. They know which firms are fair and equitable, and which are not. They know which pay fairly with a fair per diem policy, and which skim money off of the top of the per diem allowance. In short, the project-hire population has a better idea of what is going on in the archaeology of the country than any other population, even other members of the professional community. Their knowledge is the knowledge of the Help; they get the image before it has been sanitized. And, they are being unionized.[4]

Although there is a second source of project-hires for projects, it is rare that they will be used in a Phase I project. That second source is the general labor population available through the unemployment office for the region where the project is located. This labor source, along with the need for specialty professionals, such as heavy equipment operators and so on, is more often found in Phase III projects (see Chapter 7; however, it is common to use heavy equipment as part of Phase I investigations in urban environments and in situations where deep-testing of floodplains is needed). By the way, this should underscore the intensely professional nature of the Phase I process: In many cases, the lowest level of expertise for field operations will be a person with a college background in anthropological archaeology; it is not unusual for some Federal contracts to specify that field workers have a completed college degree along with a year or two of supervised field experience.

5.2.5. Field Logistics: Housing, Per Diem, Transport

Most Phase I projects are done within a couple-hour round trip of the main office. In situations where the project is at too great a distance to commute, issues of housing and per diem come up.

"Per diem" refers to a set fee paid to field workers as a kind of reimbursement for room and board costs while in the field. Per diem will be (or is supposed to be) paid out, when circumstances warrant, to all field people, be they salaried employees or project-hires.

The fee and how it is paid varies by region, by compliance contractor, and to a lesser extent by firm. For example, Federal guidelines in the early 1990s set the per diem rate for Federally contracted field work in the Middle Atlantic at $80 per day. That was and is a sizeable sum; as might be expected, sums that size produce all sorts of interesting behavior for those involved.

Per diem is meant to cover the costs of room and board, to allow the field person to live comfortably, since the work often is exceptionally rigorous. It exists for the convenience of the employer, in part for that reason but also in part because it is a less expensive accounting procedure than collecting and documenting lodging and meal receipts for each employee. Thus, at least the people in the field will be well fed and have good accommodations, and, as a benefit to the firm, the quality of each day's work is much better than it might otherwise be.

In reality, per diem often is viewed as additional funds, both for the field person and for the firm. For the field person, anything that can be done to cut down the field living costs below that $80 a day (or whatever the figure actually is) will be a net savings that will not be taxed.[5] As a result, one finds field crews in motels

---

4. However, the extent of unionization of archaeological field technicians is not great, with estimates ranging from five to 25 percent of those who would be eligible. Our industry contacts are not aware of any firms that have union contracts as of this writing (March 1999).

5. After having spoken with three private-sector archaeology firms about this, we found that none of the CFOs knew the correct answer to per diem and taxes. Since the IRS levies penalties for mistakes in this area, it seems like a good idea to give some sense

forever smuggling in hot plates and coolers and who-knows what else in an (usually successful) effort to cut down on the foods costs. By the way, it is illegal in most places to have and use a hot plate or similar device in a motel or hotel room.

One also finds some firms too mesmerized by the apparent cash flow not to, sooner or later, want a piece of the per diem action. The field archaeologist should expect only 90 percent of the announced per diem rate to actually be paid: A number of firms will withhold as a processing charge around 10 percent of the per diem due to the field worker. This is one of the weaknesses of the project-hire position: Because the project-hire is not permanently affiliated with a given firm, the only grievance procedures that exist, exist at the Federal level (Department of Labor, Internal Revenue Service, National Labor Relations Board).

There is a second aspect of per diem that every entry-level professional archaeologist needs to know: In many cases, the per diem -- well, okay, 90 percent of

the expected per diem -- will not be sent until long after the project has ended. That is, those firms will wait until they have been paid by their client before the per diem cheques are cut and mailed out.[6] This means that the person in the field will have to provide funding for food and lodging, in effect providing for the benefit of their employers a loan for personnel support costs for the duration of the project. However, unlike the banking industry, it will be the person providing the loan who will pay the 10 percent fee for service on that loan, the 10 percent withheld by the firm for processing the per diem cheques.

How is housing arranged? This varies by the firm. Some firms will arrange housing beforehand. This becomes the responsibility of the project manager, who will call ahead or visit the communities near the project area, check rates, and make arrangements accordingly. In cases like that, the firm will cover for housing costs out of the per diem budget line; with the balance then going to the project members as a meals allowance. Other firms leave it to the employees, or at least the project-hires, to find lodging for themselves.

Transportation to the project area on a per diem project usually is the responsibility of project-hires, although this varies by project. For permanent employees, the firm is required to provide transportation, or to reimburse transportation costs to and from the project area if a personal vehicle must be used. Once at the staging area for the per diem project, the firm is responsible to getting crew to and from the actual site of field work. By the way, in situations with project-hires but a non-per-diem project, how the field worker gets to the project area will be worked out beforehand with the employer. It often is identical to that found in any construction project: The field worker need only be present in the field at the time assigned; how they get there is their problem.

---

of how taxes and per diem work. The following is based on remarks by Ms. Peggy Nordman (Breen, Winkle, and Company, Inc., Columbus, Ohio).

Per diem and the savings accrued usually are not subject to Federal income taxes. The employee is not required to include in gross income the portion of a per diem allowance received from a payer that is deemed substantiated when the arrangement otherwise meets the business-connection and return-of-excess amounts requirements, because the amounts are treated as paid under an accountable plan [Rev Proc 97-57, §7.03, 1997-52 IRB 31; see IRC (Internal Revenue Code) §1.62-2 (h)(2)(i)(B) and §31.3401 (a) - 4(b)(1)(ii)].

Deemed substantiated means that a per diem satisfies adequate accounting requirements, which in turn means that all four of the following apply (Internal Revenue Service 1998:183): (1) the employer reasonably limits the amount to ordinary and necessary expenses for the conduct of the trade or business; (2) the allowance is similar in form to and not greater than the Federal rate (see Internal Revenue Service 1999); (3) the employee can prove dates, place, and business purpose to employer in a reasonable amount of time (e.g., time sheets, field notes, travel journal); and (4) the employee is not related to the employer (cutting through the reasoning and code, in those situations, the person needs to keep receipts).

Each year, the Internal Revenue Service computes the reasonable amounts needed for per diem expenses for all parts of the country (e.g., Internal Revenue Service 1999). By the employee keeping expenses within the limit or rate for the given area, the incurred expenses are *deemed substantiated*, meaning that receipts are not required to justify the reimbursement represented by the per diem cheque. This allows the employer to substantiate the expenses and not fuss with tracking a myriad of employee receipts when computing corporate taxes.

The Internal Revenue Service each year publishes a locale rate guide for per diem (e.g., Internal Revenue Service 1999; do not ask about how per diem and truck drivers work. Please.). Employers are not required to pay that rate, although we have worked with DoD contracts that required that rate to be used as a condition of the contract. Any savings that can be done within the bounds of that rate are not taxable; any savings from an employer that is paying beyond that rate *are* taxable. Thus, if the Federal locale per diem rate is $121, and you spend only $100, that $21 balance is tax-free. Hence motel hot-plates. However, if the Federal locale per diem rate is $121 and the firm -- beyond all imagination -- pays a per diem of $125 while you spend only $100, the $4 balance *is* taxable.

---

6. Although we had remarks from reviewers that they were unaware of any firms that either retained a percentage of the per diem or that waited until the end of the project to cut the per diem cheques, we are personally aware -- first-hand -- of a number of large archaeology firms/divisions in the eastern United States that follow this as a regular practice. However, our reviewers noted that in the cases of their own firms or institutions, and in the cases of similar firms or institutions in their regions, per diem was paid at times on a weekly basis, the week after the expenses were incurred, and without any "surcharge" taken before hand. We have found that the first kind of practice is common enough that the project-hire should be prepared for it to happen; if it does not, then it can be considered a pleasant case where our concern was overstated and unnecessary.

5.2.6. Equipment and Supply Needs

For those entering into professional practice, one of the most often overlooked and unknown aspects of the field is also the most basic: Equipment needed to accomplish basic Phase I goals. The seeming triviality of this is implied in the historic lack of mention in college texts of what it is that is needed or used (however, see Feder 1997:63). This is like trying to explain how to cook without indicating at all the utensils needed or the units of measure involved. Tables 5.2 and 5.3 summarize what is used.

Some firms issue to each crew member most of the equipment listed in Table 5.2; other firms expect that the crew member will possess some or all of the equipment, much the way a construction worker, auto mechanic, or machinist is expected to provide the tools of trade.

Table 5.2   Equipment Required by Each Crew Member for Phase I Subsurface Survey

* range-finder kind of compass
* two colors of flagging tape
* bags
* indelible, write-on-any-surface, ink marker
* retractable metric hand tape (3-m, locking)
* shovel testing or surface survey field note forms (preferably something that will go into a notebook)
* pencil
* clipboard (shielded metal)
* trowel
* round-nose shovel[a]
* small screen (mesh size varies by state, site, and field conditions [soil/sediment, temperature, wetness][a]
* simple hand-held calculator
* hard-hat if working on a construction site; hard-hat and safety vest if working along a highway (usually required for DOT-type contracts)[b]

---

a. Applies to regions/projects where shovel testing is done.

b. Hard-hats and safety vests may be new equipment requirements to many workers; it does not hurt for the firm to have an extra supply of these on hand. By the way, such equipment socially validates the field archaeologist in a construction setting. We have had fewer challenges to our people in the field when they have been wearing hard-hats (and of course even fewer if they also have been carrying the authority-conferring clipboard, pencil at the ready).

Most of the listed material is meant to be carried in a backpack, one identical to the nylon-with-padded-straps type used by undergraduates to cart books around campus. Some firms even provide such packs along with the equipment. The reality, though, is that the shovel, screen, and clipboard are carried in the hand, the tape measure is clipped to a belt, the compass is hung about one's neck or stuck in a pocket, and everything else is stashed away in pockets. Most veteran field workers dress with the same kind of multi-pocketed vests and garments associated with trout fishermen and photojournalists, and for the same reasons: To have categorized and immediately at-hand what their profession demands.   Most often the backpack is used to carry artifacts, but even that is not always true.

Table 5.3. Equipment Carried by Crew Chief or Field Supervisor

*   Munsell soil colors book
*   project map or copy showing planned shovel test or collection area locations
*   first aid kit if the crew is going to be far from the field vehicle
*   GPS (as needed)
*   cell phone
*   camera (not always needed for Phase I; however, some states require soil profile or general landscape photographs)

Supplemental materiél varies by project and regional needs. Lunch may have been packed; it probably *will* be in the backpack, along with a canteen. Rain gear may be stored there as well.

Depending on the area and terrain, it may be important to have an extra set of vehicle keys, a good road map, and an idea, known to the crew, of how to get emergency help. It is assumed that the crew had first aid training, including CPR; for some Federal contracts, it is required that someone with that kind of training be present.

5.2.7. Setting Up

After the project has been awarded, and a budget and schedule are in place, the Phase I project must be set up. "Set-up" refers to all of the preparatory steps that need to be taken to make sure that the project is done properly, and within time and budget limits. Phase I projects are budgeted with very little margin for error. Phase I projects also are a major source of corporate cash flow. Knowing what to do and how to do it are key to corporate survival.

5.2.7.1. Project Maps

Most Phase I projects will be provided with a project area map. These maps will have been prepared, either by or for the client, to be presented to the local planning board. Usually, these maps are done at a 1 inch to 50 ft, 1 inch to 100 ft, or 1 inch to 200 ft scale, and usually they show what will be done as part of the construction project. Such maps will show landscape features like roads, utility poles, fences, as well as other survey marks.

How the project maps are prepared varies from project to project. For large projects, such as pipe line corridors or U.S. Army Corps of Engineers floodplain projects, an engineering firm may be used to prepare the basic property maps. That firm will use aerial photographs for the preparation of the map, sometimes flying the project area themselves. The plans for small housing developments may have been done by a land surveying firm hired specifically for that purpose.

There is a caveat that attends project maps, primarily blue line renderings. These often will contain errors. The practicing archaeologist should not be surprised if his or her field measurements contradict the information on the project map supplied by the client. While archaeologists also make mistakes, in our experience about 80 percent of project maps supplied to us by clients have had errors of varying degrees, such as mistakes in distances or feature locations. The

proper procedure is to verify one's field measurements as closely and as well as possible, record that verification in notes, then continue while informing where important to the client (see "*We learned about archaeology from that ...* The Power Line Corridor").

5.2.7.2. Subsurface Survey: Planning Shovel Test Transects

The purpose of the Phase I survey is to make a reasonable and good faith effort to see if archaeological sites that might be eligible for listing on the National Register are present within the area of potential effects; that is, to make a good faith effort to identify potential *historic properties*. To accomplish this purpose usually means first trying to identify if any kind of archaeological site is present, working out something of the horizontal limits of such sites, then getting some sense of the age and cultural affiliation of the located site.

In the western and southwestern parts of the country, where surface visibility is good, aggradation is rare, and soils are sufficiently inactive that they do not behave as fluids, subsurface testing seldom is needed. However, for most of the country, Phase I site identification will involve subsurface testing of some form. And that form usually is shovel testing. Generally, Phase I subsurface testing like shovel testing can assess site depositional integrity in the sense of if extensive disturbance, such as plowing, has occurred. That can

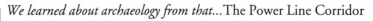

We learned about archaeology from that... The Power Line Corridor

A situation that illustrates well the errors that can exist in a project map concerns a power line corridor project we did in the Southern Piedmont a number of years ago.

There are basically two kinds of Phase I projects: Those that examine large parcels, and those that examine corridors. Of these, the corridor project is the one where errors in the project map can present the greatest potential problem for the client. With a corridor, any error in bearing or distance along the course of the corridor not only grows as distance in-creases or bearing changes, but also can result in the wrong property owners being contacted or land, purchased/cleared.

The proposed corridor ran through cropped and abandoned tobacco and maize fields, active pastures and hay

fields, 20 - 50-year-old secondary growth, and across state and local highways as well as gravel access roads. The distance was around 10 miles, with seven changes in bearing over that distance. The firm putting in the corridor had had the project flown – there was a lovely aerial photograph to work with – and had had a surveying company hack out the center line. Thus, the project came not only with a very thorough and detailed project map, it also had a multiplicity of corridor stakes and field marks to allow anyone coming in after the surveying crew to find their way along the entire corridor's length.

Most of the corridor testing went as easily as these kinds of projects ever do: Corridor projects require a lot of leap-frog testing as crew pass each other testing the next place along the corridor, and they require moving a field vehicle from one end to another so that crew do not have to walk back over the land. The excellent map

made planning – both shovel test location and basic field management – very easy. Further, with the roads, stakes, and bearing changes, combined with the aerial photograph and USGS 7.5' maps, maintaining ground truth was extremely easy.

Thus, we were quite startled when we came to a portion of the project, about seven miles into the exercise, where our paced field distance did not match what was staked out in the field, but *did* match the project map. The error was around 10 m, and was apparent because the project map, as interpreted by our pacing and by our pre-field shovel test planning, suggested that the corridor made a 90° turn 10 m beyond where the land survey crew had made that same 90° turn.

What to do?

We of course double-checked our field distances, using a tape measure. Fortunately, the corridor had just

allow for the *exclusion* of a site from probable Register-eligibility due to lack of matrix integrity.

Phase I subsurface sampling that uses shovel testing or, in alluvial settings, backhoe trenches is in most cases systematic sampling. For shovel testing, the sampling unit is a shovel test unit or shovel test pit (abbreviated ST or STP); the activity is "shovel testing." Shovel tests are set out in straight line transects, with the shovel tests placed at intervals. Intervals vary by two factors: government review agency protocol and budget. Table 5.4 gives a sense of what is expected for Phase I exercises by state and territory. The practicing archaeologist must contact the appropriate government agency for Phase I protocols within its jurisdiction; since requirements change and, in several cases, are under review, Table 5.4. should not be used as a substitute for direct agency contact.

Ten states currently (Spring 2000) require little if any subsurface testing during Phase I:

Arizona	North Dakota
California	Oregon
Hawai'i	South Dakota
Nebraska	Utah
Nevada	Wyoming

The need for subsurface testing in those 10 states is precipitated mainly by surface visibility combined with presence or absence of alluvium.

Another eight states currently (Spring 2000) have discretionary subsurface testing protocols, where shovel testing -- both if it is done as well as how it is set up -- is to some extent left up to the project design. Those states are:

Idaho	Missouri
Kansas	New Mexico
Massachusetts	North Carolina
Mississippi	Wisconsin

The remaining 32 states require shovel testing to be done in some kind of interval fashion, or require such testing when certain terrain conditions -- say lack of surface visibility, as in Texas or Minnesota -- apply.

When used, shovel tests normally will be set out in a grid-like pattern. For example, most areas in Maryland will be tested with a 20 x 20 m grid of shovel tests. These grids are comprised of parallel shovel test transects. Occasionally, radial shovel test patterns -- where transects radiate out from a common point, like spokes from a wheel-- have been used. Such a testing pattern is not common.

Phase I shovel testing is premised on the assumption that archaeological debris will be spread about in a sheet, referred to as SHEET LITTER. The individual shovel tests puncture that sheet, documenting the horizontal extent of any site present. The shovel tests represent individual points from which a coarse image of the site can be discerned. Those points are treated

crossed a local asphalt road, and the surveying crew had hammered a reference spike into the pavement. Our pacing had come out right on that spike, so we knew we were in agreement to that point (and while it should work that way, still had us smiling with pleasure at our field accuracy).

The next 15 or so shovel tests continuing beyond the road could be easily measured; these, too, were found to be correctly spaced. By the time our checking was done, it was clear that either the project map had been drawn incorrectly, or the land surveying crew had made its turn 10 m too soon. In any case, our field crew was where it was supposed to be; the issue now was how to best serve the client, who was blissfully unaware at the moment that any problem existed, and instead was presumably enjoying the weekend.

The immediate field solution was to shift the testing pattern in such a way that the project map corridor as well as the possible real corridor both would be tested. This fortunately was simple to do, and did not materially increase the number of shovel tests nor send crew very far afield. The testing was continued from that point, and over the next two days for the project the two corridors began to spread away from each other, as the original 10 m error compounded itself.

An attempt was made to inform the client of the problem the day that the error was discovered. However, by the time any action could be taken – which meant double-checking both project maps and land survey notes – the Phase I testing was completed. We had, though, managed to adjust the Phase I testing pattern so that, regardless of which was correct, the project map or the surveying field stakes, the client's project corridor was tested.

(The alternative – to suspend testing until the client could send a survey crew into the field and sort the problem out – was not viable in this case. Corridor construction already had started, our crews already were in the field, a stand-down on our part would idle the field personnel for the weekend, and the delay in getting a land survey crew out would result in overall construction/clearance delays and added costs that the client wanted to avoid. The solution developed allowed the client to continue the overall project, covered the archaeology well, and permitted time for the land survey crew to act.)

The point here is that pre-project planning of shovel test location is vital for a Phase I project. Errors happen, and they can be with the project map, the land surveying crew, the Phase I pre-planning, or the Phase I testing crew. But, there WILL be errors at some point. It is the project manager's responsibility to be alert to those errors, since the client is depending on the accuracy of the Phase I work.

Table 5.4. Phase I Shovel Testing Protocols by State, Territories, Commonwealth, Protectorate, and District. Shovel tests are a standard 30 cm diameter, either 40 cm deep or 10 cm into culturally sterile subsoil, unless otherwise indicated. Most states require a drawing of at least one shovel test profile in any report. This table is only an approximation of requirements or suggested practices. More detailed information is available from each state; many of them issue extensive guidance documents. Most state transportation agencies, due to the greater volume of contracts, will have more specific shovel-test requirements in their SOWs and RFPs (Scopes of Work and Requests for Proposals). (Sources of table information included telephone contacts and web site contents in addition to printed material cited.)

Jurisdiction	Default Interval	Default Pattern	Slope Limits	Default Screen	Comments
Alabama	30 m	-	-	1/4"	Testing interval can be up to 60 m in areas of low probability. Site boundaries should be established through 5 - 10 m testing. Depending on field conditions there can be other variances from protocol.
Alaska	-	-	-	-	Archaeology undertaken by the state conforms to Federal standards.
American Samoa	15 m	-	-	-	Shovel tests not required on Tafuna plain. An involved, individualized scope of work is prepared, with project-specific spacing and testing requirements.
Arizona	-	-	-	-	Phase I surveys usually do not involve ground disturbance. If vegetative cover or other circumstances warrant subsurface testing then the protocol is specific to the project. Backhoe trenching is most common in alluvial situations.
Arkansas	5 m	grid	-	1/4"	Soil can be hand troweled and sort instead of being screened, but method should be explained in the report. Shovel tests can be at 10 m intervals in areas of heavy ground cover. Shovel tests recommended but not required in plowed land (about a third of the state).
California	-	-	-	-	Generally, surveys do not test subsurface unless evidence of buried soils or other geomorphology warrants.
Colorado	-	-	-	-	Field component is primarily a surface survey. Phase I is termed "Class III Cultural Resource Inventory."
Connecticut	-	-	-	-	Assessment and reconnaissance are divided into two stages within the Phase I. *The Environmental Review Primer for Connecticut's Archaeological Resources*, by David Poirier, 1987, Connecticut Historical Commission, provides basic guidelines and policy.
Delaware	-	grid	5%	1/4"	Protocols are guidelines only, other than the policy of requiring screening of all excavated soils unless otherwise agreed upon.
District of Columbia	-	-	-	1/4"	Phase 1 subsurface testing usually involves trenching and other large-equipment activity, due to the urban nature. If there is Phase I excavation it will usually continue into a Phase II operation. Shoveled units are screened.
Florida	25 m	-	-	1/4"	Usually a grid pattern is employed. Areas should be ranked "high," "medium," or "low" site probability. Moderate- and low-ranked areas may be tested at 50 m intervals, with at least ten percent of low-ranked areas tested. Subsurface tests should be 50 cm in diameter and at least one meter deep. A 50 cm x 50-100 cm unit recommended for every 900-2,500 square meters coastal shell midden areas, and for every 400-900 square meters of dark earth midden areas and deep sandy interior environments.
Guam	-	-	-	-	Determined on a case-by-case basis. Subsurface investigations, if required, may be by shovel, core, or backhoe.
Georgia	30 m	-	10-15%	1/4"	Georgia standards are not specific. Most consultants use grid or transects with 30-m intervals rather than just examining high-probability areas. Surface inspection adequate where ground visibility exceeds 25 percent. Maximum depth is generally 75 cm (only feasible in the Coastal Plain).
Hawai'i	-	-	-	-	Surface surveys usually suffice; design is on a case-by-case basis.
Idaho	-	-	-	1/8"	There are no requirements for shovel testing. The state recommends 1/8" screen mesh for any subsurface testing.
Illinois	15 m	grid	-	-	Shovel tests are 40 x 40 cm and must be screened. Surface inspection intervals must be 5 m and are the norm with good visibility. Augment surface inspection with shovel test when surface visibility less than 25 percent, and with a shovel test grid when less than 10 percent. Shovel test grid interval decreases from 15 m to 5 m when cultural material is encountered. In addition to the state *Guidelines*, the Illinois Archaeological Survey's *Professional Standards* (1983) govern archaeological work. State archaeologist memorandum of 18 December 1996 serves as addendum to *Guidelines*.
Indiana	10 m	-	20%	1/4"	Shovel tests should be at 5 m intervals if the soil is unscreened. Shovel probes used when ground visibility is less than 20 percent. As of Spring 1998, revised draft guidelines were under review.

Table 5.4. Phase I Shovel Testing Protocols by State, Territories, Commonwealth, Protectorate, and District (con'd).

Jurisdiction	Default Interval	Default Pattern	Slope Limits	Default Screen	Comments
Iowa	15 m	grid	15%	1/4"	Transects are usually rectangular but can be staggered triangles. Transect intervals are usually 15 to 10 m. The "shovel test" here means a 50 x 50 cm unit dug in flat-bottomed 10 cm levels. However, there are no depth or diameter requirements. Subsurface testing begins when surface visibility is below 30 percent or there is apparent alluvial or colluvial deposits.
Kansas	-	-	-	-	The testing procedure is at the discretion of the consulting archaeologist
Kentucky	20 m	-	-	-	Interval transects are at 20 m. If a site is encountered, the STPs must be screened, otherwise trowel-sorting is sufficient. Raking or plowing is encouraged as a means of improving surface visibility. The state's *Specifications for Archaeological Fieldwork and Assessment Reports* (1991) applies.
Louisiana	30 m	grid	-	1/4"	Shovel sort acceptable in some cases. Transects normally 30 m apart, 50 m in low probability area.
Maine	10 m	grid	-	1/4"	Default pattern for prehistoric site surveys is linear.
Mariana Islands	-	-	-	-	These small islands primarily follow Federal guidelines.
Maryland	20 m	grid	10%	1/4"	interval and screen size varies by probability and nature of site
Massachusetts	-	-	-	-	A state permit is required for "archaeological reconnaissance surveys"; a research design is required that gives a high probability of finding the types and sizes of expected resources in a project area.
Michigan	-	-	-	-	
Minnesota	15	-	-	1/4"	Transects are 15 m apart and shovel testing is done when vegetative cover prohibits adequate surface visibility. Shovel tests are 40 x 40 cm.
Mississippi	-	-	-	-	Each situation is handled on an individual basis.
Missouri	-	-	-	-	Although the individual archaeologist has discretion, the state provides a detailed outline for survey reports. The *Guidelines for Contract Cultural Resource Survey Reports and Professional Qualifications* by Michael S. Weichman, 1986, Missouri Department of Natural Resources, is undergoing revision.
Montana	5 m	grid	-	1/4"	The Historic Preservation Office prefers $\frac{1}{8}$" screening. Shovel testing is not considered particularly accurate in locating features or diagnostic tools and is only recommended to delineate boundaries based on moderate-to-high surface densities of artifacts or when surface visibility is poor, impact areas are small, and site probability is at least moderate.
Nebraska	-	-	-	-	Shovel testing is only employed when surface visibility is poor. In the rare instance of use, protocol is on a case-by-case basis.
Nevada	-	-	-	-	Shovel tests are seldom used.
New Hampshire	8 m	-	-	1/4"	Shovel test units are 50 cm x 50 cm.
New Jersey	-	-	-	1/4"	Area of potential effects must be tested with an average of 17 one-foot probes per acre (equivalent to 50 ft intervals in a rectilinear grid). Highway and other linear projects should be tested at least every 50 ft. Guidelines issued 1996 by Historic Preservation Office.
New Mexico	-	-	-	-	New Mexico is in the process of developing a shovel testing policy.
New York	15 m	grid	none	1/4"	The protocol is contained within the *Standards for Cultural Resource Investigations and the Curation of Archaeological Collections in New York State*, New York Archaeological Council 1994.
North Carolina	-	-	-	-	Protocol is left to the discretion of the archaeological consultants for both Phase I and Phase II surveys.
North Dakota	-	-	-	-	Shovel tests seldom used.
Ohio	30 m	-	15%	1/4"	*Archaeology Guidelines*, Ohio Historical Society 1994, contains a "suggested minimum" for subsurface investigations; alternatives are permissible but must be justified in the report. Deep testing of screened 1 x 1 m per 30 m interval is required for buried soil horizons. Hand excavation of 50 x 50 cm screened units at 15 m intervals is specified where plowing, disking and washing is not feasible for formerly plowed fields or if in undisturbed soil.
Oklahoma	-	-	30%	1/4"	Shovel test unit is 0.25 square meter. Spacing and pattern are at the discretion of the archaeologist.
Oregon	-	-	-	-	Oregon does not have testing protocol. The Association of Oregon Archaeologists is considering developing guidelines similar to those of California.
Pennsylvania	20 m	grid	8%	1/4"	50 x 50 cm units, testing to go to top of Pleistocene sediments, regardless of depth below surface
Puerto Rico	15 m	grid	15%	1/4"	Shovel test pits are 50 x 50 cm. Medium probability areas can be at 25 m intervals, low probability areas at 30 m (4 per acre). Deep testing with 1 x 1 m pits required for alluvial or colluvial areas.

Table 5.4. Phase I Shovel Testing Protocols by State, Territories, Commonwealth, Protectorate, and District (con'd).

Jurisdiction	Default Interval	Default Pattern	Slope Limits	Default Screen	Comments
Rhode Island	-	-	-	-	Shovel test procedures are detailed in individual Phase I permits. There are three Phase I types: disturbance assessment, reconnaissance, and intensive surveys.
South Carolina	30 m	-	-	1/4"	Shovel and Auger tests must be at least 30 x 30 cm and be screened. If a site is "probable" then testing interval is no more than 20 m. Testing pattern is site- and project-specific. The guidelines are currently being rewritten.
South Dakota	-	-	-	-	No protocol for shovel testing. Very little subsurface work is done. Surface survey transects are to be no more than 30 m apart. The state is considering revising the guidelines for archaeological surveys and reports.
Tennessee	30 m	-	-	1/4"	Tennessee Division of Archaeology prefers methods based on specific site conditions. Intervals should not exceed 30 m and ¼" mesh screen is the standard.
Texas	30 m	-	20%	-	Shovel testing required when less than 30 percent of surface visibility. Interval is 15 m in far West Texas. At least 6 tests are needed for site boundaries unless surface is visible. Shovel test/acre is 1 for projects under 10 acres, ½ for 10-100 acres and ⅓ for 100-200 acres.
Utah	-	-	-	-	In most areas of the state visual surface inspections are the predominant means of gathering archaeological data in Phase I. Shovel testing is recommended on a case-by-case basis in alluvial areas, heavy ground cover, and areas where cultural remains are likely.
Vermont	8 m	-	-	1/4"	Shovel tests to be 40 x 40 cm squares. Bracket or cluster shovel test pits are required around isolated test pits that contain cultural resource materials and within a 200-foot zone around visible historic ruins. See also the state's *Guidelines for Archeological Studies*, which has just been revised.
Virginia	15 m	grid	8%	1/4"	All shovel test profiles must be "fully documented."
Virgin Islands	10 m	-	-	-	Most land is subject to Federal jurisdiction and thus is surveyed by NPS guidelines.
Washington	-	-	-	-	Protocol is at the discretion of the archaeologist in the field.
West Virginia	15 m	grid	20%	1/4"	The 1991 guidelines are currently being revised. Intervals decrease to 5 m if shovel tests positive.
Wisconsin	15 m	-	-	1/4"	Shovel tests of 10 m intervals and 10 m between transects are highly recommended. The *Guidelines for Public Archaeology in Wisconsin* were revised in 1997 and are available from the state historical society.
Wyoming	30 m	-	-	-	Protocol is at the discretion of the archaeologist in the field. Phase I surveys are called "Class III Inventory." The field component is primarily a surface inspection.

TIP: Project Area Features for Verifying Location

The Phase I crew is often the second or third party to go over the landscape. The first usually is the land survey crew. They may clear corridors and set stakes, the latter being recorded on the project map. Certainly other major landscape features, such as streams or building foundations, generally are noted. When setting out shovel test transects on paper, the locations of these items should be noted along with distance from a given shovel test position; this allows verification and control of the testing pattern.

Sometimes the people who do the water percolation tests (perc tests) get in before the survey crew does, which is helpful in the field since survey crews often map in the perc tests to meet septic system and other drainage permit requirements. Groundwater monitoring wells may have been installed for the same reason. Perc tests result in small,

foot- or two-foot high piles of fill around a hole maybe eight- to 12-inches in diameter. Often these as well as monitoring wells are marked and numbered with a stake, and the number will also be found on the project design map. The field crew can use these mapped features to verify shovel test positions.

However, as a caution, it must also be remembered that often surveying crews take a series of point-elevation samples, then interpolate landscape topography either from those points or from aerial stereo-photographs. Archaeologists work at a greater level of landscape detail and resolution than usually required for land surveying.

like the points making up a half-tone newspaper picture. The denser the points, the better the resolution and definition of the image. This becomes one of the advantages of a formal grid pattern as opposed to haphazardly distributed shovel tests.

There are several implicit assumptions about archaeological sites contained in this. The first is that cultural materials will be distributed about a site as a sheet litter. Second, that sheet, as a (mathematical) topological plane is (mathematically) continuous. There might be areas of high artifact concentrations and of low concentrations, but the transitions from one to the other are assumed to be gradational, not discontinuous. More often than not, these first two assumptions closely approximate reality, because more often than not the deposit has been plowed; the assemblage, as an image, has been slightly blurred (generally no where near the extent that people often think of [Odell and Cowan 1987]) and extensively augmented from a manure spreader (see *"We learned about archaeology from that ...* The Manure Spreader Example").

The third assumption is that there is a threshold density for sites that would meet the data potential criterion in **36 CFR 60.4**. One artifact recovered from a 30 cm diameter, 40 cm deep shovel test (area: 0.07 m²; cylindrical volume: 0.028 m³; more common parabolic volume: 0.019 m³) represents an artifact density of about 14.1 artifacts per square meter, or 52.63 artifacts per cubic meter.

The fourth assumption is that there is a threshold area for sites that would meet the data potential criterion in **36 CFR 60.4**. The largest closed-curve, contiguous area that can be missed by a grid of points is ½π times the square of the shovel test interval. For a 20 m testing interval, this comes out to around 628 square meters, an area about 10 percent greater than a small, 50 x 120 foot suburban residential lot.

Shovel test transects should be lined out on the project map *before* the testing is started; this permits making a note of the number of shovel tests for each transect, which will tell the individual crew member when to stop (see box: "Tip: Setting Up Shovel Test Transects on the Project Map"). It also allows for the quick deployment of personnel when in the field: Knowing roughly where in the project area to begin each transect, as well as how long each should be aids greatly in getting the work done in a quick, thorough, and professional way. The landscape features shown on the project map will be used by the practicing archaeologist to establish ground truth and to relate the Phase I testing pattern to places in the project area.

Often, there is no clear idea in the field where the project boundaries are. Although the client or the subcontracting surveyors are supposed to flag project boundaries, this rarely is done. Thus, knowing how far to go along the transect is important. Knowing

how many transects there will be, how many units will be needed in each transect, and where all of the transects are located serves to give direction to the field crew and to execute the field work efficiently.

Setting out the shovel test transects on paper must take into account ease of setting up the transects once the crew is in the field. If there is a straight stretch of road shown on the map, that stretch of road should be used as a base line and shovel test transects placed at right angles to it. The advantage of a marked road, a widely spaced pair of utility poles, or some other linear feature, is that one can sight along the feature with a compass, then turn 90°. It is vital that the practicing archaeologist identify some kind of straight line on the project map that also exists in the field; that straight line, however defined, will serve as the reference line for the entirety of the Phase I testing regime. It is as close as the Phase I testing program is likely to get to a datum. All Phase I exercises must be set up and prosecuted as if someone else will have to come back in and relocate the shovel tests.

Over very large project areas, it sometimes becomes necessary to change bearing for a transect or set of transects. That bearing change needs to be worked out beforehand. Crew members need to know that, for example, after shovel test 8 on transect 5, they will continue on the original bearing for 10 more meters, then set out on a new bearing to their right/to the north/to the whatever by so many degrees. Compound transects are tricky, because even the best crew with the most consistent pace still has errors; adding a bearing change somewhere along the transect can compound position error. However, it is much more dependable than trying to establish a second base line in the middle of a project area, without any baseline or locational referents.

Ironically, the Phase I work also empirically verifies the ground-truth of the project map. For areal projects, this rarely matters much in the larger scheme of things: If the property line is off by a few feet, there still is enough "play" in land use and property lines for the adjacent property holders to eventually work things out without the land itself having been physically committed to one agenda or another. However, for corridor surveys, where an error in position compounds each time direction changes, the potential legal problems for the client are enormous: Most corridor projects represent purchases of right-of-ways; errors in position can result in the failure to clear the true right-of-way.

All of this is why using the project map to verify position is so important. From an archaeological perspective, the project map will need to be corrected before the report is prepared; that corrected map showing shovel test locations will be in the report; the original will be in the field notes presented for curation.

We learned about archaeology from that... The Manure Spreader Example

The presence of artifacts does not always indicate the presence of a site, even if those artifacts are spread over a large area in great density or are concentrated in particular areas. This is known as the Manure Spreader Example, and ended up restructuring Maryland assessment protocols. It came about in the following way.

A once-cultivated field, since overgrown, was to be used for a residential development. The property was bounded on one side by a small stream, and on the other by a road that had been in use since the early 1800s. During the 1800s, a little community had grown up where the road crossed the creek, a community now long gone. As recently as the 1960s, a local kiln had operated adjacent to the property, on a parcel between the field and the road that was outside of the project area. Because of the proximity to water and the high probability for prehistoric as well as historic archaeological remains, local code required a Phase I survey.

Phase I shovel testing was done at 20 m intervals along 11 transects over the 3.5 hectares that were involved. Testing revealed that there was a light scattering of historic artifacts – bottle and plate glass along with common nineteenth-century ceramics – over the entirety of the project area, along with a few prehistoric artifacts and three heavier concentrations of historic artifacts, again the mix of bottle glass, ceramics, window glass, nails (more often cut than wire), lamp glass, some meat bones, coal and coal-cinders, and some kiln-related artifacts. Nearly all of the historic artifacts came from the plowzone; all datable material fell between 1880 and 1925. The dates corresponded to the landscape history indicated by the vegetation, which was consistent with an episode of farming that had started in the late

1880s and continued into the early 1930s, when it appeared to have been put into pasture. The land seemed to have been finally taken out of production in the 1960s.

The artifacts, both as a suite of materials and as a distribution across the project area, had some interesting characteristics. The first and most telling was that each of the three heavy concentrations was located near a corner of the farm field: one near the road, another near where the kiln property was, and a third opposite the parcel that contained the original farm house (still standing but, like the kiln property, not part of the project area). The second characteristic that the three concentrations had in common was size: The distribution of artifacts as plotted on a map of the shovel tests were all about the same oval size that, with intra-transect testing, gave a size of around 50 x 70 m. The third characteristic involved contents of those three areas: True, the artifacts were bottle glass, ceramics, meat bones, plate glass, lamp glass, and so on, but statistical comparison based on frequency and type indicated that they all were quite the same in relative proportions of material present (the same ratio of bottle glass to ceramics to bone to plate glass to lamp glass). Further, while there was an assortment of common – and rarely more expensive – ceramics present, there really was no repetition in ceramic type.

Testing itself had not located any soil discontinuities. Instead, there was the standard 25 - 30 cm thick Ap horizon over a C horizon (the soil was an entisol); no foundations and, excepting one piece of wall plaster, the cut nails, and some brick fragments, no evidence of other architecture-related artifacts such as bricks, foundation stones, or mortar.

Because of the possibility of unknown historic sites, a history of a nineteenth-century community, and an artifact inventory consistent with that of a

residence, the agency reviewer requested that additional testing be done around the artifact concentrations. However, it was clear at this point what had caused the artifact spread and the occasional concentrations: a manure spreader. Although more testing was done, this explanation was subsequently accepted.

A standard part of nineteenth-century and early-twentieth-century farm equipment was the manure spreader. On farms with livestock, barns would be cleaned out and the animal waste tossed into the spreader. Seasonally, the contents would be spread over the adjacent fields. However, the manure spreader also collected kitchen scraps and waste, and occasional small bits of household trash and debris. In many ways, manure spreaders served – and in places where they still are used, serve – as a sort of dumpster for the farm compound.

The agency reviewer was right: The debris over the project area was the signature of a residence. However, the debris had been transported into then spread over the field. The concentrations represented starting, crossing, and excess dumping points for the spreader; the similarities in artifact assemblage represented the blurring together, over about 50 years, of the common kinds of household accidents that would individually be distinct: a broken window pane this month, a shattered plate at Thanksgiving, the remains from a Sunday roast, empty medicine bottles from Aunt Marcy.

The Manure Spreader Example illustrates the importance of understanding the behavior that took place on the land when it was in use, as well as the signatures of such behavior.

5.3. Field

Although Phase I is termed "shovel testing," "reconnaissance survey," or even misleadingly "cultural resources inventory," much is done during this stage of the field work. The order in which the work is done does not matter too much since all of the work is done in such a short time. Most non-Federal Phase I surveys involve comparatively small areas and can be done within a week; many actually can be done inside of three days, depending on crew size relative to project area. Phase I surveys over large tracts, such as Federal forests or military installations, take considerably longer.

Three sets of data are retrieved during field work: vegetational, pedological, and archaeological. The first two, which chronicle depositional integrity, will indicate if the third has any meaning in terms of the National Register criteria.

5.3.1. Landscape History: Vegetational and Pedological Data

Landscape history is derived from two data sets: Vegetation and soils. Together, these data can answer most initial questions about past land use and therefore the likelihood that the project area lacks near-surface depositional integrity. The vegetation, especially tree cover, records the sequence of land-use events over the last 100 years or so; the actual time depends upon the part of the country. The soil augments the interpretation of the vegetation and serves as a bridge to understanding the impact of past land-use activities on the archaeological deposit, if such is present.

5.3.1.1. Land-Use History Based on Vegetation Succession

Almost no forested area in the eastern/midwestern United States and few in the western United States escaped lumbering activities sometime in the last 200 years. East of the Mississippi for example, there are few stands of trees present that are older than 100 - 150 years; most are less than 50 years old. Nearly all of the landscape, then, represents vegetation communities that have emerged subsequent to land clearance. The original land clearance could have been from lumbering, cultivation, pasture, charcoal production, or even military encampments like those east of Manassas Junction in Virginia. Subsequent land use activity often included cycles of use that resulted in land disturbance.

The vegetation community present at the time of the Phase I survey represents what has succeeded over the landscape *since* the last land use took place (Figure 5.5.). Some of the plants present would come from locally available seed sources; others would come from intentional plantings, as in the case of many of the even-aged stands of longleaf and loblolly pines in the Georgia Piedmont, put in as seedlings for erosion control. Knowing what plants represent what situations goes a long way in reconstructing what has happened to the landscape and, in turn, the nature of the soil development and depositional integrity.

We have found that the easiest way to reconstruct the land-use history is to document that vegetation succession for the project area (Neumann and Sanford 1987). Different vegetation communities, especially forest communities, are associated with different uses of the land (e.g., Watts 1975, Russell 1997, Wessels 1997; for an extensive, albeit dated, list of sources, see Firth 1985; one of the many nice things about the Firth source is that the Internet cut-off in many source-searches of 10-years in effect is avoided). The vegetation and the sequence or order in which types of vegetation take over a given piece of land vary by area of the country. It is the practicing archaeologist's responsibility to become familiar with the types and land-use associations of those plants found in the region where work is being done. This does not mean learning all of the subtle nuances of species classification; it does mean learning about the more common plants likely to be encountered under project conditions, as well as the land-use situations with which they are associated. Every part of the United States has not only handbooks and manuals on local plants, every part of the country also has pleasant little discourses on the land-use history associated with those plants. Sometimes, they are both the same book.

Areas that are forested, or naturally forested, offer the most potential for reconstructing land-use history because trees are comparatively long-lived while often associated with particular land-use patterns, woodland communities change out more slowly, and the general age of trees can be estimated rather closely. However, it is possible to apply landscape history interpretation methods to prairie and non-wooded environments (e.g., Neumann, Sanford, and Warms 1993), it is just usually some interpretive information -- such as a demographic profile of the plant community -- will not be available.

Recording in some regular detail the vegetation of the project area, with the intent to sort out the land-use history, is really very easy. It also is remarkably useful and powerful for the practicing archaeologist, both as an interpretive instrument and as a demonstration to the client and the review agencies of the firm's fundamental concerns for the resource and the appropriate treatment of it. There is probably no better way to support an argument that a now-forested area was once plowed or otherwise severely disturbed than by documenting that the forested community is comparatively young and made up of trees associated with plowed land that was since abandoned. This is

Tip: Setting Up Shovel Test Transects on the Project Map

Setting out the transects on the project map requires using an engineer's ruler, a protractor, and a divider. The engineer's rule provides a scale and the capacity to draw straight lines. The protractor helps in setting out bearings. This seems self-evident; it is not. Very few people are aware of this before entering private practice. About half of the firms we have dealt with over the years instead went directly into the field with a project map, somehow hoping to figure out there where shovel test transects should be positioned.

Setting up those transects on the project map requires identifying the linear feature that will be used as the baseline once in the field. With that linear feature/baseline identified – a line of utility poles, a straight section of highway – the protractor is then used to figure the right-angle turn relative to the base line, which allows the transects to be ruled onto the map. The protractor also allows figuring degrees to be added or subtracted in compound transects, where the bearings change.

A right-angle or 90° turn is safest since it avoids the confusion of trying to start people off at staggered intervals along that baseline. That sort of thing is possible, of course, but would be considered seriously advanced field project management. Only a veteran project manager will be able to do that sort of thing. It is always better to keep things as simple and uncomplicated as possible.

The project map received from the client, more often than not, will have north set out as a true – as opposed to magnetic – bearing. It is tricky, and not really more efficient, to try to figure out from the project map the true bearing of the baseline or of the transects set at right angles to it. It is better to wait to get into the field, then simply use uncorrected, magnetic bearings, working off of large-scale landscape features that the land surveyors already have recorded (and recorded at a level of resolution better than possible using a hand compass or a GPS instrument).

A second tip is to make use of a divider, the kind used in nautical or aviation navigation. The dividers can be set at given distances, say 20 m (conversion from feet to meters, graphically, requires the engineer's rule), then moved along the pencil line drawn on the map showing the planned shovel test transect. Using dividers is infinitely faster than trying to compute the exact feet-to-meter-to-feet conversions for each shovel test location, something that we also have seen project managers attempt, many of whom eventually gave up in frustration, handing the project map off to their crew chief to figure it all out in the field.

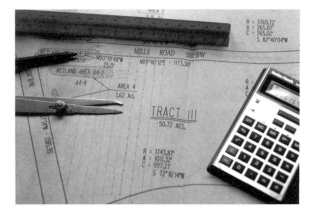

Figure 5.3. *Setting Up Phase I Shovel Test Transects on a Project Map. The first steps include locating on the project map some feature – in this case a local road – that has a long, straight stretch that can serve as a field baseline. Transects will be drawn on the project map at right angles to that field baseline. In the field, an uncorrected compass bearing will be taken for that straight line, then a 90° turn will be made corresponding to the lines drawn on the map. Spacing of those transects on the map is done using dividers.*

Figure 5.4. *Detail of Phase I Transect Plan in Progress. The pencil tip is at a point that can be located readily in the field, a point that will serve as a starting place for spacing the shovel test transects. By setting out the number of shovel tests per transect beforehand, crew are made aware of just how many shovel tests should be present in a given transect before the edge of the project area is reached. Often that number can be compared with where project area actually does stop.*

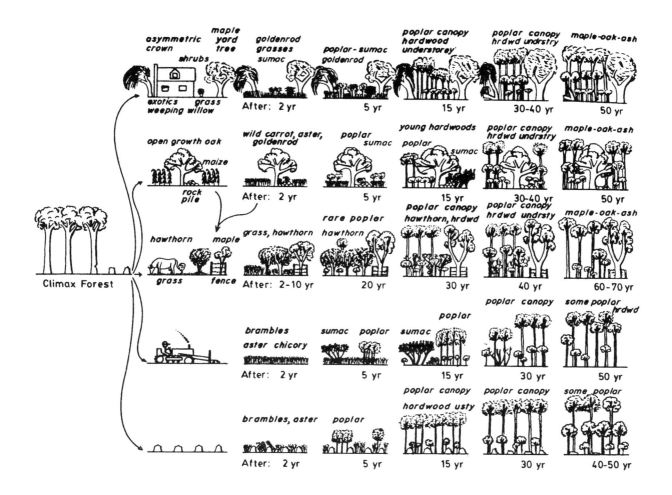

Figure 5.5. Generalized Categories of Vegetation Succession for the Northeastern United States (after Neumann and Sanford 1987:121; see also Sanford, Neumann, and Salmon 1997, Sanford et al. 1994). Similar sequences have been developed for then used in the Middle Atlantic (Neumann 1989a, Neumann and Williams 1990), the Southeast (Neumann and Williams 1991), the Ohio Valley (Neumann et al. 1990), and the Southern Plains (Neumann, Sanford, and Warms 1993), and are invaluable, cost-effective models of particular value to the practicing archaeologist.

especially true since most of the physical as well as visible evidence for a plowzone will disappear after 40 years under tree cover. It is in everyone's interest -- the client's, the review agency's, the resource's, and the firm's -- to get the issue of past land disturbance right.

Other vegetation and landscape features also are recorded during the Phase I exercise. For example, raspberry, greenbriar, thistle, and pasture rose all are associated with pasture activities as well as land disturbance resulting in topsoil loss. Vinca (periwinkle) is a shade-tolerant ground cover associated with cemeteries; it was an intentional planting. Boxwood is an ornamental hedge row plant around residences.

Evidence suggestive of former fence lines and roads should be recorded at this time. For example, a line of

old, open growth cherry through a woodlot in central New York is a good indication of an old fence line; a line of 1.5 m diameter sugar maples going across front yards of houses built after World War II is a good indication of an old road course in the Northeast. In Neumann's front yard east of Atlanta, there are three 40 - 50 cm dbh loblolly pines. The house was built in 1980; the house next door has a 1.2 m dbh water oak, a big old open growth thing similar to two more behind the houses and another up the hill in a neighbor's back yard. The pines represent erosion control plants from around 1940; the oaks date from the late 1800s when the land served as crop land and pasture.

The purpose of recording the vegetation in the above fashion is to get some sense of what has happened over the landscape since it was last cleared, and how it may

Tip: Recording Tree Demographics for Analysis of Succession

In areas that are naturally forested, or areas that at least have trees growing in them, the most accurate and cost-effective way to document vegetation succession comes from recording the tree demographics. Recording woodlot demographics is driven by a few simplifying assumptions that will be mentioned in a moment. The field work itself consists of noting the *diameter at breast height* (dbh; about 1.2 m from the ground surface) of the tree, the kind of tree (genus and, if useful or possible, species), and the form of the tree (open-growth or closed-canopy growth). It is necessary only to record diameters in 10-cm increments.

When is this done; how is this done? Obviously a tree survey could be done at any point in the project, but it is most efficient to obtain the information of the sizes of the trees present during the Phase I survey, especially in those situations where a systematic shovel test sample is being done. (There is a strong correlation, by the way, between extent to which a state is forested and the expectation for shovel testing to be done during Phase I.[a]) This is done by collecting information on ALL SIZES of the trees within a given radius, say 3 m, of the shovel test unit being excavated. "ALL," in this case, means those numerous little saplings just as much as the larger trees. This is a point sample, similar to how foresters survey a stand of timber. The advantage of tying the tree and vegetation data to the shovel-testing regime is that it allows the investigator to discern changes in past land-use activities *within* the project area. Many Phase I exercises involve project areas larger than 20 ha; often, those project areas once were farms where some of the land was pasture and some of the land was cropped. Having the information on vegetation linked to the embedded grid that comes with a Phase I shovel-testing program enables the practitioner to reconstruct the local cultural geography as it pertains to the project area, including areas that may have been plowed and areas that may not have been.

How will these data be used? Figure 5.6a shows a shovel test record sheet with vegetation data recorded, then a hand tabulation of the trees present relative to diameter class, then a final graph based upon that data set. Unless it is important in the region or the crew has the expertise, usually recognition at the level of genus will be enough. Trees will be classified by diameter class; usually 10-cm dbh increments is sufficient resolution. Under most circumstances, it can be assumed that the age of a tree, in years, is about the same as its diameter in centimeters. In some cases, this rule does not hold. Fast-growing, high water table trees like cottonwood, sycamore, tuliptree, and willow, tend to be half as old as their diameter in centimeters. Trees that emerged under closed-canopy conditions, like oak or holly or dogwood in a forested track, may be half again to twice as old as their diameter in centimeters. Wherever possible, stumps and other cuts – even limb cuts – should be used to estimate growth rate relative to age rate.

a. Proportion of forest cover based on Espenshade, Edward B., Jr., and Joel L. Morrison. 1980. *Goode's World Atlas.* Fifteenth edition. Rand McNally & Co., Chicago, pp.82-83. Shovel test requirements from sources Table 5.4. Sample used 41 states from continental United States: r = +0.8499, t = 10.07, df:39; p << 0.001 that no correlation exists.

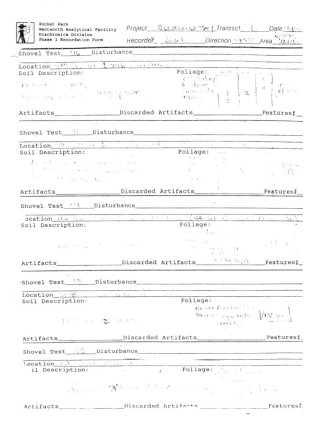

Figure 5.6a *Example of a shovel test record form with information entered on tree types and size classes observed within 3-m of the particular shovel test. These data represent what in forestry is called a "point sample," a common and efficient way to measure forest community structure.*

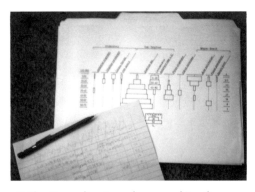

Figure 5.6b. *Recording tree demographics then assessing what has happened over time requires first that the field data be converted to percentages then somehow graphed. What is sought is what proportion each tree type makes up for each 10-cm diameter class. This is a seriation exercise. The figure here, for example, shows how oak and pine steadily declined in proportion at the expense of sugar maple. The sugar maple began appearing around 30 years before the data were collected; most of the common understorey trees began emerging around 10 years later.*

Also recorded are growth characteristics and patterns. For example, the trees will be open- or closed-canopy in their growth habit. Trees that emerged along fence lines when the land was open and under cultivation will be open-growth, with spreading limbs relatively low on the bole. The age of those trees gives an estimate on the age of the fence line; the age of the surrounding woodlot community gives an estimate on when the field was abandoned.

Plotting out the above information in matrix form is the first step, as was shown in Figure 5.3. The next step is assessing what that information means, and using the summary of the data as a vehicle to support the Phase I conclusions (Figure 5.7). This really is a seriation chart, where the tree genera are like ceramic types and the changes in their frequency represent changes in the use of the land. Since the diameter of the trees is strongly correlated with the age of the trees, the diagram can be used to approximate just WHEN those changes in the woodlot community structure took place. We have found, by the way, that this is accurate to within plus or minus five years, checking our interpretations with informants, photographs, and local histories.

See:

Sanford, Robert M., and Thomas W. Neumann. 1987. The urban tree as cultural artifact. *Northeastern Environmental Science* 6:46-52, which provides details on assembling such demographic profiles while showing how they can be used in an urban forestry situation.

Good examples of how such demographic profiles can be used to reconstruct past land use may be found in:

Neumann, Thomas W. 1989. *Phase I Intensive Archeological Investigation of Catoctin Furnace (18 FR 29), Cunningham Falls State Park, Frederick County, Maryland.* Maryland Department of General Services, Baltimore; and

Neumann, Thomas W., William C. Johnson, Jennifer Cohen, and Neal H. Lopinot. 1990. *Archeological Data Recovery from Prehistoric Site 36Fa363, Grays Landing Lock and Dam.* U.S. Army Corps of Engineers, Pittsburgh District.

Figure 5.7. Presentation of Field Data. The figure at left shows how the final product relates to what was originally seen in the field. The data here came from a residential lot in south Texas, where the largest trees present were 20-30-cm dbh cedar elms (Ulmus crassfolia). These were joined about a decade later by various live oaks (Quercus virginiana and Quercus fusiformis) along with a mix of secondary species. In this case and using the tree demographics, the land was taken out of pasture for development around 20 - 30 years before the photograph was taken. In point of fact, the land was developed into a residential community around 24 years earlier.

Fig. 13. Residential yard cut from abandoned pasture. Isolated trees are live oak; specimen in left foreground around 20 cm dbh. Pasture associates include prickly pear and, along right margin, Ashe juniper growing in a straight line.

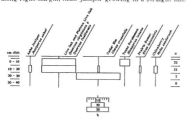

Fig. 14. Demographic profile of trees on a residential lot developed from abandoned pasture. The elms in this sample probably were closer to 20 years old than to 30 years old; the pasture probably was taken out of use in the 1970s. Most of the junipers originally present were removed; residents in this part of Texas prefer oaks over junipers, and the latter usually are removed. In a natural, emerging stand, the number of trees decrease exponentially as the diameter increases. Here, the fact that the largest number of trees is in the 10-20 cm dbh range suggest selection against the saplings that would otherwise be present.

have been used before being abandoned. This is a vital step in ascertaining depositional integrity, since it will help answer the question of if the project area once had been plowed. After 30-40 years under forest cover, a plowzone horizon (an Ap horizon) will no longer be discernable based on soil characteristics (technically, it no longer exists). However, vegetation characteristics associated with a formerly plowed field may well exist, prompting the practicing archaeologist to look for supporting evidence, such as the concentration of artifacts at 25-35 cm below the surface, the common depth to which smaller artifacts settle in an often-plowed field, since it is the basal depth of most plowzones.

5.3.1.2. Land-Use History and the Soil Profile

An application of soil development principles becomes essential in confirming the land-use history developed with the vegetation survey in those parts of the country where Phase I involves shovel testing (Table 5.4.). The character of the soil is a critical data-set obtained during this step, since it often will be needed to justify arguments about a lack of depositional integrity in the project area.

Soil formation depends on several variables: mineral component, local climate, vegetation present now and in the past, and land use. All of these have a bearing on reconstructing the land-use history and therefore on factors influencing depositional integrity. Elementary knowledge of soil dynamics therefore is critical.

Just as most of the land east of the Mississippi has been cut over, much of that land also was once plowed. It should not be assumed that the land, because it looks untillable today, had not been plowed in the past. The reason lots of land no longer is farmed today is because people learned in the past, through the failure of farms, that it could not be used. For example, the Root River basin in southeastern Minnesota is filled with abandoned farmsteads, left from people in the 1870s-1920s who plowed the 40°-60° slopes, only to have the hillsides wash into the bottomlands. This is a good place to also note that many of the small stream valleys in the eastern and midwestern United States have over (sometimes an order of magnitude over) one to two meters of sediment deposited within the last 120 years as a product of those erosion-prone farming practices. Thus, over much of the area east of the Rockies, the land surface seen now may not be the aboriginal surface, and lack of any evidence to a depth of 30 cm -- typical plowing as well as shovel testing depth -- of aboriginal occupation is misleading.

Evidence of plowing will be masked, in time, by the development of a new soil profile in response to subsequent land use and its associated vegetation community. Recognition of that past plowing is

Review of Soil Horizon Descriptions and Nomenclature

There are actually two soil horizon description systems used by archaeologists and present in the literature. One represents a system that began well before 1938 and continued through 1981 (Rice and Alexander 1938:889; see also Soil Survey Staff 1951, 1975; Olson 1976). The second is a modification of that system that was set out in 1981 (Soil Survey Staff 1981:4-39 - 4-50; see also Foss, Miller, and Segovia 1985:5-7). The basic aspects of these two systems compare in the following ways:

Pre-1981 Designation	1981 Designation
A1	A
A2	E
A3	AB
B1	BA
B2	B
B3	BC

In the pre-1981 system, the initial Arabic numeral following the horizon letter was alphanumeric and referred to a particular characteristic of such a horizon. The second Arabic numeral, if one was used, had ordinal meaning. In the 1981 system, Arabic numerals exist for purposes of order only. Subordinate distinctions in horizons, previously designated by numerals, are now represented by one of 22 lowercase letters (Soil Survey Staff 1981:4-43 - 4-47). The only major horizon designation, commonly encountered or needed by archaeologists, that did not change was "Ap," which still means a plowed horizon.

The majority of county soil survey books use the pre-1981 system, primarily because the data were assembled well before the 1981 changes. Much of the archaeological literature and most of the engineering reports treated by the practicing archaeologist will also use the pre-1981 system. Recently trained archaeologists of course will know and use the current descriptive system. It is necessary for the practicing archaeologist to be fluent in both systems, and to be very specific about which of those systems is being used in the field notes, bag labels, and reports.

A manual written by soil scientists for the practicing archaeologist is

Foss, J.E., F.P. Miller, and A.V. Segovia. 1985. *Field Guide to Soil Profile Description and Mapping*. Second edition. Soil Resources International, Moorhead, MN. Segovia, a gentleman and scholar whose answering machine graciously greets the caller in three separate languages, has a great deal of experience working with professional archaeologists, and the manual reflects this.

A classic soils text that works well as a desk reference:

Brady, Nyle C., and Ray R. Weil. 1998. *The Nature and Properties of Soils*. Twelfth edition. Prentice Hall, Upper Saddle River, NJ.

Tip: County Soil Survey Books

About half of the 3,066 counties – mostly agricultural counties – in the United States have had a soil survey done; such surveys having been undertaken regularly at least since the 1920s. That is, the different types of soils present in the county have been carefully classified and described, with the distributions mapped and their engineering characteristics determined. This information is contained in a county soil survey book published by the US Department of Agriculture and distributed through the county soil survey or extension service. These documents, traditionally available for free, are required tools for the practicing archaeologist.

The county soil survey book will have a large-scale map based on aerial photographs of the county, along with the boundaries of each soil body lined off. Those soil bodies are classified not only by type of soil but also by slope of the land, making the information a powerful planning tool for Phase I projects. The surveys also provide generic profile descriptions – color, texture, boundary characteristics – for each soil type. Thus, the practicing archaeologist can know, before entering the field, what to expect as far as soil characteristics in the project area.

It should be remembered, though, that soil body distributions are not always exactly as shown on survey maps. Local archaeological testing may yield different results than what is expected.

important. Plowing has a critical impact on site depositional integrity; unplowed, open air archaeological sites are extremely rare in the eastern United States, as well as in the cropped areas of the midwestern United States.

It could be argued that almost any kind unplowed prehistoric site in agricultural parts of the country would satisfy criteria for listing on the National Register of Historic Places, simply because of the rarity of such data potential. If it is thought to be unplowed, the SHPO or equivalent agency most likely will request Phase II testing and evaluation. One of the great dangers then facing any Phase I survey in an agricultural region is the failure to recognize that a given deposit had been plowed, resulting in a call for further testing and expense for the client. Since such situations can easily be avoided, those kinds of errors represent professional negligence.

The danger of failing to recognize a past plowzone comes from two sources. The first source is that field crews will be trained to recognize fresh or comparatively fresh Ap horizons only. Crew members have an expectation of what an Ap/B horizon interface will look like, and they will be sensitive to that, almost to the exclusion of everything else. The second source of danger comes from supervisory personnel forgetting that over time the Ap horizon will take on the

characteristics of the solum typical of the vegetation cover now present in the project area.

Recognition that horizons and horizon boundaries change solves most of these problems; remembering as well that forest soils generally have A horizons only 10-cm thick or so, and that historic plowing usually was 20-30-cm deep (8-12 inches) helps to serve as a control in assessing the test results. The transition from a farm field soil profile to a forest soil profile can occur within 30-40 years; knowing or even suspecting the landscape history of the project area assists here.

The last issue under the topic of soils is the vertical location of recovered artifacts.

How do things get buried? There are two logical options: either fill or sediment of some kind is placed over the objects, or the objects sink. For the vast majority of situations in the United States, the practicing archaeologist will face one of two situations: artifacts buried either by alluviation or by human activity, such as in an urban setting; or by sinking. Of these logical options, the second is the more important to understand.[7]

Soils are biologically active, three-dimensional matrices. Those matrices contain a host of organisms including ants, worms, and burrowing mammals of various descriptions. These creatures are constantly digging and bringing fill to the surface; over time, tunnels collapse and new ones are dug, with fill again deposited on the surface. The soil is like a vast, very slow-motion fluid with a convection current. It also is, at a larger scale, much like a liquid.

Liquids are made up of particles -- molecules -- that are free to move and not locked into place. Soils can be thought of in somewhat the same way: as made up of soil particles that also are in motion, the motion being provided by the soil fauna. It is that freedom to move, that agitation of particles that causes the soil to behave like a fluid. Thus, a large coffee can filled with clean sand will support a quarter placed on the surface of the sand because all of the sand grains are motionless, locked into place by friction. However, if lots of small holes are put in the side of the can, straws inserted, then air blown in through the straws, the grains of sand will move and the quarter will drop to the bottom of the can. This, by the way, is an old high school physics demonstration that many probably recall. In practical terms, a soil is behaving the same

---

7. For additional references as well as a detailed discussion of soil fluidity as it applies to archaeological deposits and the sinking of artifacts through soil horizons or cultural sediments, see Neumann, Thomas W. 1993. Soil dynamics and the sinking of artifacts: Procedures for identifying components in non-stratified sites. *Journal of Middle Atlantic Archaeology* 9:94-108. The mathematics for flotation-sized particle movement are given in: Neumann, Thomas W. 1978. A model for the vertical distribution of flotation-size particles. *Plains Anthropologist* 23:85-101.

We learned about archaeology from that... The Missing Feature

One of the more interesting cases we have experienced regarding misread soil profiles involved a Federal project in the Ohio River drainage. Phase I testing of the floodplain had indicated the presence of a large village complex and, about a mile downstream from the village, an undisturbed site of the same Late Prehistoric/Late Woodland type. The combined Phase I/Phase II report indicated further that large archaeological features were present, beginning about 10 cm below the surface. We were to re-establish the surveyed baseline, complete Phase II testing, then complete the Phase III data recovery prior to destruction of the site. Particular attention was to be directed toward the two enormous archaeological features that Phase I/Phase II subsurface testing had located.

Entering the field revealed that the woodlot covering the site consisted of an even-aged stand of secondary growth trees roughly 30-40 years old, with the woodlot bounded by an old, deteriorating barbwire fence. None of this information had been given in the Phase I report, which had provided a section on what the "natural" vegetation was suppose to be, instead of what was actually there (a very common although careless, and therefore unprofessional, practice).

The mix of species we encountered suggested that the field had last been used for pasture but, before that, had been plowed extensively. This obviously contradicted the Phase I report of an undisturbed site with features surviving within 10 cm of the surface, and served as a warning to us.

The original base line was re-located and easily re-established: Labeled stakes were still present and the backfilled Phase II test units could readily be seen. When testing was done around those in which the features had been defined, though, no feature was found. Instead, what was present was a 10 cm thick E horizon [A2 horizon] over an AB or BA horizon [A3 or B1 horizon] that extended to maybe 25 cm below the surface. Below that was the undisturbed B horizon. In some places, the AB horizon [A3 horizon] stood out like a stain relative to the lighter colored B horizon matrix; artifacts would be present within that darker colored fill.

What the soil profile represented was simply the transition, after 30-40 years, of an Ap horizon to a standard forest soil, with its thin E horizon [A2 horizon] over horizons that were fading from the lower part of an Ap horizon, through temporally transitional horizons, back eventually to a B horizon. The presence of artifacts in that darker "fill" came from the plowing and mixing that had occurred when the field was cultivated; the concentration of some artifacts at 25 cm below the surface represented the settling out of artifacts at the Ap/B horizon boundary. Such abrupt horizon boundaries represent changes in soil viscosity, and material settling through the soil will build up at that horizon boundary, much the way that particles will build up at the boundary of two fluids of different viscosities, which in fact is how flotation use to be done before Struever's use of water (which is also why the seeming redundancy in the name of the original process: "Water flotation"; the process originated among geologists and used oils of differing viscosities to separate out microfossils).

The upshot of all of this was that there was no feature, only a plowzone remnant. The vegetation and thickness of the Ap horizon told a story of land plowed, some topsoil loss from sheet erosion (a separate issue), then field abandonment sometime in the mid-1950s, an interpretation that was verified a couple weeks later when the original landowner was located and interviewed.

The misinterpretation of a remnant Ap horizon for a feature because of the darker color, thinness of the darker band, and concentration of artifacts had been reinforced by the general absence of a clearly recognizable Ap horizon over much of the project area. This was because the 30-40 years of emerging forest cover had brought with it a new soil horizon regime, one reflecting woodlot conditions. Where once there had been an Ap horizon then a B horizon, there now was an E horizon [A2 horizon] grading into an AB/BA horizon [A3/B1 horizon] that had a faint but even and straight boundary with the underlying B horizon. Knowing what to look for helped in recognizing this, but knowing to look at all came from the recognition that the land was covered with vegetation that was only around 30-40 years old to begin with. Logic suggested that, 40 years ago, the field was clear and, given the species mix, plowed.

This turned out to be a difficult issue to grasp for the state's SHPO as well as for the government agency enabling the construction. Like a large number of archaeologists, they were unaware that soil horizons change as vegetation cover changes. Further, they naturally trusted the results of the Phase I/Phase II report. A statement contradicting not only that report, but in effect declaring that there never was a need for the Phase III data recovery scheduled for the site, was clearly embarrassing.

Much of this could have been avoided had an interpretation of the landscape history been made at the start, and had an understanding of soil horizon formation been present on the part of the initial Phase I project.

way, and objects dropped on the surface will, given enough time, sink.

Each soil horizon may be thought of as having a different viscosity, depending as much upon the texture of the soil as upon biological activity in the horizon. The A or E horizon is more fluid than the B horizon; a plow zone -- the Ap horizon -- is more fluid than a pasture soil. For this reason, one will observe in the field that artifacts will tend to "bunch up" at an

We learned about archaeology from that... Site Disturbance and Soil Profiles

In 1989, we directed the Phase I and Phase II investigations of a proposed residential development north of the District of Columbia. One part of the area was covered by a 50-year-old woodlot; successional evidence combined with the presence of an old barbwire fence suggested that the field had probably been rotated between pasture and crops. The last use most likely had been as a cultivated field.

Maryland Site files indicated the possible presence of a prehistoric archaeological site; site maps showed tentative eastern boundaries extending into the western part of the project area. Those boundaries had never been confirmed.

During shovel testing, prehistoric materials were recovered, indicating a sporadic distribution of materials over the west half of the woodlot. Shovel testing also provided information on soil development. In pre-1981 soils terms (as used in the report), there was a 5 cm thick A1 horizon over a 10 cm thick A2 horizon over a 12-15 cm thick A3 or B1 horizon, depending upon area. The boundary of the A3 or B1 horizon with the underlying B2 horizon was even, albeit hard to see. No artifacts came from the B2; few artifacts were coming from depths that would put them in the A3 or B1 horizon.

Did the site have depositional integrity? The soil profile suggested that the area had once been plowed to a depth of 30 cm or so below the current surface. The unused Ap

horizon, left under an emerging woodlot for 40 years or so, now had a profile sequence of A1-A2-A3/B1. The mechanical disruption of the archaeological deposit was reflected in the restriction of the artifacts to the old plowzone. Had the area not been plowed, then a profile sequence of A1-A2-B2 would have been expected, with the A1-A2 sequence having a combined thickness on the order of 10 cm or so.

In the case of this proposed residential development area, the pedological information was combined with the vegetational succession information to argue that the area probably had been plowed, and therefore the prehistoric artifacts were located in a disturbed matrix.

E/B horizon [A/B horizon] interface. There is another issue here: Because artifacts sink, and because prehistoric sites existed in an area long before plowing was present, finding artifacts below the Ap horizon is no indication that one is dealing with a second, undisturbed component. Rather, it is just as likely that the top of the deposit has been clipped and churned by plowing, while the lower end of the vertical spread of artifacts, slowly sinking over the centuries, has not been disturbed. Whether or not a sub-Ap horizon assemblage represents a separate occupation can be easily tested statistically; if such a spread of artifacts between plowzone and sub-plowzone is found in the field, then that vertical distribution must be tested statistically for independence before the Phase I report is submitted.

5.3.2. Field Methods

There are three general categories of field methods used to collect field data during Phase I investigations: (1) shovel testing, (2) ground-surface examination, and (3) heavy equipment testing. Shovel testing is the most common, being used over most of the eastern and midwestern United States, as well as in settings where ground-surface visibility is restricted. Ground-surface examination is common in many areas of the western and southwestern United States where the ground surface is visible and soil/sediment aggradation rates are not considered issues. Heavy equipment testing, usually using a backhoe, is generally used in urban areas as well as in situations where deeper testing through sediments, as in a floodplain, is needed.

Archaeological surface reconnaissance has been discussed often in the literature (see Renfrew and Bahn 1991:63-69; Sharer and Ashmore 1993:186-192, 196-201, 237; Feder 1997:54-55; see also Fish and Kowaleski 1990), with topics ranging from essential if mundane issues of field procedures to equally essential and far from trivial issues of regional sampling. There is no need to try to do again here what has already been done -- and done better than we would do -- elsewhere.

Archaeology involving large structures and urban or built-up settings also has been discussed, although perhaps not as often in terms of using heavy equipment in urban areas (see Renfrew and Bahn 1991:91; Sharer and Ashmore 1993:25-276; Hester 1997:73-77). However, there is more than enough information available already to make repeating it here superfluous.

This is not true, though, for shovel testing. Of the three common Phase I procedures, we have found that shovel testing is rarely discussed with the same attention given to more tradition archaeological methods. Given its widespread use and importance as a data collecting method for Phase I investigations, it seems useful to go over shovel testing in some detail.

5.3.2.1. Subsurface Testing by Shovel Testing

The primary procedure for collecting field data during Phase I surveys in the majority of states is shovel testing (Table 5.4.). Even in those states where most

We learned about archaeology from that... One Component or Two?

An excellent example of the importance of being aware that artifacts sink in an active soil comes from an urban floodplain project we directed in West Virginia. In this case, the Phase I work had been done by another firm.

Most of the area around the small town was under cultivation, to the point where some of the fields were literally adjacent to the backs of buildings in the business district. Several of those fields contained prehistoric artifacts, and a series of new sites had been identified for the overall project area. Our responsibility was to provide Phase II testing for some of these, primarily because the Phase I report noted that many had undisturbed, sub-plowzone components.

How was it known that these were separate, undisturbed prehistoric components? To be truthful, the Phase I report had not been specific about this, but instead followed a common assumption made by archaeologists in

the eastern and midwestern United States. That assumption in effect holds that the material found in the plowzone could have come from anyplace between the surface and the maximum plowing depth. A safe and obvious assumption. Any material found below the plowzone would be in an undisturbed context, a not unreasonable assumption. That material in the undisturbed subsoil therefore represents a separate and undisturbed component, clearly NOT a safe assumption, much less a conclusion that follows logically from the previous two arguments. However, it is that reasoning that is *partly* responsible for the guidelines of many SHPOs that specify excavation through the Ap horizon into *culturally sterile* subsoil. The hidden assumption is that prehistoric artifacts, between the time they were deposited and the time the site was plowed, did not move down through the soil. Further, it assumes as well that the artifacts could not have moved from the plowzone into the subsoil after plowing commenced. Both assumptions are wrong.

In the situation of the small town and the myriad of prehistoric sites with

undisturbed components, it proved relatively easy to demonstrate that the artifacts that came from immediately below the Ap horizon actually had originated among the assemblage still located within the Ap horizon. This required nothing more than subdividing the artifacts into functional classes and raw material classes, then running a chi-squared statistic between the Ap and the upper B horizon populations. In all cases, it was found that there was no reason to consider the two to be independent sets.

The point here, among many, is that it is vitally important not only to remember that artifacts move through the soil and that they have had a lot of time to do that before plowing commenced, but also that before a recommendation is made that the artifact population is independent – a separate component – from that found in the plowzone, the supposition *MUST BE tested statistically*. In this case, then, there usually was only one component present, and the artifacts recovered from the B horizon actually were not located in their original vertical positions.

Phase I data collection involves surface survey of some kind, shovel testing will be used in areas where ground visibility is less than 30-40 percent, or where there is some concern that conditions have concealed archaeological evidence. While it should not be thought that the only way in which Phase I archaeological field work is done, shovel testing is the most widespread procedure nationally.[8] However, it is anything but standardized. We will go over some details for shovel testing in a moment.

A shovel test is a limited subsurface excavation, the purpose of which is to provide information on the presence or absence of artifacts while doing minimal damage to the site and requiring minimal labor. It emulates the effects of a plow, and historically is derived from that and the associated data retrieval that would come from surface collecting a plowed field.

Usually, a shovel test is a circular excavation about 30 cm in diameter and about 40-cm deep. These normally will be dug along straight-line transects at some pre-set interval, such as 15 m, 20 m, or 30 m (Table 5.4.). Nearly all distance determinations in the field will be done by pacing; all transect directions will be done using a hand-held compass. Verification of position within the project area will depend upon the relating of those distance and direction determinations to a project map, usually supplied by the client.

In reality, shovel test size varies, both by state requirements and by what people actually end up doing in the field. Shovel tests that are circular at the surface are suppose to be cylindrical throughout their depth. Usually, though, people digging them deliver a shovel test unit that has the form of half an egg; that is, it is sub-conical. In Iowa, New Hampshire, Ohio, Pennsylvania, and Puerto Rico, shovel tests are to be square, 50 cm on a side, and at least 50-cm deep; in Illinois, they are to be 40 x 40 cm. In Florida, they are to be 50 cm in diameter, an initial area about 27 percent smaller than those square 50 x 50 cm units. In New York or Maryland, they are to be around 30 cm in diameter and 40-cm deep. In terms of volume, the

---

8. States whose areas are less than 50 percent forested tend not to require shovel testing as the default Phase I field procedure (see Table 5.4.; see also fn. a in "Tip: Recording Tree Demographics for Analysis of Succession"). We found, in doing the background research for Table 5.4. particularly, that there is a degree of unease among archaeologists in those states that do not require shovel testing, or that lack some kind of default shovel test protocol.

Iowa shovel test is around 6.6 times as much as the Maryland shovel test; the Iowa shovel test threshold of artifact recovery is 4.0 artifacts per square meter, or 8.0 artifacts per cubic meter.

As noted above (Table 5.4.), many states have established default protocols for shovel testing. These specify the size and form of the shovel test, the kind of screening to be done, the default shovel test and transect intervals, and the maximum slope on which testing must be done. It is the responsibility of the practicing archaeologist to be conversant with the particular state's requirements in this regard. The state regulatory agency will be only too happy to supply a copy of the regulatory guidelines, and of course such information is increasingly available from the Internet.

Shovel testing is premised on the assumption that artifacts are distributed as a continuous sheet, referred to as *sheet litter*. This is why it is important to remember that the common sub-conical, 30-cm diameter shovel test 40-cm deep removes 0.018 cubic meters of dirt over an area of 0.07 square meters; if artifacts were distributed continuously and evenly over an area, they would have to have a density of 14.1 per square meter within that 40-cm depth (about 53.1 per cubic meter) for a shovel test to catch one.

Most states require that shovel tests be at least 40-cm deep or to go 10 cm into culturally sterile subsoil. If anything more is done, it will depend upon field circumstances and the company's protocol.

How is the fill from the shovel test processed? In some states, such as Arkansas, Louisiana, and Kentucky, it has been acceptable to shovel-sort the fill; in most other states where screening is expected, fill must be screened through 1/4-inch (0.635 cm) mesh, although in Idaho and Montana, 1/8-inch (0.318 cm) mesh is required, while in Maryland 1/2-inch (1.270 cm) mesh may be used on industrial sites. To put this into some perspective, we have found that shovel sorting recovers approximately 20 percent of what would be recovered with a 1/4-inch screen (Neumann and Sanford 1985a).

In most states, shovel testing is done as a systematic sample. That is, shovel tests of a certain size are placed at a pre-specified distance from each other. In Maryland, for example, the default shovel test intervals are 20 m for low and moderate probability areas, and 10 m for high probability areas. In any area, the regulatory agency may change the intervals depending upon the situation. Shovel test intervals of 3 m are not unknown, although such small intervals usually are for sites already judged to be eligible for the National Register. Such small intervals are also very expensive. The practicing archaeologist must remember that the work is being done in a way that, when reported, will allow the regulatory agency to make decisions about the veracity of the archaeologist's conclusions.

If cultural materials are found during shovel testing, good professional practice is to return when all of the transects are done to place more shovel tests midway between those in which something was found, and those adjacent in the transect pattern that did not contain any material. For example, if a 20-m interval was used, and if some flakes were found in a shovel test, then shovel tests should be placed at 10-m intervals around that positive shovel test. One purpose of shovel testing is to get an idea of site limits as well as extent; testing between shovel tests that contained materials and shovel tests that did not contain materials helps assessing if the materials are a spot find. If there is an extensive spread of material, such half-interval testing helps refine site limits.

The review agency will want site limits verified sooner or later anyway. Anticipating the review agency's needs and questions in this way generally hastens the review process. This means that the Phase I report is cleared faster, which means that the client goes through the entire process faster. The faster the client legitimately goes through the review process, the less the client is paying in interest on loans and the happier the client is. Everyone benefits: The review agency is assured that the resources in the area have been documented to the best of the Phase I capacity; the client is delighted to get through another regulatory step; and the practicing archaeologist develops a reputation for competence with the review agency and with the development community.

This supplemental testing, or second-pass testing, should be done after the main transects are completed. The purpose is to refine the edges of an artifact spread; it is pointless to be testing around shovel tests that turn out to be in the middle of a site.

5.3.2.2. Setting Up Shovel Testing in the Field

How many people are involved in a Phase I survey? How much time does it take, or should it take if shovel testing is involved?

The minimum crew is two regardless of the Phase I field method; larger crews require one supervisory person for every 10 people, again regardless if surface reconnaissance or subsurface testing is involved.[9] Where fill is screened and the interval is 20 m, 30-35 shovel tests can be excavated per day per person. Where fill is shovel sorted and the interval is 20 m, approximately 50 shovel tests can be excavated per day per person. We have performed Phase I testing under all weather conditions and have found that these rates hold regardless of weather or landscape.

---

9. IBM and AT&T maintain corporate policies that limit the total number of people under any one supervisor or manager to seven. Seven is considered the maximum number that can be effectively managed.

Tip: Cautions on Using Compasses

Although GPS (global positioning system) instruments are increasingly used for Phase I positioning, the standard hand-held, range-finder compass remains the most common piece of positioning equipment. Compasses are inexpensive, accurate, dependable, and robust; they are part of standard crew issue. However, two sets of cautions are in order for their use, above and beyond those mentioned in manuals or taught in field training courses: interference in the field that alters readings, and idiosyncratic patterns of actual use.

The most important caution has to do with external interference with the compass. Beware of the effects of power lines; this is important when a road is chosen for that Phase I baseline. Road segments are wonderful references: On getting to the field, while the crew is sorting out gear, the crew chief or project manager will be locating project boundaries then sighting down the road to get an uncorrected compass bearing. The transects for testing probably will be going off at right angles to the road, and having made determinations of what transect bearings will be, and having located where each of the transects should start, the crew is turned loose.

Problem? Always remember to look UP before choosing the road as a reference, or at least choosing where to stand to take that bearing. Power lines run along road corridors; power lines make mayhem of hand compass readings. Stationary transformers also will alter compass readings: One project we ran involved a parcel of former pasture that was to be converted to a housing development. The project baseline and staging area were the edge of the parking lot of an adjacent fire house. This was around Christmas, with a foot of snow on the ground and more coming down while the project was being set up. (This was one of those situations where the project had been awarded while everyone was in the field. Crew brought the map down, and the Phase I transects were worked out on the hood of the car while snow swirled around.) It was not long before the actual start of the testing that it became apparent that everyone's compass bearings were messed up. The open pasture setting and sound project map allowed for double checking of bearing with actual physical features: Things kept getting repositioned. It turned out that the problem came from the initial setting out of the baseline bearing: Around the side of the fire station, actually very close to

where the initial bearing was taken, were a pair of transformers, which evidently had just enough electromagnetic field strength to disrupt the local compass readings.

A second, and somewhat less serious caution involves idiosyncrasies in compass use. People sight along the compass in individual ways. This is complicated by the short distance one has with a range finder compass: The four to six inches of sighting distance between one end of the compass and the other is too short of a straight line not to be fraught with the same difficulties in accuracy that attend the performance of a short-barreled pistol with that of a long-barreled rifle. It is important to make sure that crew members know what the ground truth referent will be for points along the transect. For new crew members, the crew chief or the project manager needs to figure out if the person "lists to port or starboard," as it were. Standing everyone on the same point and sighting at the same thing should do this. With a known crew, it is a managerial responsibility to know the crew's peculiarities.

For example, in the situation with the fire station, even with the baseline set out, the project manager and the crew chief stood together and sighted out the point in the distance that would be the ground truth referent given the 90° bearing turn. They chose points that were, when finally reached at the end of a 38 shovel test transect (and a long, tiring day given that foot of snow) about 20 m apart. The project manager had finally declared his reference to be THE referent, everyone knowing that it was just getting an agreed upon point that was the issue. The area would get tested properly regardless.

There is the possibility that the two compasses were functioning differently, although this normally is not the way to bet. The compasses both were set with 0° declination. In situations like this, compasses should be checked or some kind of decision should be made about whose is correct. Generally, a good rule of thumb is to argue that the correct reading will be that of the senior supervisor in the field.

For area surveys, it is best to space crew members at the start of every other transect then send them out.

When they reach the end of their first transect, they would go to the next transect and work their way back to the starting baseline. The shovel tests would still be numbered sequentially, in order actually dug; the notation on transect bearing that will be made in the field notes and so on (see captions Figures 5.13 to 5.15) tells at what end of the transect the digging actually began. This is why bearing is so important on the field notes, and why the overall field notes are so important.

For corridors, the procedure is different. Corridors are inherently inefficient, since at least one person will need to walk back over the way they came without doing any testing. Unlike an area survey, where the distance each person walks approximates the distance that will be tested, in a corridor survey, everyone will walk the same distance over the segment of the corridor they are, collectively, testing. However, they will actually dig only a fraction of the shovel tests.

Where the number of transects of shovel tests along the corridor is less than the number of crew members available, it usually works best to divide the crew among the transects. Crew members then leap-frog, digging every other or every third shovel test unit.

The field supervisor or the project manager will be responsible for identifying stopping places along the corridor where the field vehicle can be brought in close to the crew. This is as much for safety reasons as for work efficiency. In the more built-up areas of the eastern and midwestern United States, few corridors go very far without crossing a road or a farm field with a tractor path. The testing procedure needs to be planned well enough beforehand to know how far the crew will get and to where the vehicle should be driven.

It is the field supervisor's responsibility to check at the start that everyone is spaced at the proper interval and that the initial shovel tests are coming out at the proper interval. When transects reach an end, that is a good time to double-check spacing. Experienced field crews tend to have very accurate paces; they also have a very good sense of how far away, visually, their co-workers' transects should be. Since each shovel test has a number, the crew members should be asking adjacent workers what number shovel test that member is on, to make sure that the interior of the testing pattern is square and true.

The shovel test transect has a direction or bearing; the crew will be using hand-held compasses to determine the direction to go for the next shovel test. What bearings to use: magnetic or true north?

Unless the particular project somehow requires it, or because it is infinitely easier to do so, making corrections for magnetic declination on a hand compass that cannot be read any finer than a degree and, in fact, is ruled off in two degree increments, is absurd.   Unless there is a good reason (and convenience is the basic good reason; this is translates into cost-effectiveness), current magnetic north should be used.

The field supervisor should make sure that each crew member has the compass set to zero declination. If, some day in the distant future, it becomes important to re-do or re-establish the transects, there are ways of computing changes in declination. For example, all land surveying books regularly publish a figure of the United States showing the rate at which magnetic declination changes per year. If it is that important in the future, then the time and effort needed to figure out what direction the Phase I transects went in will not be viewed as a real problem.

Going with a magnetic bearing at a known time is more accurate in terms of documentation that trying to guess a magnetic declination, getting everyone on the crew to set the compasses up right, then going off and doing it.

5.3.2.3. Doing Shovel Testing

Although the Phase I process is arguably the key exercise in archaeological compliance work, it is not often taught. This seems to hold very much for doing shovel testing. Again, archaeologists generally get a thorough grounding in surface survey methods, and it is not at all unusual for students to have a lot of exposure to large-scale and complex excavations. Not a few of us got into archaeology in part because of the fun of those formal excavations. It is doubtful, though, that many really got into archaeology because they were enamored with the image and romance of shovel testing woodlots.

This has resulted in something of a problem for the private sector. New hires, be they temporary or permanent, with bachelor's or advanced degrees, generally have some sense of how to do a surface survey or to do basic excavation. But we have found that many do not have much of an idea of what is expected of them for a shovel-testing regime. This puts the private-sector community -- and not infrequently the public-sector community -- in the bind of having to provide that training. However, firms are not in the business of training employees in the tasks for which they hold college degrees. That is the responsibility of the college or university community.

Given the lack of coverage in the literature of this kind of Phase I process, we briefly illustrate how shovel testing is done on pages 144 - 147 (Figures 5.8 - 5.16). This should also help those in government review positions who may not have had much in the way of Phase I shovel testing experience, yet are required to assess whether a Phase I project has been correctly and adequately performed. Hester (1997:98-101) did something similar for more formal excavations when he described "Excavating a 'typical' unit." Being able to visualize what goes on can be a great deal of help.

5.3.3. Field Notes and Records

Like all field notes, Phase I field notes are kept in a D-ring (slant-ring) binder. Round-ring binders should be avoided since the back pages get torn due to the shape of the rings and how the pages move -- or do not -- as the binder is set flat and opened.

Phase I field notes have four categories of information:

* general project information, maps, scope of work;

* the general field notes kept by the field supervisor;

* the specific shovel test field notes kept by the crew and the supervisor; and

* the field specimen sheets (bag inventory).

Some Images of How Phase I Shovel Testing Is Done

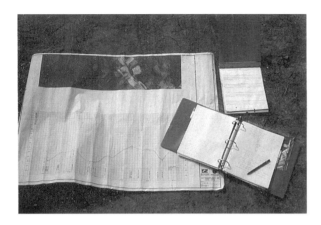

Figure 5.8 (top) and Figure 5.9 (right). The first step on entering the field is to locate where in the physical world the project area actually is. The Phase I transects will have been set out in the office first, and done so with reference to some kind of in-the-field feature that will serve as a baseline (see also Figure 5.4). The trick, now in the field, is to locate that mapped baseline.

The idea is to get the field crew set up just as quickly as is practical. This means locating where each of the crew members will begin testing, and making sure that each knows the compass bearing that will be used as well as how many shovel tests are planned for each person's transect.

Figure 5.10 (left). Standard Phase I shovel-testing equipment includes a round-nose shovel, a small screen, a locking tape measure that has a metric scale along at least one side, a trowel, two colors of flagging tape along with a permanent ink marker, a clipboard along with shovel test forms and a couple pencils, and a backpack containing empty bags for possible artifacts, water, and any other materials needed or required for the project in question.

All of this paraphernalia will be carried by each crew member, and while it is tempting sometimes to place a lot of it in the backpack, usually most stays out at-hand since it needs to be used. Thus, the rolls of flagging tape will be stashed in pockets; the tape measure, clipped to a belt or in yet another pocket along with the ink marker; the trowel, in one of the back pockets as nearly all field archaeologists carry them; and the shovel, screen, and clipboard – usually with the pencil clipped to the pages – lugged along in the hands while the compass is hung about the neck or stuck in yet another pocket.

with their crashing through brush, all of the chaos, the exhaustion, the different ways of pacing, the different ways to read the compass, and everything else, is that they generally come out within a meter or two of where they belong – even after a 600 m transect. Given the purpose of the Phase I exercise, this is an acceptable error rate.

Figure 5.11 (above). Going from one shovel test location to the next will require that the person go in a straight line, regardless of ground cover. It also requires that the shovel, screen, notebook or clipboard, flagging tape, and other things be carried all at the same time. To go back for a second trip to carry things forward doubles the field crew walking time and is unnecessary.

 (It also can result in lost equipment. Crews can easily become disoriented in second-growth woodlots, especially in the early afternoon, after lunch and a strenuous morning. If the previous shovel test or its flagging tape are out of view, it is not unusual for people to wander about trying to find things left behind at the previous shovel test. This is why, for example, some firms paint the handles of their shovels red, or some crew members will tie fluorescent pink flagging tape to their shovels.)

 Crew members develop a routine or rhythm for doing Phase I work. To get from the present shovel test unit to the location of the next requires first that the individual use the hand held compass to determine the direction in which to go. In open areas, a distant point should be identified toward which the individual will walk. In woodlots and other areas of limited visibility, a distant tree or feature should be identified, reached, and, if the location for the next shovel test still has not been reached, another feature identified and the procedure repeated.

 Distances are measured by pacing, not with a tape measure. Although most crew members have a dependable pace, it is a good idea with a new crew to check shovel test and transect spacing with a tape at the start, just to verify field quality. Experienced crews have remarkably dependable paces: What is amazing about Phase I transects,

Figure 5.12 (above). After reaching the location of the next shovel test unit, the field archaeologist drops the equipment, turns, and takes a backsight with the compass on the flagging tape marking the previous test. The backsighting serves as a quality control, keeping the transects true and parallel. The colored flagging tape stands out, and while it may not be tied off on tree branches or pasture herbs with transit-like precision, a series of such flags still indicates visually whether or not the field worker is going in a straight line.

 Most areas of the eastern and midwestern United States have been plowed at least once. If an Ap horizon is or known to have been present, then the first shovel test level should be all of that plowzone material. In unplowed tracts, or where it is not clear if the land had been plowed, 10-cm arbitrary levels should be used. This holds for volumes below the Ap horizon.

 Fill is removed by shovel and put into the small, single-person screen carried by each crew member. The shovel test fill is raked across the screen until most has dropped out. It is not important to push all of the fill through the screen; the purpose is to see if cultural material is present in any reasonable density. By the time most of the fill has been moved back and forth across the screen with trowel or hand, it will be apparent if any cultural materials are present. [The only major exception is in areas with large quantities of gravel; even then, the screen becomes a sorting table, not a filter.]

The recovery rate in going through the remaining 30 percent of fill in the screen is around 90 - 95 percent. That is, in 9 cases out of 10, if the shovel test fill has cultural materials in it, those materials will be found.

of soil horizons should be given for each shovel test. Soil profile characteristics serve a crucial role in reconstructing the landscape history of the project area. Nothing is more frustrating than to have a collection of shovel test records that state only depth of level and soil color.

This admonishment holds for labeling bags as well. If material is recovered, then the material is bagged by shovel test and by level. Written on the bag while the person is on the transect, will be the project or site name, the transect number, the shovel test number, the soil horizon from which the material came, the upper and lower bounds of the depth of the level below surface, the date, and the name of the crew member.

Finally, often the project map will show landscape or surveying features that can be used to check transect location and accuracy. When such features are encountered, their location relative to the particular shovel test involved should be noted.

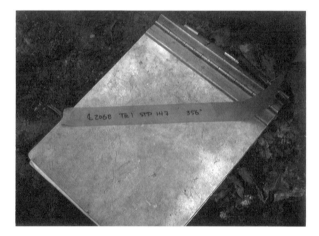

Figure 5.15 (above). After backfilling, the last step is to record the transect number, shovel test number, and bearing on a strip of flagging tape. Each flagging tape strip at each shovel test location should have the following information written on the tape:

*   the transect number or designation;
*   the shovel test number; and
*   the magnetic compass bearing that is being used.

(In open areas, pin flags are useful, and might be used with the flag labeled, or along with flagging tape. However, it is just as easy to use flagging tape in open or grassland areas, with the tape held in place by fill or sod, or tied off on hand-gathered bunch of stalks.)

Shovel tests that contained artifacts (*positive shovel tests*) should be flagged with a different color tape from those shovel tests that did not (*negative shovel tests*). The flagging tape marking a positive shovel test should have a remark written on it, stating the character of what was found. Usually something like "Historic," "Prehistoric," or "flakes" will suffice.

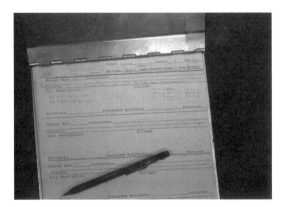

Figure 5.13 and Figure 5.14 (above). With the screening completed and any recovered material bagged, the shovel test should be recorded. This is done before the unit is backfilled. How the notes are kept for each shovel test will be discussed more below, since there are differences among firms; however, this is a good point to note that a description

It is critical that each shovel test, positive or negative, be marked, especially in those 50-year-old woodlots found over most of wooded parts of the United States east of the Rockies. The purpose of the marking is to allow the Phase I crew to return to positive shovel tests for supplemental testing and to resume work in the project area on the following day, and for Phase II crews to locate areas within the Phase I testing scheme.

The best flagging tape color is fluorescent pink in all settings; blue is the next best in forested settings, while red is good in pasture settings. Neither orange nor red work as well as one might think in forested settings, since they get lost against the leaves, especially in the fall. It saves time to flag positive shovel tests with a second color, since it is possible that the crew is going to have to go back to these when re-testing is done. Each and every shovel test should be flagged.

Figure 5.16 (below). After being labeled, the strip of flagging tape is tied to an overhanging branch, an adjacent clump of grass, or even stuck under the piece of sod removed from the yard. Having the shovel test number, transect, and bearing recorded not only helps crew members keep track of where they are along a transect, it also allows for shovel tests to be easily re-located for supplemental testing.

Flagging the locations of shovel tests also is important because in part it is likely that the group that comes in to do the Phase II will not be your company, and in part because the points represented by the shovel tests are used when people are wandering through a project area as if those shovel tests were the grid points on a map, which of course they should be.

The entire process is then repeated: Thirty-five times per person in an eight-hour day if fill is screened to meet budget; fifty times per person in an eight-hour day if fill is shovel-sorted.

We learned about archaeology from that ... The Ft. Belvoir Incident

External interference may also come from sources that are unexpected. This is known in the Middle Atlantic as the Ft. Belvoir Incident.

Briefly, the Corps of Engineers intended to expand a portion of the base into a section of the fort that had last been used for field infantry training in the 1940s. Ground cover was typical for northern Virginia, a tangled mixture of emerging climax trees under a secondary-species canopy, along with a riot of cat brier, Virginia creeper, trenches, foxholes, swamp, and abandoned command trailers. Access to this part of the fort was by standard public roads, off of which ran a short asphalt drive to a rapidly deteriorating parking lot and long-abandoned 1950s-era structure, one of those flat-roofed, two-storey red-brick sorts that one associates with post-War construction. A chain link fence ran along one side of the project area, with a gravel walkway inside that was heavily patrolled by dogs as well as occasionally bored guards (spent cartridges could be seen littering the ground on both sides of the fence). Behind the fence in the woods on the

crest of a small rise was a white geodesic dome. The remainder of the project area had a pair of lightly maintained gravel roads, roads that originally had served residents displaced in the 1930s. Most military installations have such roads, which augment access into the more remote or less used parts of the base.

The project was a standard Phase I survey, but became a nightmare. Crews would return each day exhausted, they said, from fighting the tangled undergrowth. Visibility was limited; veteran field personnel would end up with transects literally zig-zagging through the woods, actually crossing over the transects of fellow crew members. Equipment got lost all of the time: One person lost her hair-bandanna and did not notice, even with the hair dangling in her face, until the end of the day; another person lost three trowels in as many days, something unheard of for a practiced archaeologist (bandannas are inexpensive and easily purchased; however, most archaeologists still have the trowel they used in their first field school).

The project, not surprisingly, was not moving along well and was starting to go over budget, and this with a sizeable part of the land left to be

tested. In an attempt to overwhelm circumstances and put the project to rest, the entire office was emptied and eight people went into the field to finish the testing.

This last stage of the Phase I would use one of the lightly maintained gravel roads as a reference. Project maps showed that this road ran right across one side of the rectangular area remaining to be tested; it was an ideal candidate for a baseline. We all lined up along that road, spaced 20 m apart, with one person 10 m out from the chain link fence on the left and one of the authors at the other end of the ranks, 150 m away. And off we went at 90° to the road to do our transects.

The field worker nearest the fence used that as the basic guide, since it was parallel with the intended transect. She had found early on that her compass was not responding correctly, which she attributed to the closeness of the fence: The needle tended to drift in that direction. The rest of the crew used compass bearings. The person farthest out from the fence also began by using his compass. As the testing went along, that eighth person noticed after a while that trees identified by compass then sighted on in the distance when

---

Each of the above categories have sections within the notebook. The sections are separated by labeled binder separators. Not always, but often the field notebook will become the project notebook. That is, it will be the core referent for completion of the project, and will include most of the project documentation that will be turned over to the client at the end of the project.

Included within the project notebook will be the SOW (scope of work), draft figures for the final report, and other bookkeeping and project management items -- tables, figures, list of tables, list of figures, contact sheets, other maps, pretty much anything made out of paper that has even a passing bearing on the project. These will be added into the notebook after the project has come out of the field.

The following gives the core information that should be in the field notes, arranged in the recommended order. Unless indicated otherwise, these notes will be kept by the project manager or field supervisor; the project manager is responsible for the field notes, even if those notes are kept by the field supervisor.

Section 1. General Project Information

* SOW (Scope of Work):

Include those sections of the SOW pertaining to what kind of work is requested, where it is to be done, and similar work-order-like specifications. These sections are photocopied then placed in the notebook. The germane work requirements should be highlighted or underlined.

* Logistics, including work orders from management and hour allocations for the tasks concerned:

For the purposes of the field notes, the logistics should break out how many person-hours have been allocated to the particular project, based upon specific tasks. Some firms help manage this by having *Work Request Forms* specifying the tasks needed and how many hours were allocated in the budget to complete those tasks.

one shovel test was paced out, would not be the tree the compass pointed to for the next shovel test. Person Eight decided, off there from everyone else, to focus on the original tree that had been the constant for the first couple shovel tests and NOT depend as much on the reading of the compass.

When crews work, they keep voice contact, especially in overgrown areas. And the Ft. Belvoir project was sufficiently bizarre anyway that this normal practice was enhanced. Though the morning there were the occasional calls. For Person Eight, out on the far right flank, those voices began to fade. And fade. And finally end altogether.

The morning passed to noon then a little after, the 27 requisite tests completed along the transect. Alone in the woods, Person Eight wandered back to the staging area, that crumbling asphalt parking lot behind the 1950s building. Reached. He waited. And waited. And had lunch. And waited.

Finally, the other seven came in, annoyed and bemused, with the person who had been in constant visual contact with the fence irritated with her co-workers. What had happened was that the interior six people had pivoted, swinging like a gate as they all followed their compass bearings, ending up not just crossing the first person's transect, but coming up face-to-chain-link with the fence, its gravel path beyond, and lots of spent cartridges. Person One's irritation, still visible, came from being chastised for being in the wrong place – such is the confidence that all field people have in their ability to read a compass and pace out a transect in the densest of brush. Her confidence not only was equal, so was her evidence: At least SHE had had the fence in sight all along; what were you idiots doing over here anyway!!??

Examining the project and USGS maps showed that only Transects 1 and 8 were perpendicular to the road and parallel with the chain-link security fence. The other six had drifted. It was later learned that the geodesic dome housed powerful microwave transmitters used in satellite monitoring and intelligence operations – hence the guards. And hence the project's history of serious disorientation and confusion whenever experienced crew would try to do even the most trivial of tasks.

One byproduct was a disruption of the hand compasses. Given the way that "gate" swung, the disruption was also a sound demonstration of the "Right-hand Rule" about how the lines of force in an electromagnetic fields are oriented.

(A similar kind of disorientation was reported by personnel at the U.S. embassy in Moscow in the 1970s and 1980s. The KGB constantly bombarded the embassy with microwaves as part of their intelligence operations. United States personnel would report headaches and confusion, which eventually was attributed to KGB microwave activity.)

Project maps can be used for ground truth. More importantly, they should be used constantly to verify position. This is always the case, regardless of the problem or even if there is no problem.

Project maps and figures:

Reduced versions of project area maps, including those showing shovel test locations and transects, are put in this sub-section. Often the SOW will have project area renderings; copies should be included in this section. Sometimes the reductions will have to be made from the original blue line project map; at other times, a reduced version may already exist. The goal is to provide the field notes with an 11 x 17 inch fold-out map that can be easily handled in the field.

Project blue line maps seldom are provided with bar scales. Rather, the architecture and engineering community indicate original map scale as a ratio. The project manager will need to draw a bar scale, preferably in meters, onto the original project map *before reduction*. In fact, given parallax problems with photocopier reductions, a few bar scales scattered around the perimeter of the map may be useful (see box Chapter 9: "Tip: Photocopy Reduction of Project Maps").

Additional maps in this part of the field notes include a photocopy of the appropriate section of the relevant USGS 7.5' quadrangle, along with a copy of the distance scale. It also is useful to have a photocopy of the appropriate sheet from the county soil survey.

Sketch maps of the area go here as well. These will be referred to during the field work for ground truth.

Right-of-entry materials:

Rights-of-entry are needed from property owners in Phase I surveys where the client does not own the land to be tested. For example, COE flood protection projects cross the land of many owners; the COE normally will have sent out a form letter asking that the owner grant right-of-entry to survey crews. The project manager should have in this part of the notebook copies of returned and signed right-of-entry letters; whenever possible, whoever is in the field should make certain that the landowner is contacted again just prior to entry onto the property. In any case, property generally should not be entered for Phase I purposes unless some form of permission has been obtained.

Records of interviews and communications:

Any kind of discussion that occurs between project personnel and people commenting on the project should have a written summary that is put in this section of the notebook. This includes telephone communications from the project manager to the field supervisor. The record of the interview or communication should include person and title/occupation, date and time, phone number and location, and a brief summary of what was communicated.

Some projects involve detailed project area interviews. The summaries of these interviews are placed in this section.

This is a good place to note that what is written in the field notebook has the strength of primary evidence if any issue involving the field work comes to trial. The notebook is a "discoverable document" in a legal proceeding.

Section 2. General Field Notes

* overall narrative, environmental description, general day-by-day bookkeeping; and

* collection area/transect or shovel test transect descriptions, telling how much of what was done by whom on what day.

The general field note section is the most neglected part of the field notes. One of two people will directly supervise the field part of a Phase I project: either a field supervisor, whose job it is to handle field projects but who does not write the report; or the project manager. Project managers frequently supervise Phase I field work during slack times or in small companies. One of these two individuals will be responsible for writing the daily narrative.

The narrative part of the field notes does two things: It helps tie things together by giving an idea of what transpired; and it separates the essential from the non-essential. Each day, the following information should be recorded:

* day and date;

* location if the project involves multiple locations;

* weather conditions, including 1) temperature in degrees centigrade, 2) wind direction and velocity in km/hr (see box: "The Beaufort Scale"), 3) cloud cover, 4) precipitation/snow cover;

* crew present (first entry for each individual should include full name; there after, use surname);

* who collected or dug which transect or area, and how many transects or areas were done; and

* positive transects and nature of positive ("positive" referring to transects or places/shovel testings along those transects that contained cultural evidence).

In addition to the above, the narrative section of the field notes will have a detailed description of the landscape as encountered in the field. This description includes overall information on the following:

* tree distribution and growth characteristics, should such be present;

* other understory vegetation or ground cover;

* fence lines, non-random distribution of trees or herbaceous vegetation;

* other built environment;

* soils and soil changes;

* exposed rocks, nature of stream beds; and

* gullies, steepness of gully sides, lineality of gullies.

Attention to detail and keen observation are essential.

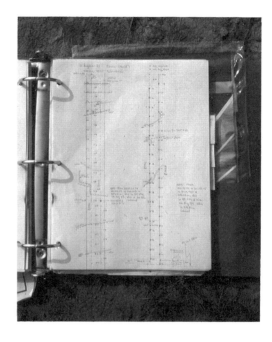

Figure 5.17. Field note page showing arrangement of shovel tests relative to a corridor survey. Annotations include streams and roads crossed, as well as woodlot edges and plowed fields.

The Beaufort Scale

A useful field tool for estimating wind velocity is the Beaufort Scale, named for Sir Francis Beaufort, who served in the 1820s as admiral of Great Britain's Mediterranean fleet. Consistent with his naval background, his was a wide-ranging and fundamentally practical intellect; he was partly responsible for the surge of interest in classical philology, for example, coming from his time spent in the Mediterranean basin.

The Beaufort Scale estimated wind speed based upon observation of the wind's effects on common, everyday objects, or at least everyday objects found among the nineteenth century English middle and upper classes. The Scale is reproduced in countless dictionaries and encyclopedias, and has been since the late nineteenth-century. Amusingly, the wording has not been changed since the scale was first published in the 1850s. The descriptions still remark on the behavior of smoke coming from chimneys, chimney pots, roofing slates, and the sound made by the wind going past *telegraph* – NOT telephone or utility – lines. The Scale is transcribed below, with some wording changes so that the lines would fit, from the version in *Webster's Ninth Collegiate Dictionary*, 1989, p.138:

Beaufort Number	Name	Approximate Speed	Signs or Effect
0	calm	< 2 kph	smoke rises vertically
1	light air	3 - 5 kph	wind direction shown by smoke but not by wind vanes
2	light breeze	6 - 11 kph	wind felt on face; leaves rustle; wind vanes move
3	gentle breeze	12 - 19 kph	leaves and small twigs in constant motion; light flags extended
4	moderate breeze	20 - 29 kph	dust and loose paper raised; small branches moved
5	fresh breeze	30 - 39 kph	small trees in leave begin to sway; crested wavelets form on inland waters
6	strong breeze	40 - 50 kph	large branches in motion; telegraph wires whistle; umbrellas used with difficulty
7	moderate or near gale	51 - 61 kph	whole trees in motion; difficult to walk against the wind
8	fresh gale or gale	62 - 74 kph	twigs break from trees; progress generally impeded
9	strong gale	75 - 87 kph	slight structural damage; chimney pots and [roof] slates removed
10	whole gale	88 - 101 kph	trees uprooted; considerable structural damage
11	storm	102 - 116 kph	very rarely experienced [in Great Britain, not Florida]; accompanied by widespread damage
12	hurricane	117+ kph	devastation occurs

Section 3. Specific Field Records

* *Individual shovel test records, arranged by transect:*

If shovel testing was done, those tests are described individually; these records are kept by the individual crew member who excavated the shovel test. Each company has its own form for completing this. Some forms require a fill-in-the-blank approach; other forms give a blank but scaled wall profile, and one merely draws lines across at the different levels representing sediment or soil-horizon changes. Some states require that at least one "typical" shovel test wall profile be included in the compliance report; usually, though, these records serve more the needs of the project manager when considering the overall tested area. Since these notes are kept by the crew for the use, in the end, by the project manager, the project manager should periodically review these, to make sure that the information needed is being recorded correctly and neatly.

General Comments on Photographs

The need for photographs during the Phase I survey varies by state. In some, there is no requirement at all. In a number of others, though, a general photograph of the project area is required, as is a photograph of a typical soil/deposit matrix profile from a backhoe trench or shovel test unit. Landscape features such as building foundations or mill races, as well as archaeological features, normally will be photographed in all states. In some cases, such as work performed for the Missouri Department of Transportation or the New York State Department of Transportation through the SUNY Research Foundation, a general architectural survey also is done as part of the Phase I exercise. In those instances, photographs are taken of structures along the project corridor, and of the corridor itself.

Traditionally, field photographs involved film cameras, although this is changing as electronic cameras with digitally recorded images become affordable and the images achieve film-equal quality. In situations with film cameras, it is important to physically label the roll canister that is loaded into the camera, then have a corresponding photo record log. When developed, the package containing the prints or the sheet of contact prints will also have that roll number transcribed to it.

Photo records should have the following: Roll number, number of exposures, speed and type of film; frame number, date, what was photographed, direction of photograph.

Many film cameras now are automatic in some way. If there is any manual control, pictures should be taken at 1/125th of a second or faster, with the highest f-stop value relative to speed possible.

Field cameras can be real headaches, and usually the less fancy the better. The best camera is the old-fashioned pentax with the needle-and-circle light meter – it is inexpensive, it is surprisingly robust, and it works.

The increasing availability and affordability of digital and electronic cameras eventually will make these preferable, since film costs will no longer be an issue and since the image could be loaded directly into the report. However, current equipment still lacks the image density of film, providing instead a true image record equivalent to a standard television screen, with the image interpolated through fractals ("image smoothing"). When these problems are solved and such cameras become standard, a hard copy of archival quality will need to be produced of all images retained. This is partly because laser-accessed CDs storing photographs have a half-life of about 10 years. That is, the images will begin to fail even more quickly than the color fails from a standard photographic print. This is also partly because the technology to access those CDs will change, rendering the information inaccessible.

When taking field photographs, a menu board should be used where possible of detail – as opposed to general view or landscape – photographs. Unless specified in the contract or in the pertinent state regulatory guidelines, it does not matter in many cases if the film is black-and-white or color. Color film is less expensive and easier to process, and gives better definition for most needs; usually an ASA 200 film will work just fine. *However, it must be remembered that color images and film negatives are NOT stable, and that the colors will deteriorate in a few decades.*

The record for each shovel test should include the following: 1) transect and shovel test number; 2) bearing or direction of transect; 3) soil horizon description (horizon, color, texture, depth); 4) positive or negative; 5) vegetation, if trees species, number by dbh, within some distance, say 5 m; and 6) landmarks and distance from landmarks, including direction.

* Feature inventory:

It is rare that a Phase I project will expose features. In situations where that occurs, a separate section containing a detailed description of the feature is needed. Features and feature forms are considered in detail under Phase II testing in Chapter 6.

* Photograph records:

A photograph record sheet should be included. This will tell the date, location, and subject of the photograph. Each record sheet should have the name of the project and the kind of film used. Some firms provide parts for f-stop and exposure time; this is left

over from the era of separate light meters and manually set cameras and seldom now is needed. As with features, photographic records seldom are needed for a Phase I exercise (except in states requiring a picture of a shovel test profile), although they may be useful for marketing or public relations.

Section 4. Bag Inventory/Field Specimen Sheets

The last section represents the list of bags of artifacts recovered during Phase I testing, the list being called a "bag inventory" or a "field specimen list." Each bag of artifacts is assigned a number. That number, as well as the transect, shovel test, depth, and contents of the bag will be recorded. A competent field specimen inventory serves as a short-cut for identifying positive shovel tests within the project area.

Different firms record bags from the field in different ways. There are three basic systems: 1) bags numbered in sequence as recorded; 2) bags numbered based upon a state based numbering system; and 3) bags numbered based upon date and sequence. However it is done, it is critical that bags be labeled each day, every day.

Bag inventories are notorious for getting confused. Assignment of numbers usually will occur at the end of the day, at a time when field crews are tired and everyone is susceptible to befuddlement. Just as each person has a way of carrying equipment and conducting Phase I excavations, so too does everyone have a way of carrying the various bags of artifacts. They may be placed in backpacks, in jacket pockets, in pants pockets.

It is helpful if each person goes through their notes and counts how many bags they should turn in, then how many they have. This helps finding that one bag stuck in the back pocket. Anyone who has done a number of Phase I surveys knows that, sooner or later there is that one small bag stashed in the front pouch of the field pack or in the left pocket of the fatigue jacket that is going to surface.

5.4. Post-Field

Phase I surveys are the bread-and-butter of most archaeological firms. To be cost-effective, several things need to be done at the same time. This does not impinge on quality; it does require attention to logistics to make sure everyone knows what their responsibilities are. Usually, the project budget will indicate how much time or money is available for laboratory analyses, report preparation, figure production, and the like.

On returning from the field, several tasks are done, generally at the same time:

* the artifacts, along with a copy of the bag inventory, go to the lab, and analyses will begin (see Chapter 8);

* draft figures for the report are prepared then submitted to the graphics division or staff (see Chapter 9);

* if needed, site forms are prepared as quickly as possible and submitted to the state so that a site number will be available for the report; and

* the body of the report, such as the general opening, cultural and environmental background, and similar sections, is started (see Chapter 9).

Although it depends upon the size of the firm and the nature of the project, it rarely is necessary for the project manager to be involved in artifact analysis at the Phase I level. There usually is nothing analytically demanding that cannot be done better and more quickly by the laboratory staff. All that the project manager needs is a summary of what was found, how common such material is or is not, and what sorts of cultural behavior such things are associated with.

Most of that will be known to the project manager anyway, so just knowing what was recovered where in the project area is close to all that is needed. Thus, from the perspective of the project manager, the lab serves as a black box, or should if the people are any good.

5.4.1. Level of Analyses Expected

The Phase I exercise is not meant to be a sustained, interpretive analysis of the archaeology or the history of the project area. Rather, it is meant to provide sufficient information to reviewers to allow *their* determination of National Register potential. It does not hurt to repeat once more that the practicing archaeologist is serving as the eyes for the review agency archaeologists, especially for the SHPO/THPO. The practicing archaeologist provides the evidence along with a professional assessment of what was found (or not found); however, it will be the government archaeologists who will make a determination, and they will do so based upon the evidence provided in the Phase I report.

The principal interpretative analysis that will be done will take place within the report, and will involve those two broad issues that are required to assess the eligibility of a site for listing on the National Register, as specified in **36 CFR 60.4**:

* integrity of the archaeological deposit, should such be present, along with

* association with a nationally, regionally, or locally important person or event; example or product of a nationally, regionally, or locally recognized artisan, designer, or similar person; and/or potential to contribute information important to the understanding of history or prehistory (i.e., "data potential").

Phase I is *not* a site evaluation process in the sense of seeing if a deposit is eligible for listing on the National Register. Rather, the Phase I survey is meant to be a good faith effort to identify archaeological sites within the area examined. However, the information collected during the Phase I survey often is capable of dealing with some evaluation questions. Just because a site is found does not mean that it is eligible for listing on the National Register; often the information available from Phase I field work is enough to exclude that site from future Phase II testing and evaluation.

While sometimes the information may be more than adequate to make a positive statement, in reality the Phase I project is directed toward seeing if either of those sets can be *excluded*. That is, in almost all cases, a Phase I assessment is sufficient only to allow review agency archaeologists to determine that the archaeological deposit does *not* satisfy the criteria for listing on the National Register of Historic Places. The level of Phase I analysis, then, is commensurate with this.

As mentioned in Chapter 2, "integrity" is a relative concept when condition of archaeological deposits is considered. In practice, it refers to "integrity relative to similar, currently known and understood examples." In most regions, a heavily plowed late prehistoric archaeological site probably would not be considered to have depositional integrity; after all, there are innumerable, relatively undisturbed late prehistoric sites already known. However, in most regions, a heavily plowed Paleoindian or even pre-Paleoindian archaeological site will probably be considered to have sufficient depositional integrity to warrant further examination. This is because the number of such sites in any condition is small.

Most prehistoric archaeological sites are evaluated based on their potential to further extend the archaeological knowledge of the region. This is referred to as "data potential." That assessment -- and the associated research questions -- have been set out beforehand in the State Plan, as explained in Chapter 2. Phase I data provide basic information on artifact density and cultural-historical affiliation.

In addition to data potential, historic archaeological sites may also be eligible for listing on the National Register based on association with known, important events or personages. Battlefields fall into this category; an early historic archaeological site associated with, say, the De Soto expedition through the Southeast would as well, as would be any of the Spanish military reconnaissance camps that may have penetrated into Montana in the sixteenth or seventeenth centuries. Phase I research provides information in two steps under these circumstances: Did historic research indicate that such an event or person was associated with the deposit; and do Phase I field data indicate archaeological evidence associated with that event or person?

While it is possible for archaeological work to examine questions regarding master artisans and designers -- the lay-out of a major eighteenth-century garden set out by a master gardener or landscaper would be one example -- the nature of Phase I work is such that it usually will not yield the kind of information needed. Generally, such projects would have had some indication from historic background research of such an association, then will have been combined as a Phase I/Phase II investigation, with the Phase I step being the shovel testing to get some feel for artifact distribution and structure of the deposit, then Phase II being a shallow, areal excavation should the issue be one of gardens or landscaping.

Generally, artifact analysis will not go beyond identification/typological classification, frequency count, and distribution across the site or project area. At this stage, there is little need to do anything else with the artifacts as artifacts.

For the historic artifacts this is conceptually clear: For example, following South's (1977) clever approach of classifying historic artifacts in terms of activity sets means that all that really is needed is classification of the historic assemblage into like sets, counts of same, then consideration of how those artifacts are distributed over the project area (frequency contour maps are excellent for this; see Figure 5.18).

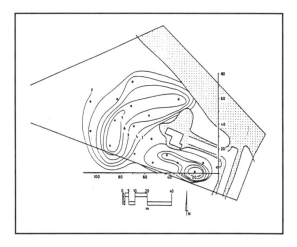

Figure 5.18. Example of an Artifact Frequency Contour Map, Using Shovel Test Units as Points. Such distributional maps follow the assumption that archaeological materials are distributed as sheet litter, which is the same assumption that justifies shovel testing. Frequency contour maps serve as heuristic devices for understanding the nature and extent of the archaeological deposit. Thus, in this case, there was a high concentration of materials in the southeast corner of the tested area.

Like the historic artifacts, what is needed for the prehistoric artifacts is an idea of what is there. Unlike historic artifact classification, some of the prehistoric artifacts will require examination under low magnification to correctly assign function. This refers specifically to using a dissecting microscope to separate the microliths in an assemblage from the unused flakes, especially those under a gram. However, anything beyond simple recognition is over-doing it; if the site is that important, more will be evident during the Phase II testing and either the present firm or another company will amuse themselves doing the microscope work. If it is not important, then some poor graduate student 150 years from now can amuse himself or herself or itself looking at the stuff; all that is needed is to tell them where the material came from and the circumstances of its recovery. Thus, counts, depths, soil horizon (correctly identified), and rough classification are all that are needed. The purpose is merely to figure out what is there and roughly how much is present; with the project area map, the location of the material can be plotted.

5.4.2. Addressing Basic Phase I Issues

In our experience, 19 out of every 20 Phase I projects do not contain archaeological sites worth fussing about; that is, even if archaeological materials are present, they do not satisfy **36 CFR 60.4** criteria for listing on the National Register. In most cases, it is not so much that archaeological materials are lacking as it is that those materials are sporadic, common, undiagnostic, or contained within disturbed matrices. However, in those situations just as in that one project in 20 where the possibility of a Register-eligible site cannot be excluded, it is critical that the case be made.

Making a case against or for additional -- that is, Phase II -- testing is done in three ways:

1) by reference to the integrity of the deposit (based on soil and vegetation work);

2) by reference to what is already known (historic and prehistoric background); and

3) by statistical tests for patterning.

Of the National Register criteria, depositional integrity is the most important. If a site does not have depositional integrity, it does not satisfy Register criteria and therefore is not eligible for listing on the National Register. Therefore, the site or deposit or artifact concentration is not significant in that professional, technical sense (see also Chapter 2), regardless of how alluring that fluted point found in the bulldozer backdirt pile might be.

Assessing depositional integrity at the Phase I level, to the extent that it is possible, will depend upon any available soil profiles and upon the vegetation reconstruction. The first question is what evidence, if any, is there for a plowzone? This is more a question in the eastern and midwestern United States, where nearly all of the landscape was plowed at some time or another. (By the way, this also includes land now under a couple meters of sediment along the valley trains. One site we dealt with in the Root River basin of Minnesota had a plowzone 2.3 m below the current -- and actively plowed -- surface. For another cautionary tale about Phase I testing, results, and historic alteration of the landscape, see Chapter 6: *"We learned about archaeology from that...Secondary Deposition and Cowanesque"*). Similar questions hold for agricultural areas in the western United States.

If historic artifacts have been recovered down to 20 - 30 cm below the surface, but no deeper, then the area may have been plowed. If there appears to be a concentration of artifact-sized materials -- artifacts or just gravels -- in a seeming band at such a depth, again the deposit may have been plowed. Both cases result from the sinking of artifacts through the less viscous plowzone horizon (when and just after it was plowed), combined with the same kind of size-sorting that occurs when salt shakers or boxes of children's blocks are shaken, with small objects accumulating at the bottom.

Does the project area have an iffy AB or BA horizon [A3 or B1 horizon] below a 10-cm thick E horizon [A2 horizon]? Did that AB or BA horizon [A3 or B1 horizon] end at 25-30 cm? Are the trees over the project area around 40 years old or so? Are they what would be considered young climax-stage trees, or older secondary-succession species? If those questions can be answered "yes," then it is likely that the AB horizon [A3 horizon] is a remnant of an Ap horizon, over cultivated land that has been abandoned for at least 40 years. This is where the field notes are needed.

The crew should have recorded the trees and vegetation over the project area. If there are trees in the project area, a matrix should be prepared, with tree dbh in 10-cm increments going down the left side, and genus/species going across the top. The matrix is then filled in with numbers of trees observed for each diameter category for each kind of tree mentioned. The percentage that each type of tree makes up for each 10-cm class are then computed. This *is* a seriation chart, albeit for trees (see also box "Tip: Recording Tree Demographics For Analysis of Succession"). And it works very well in reconstructing what has happened on the landscape. In effect, plant succession is being reconstructed, as discussed earlier. This should help give an idea of how long a project area was open or cropped; it should also tell if it was in pasture. The advantage is that such interpretations not only help the practicing archaeologist get a sense of how land use and associated disturbance has changed, *it provides replicable, detailed empirical evidence for the interpretive conclusions.* This is extremely important to the review agencies.

Integrity is relative; it depends upon how intact other sites of the same sort historically have been. This is related to a broader issue of what is already known about the historic and prehistoric archaeology of the area. All states are required by Section 101 of the National Historic Preservation Act to have prepared and presented what is known as a "State Plan" (see also Chapter 2); every professional office should have copies of the plans from each state in which the firm practices. The State Plan lists the major research issues for the state. Research potential and the significance (technical sense, of course) of an archaeological deposit are to be seen in this context.

Evaluating the importance of an archaeological deposit requires intimate familiarity with the history and prehistory of the region in which the project area is located, knowledge as well of the State Plan, and knowledge of what already is known about the particular cultural historical period to which the archaeological deposit would belong. While the historic and prehistoric backgrounds presented in the Phase I report may seem formulaic, and may seem like some kind of procedural hoop through which the compliance archaeologist must jump, they in fact represent critical assessment steps in the entire assessment process.

Phase I results rarely provide an outright indication that a previously unknown site should be considered eligible for listing on the National Register; more often, there are indications that the site should not *not* be excluded from further testing. This is identical to the Popperian approach to science, wherein one does not demonstrate or "prove" a hypothesis, one merely fails to falsify the hypothesis.

Statistical testing and assessment of patterns may become critical in the Phase I analysis. Most often, this will involve testing if the archaeological materials found below an Ap or suspected Ap horizon are independent of the assemblage found in the upper levels. Such situations were discussed above (see box "*We learned about archaeology from that ... One Component or Two?*"), and require little more than selecting a series of artifact classes, dividing the deposit into Ap or non-Ap-horizon, then using a chi-squared statistic to see if the two sets are independent. The chi-squared statistic is excellent for compliance archaeology issues, since questions of depositional integrity are those of disturbance, and questions about disturbance are questions about if portions of an assemblage retain their identity (that is, are discrete and independent of the rest of the material recovered) or not.

Related to assessments of depositional integrity, sites, and artifact distributions is the issue of artifact patterning over the project area. This is done in two ways. The first is qualitative and visual, and makes use of the Phase I project map that shows where the shovel tests were located. This presents an evenly distributed, pixel-like image that becomes ideal for presenting the distribution of artifacts over part or all of the project area.

Allowing for the assumption that archaeological materials exist as a sheet litter, then the points represented by shovel tests represent a point sample of what would be, in topology, a smooth, gradually changing gradational surface. Given that (and Phase I shovel testing is premised upon exactly that), then it should be possible to approximate the density distribution of artifacts or classes of artifacts across a series of position shovel tests simply by using the shovel test artifact counts as points controlling a

surface contour map (Figure 5.18; see Neumann and Sanford 1985b).

Such distribution maps are heuristic devices, and can be worked up using information supplied by the Phase I laboratory analysis. These work well for prehistoric as well as for historic materials, and give review agencies some sense of the distributions and concentrations involved. For historic artifacts, the information probably should be given as total of historic artifacts, then of architecture artifacts only, then of kitchen artifacts only (South 1977). This should be sufficient to isolate historic habitations (however, see above "*We learned about archaeology from that* ... The Manure Spreader Example"). For prehistoric artifacts, the information should be given as the total number of prehistoric artifacts, then the total number of flakes, the total number of microliths (if the laboratory has isolated these), the total weight of fire-cracked rock, then the total number of ceramics.

Each of these contour maps should be presented as a separate figure in the report, and obviously this is done to make the point that the practicing archaeologist feels strongly that testing beyond Phase I is needed to assess the Register eligibility of the deposit. (Correlation coefficient matrices may be useful in extreme cases; see Chapter 6, section 6.4.2.).

5.4.3. General Structure of Report

The general structure of archaeological compliance reports is given in Chapter 9. The purpose here is to mention those elements unique to the Phase I report. This will help in understanding how the various steps of the Phase I project will come together in the report. Table 5.5. gives the basic contents of a Phase I report.

The Phase I project report is a form of analysis, just as the work in the laboratory -- if it was needed -- was a form of analysis. In the "Results" section, evidence is given and then interpreted to present reasons why the review agency and the SHPO/THPO should or should not continue with a Phase II investigation.

5.4.4. Additional Tasks: Site Forms

After coming in from the field, and about the time that the laboratory is starting to clean and catalogue, site forms have to be handled. If a site was already recorded for part or all of the project area, then an updated site form should be provided to the state. If a site has been found that is not recorded (and project preparation should be sufficient to tell whether sites are known for the project area), then a site form must be prepared.

Review agencies prefer, and at times require, that the site number be used in the final report. This means

Table 5.5. Basic Contents of a Phase I Report

Abstract: Summarizes the nature of the project and its conclusions; this will be the first section of the report that the agency reviewers will read, with the second section being the "Conclusion" section.

Acknowledgments: Lists the agency and client personnel contacted, along with local individuals and resources checked; provides as well a list of professionals involved in the project.

Introduction: States where project is located, what kind of impact activity is planned, and who the contracting/review agency or agencies are. The research design may be included here, and/or in the Methods section.

Environmental Background: Summarizes the vegetation, soils, geology, and other non-cultural elements of the region and the project area. The focal point is always the project area, and this is essentially an exercise in physical geography.

Cultural Background: Summarizes the history and prehistory of the region, with special reference to the project area; it may include a map and table showing locations and nature of known historic and prehistoric sites/structures within a set distance -- usually 2 km -- of the project area.

Methods: Outlines the field and laboratory methods, and also states where materials, project documentation, and other items will be curated.

Results: Presents in details the results of the background investigations and of the field work as they bear upon the Phase I exercise; there will be an interpretive discussion here as well.

Conclusions and Recommendations: Summarizes the report's conclusions and reasoning leading to those conclusions; this section will be the second section agency reviewers will read in the report.

References Cited: References usually are cited in standard anthropological literature format, and will include informants and maps along with the more traditional types of sources used.

Appendices: Includes new or amended site forms; tabulation of artifacts recovered (if any); and for some projects, summary of interviews, a copy of the scope of work, and qualifications of project personnel.

---

that the site form needs to be completed and submitted *as soon as possible after coming out of the field.* A few states would like to have the collections labeled with the site number; this means that the site number needs to be obtained before the laboratory people begin labeling. The turn-around time for getting a site number varies by state and by work load; the practicing archaeologist should have some idea of how long it will take to get new site numbers for the particular state in question.

Dealing with site forms raises two issues: 1) determining if what was present was a site; and 2) mechanics for amending, updating, or completing then submitting site forms.

Although **36 CFR Part 63 (IV,A, 2)** defines a site as any "location of prehistoric or historic occupation or activity" (see Chapter 2), there is no firm definition of what this actually constitutes. After all, this is hardly a precise definition. However, Phase I surveys are intended to identify if sites are present that might satisfy criteria for listing on the National Register of Historic Places. This means that a consistent, operational definition is needed. For example, does one shovel test having five artifacts in it mean a site? How about one shovel test with one artifact? Two artifacts? How about two shovel tests 20 m apart with artifacts (pick a number of artifacts), but nothing found in shovel tests between them? How about two shovel tests 10 m apart, but the shovel tests out 20 m are free of artifacts? Just exactly WHAT constitutes an archaeological site, as opposed to incidental litter?

The point is that a decision needs to be made. Further, the decision should be one that is consistent with the needs and opinions of the state. Some states do have definitions of what constitutes a site (e.g., Alabama, Louisiana). More often, though, the state will not be very clear about thresholds for the presence of a site. The entire Section 106 process still is very new; no one really has been trained to operationalize much of the day-to-day archaeology in the country, at least in such a way that management decisions can be made.

By way of an example, we have used the following criteria for satisfying the bookkeeping definition of a site:

1) If a feature is found, even in one shovel test, call the area a site; or

2) If at least three shovel tests, meaning at least two at 20-m intervals and the intervening ones, have more than two artifacts each, call the area a site.

Calling the deposit or spread of artifacts a site does not mean that it is significant in National Register terms. It is merely a way of keeping track of clusters of debris over the landscape. It allows the practicing archaeologist to decide if site forms should be submitted. In this respect, if the state disagrees with the archaeologist's definition or threshold, then the state can provide operational criteria.

Most states have a state site form. Some, like those for Maryland, are easy to fill out and are meant to be partially encoded into a computerized file. Many state expect that a photocopy will be attached of that part of the USGS 7.5' quadrangle where the site is located.

Most states now require that a completed site form be submitted and be in their possession before a site number is given. The practicing archaeologist should have blank site forms on-hand. Getting the forms, if such already is not present, is easy: Just call the state review agency or visit the agency's Internet Web site.

It is possible that in the near future filing site forms will be done electronically. This will speed up the process in terms of submission; it remains to be seen if this also speeds up the turn-around time for getting site numbers, since the limiting factor on turn-around time is staffing at the state site files and review of submitted forms, not submission of the forms themselves.

6: The Phase II Process: Testing and Evaluation

6.1. Intent and Goals

The purpose of Phase II testing and evaluation is to see if the archaeological site identified during the Phase I survey satisfies criteria for listing on the National Register of Historic Places. As will be recalled from section 2.2.3.2., those criteria consist essentially of two parts as far as archaeological sites are concerned (**36 CFR 60.4**): (1) the eligible site is associated with important persons; associated with important events; exemplifies well the craftsmanship of a master, or design of a period or craft; or contributes to the understanding of the period or culture represented; *and* (2) the eligible site has integrity. Phase II testing seeks answers to the following:

* Is the site associated with nationally, regionally, or locally important persons or events?

* Does the site exemplify well or even chronicle the work of a renown craftsman, or a particular form of landscaping, construction, or "building"?

* Does the site contain information that can contribute to the knowledge of the associated period or culture?

* Does the site have integrity, usually in the sense of depositional integrity?

* If there is a question about depositional integrity: Does the site at least have deposits that are equal or more intact than others known for the same kind of site?

* What are the spatial and temporal limits of the site?

Phase II testing is an evaluative step. Following from the Secretary of Interior's Guidelines for Evaluation [48 FR 44723], the results are meant to provide the review agencies with enough information to determine whether or not the site could be listed on the National Register, as well as the physical extent of that site. Phase II is concerned both with the nature of the site itself, as well as how that site might relate -- functionally and temporally -- to other sites in the region. It is analogous to abstracting a book. Thus, it can also yield substantive data in its own right, even if the site itself turns out not to be eligible for listing on the National Register.

It is well to repeat at this point that the professional archaeologist does not make *determination* of eligibility; rather the archaeologist assesses whether or not the site *satisfies* the criteria set for in **36 CFR 60.4**. Only the Lead agency can make what is called a determination. The archaeologist can state only that the site *appears* to satisfy or not satisfy the criteria for National Register-eligibility, then proceed, in the submitted report, to argue the case (see section 2.2.3.3).

Phase II is a testing exercise. When this testing involves excavation, only enough of the site will be dug to enable a determination to be made. The excavations may be done as small test units, exposing no more than 0.2 - 0.5 percent of the site area. They may be done as larger area tests, exposing more of the site but not as deeply. Or, the site may be plowed; a controlled surface collection done; and a small portion of that plowzone, stripped to expose and map features. On rare occasions, deep backhoe trenches will be dug, primarily to see if what might be occupation layers are deeply buried. The idea is to get just enough information on the site that its Register-eligibility can be determined.

How much and what kind of testing actually is done depends on a host of factors. These range from the suspected nature of the site and protocols in the given states, through funds available, to formalized agreements between the SHPO/THPO and the agency or client. The purpose of Phase II testing is to refine or clarify impressions of depositional integrity, cultural affiliation, vertical extent of the cultural deposit, and site function that came from the Phase I survey work. Phase I field work, especially when it involves shovel testing, often will yield enough information on a particular site for agency reviewers to confidently *exclude* from the need for the more comprehensive Phase II evaluation process. But in those situations where Phase I has located an archaeological site and preliminary indications cannot exclude the possibility that it might satisfy the quality of significance as defined by **36 CFR 60.4**, then more work will be needed. The idea of the Phase II testing step is to access just enough of the information content of the site to make a judgment about its contents. It would

be analogous to reading the back of a paperback book to determine the importance or relevance of what the book contains.

Phase II testing is similar to site testing in field manuals and archaeology texts. However, it differs in three ways:

(1) there will be a previous study, equivalent to a Phase I survey, indicating the general horizontal bounds of the site and general artifact distribution;

(2) a predetermined number of test units of a predetermined size will be excavated; and

(3) the goals of the testing are to refine earlier impressions of site contents as they would pertain to a nomination of the site to the National Register.

Site testing as performed in a university or museum environment either serves to abstract a previously reported site, as Phase II testing does; or it serves as a preliminary, exploratory step done immediately before full-scale excavation. The difference between academic and professional testing, then, is that third point: Phase II testing has specific questions relating to Register eligibility that need to be answered.

Phase II testing usually involves 1 x 1 m, 1 x 2 m, and rarely 2 x 2 m units. In parts of the country where plowing is common, controlled surface collections may be made and/or mechanical removal of parts of the plowzone may be done. Backhoe testing is occasionally used, especially in floodplain settings, although this helps only in locating/confirming deeply buried deposits and not so much with the contents of those deposits.

The depth of test units varies by several factors, including state requirements, agency protocols, nature of the deposit, and nature of the project and its possible effects. For example, 1 x 1 m units seldom can be excavated deeper than 1.0 m, simply because of the limitations imposed by the length of the shovel handle, which bangs into the unit walls when drawn back to remove fill. However, digging much deeper than 30 cm may be pointless if the site involves the backyard of a historic structure, since what will be of concern or interest may be the lay-out of garden beds and walkways, and the past presence of wells and outbuildings. The U.S. Army Corps of Engineers (COE), in some districts, requests testing to 2.0 m below the surface, which requires at least one horizontal dimension of the unit to be around 2 m for excavation by shovel. Beginning at 4.0 - 5.0 ft (1.2 m - 1.5 m), depending upon jurisdiction, state safety and OSHA (Occupational Safety and Health Administration) regulations require some kind of shoring of the walls; these are spelled out for example in the Corps of Engineers's *Safety and Health Requirements Manual* (the most recent edition can be viewed at http://www.hq.usace.army.mil/ceso/cesopub. htm). Thus, such units need to be able to accommodate shoring hardware.

In short, while many Phase II exercises involve small test units, any method is used that will answer the necessary questions regarding Register-eligibility with a minimum amount of damage to the site.

Phase II testing best assesses site depositional integrity; Phase I investigations normally can only tell, at best, if a site has been extensively disturbed. Thus, with the Phase II testing is the first opportunity to study the structure of an archaeological deposit, because a sizable profile or window on that deposit is opened. It is helpful to remember that archaeologists dig to answer questions: If the site is so limited and fragile that testing eradicates most or all of the deposit (called "testing out-of-existence"), then a good argument could be made that it did not possess the quality of significance as defined in **36 CFR 60.4**. None of the statutes treat this, but in effect, to be Register eligible implies that the site data are sufficiently robust and redundant to withstand Phase II testing.

6.2. Project Structure and Pre-field Preparation

6.2.1. Phase I Investigations and Recommendations

Phase II testing is initiated in response to one of two situations:

* A Phase I survey that identified an archaeological site of sufficient size, character, or depositional integrity that further examination was needed to see if it could be listed on the National Register; or

* The site already was known and, perhaps, listed or considered eligible for listing on the National Register, and the questions involve getting further details on the nature of the deposit in preparation for Phase III data recovery.

The vast majority of the cases will be where the site was first encountered during a Phase I survey. This means that the data and results from that Phase I report are critical to structuring the Phase II testing effort.

The Phase I report should have provided the following information:

* land-use history based upon current vegetation cover;

* history of the project area, especially in terms of potential disturbance, previously reported sites, and reported extent of those sites;

* nature of the soils as reported by the NRCS (Natural Resources Conservation Service) or equivalent agency, as well as how that report compares to what was encountered during shovel testing;

* if shovel testing had been done, a shovel test map showing which units contained what kinds of artifacts, sufficient for the person doing the Phase II project to construct an iso-frequency artifact contour map;

* a list of what artifacts were recovered, as well as where those artifacts are curated;

* a copy of the site form submitted to the state, along with site number;

* a clear statement about why the site could not be declared ineligible for listing on the National Register; and

* suggestions or recommendations for Phase II testing.

Phase II testing will be done on an archaeological site. This means that there has to be a site form, either submitted or already recorded by the state, for the site. By the time the Phase II testing is started, there should be a site number as well; that site number really should be assigned by the time that the final draft of the Phase I report is produced.

The Phase I report should provide detailed information on the project area -- vegetation, land-use history, soils -- along with a general overview of the history and prehistory of the area. It also should provide a very good map of the horizontal distribution of archaeological materials as well as sufficient information for the Phase II archaeologist to relocate any subsurface testing or surface artifact concentrations.

The Phase I report will also explain why it is that the site appears to warrant further testing. It may be due to the nature of the material found or the density of that material. Or perhaps it was because the site was associated with some important event or person, making the question of if more information is contained in the deposit a good one to have answered; battlefields and related troop movements would be an example. It is even possible that Phase I background research indicated the presence of excellent examples of landscaping; Phase II testing may well be able to answer if signs of planting beds and paths remain.

In situations where Phase II testing is recommended, the Phase I report will also provide some suggestions about how that Phase II testing might be done, as well as what questions, exactly, need to be answered.

6.2.2. Research and Sampling Strategies

In many cases, Phase I investigations will have established horizontal site limits for cultural deposits within about 40 cm of the surface and given some sense of site depositional integrity, land-use history, and cultural contents. Phase II testing continues this investigative trajectory by expanding on the Phase I results. Phase II testing examines more of the deposit, be it area or depth as the site warrants. Phase II testing has a greater chance of exposing features, which means a greater chance of finding diagnostic artifacts in association.

Phase II testing is, in many ways, not unlike much of the cultural-historical archaeology done in the United States prior to the 1960s. That is, the issue is to see what range of materials the site might contain, how abundant those materials might be, what their cultural and temporal affiliations are, and how intact the deposit is. The sampling strategy is one of locating then exploring what appear to be the richer or more artifact-ladened parts of the site, in part because these will be more likely to contain the temporal/cultural diagnostic artifacts needed.

The Phase II sampling strategy normally is built upon the Phase I results. This requires an awareness of the limitations of Phase I investigations. In the eastern and midwestern United States, Phase I subsurface sampling normally examines the first 40 cm below the surface, depending upon the jurisdiction and protocol. It may have been a surface collection of a plowed field; it often will be the results from a shovel testing regime. In the western United States, subsurface testing during Phase I probably was not done. The presence of a site would have been indicated by artifacts or land features visible on the surface. In both case, then, the physical sample comes from relatively near if not on the surface.

Archaeological sites over most of the United States can be divided into two sets:

(1) sites located in aggrading settings; and

(2) sites located in non-aggrading or even deflating settings.

Both surface survey and shovel testing often will work to delimit archaeological sites in non-aggrading settings. Not always, of course, since areas with well-developed soils (meaning deep solums) may have prehistoric materials that, over a few millennia, have sunk deeper than plowing or shovel testing normally

reach (see also section 5.3.1.3). But most of the time, Register-eligible sites in non-aggrading settings will be identified, especially if shovel testing is used and the site has a reasonable density of material remains.

Sites in aggrading settings are less likely to be encountered by shovel testing. Most settings involve floodplains, although locations susceptible to colluviation -- slope wash, in a phrase -- also qualify. Although this varies by how deep state protocol require shovel tests to go (see Table 5.4), shovel testing or plowing often only identify any occupations since the last 30 or 40 cm of sediment was deposited (it will even identify the material transported *in* that 30 - 40 cm of deposited sediment; see below "*We learned about archaeology from that ...* Secondary Deposition at Cowanesque"). It normally will identify no more. This influences sampling at the Phase II level, as well and decisions involving how to spend testing volume.

Phase II activities involving digging really are activities that have a given amount of *volume* for the archaeologist to spend. That volume can be placed in test units that have small areas but are deep, or that volume can be placed in test units that have large areas but are shallow. It can even involve plowing then mechanical removal of some of that plowed area. The decision will need to be based upon the Phase I survey results, but also upon the alluvial/colluvial possibilities of the setting as well as what is known for other sites in the region.

In situations where Phase I investigations encountered archaeological materials, Phase II test units should be placed in areas that have higher-than-average artifact concentrations or higher-than-average concentrations of certain culture indicators. This procedure, by the way, corresponds to a normative-culture approach attacked by the New Archeology during the Methodological Debate in the 1960s and 1970s.

There are two reasons for locating test units in areas with high artifact concentrations. The first is to get a sound idea of the potential range of artifact contents in the site while disturbing as little of the site as possible. The second reason is that areas of high artifact concentrations often are associated with heavily used areas of an archaeological site, and often those areas also contain features. Features -- those non-portable human alterations of the site fabric -- show site depositional integrity while also serving as repositories of wide assortments of data that presumably all belong together: That is, features have very high behavioral-information contents. It is not that one wants to find features because they will have a lot of neat things in them as it is to learn if features still survive at the site.

Phase II is not meant to be an excavation of a site in the sense of getting a complete understanding of the site; Phase II is a testing exercise. If the issue was to learn as much as possible about the site at this stage, then a probabilistic sampling strategy probably would be a good strategy, although that would depend upon knowing that the deposit for which bounds were set during Phase I reasonably approximate what is being sampled during Phase II. And having the money to do it.[1]

For prehistoric sites, a common indicator for the presence of features is fire-cracked rock. If Phase I testing indicated a confined area in which fire-cracked rock was located or higher than average, such an area would benefit from testing. This is because there is a correlation between fire-cracked rock and features; where there is fire-cracked rock, it is possible that there are features. The reason for examining such an area is not necessarily to find features; rather, it is to see if features survive at the site. The issue is site depositional integrity. All issues in archaeological resources work involve issues of site depositional integrity.

For historic sites, the range of indicators for features is greater. For example, signs of structures include remains associated with buildings, such as daub, plaster, nails, mortared brick, tiles, roofing nails or slate fragments, and plate/window glass (however, see Chapter 5 *"We learned about archaeology from that ... The Manure Spreader Example"*).

In situations where the site is located in an aggrading setting, the Phase I examination more than likely encountered the shallowest cultural deposits. It may or may not be true that deeper cultural materials exist. The only ways to find this out will be either to dig or to use some form of remote sensing to identify features. Even then, though, sooner or later some kind of physical verification of the remote sensing results probably will be needed, which will mean

digging through a reasonable volume of the deposit's matrix.

It is important to remember that Phase II testing has goals different than the excavation of the site. Phase II testing serves to see if a site has depositional integrity and, most often, if the site has data potential. Phase II testing is not meant to replace data recovery. Thus, sampling is entirely different than with a Phase III data recovery exercise. This is where an approach technically identical to that of a normative-culture, cultural-historical approach is the one that works best. The question is one of what might be or possibly is present, not what is -- plus-or-minus -- present.

While a probabilistic sampling strategy is possible in non-aggrading settings, where the Phase I survey may well have provided a reasonably well-defined border for the site, it is far less likely to get back the kind of information needed to address Phase II issues. More often, only part of a site will be in the project area, be it a tract of land or some kind of project corridor. But all of this is more of a situation-by-situation issue.

The sampling strategy will be built on Phase I results. Usually, the Phase I survey will have involved shovel tests. The Phase I report should include a map showing the distribution of those shovel tests as well as which shovel tests contained materials. The Phase I report may or may not have presented the testing results as artifact iso-frequency plots; in any event, the Phase II archaeologist will need to have such a plot (see Figure 5.18).

6.2.3. Site and Region Documentation

Phase II testing is initiated because a site has been located, and Phase I examination was insufficient to answer the question of if the site should be excluded from the National Register. Part of the Phase II process, like the Phase I process, will require review of what already is known, archaeologically, about the site and the region that it is in. This will require examining the state site files.

The process here is similar to that outlined in Chapter 5, section 5.2.1. for Phase I background documentation. As with Phase I site and regional documentation, Phase II background work will include accessing state site files, then constructing a list of sites and site features located within a given distance of the Phase II site. That information will include:

*   site number (and name, if any);

*   cultural historical affiliation;

*   associated reports/publications; and

*   National Register-eligibility.

---

1. Anything that increases what is known about any subject -- including what might be known about an archaeological site -- has a commensurate energy cost. This is basic Information Theory: Increases in organization -- and knowing about something in greater detail than it is known now is just that -- have corresponding increased energy costs. Increased energy costs are directly proportional to increased fiscal costs. Probabilistic samples provide a great deal of new information, but are also more expensive than non-probabilistic samples. One needs always to determine if the additional information is worth the cost, and to be aware that any request for additional information must, according to basic physics, require an increased expenditure in resources to get that information. This is one of the applications of physics to basic business practices. The earliest treatment of information and cost was: Shannon, Claude E. 1951. Predication and entropy of printed English. *Bell System Technical Journal* 30:50-64. For discussion of relationship to knowledge in the colloquial sense, see Tribus, Myron, and E.C. McIrvine. 1971. Energy and information. *Scientific American* 225 (2):179-188; Costanza, Robert. 1980. Embodied energy and economic valuation. *Science* 210:1219-1224; and Neumann, Thomas W. 1998. Early Holocene climatic warming and the energetics of culture change: The ecology of Early - Middle Archaic transitions in Georgia and South Carolina. *Journal of Middle Atlantic Archaeology* 14:65-93.

The Logic Behind Digging the Richest Part of the Site

Phase II sampling, with its focus on digging in the most artifact-rich part of a site, is similar to the way excavation units were placed prior to the Methodological Debate and emergence of the New Archeology in the 1960s. The logic behind this kind of judgmental sampling differs, but the procedure appears the same. It does not hurt to explain what that pre-1960s logic was, and to summarize the objections.

Archaeology's Great Methodological Debate, which began in 1962 and remained a major issue into the early 1980s, was concerned with how best to do diachronic anthropology. Part of the issue involved how to structure research questions ("methodology" in the strict sense); part of the issue involved examining why what currently was done was not the best way to do diachronic anthropology.

There is a huge literature on the Methodological Debate just as there is of that Debate. With and from it emerged the New Archeology. It is important in understanding professional archaeology, how it is done, and why it sometimes is denigrated by the academic community.

The core of the Methodological Debate grew out of the Willey and Philip's (1958:2) paraphrase of Maitland's remark that "archaeology is anthropology or it is nothing." Examination of archaeological research indicated that, progressively since the turn of the century, archaeologists had become less and less concerned about using archaeological data to talk about how people had lived in the past, and had instead become more and more caught up in talking about the artifacts themselves. That is, a report on a large prehistoric village site would in effect be a long and torturously dull explication of the myriad of subtleties to be found in different styles of broken pots. There would be little in the way of discussion about how it is the people themselves lived, what they might have been doing, and why they should have had all of those pots anyway. Reports did not speak of people, or of one generation melding into the next; rather, they talked of one kind of pottery type being replaced by another, of differences in surface treatment and

decoration and temper and so on. The issue was artifacts. And this appeared – and was, albeit not thought so by those doing it – to be missing the point of archaeology-as-anthropology.

Part of the field methods of that earlier approach involved digging the part of the site that was most likely to yield an abundance of artifacts. Or digging sites that would do that, such as burial or mound sites. This excavation tactic became in the Methodological Debate synonymous with the kind of artifact-rich/behavior-poor archaeological research that was just the thing that should not be done. And since the Methodological Debate was not just a debate but a rhetorical campaign waged to win the hearts and minds of the research community, such an artifact-focused excavation tactic was held up as a sign that the person involved was not doing true, anthropologically oriented archaeological research. This new archaeology was called, imaginatively, the New Archeology. From it would come the archaeology that is done today in both the professional and academic sectors.

In point of fact, there was a theoretical logic to digging the richest part of the archaeological site, and it probably does not hurt to mention it now.

The core concept of Anthropology is "culture." Culture generally is seen to be a mental set of standards, shared with other members of the culture, for how to live and understand the workings of the world. It serves as a behavioral adaptation for a given human population. The idea of a multiplicity of cultures, each representing the way in which a people go about living their lives, was the result really of Franz Boas and his students. That idea of culture dates from around 1916. From around then forward, culture was seen to be entirely mental in nature; that is, it was a shared pattern of beliefs, of customs. It is what was held in common with others; in fact, it was what was shared, the norms of the culture. Not surprisingly, this view was called the *Normative View* of culture.

It is very important that two other sets of information be obtained:

*   depth and nature of deposit of sites of similar cultural-historic type and physical geographical setting within that same range; and

*   nature of surviving features and other cultural contents for those similar sites.

The site file review, as well as the other background research, is meant to do two things. The first is to provide the project manager with detailed information about what the deposit itself might be like: What should be expected? What have others encountered in the past? What should be planned for?

The second thing that the background research needs to work out is what already is known. Phase II testing

is meant to yield the information to decide whether or not the site should be listed on the National Register. This is to some extent a comparative decision, and the comparison is with what is already known. The site files hopefully will have that information. Remember that comparative "what is known" normally will be on a state-by-state basis, since the archaeological sites are considered resources at a state (less often local government) level. That is, while the Olsen-Chubbuck Site (Wheat 1972) may be the grandest discussion and exposition on a late Paleoindian bison kill, that does not mean that a site like it in Nebraska also would not merit listing on the National Register for Nebraska. Or the Itasca Bison-Kill Site for Minnesota (Shay 1971).

An ethnographer or archaeologist did not study culture; direct observation of that mental template of beliefs and values of course was impossible. Rather, they studied the cultura*l* behavior, the products of that culture. The nature of the culture itself was then inferred.

Since culture was a shared mental template, it stood to reason that one well-informed person could tell an ethnographer a lot, and that informant's account could then be built upon by other accounts. For ethnographers, that led to the idea of cultivating one or a few main informants, individuals who had a vast and detailed understanding of their culture. For archaeologists, it meant gathering as much as possible of the widest variety of cultural debris.

Artifacts were the products of cultural behavior. Thus, artifacts reflected, second-hand, ideas or parts of the culture that were present in the maker's mind. Like the Neo-Kantian Movement that molded Boas's ideas of culture (and gave rise to the idea of cultural relativity and, in its present form, ethnic or multi-cultural sensitivity), objects represented mental images, ideas, or metal templates of their makers. They were the shadows on the back wall of the cave.

The more artifacts, and the greater the variety among them from a single site, then the wider the range and better the approximation of that mental template that could be made. It was sort of like collecting vocabulary: The greater the list, the closer one came to having the language. (Later, to continue the analogy, the New Archeology would argue that it is just as important to know how that language is put together; having only a vocabulary does not tell about syntax nor enable communication.)

This approach led to a focus on the prehistoric burial mounds in the eastern United States. It also led to the inventorying of site contents – called *trait lists* – that would prove diagnostic of a given culture. That is, the more traits held in common by two sites, the more likely it was that they shared enough of the same ideas to represent a related

or the same culture. Thus, a trait list – a presence-absence inventory of artifacts from a site – would be diagnostic of a given culture. These trait lists drew on the inspiration of the ethnographic trait lists Kroeber – Boas's first student – was having *his* students, like Phil Drucker on the West Coast or Harold Driver in the Southwest, do.

There was an added advantage of trait lists: They could be used to compare sites temporally and culturally. That is, if the two vocabulary lists are similar, then the language and probably the culture were the same, or shared a common origin.

What happened from that – an increasing focus on the things that made up those artifact inventories, and how those artifacts themselves changed over time or space – perhaps was to be expected. In any case, by the mid-1960s that digression was called to task. And the digging of the richest part of a site, as opposed to taking a statistically representative sample from the site, became synonymous with non-scientific, non-anthropological archaeology. Since Phase II testing often involves locating and examining the areas of a site with the highest concentration of artifacts, it has been viewed by many academic archaeologists as a return to that pre-Methodological Debate era.

Phase II testing now is an assessment of what the site potentially may contain, at its maximum. It also is seen to be the first of a two-step process to learn if the site – or portion of the site – actually needs to be fully excavated. It will be that third step – Phase III data recovery or mitigation – that will build on the information provided by Phase II testing to know how to best allocate excavation resources both to reassemble what took place on the site, or the portion threatened.

Willey, Gordon R., and Philip Phillips. 1958. *Method and Theory in American Archaeology*. University of Chicago Press, Chicago.

6.2.4. Contacts, Public Relations

Phase II testing involves a greater amount of excavation than Phase I survey work; it tends to open larger areas and to go deeper. As with Phase I work, Phase II testing requires two sets of people to be contacted prior to field work: landowners and utilities.

Phase II testing can be extensive and disruptive: While some people may have little trouble with the thought of a 1 x 1 m unit being placed in their yards, they often will be uneasy when they actually see the size of the associated backdirt pile. In situations where a farm field will be examined, the farmer may be very concerned that testing activities will destroy crops or endanger livestock.

Contacting landowners becomes a three-step process for Phase II:

* actually contacting and speaking face-to-face with both the landowner and whoever is resident on the property;

* a clear explanation about what it is that will be done, the extent of disruption, and how long that condition will last; and

* a clear explanation of what will be done to restore the land back to its original condition and, in farm field situations, compensate for damages.

In Phase II situations where the client is seeking to develop property, the client already is aware -- or

We learned about archaeology from that ... Random Sampling, Target Populations, and Sampled Populations.

We were once asked to complete the Phase II testing on a project in Pennsylvania that was already scheduled to go to Phase III. Phase III was to include stripping of the plowzone. A university field program had done the Phase I survey; a second firm then had been brought in to provide an "intensive survey/testing program." This was a Phase II testing regime, the SOW calling for 55 1 x 1 m test units. The SOW, developed by the SHPO, also had required that those units be distributed as a nested random sample.

Twenty-three of the test units were excavated within the 1,725 m² of the site, and encountered four prehistoric features. Our responsibility was to finish the Phase II testing by raising the final random sample to 3.0 percent, since part of the research was meant to test the usefulness of a hierarchical or nested random sampling strategy, proposed by a University of Pittsburgh student to assist cultural resources work (Drennan 1987).

Although the sampling program had not been completed, the previous firm still could use the results of the sample to predict what would be encountered when plowzone was stripped during Phase III. Since four of the 23 test units (17.4 percent) contained prehistoric features, it was argued that 293 of the total of 1,725 (17.0 percent) 1 x 1 m units possible at the site would contain features. Further, since the features identified were estimated to extend into an average of 5.5 1 x 1 m units per feature, it was predicted that 53 prehistoric features (293 units/5.5 units per feature) would be found at the site. However, later, when the plowzone was removed during Phase III, only 12 prehistoric features were found. The SHPO was outraged, arguing that the Phase III was fundamentally flawed. What happened?

The difference between what was predicted and what was encountered was due to confusion between target populations and sampled populations. A *target population* is the set of things or the topic about which more information is desired. The target population for the SHPO as well as for the firm testing the site was features: How many features were present at the site, given the sampling done to date? The target population, though, was not the population that being sampled. A *sampled population* refers to what the sampling program actually samples, regardless of what the investigator intends to sample. The Phase II sampled population was not the number of features; rather, it was the amount of *feature area exposed* by test units.

There were some other problems with field interpretation that are incidental to the point here. The upshot, though, was that in the area where the previous firm had finished the 3.0 percent random sample, testing had exposed 0.20m² of feature *area*, suggesting that perhaps 6.67m² of feature area (33.3 x 0.20) would be exposed when the plowzone was removed. In another part of the site, where only a 2.0 percent random sample had been taken and 0.18m² of feature area was exposed, there should be another 9.00 m² of feature area (50.0 x 0.18) would be exposed when the plowzone was stripped during Phase III. In the end, the sample would have predicted not 23 features (the target population), but the presence of around 15.67m² of feature area to be present (the sampled population).

Phase III stripping of around 1,550m² exposed 14.32m² of feature area; monitoring during construction clearance identified another 1.57m² between two more features. That is, the predicted feature presence was around 15.67m², the observed was around 15.89m².

Pretty close, right? No, just very lucky. The results mollified the SHPO, which was legitimately upset anyway because of serious field management problems, and therefore understandably skeptical of any research results. However, the larger issue of sampling error was avoided.

The original sample consisted of 23 units over 1,725² of site area, roughly a 1.3 percent sample. (Actually, because it was a nested or hierarchial sampling design, part was sampled at 3.0 percent, part at 2.0 percent, and part at 1.0 percent; we were brought in in part to get the entire sample up to the desired 3.0 percent.) A sample of 23 is too small to be meaningful; even a sample of 55 is way too small. The 95 percent confidence interval on a sample of 55 units is around 26 percent. This means that if a 55-unit sample was repeated across the site 100 times, the results in 95 of those test runs would vary plus or minus 26 percent (15.67 ± 4.07m² for the feature areas in this case). Just because 3.0 percent of the site was sampled did not mean that one could multiply the results by 33.3 to arrive at what the entire site contained.

The core lessons here are to be aware of what it is that is sampled when a probabilistic sample is done and to make sure that the error rate for the sample size is known.

See also

Anderson, T.W. 1984. *Introduction to Statistical Multivariate Analysis*. Second edition. Wiley, New York.

Drennan, Robert D. 1987. Sampling to estimate whether in situ features are present. Ms. on file at the Cultural Resource Management Program, University of Pittsburgh.

Hamburg, Morris. 1970. *Statistical Analysis for Decision Making*. Harcourt, Brace, & World, New York.

should be -- of what the Phase II work will involve. In situations where private property is involved in a project corridor or area due to government undertaking (such as a highway corridor or flood

control project), the people whose property may be involved may not be aware of what is going on. It is the client's responsibility to obtain written permission from the landowners (called "right-of-entry forms") to allow archaeological work to be done. The archaeologist should have copies of those completed forms, as well as the names of owners and locations of their property.

Before any Phase II field work is done, the professional archaeologist should contact the property owner and discuss what is going to happen. This normally requires phoning ahead to set up a meeting time, then driving out to the landowner and spending time -- at their pace and sensitive to their schedule -- making sure that everything is still okay and explaining what is involved in Phase II testing on their land.

How all of this is done will vary by the part of the country, or even part of the landscape, one is in. In an urban residential area it may be strictly fact-related and rather straight forward; in a rural area it may involve time getting acquainted and asking after community matters.

In speaking with the landowner or resident, it is important as well to ask about any archaeological collections that they may have from the site area, or any previous knowledge that they may have about land use. Contacting the resident or owner is an interview opportunity, and it should be used to fill in more about the site area. For farms and for lots with substantial gardens, it is possible that the household has artifact collections from their property. These should be examined, both for their own value and also because, if the people have bothered to gather and curate them, they are important to the people themselves. The collection may be sufficient in size to warrant a separately scheduled trip to document the material.

Landowners need as well to be asked about past buildings, gardens, and other land-altering activities. This holds particularly for questions in rural and suburban areas: locations of sewer lines, of septic field lines and tanks, and of field tile systems. In floodplain areas, questions about floods and flood deposition should be asked. It is not at all unusual for farm fields to accumulate half a meter of sediment during a single flood event.

The major concerns of the landowner and resident will be what is going to happen, and what provisions have been made to put things back they way they are now. The kind of work that is going to be done needs to be explained clearly: the size of the hole that will be dug, any screening that will be done, the size of the backdirt pile that will form. If the utilities will be contacted to check for locations of subsurface pipes and lines (see below), then that needs to be mentioned along with explaining that those utilities may well spray paint lines across the lawn. Remember, too, to explain what will be happening to any artifacts recovered, again just to make sure that there is no miscommunication. The owner or resident needs to

Tip: Face-to-Face Contact

Usually it will be the field director or project manager who will be contacting the landowners or the resident. Although there are some differences around the country – and one needs to be sensitive to those differences – it is generally important, when the door is answered, that the archaeologist identifies himself or herself and extends his or her hand, especially if the person has already been spoken with on the phone. Shaking hands is very important in the extra-academic world, and is something that, in our experience, is hesitantly done in academic settings. Equally important is to be sensitive to appearances: One should not be contacting property owners for the first time after having spent the morning mucking about sweatily in the fill. In the United States, one's appearance always indicates one's sense of respect for another. This does not mean being overly dressed – an equally idiotic thing to do – but does mean being clean and presentable.

Remember, too, to make sure that a business card is given to the person. It should have the archaeologist's name on it, the name of the firm, and in addition to the firm's phone number, a local contact number where the project director can be reached should be penciled in. (By the way, since many states require educational outreach as part of the compliance project, this is a great time to do some of that.)

be aware of the time of day that the field crew will show up, and generally when they will leave. All of these things are basic courtesies.

Equally important is to reassure the owner or resident how the land will be restored, and what to expect as it goes back to normal. Phase II test units can generate a substantial amount of backdirt, at least when viewed on an in-town residential lot 50 feet wide. It needs to be explained that there will be a small mound over the test unit, and that it will take a given amount of time for that mound to settle. It is not a bad idea to have documented the subsidence of other backfilled units, and to bring photographs along to show what happens as well as how long it takes.

Sometimes firms working in urban and suburban areas will retain local landscaping firms as part of the project. If that will be the case, then the name and contact number of that firm need to be provided, while it is explained that all landscape-restoration costs will be covered.

Phase II testing on cultivated fields and in pastures presents additional problems. Working in cultivated fields may result in damages to standing crops. While care always should be taken in a cropped field, it is inevitable that crops will be lost, usually over an area about three times that of the test unit itself. The owner or resident needs to be told that crop damages will be compensated, as well as how that compensation will be computed.

Some Federal agencies set the rate for reimbursing crop damages as the market price of the crop itself. The professional archaeologist needs to be aware that that rate may be considered unfair by the farmer because the farmer uses the crop differently. For example, years ago we did a project for the Corps of Engineers that resulted in damages to feed corn (maize). The COE District's policy was to compute average yield per acre, then reimburse at the going rate for a bushel of corn. The problem was that the farmer used not just the ear of corn, but the entire plant, since it served as feed and silage. A fairer rate would have been three times the COE District's rate. The farmer was irritated, and felt frustrated and powerless. And since it was during a couple-year span when silage and winter feed were short, the entire crop damage situation was viewed as threatening. The amount of damage probably was not all that much, but that was not the issue. The farmer felt bullied.

Pasture situations will require reassuring the farmer that the test units will be fenced off. Cattle are notoriously curious but not intellectually gifted; the last thing anyone wants is for the crew to come out of a morning to find that a prime dairy cow had somehow fallen into the test unit late the previous afternoon.[2]

The first set of people to contact are landowners and land residents. The second set of people to contact are local utilities. This is more an issue in urban and suburban areas, and along highway corridor right-of-ways, than it is on farm land.

Phase II testing tends to go much deeper than Phase I shovel tests; the potential to cause damage is much greater. Most states have clearinghouses where the person planning to dig -- contractor, archaeologist, whoever -- can or even must call. The clearinghouse then contacts the various utilities, and crews will be dispatched to mark the locations of any underground service lines in the project area. For example, in Pennsylvania, there is the *Pennsylvania One Call System, Inc.*, where with one call all of the utilities possibly involved can be contacted to see if there will be a problem. Such clearance is required by Pennsylvania law; Pennsylvania Act 172 of 1986 requires three working-days notice. Many other states have similar requirements; it is the professional archaeologist's responsibility to check about this.

---

2. One of the best stories we have heard that illustrates problems with cattle is told by a person who was doing Phase II and Phase III work along the Ohio River on behalf of the Corps of Engineers - Louisville District. Evidently deep backhoe trenches were being dug, with the far end taken down a couple meters, but with the floor sloping back up to grade. The testing was in a pasture. One morning, the crew arrived to find a cow in the trench. At the deepest end. Facing the wall. It evidently had spent the evening relieving itself as well. Livestock have not been bred for wits; the concept of backing up is not something that occurs to the standard-issue cow.

6.2.5. Labor Estimates

Labor estimates for the Phase II project will have been made at the time the proposal was developed for the client. Those estimates will have been based upon the firm's previous experience with such projects and will be structured in a way that is both competitive and realistic. Should the project be awarded to the firm, the labor estimates used for the proposal budget will become the actual labor available for the project.

Phase II testing projects have the same five broad budget categories found for Phase I projects:

1. start-up;

2. field work;

3. analysis;

4. draft report preparation and delivery; and

5. final report delivery and turn-over.

As explained in Chapter 3 and again in Chapter 5, each of those five budget sets involve three variables: the level or pay grade of assigned personnel, the number of hours needed by an individual to complete his or her part of the task, and the hourly pay rate for those personnel relative to that number of hours. While computing a budget for bid eventually will involve all three, for execution of the project is really becomes a matter of who will be doing the work and how much time they will have to do it.

"Start-up" refers to what is done to prepare to go into the field. This will require assembling equipment and supplies; it also will require scheduling or arranging any power equipment, land-survey and/or mapping equipment, and possibly billeting. A health and safety plan specific to the site will be prepared, and a site safety officer will be designated. Phase II may well require an extended field stay far from the home office, and arrangements may be needed for where the crew will stay.

Start-up for a Phase II project will also require preparatory work at the office for where the site is located, how to go about re-establishing Phase I survey transects (if a Phase I had been done), and requesting or securing a copy of the county's soil survey report.

Personnel involved in the start-up phase of the project will be the project manager, a crew chief or similar senior field person, and possibly a field technician or the secretarial staff. Making arrangements for equipment will be done more often by the project manager, who may also find it advisable to go to the community at least once to make sure that things are properly arranged, local government contacts are established, and the property owner or tenant has been briefed about the pending work.

Excluding trips into the field to make arrangements, the start-up aspect for most Phase II projects will be on the order of two person-days for each of the three individuals listed.

By the time the start-up portion of the project is done,

(1) all of the equipment should be secured and in the field vehicle;

(2) contacts and other arrangements will have been made with the local community, including at least locating a subcontractor for heavy equipment and landscaping if the SOW requires these; and

(3) the site will be located.

"Field work" estimates do vary by the region of the country and the type of site. Most firms will have maintained the equivalent of time-motion studies that allow accurate bidding on Phase II projects. Personnel at this stage in the project will include the core field work team -- the project manager, a crew chief or field supervisor, and field archaeologists -- along with others hired for specialized work, such as backhoe operators or geomorphologists.

There are several factors that will influence field work labor estimates, including:

* if mapping is needed and the nature of the land relative to any mapping;

* the number of test units or size of the field to be collected;

* how deep the test units are to be dug;

* how heavy the soil and what the screen size requirement is;

* the type of site and the abundance of artifacts -- and kinds of artifacts -- located on it or in it;

* density and nature of any features that may be present; and

* weather.[3]

Labor estimates for mapping depend upon the characteristics of the site, the kind of equipment used, and field conditions. Using an optical transit, two people can secure around 90 readings in a day in an open setting. Using a total station instrument, the same amount of work can be done in about half the time.

For standard test units where the fill is screened through 1/4-inch (0.635 cm) mesh, a fair estimate for labor will be around 1.3 - 2.0 person-days per cubic meter, but again such a figure will fluctuate depending upon the nature of the soil (indurated soils, for example, may well triple the amount of time needed), site, and weather conditions. We have found that that number is a good place to start for most areas in the eastern United States, and we have then proceeded to modify it depending upon possible field conditions. For example, we found treating a historic site in Maryland that 5.0 person-days was needed to excavate and process a cubic meter of test unit fill, but that project was complicated by extraneous factors independent of the deposit. And in one particularly appalling Phase II project, done during the winter in compacted soil on a prehistoric site, 4.9 person-days were needed per cubic meter of fill.

Labor estimates for controlled surface collections will depend upon the collection method used and the abundance of artifacts present to be collected. Most of the labor involved will be either in setting out control points for the collection, or in picking stuff up from the surface. We have found that a controlled surface collection with 20 x 20 m collection areas where the collection area corners are triangulated in will require up to one person-day labor for every 0.25 ha of collection area (see also Table 5.1). As with test units, such numbers will vary by region, site type, and other variables. The number, though, should give some sense of scale for the work involved.

By the time the field work is completed, there should be a project grid map showing the locations of the test units or surface collection areas relative to a datum or similar benchmark, a project binder containing unit-level forms and feature forms for all units and features, and a backfilled or otherwise restored landscape.

Labor estimates for "Analyses" vary by region, type of site, SOW and SHPO/THPO or equivalent agency

---

3. It is worthwhile noting that most firms will perform field work under most field conditions, and will simply try to adjust work to off-set the weather. Cold is a problem, but many firms will continue working through sub-zero (Fahrenheit) conditions, either thawing the ground on an as-needed basis or keeping it thawed with some kind of unit-specific shelter. Snow rarely is a problem if the air is cold, since it behaves more like dust that can be blown off of notes. Extreme heat hampers field work in part because of the associated heat stress, but also because the ground will be baked

and difficult to dig or screen. Few will work in sustained rain, and that really is the only across-the-board situation we know where field work will be postponed. Even then, we have run a number of Phase II projects in substantial, non-nonsense, torrential, unrelenting Nor'easter rains that lasted for *days*: The water actually helped in the screening; we worked out a way to keep most of the water out of the unit when digging was not being done; and notes were kept in the field vehicle. Professional archaeology is also a business for many, and is part of a greater business-development processes. Weather is something that is worked around.

requirements for labeling and curating, and specialized analyses. Estimates we have seen have allowed a person-hour of analysis time for every 2.0 - 3.0 person-hours of field time. But that is very rough and is only meant to give a sense of scale.

In most cases, the budget will have three pay grades assigned to the analysis step: the project manager, doubling as the project's generalist analytical expert; the laboratory director; and a laboratory technician, who may be a full-time lab person or just as likely one of the people who had been working in the field. The project manager and the laboratory director will have a reasonably good sense of how much effort will be needed to do the analyses required of the SOW. There may be a considerable amount of time expended by laboratory technicians cleaning, labeling, and cataloguing artifacts.[4]

Specialists will have their own time scales and estimates, which will have been worked into the budget either as a line-item cost estimate or converted for the sake of the bid into some kind of hourly rate.

The analysis step is meant to provide all of the basic measurements and descriptions of artifacts and of the deposit. It is labor intensive, as the numbers suggest and as Information Theory would predict: Information in the strict sense of the term is being produced, and the more information desired, the greater the effort required. The analyses themselves will generally be at the level one would expect of a graduate thesis: the full range of descriptive measurements; low-magnification examination of prehistoric flakes for microliths; use-wear analyses; typological classification of diagnostics, including all of the subtle variations in colored glass and glazed ceramics; and even flotation processing if the SOW so requested.

By the time this step is finished, the artifacts should be labeled and bagged, and there should be a detailed artifact inventory available. All measurements, weights, counts, and typological decisions should have been made. The artifacts themselves should be at the point where they are in acid-free boxes and are ready for turn-over to a curatorial facility.

The fourth step in the Phase II project involves assembling then delivering the draft report. This will involve four basic tasks:

* background literature research and report writing;

* figure/illustration preparation;

* report production; and

* physical delivery of the draft report.

Most of the work on the text and tables of the report will be done by the project manager. The amount of time needed for this varies greatly by the nature and scale of the project. Writing the report will also include the data analyses themselves, meaning the assessment, interpretation, and syllogistic application of the analytical data. Any statistical tests will be done by the project manager at this point; most tables will be compiled at this time as well.

Figure and illustration preparation will have been underway, since things like the site location map, perhaps the site and project maps, and unit profiles, all could have been started as soon as the people returned from the field. Artifact photographs also will be taken at this time. The basic rule is to photograph at least examples of all diagnostics. Most firms allow the graphics department three person-hours per illustration.

Report production represents a desk-top publishing exercise. The amount of time will depend upon the complexity of the report, and may involve the project manager along with someone from graphics and someone from the secretarial staff. Some firms maintain a permanent desk-top publishing person, assigned either to graphics or to a general administrative staff, who will merge texts and illustrations and assemble the document. Other firms will leave this process up to the project manager and whoever has been delegated to assist in the process.

The final product will be a bound report, usually in an 8½ x 11 inch format, that runs around 50 - 100 pages (not infrequently well over 200 pages) single-spaced with 10- to 12-point type. The document will be produced as a hard copy, even if submission can be done electronically. The report really represents a condensed and elaborated set of field notes and analysis notes for the site. In effect, the report will become a curated part of the collection for the site; for Section 106 projects, **36 CFR 79** *requires* the final report to be a curated part of the collection.

The final step in the Phase II project will be production of the final report and the turn-over of artifacts, field notes, and analysis notes. Usually the review agencies will have comments on the report, and will request that those comments be "addressed" in the final report. Sometimes these are cosmetic; sometimes they are extensive. The project budget usually allows about one or two person-days for each of a secretary and the project manager to deal with these things. Turn-over will include submission of the final report

---

4. It depends upon the agency, the SHPO/THPO, the eventual curatorial facility, and the firm's practices, but often all diagnostic artifacts will be labeled individually, while some percentage of non-diagnostics will be labeled for each unit-level artifact class. For example, all projectile points from a prehistoric deposit will be labeled, but perhaps only one in 10 of the unmodified flakes will be the labeled. Those will be mixed in with the unlabeled flakes in the bag used to curate the material, along with a labeled piece of acid-free paper. See also Chapter 8.

(sometimes with multiple copies, as specified in the SOW), as well as some deposition of the artifacts and project notes. That turn-over of collection material may be to the agency or to an approved curatorial facility. It should be noted that, in most states, the artifacts are the property of the client and/or the landowner, as they are under Section 106 [see **36 CFR 79.3(a)(1)**]. More often than not, they are more than happy to get rid of the stuff.

6.2.6. Staffing Needs

Just as with Phase I projects, Phase II staffing will require both field and non-field personnel. In larger firms, in-house staff may be available for all tasks; in smaller firms, individuals may be required to perform a series of tasks. Generally, though, the broader the archaeologist's expertise, the more roles he or she can play in the Phase II process. "Adaptivity" in the private sector corresponds to being an "expert generalist," and that holds for large as well as small firms.

Phase II needs require a wide range of skills, but rarely come with a budget equal to buy those skills. The goals of the exercise as well as the professional requirements -- satisfy questions of Register-eligibility on one hand but provide a sound analysis of an archaeological deposit on the other -- result in needing people with a tremendous breadth of archaeological expertise.

Staffing needs correspond to the task needs outlined in section 6.2.5.:

* personnel able to handle logistical support, including start-up aspects of the project;

* personnel who can do the field work needed;

* personnel who can do the laboratory analyses required; and

* personnel who can produce a complete, peer-immune professional monograph quickly and under deadline pressures.

Most firms have the in-house staffing capability of supplying the core needs for a Phase II project. Those people will include:

* *project managers*, who will have the responsibility of overseeing all aspects of the project from its inception until turn-over, and who will be responsible for coordinating all field, analytical, and report tasks;

* *laboratory staff*, managed by the laboratory director and responsible for each firm's project needs, and for the management of all material products of the project;

* *field labor*, including both field supervisors as well as basic technicians, who will be responsible for the extraction of the informational contained within the archaeological deposit;

* *graphics*; and

* *secretarial and administrative*, who will be responsible for coordinating the production of the Phase II report as well as for all of the managerial paper work approved by the project manager.

6.2.6.1. Non-Field Support Personnel

Non-field support personnel are those who assist with the start-up of the project, who do the laboratory analyses as well as preparation of the collection for curation and turn-over, who prepare the figures and illustrations, and who produce the report. Those individuals almost always are permanent members of the firm whose tasks can be divided into administrative (start-up and report production) or analytical (analysis, curation, turn-over).

As in-house staff, those people will have several other projects for which they are either responsible or are participants. The project manager is responsible for issuing precise instructions for what he or she needs to have done, for providing a clear number of person-hours that are available for the task, and for monitoring the progress of those tasks relative to the amount of time allocated. Some firms handle this by using *Work Request Forms*, which actually results in a level of managerial organization above that for which the requests were issued (someone is needed to monitor those task requests). In large firms, this is necessary; in small firms, it may create more confusion than order.

Most tasks that involve office-based work, be it setting the project up, doing the analyses, or producing the report, will be tasks that use in-house personnel. The only exception -- and it is an important exception -- will be the use of specialists for particular aspects of the Phase II analyses.

Specialists may be needed for three basic sets of information:

* structure and interpretation either of the soils or of the sediment of the site;

* detailed analyses, such as hydration analyses, ethnobotantical analyses, faunal analyses, or the basic high-magnification use-wear analyses of the prehistoric lithic applications industry; and/or

* statistical analyses, especially as these pertaining to site depositional integrity and presence/absence of components.

Each of these people will have been solicited and hired on as subcontractors, sometimes for the duration of the project. There are firms that have in-house capabilities for such tasks, but most firms will need to locate specialists outside of the firm.

The specialists will have a rate schedule. That rate schedule should have been solicited during the bidding process so that the project manager has some sense of how much of the project budget will be used. The subcontracting specialist will do whatever the task requires, and generally will return a hard-copy written report along with photographs, illustrations, along with a word-processing file in the firm's preferred word-processing program, an ASCII file, or, if needed, both.

Some firms will reproduce the specialist's contribution as an appendix; others will incorporate the results into the appropriate analysis section and make the proper references. Some firms will list the specialist as a co-author on the report. All of this is a matter of firm protocol combined with a sense of how much the specialist has contributed.[5] We have generally followed a policy that, if the contribution to the report is over five percent, it probably is fair to list the specialist as a contributor if his or her contributions have not already been isolated with a by-line; over 10 percent, the author definitely should be considered a co-author. (Conversely, editing or ownership of the firm does not warrant listing as co-authoring.) In all

---

5. Listing who is an author is a matter of professional ethics, and not surprisingly something felt about deeply by all of us who work in a field where status is based upon, and one of the only physical products of what we do is, our publications. They probably exist, but we are unaware of fixed guidelines for assigning authorship in professional archaeology. The medical and biomedical communities, though, have a policy, and these might serve as a place to begin (International Committee of Medical Journal Editors 1991:425):

Authorship credit should be based only on substantial contributions to (a) conception and design, or analysis and interpretation of the data; and to (b) drafting the article or revising it critically for important intellectual content; and on (c) final approval of the version to be published. Conditions (a), (b), and (c) must all be met. Participation solely in the acquisition of funding or the collection of data does not justify authorship. General supervision of the research group is also not sufficient for authorship.

Similar authorship guidelines are in place for the *Journal of the American Medical Association* (Lundberg and Flanagin 1989:2003-2004; JAMA 1992:41). They are also in place for some Federal agencies, notably the Centers for Disease Control and Prevention.

In terms of "substantial contributions," it is noteworthy that the *Journal of the American Medical Association* (1992:41) limits the number of authors to six; any greater number must be justified. However, that applies to articles, not monographs.

cases, the specialists subcontracted for the Phase II project should receive copies of the final Phase II report.

6.2.6.2. Hiring or Assigning Field Personnel

While the firm will have the people needed to build the core of a Phase II project, often the needs of that project will require additional personnel, especially to accomplish the field work. Similar situations were discussed for Phase I projects in section 5.2.4.2.

The requirements of the Phase II field work may well require hiring additional people to do the basic archaeological work. This may be because the project is too large to be handled by the firm at the moment, and additional people are needed to cover for the short-term labor shortage. Or it may be because the firm does not maintain an in-house staff for larger, set-piece testing and excavation projects.

Many firms in fact maintain a core population of permanent employees, the numbers of whom are adequate for most Phase I surveys but insufficient for larger Phase II testing projects. This is a business decision based upon cash flow, and is based on the same reasoning faced when a firm chooses to rent vehicles instead of owning vehicles. It may well be less expensive to hire additional people for specific large projects because such projects are too infrequent to support the payroll of a staff that size.

As mentioned in section 5.2.4.2., there is a population of migratory field archaeologists who move from project to project. This by itself argues for the corporate structure just mentioned, since for such a population to exist requires that such a practice of hiring up for the duration of a project be relatively common. That population of migratory archaeologists are referred to as "project-hires" since they are hired for the length of the project, and may not be able to be employed by the firm when that project -- or perhaps just the field portion of that project -- ends.

The temporary hiring of field archaeologists is much more common for Phase II and Phase III projects than for Phase I. Phase II and Phase III investigations tend to be larger in scope, and tend to be of longer duration. The project-hire population is located usually through a phone network that the professional archaeologist maintains with other professionals. If a project needing additional people is coming up, the archaeologist may phone colleagues in other firms, and sometimes even the local academic archaeologist, to say that a project of a certain duration will be starting at such-and-such a time and people will be needed.

Much less often will such temporary field positions be formally advertised. Sometimes one comes across a request for field workers published in the American Anthropological Association *Anthropology Newsletter*, or in the printed or electronic versions of the *SAA Bulletin*. This happens maybe once or twice a year and reflects a firm that suddenly has been overwhelmed with work, or a firm that has found that all of the project-hire people are committed for the period in question.

There are two other common sources for project-hires used in Phase II projects. The first source is local college students. Most Federal projects would require sufficient experience as well as formal training before the person could excavate, but often college students with training can be employed on projects subcontracted through a private-sector client. More often, such students will serve as assistants in the laboratory, cleaning and labeling artifacts. College students are an available, although not often sought, temporary labor pool for private-sector firms.

Another source for project-hires may be the unemployment office. The local unemployment office will have access to the general labor pool, ranging from unskilled labor to skilled workers such as machinery and equipment operators. Making use of this source for personnel is not common for a Phase II project, since the job skills represented would serve best for backfilling, material transport, and similar efforts that are more of a problem with Phase III data recovery.

6.2.7. Field Logistics: Housing, Per Diem, Transport

Phase II testing projects are more labor- and time-intensive than Phase I projects. They also may involve work done farther from the home office. This raises the issue of crew housing, per diem costs, and general transportation.

Some firms will arrange for housing beforehand, and field crew will be billeted at that place. In these situations, the firm will cover the cost of the lodging, and many will deduct a per capita amount from the overall per diem of each crew member to cover for that lodging. In other situations, the crew -- who may consist mostly of project-hires -- will be expected to find their own places to live; their only responsibility is to show up at the site each day. This is similar to what is found among construction workers, geologists, and, in the academic world, gypsy scholars. If the firm has the policy of arranging lodging, then the project manager will need to locate suitable lodging and bargain for a weekly or monthly rate.

Per diem costs will be managed through the firm. As mentioned in section 5.2.5., per diem is a sticking point for many who work on the road in archaeology. The per diem is meant to cover room and board; the Internal Revenue Service has established expected per

diem rates for localities. Federal projects are expected to adhere to those rates as minimums (see 5.2.5. fn. 5 for details of Internal Revenue Service regulations on tax liability and other information).

The per diem funds will come from the client or the Federal agency to the firm, which will then disburse those funds to the project's field personnel. *However*, few clients or agencies will be billed for or pay for any portion of the project until after certain "milestones" or portions of the project have been finished (see also section 3.2.3.5.). One of those milestones will be the field work. This means that the funding for the per diem of a crew will be coming out of the cash reserves of the firm until such time as the client can in effect reimburse the firm.

While there are firms that pay out per diem on a weekly basis, nearly all firms in our experience will not disburse any per diem funds until they absolutely need to, and that usually means not until the first payment from the client is received and the cheque has cleared. This in turn means that it will be the crew member in the field who will have to provide the money certainly to cover food, and if the firm is one where the crew members are left to their own devices to find lodging, then they will need to pay for that as well. Industry reviewers reading this paragraph were very annoyed by this, but it is best to plan that the first per diem cheque for a project probably will not show up to the field archaeologist until three months after the field part of the project has been finished. (It is our good fortune that our industry contacts have what we consider ethical per diem policies.)

Per diem represents substantial cash flow through a firm, and many firms will hold back five to 10 percent of each person's per diem as a "processing fee." What this really does is covers any interest that the firm may be facing if it is paying up front for crew billeting and has had to take out a loan or start drawing on corporate cash reserves, which can be argued as fair. More often though, it becomes an excuse to pick up some of that cash flow. In effect, most field crew people, and particularly project-hires, provide their employers with a short-term business loan that actually pays the recipient of that loan between five and 10 percent interest.

To keep per diem outlays down, many firms have adopted the construction industry's practice of working for 10 straight days, then taking four days off. For any project, Federal labor law will require that hourly pay workers receive overtime pay for the sixth and seventh day of work in a week. Many firms -- construction just as much as archaeology -- work around this by giving the first two days of Week One and the last two days of Week Two as "weekend days" to the crew. In practical terms, this means that the person will be working for 10 straight days (this is called a "10-on/4-off" or a "10 - 4" work regime).

Observations on Eating Out on a Per Diem Project

Everyone seems to approach per diem projects a bit differently. Young crew members, out of college for a couple of years and, as project-hires, engaging in the turn-of-the-century's version of the 1920s European *Grand Tour* by traveling the back roads of rural America, tend to spend their time more in the lodgings to eat. Their concerns are cash flow, just like the firm, and preparing their own meals is a cost-cutting strategy that serves to supplement their pay.

Older crew members, especially those who have been bottled up in the office for the last couple of months, view a per diem project more as a vacation of sorts. Cash flow is less of an issue; instead, it is sort of nice to be able to eat out each night, and to have a quiet room to oneself.

There are advantages and disadvantages in these two approaches. The disadvantage – aside from additional cash outlays – generally is the potential for really boring dining. Some communities may have a wide range of eateries open for breakfast, lunch, and dinner, at least enough and with enough menu variety so that the mind does not become numb. It is pretty hard, on the eighth evening of a 10-day work span, to come back as the evening dims in the Northeastern late autumn where the cold has drained the body, to shower *then* to go back out and find a place to eat. The real desire is to sleep, especially as the room is filled with the dry warmth so at odds with the moist, frost-ladened cold. Oddly, the younger the crew person, the more likely it will be for them to do this.

The advantage is, as any anthropologist knows, GOSSIP! For long-term per diem projects in small communities, the archaeology people are known and curious outsiders. People love archaeology, and they have a wealth of information on the world around them. Eating breakfast at one place, lunch at a second, and dinner at several, often will reward the archaeologist-as-anthropologist with considerable insight into the community and its history. It works both as scholarship and as public relations.

Probably the best decision that a project manager can make on a per diem project is to select a good, unobtrusive place to have breakfast, and to go there regularly during the course of the project. Those small, unadorned diners that have cars and pick-ups around them at 0600 are the places that have maintained a clientele, and that clientele will represent a social network. It is as close as the United States now has to the social network of the English pub.

Breakfast people are regular people: They sit in the same places, eat the same thing, show up at the same time. They form a small community over the years, such that the first in will go around behind the counter and fetch the coffee pot, and will pour for the others as they arrive. They also are morning people, who for reasons unknown to civilized humans tend to be viewed as more responsible. It takes no more than a week to be viewed as a regular, to know people's names. Pouring coffee for the others of a morning seals this. In the right time of year – say around the autumnal holidays and festivals – a camaraderie emerges that can sustain the spirits of a person away from loved ones and suffering from a mixture of sunlight depravation and simple physical exhaustion.

And, the people will provide insights into the history and workings of the community that will not be available to a person hiding out as some culture-shocked foreigner in a motel room.

Lunches are as likely as not to provide a similar kind of information access. Many small towns have a place where community leaders eat on a regular basis; this is especially true of county seats. However, the crew coming in from the field to eat will be ... well, the polite term is either "ripe" or "seasoned." The opportunities for information transfer and interaction are less. Usually, the field crew just wants to eat, rest, drink as much water as possible (and in the winter, soup; unmentioned in the world's scriptures is the Deity's creation of the ultimate cold-weather food: soup), and, oh yes, rest. The information node in these instances will be the person who owns the eatery or who waits the table, and the place to eat as often as not is the standard in-town diner.

Unlike breakfast, lunch will be less a community interaction affair and more a table-set-to-provide affair. The communication web is that of a chiefdom, going to a center point – whoever is waiting the table – before being sent out again. Still, it often is a better thing to do than to sit around in the field with the other people.

Dinner we have found is a treat, but it does require dragging oneself out into the dark of a winter night, when the field vehicle is all of cold and stiff vinyl, with that curious artificial smell, and the unfamiliar world is one of yellow-white lights and unfamiliar places. The people who stay inside and eat before the television may actually have the advantage here. We have always gone out of an evening, in part to explore what the community has to offer in the way of food (dinner is the community's "best gastronomical foot forward," to abuse Fussell's [1983:87] paraphrase of Russell Lynes), but mostly just to have something to eat. There rarely is any kind of information transfer about the community that takes place in an American restaurant at dinner time. Tables are cloistered and set apart; those serving are perfunctory. The advantage, though, is if the project manager or field director has dragged along crew members, he or she can learn more about those people. That in turn helps in basic project management. Oh yes, and one gets to have the camaraderie of a shared meal.

Looked at in terms of per diem, though, this means that instead of paying out for 10 days of per diem over the course of two calendar weeks, the firm need pay out for only nine (the evening before the work week begins is covered, the last day of the work week is not). That is a 10 percent reduction in proposal bid for the per diem line item.

Per diem jobs are viewed by many as opportunities to pick up addition pay. Even with the firm's "processing fee" and all the other accounting shenanigans, the per diem can represent roughly another $10 - $30 a day in wages, depending on how much lodging costs. Additional funds, by the way, that usually are tax-free (see again section 5.2.5. fn. 5). As a result, many field crew people will share rooms, shop at the local food markets, and fix their own meals: Breakfast will be in the room where they are staying, lunch will be bagged, and dinner more than likely will be something heated on the hot plate that the motel has sternly and repeatedly said is illegal to have.

Transportation costs and arrangements depend upon the firm. For project-hires, it is their responsibility to get to a staging area if not work site on time. Transportation to that staging area -- say the motel where the crew is billeted -- usually is not an obligation of the firm, although transportation into the field from that point usually is. For permanent staff, transportation to and from the job site relative to the office usually *is* a corporate obligation. Further, it almost always is necessary to have a field vehicle to transport equipment and collections to and from the site. Transportation, then, is a logistical issue, one solved in three ways.

The first way of dealing with field transportation is for the firm to own its own field vehicles. This has advantages and disadvantages. The advantage is the transportation flexibility and per mile cost. The disadvantage is maintenance. We have almost been killed ("almost" being the two feet between us in the driver's seat of the forever-stalling field vehicle and the now-stopped gasoline tanker truck with the smoke rising from its brake pads as it decelerated from 55 mph with 13 passenger vehicles stacked up behind it) on two occasions in corporate field vehicles that were not properly maintained.

Many firms expect employees to provide use of their vehicles for the firm. The employee will be reimbursed for mileage, but the vehicle will be expected to be used to transport personnel, equipment, and collections. Any insurance issues will ultimately devolve to the car owner. Insurance firms will consider the business use of a private vehicle in this way a new and increased risk exposure requiring re-rating of the policy, which makes sense of course. In most cases, the employee using his or her personal vehicle on behalf of the firm will not have that vehicle covered under the firm's policy (the firm may have added the vehicle under their coverage, but that is not common). If a claim is filed by the employee against his or her policy, and it is clear that the vehicle has been used in this way, the insurance firm probably will cover the claim *ceteris paribus*, but it will want to re-rate the coverage.

The third way to deal with field transportation is to rent a vehicle as situations demand. The advantage is

that the vehicle is safe and well-maintained; the disadvantage is cost if this is done very frequently. Many firms in our experience rent vehicles for extended projects.

6.2.8. Equipment and Supply Needs

The equipment of a Phase II project is the same as that of any archaeological excavation. Any number of standard textbooks supply lists of needed equipment, and the reader is directed to those sources.

Nearly all firms supply the basic field equipment needed for the Phase II project. This will include the excavation tools, the screens and/or sorting tables, the bags and indelible markers, and the record-keeping materials.

Field archaeologists, and especially project-hires with more than a couple years of experience, take tremendous pride in their excavation skills. Most will come with their own trowel, and many also maintain specialized tool kits that include dental picks, lines and line levels, plumb bobs, different sizes of trowels, paint brushes and whisk brooms, colored tacks, indelible markers, different sorts of tape measures, and other small hand tools. The firm will have a general tool box with similar kinds of equipment, but it is rare for it to be as elaborate or refined as that found among the professional field archaeologists. This supplying of one's own tools, or at least ownership of them, is found in the construction, auto repair, and machinist industries, for example, and reflects the importance of the person's manual skills for continuance of his or her livelihood.

While excavation equipment will be owned by the firm, or purchased if suddenly needed for a given project, more expensive pieces of equipment may not be. This is especially true for surveying equipment. Some firms do have theodolites, for example; many do not. In our experience, as often as not the theodolite owned by the firm is out-of-level and needs maintenance.

Most firms confronted with a Phase II project requiring mapping will rent a theodolite and leveling rod, or comparable equipment. The costs usually are not terribly great, and there are no issues of equipment condition.

6.2.9. Setting Up

Setting up the Phase II testing operation requires attention to crew logistical and equipment needs, and to field needs. Logistics and equipping have been discussed. Field needs include mapping and deciding where testing will be done. That testing may be actual test units, in which case decisions need to be made about where to dig, or the testing may be plowing and limited plowzone removal, in which case the field will need to be prepared.

6.2.9.1. Project Maps

Phase II testing is sufficiently formal archaeologically that mapping is required. That mapping may be based upon existing project maps, may require making a map better suited to archaeological needs, or some combination.

Most project areas will have had a topographic map prepared by the client. This will be done using English measurements, which usually is not a problem. The contour intervals often will have been interpolated from aerial photographs with a few ground checks, which may *be* a problem. It is sometimes possible to use a project map for the Phase II excavation map: After all, the land will have fixed property stakes while the land survey will have been tied into a permanent datum. If the archaeological test units are tied into project map benchmarks, then the archaeologist will have the excavations tied into a replicable physical location.

Remember, if the site is extremely important, people in the future will be willing to take the trouble to work out where things were, provided there is a sound record of where things *are* located. Thus, we have used building corners, highway right-of-way markers/mile posts, and similar often-mapped physical features to serve as points from which test units have been triangulated. Because those physical features will appear on several different maps over many years, they are in effect permanently recorded with sufficient resolution to allow someone in the future to re-establish their precise location, should that be required. The more mapping redundancy associated with what will be used as a field datum or referent, usually the better.

In many cases, a topographic map will be needed. It may even be specified in the SOW. There should be someone on staff who can do a topographic map.

6.2.9.2. Relocating Phase I Testing Pattern

Most Phase II testing programs are based on Phase I results. This means that it is important to relocate the Phase I mapping referents, at least close enough so that the testing done will be in the general area of the artifact concentrations identified during Phase I.

In most cases, the Phase I survey can be relocated in one of three ways:

* looking for surviving, labeled flagging tape;

* using the original project map and working back with compass bearings to the original shovel test transects; or

* using the GPS system to return to the general vicinity, then working around to find an emplaced ground-truth referent.

Mapping

The maps needed by archaeologists are different than those produced for construction projects. The differences usually are in the details and resolution: Construction projects will give a general lay-of-the-land; the archaeologist will note every small rivulet on the surface. It almost always is a waste of effort to hire a land surveyor to do a topographic map of a site if there is an archaeologist available for that. And all archaeologists are supposed to have been trained to prepare topographic maps.

Normally all that one needs is a couple position references -- labeled flagging tape markers for shovel tests, pin flags to re-locate surface finds -- to work out the rest of the Phase I grid, provided one also has a copy of the appropriate parts of the Phase I report. We were even fortunate in one case to have a project area where the Phase I people had put in *labeled wooden stakes using a transit*. Amazing. And very rare.

In situations where the shovel testing was done but the firm did not mark its units, the problem is a bit trickier. (Some firms, to reduce costs, only mark positive shovel tests, which must be a nightmare to relocate when intra-grid testing is done.) It will require re-establishing the original shovel test system, using the same markers and orientation that the original Phase I field team used. This may require examining the Phase I field notes and project map, or it may be possible to get that information from the Phase I report's "Methods" section, combined with the copy of the project map produced in that report. This is where the professional archaeologist really hopes that the Phase I people knew what they were doing. By the way, this is why it is so vital to keep accurate and detailed field notes -- "detailed" in the sense of physical terrain characteristics. Someone else may well be coming back to re-establish the Phase I shovel test locations.

Fortunately, most Phase I shovel test regimes are properly spaced, or at least are so within a meter (still much better than GPS, even with the military restrictions on accuracy lifted). It can be aggravating, tiring work to re-establish where what numbered shovel test actually was, but it can be done.

Phase II testing based upon Phase I surface collections can be difficult. Often, the collection areas are not so well marked that they can be relocated a year or two later. Further, unlike shovel tests, which *do* leave feature-like traces than can be identified, Phase I surface collections often provide no physical evidence. Re-establishing where what was collected will have to be handled on a case-by-case basis. If the professional archaeologist is lucky, the person who ran the Phase I will have kept notes with an eye toward the likelihood that someone would have to come back and relocate everything. If not, the old adage of "do the best you can" holds.

This then, should be a caution for people thinking about Phase I surveys: Always set up field notes and field work in a manner as if the entire process will need to be reconstructed for a Phase II exercise.

6.3. Field

6.3.1. Landscape History: Vegetational and Pedological Data

The Phase I survey should have provided a detailed account of vegetation in the project area, land-use history based upon that vegetation, and discussion of the local soils. Our experience has been that many firms do not do this, or their personnel are not able to do this. If the Phase I report does not contain this information, the professional archaeologist will need to do this work.

6.3.1.1. Land-Use History Based on Vegetation Succession

The specifics of land-use history based upon vegetation were given in section 5.3.1.1.

If the Phase I survey report did not provide a summary of the landscape and a general outline, based upon it, for the land-use history, then that work will need to be done. This is nothing more than being able to recognize different plant species -- especially trees -- and, using their growth habit and the successional stage, work out how the land was used prior to the appearance of the current vegetation cover. No professional archaeologist should be unable to do this. The methods are outlined in Chapter 5.

Remember that providing a generic summation of what native vegetation may occur in an area is not a substitute for this. One is providing a detailed description of the vegetation present on the site, *as well as* the implications that *that* particular plant community has for how the land was last used and, possibly, the site's depositional integrity compromised.

Land-use history based upon the vegetation is critical to the Phase II process. It is not unusual to have Phase I surveys conducted where such features are ignored. This often results in a declaration, in the Phase I report, that the landscape is undisturbed. *That* declaration then prompts the review agency to require a Phase II or even a Phase II/III examination of the project area. This all because the Phase I project director failed to examine the vegetation and its implication for land use over the last 30 or so years.

6.3.1.2. Land-Use History and the Soil Profile

As with vegetation and land-use history, the application of soil development principles and soil mechanics to understanding land-use history was considered in section 5.3.1.2. These apply with greater force for Phase II testing.

Phase II testing opens up a larger volume of a site; it also tends to go deeper, and provides a much clearer sense of the soil and sediment structure of the deposit. Because soil information especially can be determined better during Phase II, and because the artifact sample is so much larger than with Phase I, questions about vertical distribution of artifacts and site disturbance are more easily addressed.

Phase II testing requires that the soil horizons be recorded for each test unit. That is, in addition to indicating where excavation levels were, it is important to describe the soil profile in soil science terms, at least to the extent of a field determination of horizon.

In theory, this should be done to confirm the information provided in the Phase I report. In reality, many Phase I reports will have neglected to provide any information about actual soils horizons. Instead, they will assign Roman numerals or capital letters to each apparent change in soil color, usually without understanding what is meant by soil horizon development. (There really is no excuse for this.)

The importance of understanding soil development -- and distinguishing soils from sediments -- cannot be over-emphasized. If achieving this requires calling in a county soil agent for a spell just to provide field descriptions, then do that. It is much better that the archaeologist do this, and professional training should not have allowed the archaeologist to graduate without those skills, at least at the master's level.

We learned about archaeology from that ... Heather Heights

A few years ago, we were retained by a Middle Atlantic firm to provide the analysis and interpretation for a Phase II testing exercise in Maryland. It was instructive.

The firm had conducted a standard Phase I survey. The project area was a woodlot filled with 30-40-cm dbh oaks and hickories, and generally appeared undisturbed. The Phase I survey was well-executed. The soil profile, when we managed to work it out from the field notes, indicated a standard 10-cm thick A2 horizon [E horizon] over a 15-cm thick A3/B1 horizon [AB or BA horizon] that then continued into a B2 horizon [B horizon]. Shovel tests returned Late Archaic – that is, prehistoric from around 4,000 years ago – artifacts from two distinct loci. Two sites were clearly present and, based upon the amount of material and location, Phase II testing recommended.

The initial interpretation by the firm was that the sites were undisturbed, which was the main reason Phase II had been recommended. Eight 1 x 1 m units were placed in each of the two sites, then excavated into culturally sterile subsoil. Most of the artifacts were recovered from within 30 cm of the surface; some were found between 30 - 40 cm below the surface, and artifact frequencies decreased exponentially from there. The soil profiles described for the Phase II test units corresponded to what had been described for the Phase I.

Our conclusion, based upon the size and probable age of the trees, the nature of the soil profile relative to those trees, the vertical position of most of the artifacts, and the exponentially decreasing frequency of artifacts below 30 cm, was that the sites had been extensively plowed. Further, since the land was on a three percent slope, there probably had been considerable sheet erosion, certainly sufficient over the years to have allowed plowing to cut into whatever features may once have been present. Our conclusion, then, was that both sites were plow-truncated, and that Phase III was not warranted.

We wrote up our results; the firm incorporated them into a larger report then submitted the report to the SHPO. The SHPO responded by saying that the case did not appear to be proved. As near as they could understand, the site appeared to be undisturbed based upon the submitted Phase I report; the Phase II testing had produced a fair quantity of material; and since the two sites were located in an undisturbed woodlot, Phase III data recovery still seemed to be the best decision. Late Archaic archaeological sites are very common in the eastern United States; undisturbed Late Archaic sites, especially in upland settings as this one was, are very rare.

Usually the greatest issue for a prehistoric archaeological site is the integrity of the site, since data potential almost always is the criterion of significance invoked when Register-eligibility is recommended. If the integrity of the site is compromised, then often too is the data potential of that site.

The Phase I survey had provided a description of the tree cover and of the soils, but had not reasoned beyond those to address land-use history. Instead, the Phase I report had suggested the site was in an undisturbed woodlot, and that was taken by all concerned, the firm as well as the SHPO, to mean that the land itself was undisturbed.

Clearly, if the tree cover consisted of 30-40-cm dbh oaks and hickories, then the woodlot itself probably was around 40-50 years old. Since no stumps were present on the landscape (something we asked when we spoke with the firm), and since no other larger trees were present, then obviously the woodlot itself could only be as old as the trees on it. It seemed likely that the woodlot began emerging around World War II or a little after, which in turn meant that the land was unwooded before then.

The soil profile was not that of a forest soil. A forest soil has a thin A horizon [E horizon] over a B horizon. A transitional series of horizons that, added to the extant A horizon, would be close to the depth of a plow zone, was suspicious. Knowing that it takes maybe 30-40 years under continuous forest cover for an Ap horizon to be pretty much lost, helped. And knowing that the trees themselves were about that age, and that the A3/B1 [AB/BA] horizon transition is what is encountered in those changes, all suggested that the sites had been plowed.

The final proof involved a discussion of soil mechanics – artifacts sink through the soil, as was explained in Chapter 5 – combined with a simple series of statistical tests. Those tests – chi-squared to show the lack of independence, correlation coefficients as a surface trend analysis to show that the proportional vertical distribution of artifacts was the same across the sites regardless of unit – demonstrated that all of the material encountered in the B horizon had originated in what had been an Ap horizon.

The reasoning was presented to the SHPO. The result was that the Phase III requirement – which in 1991 would have required another $50,000 of work – was waived. The client, of course was grateful, and the SHPO was impressed with the firm; both situations were good for business. The lesson here is to always make sure that the vegetation and soils are taken into account in formulating a land-use history of the site area.

Soil Development and Applicability of County Soil Surveys

One danger that does exist with having county soil agents work up the soil profile is a conceptual bias that exists in agricultural soil survey. That bias is that soils have not developed out of recent sediment accumulations.

We would not be aware of this were it not for having dealt with a deep prehistoric site as part of a Phase II. As always, we had picked up a copy of the county soil survey report and had identified the type of soil for the site. This had also been mentioned as part of the Phase I. What the soil survey assumed, though, was that the soil had developed *in situ*, over some parent material that had been in place for a very long time.

It turned out that the site had 40 cm of 150-year-old overburden resting on the original seventeenth-century floodplain soil. That soil, we discovered, was only a half-meter thick, having developed from sediment that built up over a previous floodplain surface ... and prehistoric occupation. In the end, we found that there were several distinct soils, each developed during periods of sedimentary homeostasis from sediment piled up during periods of aggradation. The soil types, as reported in the soil survey report (and as used by regional archaeologists to talk about prehistoric site selection based upon crop suitability), were entirely different below about 40-60 cm. This, by the way, is one reason why attempting to develop a prehistoric settlement pattern based upon modern soil distributions is invalid: The modern, mapped soils are rarely the soils with which prehistoric peoples had to deal, or even had available.

Soil survey books are assembled over years, and they involve sending crews out to put in sampling pits. Those soil test pits are not unlike archaeology Phase II test pits, although the fill is not screened and the units are not as neatly dug. The entire landscape of a county will be sampled and spot-checked, with the soil profiles being described in detail. Those soils then are assigned to soil types based on several criteria, and the county will be mapped in a way that shows "soil bodies" spread over the landscape.

The assumption is that the near-surface soil is the same as what is underneath; that is, there is no pedological discontinuity, as it were. True, many floodplain soil types are described as "undifferentiated," but the important thing to remember is that, for the soil scientists and for the county soil agent, the issue ends when a soil/sedimentary discontinuity is encountered. This is just the opposite for the archaeologist worried about prehistoric behavior: Not only is the modern soil an issue (since it influences the structure of the deposit), so too is the nature of the prehistoric soil, since past people had to live with that and since the properties of *that* soil influence the archaeological materials within its matrix.

6.3.2. Field Methods

6.3.2.1. What is Going to be Done: Testing

Phase II testing will usually involve one of two basic approaches:

(1) excavation of test units; or

(2) controlled surface collection of a plowed site, with limited plowzone removal.

The excavation of test units is straight forward, with most basics taught in standard academic field schools. Test units normally will be 1 x 1 m, 1 x 2 m, or 2 x 2 m, depending upon project needs, especially the site's structure. The units, more often those evaluating prehistoric sites, will tend to be taken to 30 cm below the last level containing cultural materials, or until C horizon material is encountered. The phrase often used is "30 cm into culturally sterile soil." The actual final depth will depend upon the nature of the site as well as SHPO/THPO or agency testing policy, and will be specified in the SOW.

The second common Phase II procedure is a controlled surface collection, accompanied with some kind of selective plowzone removal. In most cases, this will mean that the field itself will need to be plowed; the boundary of the plowed area mapped; the plowed area itself gridded off somehow; and the field itself collected. Then, based upon the results of that surface collection, a portion of the plowzone will be removed. In these situations, what the Phase II testing is doing is seeing if there is any abundance of cultural remains, if those remains have any concentrations, then if any features -- trash pits, hearths, postholes, foundation markings -- survive beneath that plowzone.

6.3.2.2. Setting Up in the Field

Setting up the Phase II project in the field is similar to setting up a standard archaeological excavation. The only major difference is that the Phase I survey results need to be considered, which in turn means that the original Phase I sampling pattern has to be relocated. This was discussed in section 6.2.9.2.

For Phase II projects involving test units, a baseline of some sort may be set out relative to a datum, then units placed relative to the results of the Phase I survey. In places where there is a sound project map and readily used mapping features, such as a house corner, the units may be oriented using a hand-compass and unit positions triangulated in from the mapping features.

We learned about archaeology from that ... Providing Adequate Soil Descriptions.

We directed a large Phase II project several years ago on a site where the deposit reached at least 4.0 m below the surface. There was no question that the site was going to go to Phase III data recovery: It had been listed for several years on the National Register. The purpose of the Phase II was to get information on the deposit in preparation for full-scale excavations. It proved to be a very instructive exercise indeed.

This was the entrée project for the firm that retained us, and had been bid with no margin of error to gain access to that market. Fifteen 1 x 2 m test units were dug, with the SOW specifying that these be taken in 10-cm arbitrary levels to 2.0 m below surface, or 30 cm into culturally sterile subsoil, whichever came first. Six of the units were paired up, allowing a backhoe to extend the final depth in those three cases to around 4.0 m below the surface.

The National Register nomination form, as well as the site files and the SOW, all had indicated that the site matrix consisted of a rather wonderful, fertile, and quite workable floodplain soil, homogenous to an unspecified depth. This soil, in fact, was being used by some regional archaeologists as part of a predictive model for where Late Woodland sites would be located. And the firm had bid the project assuming that the soil descriptions were accurate. However, this turned out not to be the case: that defining surface soil ended 60 cm below the surface. Instead of a homogenous deposit, the site turned out to be a series of prehistoric occupations contained within a series of buried soils.

Cultural materials were recovered down to 2.0 m in most of the hand-excavated units; sporadic cultural material came out as deep as 4.0 m from the units that were extended using a backhoe. The water table, by the way, began around 1.8 m below surface. Or would have, if it was not so cold.

The field work was arduous, done in the open lawn area of a local airport over a Pennsylvania winter. It was cold. There is no other way to describe it. We saw the West Branch of Susquehanna River freeze over in a day, bank to bank. And at one point, field crews were working when it was -30°C (-22°F), simply to stay on schedule and within budget. Removing fill under such conditions was torturous. The project actually was finished exactly within budget, but the time and effort expended was numbing. The field portion of the project lasted four months.

We did detailed unit profile drawings. Since this was a situation where Phase III was planned (the Phase II was a testing exercise in the sense of working out just what the deposit was like), and since the firm we were involved with planned to bid on this, we decided to spend the extra time and effort to work out a detailed field description of the soils. That soil profile work was not requested of the SOW, and in fact was done as an additional effort, just to keep matters straight. (Indeed, the firm was against the extra work. It took about three hours each evening for two weeks to work out the detailed profile description, then another week back at the office speaking to soil scientists, to finalize that description. All of that was unbudgeted.)

In situations where mapping is to be done, a permanent datum will be needed. It becomes the archaeologist's responsibility to tie that datum in with another, permanent map reference feature. This may be done by using a transit to tie the site datum into a USGS benchmark; it may be done using some kind of GPS referent.

For Phase II projects involving controlled surface collections, the field may be overgrown and need some kind of clearing. This will require locating then hiring someone with a brush-hog to mow the field, then some kind of provision to get rid of that brush before the land itself is plowed. Plowing will have to be arranged as well, and some idea of plowing depth also determined.

How the surface collection is controlled will depend upon SOW specifications. Some situations will have the plowed area gridded off into 10 x 10 m or 20 x 20 m areas, each corner marked by a pin flag. Other situations may involve a series of stakes tied into a datum with a transit, a string tied to the stake, and a surface collection done throughout the reach of that string (a tethered surface collection). Regardless of how the collection is controlled, the control points will need to be mapped into a permanent datum for the site.

For Phase II testing projects, it also is expected that the project area and its setting will be photographed. A number of different photographs from different perspectives are useful. Taking a panoramic view by overlapping a series of exposures is an excellent way to provide a sense of how the project area looked at the time the Phase II work was done.

It turned out that the entire site had around 20 cm of recently plowed silt deposited over a previously plowed field. That field had a 30 - 40 cm thick Ap horizon that continued down into a B horizon to around 80 cm below the surface. Below that was another A horizon - B horizon set; below that, yet another. In all, there were six buried soils located at the site, each containing prehistoric materials and some features, making the site a very interesting exercise indeed.

Most of the description would be tangential to the issue here. We learned the nomenclature for buried soils: a series of apostrophes, by the way, with the B horizon for each being indicated as a "Bw," meaning infused with clay. Indeed, clay illuviation was one of the dominant pedological factors at the site. The result were soils with horizon characteristics that are called "indurated," the technical measurement of which is "a soil that needs the blow of a hammer to break." (True.) Imagine dealing with this when the wind is howling, the still-air temperature is somewhere below zero, and this stuff is resting in the screen.

We worked up the soils description,

and presented the Phase II results for the site in terms of the buried soils. We even set out an appendix explaining soil processes and nomenclature, and how they applied to the site.

The archaeologist at the time for the Lead agency demanded that the soils appendix be removed from the draft report. With a series of other amendments, the report was produced. In time, we did the data recovery plan for the site, worked up a sound Phase III data recovery proposal, and sat back as another firm received the award.

That firm, unfamiliar with the determining feature of the deposit – that indurated nature of the soil – ran into cost overruns of a seven figure range. It was a true disaster. Incensed, they filed a suit against the Lead agency, arguing that the Phase II report was lacking in its description of field conditions.

An international panel of soil scientists, sedimentologists, and fluvial geologists was assembled. While the appendix had been removed, the other bits treating the soils and their characteristics had survived the editing process, mainly because they were

embedded in profile drawings and their legends, and in the text. The panel's conclusion was that the report was excellent, especially in terms of the discussion of the soils, and that the plaintiff had no grounds for complaint. The firm lost its case, and presumably absorbed the costs, since it is still in business (although the entire cultural resources division was restructured).

Ironically, the appendix that had been cut out of the report, and that had been garbled by office editing (the word "illuviation," for example, had been changed to "alluviation"), was later requested by the new Lead agency archaeologist. We learned this second-hand. We only hope that he had the understanding to figure out that "illuviation" was meant.

The lesson here, among many, is that just because the budget or SOW does not request something to be done, does not mean that it should not be done. There was no provision in the SOW for a detailed soils description of the site. That description was done because it was considered a professional necessity. As a result, the client as well as the firm was protected from enormous and – knowing the finances of the firm in question – bankrupting lawsuits.

6.3.2.3. Execution of Field Work

Field work often will involve digging test units, doing a controlled surface collection, and/or mechanically stripping a portion of a plowed site.

The excavation of test units for Phase II testing is similar to the excavation of any archaeological test unit in the United States. The differences involve more what is or is not essential to the excavation process, and that in turn is driven by what Phase II is meant to accomplish in the overall compliance process.

Probably the greatest differences in excavation procedures between a Phase II exercise and an academic testing exercise is the speed. This certainly caught us when we went from the academic sector to the private sector. While this was mentioned above, it does no harm to repeat here that, for most areas of the country, a standard 1 x 1 m test unit in an unstratified deposit will be taken down to 100 cm and backfilled in a day. The speed is based mostly on the crew knowing what to do, as well as well-developed motor skills along with crew members being in good physical condition, but it is also helped by knowing

what is or is not needed. For example, the unit walls will be cut with a shovel; only one will be troweled, and that will be done when the base of the unit is reached.

Test units will be set out most often by setting large nails or spikes into the ground, then stringing the bounds of the unit around those nails. Less often will wooden stakes with grid labels be used. The unit corners will be either triangulated in from a mapped reference point, or will be tied into a site datum using a transit. If a transit is being used and if a topographic map is being prepared, then elevations (above mean sea level) will be taken for each of the unit's corners, and those elevations will be recorded on the unit excavation form. If elevations are not being taken and a previously prepared topographic map is being used instead, an estimate should be made of what the elevation of at least one of the unit corners is.

Fill from the units usually will be screened. Screen size will vary by SOW requirements and SHPO/THPO protocols, and will vary by jurisdiction and nature of the site. For example, prehistoric sites over the Midwest and the eastern United States often will

Figure 6.1. Panoramic view of a project area. Panoramic views are made by overlapping photographs, emphasized here by the contrast between the left and right halves. Doing the image this way gives a much better sense of the landscape than do photographs taken with a wide-angle lens.

use a 1/4-inch (0.635 cm) mesh. Sites located in heavy clay soils may use 1/2-inch (1.270 cm) mesh, and this may be recommended for industrial sites as well.

Screening protocols also vary by other situations. For example, we directed a Phase II over a site that turned out to be the land-fill midden for a community. In the late 1860s, the town had burned down (something, we have noted, that seemed to have happened in the mid- to late 1860s to most small towns in the East and Northeast). All of the trash was gathered up and dumped along the river bank, in this case in front of the courthouse. A few years later, the local Ladies Auxiliary had it landscaped into a park, which is what it is now. Putting test units into the park resulted in recovering all of the broken window glass from that 1860s fire. There were actually 15-cm thick strata of nothing but shattered window glass. While a 1/4-inch mesh was required by the SOW, and while regulations required that ALL cultural artifacts be retained, we managed to convince all concerned that retaining the equivalent of 2.5 m³ of broken window glass (equivalent to 6,240 kg) probably was not necessary.

Fill will be screened until there is a lot of material rolling around *on* the screen. That material will be sorted through, then the screen contents will be dumped. As with Phase I, the screen for Phase II is as much a sorting table as it is a sieve.

Fill will be removed by arbitrary levels within natural levels. Although it depends on the area, site, and SOW, usually the Ap horizon will be removed as one level, and soil horizons below the Ap will be removed in 10-cm levels.

Depth will be measured from the ground surface. Unless circumstances require otherwise, all unit depth measurements should be taken relative to the original land surface, with the unit floor being at the same depth at each of the four corners as well as in the midsections of the unit walls. That is, the planes of all unit floors should be parallel with the original land surface of the unit, or with the next deepest natural surface exposed.

Each level will be given at least one artifact bag. Most firms will use paper bags; some will use zip-lock plastic bags both in the field and again in the laboratory. This is a cost-effectiveness decision, and depends as much upon field conditions as it does upon cost. Inclement weather makes using plastic bags sensible, as does material being recovered from below the water table.

Each bag will be labeled with the following:

* site number;

* excavation unit number or coordinates;

* soil horizon if known;

* depth below surface (cm bs);

* initials of excavators; and

* some bag or field specimen number, added at the end of the day.

Some projects will assign a number to each excavation unit; others will use grid coordinates. If both are available, use both. Where grid coordinates are used,

Figure 6.2. Example of a labeled artifact bag. Note especially that the "field specimen" bag number has been added to the upper right-hand corner. All bags will be labeled sequentially for the duration of the project, with the labeling done each day. It might also be noted that an economical practice is to use paper bags for the field, then transfer materials to plastic bags during laboratory processing. Paper is less expensive than plastic and, unless conditions warrant otherwise (such as work done during rain), a better choice.

ALWAYS provide ALL coordinate numbers, and not the coordinates of just one stake. For example, that 1 x 1 m unit placed roughly 50 m north and 20 m east of the datum should be labeled on the bag and in the field notes as N50-51/E20-21. This leaves no room for confusion for the person who will be working with the data five weeks from now, or five decades from now. Always err on the side of information redundancy. Always.[6]

---

6. This admonition is prompted by a common practice over most of the twentieth century of using just one of the unit's corner stakes as the "label" for the unit, presumably to save the incredible effort of writing out six more characters. Sometimes it was the southwest stake, sometimes it was the southeast stake. For one investigator, it was the *north*east stake. The stake chosen depended upon practices in the part of the country where the work was done, or on the part of the country where the field director received training. As a practice to increase potential ambiguity and confusion, few have been developed to rival this. Looking at labels years later, one never knows just *which* corner stake the person chose to use, a problem we have seen compounded by the survival of the artifacts (labeled by grid coordinates and site number) and published site maps but premature demise of the field notes and actual field maps.

Each level should have a completed bag, even if nothing was found. This is for bookkeeping purposes. A labeled bag is a physical object that allows the person tracking all of the test units to keep abreast of which levels did or did not contain cultural materials.

In unstratifed sites or sites with relatively thick natural strata, the sequence for removal of a level is straight-forward: For a 10-cm level, the fill more often than not will be taken out in angled cuts that remove a shovelful close to 10 cm below the current floor level. The person digging will be tracking changes in texture and color visually; the person screening will be tracking changes in texture and color by feel. The screener's job includes monitoring what is coming out of the test unit; if there is a sudden change in artifact numbers or fill character, the screener advises the person digging, should that person not have noticed already.

Despite the seeming danger of damage to a feature in this, such rarely happens because each shovelful is being checked to make sure that it *does not* happen. Professional field archaeologists take great pride in their excavation skills, much the way that artisans take pride in their work.

Most people digging can keep well ahead of the person screening, and most testing pairs -- units tend to be dug by two people, one moving dirt and one screening -- will trade off one level to the next. When most of the 10-cm level has been removed, the person digging will check the four corners to see just how close the present floor is to how deep it should be. (Remember, depth will be measured "below surface," and usually the referents will be the corners, with quick checks along the centers of the unit walls.) After that, a portion of the floor will be worked down to the proper depth, then the rest of the floor will be removed and prepared using a flat-nosed shovel. Thus, something else that is rarely done during Phase II work is the troweling of a floor. A sharpened flat-nose shovel normally will do just fine.

The final product for each level will be floors that are the correct distance below-grade, with the floor itself having been cut cleanly enough to identify feature stains should they be present. The fill will have been gone through, and the walls will be vertical and plumb, so much so that the floor will be the same size as the surface, stringed opening. What has not been done has been troweling all four walls, troweling the floor, or trying to push every piece of soil through the screen.

Unit notes will be updated after each 10-cm level, or at the base of the Ap horizon, should there have been one. Most procedures will call for measurement below surface at the four unit corners, and that will be recorded, along with the soil color (Munsell determination) of the floor. Any color patterning or

Tip: Measuring and Controlling Unit Depth

One of the more aggravating things to encounter is a Phase II project where the floors of test units, placed on sloping land, are at right angles with the earth's gravitational field. We have encountered projects where units were placed on slight slopes, and where the upslope end of the unit floor was 40 cm below the surface, while the down slope end was only 30 cm below the surface. Since there was a plowzone, this resulted in the upslope part of the 10-cm level being entirely in sub-plowzone materials, while the downslope was still within the plowzone. This kind of excavation procedure often uses a string and line level stretched out from some control point that serves as a depth datum for the given unit. One knows that the unit was excavated in this fashion when the field notes, unit notes, or artifact bag have a depth indication accompanied by "bd," such as "30 - 40 cm bd." The "bd" means "below [this particular excavation unit's] datum."

Unless there is reason to believe otherwise, such as readily defined natural/cultural strata, virtually all archaeological deposits, and especially those in active soils, will be parallel with the land surface as it currently exists. Certainly, an excavation unit's floor that is so excavated will be closer to what things were like in the past than will something dug normal to the planet's gravity. Thus, in the situation above, each corner of the unit should have been 40 cm below the surface, duplicating on the unit floor the original surface slope of the test unit. One will know that this procedure has been followed when, in reviewing field notes or looking at the artifact bags, the level depth is accompanied by "bs," such as "30 - 40 cm bs." The "bs" means "below surface."

In most Phase II situations, then, it is also beside the point to set out some kind of unit datum, stretch a string with line level out over the unit, then attempt to measure the depth of the floor relative to the string. Again, this tends to be done in situations where – for reasons we do not quite follow – the floor of the test unit is to be kept normal to the planet's gravitational field, even though the deposit and everything else slopes. The use of a string-line level in this fashion in most open field test unit cases is not going to be needed, and just adds to time and labor. Instead, measuring from the surface down, usually at unit corners, should be adequate.

artifact array found or left intact in the floor will be sketched in. Comments will be made about texture, fill, and anything else that the project manager has asked the crew to record.

Something rarely done is having the floor of each level photographed. The only time photographs and additional drawings will be made of the test unit will be when features are encountered. Unless there is something to cause comment -- and remember again, the field crew is generally skilled and experienced,

Tip: Unit Walls

In excavating test units especially, it usually is necessary only to trowel one unit wall. That wall will serve for the profile photograph and drawing. The other unit walls will be shovel-cut. Experienced field crews can keep an excavation unit wall clean and plumb with a flat-nose shovel; many, indeed, can do it with a mattock. In most situations, the entire unit will be dug out, with all walls cleaned using a shovel. After the base of the unit is reached, *then* one of the unit walls will be troweled or "cleaned."

although *not* as experienced as the project director -- there *normally* is no reason to photograph each unit level. The final decision is up to the project manager.

When a unit reaches its final depth, which will be pre-determined by instructions in the SOW, unit records will be finalized. By that point, there will be a collection of what are called "level forms" for each of the excavation levels taken out. Now, what will be needed is a profile drawing of the test unit as well as a photograph or series of photographs of that same wall profile.

One of the unit walls will be selected to be troweled clean, variously referred to as "troweling the wall" or "cleaning the wall." The unit profile will be photographed before it is drawn.

There are two things involved in photographing the unit profile. The first are standard picture definition things: Metric scale, indication of compass north (for most parts of the country), photo menu board. The photo board should indicate the site number, unit number, unit grid coordinates (ALL coordinates), floor depth below surface, and date. Chalk boards are acceptable albeit unprofessional; black-with-white-letter menu boards are preferable.

The second thing involved in unit photographs is neatness. The area that will be in the photograph should be clean and tidy. The string that has served as the unit edge all of this time should be removed (if it has survived intact). Any extraneous leaves, twigs, clumps of dirt, and similar bits of debris should be removed from around the surface. Sometimes this is not possible: Sometimes the only photograph available will be the one with the toe slope of the backdirt pile in it. Still, as much of that backdirt pile toe slope should be moved or, if that is not practical, groomed.

There is a reason for this. Rightly or wrongly, the subconscious assessment of the quality of the work done will be based in part upon how neat and tidy the unit photographs are. Many of the unit profile photographs will be presented in the Phase II report,

Photo Menu Boards

Black slotted menu boards around 16 x 20 inches are preferred for in-photograph labeling. These will require the white plastic letters that are used to spell out the site, unit, and other information of importance.

Photo menu boards are used for unit profile photographs and for feature photographs. When a feature is being documented, the labeling on the menu board should say "Feature __," giving the feature number as well as any information pertaining to depth or, if proper, horizontal location. When a profile is being shown, then the compass direction of the profile should be given. Usually, the menu board will be set up to read:

Site number
unit number
unit coordinates
Feature [number] *or* [compass direction] Profile
depth cm bs
date

Photo menu board letters tend to be about 1.5 inches high. They exist as uppercase and lowercase. They tend to get lost a lot. We suggest the following, if this is not being done already.

Photo menu board letters should be kept in a small tool or tackle box. There should be plastic bags each containing the letters for commonly used words: Feature, Posthole, Hearth, Unit, North, South, East, West, Profile, cm bs. The photo board may well have the site number kept on it for the duration of the project. Professionalism suggests that this should not be a problem; decades of dealing with field work indicates that some of the letters or numbers will get knocked off anyway. If the site number is not kept on the board, the necessary letters and numbers should be bagged separately.

All of this separation of individual words is to bypass the fumbling around that a person will need to do to set up the menu board prior to a photograph. The more that that kind

of work can be simplified, the faster the process will go. Letters should be in labeled bags, usually three different letters per bag, and there should be a surplus of letters. More importantly, when the letters are taken off of the menu board, they should be placed back in the correct bag. We have seen crew members spend 15 minutes fumbling about trying to set up menu boards; that is 15 minutes of billable time spent on an exercise that can be managed much better. In bad weather, having things set up beforehand is quite a blessing: We have run Phase II testing projects often in sub-zero weather and in weather well over 42°C with 50 percent humidity. Any decision making that can be done ahead of time really helps people who are tired, cold (or swelteringly hot), and not thinking clearly. Setting up the letters for a menu board is one such exercise that can be done ahead of time.

Figure 6.3. *Placing the letters for frequently used words, like "unit," "wall," "profile, or "feature," in separate bags is a great deal better than trying to sort through and re-form the words each time the photo menu board is composed.*

and unlike the profile drawings (which will be re-drawn at the office), the photographs taken in the field will be the ones used. While it is possible with digitizers to edit those pictures, it is more cost-effective to get as much of it right the first time, when the picture is taken in the field.

After the photographs are done, the wall profile will be drawn. Unit profiles will involve two people drawing, and this again is not much different than what student archaeologists learned in the field schools. There will be a string line with a line level. Measurements will be taken relative to that line of the surface as well as the floor and intervening profile features.[7] Dominant soil

colors, including mottling, will be noted, as will texture. It is also important to indicate soil horizons and horizon boundaries. The other features of the profile drawing -- scale, grid coordinates, legend -- are all commonly explained in standard archaeology field schools and methods texts, and need not be repeated here.

After the unit is finished, it will need to be backfilled. Scheduling this depends on the nature of the project as well as immediate circumstances. Sometimes, it being near the end of the day and setting up another

---

7. We mention the surface here. Years ago, working as crew members on a TVA (Tennessee Valley Authority) project, we produced a rather fine profile drawing of a complicated feature. We

passed it along to the project director. The project director looked it over and calmly remarked that, it looked really fine (we beamed), but we had forgotten to put in the string level as it related to the land surface (groan). So, while the rest of the crew ate dinner, we toddled back out to the site and redrew the feature correctly.

Tip: Dealing with Cold and Inclement Weather

To remain competitive, private-sector firms need to do field work under conditions that the academic sector can safely avoid. This includes rain as well as cold. Over the years, different firms have come up with solutions for dealing with archaeological field work in extreme weather.

The only major problem with cold weather is that the ground freezes. Field crew can dress well enough to stay warm, and while working in the cold is tiring because the body is both trying to warm itself and also is fighting the restriction of additional clothing, there rarely are major health problems due to the cold itself. Indeed, when it is really quite cold – in the -20°C range – one will still find that the person doing the digging is generating enough body warmth that jackets and sometimes even gloves come off.

Cold weather presents two basic problems for the field archaeologist, based upon daily temperature range. In situations where the temperature goes above freezing during part of the day, the near surface soil will thaw, resulting in both a slippery footing as well as mud. Further, that freeze-thaw cycle will cause the unit profile walls to begin spalling off. This creates a major problem if the unit walls were cut too finely, since a respectable profile photograph may be impossible.

In situations where the temperature stays below freezing throughout the day, excavation is difficult. The ground may be unfrozen below the depth reached by the shovel, and may land in the screen unfrozen. However, unless it is processed quickly, it will freeze and become very hard to work. Avoiding this is done by slowing down how quickly the fill is tossed into the screen, as well as making sure that the person digging chops up the fill as much as possible.

If the ground is frozen and features need to be handled, often firms will spot-thaw the portion of the ground over the feature, scrape it back, photograph it, then remove the fill before everything freezes back up. It is not unusual for work in cold areas to use a 30-gallon metal trash can, a lidless oil drum, or something similar, move it over a section of ground, build a fire in it, and let it thaw the earth beneath it.

One problem with frozen earth is that it is frozen. This means that a hand trowel will not have much effect, and examining things like posthole stains can become very

difficult. One approach that is commonly used is to take a machete and a small three-pound hammer, place the machete across the possible posthole stain, then section the stain with a sharp blow of the hammer across the back of the machete blade. Since the stain will already be recorded and mapped, the only issue will be processing the fill, which will now be available as a chunk of frozen earth. It is ugly, but it works, and more to the point, does not do any damage to the data base. The only caution is that if it is sufficiently cold, the blade may shatter; we have had that happen on a few occasions.

In some situations, it may be possible to erect small shelters over test units. This depends upon any number of circumstances, not the least of which is how deep the test unit will be. There are few solutions for shallow test units, unless a camping tent of sufficient height is used. Even then, the issue is one of adequate light to do the work.

What actually is done will depend upon where the site is, and just how cold it is getting. We have done several Phase II projects in severe cold, where units went down over a meter. We built small pup-tent-like frames with 2 x 4 lumber, covered the frames with translucent plastic, then placed them over the units . During the day, the body heat of the person working inside kept the air above 10°C, even though the outside temperature was around -15°C. The clear plastic allowed enough light in to see what to do. At night, we dragged a sheet of plywood over the unit, then put the tent-like contraption over it. That trapped the day's heat inside enough so that, at levels deeper than about half-meter, the floor remained thawed.

Phase II testing and surface collections can be done in rain; certainly surface collections can with no major difficulty. Hand excavation requires that the unit be protected, both from direct rain coming into the unit as well as from surface run-off that can enter the unit. That second danger can be more of a problem, since it can destroy the unit walls. Fortunately, in most parts of the country, rain storms normally do not last more than a day, and often less than an hour, so work can be postponed. If the work cannot be postponed, then it may be required to jury-rig some sort of temporary shelter for the unit (the person screening gets to stand in the rain regardless).

Figure 6.4a. Example of a temporary shelter placed over a Phase II unit. Such shelters keep the unit warm in the winter and allow field work to be done under conditions where it might not be possible otherwise.

Figure 6.4b. Temporary shelters allow testing even in sub-zero conditions.

test unit not being possible, it makes better sense to fill in a unit. In other cases, where access is possible and safety is not an issue, it may be possible to leave the units open then hire a backhoe with an endloader to come in, or even rent a Bobcat™, and fill the units. In yet other cases, it may be that the area is too accessible to people or livestock, so that each unit is to be backfilled when completed.

Establishing control for a controlled surface collection can be done in two basic ways: gridding off the area somehow and collecting from those areas; or piece-plotting, which is normally done using a transit.

In parts of the country where ground-surface visibility is good and soil or sediment accumulation is not an issue, the site can be collected as is once the control system is set up. In other parts of the country where ground visibility is not good, or where there is an active soil, the site may be plowed, then disc-ed or harrowed first. This usually will be done only if there is evidence that plowing had once been done, and only if it is reasonably possible to do.

Once the site has been plowed, setting up a collecting grid can be done in several ways: The collection unit corners can be "shot in" with a transit, they can be sequentially triangulated in, or they can be set out by eye. Most systems either are overly exact and correspondingly expensive, or rather inexpensive and unacceptably inexact. The final decision will depend upon circumstances, and hopefully this will have been foreseen when the Phase II budget was worked out.

A controlled surface collection may well serve the needs of a Phase II testing regime. Often, though, in areas where plowed land is common it is the first of a two-step process to see if the site retains depositional integrity, here in the sense of retaining features and structure indications like foundation trenches or posthole stains. The surface collection then becomes an instrument that is used to help locate areas of the site where such features may survive. The second step, then, is to peel back that plowed matrix and look at the unplowed surface.

Removing the plowzone often is best done mechanically, and most SOW that request plowzone removal are written with this provision. It is not that information is not contained in the plowzone. Rather, the information content relative to the needs of a Phase II testing exercise and to the overall needs of the compliance project are such that loss of that information is secondary to what will be gained by stripping.

Most sites plowed for a controlled surface collection have a history of having been plowed. Thus, the artifacts already are a bit out of horizontal and a lot out of vertical context. If one wants to imagine artifacts as pixels in an image, then that image is blurred. Pulling back the plowzone to see what, if any, features may have been associated with -- or even been a source for -- those artifacts becomes an exercise in documenting site depositional integrity and a first step in assessing the behavioral-information potential of the site.

The SOW will indicate if any features are to be recovered. Most Phase II testing exercises that have the controlled surface collection followed by a stripping of selected plowzone areas only request that the features be mapped in. The best way to do this is simply using a transit and plotting a point on each feature relative to the site datum. The feature -- pit, foundation trench, whatever -- will then be drawn with the surveyed point or points indicated. Features will be photographed, and this will make use of the photo menu board, scale, and directional indicator.

Mapping will be detailed and precise. Most Phase II exercises of this kind will require that the stripped area be backfilled. It may be a year before anyone -- and it may well be another firm -- returns to the site. Locating those re-buried features will be difficult enough even with sound field notes. High-quality mapping will be recognized and noted by that firm, by the Lead agency, and by the SHPO/THPO. It never hurts to do things that enhance the reputation for quality of one's own firm.

6.3.3. Field Notes and Records

The field notes for the Phase II testing exercise will be kept in a three-ring, D-ring (also called slant-ring) loose-leaf binder. Using a round-ring binder is not a good idea. Round rings tend to trap the back pages; opening the binder often will tear punch-holes of those pages. Round-ring binds are much harder to use than D-ring binders.

Phase II field notes contain five sets of information:

* general project information, including maps and SOW;

* general field notes as kept by the field supervisor;

* specific unit and unit-level notes kept by each test-unit crew;

* feature records; and

* other records, inventories, and logs.

Each of those information sets will be a general sub-section within the field note binder, and will be set off by some kind of tab-labeled divider. At the end of

Comments on Safety

All Federal projects we have directed have required, as part of standing OSHA requirements, that there be a developed safety plan known to all employees, along with a designated safety officer. This has held even for projects where excavations are shallow: People can get seriously hurt in any number of remarkably imaginative ways. Personnel need to know hospital locations and emergency phone numbers; most firms make sure that the first-aid and CPR training of all employees is current.

For test units opened in pastures or in residential areas, it is important to cover the units over each evening and to somehow fence those units off. Generally, half-inch plywood will be adequate to cover the unit; quarter-inch plywood will be too weak to support a person's weight, while particle board will come apart in the wet.

Where the problem may be pedestrian traffic, usually 36- to 40-inch high posts with yellow caution tape bounding the unit or the area being tested will be sufficient for insurance purposes, combined with the plywood over the units, and the screens set on the plywood. Such tape is available in hardware and home supply centers. Urban environments may require more formidable barriers, and at times a security guard. This will depend upon circumstances, insurance liability requirements, the community, the Lead agency's procedures, and perhaps even the SOW.

In pasture settings, a piece of plywood over the unit is helpful, but any livestock larger than a goat will go through it if it steps on it. Livestock may be dumb, but they *are* curious. A fence that can serve to discourage inquisitive cattle usually is needed. Yellow caution tape generally is not effective: Livestock often are illiterate, and in any case tend to try to eat the tape, usually with less than pleasant results.

In woodlot areas in the fall, and in some states in the spring as well, it may be important for all crew members to wear flame-orange vests. This serves as protection – to some extent – from hunters. It is always important to know when the hunting seasons – especially the elk, deer, boar, and bear seasons – are. Since some states already have a doe season, and since most wildlife managers are recommending that all areas with deer have a doe season, the project manager especially needs to know if there is a spring hunting season.

Figure 6.5. *Example of Phase II project in a public area. Here, the project could be secured with the fence and gate. Normally, corporate insurance policies as well as Federal regulations require yellow caution tape and other barriers be placed around the test units. It usually is best to cover units with plywood as well.*

field work, when the project has moved to the office, the field note binder will become the project binder. At the end of the project, the binder will have proprietary corporate information removed, the rest of the information copied, then the original notes will be turned over to the client, or a suitable curatorial facility, along with photographs, artifact collections, and a copy of the Phase II report.

Like Phase I notes, the Phase II notebook may end up containing draft figures and tables to be used in the final report, progress reports, management summaries, and often anything written on paper that has a bearing on the project. Unlike Phase I notebooks but like Phase III, the Phase II set of notes may come to include a second or even third binder devoted to photographs, slides, and drawn figures, and perhaps even tables. This will happen if there is an abundance of such material; otherwise, those images and tables will be placed in a back section of that growing project binder.

As with the Phase I field notebook (see section 5.3.3.), the following generally should be in the Phase II notebook, probably in the indicated order.

Section 1. General Project Information

* *Scope of Work (SOW):*

A copy of the SOW will be placed near the front of the project notebook, along with any other explanatory correspondence. Specific project requirements -- number, size, and depth of test units, for example -- will be highlighted or underlined.

* *Portions of the Phase I report:*

Copies of the essential parts of the Phase I report will be present. These will include the map or figure showing artifact clusters or shovel test distributions, perhaps a table or list of what material was found where, and any other documentation that will be of use in setting up the Phase II testing regime.

Deep Units and Shoring

Phase II testing can involve excavation units that go well below the surface. OSHA regulations require that any excavation unit deeper than 5.0 ft (about 1.5 m) must either be shored or stepped back; in California, CAL-OSHA requires shoring in units deeper than 4.0 ft (about 1.2 m), and a permit for units deeper than 5.0 ft. "Stepped back" means clearing back a floor or ledge of a given distance (depending upon the engineering properties of the soil) for every 1.2 or 1.5 m of depth in a unit. In effect, it is like making steps. Such a process could become expensive, and in some settings may not be possible because the room just might not be there. For example, if the soil or sediment matrix could support a shelf of 1.0 m width for every 1.5 m of depth, a 4.5 m deep 1 x 2 m test unit might require opening a 5 x 6 m unit area at the surface to accommodate the stepping.

The second solution is to shore the walls of the test unit. There are any number of solutions, ranging from using adjustable steel columns as lateral braces to hold wales and the vertical sheet piling in place, to formal shoring "cages" that may be placed in the unit or trench. The U.S. Army Corps of Engineers *Safety and Health Requirements Manual.* (EM 385-1-1, Rev. October 1996) provides specific instructions, diagrams, and notes for different shoring options, and the minimum requirements for shoring relative to soils and excavation depth. (The most recent information with respect to these and related field safety issues can also be accessed at http://www.hg.usace.army.mil/ceso/cesopub. htm, which is a convenient source for field-planning information.) If shoring is anticipated, then the proposed Phase II budget will also need to make allowances for this.

In shoring situations, the unit profile is drawn sequentially: Every level or two, another band of the wall profile is drawn and photographed. If the camera can be kept the same distance out, at the same angle, and in the same vertical axis, it actually is possible to reassemble a photo mosaic of the unit wall.

One other item here: Safety. When units begin to go deep, safety becomes a major issue. Trenches collapse; people get killed. If a unit or trench is at a depth requiring shoring, then the unit or trench needs to be shored. People are not to be in unshored trenches. If the test unit is going to have any depth, hard hats are required. For some projects located

in areas of active construction, the wearing of hard hats may be mandatory even for walking across the surface of the project area. The area will be posted as a "Hard Hat Area," and the firm will be required to supply all personnel as well as all visitors with hard hats.

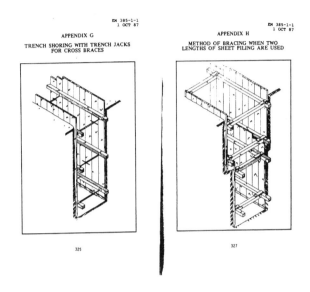

Figure 6.6. *OSHA regulations require shoring whenever units reach 5.0 ft (about 1.5 m) below the surface; in California, shoring is required when depths exceed 4.0 ft (1.2 m). Unit walls can be braced in any number of ways; the above figure presents two systems diagrammed in the US Army Corps of Engineers Safety and Health Requirements Manual (EM 385-1-1. Rev October 1987).*

* *Logistics, including budget and hour allocations for tasks:*

The logistics section of a Phase II field notebook will contain the standard number of person-hours available for field work and often for the entire project. That section also will contain the amount budgeted for rental of backhoes, endloaders, or other heavy machinery that may be required. Hopefully, when the budget was prepared, the people doing that had had the foresight to call the area where the site is located and get names and price quotes for the rental of such machinery. That information, too, should be in this

section and again written down in the records-of-communication (see below).

Some firms will use *Work Request Forms* or similar quasi-memoranda to help project managers keep track of how many people will be needed for how long on which projects, including field and laboratory work. This is particularly important in larger firms, where many projects are running concurrently. Scheduling everyone becomes critical. Such forms will be placed in this part of the notebook as well.

Schedules, too, may be needed, along with some sort of work-flow time-line diagram. Some Phase II testing exercises are small; some can be very large and last a couple months. This means that some sort of schedule is needed to keep the project on track. A copy of that schedule will be placed in this section.

Any vehicle mileage records or per diem requirements should also be placed in this section.

Project maps and figures:

Copies of project maps, copied sections of county soils maps and USGS topographic maps, and related diagrams and figures will be placed in this sub-section. This will also include mapping information, specifically where the site datum is or will be, where the nearest USGS or similar benchmark is, and similar information. It is just as likely that the Phase I shovel

test map will be located in this section as in the section above.

Unlike Phase I survey, Phase II testing will result in a site map showing the locations of test units, controlled-surface-collection areas, and so on. Depending on the scale of the project, that map may be kept out and separate, or it may be located on a fold-out sheet in this section.

Right-of-entry materials:

A letter indicating permission to excavate from the landowner should be included. In Georgia, for example, it is state law that such permission be in written form, and the state must be notified as well that such excavation will take place. Any permitting letters and other operating agreements should be placed here.

Phase II and Landscape Archaeology

Phase II testing of historic-period properties often is better achieved by opening larger areas relative to unit depth. This holds especially for the areas around historic buildings.

Much archaeological information on a historic-period property is in the past landscaping and building foundations, and that information is contained in the first 30 cm or so of the deposit. Rarely does one actually recover lots of artifacts from the yards of historic residences (wells and privies, though, generally have a lot), and it does not make much sense to open a small "excavation window" like a 1 x 1 m or 1 x 2 m unit, then go deep into a landscape where most of the material and associated features will be closer to the surface. It makes better sense to do landscape archaeology, spend the budgeted excavation volume more on shallower units that open a larger area, and thus get a sense of if signs of planting beds, paths, outhouses and other outbuildings, and so on remain.

This is the Phase II application of "Landscape Archaeology." Landscape archaeology focuses on the cultural lay-out of the landscape, most often in terms of gardens, compounds, and similar landscaping and outbuilding exercises. Remember that archaeology is concerned ultimately with understanding how people lived in the past, and thus needs to look at the patterning of the world that people left behind. For many historic sites, that patterning will not be artifacts only, but also the features in the landscape. For excellent introductions, see Kelso, William M., and Rachel Most, editors. 1990. *Earth Patterns: Essays in Landscape Archaeology.* University Press of Virginia, Charlottesville, and Yamin, Rebecca, and Karen Bescherer Metheny, editors. 1996. *Landscape Archaeology: Reading and Interpreting the American Historical Landscape.* University of Tennessee Press, Knoxville.

Figure 6.7. *Example of shallow Phase II testing defining garden features in the yard of a documented historic residence. Historic archaeological deposits often are shallow, and evidence of past site use can be seen when the upper 30 cm of the deposit is removed. (Photo courtesy of R. Jerald Ledbetter and Southeastern Archeological Services, Inc.).*

* Records of communications:

Any kind of conversation or discussion held with non-project people, or any managerial discussion held with corporate personnel, should be accompanied by a written summary of the discussion. That summary should include the name and title of the person, corporate affiliation, date of discussion, phone number and/or location, and a brief summary of what was discussed.

Interviews with the landowner or resident will be placed under records of communication. So, too, will any discussion with firms renting equipment. Eventually, as the project moves from the field back to the office, conversations with analytical specialists and curatorial facilities will be recorded here as well.

Section 2. General Field Notes

The general field notes contain notes on two sets of information:

* an overall narrative of the project, including nature of the project environment and general day-to-day bookkeeping; and

* summary details on test units or on the controlled surface collection.

The general field notes section often is the most neglected of any of the archaeological record keeping, matched only by the neglect of records-of-communication. Where other parts of the field notes represent pieces of paper composed or drawn by others that can be inserted into the binder, both the communications summaries and the general field notes are composed by the person managing the project in the field.

The general field notes require a detailed recounting of the project area. This will need to include details on vegetation cover and on the kind of soil present. It will be in this section that a vegetation survey, similar to what should have been done for Phase I, will be given, should it be missing from the Phase I report. Even if it *is* in the Phase I report, the results of that work should be verified. How to do this is explained in section 5.3.1.1.

This section also requires detailed descriptions of where, precisely, the site and its mapping referents are located. It needs to be written out with the assumption that 50 years from now someone will have to come back to the area and relocate the test units, and further assume that the landscape may be greatly changed. That is, a reasonable attempt needs to be made to allow someone in the future to relocate the site. This can be done by triangulating in a site datum

Setting Up Controlled Surface Collections

The two most common ways to quickly set up and do a controlled surface collection are the *triangulation method* and the *band method*. The triangulation method requires setting out a baseline of some sort along one side or down the long axis of the area to be collected, along which will be placed pin flags or similar markers at collection grid intervals. The crew will then work off of the grid unit markers, triangulating in the other corners of the collection area. It may be tedious at first, but once the rhythm is established – including knowing what the diagonals for the grid unit should be (amazingly, just about always equal to $\sqrt{2}$ times the length of the square unit's side) – setting out the markers goes quickly. The system is accurate and normally cost-effective. A transit generally will be used to tie in some of the unit markers with the site datum, which gives fine horizontal control.

A variant on the triangulation method is the *band method*. This is a bit less exact, but somewhat faster. It does require a collection area that is relatively narrow. The band method sets out a baseline of grid corner markers at one end of the collection area, like the triangulation method. Then two sets of markers on either side of the plowed area will be set in, forming lines that are at right angles to that first baseline. In effect, three sides of a rectangle will have been set out, bounding the plowed area. Then a tape spanning the area is set between the two side sets of markers, and people "eyeball" where collection units begin and end, based upon reading the stretched tape measure. This system is fast, but not as exact as a triangulation method. With pairs of tapes stretched across area being collected, it is simply a matter of lifting one tape up and over the other to do each collection band.

In both cases, bags labeled with the site number and grid number or coordinates will be used for each collection area. Again, as with test units, it may be well to make up a bag for every collection area, even if nothing was recovered from it. The bags themselves, empty or not, will assist in bookkeeping.

Piece-plotting and similar location-measured collection activities are not as common. The crew will walk the area and place pin flags or similar markers at artifacts or artifact clusters. A transit will then be used to plot in each locus of artifacts (GPS positioning is currently too inexact). Those loci will be numbered, and the number will be recorded both on the bag and on a master set of notes. Later, a map will be prepared showing the locations of artifacts. Piece-plotting is best done if the artifact count is low, or expected to be low, since keeping adequate notes can be tricky.

from a number of reference points that are known to be mapped with their positions widely and redundantly recorded. More and more often, it is done using a GPS; however, GPS positions still are not as precise as traditional land surveying.

Tip: Small Backhoes and Stripping Plowzone

Phase II and Phase III compliance projects may require using heavy earth-moving equipment. This varies by project. In areas where plowing is common, often what is needed for Phase II is the selective stripping of the plowzone.

There are some things to remember in using heavy equipment. The first is to locate machinery that not only is within budget (but then that should have been foreseen when the budget was worked out), but is of the size and type needed.

The second is modifications. The most common piece of equipment used by an archaeologist will be a backhoe. "Backhoe," for an archaeologist, is the comparatively small, scorpion-like device that has a bucket endloader at one end and a 60-cm-wide bucket on a 4-m arm at the other. "Backhoe," in the construction industry, ranges from those small Bobcat™-like things that fit on the end of a pick-up truck to the large, track-tread machines used to dig foundations and move ore out of strip mines. The machine that is desired is a "backhoe-loader," the kind of backhoe, with tires, one would use to put in a sewer line.

Most backhoe buckets are toothed. This is not good. Using the bucket with teeth will result in a series of parallel grooves 2-inches deep. Ugly, and makes review agency people really mad. It also makes dealing with the deposit a problem. Those grooves can be worked around, but there are better ways to handle this.

Generally, practicing archaeologists will request that the backhoe owner or operator spot-weld a plate or clean-up blade to the teeth of the backhoe bucket (it is possible to pop those teeth off; much easier just to spot-weld a blade of metal on). Doing this in effect converts the machine to the equivalent of a Gradall™, but at one-third the rental cost and with considerably greater maneuverability.

(A clean-up blade is a 90-cm or so long, 30-cm high convex steel blade that usually is set in the front of a small piece of earth-moving equipment. It is meant to just push fill out of the way, hence the term "clean-up blade." A piece of quarter- or half-inch steel 90 cm long and 30 cm wide will do the same job, and can be easily spot-welded or tacked to the teeth of a standard 60-cm-wide backhoe bucket. Our impression has been that experienced operators prefer that piece of steel to a manufactured blade, since it behaves like the detailing hand planes/scrapers used by woodworkers.)

People are fascinated by archaeology, and it is not unusual for a firm to give the task of working with the archaeologist to the senior equipment operator. The capacity of the operators we have worked with to use a backhoe with a clean-up blade is remarkable. We have seen them shave a centimeter from a 3-m strip. They are very, very good at what they do.

Figure 6.8. Small backhoes often are used to dig deeper test units, strip areas, and even help backfill. Rental usually is by the day or half-day, depending upon the area, with the cost including both the equipment and the operator. The kind pictured here is the type most commonly used. The bucket arm will read a maximum of 14.0 ft (about 4.3 m). Bucket widths vary, but usually are around 60 cm. (Photo courtesy of R. Jerald Ledbetter and Southeastern Archeological Services, Inc.)

Figure 6.9. To be effective for stripping, the backhoe bucket needs to be modified: Either the teeth should be removed, as in the case here, or a strip of metal attached over the teeth. This avoids the gouging of the site that the teeth would make. A common solution is to spot-weld either a clean-up blade or a sheet of steel to the "inside" of the backhoe teeth. (Photo courtesy of R. Jerald Ledbetter and Southeastern Archeological Services, Inc.)

Figure 6.10. *Backhoe stripping plowzone from a site. The procedure for stripping has the backhoe moving over the unexcavated surface and placing fill to one side. Crew members then use flat-nose shovels to remove the last bit of plowzone to expose the unplowed B horizon. (Photo courtesy of R. Jerald Ledbetter and Southeastern Archeological Services, Inc.)*

Most operators will already know – intuitively, because this also holds for other backhoe work – to position themselves to move over the unexcavated surface. The professional archaeologist needs to explain clearly what needs to be done. This must include showing – not just saying – how deep to dig, and that will require monitoring. Also, it is important to explain where the fill is to be placed, and just as important to provide markers so that the operator knows what area of the plowzone to remove. And, when working with backhoes in this fashion, *always* stand where the operator can see you, and make sure that eye-contact is frequent so you both know you are aware of the other.

As with any management situation, starting out by explaining what you are trying to do, and what you have done or planned to do to help out, will result in a person with a couple-three decades of heavy machinery operation working with you to achieve the project's goals.

The backhoe operator will remove most of the plowzone, perhaps all but a centimeter. However, it will be the field crew, using flat-nose or cut-nose shovels, who will shovel-scrape away the remaining plowzone and define features, should they exist.

In situations where long strips are being exposed, as may be the case when plowzone is removed for a Phase II, the idea will be to have the backhoe operator strip the plowzone back, and progress along the pre-determined path. As the fresh area is exposed, the crew will need to shovel-scrape that area down, then mark the center of every possible feature with a pin flag. After an hour or so, most readily visible features will be lost to view because the ground dries. The idea is to mark features, then to come back and examine each one in detail.

Figure 6.11. *As crew members shovel-scrape, they are expected to recognize feature stains or patterns, then to place pin flags or similar marking devices in those stains. It will be after the area has been stripped that crew members will return to those markers, clean up the area, and photograph then map in the feature. (Photo courtesy of R. Jerald Ledbetter and Southeastern Archeological Services, Inc.)*

The field notes will also keep a running daily narrative of work at the site. That narrative will include the following:

* day and date;

* weather conditions, including (1) temperature in degrees centigrade, (2) wind direction and velocity in km/hr, (3) cloud cover, and (4) precipitation/snow cover;

* field crew present (the first time names are entered, the full name will be given; there after, use the surname); and

* progress or activity on each test unit or with the surface collection areas.

The test units will be set out in numerical order as discussed. For each unit, the names of the people working on that unit need to be recorded, as do the beginning and certainly the ending depths for the day and anything of interest that may have been exposed.

The daily narrative helps piece back together the progress of work on the site. It also helps in making labor estimates for future projects, since all of the information needed for a time-motion study will be recorded.

Section 3. Specific Unit Records

Where test pits are being dug, each test unit will have a specific series of field notes particular to it and maintained by the crew members assigned to that unit. Those records tend to be formalized, and often consist of a cover sheet for each level. That sheet will have blanks to be filled in, indicating site number, date, unit number, unit coordinates, level number, level depth, soil color/texture, associated features, notable artifacts, photograph numbers (if any), and recorders. Somewhere on the form the actual elevation above mean sea level for the corner stakes should be entered. This will be based either on a direct transit reading, or on interpolation from a topographic project map supplied by the client.

At least half of the page will be devoted to filling in specific information about the level. This is done to make sure that important information is not forgotten. The remainder of the page, or sometimes the back side, along with any additional continuation sheets, will be available for unit floor or wall drawings and explanatory notes. Often, those open areas of the page will be gridded. The continuation sheets will have blanks asking for site number, unit number, unit coordinates, and level.

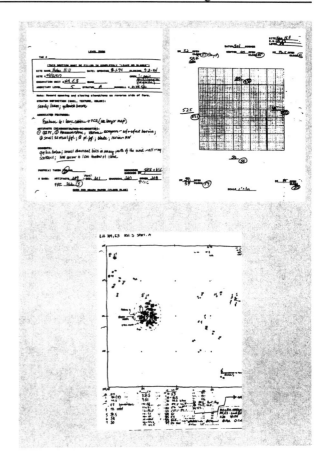

Figure 6.12. Example of a test unit/excavation unit record form. The reverse side is gridded for providing a map of the unit floor. Graph paper serves in this case as a continuation sheet.

Where controlled surface collections are being done, unit forms should be used for each of the surface collection areas. This again is more a bookkeeping exercise, but that form should record the collector's impression of where within the surface area the larger concentrations of artifacts were.

Section 4. Feature Records

Feature records may be placed in a separate section, or they may be placed with the unit notes. On large sites, or with large Phase II projects, it generally is better to keep the feature notes together in one place. This helps in quality control for the records, and also helps to keep track of numbering. While test units may be labeled by numbers or by coordinates -- and using coordinates is better -- features tend to be labeled numerically and in sequence. There is always the danger that the counting will get mixed up.

To avoid bookkeeping and counting errors, the feature section of the field notes will contain a general feature inventory sheet. The feature inventory sheet will list feature number, unit location, level and depth where first defined, and nature of feature, and date.

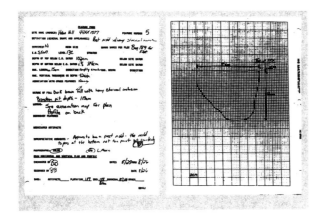

Figure 6.13. Example of a feature form. The reverse side is gridded for planview and cross-section drawings.

Figure 6.14. Example of a field specimen or bag inventory form.

There will be specific fill-in forms for features, just as there are for test units. Again, like test units, these will have spaces for site number, test unit number and coordinates, date, level and depth where first recognized, photographs taken, flotation or soil samples retained, and names of the recorders. A plan view of the feature will be made; where appropriate, profile drawings also will be made. Recordation of the feature will be like that taught in most field schools, and need not be repeated here.

The reason the features are all placed together in one section generally involves bookkeeping. However, it also will help when the time comes to write the Phase II report. When the testing results are discussed, often the discussion will begin with the features before moving on to the general results of the units. Having all of the features set out in order makes that task a bit easier.

Section 5. Other Field Records, Logs, and Inventories

The remainder of the field notes consist of formal bookkeeping records. Each firm will have forms for these, and there will be a file box on-site where blank forms are stored. Hopefully, those forms will be pre-punched; if not, a three-hole punch should also be kept with that file box.

Four sets of records may be located in this section:

* mapping and land-survey notes;

* photo log;

* bag inventory; and possibly

* soil or flotation sample inventory.

Although it varies by how the archaeologist was trained, often it is best if the transit and mapping notes can be kept on forms that can be placed in the project notebook. Formal land survey courses will teach the student to use a smaller, bound surveyor's notebook, which is how such records are kept in the profession. We have found that it is better to make up a standard page form that can be punched and placed in the project binder. This keeps all of the information together and avoids the danger of having the mapping booklet, because its size is so much different than that of normal archaeological records, from getting misplaced. However, this will depend upon the firm and often the project manager.

A standard photo log will be needed. Most Phase II testing exercises generate a large number of photographs. Those photographs include general views of the project area as well as specific photographs of unit walls and of features. The photo log needs to include roll number and film type (for film cameras), exposure number/frame number, and nature of image. Direction of view should always be indicated, as should what the scale the metric scale in the image is. In situations where film is used, the site number and roll number should be written with an indelible ink marker on the plastic case of the roll itself before it is loaded into the camera. This avoids potential confusion later.

A bag inventory is essential. Each artifact bag should be assigned a bag number or field specimen number. There should be a master list in the field notebook that coordinates those numbers with the unit, level, and/or feature.

As with Phase I survey projects, the bag inventories for Phase II projects have a habit of getting muddled somewhere along the line. Fortunately, Phase II often generates substantially fewer bags than a Phase I project. We have found that it helps to avoid confusion to include empty bags on the list, with a note alongside saying "empty" or "no artifacts recovered." This forces each test unit to turn in a number of artifact bags equal to the number of levels removed, and helps avoid bags being misplaced. Every project manager has a way to deal with this, and that will be the procedure used for the given project.

In some Phase II projects, the SOW may request soil samples or flotation samples. These may be collected from features only, from the screened backfill of a unit's level, or from increments down the column of a test unit. These will need to be tracked, just as the artifact bags are tracked.

6.4.   Post-Field

The Phase II testing project is a formal investigation of one or more archaeological sites. The post-field phase of the project is similar to that of any traditional archaeological research effort, except that it must be finished by a fixed date, with many people working on different parts of the project at the same time.

On returning from the field, the following tasks will need to be done so that a draft report can be delivered by its scheduled date:

*   The artifacts, along with a copy of the bag inventory, will go to the lab, and general analyses will begin (see Chapter 8);

*   any specialized analyses, such as high-magnification use-wear on diagnostic artifacts, or flotation processing, will need to be scheduled with the samples shipped to the subcontracting specialist just as soon as the laboratory staff has processed the materials;

*   film or other images will be processed;

*   draft figures for the report will be prepared then submitted to the graphics department;

*   a site map will be prepared if needed, and that too will be submitted to the graphics department; and

*   the writing of the report will be started (see Chapter 9).

While most of these tasks will be done at the same time, as they were with a Phase I project, there also are major differences. The first will be in responsibility for analysis. While much of the analytical work can be done initially by laboratory staff, much of the more important work that treats data potential and site structure will be done either by the project manager or by sub-contracted specialists. Whereas a simple count and categorization of artifacts was sufficient for Phase I, basic and sometimes detailed mensuration may be required for Phase II analyses.

The second major difference will be the level of background research and citation of current research literature. For a Phase I report, a general summary of the history and prehistory of the region is appropriate. For a Phase II report, a summation of the current understanding and status of research relative to the type of site and the region is expected. This task, too, usually will be that of the project manager.

6.4.1.   Level of Analyses Expected

The major difference between preparation of the Phase I report and the Phase II report is the level of analysis and literature research required. The issue is to provide information to allow the Lead agencies and the SHPO/THPO to determine if the site is eligible for listing on the National Register. The research information provided needs to address questions about site depositional integrity and about information content of the site, or about association of the site with important persons, events, or craftsmanship/design.

The Phase II analysis is a detailed interpretive analysis of a given archaeological site, in terms of its depositional structure, its archaeology, and its place in local and regional culture-history. The testing performed rarely is sufficient to provide final answers to standing research questions as set forth in the state historic preservation plan or present in the literature, but the results *are* sufficient to contribute to the basic understanding of the region's history or prehistory.

To give some sense of scale, the level of analysis for a Phase II project is generally at the level expected of a short doctoral dissertation or a refined master's thesis. True, the goals of the Phase II report are different than those of graduate theses, but in terms of literature review, data analysis, and interpretation of those data, the two kinds of documents are not all that different. New knowledge will be produced and presented in the report, knowledge that furthers understanding of the area's past. It is possible that that information will be redundant and does not have the potential to provide an important contribution to our understanding of the past; that is, the site appears to be another example of a mid-nineteenth-century farm house (see Chapter 2 box "Integrity" for comments on comparable examples). It is just as possible that it does have such potential: The only way that that will be known is if the analysis itself is sufficiently detailed.

The following will have to be done so that the ultimate purpose of the Phase II exercise -- addressing Register-eligibility -- can be done:

* A detailed treatment will be needed of the site matrix so that questions of depositional integrity can be addressed;

* diagnostic artifacts will need to be identified, related to a specific period or culture, and placed within depositional context;

* basic measurements will need to be taken and descriptions presented of appropriate artifacts;

* components will need to be delimited vertically and/or horizontally across the site, with the distributions verified statistically;

* basic relationships among behavioral indicators within the artifact collection will need to be shown statistically, then plotted horizontally to the degree allowed by the testing protocol; and

* the contents of the site and its components will need to be related to the larger body of research about region's history or prehistory, and that in turn will need to be tied both to standing research questions in the literature and in the state plan.

Sometimes specialized analyses will be done to advance particular analytical sets. For example, high-magnification use-wear analyses may be done on the lithic applications industry to relate tool use to site function and to intra-site activity areas. Questions of seasonality and settlement pattern may be handled through the specialized analysis of flotation samples, should the SOW have requested such work. It is even possible that radiocarbon dates were requested. All of these, though, as simply refinements of the analyses sets mentioned above.

Phase II analyses inevitably will involve comparative questions. These will be of two basic types:

* Are the materials present in one level or component independent of those in another level or component?

* Does the horizontal distribution of artifacts show internal behavioral patterning?

The first question will involve that of site depositional integrity and of single versus multi-components. Often in areas where plowing is common, a site will have been plowed but the Ap horizon has long since disappeared, replaced by an A2-A3/B1 horizon sequence [E-AB/BA horizon sequence]. Or perhaps that Ap horizon is still discernable. Are the artifacts located in the B horizon derived from the same population as that of the Ap horizon? If the answer is yes, the site is disturbed and may well be considered ineligible by the agency or the SHPO/THPO for listing on the National Register.

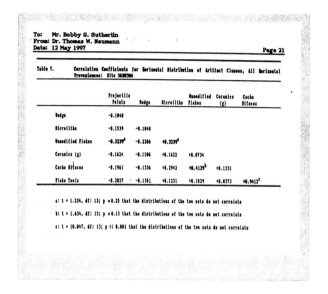

Figure 6.15. Example of a correlation matrix used to get some idea of artifact associations and depositional patterning. The artifacts came from the same component in widely dispersed test units. The results suggested a non-random distribution of artifacts based upon function.

Again, if artifacts are found in an active soil 10 cm below the surface, and others are found 50 cm below the surface, do they represent separate occupations, or just the sinking of older material deeper into the solum? We faced this question at the 300-year-old Friends' Third Haven Meeting House in Easton, Maryland. The answer was that the material had sunk (Neumann 1993). Again, statistical comparison of assemblages for each 10-cm level was done to show that the artifact sets really were not independent, but instead proceeded from a common surface origin.

There are two statistical tests most often used to establish basic arguments for Phase II analyses, a correlation coefficient and a chi-squared. A chi-squared test is used to decide if two populations of things came from the same set or not. It will be used to argue if the material from one level or place in the deposit is independent of that in another.

The best way to accomplish assessing behavioral patterning is the *correlation matrix*. This is a simple and efficient way to summarize level-artifact information from disparate test units, while also providing an insight into behavior patterning. All that is requires is setting out a matrix, where each side consists of artifact categories (e.g., for a prehistoric deposit: unused/waste flakes, microliths, bifaces, projectile points, ceramics, steatite, fire-cracked rock), then running a Pearson's r correlation coefficient against each of the pairs in the matrix (Figure 6.15). This gives some sense of how the distributions of different artifact classes covary with the distributions of other artifact classes. The correlation coefficient merely states that the topological plane based upon the frequency points of one artifact class is parallel with

We learned about archaeology from that... Secondary Deposition and Cowanesque

The Cowanesque Reservoir in extreme north-central Pennsylvania is maintained by the U.S. Army Corps of Engineers. Beginning in 1987, the Corps of Engineers began the process that would expand the reservoir to its final design capacity. This involved several Phase I, Phase II, and Phase III projects, most of which were conducted by different firms. We directed one Phase II project that is of interest here.

The site was located on a T1 terrace approximately 50 m south of the Cowanesque River, a 20-m or so wide, two-meter deep stream that ran around 2-3 m below the level of the floodplain terrace. Phase I testing, done on two separate occasions by two different firms (once with shovel tests and a second time with a backhoe), had indicated the presence of a prehistoric site. The Phase II exercise was to determine if the site had integrity and to confirm data potential. Based on the Phase I report, the Pennsylvania SHPO had already tentatively determined that the site probably had data potential (a shovel test had actually recovered fragments of a nearly entire prehistoric pot, something unheard of by the late

twentieth century in the eastern United States). Our work in many respects was probably unconsciously seen as *pro forma*: Everyone pretty much felt that this was a legitimate, Register-eligible prehistoric site.

The Phase II assessment involved further shovel testing of the terrace, then a series of 1 x 2 m excavation units, taken in 10-cm levels to 30 cm below the deepest occurrence of cultural materials.

The results were interesting. Only a couple of the shovel tests – and these were the ones closest to the edge of the floodplain terrace – recovered any cultural material, which consisted of prehistoric waste flakes, or historic coal, window glass, or ceramics. This was also true of the 1 x 2 test units. The material recovered all came from within 30 cm of the surface. Because of the absence of features, the absence of anything more than apparent lithic manufacturing debris (waste flakes), and the apparent confinement of these items to what probably would have been a plowzone, the site was assessed as having no data potential or integrity.

These results contradicted the original Phase I reports, and resulted in a legitimate challenge from the Pennsylvania SHPO: How is it that

TWO Phase I reports had each concluded that the site had data potential and integrity, while our Phase II assessment concluded that it probably had neither? The draft report was returned with (lots and LOTS of) comments, to be revised in accord with Phase I conclusions.

Our initial assessment had simply been that, because all of the cultural material had come from the plowzone, and because all of it was waste debris, that the site had neither data potential nor integrity. Clearly, more needed to be said.

A total of 20 prehistoric waste flakes, 11 pieces of historic ceramics, 8 pieces of window glass, and 14 pieces of coal (historic) had been recovered during our excavations. Fifteen of the flakes, 8 historic ceramic sherds, 5 pieces of glass, and 13 pieces of coal had been recovered from the Ap horizon. The flakes had been weighed; everything else had been counted. We went back and weighed the other items. All of that material – regardless of whether it was a prehistoric flake, a historic piece of glass, or a hunk of coal – had an average weight between 0.1 - 0.2 g. Further, everything – historic or prehistoric – all weighed within 0.01 g (flakes) to 0.3 g (the coal) of the same weight.

that of another; that is, that certain sets of things tend to be found in the same area as other things. To picture this another way, if a frequency graph was made of the two artifacts classes, the lines for each class (following an x-axis arranged by unit) would be nearly parallel. In anthropological terms, this means only that the distribution of one set of artifacts correlates positively or negatively, or not at all, with the artifacts of another set. To paraphrase Runyon, whom Thomas (1976:95) quoted, it may not be causality, but it sure is a good way to bet.

6.4.2. Addressing the Basic Phase II Issues

The Phase II project is meant to provide what is needed to answer questions about the eligibility of the site for the National Register. Those questions really come down to two basic issues:

*   Does the site have depositional integrity?

*   Does the site contribute or have the potential to contribute to our understanding of the country's past?

In treating the Phase II analysis, those are the two questions that really need to be addressed before the professional archaeologist chooses to recommend to the agency if the site should or should not be considered eligible for listing on the National Register.

Site depositional integrity usually is the independent criterion. That is, if the integrity of the deposit has been compromised, then often the information potential of that deposit also is compromised.

Integrity, though, is a two-variable issue. The first is physical disturbance, which would include plowing, fill events, and similar disruption (we dealt with one site in Minnesota, located on a sand terrace along a river, that turned out to have been cleared of large oaks in the 1920s using winches and oxen teams to

This was pretty much the only information we needed: We argued that the cultural materials, prehistoric and historic, had been deposited on the T1 terrace during a flood event, that they had originated from upstream, and that their deposition had occurred subsequent to valley clearance and the start of cultivation. Further, none of the previous materials recovered from the terrace, with the exception of the fragments of the pot, were in their original context.

(We later found the weights for the flakes recovered during the Phase I testing. Those weights also were the same as the weights of the material we had recovered.)

The solution, obviously, involved stream transport and re-deposition of such materials. The reason that all of the materials, historic or prehistoric, ceramic or coal, were of the same weight was that they had been size-sorted during a flood, and deposited at the same time. The governing formula for particle movement is the Manning Formula, which in effect makes size of an object and its movement by a fluid dependent upon the velocity of the fluid that picks it up and moves it. (Interesting tidbit: It takes the same force or "head" of water to detach and move a *clay-sized* particle [0.002 mm diameter] from its matrix as it does to

move a rock the size of a softball [110.0 mm or so in diameter]. Sand- and silt-sized objects, like the flakes, glass, ceramics, or coal, all move in response to substantially less force.)

The reason all of the materials were found *together* (an important point as well) in the plowzone was that historic land clearance has increased flood discharge rates sufficiently to produce enough head during a flood to pick up and move cultural materials. Flood waters are notoriously indiscriminate, and being unable to distinguish between particles that are natural and particles that are artificial, picked up all within a size range and carried them downstream. When flood flow velocity decreased, the force needed to keep the particles in suspension disappeared, and the larger particles dropped out. Water crossing a T1 terrace would result in just such a decrease in local flow velocity at the end stages of the flood, since the terrace would produce friction against the movement of the floodwaters. This also explained why everything was in the plowzone: The event or events carrying the prehistoric as well as historic materials downstream had happened *after* Euroamerican settlement of the watershed; of course the stuff would have been dropped onto a surface that was or would soon be plowed.

This is a cautionary tale. The Phase I reports as Phase I reports were sound and logical. Phase I analyses are not expected to do things like weigh each flake or piece of broken window glass, not to mention coal. The response of the SHPO to the Phase II conclusions, presented as they were in the draft report without such explanation, also were proper. While we had a suspicion, because of the plowzone restriction of the materials as well as their non-diagnostic nature, that the site was not eligible for the National Register, and while that might have been (or actually was, as it turns out) a really sound gut reaction, it still was NOT adequately documented relative to the needs of the SHPO. The Phase II responsibility is to document thoroughly.

Two points, then: Always document as if for an adversarial audience why the Phase II results are as they are; and always remember those college physics and hydrology classes, taken for just this purpose.

Neumann, Thomas W. 1988. *Phase II Investigations at 36Ti31 and 36Ti47, Tioga County, Pennsylvania.* U.S. Army Corps of Engineers, Baltimore District.

twist out stumps and, when that failed, gun powder; we concluded that the deposit probably had been disturbed).

The second issue for integrity is that of relativity. How disturbed is the site *relative to* other examples? A heavily plowed Late Prehistoric site in Alabama, where only the bottom 10 cm of some posthole stains survive and everything else is in the plowzone is disturbed and probably not eligible for listing on the Register; a site with exactly the same physical attributes but with Paleoindian artifacts would clearly be eligible. Depositional integrity is a relative issue, and it is relative to what is known about similar kinds of site within the jurisdiction of the SHPO/THPO. Culture resources are managed at the state, tribal-land, or local government level, and comparisons need to be made based upon those bounds.

Statistical tests establish the metrics for how to argue a case. The final answer to the question of depositional integrity will depend upon a thorough

understanding of the historic or prehistoric research literature, and how the site may or may not fit into gaps within that literature. Part of those gaps will have been identified in the state historic preservation plan, although not all.

After treating the question of site depositional integrity -- and it is possible that deeper components have depositional integrity while the surface has been seriously disturbed -- the second broad issue is if the information content of the site has the potential to contribute to what is known about the past, be it people, events, ways of making or doing things, or just understanding of life-ways in general. Historic sites usually involve any of those four options; prehistoric sites involve usually only the last, also called "data potential."

The information content of the site also requires knowing the research literature for the region. It also requires having some sense of what the site in question actually *can* say regarding past human behavior. This probably is where Phase II work differs most from the cultural-historic approach of pre-1960s normative archaeology: The cultural-historical material will be used to get some sense of cultural association, but from there the issue will be trying to get a sense of what human activity took place on the site, and how that activity fits into what is known about how people in the area were living at that same general time.

Establishing the general nature of the information content of the site -- making an abstract of the site's information, to return to that analogy -- should include both statistical tests for behavioral patterning as well as behaviorally sensitive analyses (e.g., South's [1977] functional groups or, for prehistoric materials, use-wear analyses) that are then tied into the larger sense of what people were doing during the period in question.

The professional archaeologist *does not make a determination*. However, the professional archaeologist will make a recommendation of what the Lead agency should do, and that agency generally will follow the archaeologist's advice.

6.4.3. General Structure of Report

The Phase II report has two parts:

* the basic report itself, consisting of background information, methods, analyses, and results; and

* recommendations.

The general structure of a report is considered in Chapter 9. For Phase II, it will simply consist of an introduction in which the project is explained, a discussion of the environmental and cultural context for the site, research and analytical methods, data analyses, discussion of results, and recommendations. The most important part will be recommendations.

There are two options. The Phase II report can argue that the site does not satisfy criteria for listing on the National Register, or it can so argue. If is argues that the site *is* eligible, then it can argue that the current project will or will not compromise Register-eligibility (for example, putting an asphalt parking lot over a site that is 40 cm below the surface probably would do more to protect the site than damage it). That is, will there be adverse effects (remember, an adverse effect is only possible if the property is eligible for listing on the National Register)?

If the site is argued to be eligible for listing on the Register, and if the project as currently designed would compromise the information potential of the site, then the options are either to re-design the project

to avoid damaging the site, or to recover enough information from the site so that the continued existence of what remains will be redundant. That is, mitigation either through project design or through data recovery.

The end portion of the report, where the recommendations are presented, is the reason behind all of the Phase II work. The field work and analysis of course contribute to an understanding of the past of the region. And that information may be -- and very often is -- of immense interest and of primary research value in its own right. But that information was gathered to help decide something else: Should a project that people depend upon be redesigned at significant cost, or should the part of the site that will be destroyed be excavated, also at significant cost?

If the answer is to re-design the project, the archaeologist must have a realistic sense of the engineering and design needs for that. Maybe it only would require moving a pipe line corridor a little ways to the left or right, bypassing the site at a cost less than that of having to dig up the site. Or again, perhaps re-drawing the lots so that the portion of the site ends up in the resident's backyard and not under the house foundation or in the septic field is a realistic solution. Combined with a plat notation about future land use, this may suffice, and everyone comes out a winner.

Sometimes, though, the decision options will be to allow the town to continue to be flooded, to move all the people in it, or to just dig out the part of the site that the flood protection structures will destroy. In that situation, the archeologist will need to provide an outline for a *data recovery plan*, since in most cases it makes better sense to recover the information contained in the site rather than allowed people to have their houses and businesses destroyed every year.

A *data recovery plan* is a basic outline of the research questions and field procedures needed to extract the data from the archaeological site, or portion thereof, that will be destroyed by the construction project. The data recovery plan may end up as a separate document, and contracted by the Lead agency, but the Phase II report should provide a brief synopsis of what the project manager envisions as the best solution to the problem that the agency faces. At this point, the world's expert on the site and its physical and cultural characteristics will be the project manager. That person will have the best idea of what the next step should be.

Details about data recovery plans are given in Chapter 7. For the Phase II report, it usually is only necessary to give a general idea of how a Phase III data recovery project should be approached. A data recovery plan is, in effect, a proposal for a Phase III SOW.

7: The Phase III Process: Mitigation through Data Recovery

7.1. Intent and Goals

With the determination at the end of Phase II testing that the archaeological site is eligible for listing on the National Register, the Section 106 Process becomes more formal. Even though the process has been, until this time, expected in the Federal (and most state- and local-level) statutes, it is the determination of Register-eligibility that triggers a series of formal steps leading to Phase III data recovery.

That series of formal steps is set out in **36 CFR 800** (see Chapter 2 sections 2.2.3.4. and 2.2.3.5.):

*   determinations of adverse effect [**36 CFR 800.5**];

*   provision of what in effect are the Phase II results to all consulting parties and invitation for public comment [**36 CFR 800.6 (a) (2)-(4)**];

*   production of a Memorandum of Agreement (MOA) that specifies what steps will be taken to mitigate or resolve the adverse effects of the undertaking [**36 CFR 800.6 (b) - (c)**]; and

*   mitigation of those adverse effects either through redesign of the project or through archaeological data recovery.

If mitigation or resolution of adverse effects can be done only through excavation or similar archaeological investigation, then Phase III data recovery will commence.   Phase III data recovery has one fundamental goal:

*   recovery, analysis, and dissemination of the anthropological (human behavioral) information stored within the part of the site matrix that will be compromised by the undertaking.

What all of this means is that a site eligible for listing on the National Register will be compromised by the undertaking as it is currently envisioned, and that those effects need to be mitigated. Sometimes the adverse effects are mitigated by re-designing the undertaking so that the site is not altered. But most often the only practical solution to off-set the expected impact will be to conduct a full-scale, set-piece excavation of that portion so compromised. That action, then, becomes mitigation of adverse effects through data recovery. The MOA merely spells out that the signers -- the agency and the SHPO/THPO -- agree that this is the case, and what in a general sense will be needed to off-set the adverse effects to the site.

(Sometimes it can be argued that there will be no adverse effect, or that mitigation is not needed, because a comparable or better example of the site exists elsewhere, or may even have been investigated already. That is, the Federal agency may determine that there will be no adverse effect because a better example already exists. Eligibility for listing on the National Register does not depend upon existence of other, similar sites *per se*; in a somewhat round-about way, existence of comparable sites may influence how the integrity of the resource is seen [see Chapter 2 "Integrity"], but that is a different issue. Eligibility for listing on the National Register also does not automatically mean that the site will be excavated. The Section 106 Process is meant to make sure that the existence, within the area of potential effect, of Register-eligible sites is taken into account by the Federal agency. The agency will make the initial determination of if those effects will be adverse.)

The idea of the Phase III process is to make the continued existence of the portion of the site threatened *redundant* (see for example the architectural equivalent, **48 FR 44730** in Appendix A; the HABS/HAER process is meant to generate the documentation that makes the continued physical existence of the structure redundant; if another building is desired, it can just be built from the notes left after Phase III). Starting from when the Phase III process has ended, all of the information potential of the portion of the site that is damaged during the undertaking will exist in what was produced from that Phase III exercise. That information base will be the archaeological assemblage, field records, laboratory analysis records, and report.

Achieving Phase III data recovery by the private-sector or government archaeologist is similar to the formal, full investigation of a site conducted by an university or museum research unit. In both cases, a research design and set of research questions are prepared, and a sampling strategy specified. For Phase III, much more of the site is examined than in Phase I or Phase II; the level of analysis is more detailed.

The differences between the professional setting and the academic setting, and the responsibilities attending those differences, are important. The failure to recognize those differences has resulted in some universities and museums, attracted by the financial benefits of a Phase III operation, and selected to do the work because of their institutional resources and low labor or overhead costs, failing to complete the work anywhere near the deadline specified in the original contract. Those differences also result in serious misunderstandings between the two aspects of archaeology, the professional practitioner and the academic researcher. The former contends that the academic unit cannot complete the work in "real" time, and in accordance with the spirit of the compliance legislation. The latter contends that the professional archaeologist is damaging the site in the perceived rush to get the job done on time. Both positions are overstated and essentially false.

However, there are differences in how the professional archaeologist approaches Phase III excavation compared to how the academic archaeologist approaches a set-piece excavation; the perception that differences exist colors the training the nascent archaeologist will receive, since this training will come first from an academic setting. How the professional archaeologist handles the Phase III data recovery is how the professional archaeologist will be judged by others in the field, both academic and extra-academic.

The first difference between the professional and academic settings is that, in a professional setting, the site has been selected by circumstances for data recovery; the site usually was not selected because it could address a pre-existing research design held by a particular investigator. True, each state has (or is supposed to have) a state plan that includes a detailed rendition of research needs, questions, and designs. However, the site tagged for Phase III work will be examined because it, or part of it, soon will be destroyed.

(The compliance process was not brought into existence to serve the research needs of the archaeologist; it was brought into existence to lessen the impact of damage on the cultural resource, to at least give the society the right of first refusal on the information contained within that site. The process provides data; the process provides a wonderful research opportunity; but the process *does not exist to provide* a research opportunity. Rather, it *affords* an opportunity to do research.)

The second difference between academic and professional settings reflects the circumstances surrounding the data recovery project. The site will be destroyed -- there are construction and development schedules built around the data recovery schedule. Funding is limited by many non-statutory factors and depends not only upon whether Phase III is required by Federal, state, or local statutes, but also upon how much capital the developer or contractor has available and the perceived cost-benefit ratio.

Not only is funding limited (all archaeologists face this), so too is the time available to work on the data recovery project. Not everything that one might want to do can be done, be it during excavation or during analysis. Instead, it almost always is best to stick to what was outlined in the SOW, since the work or level of analysis stipulated there should be able to be done within the time and funding limits of the project.

The issue of deadlines and schedules is what renders archaeology in the private sector so much different than in the academic sector. This is not to say that university researchers do not have deadlines: Untenured faculty seeking tenure have very harsh deadlines indeed. Rather, the private-sector project time table is much more compressed, and the deadline is -- as is often the case for an undergraduate, too -- fixed with no option of an extension. The archaeologist then does the best that can be done given the time available.

All of this also reflects the legacy of WPA archaeology mentioned in Chapter 1. It is better to have something analyzed and written up than to have nothing at all. The Phase III analysis is to be a complete and thorough excavation effort, but it rarely can be an exhaustive effort. If someone feels that more could be done with the data, then those data as well as the original records will be available for the work on the site to be continued.[1]

There are two other differences as well, both related to the circumstances just mentioned. One is that the source of the funding is the client, be it private or public sector. The amount of money available is limited. For Federal undertakings, that limit often is whatever is left of the up-to-one-percent of overall project costs the agency can allocate to the Section 106 Process (see also Chapter 2 section 2.2.4.).[2]

The other major difference is that mistakes made by the professional archaeologist may well result in penalties. Like those in a university or museum the private-sector archaeologist accepts responsibility for what he or she has produced. Unlike them, though, errors in the private sector, even errors made in good faith, can result in immediate and tangible penalties, ranging from delays in final payment on the project to, as with the Transco Incident, major suits and fines. Similar penalties exist for failure to finish a project within the schedule outlined in the SOW.

7.2. Data Recovery Plan

The *data recovery plan* is what the name says: A plan for recovering data from the site determined, through the Phase II process if not earlier, to satisfy criteria for listing on the National Register of Historic Places. The reasons for listing can be varied, and those will determine the particulars for the data recovery process. The determination, to repeat again, was made by the Lead agency and not by the practicing archaeologist.

The data recovery plan may have been required by the Phase II SOW and presented as part of the Phase II report; or it may be a separately assembled, stand-alone document. If the latter, then it may have been solicited through a competitive RFP. The data recovery plan will become the basis for the Phase III SOW.

Some Phase II SOW will request that the professional archaeologist develop a data recovery plan; in situations like that, the Phase II testing was done more to get an idea of what a data recovery plan might entail than to provide the information needed for a review agency to make a determination of eligibility. The Phase II report then may contain an outline for a data recovery plan, or at times may even contain the details of such a plan. A pre-structured data recovery plan then becomes part of the Phase III SOW; the professional in another firm that has been awarded the Phase III work then must come to terms with, at times, ideas and procedures at odds with company protocol.

The data recovery plan addresses six topics, usually in this order:

---

1. It could be argued that this factor presents an ideal opportunity for an industry-higher education alliance in research. The core analyses will have been completed as part of the Phase III work by the firm, perhaps even using academic-sector researchers as subcontractors. Continued work on the assemblage after the Phase III project itself ends could be done by the academic community, which will have the time and sometimes the wherewithal for more detailed or subtle analyses.

2. We are aware of projects where nearly all of the obligated funding was used at the insistence of the SHPO in fussing about

with overly elaborate Phase I and Phase II exercises, only to find that very little funding was left to adequately document Register-eligible sites at the Phase III level. The Federal agency, by the way, was not in the mood after years of haggling with the SHPO to cut slack nor, given Congressional oversight relative to the final needs of the project, inclined to provide more for a state that had mismanaged its budget and ignored the Federal statutes. This does not happen often. To avoid this sort of problem, a good rule to follow is for the SHPO to think in terms of one percent of project funding as potentially available for cultural resources work, and to plan accordingly with that as a kind of limit of what can be done.

Responsibilities and Perspectives

It is important at this point to note that the client is the entity underwriting the data recovery exercise; the client is doing so – from its perspective – as part of the overall permitting process. Costs are not being borne by a bottomless well devised to satisfy the archaeologist's intellectual whims of inquiry; costs are being borne by the operating margin built into the client's overall financial structure. Sometimes a plat notation or a protective covenant, resulting in no further construction, will make better economic sense than funding a Phase III exercise in order to continue the project. In cases like that, the developer or contractor can take the reduced value of the property (because its development potential is limited) as a business loss. But it must be remembered that any developer or contractor is not in the business of taking losses; such a devaluation is not appreciated. Further, the line between built-in operating costs and profit margin is very thin; some Federal agency contracts, for example, limit the profit that government contractors can take. If costs become prohibitive, the client may just cut and run. This is, perhaps, a real world application of Lewis's *limited good*: There will come a point where every dollar spent by a client to work around a compliance problem will be a dollar taken from payroll. No company wants matters to reach that point. A good company manager will want to avoid endangering employees.

Scheduling and finance limits result in the data recovery being designed to get the maximum information from the imperiled resource with the available means. Into this will enter the SHPO/THPO or analogous agency, charged with protecting the cultural resource data base. The SHPO/THPO is made up of people with agendas often at variance with those of the developer, sometimes at variance with those of the private-sector archaeologist and the Federal agency, and – rarely – even at variance with those of the ACHP.

Professional archaeology has been at a cross-roads ever since the Section 106 Process emerged. There are serious issues involved, and this is as good a place as any to mention them. A common statement among the academic community for many years, seldom mentioned in print, was that the professional was "in the pay of" a particular client and therefore would do what needs to be done to get the client to avoid paying any more than necessary. While it is still heard on occasion, that charge reflected an ignorance of how the entire process works. This danger was anticipated when the legislation was first worked out; it has never really become a problem.

How is this potential conflict of interest avoided? It is avoided primarily through the review process. There are two issues here that get mixed up: Doing what is best for the client in terms of costs, and doing what is best for the client in terms of how the client's actions will be judged by the review agencies. The potential conflict is avoided by separating the steps in the decision-making process, while at the same time keeping the client's interests and needs at heart.

What is best for the client in terms of costs is ALWAYS what is best in terms of how the archaeologist's work, as a subcontractor, will reflect on the client. For the client's project to continue requires that the archaeological work performed by the professional archaeologist be completely approved by the state's or the tribal land's apologist for the cultural resources: the SHPO or the THPO. The review agencies have the power to pull permits; the review agencies have the power to stop the client. The client already has locked into bank loans, and has people on payroll. The client cannot afford to sit still. The professional archaeologist must provide a research design (for the Phase III data recovery), an analysis, and a report that will meet the requirements of the review agencies. The better the report, the faster the review and consequent permitting. The final arbiter in the compliance process is the government review agency; the archaeologist works and writes not for the client, but for the review agency, which then will decide the client's fate.

(1) an outline and background of the project history;

(2) a brief review of the environmental setting for the site and project area;

(3) a summary of the discovery and exploration of the site thus far;

(4) a summary of the prehistory or history as it pertains to the site (this is an intellectual context that presents the status of the research information that the site is seen to partially store);

(5) a detailed description, probably repeating the Phase II arguments, of how this particular site addresses the research questions listed; and

(6) a plan for actually getting the data from the site to address the research questions.

If the Phase III data recovery plan is meant to be a stand-alone document, then these parts will become chapters, or will be joined together as a single chapter, in that document. It is well to go over each of these. It should be noted that here and below it is assumed that the site is contained within a volume, and that subsurface work will be done.

7.2.1. Project History and Background

Phase III data recovery exercises do not exist in a vacuum; matters have reached the point where data recovery is needed because of the undertaking itself. What is the nature of that undertaking? Is it a PUD (planned unit development)? Is it a sewage treatment plant? Is it a drilling platform for oil exploration? Is it a sewer line? Is it a levee?

Memoranda of Agreement (MOA)

A Memorandum of Agreement or MOA is a signatory contract regarding the continued pursuance of the cultural resource process. It is meant to be a formal agreement, between the Federal agency and the SHPO or the THPO,

(1) stating that a Register-eligible site or sites were identified during the Phase II process (or agreeing that the site already is listed or eligible for listing on the National Register),

(2) considering if the planned undertaking will have an effect on that site or sites, then

(3) summarizing what needs to be done to mitigate the effects on the site or sites from the undertaking, should those effects be considered adverse.

An MOA is executed when cultural resources eligible for listing on the National Register were identified within the area of potential effects during the Phase II testing process. In such a situation, the Criteria of Adverse Effect [36 CFR 800.5 (a)] will be applied. It will be the Federal agency, working with the SHPO/THPO, that applies the Criteria of Adverse Effect. This ultimately results in one of two conclusions: The undertaking will significantly change the character of the resource (that is, have an adverse effect), or it will not.

If the agency and the SHPO/THPO agree on the effects of the undertaking (adverse or not) as well as on any necessary actions, then an MOA will be composed, a copy along with any other summary documentation sent to the Advisory Council for Historical Preservation (ACHP), and the undertaking will continue. In this situation, the agency and the SHPO/THPO are signatories to the MOA.

If the SHPO/THPO disagrees on the terms of the MOA or refuses to sign the MOA, then the agency will ask the ACHP to join the consultation. The ACHP must receive documentation relevant to the situation for a 30-day review period while the Federal agency advises the SHPO/THPO.

In the case where the SHPO/THPO cannot agree and/or refuses to sign, the ACHP will become the final arbiter. If it agrees with the Federal agency (or suggests changes that the Federal agency accepts), then the Federal agency needs only to comply with whatever it was the MOA (with any changes) set out. The ACHP instead of the SHPO/THPO becomes one of the two signatories to the MOA, and in effect the SHPO/THPO will be overruled. However, if the ACHP objects to the Federal agency's conclusions and the agency does not agree to the proposed changes, then the effects will be considered adverse and some kind of mitigation of those adverse effects will be required.

Only the signatories – the agency, the SHPO/THPO, and/or the ACHP – have the power to amend, execute, or end an MOA. Other of the consulting parties may be invited to sign, too ("invited signatories"), but their refusal to concur or to sign the MOA does not invalidate the MOA.

In nearly all cases, the Federal agency and the SHPO/THPO will be in agreement. Both will work together to develop a way that off-sets what otherwise would be adverse effects to the character of the cultural resources. That solution may be a re-design of the project, or it may be some kind of data recovery. It will be that agreement that is set for in the MOA, and which will initiate the formal process of Phase III data recovery, if so required and agreed.

Sources for and details about the project history will be located in three places:

* the SOW;

* the Federal agency; and

* the Phase II report.

It is important at the very start to outline how matters have reached the point that they have. Doing this chronicles what measures have been taken that would have avoided the entire data recovery issue. In effect, the capacity for redesigning the project to avoid the site will be apparent. This section shows that alternatives for the planned undertaking have been considered, and have been found wanting.

For example, when the data recovery plan for Lock Haven was submitted, a review was conducted of all of the history of flood control for the West Branch of the Susquehanna (see box Chapter 4, "*We learned about archaeology from that ... The Lock Haven Flood Protection Project*"). This summarized the known pattern in flooding, beginning in the 1600s. It went

over studies done by the U.S. Army Corps of Engineers in the late 1920s and early 1930s showing that a series of dams upstream would not solve the problem of flooding in Lock Haven. The final options were to either build a flood control structure around the city or not to build such a structure. If such a structure was not built, the options then were to suffer through the periodic losses caused by flooding, to move the town, or to move the river. None of those options were practical. However, building the levee and floodwall system would destroy sections of sites either eligible for listing on, or actually listed on, the National Register of Historic Places.

The summation of the project underscores that alternative mitigative measures have been explored and have been found wanting.

7.2.2. Environmental Background

The second part of the data recovery plan presents a synopsis of the environmental setting. What is the nature of the vegetation? The faunal community? The soils? The geology? What were these like in the past, especially around the time the site was occupied? What are conditions like now?

Information on the environmental background will be found in three basic places:

*   the Phase I and Phase II reports;

*   the county soil survey report, if there is one; and

*   the environmental and ecological literature.

The environmental setting will treat the climate (past and present), the general and specific ecological system (again past and present, and including current vegetation), and edaphic/geologic factors as they are currently thought to exist.

The environmental background addresses two issues. The first involves research and understanding of the archaeological site. Extra-academic archaeology in the main is governed theoretically by cultural ecology. The core premise of cultural ecology is that human culture serves as a behavioral adaptation for a given human (breeding) population.   Because that adaptation is behavioral, it has great flexibility in its ability to respond to changing environmental/ ecological conditions; moreover, it *does* respond to those conditions. Any understanding of how people lived in the past therefore requires knowing the circumstances under which they lived.   The environmental background is meant to present the general conditions under which that culture existed and to which the values of that culture must have responded.

Some of this will involve resources needed by people, say the quality of the soil for a seventeenth-century tobacco farmer or the availability of suitable stone for tools for a seventh-century Indian. Some of this will set the conditions to which the people had to adjust, such as deep upland snow packs in the winter requiring people either to have snow shoes or to spend the season in the bottomlands along the rivers. It must be remembered that this section *must* be adjusted for conditions as they were in the past, when the site was used. We have seen environmental backgrounds that simply described conditions as they exist today, and assumed that things had pretty much always been like that. Such ecological naiveté should be avoided.

The second issue that the environmental background addresses is the present structure of the site and the integrity of the deposit. The results of the vegetation successional survey done during the Phase I, and the nature of the soil conditions presented during Phase II, become crucial for considering the structure of the site and its integrity. These modern conditions also assist in engineering the archaeology of the data recovery plan (section 7.2.6.): How deep is the water

table? How much rain falls during the normal season when the work is to be done? What is the character of the soils?   How deep is the top of the Pleistocene sediments?

The environmental background may be presented as a separate second chapter, or as the opening of a second chapter that also treats the specifics of previous site investigations as well as the historic and/or prehistoric cultural background for the site.

7.2.3. History of Site Investigations

The third part of the data recovery plan summarizes the nature of the site. What work has been done at the site? When was it done? Who did that work? What were the conclusions? What was the nature of the deposit?

The history of the site investigations will be found in four places:

*   the Federal agency's records, which should have been provided at the time the project was awarded;

*   the SOW;

*   the state site files or SHPO/THPO, which will have records of who performed what kind of research on the site (this includes the National Register nomination forms, if the site has been so nominated); and

*   the Phase II report, which is supposed to contain a summary of the previous research done at the site and should also be available at the SHPO/THPO or the state site files.

The discussion of the particulars of the site are critical, since they contain two types of information: (1) nature of the archaeology, and (2) structure of the deposit. Both influence how the site should be approached in the field, and what questions may or may not be answerable given the probable data stored within the site matrix. It is the nature of the archaeology that will be considered in this section; while the details of the field work will be recounted, most of the details about the site matrix will be considered when the site itself is described and the mechanics of the data recovery plan explained (see section 7.2.6.).

This section of the data recovery plan generally is not very long. It naturally organizes itself, since it is best presented in chronological order of the investigations of the site. Thus, the Phase I work will be considered first, along with how that work was done, what was found, and where it was located. (Remember to examine a copy of that Phase I report, too.)   The

Phase II work will then be considered, again with how that work was done, what was found, and perhaps how deeply the deposit was seen to go.

It is important that the methods used during previous work be covered: What was the nature of the Phase I or Phase II programs? What are the field conditions for the site? If prior subsurface work was done, how much was excavated to what depth and in what way? How and where were the test units or shovel tests placed? How was the fill processed? What was found or perhaps not found when the work was done?

This section is, in effect, a review of all that has been written and discussed about this particular site. Major issues about eligibility have been settled; it is uncommon to find that a site recommended for data recovery actually was misdiagnosed. (Mistakes occur; mistakes of this nature should not happen.) In any case, the professional archaeologist formulating the data recovery plan is relieved of making such a judgment; actually, it is inappropriate to come right out and address that issue.

7.2.4. Place of Site in Overall History/Prehistory

The fourth part of the data recovery plan details how the site fits into the overall understanding of the greater area's history and/or prehistory. What kind of site is it? How old is it; or more specifically, with what cultural-historical period is its Register-eligibility associated? How does it relate to standing questions about the past, such as seasonal movements, expansion of settlement frontiers, or structure of emerging social classes?

This step involves assembling a refined background on the history and/or prehistory that pertains to the contents of the site. This will require

* reviewing the standard local, regional, and national journals for apposite articles;

* examining monographs and other book-like publications housed in professional or academic libraries;

* contacting the local libraries for manuscripts and other records that may have a bearing on the site; and

* accessing the compliance reports, located at the appropriate SHPOs/THPOs or state site files, of similar sites (a substantial part of the existing literature on the archaeology of an area is now located in compliance reports).

This information will be found in four basic locations, often in this order: The professional libraries,

including journal holdings, of the staff archaeologists; the SHPO/THPO or state site files; the public library located nearest the project area; and the local university or college library.[3]

There are two core issues for the site being considered for data recovery: (1) its data potential, and (2) the uniqueness of its information contribution. If the site has integrity (established during Phase II if not before), the default questions are what data are present, and how do those data bear upon standing questions about the past.

The third step in considering the data recovery plan involves placing what the site represents into the overall framework of historic and/or prehistoric understanding for the area of concern. This is a classification issue: Where exactly do the data fit into the overall structure of our understanding of the past? Or where do those data fit into our understanding of the person or event with which the site is associated and has made it eligible for listing on the National Register?

The basic answer to this should have been presented in the Phase II report, and should also take into account the state historic preservation plan. The Phase II report should have reviewed the historic or prehistoric literature, assessed what was known about the site, then argued for how the two sets fit together. The data recovery plan continues that line of reasoning, considering the site in the context of the past.

This comes back to the historic and prehistoric background research that was done, especially for the Phase II project. That research will have to be confirmed -- read "repeated" -- by whoever is

---

3. Major land-grant universities as well as many other state universities often have adequate, and sometimes outstanding, archaeology holdings treating the United States or the region in which the school is located, at least at the level needed by the professional working on a Phase III project. It has been our experience that many private colleges and universities, for some reason, do not, although they often have exceptionally fine historic map collections.

For those working within colleges and universities, access to the regional archaeological literature is not much of an issue, in part because inter-library loans in effect create a much larger virtual library to which all college faculty can have access (although the relevant compliance reports filed with the state in all cases *must* be read, which usually means sending someone over to the SHPO or wherever those reports are kept).

For the extra-academic archaeologist, though, access to those holdings will either be through the local public library (some states have inter-library loan agreements between the state university system and the local public libraries), or through physically visiting the holdings.

There is also the growing danger for Internet-accessed journal holdings: Many access programs will only carry journal issues back 10 years, which often compromises the archaeological literature review. That the decision for such a cut-off on the professional was made by a non-archaeologist is also a matter of growing concern within the field.

assembling the data recovery plan, even if it is the firm that did the Phase II.

There are no specific instructions for assembling this part of a data recovery plan, short of a standard scholarly literature search. The data recovery plan requires a detailed discussion of what is known about the archaeology for the cultural-historical period with which the site is associated. For single component sites, this is comparatively easy. For multi-component sites, this approaches a sustained synopsis of what is known for the period -- and associated cultures -- represented by the site. It is no mean feat. As a result, by the way, some of the nation's most thorough summaries of regional history and prehistory are located in data recovery plans, or in the cultural-historical backgrounds of the consequent Phase III reports.

The literature review for the data recovery plan requires not just locating and sensing the contents of previously written material, but also drawing that material together into a cogent whole relative to the site being considered. Further, it requires accessing the information contained within the compliance reports for similar sites within the region. For example, a site located in northern Kentucky will require accessing comparable site reports -- Phase II and Phase III reports -- for Kentucky, Ohio, and Indiana. That in turn means sending people to Lexington, Columbus, and Bloomington to review those reports, if they are not already accessible over the Internet.

Private-sector and government archaeologists are aware of that literature; the academic community normally is not, since the research interests of the majority are outside of the United States. Almost all recent field research is located in those Phase II and Phase III reports, and since the reviewers will be government archaeologists, it will be familiarity with *that* literature that they will use to assess the legitimacy of the data recovery plan.[4]

7.2.5. Research Issues and Reasons for Significance

The status of the historical or prehistoric archaeology as it relates to the site only sets a context. How does the site itself relate to that context? What questions does it appear capable of answering? Remember that an archaeological site usually represents a three-dimensional information storage matrix that the archaeologist is best -- if not only -- qualified to access.

There are two issues addressed at this point by the data recovery plan:

*   the nature of the site relative to standing research questions; and

*   the core reasons why this particular site is considered significant in terms of the Section 106 Process.

Having reviewed what the site is known to contain, then the general status of the history or prehistory relevant to the site, the next step is to explain what the site is seen to be able to do in terms of expanding our understanding about the past. This will rest heavily not only on what has been learned from the literature search, but also on what questions exist in the state historic preservation plan.

The reasoning for why the site should be considered eligible for listing on the National Register will be given in the Phase II report. If the site actually is listed on the Register, then the nomination form will provide details, although in theory the Phase II report should have examined that material and reported on it. Good scholarship will require the Phase III archaeologist to look at a copy of that nomination form anyway.

In addition to summarizing why the site is eligible for listing on the National Register, the Phase II report should have also suggested how the site can contribute to understanding the past. That is, there should be some sense contained in the report of research questions the site is well suited to address. That information should be contained in the "Recommendations" chapter (see also Chapter 6 section 6.4.3.; Chapter 9).

It is at this point in the data recovery plan that specific research questions not only are set out, but the data needed to address those questions are specified. The methodological framework may be inductive, specifying the sorts of things needed to be gathered to assemble an image of the past, or it may be deductive, with the particular evidence needed to address formally constructed hypotheses.

At issue, then, is the transition from "What kinds of questions can the site answer?" to "What physical information is needed to answer those questions?"

7.2.6. Physical Characteristics of Site and Data Recovery Plan

The last section of the data recovery plan sets out a detailed procedure to extract the data that will address the research questions that have been identified for the site. Two factors need to be addressed:

---

4. See again Chapter 1, fn. 12. The primary and essential importance of the compliance literature to regional archaeological research is another reason why professional archaeologists are very upset if that work is looked down upon.

We learned about archaeology from that ... The Disappearance of the Onondaga Iroquois

The importance to the completion of the Phase III project of understanding the current status of research in a given area was made apparent to us by a limited data recovery project we directed in central New York.

A local developer had sought permission to construct 16 up-scale houses on about 25 ha. The project was privately funded and no Register-eligible sites were known within or immediately adjacent to the property. Further, the setting was not considered by the New York State Department of Environmental Conservation to be environmentally sensitive. As a consequence, the Lead agency for cultural resources impact became the local township planning board.

At hearings for the building permit, the local amateur archaeology community came forward. It seemed that there *was* an archaeological site located on the property, a 3 ha late-seventeenth-century Onondaga Iroquois occupation that they had been working on for a number of years. The amateur community asked that some kind of effort be made to allow that site, known as the Weston Site, to be further explored prior to construction. Learning that such resources were present, the township planning board, the developer, and the local archaeology community devised a plan whereby limited Phase III data recovery would be done over the two lots within which the site was known to exist, while the other lots would be monitored for prehistoric remains.

Onondaga Iroquois prehistory and history are exceptionally well known, primarily through the work of James Tuck (1969, 1971) and Jim Bradley (1979, 1987). Tuck had taken, as a dissertation project, the problem of working back in time from historically

known Onondaga villages to the point where the Onondaga were first identifiable, at least in a material culture sense. To do this required tracing site locations. It was known from early records that the Onondaga maintained at any one time two villages, one large and one small, along with a scattering of farmsteads. Those villages would be abandoned and new ones established on the order of once every 30 years.

Tuck (1969, 1971) managed to locate pairs of Onondaga villages from the early 1700s back into the mid-1200s. It was a spectacular tour de force of research, demonstrating the vast potential of Steward's (1942) Direct Historical Approach. The collection that was generated remains as probably the only complete material culture documentation of the emergence of a known ethnic group in the eastern United States. However, the by-product of that research was that there really was no room for *another* Onondaga village, certainly not one the size of the Weston Site. In theory, all of the larger sites had been accounted for; all of the pieces of the puzzle were known and fitted into place.

The Phase III excavation consisted of stripping the plowzone, then identifying and mapping features and posthole stains that were resolved into house outlines. Field work exposed four house floor outlines, another four possible house areas, three projectile points made from copper trade kettles, six kaolin trade pipe stems, six trade beads, three native ceramic pipe fragments, and an appallingly unsophisticated stone tool industry. The bore diameters of the kaolin pipes suggested a manufacture date from the mid-1690s and, given lag time between manufacture and arrival among the Onondaga, probably represented a late 1690s deposit. (European kaolin trade pipes can give a rough indication of age because the bore diameter changed in known ways over the 200 or so years they were

available. For most of the period in question, the bore diameters decreased at a surprisingly fixed rate, so fixed in fact that there are linear regression equations that allow an age estimate to be made of when the pipe was made.) The absence of any other native ceramics except the native pipe fragments was consonant with the late-seventeenth-century date: Both Tuck and Bradley had noted that the very last native industry to disappear archaeologically with the replacement by European trade goods was native ceramic pipes.

Given the size of the site, and the size and density of the houses delimited relative to the area of the deposit exposed, it was estimated that a population of well over 1,500 had been present. Such a population would have accounted for nearly all of the Onondaga known to be alive in the late 1690s. However, there was no historic mention of such a village. Further, not only had all of the villages for the period of concern been identified; the quantity of material remains for a large village was puzzlingly small, especially given that such a village would have been used for 30 years.

The site was located near where another site long had been known. That site, called Bloody Hill, derived its name from the enormous number of historic and prehistoric Onondaga burials that had been exposed ever since farming began. Bloody Hill derived its name from a corruption of the translation of the Iroquois *ote-queh sa-he-eh*, meaning "It is the field of blood" and used for identifying burial grounds.

Consider, then: A large historic occupation site from the late 1690s, with extremely crude lithic technology (Tuck and Bradley both were adamant in stating that the Onondaga had long since abandoned stone tool technology by the late seventeenth century); a paucity of material remains; nearby and numerous early historic burials; and a location that was on a slight slope along a stream, sheltered by hills to the northwest. Further, it was a large site from a time when the Onondaga enjoyed sound relations with the British, and therefore a period for which the location of every Onondaga village was known. Yet this one was not mentioned.

The tentative conclusion: We had stumbled on an Onondaga refugee camp. And this began to point up the importance of tracking a sound historic background, or all of this would have been overlooked.

At the time that the Weston Site was occupied, the principal village for the Onondaga was what is now called the Jamesville Pen Site, occupied from around A.D. 1680 through its burning in A.D. 1696 to A.D. 1720. After A.D. 1720, the Onondaga moved farther west.

In A.D. 1696, the Onondaga occupied a valley 3 km west of the Weston Site, with what is now the Jamesville Pen Site being the principal or large village. At that time, the Jamesville Pen Site was stockaded and well-defended, the defenses being state of the art, designed then emplaced by British military advisors for protection from the French. The valley extending south was filled with maize fields and little farmsteads. In all likelihood, there probably were around 1,500 men, women, and children spread down that valley, with maybe 1,100 or so in the village. In July 1696, the French sent a raiding party south with Huron elements under the leadership of Frontenac to attack the Onondaga, arriving around 15 km north of the village on 1 August.

Aware of the approaching force, out-numbering that force by two-warriors-to-one, holding an intimate first-hand knowledge of the land, and having a the state-or-the-art military defense, the Onondaga – as anyone would expect – naturally burned down their village

and fort, burned *all* of their crops, and disappeared. When the French-Huron forces arrived the next day, they found complete devastation. Aside from a desultory exhumation of a few Onondaga graves by the Huron (to curse the spirits of their enemies with roaming the world forever), the raiding force returned to Quebec. The Onondaga were not reported again until an account by the British made in September 1697, when they once more were living at the Jamesville Pen Site but were in a "wretched condition."

What happened to the Onondaga? That is, where did they spend the 13-month period from August 1696 to September 1697? All of the maize crop was destroyed. There was no shelter. The first serious frost in the region comes in mid-October; the first snows not too long after. The winter of 1696 - 1697 was notable in Europe and Iceland as being the coldest since the A.D. 1300s (the winters of A.D. 1695-1700 have only been equaled by the winters of the late A.D. 1700s and the early A.D. 1800s). Climate is global; severe winters in Iceland and England usually mean equally severe winters in central New York. The estimated population for the Onondaga in A.D. 1696 was 1,489 men, women, and children, of whom 350 were adult men. In A.D. 1698, it was 1,064, where 250 were adult men. (The British counted "warriors" or adult males; theirs was a military concern. Total population in a situation like this is projected from demographic tables.)

The Weston Site, with its paucity of material goods and pathetic attempt to work out a stone tool technology under emergency conditions, appeared to us to satisfy the criteria for an early historic aboriginal refugee camp: a large but clearly short-term occupation dated to when it was known that the Onondaga dropped from the awareness of the wider world. Our ability to document this,

though, required knowing about early Onondaga Iroquois population movements, previous village locations, history, and of course climate. This should also point up the importance of being aware of other disciplines in addition to archaeology and culture history. Phase III projects provide enormous research potential.

Bradley, James W. 1979. *The Onondaga Iroquois: 1500 - 1655: A Study of Acculturative Change and Its Consequences.* Ph.D. dissertation, Syracuse University. University Microfilms International, Ann Arbor.

Bradley, James W. 1987. *Evolution of the Onondaga Iroquois: Accommodating Change, 1500 - 1655.* Syracuse University Press, Syracuse.

Neumann, Thomas W., and Robert M. Sanford. 1987. *The Weston Site: Phase III Cultural Resource Mitigation of the Southeast Area.* Prepared by Neumann & Sanford Cultural Resource Assessments, Syracuse, New York, on behalf of Goodfellow Construction, Inc., Jamesville, New York.

Steward, Julian H. 1942. The direct historical approach to archaeology. *American Antiquity* 7:337-343.

Tuck, James A. 1969. *Iroquois Cultural Development in Central New York.* Ph.D. dissertation, Syracuse University. University Microfilms International, Ann Arbor.

Tuck, James A. 1971. *Onondaga Iroquois Prehistory: A Study in Settlement Archaeology.* Syracuse University Press, Syracuse.

* the nature of the site matrix (this is the physical structure of the medium for which the archaeologist must develop a data extraction strategy); and

* the best approach or approaches for recovering the archaeological data contained within that matrix.

The first issue involves the structure of the site itself, and how the actual excavation should proceed: What has previous work revealed about the physical character of the deposit? What was indicated about the horizontal dimensions relative to the overall project area? The vertical dimensions? Will shoring be needed because deposits extend below 1.2 - 1.5 m? What is the height of the water table in the wettest season? How should the fill be processed: Dry-screening, water-screening, air-screening? What is the nature of preservation? Is the site contained within a soil, is it contained within a buried soil, is it contained within a cultural or natural sediment? Did anyone have the sense to check about particle movement?

All of the information on the physical characteristics of the site should be contained in the Phase I and Phase II reports. This may be augmented by reference to soil survey reports and perhaps engineering boring logs or percolation tests, especially if there is an issue of a shifting or high water table.

The second issue involves engineering the archaeological methods needed to extract the information stored within the archaeological site. The data recovery plan will propose specific field methods that are best suited for recovering the archaeological data contained within the site. An archaeological site is a form of information storage on past human behavior; the archaeologist is the expert in extracting that information. Extraction involves three steps: Excavation, analyses, and reporting/writing. The first, to use a computer analogy, corresponds to reading the existing code as a machine language, the second corresponds to conversion of that into an analogue language, and the third corresponds to the output.

It is at this aspect of the data recovery plan that the professional archaeologist will begin making extensive use of the method-and-theory literature as it bears upon data recognition and recovery. This is the topic of numerous texts as well as of standard archaeological method-and-theory and field courses. It is not our intention to deal with that subject; instead, the reader is directed to those sources.

7.3. Project Structure and Pre-field Preparation

Developing a concerted plan for archaeological methods best represents the kind of military-campaign approach to archaeology formulated and advocated by General Pitt-Rivers (see Daniel 1962) and Sir Mortimer Wheeler (1954). For many Phase III exercises, it is at just that scale, in terms of complexity of methods, logistics, and schedule of execution. Few university or museum archaeology programs focusing on field work in the United States approximate that scale of work anymore.

7.3.1. Site and Region Documentation

The Phase III data recovery project requires an intimate understanding of the current status of research as it would apply to the site considered for investigation. Addressing this requires that the professional archaeologist perform a two-part background research exercise prior to performance of the work.

The first part of the background research will involve the status of the basic culture-history as it applies -- or perhaps might apply -- to the site that will be disassembled. The second part of the background research involves the status of the research *questions* that the site may -- directly or incidently -- address. This corresponds to what was set forth in section 7.2.4. regarding the background needed for a data recovery plan.

For example, the core question for a region might be the impact of climatic change on population size. The site, as an undisturbed sixteenth-century example, may well indicate if the particular culture was collapsing under the combined impact of the Neo-Boreal climatic minimum and small pox. Yet, ancillary questions may include the nature of the pre-fired ceramic technology (actually, an unresolved question for prehistoric North America north of Mexico), persistence of the microlithic compound tool industry (a major issue in lithic applications technology throughout the midwestern and eastern United States), and frequency of elk in the deposits (critical for further supporting Kay's [1994, 1996, 1997] argument about aboriginal overkill relative to National Park Service wildlife management practices in the Montane West).

The professional archaeologist, as a systematist and a generalist, is required not only to know about the human history/prehistory as it pertains to the site, but also to be at least *aware* of the immediately related issues involving wildlife and plant ecology, climatic change, soil science, and similar disciplines whose research questions might be handled with the information stored within the archaeological site. While knowledge of the history or prehistory falls within the purview of professional expertise, the awareness of the possible issues of the other fields is that of awareness only, and is a consequence of broad reading of those fields, in a monitoring kind of way. The professional archaeologist pursues that reading,

Permitting

In some instances, the professional archaeologist may need permits to execute some aspects of the data recovery plan. This will vary by municipal and sometimes even state environmental and safety regulations, and have to be considered on a location-by-location basis. For example, if large areas are to be plowed and or stripped, then silt fencing will have to be installed. Or, if water screening will be used to process fill, then allowances will need to be made for a settlement pond, and very likely for some kind of water course pollution variance. That is, the idea of building a ramp and water-screening frame on the slope of a river, setting a pump up to draw water from the river to power the hoses for the water screen, then washing the soil into the river, may violate local, state, and Federal environmental ordinances.

not as much in the expectation of contributing to the field as in the need of knowing the general intellectual issues that bear upon understanding how people lived in the past, as well as in the requirement of knowing enough about the immediately adjacent fields to be able to manage specialists hired for analysis. The best analogy is with a symphony conductor: One need not be able to play all of the instruments to have a knowledge of what those instruments can or cannot do, and when they should be used.

7.3.2. Local Contacts, Public Relations

Phase III data recovery represents full-scale archaeological investigation of a particular site or sites. The scale is quite large and potentially disruptive. However, the nature of the archaeology itself often is fascinating and compelling. More than Phase II testing, then, the Phase III project requires coordination of local contacts while presenting even better public relations possibilities.

There are up to three sets of people who will require being contacted prior to the start of the Phase III project:

*   the landowner or owners;

*   the utilities companies; and

*   the local or regional government officials, including any tribal/native representatives.

The need to inform the landowner of the project should be obvious. Usually, the preliminaries for this were done as part of the Phase II testing. The issues, though, are the same: letting the person know what is being planned, the scale of what that planning could involve, and how long all of this will last.

Much of this already has been explained in section 6.2.4. The professional archaeologist will need to visit with the landowner and/or tenant and go over in reasonable detail what the Phase III process will involve. This will include not only the scale of the excavation and consequent backdirt pile (if such will be involved), but also the provisions that have been made for landscaping, the time of day during which work will be done, and how safety and/or security will be maintained. Once more, right-of-entry forms should have been completed, and the archaeologist needs to have copies of those. In built-up areas particularly, it will be necessary to contact the local utilities, or the appropriate clearinghouse, to have the presence of any underground lines marked. All of this was covered in Chapter 6.

With Phase II testing, local government officials may have been advised of the project. This normally is done only when the work is located within a town, village, or similar community. It is a basic courtesy to inform the officials of the community what is going on. Part of this also involves the nature of the work: Flood protection projects, for example, will have involved several levels of government contact already, and the archaeologist is merely one part of a larger, government-enabled process. It is important to let people know what is going on; the last thing the professional archaeologist needs to have happen is to start work without telling anyone and have the local town council go storming to the Federal agency to ask *why* they were not told that work was beginning.

This quickly raises issues of protocol, of who speaks with whom at what level of the organization relative to what level of government. That is, as a protocol courtesy, just who among the local officials is it that the project manager *should* inform of the pending Phase III work? For most Federal projects, there will be a local contact person who coordinates the overall undertaking with the community. That person already will have been involved in the cultural resources process, and usually is the person contacted.[5]

---

5. In more complex social situations, we recommend *Letitia Baldrige's New Complete Guide to Executive Manners* (1993, Rawson Associates/Macmillan Publishing, New York), pp. 299-339. To give some sense of this: It has been our experience that the CEO of the archaeology firm, as a subcontractor, ranks below the CEO of the general contractor, who in turn will rank in the same level with the mayor of the community, the president of the local college, the commander of the local military installation, and the local episcopate or sectarian/doctrinal equivalent. For those familiar with academic protocol, the CEO of a subcontracting archaeology firm ranks equivalent to an academic dean while the CEO of the general contractor ranks equivalent to a college president. Corporate managers rank equivalent to an assistant dean or a departmental chair: the firm's CFO, for example, or the head of the cultural resources division. The project manager or principal investigator, then, would rank equivalent to a faculty member. See also: Gunn, Mary Kemper. 1969. *A Guide to Academic Protocol.* Columbia University Press, New York.

Public Relations and the Media

One of the reasons why archaeology continues to exist and be successful as a private-sector enterprise is because of the exceptional history of public relations and public education that has gone on for well over a century. Professional archaeology especially exists at the pleasure of the public, since it exists as a consequence of Federal, state, and local statutes. It is a matter of professional survival writ large to maintain that quality. It also is a matter of self-preservation and, most would therefore say, of common sense.

Interaction with the public will come either informally, as people wander by to ask what is going on, or formally through the professional news people. Generally, it is part of the field director's responsibilities to deal with both groups, even though their first point of contact may be the pair of individuals working over near the edge of the site. It will depend on the nature of the project and the part of the country where it is, but usually all field crew should be reminded to be polite but somewhat unspecific in their answers, and to as quickly as possible direct the person asking to the field director or senior supervisory person on site.

For the incidental passer-by, this works well enough; but what of the local government official, or the television crew that has just arrived, with camera, microphone, and van-with-satellite-dish? That is a contingency that *needs to have been foreseen and considered prior* to the start of the Phase III work (see remarks in section 7.4.2.1. about attention to details and planning). The firm, the government agency, the SHPO/THPO, the landowner or client, and the local government representatives need to have worked out an agreed-upon set of procedures about how to formally handle publicity. It may be one where a general human-interest story for the weekend is all that is needed or desired, and such coverage may prove to be just fine. Good public relations are essential for archaeology. Or it may be that the best thing to do, because of the scale of the project and its location within a larger construction zone, will be to have a "media day" late in the project. The print and electronic media may be then informed so they can schedule. Such arrangements also allow the archaeology firm to organize itself and work out how it wants to present the information.

"Media days" will involve tours, photo opportunities, and media packets. Although they do interrupt the flow of the archaeology, they should not be seen as disruptive or counter-productive, but rather as opportunities to give something back to the community that also is going to be asked to support archaeology – through those statutes and any cost-related legislation – in the future.

Tours may involve the general public, or just a flock of government officials and local dignitaries. In either case, it is best to have planned out a course through the project area. Where necessary, boards or planking may need to be put down both to protect the site and to protect people's shoes. For the general public, the tour can be handled by crew sufficiently talented to serve as ad hoc docents. For officials and dignitaries, the tour should be guided by the CEO with the project manager in attendance.

(As a general warning: Many construction areas are advertised hard-hat zones, requiring all people to wear hard hats. Officials, dignitaries, and corporate executives often *refuse* to wear such, since it is considered a lowering of their social status. This is a delicate situation, and can only be addressed or enforced by someone considered their social equal. For hard-hat areas, always have on hand a supply of WHITE hard hats, which signify executive status.[a] Politicians, by the way, usually love to be photographed by the media wearing hard hats, since it informs their public that they are of the same order as the common people.)

Usually with tours organized for officials will be a related tour for the media. In these situations particularly, photo opportunities should be planned. These include not just neat things in the ground, or people doing archaeology things, but also some kind of setting out of the more photogenic or interesting artifacts recovered. Remember, people really do love archaeology, and they really do enjoy looking at the things: Give them the chance to share the excitement.

Where one is lucky enough to have an entourage of officials and dignitaries along with reporters, it should be possible to arrange things so that people are photographed along with the artifacts or the major site discovery. This makes the local politician happy, since this is part of his or her profession, and apprises that individual of the sensitivity and forethought of the archaeologist. That is, it is good politics to be politick and think of the needs of others in this.

Media packets will include a brief written summary of the site, some reproduced photographs or drawings, and other hard-copy, visually oriented items, gathered together in a pocket folder. Usually these will be prepared at the home office in advance and should include a one-page press release. They should always be presented with a sense of quality: Heavy paper or even clay paper, clean and crisp images, tasteful lay-out. This is the opportunity for the firm and the archaeologist to control what it is that may be said about the site as well as about archaeology in general; it is also the opportunity for the archaeologist to reinforce the image of professionalism that is essential for the survival of the firm ... and of professional archaeology in general.

---

a. Although there are no rules or regulations regarding this, hard-hat colors have come to signify status and role within the construction industry and on construction sites. White is reserved for managers and supervisory personnel; this is almost always true. This reflects the normal rule-of-thumb in the United States, where the lighter the color of clothing or apparel, the higher the social status, *ceteris paribus*. After white, the association of color and status varies a bit by region. Orange and sometimes yellow are worn by the common skilled laborer; red usually by unskilled laborers. Blue and green (sometimes yellow) are worn by specialists, such as surveyors or construction engineers. Generally, the more awkward the fit of the hard hat, the higher the social status as well, since it is suggestive of executive status.

Figure 7.1. Phase III projects can generate intense local interest, and as such are wonderful public relations opportunities. However, how such situations are handled requires taking into account the policies of the Lead agency as well as the potential disruption the added attention can cause to the client and the landowner. Phase III projects, especially in urban areas, need to have a plan for how to handle publicity, ranging from the occasional passer-by to the local television news crew, as shown here.

Phase III projects also result in public relations opportunities. How these are handled will vary by the nature of the project, its location, and the wishes or policy of the government agency, local officials, and landowner and/or client. Many people do *not* want to put up with the fuss of television reporters wandering about over their property, much less to have it widely announced that a large-scale archaeological project is being done across their backyard. Suddenly all sorts of people are traipsing through the yard at all hours of the day and life becomes unbearable, while their safety becomes a potential liability issue for the archaeology firm. Further, for many sites there is an enhanced security problem with the publicizing of the site. Collectors and looters *will* descend upon a site and pillage it.

Federal agencies normally prohibit public discussion of Phase III (or even Phase I or Phase II) projects; the Corps of Engineers maintains a general policy -- stipulated in the SOW and/or RFP -- that *no one may discuss any aspect of the project with non-agency personnel.* Exceptions to this, such as planned media days or public briefings, usually will be detailed in the SOW or the RFP. If such a policy is in force, then all project personnel, and especially project-hires, need to be told of that policy and the consequences for it being violated.

In other situations, say at the state or local level, the people may not mind or the location of the project

may be such that that kind of publicity is no problem, while the agency and/or SHPO/THPO may have agreed to publicly discuss the work. These represent public relations opportunities, and they generally need to be planned and thought about beforehand so that they can be both carefully but unobtrusively managed. Such events may involve a "media day" at some point late in the field project, where tours are conducted, media packets are distributed, and local officials have the chance to be interviewed on camera.

Phase III, because of its scale and nature, also may require expanded government contacts and public relations. Government contacts will include local or regional officials as well as Federal, state, and/or local government archaeology regulators. Local contacts need to include tribal/native representatives, especially in matters of religious or culturally sensitive sites. Some of this will depend upon the kind of site and where it is located: A large Phase III project may attract the interest of and be further facilitated by the local government officials; a comparatively small Phase III project mitigating the adverse effects of a bridge footing on a rural highway probably may be neither.

7.3.3. Labor Estimates

As with Phase I and Phase II, it will be the proposal budget prepared for the Phase III data recovery that will provide the figures for estimated labor. The firm will have basic figures applicable to Phase III work, but those figures will often serve as a scale: Each Phase III has the potential to be just different enough to make labor estimates approximate. Some of this comes from new or Phase III specific procedures; much more comes from the scale of a Phase III project. As Poe illustrated with "The Gold Bug," the quantity of an error compounds with any increase in scale, even if the rate stays the same.

Phase III projects have the same basic five project stages found in Phase I and Phase II:

(1) start-up;

(2) field work;

(3) analysis;

(4) report preparation and delivery; and

(5) final report delivery and turn-over.

As explained earlier in Chapters 3, 5, and 6, each of those five budget sets involve the level or pay grade of assigned personnel, the number of hours needed by an individual to complete his or her part of the task, and the hourly pay rate for those personnel relative to that number of hours. While computing a budget for bid involves all three, for execution of the project it is only a matter of who will be doing the work and how much time they will have to do it.

"Start-up" refers to what is done to prepare to go into the field. This will require assembling or scheduling equipment and supplies; it also will require scheduling or arranging any power equipment, land-survey and/or mapping equipment, and billeting. Phase III often requires an extended field stay far from the home office, and arrangements may be needed for where the crew will stay. Many Phase III projects also require provisioning of field crew, including hiring cooks. This in turn will mean locating someone who can cook for a large crew, as well as developing a food storage system sufficient for those provisions (usually a week's worth of food, although that varies greatly by where the project is and the size of the crew). The availability of potable water may also be of concern; again, this depends upon where in the country and the time of the year that the work is being done.

Part of the start-up phase also requires locating field crew if the firm or division does not have adequate personnel resources (normally the case for a Phase III project). This will involve contacting other firms and letting them know that there is a pending Phase III data recovery project, should *they* have project-hires that may be coming free in the near future.

Arrangements may also be needed for any environmental permitting associated with the data recovery process, plans for public education programs requested by the SOW or for public relations exercises, scheduling site security (and perhaps locating a security guard), and arranging for sanitation facilities for the crew while they are in the field. Federal projects will require that a safety plan be in place, and this will be true for some states as well as well.

Start-up will involve the project manager/principal investigator, the field supervisor or equivalent senior field archaeologist, the secretarial staff, and often the CEO of the firm or at least the head of the cultural resources division of the firm. Activities involve not only those associated with doing the archaeology, but also those associated with local government contacts. Certainly the project manager/principal investigator along with a field supervisor, and perhaps even the CEO or division manager, will need to go to the site locale (if it is at some distance from the home office) for a couple days to make needed arrangements. Depending upon the scale and location of the project, up to five person-days may be needed by each of those four individuals to make sure that the project is ready to begin.

By the time that the start-up phase is complete,

(1) all basic excavation equipment and supplies should be secured and in the field vehicle;

(2) contacts and other arrangements will have been made with the local community;

(3) all subcontracting, such as heavy equipment or sanitation, will have been scheduled;

(4) all necessary in-field equipment from local sources specific to the project, such as shoring materials, silt fences, or pumps for water screening, will be scheduled or acquired;

(5) all permits will have been physically secured;

(6) site security and safety plans will have been worked out;

(7) any required or anticipated (and unanticipated) public relations efforts will have been planned;

(8) field crew will have been located and scheduled, as will any local labor;

(9) specialists for field work also will have been located, retained, and scheduled; and

(10) all billeting and provisioning arrangements will be in place.

"Field work" estimates will vary greatly by the region, nature of the site, and Phase III SOW. These figures will have been worked out as carefully as possible during the bidding process, and will have been based upon previous Phase II and Phase III experience.

Personnel involved in the field work part of the Phase III project may include the project manager/principal investigator, one or more field supervisors, field technicians and project-hires, skilled or specialized labor hired for different aspects of the project (e.g., heavy machinery operators, security guards, cooks), and local unskilled labor. We have used a staffing rule-of-thumb of one field supervisor or crew chief for the first 20 or so field technicians, when the field supervisor was also involved substantially in front-line excavation; and one such supervisor per 10 field technicians when not so involved.

Some projects also maintain field laboratories where artifacts and matrix samples are processed as the field work proceeds; others will periodically transport the artifacts and site matrix samples back to the corporate laboratory. If that is the case, then laboratory personnel will also be involved.

Field labor estimates will be influenced by

* mapping needs;

* the complexity of the site;

* the scale and approach for excavation;

* the nature of the site matrix;

* the way in which the fill will be processed (dry screening, water screening, air screening); and

* the weather.

Site characteristics should be discernable from the Phase II testing, which was done in part to get information on the site matrix and deposit. As with Phase II, field work usually will be done in all weather conditions. Since the field work is fixed-place and of some duration, it is not unusual for shelters to be erected over the site or portions of the site being excavated.

Labor estimates for mapping and for processing fill with dry-screening correspond to those mentioned in Chapter 6 section 6.2.5., again with the caveat that these estimates can vary greatly depending upon the site. For example, in the Middle Atlantic and Northeast we have generally allowed two person-hours for excavation and recordation of each prehistoric feature. Labor estimates involving water screening can be highly variable, since the residue left in the screen may require a lot of sorting.

By the time the Phase III field work is completed, there should be at least a finished site map or maps, a project binder or binders containing excavation and feature forms, and perhaps a backfilled or otherwise restored landscape. Since most Phase III projects require matrix samples as well as feature samples for flotation, it may be necessary to bring fill into the particular site to restore it to grade; this would be even more necessary where water screening was being done. *However*, it is just as often the case that backfilling or landscape restoration is *not* needed, because construction will commence just as soon as the field work ends. Creative data recovery plans often will structure excavation in a way that contributes to the excavation needs of the construction project. All of this will have been stipulated in the Phase III SOW.

The labor estimates for "Analysis" given in Chapter 6 section 6.2.5. basically hold for Phase III projects as well, with some important exceptions. These estimates of course vary by region, type of site, SOW and SHPO/THPO requirements for labeling and curating, and specialized analyses. A realistic starting estimate for analysis time is one hour of analysis time for every 1.75 - 2.25 person-hours of field time.

The analyses expected of a Phase III project include not only complete measurements and counts of material, but also flotation sample processing and usually floral and faunal analyses. Most firms will operate a froth flotation system (see Chapter 8), and

will reduce the matrix samples down to heavy and light fractions. Our experience has been to use a person-hour per feature to estimate the labor involved. Some may continue by sorting those fractions; others may stop at that point and pass the material along to subcontracted specialists. There are many options available here, and those options depend upon in-house capabilities as well as bidding decisions (meaning cost decisions) made when the proposed budget was submitted in response to the RFP.

The labor estimates for specialists will have been based upon their individual rate schedules combined with a sense, from the Phase II work, of how much of their efforts will be needed. These estimates will often be given either as line items, set into the same general category as radiocarbon dates and other kinds of specialized processing, or converted into hourly rates for the sake of the original bid. For faunal and floral specialists, who generally will be working with material from features (and often that will be the flotation sample), around 1.5 hours of specialist time per feature will work as an initial estimate, to be adjusted relative to the site, region, and input from the specialists concerned.

In most cases, the same three pay grades mentioned for "Analysis" in Chapter 6 section 6.2.5. are required of the Phase III project: project manager/principal investigator, laboratory director, and laboratory technician. A great deal more of the technical analyses will be done by the project manager and the laboratory director than for Phase II projects. The project manager also will serve as an analytical coordinator, requesting specialized help where and when needed.

As with Phase II, by the time the analysis step is finished, the artifacts should be labeled and bagged, and there should be a detailed artifact inventory available. All measurements, weights, counts, identifications, and typological decisions should have been made. The artifacts and other remains should be at the point where they are in acid-free boxes and are ready for turn-over to a curatorial facility.

The fourth step in the Phase III project involves assembling then delivering the draft report. Like the Phase II report, this will involve four basic tasks:

* background literature research and report writing;

* figure/illustration preparation;

* report production; and

* physical delivery of the report.

Most of the work on the text and tables of the report will be done by the project manager and by any subcontracted specialists. The faunal and floral analysts, for example, will provide their results as a letter report, usually complete with tables (remember to get them to send along not only a hard copy of their results, but also a disk that has their report given in the firm's preferred word processing program, as an ASCII file, or preferably both). Writing the report will include the data analyses themselves, meaning the assessment (including appropriate statistical tests), interpretation, and application of the data to any hypothesis testing. Unlike the Phase I and many Phase II reports, the Phase III analysis should always support, wherever possible, any comparative statement with the proper statistical test.

The amount of time needed to write the report depends upon the scale of the site and the excavation. A medium-sized data recovery project (one bid in the low six-figure range) may require 20 - 40 person-days of writing time, spread among the project manager/ principal investigator and anyone else possibly involved in literature reviews or background research, plus another two to five person-days each for editing, formatting, and assembling. That time, by the way, is budgeted *billable* time, not calendar time; the writing itself will be done over a much longer period, since the project manager and others involved will be working on other projects as well.

Figure and illustration preparation will have been underway since field work ended, if not earlier. For a Phase III report, photographs and drawings/plan renderings of all features will be expected, since the report will double as a data repository of its own; many of the feature drawings can be started while field work is still going on. The scale of a Phase III project often is such that any start that the graphics people can make on illustrations will help in avoiding them from being overwhelmed while keeping the project itself on schedule. It also allows the graphics staff to stay billable, which is a basic managerial concern.

Artifact photographs also will be taken at the time that the draft report is being prepared. The basic rule is to photograph all diagnostics. Most firms allow the graphics department three to four person-hours per hand illustration, one person-hour per computer-assisted illustration or photograph mounting, and a half person-hour per artifact photograph (the labor estimate reflects two people; in settings where there is a separate graphics department, artifact photographs will require the project manager to work with the photographer in selecting and arranging the artifacts themselves).

As with all compliance reports, production of the Phase III report represents an exercise in desk-top publishing. The factors involved in this were considered in Chapter 6 section 6.2.5., and are reviewed in detail in Chapter 9.

The last step in the Phase III project will be production of the final report and the turn-over of collection, field records, and analysis notes. Usually the review agencies will have comments on the report, and will request that those comments be "addressed" in the final report. Sometimes these are cosmetic; sometimes they are extensive. The project budget usually allows about three to five person-days for each for the project manager, laboratory director, editor and publishing staff, and sometimes even the graphics department to deal with these things. How much of that time actually is needed will depend upon the scale of the project as well as the relationship with the SHPO/THPO and/or Lead agency. Most firms will budget with that in mind; if the quality of the work has been exceptional and the report, well-produced and solid, then it is very likely that the firm will have very low final report costs, and that budgeted amount will be a windfall profit.[6]

Turn-over is identical to that of Phase II: submission of the final report (sometimes with multiple copies, as specified in the SOW), as well as some deposition of the artifacts and project notes. That turn-over of collection material may be to the agency or to an approved curatorial facility.

At this point the project will have ended, except for payment of the final submitted bill. The portion of the site examined then will be stored, as information, in the Phase I, Phase II, and Phase III reports, along with their field and analysis notes, and collections. By the time the Phase III project is completed, the existence of the physical deposit of the site should be comfortably considered *redundant*. If everything was done correctly, the professional archaeologist will feel comfortable that that, indeed, is the case.

7.3.4. Staffing Needs

Phase III data recovery projects involve both field and non-field personnel. In both sets, most firms will need to augment in-house staff with people hired especially for the project. The hiring up to deal with the field work phase is not much different than that for a Phase II testing project, although there are important additions. The additional needs for the non-field, analysis and writing phase, often is critical.

In effect, the Phase III data recovery project will require construction of a virtual research team, both for the field and for the analyses that follow. There is

---

6. The project costs for the final report stage amounts to around 2.5 - 5.0 percent of a standard Phase III project budget. Even securing a portion of this without having to do the work those funds were meant to cover represents a significant profit. For the professional archaeologist with a fixed-price contract, it may be viewed as a bonus award that will accompany outstanding work, both in terms of the research and in terms of anticipating review agency concerns.

Comments on Management

Management is a defined profession; there is no way in which a short commentary could possibly cover a field that awards undergraduate and graduate degrees. It does seem appropriate, however, to make some general remarks.

Archaeology itself is now a profession, exercised in corporate and government settings. Not only is it a profession, it is also a *managed* profession. In addition to doing archaeology, the professional archaeologist both is managed and manages. For this reason, if no other, we believe that every archaeology student should take management courses (see Appendix B). At this point, though, we want to address some broad managerial themes, not just because the professional archaeologist will be involved in such a world, but because the professional archaeologist will be called upon to do this, certainly for individual projects, and possibly for the firm overall (why should the cultural resources division be managed by a non-archaeologist?).

General Managerial Responsibilities and Tasks

Managerial responsibility is to achieve strategic goals through considered tactical initiatives. That is, there is an overall goal or objective for the firm, and defined steps to get to that goal. (In business, this is called a "business plan," and normally is required before the bank will approve a loan.) The manager is part of an operating *team* that helps to plan the steps to those goals, that lines up and allocates resources, and that generally coordinates the activities needed to reach the final goal.

Managers, then, are planners, organizers, coordinators, and implementors. In those roles, they assemble and consolidate information needed for short-term decisions, long-term planning, and general monitoring of conditions that potentially influence such planning. Their resources for implementing and accomplishing those plans consist of environment or setting, matériel, and personnel. Although the specifics of the first two resources, and the training of the third, varies from field to field, the handling of those resources is surprisingly similar, which is why the degrees awarded are usually in "Management," rather than "Engineering Management" or "Management - Cultural Anthropologists," even though comparable specializations do exist at the graduate level.

All professional archaeologists are managers. As research scientists, they of course plan, organize, and implement a research strategy, and they apply the full range of resources to achieving those research goals. Their training has prepared them for understanding something of the environment in which the work needs to be done, as well as the matériel needed to achieve the needs of a given research project. However, theirs is the *only* social science field that requires having a lot of people working under their direction, as well as supplying those people, to do any appreciable field research.

The archaeologist's training usually will take into account working environment – project area or site excavation, for example – as well as the matériel needed to do the work. Specifics will be covered in method-and-theory and in field courses. What the archaeologist rarely is trained in is management and leadership of people, both in terms of specific project needs and in terms of a larger, encompassing corporate organization. Instead, as with other people-intensive/supply-intensive research fields, like Chemistry, Microbiology, or Genetics, the archaeologist learns the handling of people by imitating – or reacting to – what he or she has witnessed as a student.

Resources: People

In management there are three basic resources: the environment in which people work, the supplies they need to do that work, and the people themselves. While working environment and the matériel needed to do that work vary from field to field (for instance, the work environment and supply needs of a biochemical firm versus and engineering firm), the actual management of the third and most important resource, people, will not change.

A great deal of managerial training involves learning how to work with people, how to coordinate people as needed resources of an endeavor to achieve first the short-term and then the overall long-range goals. Personnel are the core resource of any operation. Of all the skills needed by a manager, those that involve people are the most important. Again, this is why successful managers can and will move – or be recruited to move – from one kind of firm to another. Their skills involving coordination and working with people are much more important than is their understanding of the technical nuances of the field itself. Managers work with information, coordinate information, and coordinate communication. But above all, they do all of that working with people who have the specialist skills.

Management involves working with people to achieve a set of goals. As a result, there is one core, agreed-upon precept for management in this regard: Treat employees with courtesy, respect, and dignity. In fact, the standing phrase in business is to treat employees the way that the best customer is treated.

Management involves both the act or task of management, as well as how the manager goes about doing that. While there are innumerable management *styles* (by which is meant ways in which a person actually goes about presenting himself or herself relative to managerial tasks), there are a relatively small number of things that those styles are meant to do. The following remarks are derived from that. They are not comprehensive, nor meant to be, but in our experience handling people in corporate and government settings, it does seem to cover the issues that anyone in a managerial situation must treat.

1. Treating others with respect. Nearly all remarks and instruction on managing and leading people can be condensed to a simple statement:

> Treat   people   with   courtesy, thoughtfulness, and respect.

Everything else follows from that, be it understanding how different people are motivated, acknowledging and rewarding their accomplishments in public, correcting their mistakes in private, protecting them from outrageous acts, explaining why as well as what needs to be done, delegating not just responsibility but authority, being positive, and providing a supportive and sound working environment. There are no substitutes for basic courtesy and respect; everything else managerial can be said to arise from them.

2. Honest and sincere concern, caring. People are resources; what is in their best interests will be in the best interests of the project and the firm. They must be treated with sincere care. The manager is responsible for looking after the needs of the people in his or her charge.

There are several issues involved here. The first is knowing the people under one's supervision. People are different; they have different needs. They also are motivated by different things. It is the manager's responsibility to know how the employees differ, since those differences will determine how they are to be motivated. There is an enormous literature in management on this alone.

Equally here, it is the manager's responsibility to know the strengths and talents of the supervised people. People not only represent a resource base, they represent a varied resource base. They are most effective – and therefore best to the needs of the firm – when employed where their skills are best used. Further, a good manager will help employees improve the skills they have and expand the range of their skills. In current managerial parlance, these activities overlap with what is called "coaching" and "mentoring."

Next is encouragement: Do not be hesitant to praise; always give full credit to the person who has earned it. A tremendously strong motivating factor comes from being part of a group, having not only a sense of identity in the group, but being valued as a contributing member of that group. If someone does a good job, then tell the person that they have done a good job. Sound managers praise the accomplishments of their staff, and tend to leave to them the fullest measure of credit while the manager steps to the side. There is little more damaging to employee morale than a manager who promotes himself or herself on the back of the staff's effort.

Conversely, do not mock or belittle. It is a management and leadership basic, taught in military command, that correction is done in private, is done constructively, and ends on a positive note. We have seen many supervisory situations where the manager bullies and mocks, using a near-jeering tone of voice, and does so before the entire staff in a conscious effort to humiliate. (In management, this is called "management by intimidation," a common approach in the 1950s and 1960s.) Employees are a firm's most important resource; even leaving aside basic courtesy and ethics, it damages that resource to demean it. A manager who does this needs to be corrected; if the correction does not stick, that manager needs to be reassigned or replaced.

Care for personnel involves large things and seemingly small things: The names and ages of an employee's children; the employee's birthday always remembered as an event (if the person is so inclined – some people dislike this, and the manager, familiar with the people in his or her charge, must make an effort to be aware of this) and not just a perfunctory exercise. There is no excuse for not knowing these things about one's people. It is just as important to be concerned about people's needs, and address personal problems directly – and privately – in a constructive, imaginative way. A good manager looks out for his or her people.

The manager needs to be an apologist for those under his or her supervision. This is particularly important in large organizations where resources may be siphoned off. Protecting one's people includes making sure that they have what is needed to do their work properly. Good managers make sure that their people are protected and that they are sharing in the resources of the firm.

Being an apologist also means discouraging negative remarks, rumors, and similar gossip aimed at others, be they under the manager's supervision or elsewhere within the firm.

The manager may have more responsibility, may have more authority, and may have – justifiably – access to more privilege given his or her supervisory position. However, nothing breeds resentment and drives a wedge in the team that is one's staff more than a manager who feasts at the table while his or her people receive the table scraps or leftovers. Concern for one's people includes making sure that they receive the promotions and raises that they justly deserve.

Concern for one's people also includes making sure that their needs are taken care of before one's own. There was an incident when Eisenhower was staying at the St. George on first arriving in Algiers during the War. It was raining heavily, and an aide had arranged for the General's staff car to be brought around under a sheltered portico, where it waited. The Hotel, though, was full of servicemen who had to be transported, and by putting the staff car under the portico, the troops were forced to go out another door, through the driving rain, and board. Eisenhower reassigned the aide.

(Just as important in this respect: A manager should never brag of the privilege to which he or she has access because of managerial position. It is one thing to be invited to sit in the client's box on Opening Day; it is another to return to the office saying just how wonderful it was to be entertained by the client in that fashion. If others do not have access to the privilege, then it often is better to leave the matter alone.)

3. Leading. Another basic caution, repeated in all instruction in management, leadership, and command, is to *lead*, not bully or prod. Even as a brigadier general during World War I, MacArthur shared the risks of his men, often leading raids himself (Manchester 1978:86-89). His presence, armed with only a riding crop, leading the attack on Côte-de-Châtillon is legendary (Manchester 1978:104-107). Eisenhower is said once to have illustrated the issue before his staff with a piece of string set on a table. He put his finger at one end and tried to push the string along; it of course bunched up. He then put his finger down on the other end in *drew* the string, and it all fell into line and followed. Work with people, motivate, lead, then they will put their hearts and souls into the effort; attempt to coerce and drive, and they will move along grudgingly, with no initiative, stopping as soon as the pressure is removed.

The manager has a collection of people who are meant to be working *together* and functioning as a team. This means using wherever possible first-person plural: Saying "we" creates an air of unity and shared responsibility. This also means sharing the work, looking out for how to help others on staff. The manager sets an example.

4. Responsibility must be accompanied by equal authority. Bradley (1951:20) remarked on what he learned from the command of Marshall:

From General Marshall I learned the rudiments of effective command. Throughout the war I deliberately avoided intervening in a subordinate's duties. When an officer performed as I expected him to, I gave him a free hand. When he hesitated, I tried to help him. And when he failed, I relieved him.[a]

The modern management term is "delegate." Micro-management is debilitating in any organization, and reflects managerial insecurity either in its own plans or in its capacity to hire qualified staff. Once responsibility is assigned, the individual must be given comparable authority and allowed to act with the independence appropriate to the task. Further, the authority of subordinates should never be undercut. This is a particular issue in the professional work place (see box "Managing Professionals" below).

5. Explain why it is people are doing what they are doing, and how it fits into the larger scheme of things. A core element in maintaining morale and esprit is having clearly defined plans and clearly defined orders that do not change with whim, then making personnel aware of exactly what is planned, why it is planned, and what is hoped to be accomplished. Drawing people into a project helps to make them a part of that project; they share any success. It is a fundamental management and leadership/command precept to tell the people doing the work why it is that the work is being done, and how their efforts fit into the overall plan.

People in the United States respond best to tasks they understand. Effort must be made to make sure that all understand what the overall goals of the effort are, and how their activity fits within that overall effort ("men respond more spiritedly to a task they understand" [Bradley 1951:122]).

Generally, excellent managers are excellent teachers and vice versa. They recognize what it is that needs to be known, and know how to explain that situation clearly. This overlaps then with mentoring and coaching.

A byproduct of drawing people into the goals of a project, or even the short-term objectives, is that it allows them to exercise initiative, to contribute constructive suggestions, and, when faced with a decision that must be made away from immediate supervisors, to anticipate the correct action for a new situation.

6. Collegiality. A common feature of a good manager is what might be called "collegiality." This turns up in the management and leadership literature under several guises, such as "cheerfulness," "positive outlook" or "positive attitude," and even "sociability." Sound management requires a generally upbeat and positive approach to people and surroundings. A good manager always greets the person who is passing by in the office, and does so by name. And if that person is new: then he or she will introduce himself or herself. When someone has reaped an award or claimed a success, a good manager will write a short note of congratulations. Knowing people's interests and needs, when something comes up or is read that may be of interest to another, a good manager will pass along that information. Managerial skills in knowing the needs of supervised personnel really should be a habit; one develops such a habit by exercising that kind of consideration for others at every available opportunity.

Collegiality includes looking out after colleagues within a firm, being creatively helpful when conditions warrant. If someone is walking across the parking lot with arms loaded, then get up and grab the door.

7. Workplace conditions. The last general area that the managerial and leadership literature consistently addresses is workplace environment. Good management requires looking after the well-being of one's people, and this includes the nature of the environment in which they work. The workplace needs to be comfortable, safe, and conducive to the employee's needs. It also must provide the where-withal for people to do their work professionally. This is not a recommendation for cutting-edge equipment or for luxurious surroundings; it is a recommendation for making sure that all that is needed is available to do a job properly, in an environment that supports rather than drains the employee.

Finally, we again recommend that any archaeology student considering a career in the public or private sector take one or two management courses. For those entering government work, it should be noted that courses and training in management and project management often are available through the Personnel Management Office or equivalent as part of employee development. Most firms will also cover the costs for management classes for supervisory personnel.

Bradley, Omar N. 1951. *A Soldier's Story*. Henry Holt and Company, New York.

Freidson, Eliot. 1986. *Professional Powers: A Study of the Institutionalization of Formal Knowledge*. The University of Chicago Press, Chicago.

Manchester, William. 1978. *American Caesar: Douglas MacArthur 1880 - 1964*. Little, Brown, and Company, Boston.

---

a. And a good manager, forced to relieve or reassign, will do so in a way that does not damage the individual but instead takes the skills and talents that the person has and continues to use them.

a long history in archaeology of just such an assembly of people to achieve a given end; professional archaeology in the Phase III process makes this assembly a commonplace.

The person in charge of making sure all of the pieces fit together will be the project manager/principal investigator. More than any other aspect of professional archaeology, the Phase III project requires consummate managerial-people skills to achieve the final goals of the Section 106 Process -- or the state/local equivalent -- as originally envisioned. To return to the image of a symphony conductor used in Chapter 6: The Phase III project manager is indeed like a symphony conductor, making sure that each instrumentalist works in accord with the others and the overall score to accomplish the goals of the composer (to carry the analogy, that probably would be whoever did the SOW, the score then being the SOW). The analogy continues, though: Any performance, any symphony, is finite; the work goes from beginning to end, and there is a stipulated end point. The project manager needs must make sure that the personnel involved with the project achieve that end point, in order, synchrony, and time.

It is important to emphasize this aspect of the Phase III data recovery project, since this is the major difference with an academic-sector excavation. A Phase III data recovery project has a limited amount of time, limited resources, and therefore limited personnel. Unlike an academic research project, which may continue indefinitely and do a terrifically exhaustive examination of a site (or not finish at all; all doctoral-level archaeologists personally know faculty who worked for decades on a data set, and never really finished it), the Phase III data recovery *must* be finished within a fixed amount of time. This is one of the legacies of the profession's reaction to WPA archaeology (see section 1.2.1.4.): It is better to have a formal analysis started, with all of the physical/analytical records of the site consolidated and explicated in a report, than to keep putting things off. That worry that many college students have about not having time to do a *really* outstanding job? That danger compounds when one is dealing with a young Ph.D. who has not yet adjusted to the pace and demands of the private sector. The Phase III process fortunately corrects for this.

The staffing needs of the Phase III data recovery project are similar to those of the Phase II project, corrected for the scale of the operation and analyses:

* personnel able to handle logistical support, including start-up aspects of the project;

* personnel who can do the field work needed;

* personnel who can do the laboratory and specialized analyses required; and

* personnel who can produce a monograph that will serve as the final statement on an archaeological deposit, in the face of critical reviews from government, private-sector, and even academic archaeologists.

Phase III data recovery is the last and final step in the compliance process. The site will survive only as the collection, the field records, the analysis notes, and whatever additional information that exists within the Phase III report. The Phase III process is intended to make the physical existence of the compromised portion of the site *redundant*.

Firms staffing for a Phase III data recovery balance in-house capabilities and staff commitments to other projects against the needs of the Phase III SOW. In nearly all cases, this means that additional people -- project-hires and specialists -- will need to be hired. Those individuals include:

* *Project managers*, who will have the responsibility of overseeing all aspects of the project from its inception until turn-over, and who will be responsible for coordinating all field, analytical, and report tasks;

* *laboratory staff*, managed by the laboratory director and responsible for each firm's project needs, and for the management of all material products of the project;

* *field labor*, including both field supervisors as well as basic technicians, who will be responsible for the extraction of the informational contained within the archaeological deposit;

* *analytical specialists*, who will be subcontracted to deal with particulars of the deposit or the assemblage;

* *graphics*; and

* *secretarial and administrative*, who will be responsible for coordinating the production of the Phase II report as well as for all of the managerial paper work approved by the project manager.

7.3.4.1. Non-Field Support Personnel

Non-field support personnel normally are permanent employees responsible for the administrative (start-up and report production) and analytical (analysis, curation, turn-over) tasks of the project. Although the non-field support staff for the Phase III data recovery project is an expansion of the needs identified for the Phase II testing project (Chapter 6 section 6.2.6.1.),

Managerial Communications

Management involves coordination and communication; most of managerial work is ad hoc response adjusting previous plans that is best effected by oral communication.

It is a basic axiom that there is no pattern to managerial activity. Managerial time is quick-paced and extremely committed. The manager is a communications node: Information comes in, is coordinated and digested; a response to that information goes out. As a result, not only are information contacts and networks critical, immediate and quickly delivered information will receive greater attention than will heavily referenced, long, or even routinely scheduled information. Further, oral communication almost always will take precedence over written communication. The ability to clearly state a problem becomes essential to the manager.

Managers have large and complex communications networks that are self-designed information systems. Those systems are internal as well as external to the corporation; they are both lateral and vertical in their reach. It is in the sifting through of the information moving through that network that the manager derives what is needed to make decisions or to frame out policy.

Managers need information – oral or written – to be presented briefly. The communications need to outline the situation, then present options as they relate to circumstances and short-term or long-range objectives. It is the manager's responsibility to decide.

Memos and briefings must be short, to the point, outline what the issue is, then supply the options for resolution of that situation. Thus, one does not just report a problem, one also must supply a solution or series of optional solutions to the problem.

The better aware staff are of the role of their part in the overall intentions of the firm or of the project, the more likely it will be that those suggested solutions or plans of action will be useable for the manager. This is another reason why good managers keep their staffs apprised of what overall plans and goals are.

most of the points addressed in that section also hold for a Phase III project.

Non-field support personnel commonly represent shared personnel. That is, those doing most of the administrative and basic analytical work are in-house staff who are doing the same kinds of work on behalf of other projects running concurrently within the firm. Each may have its own manager or supervisor to coordinate the multiplicity of tasks assigned it, while each set or even the division or firm may have procedures to help better schedule that staff's commitment of time.

Larger firms tend to have an administrative assistant or office manager whose role is to coordinate administrative tasks; nearly every firm has a laboratory manager or director whose responsibility is overall coordination of all analytical, curatorial, and turn-over tasks. Thus, every firm will have some sort of organization within which responsibilities and tasks are delegated. All professional archaeologists are expected to be familiar with how their particular firm is organized, to respect the chain-of-command, then to interact with that organization at the proper level and in the proper order.

In larger firms, or in firms with a tremendous amount of work relative to staff, it often is necessary to require project managers to submit *Work Request Forms* or similar memoranda outlining what tasks need to be done, when they need to be done, and how much time has been budgeted for what level of person for those tasks. Phase III projects, because of their scale, require a comparable amount of planning and organization.

Large projects often can develop a momentum of their own that, if not re-directed far enough ahead of time, can carry time and funding off of course. It is not unlike anyone running barge trains on the Ohio River, where turns, docking, and similar actions must be started far ahead of when the turn or docking is meant to be.

Phase III projects, because of their scale, also have a danger of becoming "frayed" if there is no coordinated planning and commitment of in-house staff to that plan. That is, there is a danger for small details to get set aside, overlooked, or forgotten if the project manager has not set out and scheduled needs early enough (see below section 7.4.2.1.). Phase I and Phase II projects tend to be sufficiently small in most cases that any laxness in planning can be corrected by dint of main effort; Phase III projects tend to be sufficiently large that laxness in planning then allocating work can be very difficult to correct within the schedule of the project and its SOW.

Phase III projects are likely to require extra-corporate non-field help. For administrative tasks, this often includes developing and processing photographs, producing half-tone images for reports, and sometimes even the duplication and binding of those reports. The project budget should have already identified vendors and determined rates and turn-around time for such tasks.

For analytical tasks, Phase III projects often require at least three sets of specialist tasks:

*   artifact analyses;

* floral/faunal analyses; and

* dating.

Each of those will require arranging for a subcontractor or vendor, budgeting the time and funds needed, then having the work done.

It is not uncommon for Phase III projects to also require specialized artifact conservation, historic or map research, advanced statistical analyses, and drafting or graphics preparation. All of that work needs to be scheduled in such a way that the results are available by the time the Phase III draft report is being assembled.

7.3.4.2. Hiring or Assigning Field Personnel

Most Phase III projects require hiring additional staff to do the field work. It is rare for any firm to have sufficient personnel on staff to handle any but the smallest Phase III data recovery project.

The Phase III field staff will consist of permanent employees of the firm as well as project-hires. In most cases, supervisory tasks will be assigned to permanent staff; only on comparatively large projects, or in situations where there are several field projects occurring at the same time, will field supervision also be done by a project-hire.

Unlike the non-field personnel involved with the Phase III project, the field personnel usually will be committed to one particular project for its duration. Such a commitment results in less staffing flexibility for the firm or division overall, and again requires overall planning and scheduling early enough so that the firm is not suddenly caught with staff being over-committed. (This can happen, of course, and the possibility is reflected in the request in some Federal RFPs for Standard Form 254 and 255, indicating the size of the firm, its capacity to handle the project outlined in the RFP, and anticipated commitment of staff to other projects.) Phase I and to some extent Phase II projects result in much less time commitment by field personnel, simply because the projects usually take less time; it often is possible to pull people from one project to deal quickly with another before returning them to their first assignment.

For Phase III data recovery projects, the schedule tends to be much tighter relative to possible down-time in the field (weather conditions, for example) and room to maneuver in the budget. Because of this, it is riskier to temporarily reassign field staff from an on-going Phase III to another project. It can be done, and often is done, but requires planning to protect the integrity of the Phase III project.

Most firms will build a Phase III field crew around a core of permanent employees. Those field crew additions are project-hires, the locating and hiring of which have been adequately discussed in Chapter 6 section 6.2.6.2.

7.3.5. Field Logistics: Housing, Per Diem, Transport

The logistical needs for the field portion of the Phase III project will involve arranging field accommodations and transportation for crew. There also are issues of per diem, and occasionally issues of food supplies. These needs are identical to those outlined for Phase II projects in Chapter 6 section 6.2.7., and the reader is referred to that section and to Chapter 5 section 5.2.5. for details.

7.3.6. Equipment and Supply Needs

As with a Phase II testing project, the equipment and supply needs of a Phase III data recovery project are those of any full-scale archaeological excavation. These are covered in many standard textbooks, are detailed in method-and-theory and field courses, and have been reviewed as well in Chapter 6 section 6.2.8.

There are three basic differences in equipment and supply needs between Phase II testing and Phase III data recovery:

* scale;

* duration in-place; and

* supplemental equipment or supplies.

The first difference is scale: A Phase III data recovery exercise often will require more of each equipment and supply category. For example, there will be more in the way of flotation and matrix samples, and bags or containers suitable for holding those samples will be needed. Because of the duration in-place, it will be necessary to arrange for equipment maintenance in the field, where often for a Phase II project it is possible to postpone incidental repairs until the project returns from the field. Repair and maintenance will include repairing screens and other equipment, as well as keeping hand-tools such as shovels and mattocks in good condition. Usually, the similarity between the core equipment needs of Phase II and Phase III are such that the scaling up for the latter will result in an in-house equipment surplus that will be available not just for other Phase III projects, but also to run more simultaneous Phase I and Phase II projects.

The other two equipment and supply sets generally are not interchangeable with Phase I and most Phase II projects. The second possible equipment need on a Phase III site may well be that related to its duration in-place. This can include large shelters to enable field work to be conducted free of inclement or harsh weather, ramps and other site architecture required to do the excavation, plywood for covering large open areas, and so on. Sometimes these materials must be purchased; sometimes such equipment can be rented, although it is possible that the cost of renting may be such that outright purchase makes better fiscal sense.

It also is possible that such equipment can be fabricated: We once designed a collapsible A-frame structure of color-coded two-by-fours that could be put together with carriage bolts by people wearing mittens who had not seen the contraption before, then covered with Griflin™ (a thick clear plastic with internal reinforcing of fiberglass netting commonly used on construction sites). The structure could be adjusted to cover any size area up to 15 m wide and 20 m long, and could be kept above freezing using propane space heaters even when the air temperature at night dropped to -25°C. Purchase of a pre-made structure that would do the same cost, at that time, around $5,000; ours cost $400 in supplies plus 16 person-hours labor.

The third basic difference between Phase II and Phase III needs is additional equipment normally not used in a Phase II testing project that is specific to the data recovery needs of a Phase III project. Such equipment can range from the intake hoses and pumps for a water screen, the pumps and hoses to remove water from units, shoring materials, the space heaters mentioned above, and even sprayer cans.

7.4. Field

The actual field part of a Phase III data recovery differs in four basic ways from an academic research excavation:

* The Phase III data recovery project is a continuation of previous compliance work, and is part of a larger compliance exercise;

* field technique will be abbreviated to what is essential for data recovery;

* after the Phase III data recovery is done, some if not all of what remains unexcavated of the archaeological site will disappear; and

* the Phase III project *must* be completed in its entirety by a pre-set time, and that completion *must* be within pre-set budget and supply limits.

The first difference with more traditional excavations is that the Phase III project is the continuation of earlier survey and testing on the site, work that was done preparatory to the Phase III effort. That is, there often is more continuity among the Phase I - Phase II - Phase III sequence than there is for a site identified during general site survey 40 years ago that was tested in the 1980s as part of a master's thesis, and is now being examined in detail as part of a field school.

The second difference involves field technique. Phase III data recovery is often a compromise not only in itself, but also with time relative to execution of field technique. Thus, to return to remarks in Chapter 6, it may not be possible -- nor practical -- to trowel-cut all four walls of a large excavation unit. Field techniques and overall methods will be abbreviated to that which is essential for sound data recovery. This will vary greatly from project to project and depends obviously on the site as well as on field conditions. It also requires an exceptionally fine understanding not only of proper field methods, but also of how field techniques and methods relate to recovery of archaeological data.

A third and often major difference between a Phase III data recovery excavation and a full-excavation that is part of an university or museum research project is that the Phase III site will disappear, either in whole or in part. The Phase III results, then, are meant to render -- as much as this is possible -- the continued existence of the site *redundant*.

The last major difference between a Phase III data recovery project and an academic or museum excavation is that there are deadlines that must be met. Those deadlines include when field work must be done and a draft final report, finished. Further, there will be pre-set limits on the resources available to work on the site. The professional must do the best he or she can with the resources -- including calendar time -- allocated for work on the site.

7.4.1. Preparatory

Because the Phase III data recovery effort is part of a scheduled compliance activity, certain preparatory steps need to be taken. These steps respond as well to the pending alteration or loss of the site.

There are four sets of information that need to be consolidated and understood before the Phase III field work is started or at least well underway. In theory, much of this work should have been done during the Phase I survey or Phase II testing:

(1) reconciling of previous historic and excavation maps with the current physical site;

(2) mapping;

(3) history of land use where the site is located; and

(4) site and deposit dynamics.

Together, these provide a consolidated summation of the conditions that the professional archaeologist will face as the data recovery plan is implemented in the field.

7.4.1.1. Reconciliation with Maps of Previous Investigations

Previous maps of the site need to be brought into line with the physical existence of the site itself. This is called "ground truth," a term taken from aerial reconnaissance work where the features seen in the aerial photograph are actually examined in person on the ground to make sure that it does represent what everyone thinks the image is. Since the planning for the Phase III often will be based upon where things are said to be located in the Phase II testing (and the Phase I survey), it is important to make sure where those mapped land features actually are.

This will require using whatever maps are available of the site, especially the Phase I and Phase II project maps, and relocating the land features and excavation units previously identified. Although it is not supposed to happen, we have encountered situations where the entire testing grid of a site was mis-mapped by up to 200 m.

Reconciling maps needs to be done as part of the project start-up, before one has field crew standing around being billable but waiting for work to begin.

7.4.1.2. Mapping

As with any excavation, a site map will be prepared. Even though a Phase II map should exist, unless the Phase III project is being done by the same firm, a new map will need to be prepared. Except where it is a matter of locating previous test units or where the plowzone will be removed before data recovery starts, it usually is possible to do the site mapping during or at the very start of the field work. Again, this is something that will vary from project to project. However, a site map is going to be needed.

7.4.1.3. Landscape History

As with Phase II testing, the Phase III data recovery needs information on land-use history (see also Chapter 5 section 5.3.1, and Chapter 6 section 6.3.1.). The reasons for this information, though, are different. For the Phase II testing, land-use history served with assessment of the soil as one of two tools used to help assess site integrity and assist in devising a data recovery plan. For Phase III data recovery,

land-use history is used to understand specifics about the deposit. This can range from the obvious issue of past plowing to the archaeology of how the land was used, such as formal gardens, location of pasturage, and the like.

In many ways, the Phase II use of the landscape history, that combined interpretation of soils and vegetation relative to historic documentation, is meant to provide a site-specific disturbance study (see Chapter 4 section 4.2.2.5. text box "Preservation Plans and Disturbance Studies"). At the Phase III level, the concern is twofold:

(1) the implications for the deposit of what the processes involved in the land use were; and

(2) the specific impact (or lack of impact) of those practices on the deposit.

Included in the first concern are not just archaeologically specific issues like plowing or extensive sedimentation; also included here are undocumented hazardous waste dumps either on the site, or sufficiently close to the site that the ground-water contamination may create safety problems for the crew. At this level, then, some of that Phase II testing vegetation survey needs to be interpretively equivalent to a NEPA Phase I/Phase II vegetation survey.

7.4.1.4. Site and Deposit Dynamics

The fourth body of information required by the professional archaeologist as subsurface field work proper is started is a knowledge of the physical structure of the site itself, at least as far as previous investigations permit. There are three issues that are of concern in considering site and deposit dynamics:

(1) how the deposit will effect the mechanics of excavation, both digging and matrix processing;

(2) how internal processes in the site matrix have influenced the data quality of the site; and

(3) what the engineering parameters are for the excavation.

The information needed to address those concerns should be present in at least three places:

*   the Phase I report, which provides information on the areal extent of near-surface soils and deposit conditions;

*   the Phase II report, which provides information on the vertical structure of the deposit, possible

We learned about archaeology from that ... The Mysterious Case of the French Drain

Probably the most humorous data recovery experience we have had came with the Phase III excavation of the Weston Site, the early historic Onondaga refugee camp in central New York discussed earlier. The experience is instructive at a couple of different levels: reasoning from the implications of the soil survey data, understanding how the land was used in the past, and knowing about past land-use practices.

The situation was relatively simple. A developer was putting in a series of upscale houses on two- to five-acre lots. Two of the proposed lots, together covering around 4.5 ha, contained an early historic Onondaga site that had been under investigation by the local amateur archaeology community.   When news of the development became known, that archaeology community negotiated a win-win agreement between the local town planning board and the developer: Limited Phase III data recovery would be done over those portions of the lots scheduled for construction, while a protective covenant for the rest of the land was added as a plat notation to the property itself.

The lots were located on a moderate slope of around 5-10 percent. The land clearly had been plowed: All of the landscape signatures were there, and it was at that time actually being used as a hay meadow. That it often had been plowed was confirmed by local residents, and evidence for plowing was present in the amateur archaeological investigations.   The Phase III field procedure, then, was to mechanically strip the plowzone from sections of the site, then map in and otherwise recover exposed features. The soil itself was the kind of cobble-rich soil commonly developed from glacial till by a long history of cropping and pasture. The soil survey described the type of soil (technically, a glossoboric hapludalf) on the site as seasonally wet and characterized by perched water tables (a "perched water table" is where there is an illuvial clay layer within a comparatively thin B horizon; ground water rests or perches on that clay-rich layer instead of percolating deeper).

We mechanically removed the plowzone from six 45 m long, 2.2 m wide parallel east-west trenches, then shovel-scraped those trenches to expose feature and posthole stains. There were occasional posthole stains and assorted artifacts, including datable trade goods; in the southernmost trench, we picked up five sets of posthole stains suggesting the walls of four different houses (a number of others would later be identified). In that same trench and roughly parallel with the walls of one of those houses, we also exposed a narrow cobble band. The band, about 50-cm wide, ran from one side of one of the shovel-scraped trench to the other.

Figure 7.2. *Looking east at exposed surface of cobble-filled ditch in Trench 5 of the Weston Site. Scale in distance is 1.0 m*

Suddenly, the site appeared exciting indeed! The cobble band gave every indication of cobbles set into a narrow, previously dug ditch. In a number of places instead of cobbles being present, there was dark earth, suggestive of a post mold or filled posthole. We had been involved, a couple of years earlier, with the excavation of a late prehistoric Onondaga longhouse where the walls had been constructed by first

excavating a long trench, into which were placed the vertical posts for the longhouse walls. Such "wall trenches" were known for contemporaneous sites in southern Ontario, and of course were common enough on Middle Mississippian sites, but were unknown in central New York. Now, as we stood there, with the postholes stains of House 2 showing a wall running roughly parallel with a cobble-filled ditch three meters away, we developed an image of a stockaded village, one where the Onondaga had excavated a narrow ditch, placed the main wall posts in, then packed in cobbles.   As far as we knew, something like that had *never* been reported! Wow, neat stuff!

We had one person (one of the amateur co-investigators of the site) begin taking the cobble-filled ditch apart, which he approached with incredible care and caution. Meanwhile, we attempted to trace just where this feature went. There was enough of a line that we could estimate where, if the cobble band continued on a straight line, it would appear in the next plowzone-stripped trench to the north. As we shovel-scraped that second trench, three meters away, we again exposed the cobble-filled ditch. Sighting along it, we opened a couple test units between that trench and the next, 12 m to the north, and again caught the cobble band. We were tracing quite a line, one which then appeared, as we shovel-scraped, in the third plowzone-stripped trench.

All of this was happening quickly. Then, in the fourth trench to the north ... another 50-cm wide band of cobbles seemingly set in a ditch, but much farther east and running downhill and west at a 40° angle to the direction of the first line we had found. This did *not* make sense, at least while holding the image of a trenched stockade line surrounding a village. We projected the direction of this new band, projected the direction of the one we had first found, and, as one might expect, found where they met: As a Y-intersection, just downslope from where yet a *third* such 50-cm wide cobble-filled ditch came in, this time *from the north* while also joining at a 40° angle. Suddenly, instead of an enclosure, we had a W-like dendritic pattern of cobble-filled ditches that all merged into one ditch that continued downhill.

It was on this site that Sanford observed that archaeologists dig things up to learn about how they are put together, and therefore one should not be hesitant to systematically take things apart to figure out what they are. We took 15 m of that lower section of cobbles and ditch apart, and discovered to our amusement that we had been tracing ... a French drain system.

Once we recognized this, everything else fit into place. A French drain is a type of field tile system. "Tiling" refers to placing a permeable pipe, or gravel and cobbles in a trench that is dug to a depth below the normal height of the water table. Water then flows into the pipe or permeable gravel, which is set in so that it drains the water away. The practice, used to lower water tables in soggy or marshy ground, originated with the Romans, was preserved by the Benedictines, then enhanced by the French monastic orders in the seventeenth century, whose practice of partially filling a ditch with branches set in lengthwise, or with gravel and cobbles, is the source of the term "French drain."

The English took the French concept and used it to drain the fens of East Anglia, substituting the – in their minds – silly French idea of sticks and cobbles for good honest – meaning English – unglazed ceramic drain pipes, or "tiles." Tiling was introduced to the United States with much fanfare in the 1870s, and became something of an agricultural fad well into the early twentieth century. Tiling was used to drain low-lying and seasonally wet fields, thus expanding acreage that the farmer could cultivate. It actually is rather common for farm fields to have such drainage systems in place, although most people have totally forgotten that this was a common practice, or even that sections of their land contain drain tile. The practice survives now as the preferred way for lowering water tables around foundations and in low-lying areas, and will still be called "tiling" even though the "tiles" now consist of a perforated and corrugated plastic drain pipe placed in a ditch lined with silt cloth and filled with gravel or surge stone.

A set of questions that we had not asked ourselves was how, on a soil known to be seasonally wet and characterized by perched water tables, had the developer gotten a building permit for two houses? The land would have failed any percolation test. Further, given such seasonally wet conditions, however did the field get cultivated productively anyway? Stopping and thinking about it, we should have guessed that some kind of subsurface drain system was in place. It was like a mystery novel: We had all of the clues, we just failed to put everything together. (The tile system was still working, by the way. It had been placed about 60 cm or so below grade, with a series of parallel cobbles upon which were placed flat stones. On top of those slabs was placed more cobbles. The channel under the flat stones had silted in, but the rest of the drain system continued to work well, actively carrying water down slope to a creek about 100 m away.)

The lessons include *thinking* about the implications of the landscape feature observed and recorded, but also include taking things apart. That, after all, is part of what archaeology is about: controlled and well-recorded destruction of archaeological deposits. It also reinforced the vital importance of understanding landscape history as well as historic practices in managing the land, then recognizing what the archaeological signatures of those practices are.

Figure 7.3. Detail of French drain exposed in Trench 5 at the Weston Site. The flat stones covered the drain channel, the sides of which were made from waterworn cobbles. Trowel points north; scale is 1.0 m.

Figure 7.4. Detail of French drain construction showing how the basal channel was made. The flat stones shown in Figure 7.3. capped the parallel bands of cobbles, creating the void that allowed groundwater to flow first into the drain then downhill. The volume between the cobbles had silted in, but water continued to flow across the top surface of the flat stones. Trowel points north; scale is 1.0 m.

Special Cases: Shallow Sites and Sites of Seemingly Ephemeral Events

When archaeologists think of excavation and data recovery, they reflexively think of deposits that have depth. That is, there is the image of a multi-component site with numerous natural and cultural strata. Often, though, Register-eligible sites are very shallow.

There are mainly two kinds of shallow sites that defy the image of a deep deposit and therefore warrant attention: battlefields and heavily occupied but plowed prehistoric sites.[a]

Battlefields present a special data recovery case, one that can result in tremendous data recovery given attention to basics and sound historic preparation. The deposits consist primarily of spent ordinance combined with surface land features, all located within 30 cm of the surface. Battlefields

represent places where events took place, and where there remain some traces of those events. The general sweep of events may well be preserved (if one is fortunate) in the battlefield maps prepared by the Corps of Engineers or by the Signal Corps. This certainly is true for Civil War battlefields. Since there also are exhaustive compilations of ordinance relative to troop issuance and movements (see Chapter 4 "Tip: Civil War Battlefields"), it is only a matter of *tedious* tracking of ordinance over a prepared surface map and relative to troop movement that allows the engagement to be reconstructed. It was the realization of this that allowed the reconstruction, almost minute by minute, of Custer's Last Stand (see Fraser 1983; Jordon 1986; Fox 1988).

Some prehistoric village sites also can be accessed this way. A plowed, single-component village site will have material drawn up into the swirl of the Ap horizon where, after cultivation has stopped, the artifacts will gradually settle back down into the viscous fluid of the solum.

Caught up in that Ap horizon will be all sorts of prehistoric artifacts, but most common will be the modified and unmodified flakes associated with the lithic applications industry. On prehistoric sites in the eastern United States, around 10 - 15 percent of flakes, recovered from the site and weighing under a gram, represent spent elements of compound tools and exhibit considerable edge damage from use along with well-developed use-wear. They are, actually, microliths (Neumann 1996; Neumann and Polglase 1992). For the diachronic cultural anthropologist, this represents a gold mine.

---

a. There is a third, although it is very uncommon: Military encampments and emplacements. We were involved a number of years ago with the recordation of the 1861 Confederate winter camps located east of Manassas Junction in Virginia. Back in the woods, undisturbed since they were cleared by the occupying force 130 years earlier, were all of the physical surface features of the encampments: Rifle pits, drainage ditches around tent platforms, internal hearths where all that survived were the rusted iron hoops of the chimney barrels that had dropped around the hearth stones, and paths. Data recovery consisted of raking back the leaves of the forest, photographing then drawing the features, then preparing an overall map of the encampments that later were matched to photographs found in the National Archives.

artifact movement, and details on soil horizons, potential for embedded natural/cultural strata, sedimentation rates, and groundwater conditions; and

* the county soil survey book, if such exists, which provides engineering information on the type of soil or sediment for the micro-environment in which the site is located.

The professional archaeologist, in implementing a data recovery operation, needs to have a sense of the physical characteristics of the deposit. This includes both the internal depositional structure, such as buried soils or concealed/embedded cultural strata, as well as the handling properties of the fill itself. The situation described in Chapter 6 section 6.3.1.2. ("*We learned about archaeology from that ...* Providing Adequate Soil Descriptions") should underscore the importance of understanding the handling properties of a site matrix, especially relative to other site limitations.

The physical characteristics of the site matrix will determine the rate at which fill is processed, as well as the appropriate way to process the fill: Dry screening?

Water screening? Air screening? These are tactical decisions that actually can make or break, budgetarily, a Phase III project.

The possibilities of data integrity always need to be considered. These considerations fall into two sets:

(1) preservation, be it individual artifacts or entire depositional matrices; and

(2) movement of artifacts within those matrices.

The first, preservation, concerns issues like bone or organic preservation: Is the deposit conducive to good bone preservation? Has it been below the water table and resulted in good organic preservation? What budget contingencies exist for recovery of wooden artifacts from saturated clay fill, which will preserve the external features but, because of hydrolysis from groundwater, result in the loss of the cellulose microfibrils in the S2 layer of the wood-cell walls? Answers to such questions involve groundwater activity as well as soil acidity and microbial activity.

The small flakes were moved vertically, but rarely any significant distance horizontally. Thus, they represent sort of "activity pixels," to coin a term. High-magnification use-wear analysis, which is startlingly accurate in task assignation (Yerkes and Kardulias 1993; cf. Newcomer and Keeley 1979, Keeley 1980), allows ascription of material worked and nature of working to such spent compound tool elements. Since the microliths themselves dropped (as they were pulled out of the compound tool at the time they were being used) near where they were used, plotting where the microliths are on the site, and on what and how they were used, allows working out activity areas. That is, a plowed site from which a systematic sample of such flakes was taken, has the potential to set out over the entire area the general activity sets of the people who lived there. Since people tend to continue basic activities in the same place even generation to generation (called a "standing behavioral wave," see Neumann and Sanford 1986 for how this applies to the location of small town businesses), a reasonably sound image of what happened on the site is available.

Fox, Richard A., Jr. 1988. *Discerning History Through Archaeology: The Custer Battle.* Ph.D. dissertation, Department of Archaeology, University of Calgary.

Fraser, George MacDonald. 1983. *Flashman & the Redskins.* Plume/Penguin Group, New York, especially pp. 452-455.

Jordon, Robert Paul. 1986. Ghosts on the Little Bighorn. *National Geographic* 170:786-813.

Keeley, Lawrence H. 1980. *Experimental Determination of Stone Tool Uses: A Microwear Analysis.* Chicago: University of Chicago Press.

Neumann, Thomas W. 1996. *Phase III Intensive Analysis of Site 44FX1517 (Hobo Hill): An Early Archaic - Late Archaic Resource Extraction Site.* Prepared for the Fairfax County Heritage Resources Branch, Falls Church, Virginia.

Neumann, Thomas W., and Christopher R. Polglase. 1992. The microlithic compound tool industry in the Middle Atlantic region. *Journal of Middle Atlantic Archaeology* 8:41-56.

Neumann, Thomas W., and Robert M. Sanford. 1986. *A Cultural Resources Survey: PIN 3045.29 Route 104, Mexico, New York.* SUNYC-Potsdam Public Archaeology Report 6 (5).

Newcomer, M.H., and L.H. Keeley. 1979. Testing a method of microwear analysis with experimental flint tools. Pp. 195-205 in *Lithic Use-Wear Analysis*, edited by Brian Hayden. Academic Press, New York.

Yerkes, Richard W., and P. Nick Kardulias. 1993. Recent developments in the analysis of lithic artifacts. *Journal of Archaeological Research* 1:89-119.

The second set of questions, those involving movement, hopefully were addressed in the Phase II report. Soils, be they active or buried, represent dynamic, extremely viscous fluids or semi-fluids. Artifacts move within those fluids or semi-fluids, and such movement can confound data analyses. Answers to questions in this area hopefully were provided by the Phase II testing exercise; if not, then the situation needs to be assessed and the potential, anticipated.

The third issue involves engineering the archaeological data recovery. What are the structural properties of the site matrix? This alone will determine the nature of any shoring needed. At what depth does groundwater appear? This influences both excavation wall strength as well as need for pumps. Does the ground water level rise and fall (usually indicated by the presence or absence of soil horizon mottling)? That will influence not only artifact preservation, but also the potential for ground water seepage at levels higher than perhaps encountered during Phase II testing.

The engineering characteristics of the deposit, combined with setting, will influence how the matrix is processed. For example, we bid on a deeply buried site with a particularly difficult deposit in which the SOW recommended water screening. That was a fair option, only the deposit had, according to the RFP, a series of buried soils, each with clay-saturated B horizons; the water table was within 1.5 m of the surface; and there was no place to drain the water from the water screen since between the site and the nearest stream was a heavily used highway. Water screening was an improbable possible, to quote Sherlock Holmes; there had to be a better way.

Hand screening was also not a viable option. The only solution, as one would guess, was to use focused compressed air, which was available through a Pittsburgh-based company that manufactured the Airknife™. The point here is that knowing the engineering properties of a deposit is critical to doing the Phase III archaeology. The firm that won the Phase III project found that water screening did not work, and that hand screening was impossible. Unfortunately, they were not aware of the third option.

Managing Professionals

The change in the workplace over the last 15 years has resulted in a far larger number of professionals being engaged in non-academic work than ever before. Heretofore, management of a professional workplace has occurred in the professions (such as medicine, law, or engineering), the Church, the military, branches of government, and, to a lesser extent, higher education. The shift in emphasis in archaeology from an academic to an extra-academic field requires as well an understanding of how professionals are managed.[a] Again, the following is not intended to be a review, but rather a series of guidelines and observations meant to sensitize the professional archaeologist confronted with managing other professionals ... or to being managed.

The management of professionals presents a situation that is a specialized extension of general management. General management is an exercise in long-range planning and coordination of short-term tasks, combined with supplying the wherewithal to accomplish a job along with sound skills in leadership. Management of professionals is more of a coordination and administrative exercise than general management. It is much closer to administration than to management.

Even more than normal, the professional employee is the core resource of the firm. It is the professional's expertise and/or skills that are critical to the survival of the firm, since the firm really is marketing professional services and associated skills. Very often, as in engineering, medical, or archaeology firms/divisions, that expertise is substantial and represents training in the management and support of subordinate staff. And also, in those situations, the professional often has a terminal degree in his or her field, along with considerable experience – successful experience – in accomplishing tasks and achieving goals.

In extra-academic archaeology, there are four sets of professionals within the workplace: The project-hire, the salaried employee with an advanced degree, the in-house specialist, and the subcontracted specialists. Their level of expertise ranges from the project-hire, whose experience and expertise often includes at least two years' execution of the mechanics of excavation combined with four years of college, through the generalist M.A. or Ph.D. archaeologist, to the subcontracting specialist. In many cases, there will be

a project director or project manager in charge of a team made up of those components; it also is often the case in larger firms that sets of project managers themselves are being managed by a division or branch director.

As with any basic managerial situation, it is the manager's responsibility to coordinate logistical support – the matériel, personnel, and funding – needed to achieve the specific goals of the project relative to the overall needs of the firm. The professional becomes a resource that is required by the firm to achieve those objectives. Much of what has been said about handling people in general would apply to this situation as well, with some important caveats. It works best, we think, to look at this from two perspectives: the vantage of the managed professional, and the vantage of the person managing the professional. These meld together; it is important to go over these situations.

In a professional workplace, more so than in any other kind of management situation, it is important to recognize and trust the expertise of the people who have the professional background. To put this more simply: "Explain what it is that is needed, then drop the reins." There is nothing that represents a worse use of professional expertise than having a person without professional credentials trying to second-guess a person who does. There is nothing more foolish than a non-professional trying to tell a professional how to do the work.[b]

If that level of direction is required, either the person should not have been awarded the degree or the manager made a serious hiring error. A hospital administrator or even chief surgeon does not walk into the OR to tell the surgeon what to do or not to do. The insurance adjuster would never attempt to tell the actuary how to assess the risk probability tables. The archaeology division or firm manager does not wander into a data recovery exercise and start dictating what to do or not to do.

At each level of professional responsibility, the professional should be given complete command of his or her charge. That is, the manager should only have to designate the general goals, what the professional has to work with, and when what needs to be done. The professional from that point is required to provide the deliverables within the resources allotted and by the time specified. The manager holds the professional accountable for the deliverables; how they are arrived at is beside the point, so long as it is within the resources allocated ("resources" are physical-temporal [time, matériel, personnel, budget] as well as moral [expectations of time relative to compensation]).

---

a. Management, leadership, administration, and governance are all part of a general set of behavior. Those from an academic background will be familiar with administrative activities, whereby programs are implemented. This usually involves the sharing of tasks among peers, where resources are coordinated relative to larger institutional goals. It is not managerial in the same way that it is in a non-academic setting, where orders or directions are given and expected to be followed. In academic settings, governance – the way decisions are made – will either be oligarchical or collegial, depending upon if the issue involves things like promotion or tenure (oligarchical: Only tenured faculty may vote for tenure, or full professors vote on promotion to full professor) or if they are curricular (much more collegial or at least democratic, where all at least have a voice in the decision). See: Freidson 1986:84, 211-227; Hobbs, Walter C., and G. Lester Anderson. 1971. The operation of academic departments. *Management Science* (October 1971):B134-B144.

---

b. Perhaps the most common error in managing professionals is made by non-professionals who treat the professional as an employee that somehow must be goaded to complete a task. The extent of this problem became evident in the early 1990s with the development of "flex-place" and similar "work-from-home" arrangements. Many office managers became afraid that, without the constant oversight and supervision, the person working on their own would not do the job. For anyone with an advanced degree – a triumph of self-directed, independent research in the absence of *any* remuneration – this became incredibly insulting, and resulted in high turn-over rates.

While the general rule for managing professionals is to delegate responsibility and corresponding authority – after clearly explaining what that responsibility is and how the task fits into the larger scheme of the operation – and then to stay out of the way of the actual execution, the general rules for the manager are threefold in this regard:

(1)   to monitor the *overall* exercise of that responsibility relative to the large picture;

(2)   to support and be an apologist for the professional supervised; and

(3)   to provide a professional working environment, both in terms of attitude and in terms of resources and physical conditions.

These hold regardless of the level of expertise relative to managerial oversight. Thus, for the project manager with project-hires, it becomes his or her responsibility to make sure that the work is adequately supported – in all senses – within the limits imposed on the project, and that those project-hires are completing the work within the time frame and at the level of quality required. This, by the way, applies to project-hires subcontracted for specialized work just as much as project-hires for field excavation. Again, much of this falls under the guidelines given in the "Management" section above.

For the division or branch manager, his or her responsibility is to make sure that the project manager is keeping that project within time and budget limits. If these are *not* being met, then the person in charge needs to address the situation promptly, first by advising the individual responsible of the delinquency. That advising should determine where the core problems in accomplishing the task are: They may be in managerial allocation of resources; they may be in profligate use of sufficient resources by the project manager. At this point the manager works with the professional to sort out the problems; what is desired is a win-win situation, since that is what is best for the firm.

The second point will be a close monitoring of the project by the overall manager as well as the professional project manager or subcontractor until the resources (time-funds) are depleted. The overall manager and the task or project manager will have tried to sort out the problem. Both are now trying to get the project back in line with resources. This should include *constant* feedback between the superior and subordinate relative to the project. If the task is not finished at the proper level of quality, then the manager should require the professional to provide the deliverables on their own time.[c]

If those steps – which must be tempered by considering the people and needs – fail, then the manager should consider replacing the person with someone capable of doing the job. The manager – be it the branch chief, division head, project manager, or crew chief – is held accountable for a product to be delivered within a given period. If the subordinates are unable to achieve realistic goals, even after coaching and mentoring, then the best advice is to "cut bait." Such a step always, always must be viewed as a last resort: Professionals are experts at what they do, and sometimes things *do* go awry and the best anyone can do is wince, smile, learn, and work through the problem. At other times, there really is no excuse. This becomes a core management decision, a "handling-of-people" decision that must be considered on a case-by-case basis.

In the archaeology firm or division particularly, how does the person with a master's and perhaps substantially *less* professional experience handle a person with a doctorate and perhaps many years and projects more of experience? The basic answer, which is the core of the "Management" section earlier, is with common sense, discretion, respect, and courtesy.

The person with the more advanced degree is highly trained and, with successful projects, extraordinarily accomplished. The relationship is essentially the same as a paralegal to a licensed attorney, or a nurse-practitioner to a physician. The person with the more advanced degree has earned that degree; to use military slang, that person ranks the other. *But only in the realm of the field.*[d]

The person with the more advanced degree should be aware that the manager's or director's role is one of overall coordination, and with the authority to make sure that that

---

Remember, the project-hire may be paid hourly, but in fact represents a subcontractor hired to provide a specific deliverable – a sequential series of field excavation performances that include brilliant and impeccable field notes. You, as the project manager or as the division manager, are after the field notes; if the project-hire is not providing those, then you have every right – actually, since the others in the firm are partially dependent upon the profitable success of your project – obligation to *demand* those. Your firm has already paid to have that product – the data represented by those field notes, among other records and products – delivered; you have every right to expect that that product be of first-rate quality.

d. One of the more pathetic practices we have seen is where a firm, in an attempt to elevate the professional status of its managerial staff, places "ABD" behind the name of the manager, as if this represented some kind of conferred degree. "ABD" is an abbreviation that people who have not finished their doctoral work sometimes use for "all but dissertation." It is used either because the person has yet to finish the dissertation (no shame there; most do not) or more often because the firm wants something that sounds prestigious (tremendous shame there).

Some firms put "ABD" behind the names of their M.A. archaeologists. This kind of self-conferring of a pseudo-degree is of course too poignant to be considered abhorrent, and requires patience with the evident insecurity shown by the firm that feels compelled to do this. This does happen on occasion; it also cheapens the profession, to say nothing of those who hold legitimate advanced degrees.

---

c. For example, project-hires will be expected to provide detailed excavation notes on Phase II and Phase III projects. If those notes are inadequate, or if they are sloppy or slovenly prepared (including if they are marred by rain or wet), then it is expected that those project-hires prepare, *on their own time* and *for the convenience of the project manager*, corrected and adequate documentation, even if it means transcribing those field notes on their off-hours in their motel rooms. This is regardless of project, be it Phase I, Phase II, or Phase III.

coordination sticks. There is a chain-of-command, and the professional may well be – and often is – a cog in a larger wheel. Any professional who is behaving in a fashion where that is not the case will need to be called aside and the core issue – almost always resource allocation, meaning calendar time and funds – addressed. It *should* never require addressing professional decisions. If it comes to that, it means either that the supervised professional has displayed egregious professional judgment (meaning not just that a person with, say, an M.A. can pick out an error done by a Ph.D., but that a nurse-practitioner can overrule a physician in a diagnoses; the situations are identical), or that the manager has overstepped his or her expertise. Speaking with project personnel over the last 25 years, it has almost always been the second. This bleeding over of appropriate managerial authority to also mean corresponding professional expertise is common throughout the professional workplace, and is why the "Dilbert" cartoon series continues to be successful.[e]

The greatest mistake any manager of professionals can make is to interfere in the professional's exercise of his or her expertise. This holds regardless of the relative degree involved, be it the M.A. directing the project-hire, or the M.A. directing the Ph.D. project director. Just as a core axiom of command is to issue orders and objectives then allow the person in charge to exercise the initiative and authority – and thereby morally be held to the responsibility – of the task, so too does it hold for the manager of a professional. Generally speaking, it is improper for a person with a bachelor's degree to overrule in professional matters a person with a master's degree in the same field, or a master's degree to attempt to overrule on any professional issue a person with a doctorate in that field. The temptation to do this comes from confusing managerial authority with professional expertise.[f]

In the professional workplace, the division or firm manager coordinating professionals needs to treat the situation like a cooperative or joint practice, wherein the manager is functioning as much as an administrator as a manager. To

that manager is given the responsibility – and hopefully the authority – of keeping the overall operations of those project managers in line. Theirs is one of strategic oversight along with tactical monitoring.

If one issue involves making good use of the professional – project-hire, M.A. project director, Ph.D. subcontracting specialist – then another issue involves getting something useful out of that professional. The firm or division succeeds or fails on its ability to make use of the professional. For the engineering, legal, medical, or religious fields, most novitiates are just as aware of this as are their new employers, and the transition from training to practice is rather smooth. For archaeologists, since they come out of university Anthropology environments where the goal more often is to prepare the person for an academic career, it is not smooth. The greatest managerial challenge for handling the advanced-degree professional in an extra-academic setting is getting that person to work together as part of a team and for the good of everyone.

The archaeology proto-professional comes from an academic environment in which there is great individual freedom as well as stress on doing independent work. The archaeologist with an advanced degree is an expert, and is accustomed to working individually on particular questions. Indeed, working with others on a given academic project usually will have been discouraged since childhood; instead, one worked on one's own, since to share results bordered on plagiarism. The master's thesis or doctoral dissertation is an individual work, one's own new and original contribution to knowledge; it is not group projects. Continuation into a faculty life merely reinforces this element of independence.

Working within a firm requires some adjustments. Unlike the academic world, the corporate world is not democratic in any portion of its exercise. There is a chain-of-command; there is order. There also is the expectation that the professional will work with others in the firm as part of a *team*. Teamwork means subverting one's own ego for the common good. This is actually a tricky issue.[g]

It probably works best to explain things this way: In the United States, social status and importance – prestige and power – are measured by how many people are managed or supervised, as well as by how distant a person is from primary production. This is important for the academic-turned-private-sector scientist to remember. The individual may be a brilliant and accomplished researcher, but that may be just the isolated work of one person that serves primary production. The person in charge of the results generated by several such people usually will receive a hearing, and have greater importance attached to his or her remarks, than will the single individual.

---

e. By the way, are you aware that the "pointy-haired boss" in the "Dilbert" strip was an Anthropology major in college? We find that stereotypic assessment of anthropological managerial skills in a professional workplace very troubling.

f. On the topic of managerial authority becoming confused with professional expertise: A friend once told us about a situation where the overall office supervisor was an archaeologist with an M.A., and the project manager had a Ph.D. Each had well over a decade of working in the private sector. The project involved subsurface testing of a historic-period property where the level lawn, set in a non-aggrading environment, had been in place – and in grass – for a couple centuries. The supervisor instructed the project manager to remove the 15-cm thick E horizon as a single stratigraphic level, then proceed in arbitrary levels afterwards. The project manager reminded the supervisor that the E horizon was not a stratum and it, too, should be removed as part of the sequence of arbitrary levels. The supervisor appealed to the head of the firm for confirmation of the field directive, which was given. The project manager calmly let both argue then return to the home office. The instructions were then forgotten and the deposit excavated correctly.

---

g. Sanford, in a mantra that served him well in the Navy and has worked for both of us since, observed: "Half for the ship; half for yourself," by which was meant that one commits what can be committed to the organization, but not so much that the organization become parasitic on one's self. As a good friend in Federal service was told by her supervisor: "Remember, do not love an organization, because it will not love you back."

In managing professionals, it is important to make sure that they do not lose sight of how their work fits into the larger scheme of things, be it just the project, the entire Section 106 Process, or the goals of the corporation. Each builds on the other; the continued existence of the firm depends upon the successful completion of the cultural resources compliance work in the way that it is intended to be done, and that success depends in turn on the success of the given project.

In the end, managing professionals requires that the professional be treated with respect and courtesy, and generally with deference to his or her professional expertise. The manager, though, while acceding to the expertise, must still coordinate the funds, physical resources, and time the professional is to have to make the operation a success. The professional may or may not be able to do this; the manager of that professional – regardless of if it is the corporate branch director handling the Ph.D. project director, or the M.A. project director directing the B.A. project-hires – is required to monitor those limits and keep the subordinate professional apprised of the limits. Further, that manager must also be given the authority to exercise managerial control of that professional.

See also:

Freidson, Eliot. 1986. *Professional Powers: A Study of the Institutionalization of Formal Knowledge.* The University of Chicago Press, Chicago.

Gibbons, Ann. 1994. Making the grade as a scientific manager. *Science* 265:1937-1938.

Any archaeologist thinking in terms of extra-academic work probably should look over Gibbons's article. It is anecdotal; it is insightful. Much of the article uses as a theme Dr. Ellen Vitetta, a wise and clearly sound manager of private-sector science who owns and directs an immunological laboratory. The piece has in it two of the best quotes for anyone considering managing professionals in a research setting:

"If you order 100 SCID mice at $40 each, it better be a damn good experiment"; and

"You have to provide a reasonable sandbox for your people to play in."

Although Vitetta also was quoted by Gibbons as saying that there are no books on management in the professional workplace, that is incorrect. There is a substantial literature on managing professionals; it exists not only under that label, but also under the heading of "Administration" and of course as part of military command training. However, that literature usually is not known to non-business related fields, which usually is synonymous with the disciplines found in a College of Arts and Sciences.

7.4.2. Excavation Management

7.4.2.1. General

Excavation management corresponds in all of its particulars to military campaign management, a point made time and again by Augustus Lane Fox, General Pitt-Rivers (Daniel 1962:74-76) and by Sir Mortimer Wheeler (1954). It requires

* thorough understanding of the problem being addressed (structure of the site and research issues involved),

* knowledge of the physical characteristics of the site,

* awareness of the logistical limits on excavating the site, then

* devising then *executing* a data recovery plan.

It is that fourth part -- working out then implementing a detailed plan -- that is central to any successful Phase III data recovery program. While this seems self-evident, "having a plan" for Phase III data recovery means not only a plan for *how* to get the data out of the ground, it means having a plan that gets the data out of the ground *within a specified time and budget.* That means having lined up the personnel, supplies, and support needed to do the work.

Excavation management requires having a plan, and having that plan set out in relatively specific, *scheduled* terms. It also requires that that plan

* be within budget,

* take into account contingency situations like adverse weather or unanticipated deposit characteristics, and

* afford the project manager operational authority.

A competent professional archaeologist (and the adjectives should be redundant) should have put into place the first two elements; it is management's responsibility to provide the third.

The professional archaeologist should have, in place, a plan for operations that takes into account all of the specifics of the Phase III project. These range from logistics through supply to processing the deposit. Fortunately, that plan will have been prepared, either as part of the data recovery plan that the professional archaeologist developed and now has the good fortune (because the firm was awarded the Phase III project itself) to implement, or because the professional

Neatness: Sir Mortimer meets Compliance Archaeology

Sir Mortimer Wheeler remarked (1954:80) that

It is an axiom that an untidy excavation is a bad one, whether the untidiness reside in the general layout or in detailed execution. The guiding principles are not difficult: they are 'Have a plan', a carefully thought-out scheme, and execute it in an orderly fashion.

We are more of Wheeler's mind than not: Neat-and-tidy excavations are indicative of controlled data recovery, although perhaps some sense of what "neat-and-tidy" is is required.

Cultural resources archaeology has as its goal the retrieval of information stored in a three-dimensional matrix. It is the retrieval, and the uncompromised and unambiguous nature of the retrieved data, that is of import. Those data will then be manipulated – analyzed – then presented in a final report. The data themselves will remain available for others to work with. Those data will consist of the field work records and the artifacts. Those two sets represent the primary data, data to which future workers can return to re-work and re-evaluate the research reported in the Phase III report. The excavation destroyed the site as it recorded the site: The primary data base becomes the field notes and the assemblage.

We have seen Phase III projects that had field crew shovel-scrape the last centimeter or two of plowzone from a strip cleared by earth moving equipment. As the scraping was done, features – pits, hearths, posthole stains, even stray artifacts caught in the B horizon – were flagged. Later, those features and artifacts were carefully mapped in, photographed, drawn, with a master plan of the excavation assembled. The published record – really an inked version of the field notes, with much more legible labels – presented that map, along with the individual photographs. One would never be aware of the uneven nature of the striped field, the drying earth behind the crew as it marched, three abreast, scraping and flagging possible features in the glare of the summer sun. It was untidy in one sense. But it was severely controlled and managed. What, then, constitutes "untidy"?

We have seen Phase III projects where field crew cut the walls of the scrapped strip through the plowzone, herding those walls into a straight line, with a crispness found only in a field school excavation unit. Backdirt was hauled away, sometimes quite a distance away to avoid being in a photograph. The 4-m wide trench was cut with trowels over its 100 m distance, with black plastic set down over the surface to preserve its cleaned-up character (impossible, as

any field person knows). The features were not flagged, but instead required going back over that cleaned area several times, re-scraping the B horizon surface to again define features and posthole stains. Eventually, those features, too, were photographed and drawn and mapped; the fill removed; the drawings inked then published. It was neat and tidy and would have warmed the heart of anyone to see the orderly and clean severity of stripped area. But it involved condensed moisture under plastic, turning the surface to an indistinct mud crossed by the tracks of evening beetles and snakes and requiring repeated scraping as field crew spent days re-working the same piece of land, while others moved volumes of fill away then, eventually, back to fill in the stripped area. It was, then, poorly planned and unorganized. What, then, constitutes "untidy"?

The orderliness of a Phase III excavation is a balancing act. It is a balance between maintaining crew discipline, keeping within budget, tracking data and its recordation, and creating a sense of competence for when the SHPO/THPO or Federal agency archaeologists show up to inspect. How that excavation will be judged will be, rightly or wrongly, on the neatness and tidiness of the field area. Since there is no way to anticipate such inspections, and since even knowing when they will occur would not provide the labor needed to be able to make up for the weeks of inattention, some kind of continuing policing is required.

For example, when plowzone is mechanically stripped and crew come in to shovel-scrape the remainder, it is a good idea to have them also run a string-line along the edge of the trench and use the shovels to cut a straight and "clean" wall, while also having the equipment operator drop the removed fill a meter or two beyond the edge of the trench. All of this creates an impression, actually subconscious, that details are being addressed in more important matters. It also creates a subconscious sense in the field crew of order and concern for detail.

Moving backdirt piles? We have moved backdirt piles, and have watched them moved, sometimes a furlong away, which was a bit extreme. That probably is untidy: It is fiscal mismanagement.

The goal of the data recovery project is to accurately retrieve the information from the archaeological site; there is a limit on how far a person needs to go to keep up appearances. Patton expected the troops on the front lines to shave in sub-zero weather, and sent them water to do this; they only wanted water to drink. There are limits.

Wheeler, Sir Mortimer. 1954. *Archaeology from the Earth.* Penguin, Baltimore.

archaeologist developed the core of an excavation plan when the proposal responding to the RFP was prepared. What every project manager should strive for is to have a colleague remark that "It's amazing; you've thought of *every* detail!" A project should be so well planned that is all but runs itself.

Excavation management requires knowing how many people are needed and what they will be doing, the structure of supervision, the storage and availability of proper equipment/facilities for the excavation, and monitoring of field activities. Successful excavation management requires, then, four things:

* excellent personnel management skills;

* excellent management-of-professionals skills;

* a comprehensive operational plan that provides both logistical support as well as a detailed schedule for task accomplishment; and

* an attention to detail that does not in any way become so myopic that it detracts from a sense of the overall operation and its goals.

Method-and-theory texts, and often college classes, only address the third, and only in so far as matters archaeological are concerned. College or university training in principle demands that the fourth, attention to detail, be developed as a habit in the apprentice professional. Every thing else normally is not part of the formal archaeology curriculum.

Successful implementation of the field portion of the Phase III project requires that the firm's management invests the project manager with operational authority to implement those plans. *Otherwise, unless the project manager is extremely good politically as well as managerially, the plan and the project will fail.*

The second general point under Excavation Management that needs to be mentioned involves making do with what is available for the project. This is where individuals fresh from their university training, and those supervising them, encounter a great deal if difficulty. Compliance work of any kind, but especially the Phase III data recovery project, has limited resources: There are limits on money, on various supplies, but most important, on calendar time. The practicing professional, regardless of where he or she is in the organization of the project, needs must learn to make do and produce excellence with what it is that is available.[7]

Phase III data recovery can at times be very similar to the emergency surgery found in an ER or comparable trauma-care centers. The idea is to do the job in a way that is impeccable, but also quickly and in a way that is free of frills. This is probably the most difficult aspect of compliance archaeology for those just coming out of university to accept. We variously call this approach "M*A*S*H" or "Meatball" field work, and it will be considered by the academic sector -- and even some in the private and public sectors -- as something to avoid.

Official Site Visits

Phase III data recovery projects will have site visits by Federal agency archaeologists and by the SHPO/THPO at some point during the project. The visits may well be unannounced, although that depends upon the nature of the people involved, their view of the firm doing the work, and a variety of other issues. Most of the time, the project manager will be told of an impending visit a week or so in advance.

Because the site visit can come on short notice, it is vital always to maintain the air of professionalism about the site by keeping it well maintained. We were once caught in the midst of an extremely unkempt data recovery effort, and even though the data were just fine and the site was not damaged, it really did look like a war zone. The agency archaeologists justifiably rendered a scathing review of field management. Collateral damage from that was that the agency was skeptical of the quality of the research from that point, and additional hours were needed to recover any sense of quality that had been lost.

Some Federal archaeologists will show up with video or film cameras to better record what is going on. This is quite appropriate. Their role is to make sure that the society's money is being properly used, and that the project is being performed at the highest professional standards.

At the end of the visit or, more properly, inspection, the project manager and field supervisor each should complete detailed written accounts of what occurred, which will be filed in the field notebook under "Records of Communications." We were caught in one situation where a SHPO archaeologist showed up on site, declared how wonderful the work was, assisted in some of the field work (he could work features and we were more than willing to take whatever additional skilled labor we could find), then left.   A week later there was an enormous hue-and-cry from the SHPO about the quality of the field work, so much so that six months later there was a hearing moderated by the ACHP between the SHPO, and the client and ourselves. Fortunately we had sufficient documentation not only of the field work, but also of the visit, and the ACHP concluded by praising the field work and castigating the SHPO.

The point, though, is to be aware that such visits can and will occur – and they *should* occur – and that those visits need to be documented in detail, especially if there is any hint from past interactions that the agency or the SHPO/THPO has another agenda that the visit is meant to assist.

---

7. There are cases where projects are seriously under-budgeted and therefore under-staffed or given unrealistic deadlines: These situations tend to become apparent within a week of the start of field work. Most professional archaeologists will be able to sense the difference between managerial ineptitude in support versus realistic constraints on time or matériel.

What is meant by field work that appears to be emergency surgery?   Like an ER situation, the archaeologist responsible for the Phase III data recovery is caught between the needs of the archaeological resource, and the time and resources available to satisfy those needs. Decisions have to be made about what is or is not essential in terms of field methods. To go back to the obvious example first raised in Chapter 6: There really is no reason to trowel-cut all four unit walls, or to trowel-scrape the floor of each excavation level. What is important about the actual digging is that the fill is being monitored for features or artifact concentrations, and the artifacts have the provenience originally intended by the data recovery plan.

Take a horrifically extreme example and consider it in terms of data recordation and redundancy: A feature-rich prehistoric site accessed by stripping the Ap horizon. What, then, are the data sought? The SOW, it seems, says to strip the Ap horizon (and by implication, forget the material in the plowzone, since even though a sound data recovery effort could be done based upon microliths in that plowzone, time and funding does not allow it). The plowzone is stripped; the land is shovel-scraped to the top of the B horizon; then the features are isolated, photographed, mapped, then excavated. Feature forms are kept, as is a trench and site map. Everyone knows what the feature looked like, where it was, and what it contained.

Now, given that, at what level should there be worry that, for the area two meters either side of the feature in the cleared trench, there was loose fill back on the trench floor? So long as there is a running map of the deposit, and sound documentation of the features, what matters if continued maintenance of the site ends after three hours or, as all projects will, after three months? (Actually, it does matter; see box "Official Site Visits.") In either case, all that will remain are the excavation records and whatever was recovered physically from the deposit. The hesitancy to do this, which comes from the archaeologist's initial field training, also was developed with the implicit thought to always leave open the option of going back over the deposit one more time. In a compliance situation, there rarely are second chances to re-examine previously examined areas.

All professional archaeologists are products of academic training programs where care and deliberation during the excavation process were paramount. The reflexive hesitancy many archaeologists feel about their excavations damaging the site has its source in this.[8]

Some of that care and deliberate action is appropriate; some of it is not. Where appropriateness begins and ends will vary by site, project limits, and other contingencies. It is not an easy or self-evident issue in its particulars. For example, when heavy earth-moving equipment was first used on archaeological sites in the United States, there was considerable adverse reaction. Indeed, there were articles that appeared explaining just why, in this or that particular case, such action had to be taken. Now, of course, mechanical excavation assistance is not at all unusual.[9]

Most professional archaeologists have a series of field work short-cuts that achieve the needed data in a satisfactory way but which would be viewed with trepidation by their university instructors when they themselves were students. The idea of excavating a frozen site piecemeal by thawing out sections using heat from a fire in a 55-gallon oil drum would have caused our instructors to blanche. Yet that procedure was developed in Alaska and used effectively when mitigation was done on the Trans-Alaska Pipeline. And we have been put in situations where we used that technique, and it worked just fine.

The most important thing for all practicing archaeologists to remember in this regard is to understand what archaeological data are and how they must be recorded. If that is understood, then adjusting field work from the ideal as presented in university to the practical as faced by professionals will be easy enough.

As with the Phase I and Phase II projects, the field notes for the Phase III data recovery will be kept in one or more three-ring, D-ring loose-leaf binders. Because of the scale of the data recovery effort, it is possible that a series of binders, each devoted to certain aspects of the overall project, will be used. The advantage of a multiple-binder project is a certain flexibility in handling the binders themselves; the disadvantage is an occasional awkwardness in having a number of these to carry around. The rule-of-thumb is if a single binder is going to exceed two inches, then break the project records down into multiple binders.

---

8. Recently, we spoke with a project director who, in describing the project, essentially apologized for having to use a backhoe to provide the sondages needed to better understand the structure of the deposit he was asked to disassemble. Archaeological sites may be non-renewable resources, and they may not be so robustly redundant as geological data, but most Register-eligible sites have sufficient internal redundancy that something like a sondage will gain more than will be lost. Considering that, in his case, the core of the site itself would be destroyed by a bridge abutment made such caution -- while quite understandable -- really unnecessary.

9. Of course, from the other perspective: While there was concern in the 1960s about mechanical removal of fill, there was no corresponding concern about screening fill. The use of hardware mesh to screen fill from archaeological deposits in the eastern and midwestern United States did not become common until the 1970s. Fill was shovel-sorted instead, while features were sometimes trowel-sorted and sometimes screened. Screening actually seems to have been more common among looters, at least those working the rockshelters and similar cave deposits in the mountains of eastern Kentucky. Water flotation was not initiated until the late 1960s, and was not common until the early 1980s. Now, these matters of excavation propriety are reversed: Few would not screen fill, or at least would think hard about why they were not screening; while no one has a problem with reasonable mechanical assistance in excavation.

7.4.2.2. Notebooks and Record Keeping

Phase III field notes contain five sets of information:

*   general project information, including maps and SOW;

*   general field notes as kept by the field supervisor;

*   specific unit and unit-level notes kept by each test-unit crew;

*   feature records; and

*   other records, inventories, and logs.

If it is anticipated that more than two inches of field notes, photographs, tables, and forms will be produced by the combined field and project operations (including post-field aspects of the project), then the notebooks should be subdivided by operational tasks into thinner binders. The best way to do this is by placing the general project information and the general field narrative in one binder; the specific unit-level notes and features documentation in a second; and the various inventory records in a third. A breakdown in this fashion allows the project manager to use one binder for communications, excavation management relative to operational plan, and overall communications; while the second and third binders, associated with day-to-day field work, can be maintained by the senior field supervisor. In this situation, the core project binder stays with the project manager, and he or she will review the other binders on a daily basis. (It is likely that later a fourth and fifth binder will be added for the overall project: The fourth, containing laboratory analysis notes; and the fifth, possibly containing negatives but certainly containing prints, contact sheets, additional graphics, and perhaps even summary tables. Again, this all depends upon the scale of the project.)

Separate binders allow for better delegation and maintenance of record keeping; however, with that delegation comes the requirement that they be reviewed constantly to make sure that subordinate supervisory personnel are keeping the records the way they must be kept. (Remember to label *both* the front and sides of the binders so that it is know what they are: This avoids confusion in fumbling for what is needed, of course, but also anticipates the final curation of those notes.)

As with the Phase I and Phase II field notebooks, each of the field note sets will be set off in the binder by a tab-labeled divider. And yet again, at the end of field work, when the project has moved to the office, the field note binder will become the project binder. At the end of the project, the binder will have proprietary corporate information removed, the rest of the information copied, then the original notes will be turned over to the client, or a suitable curatorial facility, along with photographs, artifact collections, and a copy of the Phase III report.

The same basic sub-sections contained within the Phase I and Phase II field notebooks will be found within the Phase III field notes. These have been discussed in Chapter 5 section 5.3.3. and Chapter 6 section 6.3.3. To these will be added sub-sections, such as one giving the specifics of the data recovery plan. To review these as they would be assembled in a multiple-binder project:

First Binder

Section 1. General Project Information

*   Scope of Work (SOW) and accompanying correspondence;

*   A summation of the data recovery plan along with the project schedule;

*   Logistics, including budget/hour allocations for tasks;

*   Portions of the Phase I and Phase II reports that have a bearing on immediate excavation questions;

*   Project maps and figures:

*   Permits, clearances, and right-of-entry materials; and

*   Records of communications.

Section 2. General Field Notes

*   An overall narrative of the project, including nature of the project environment and general day-to-day bookkeeping; and

*   Summary details on buildings, rooms, units, blocks, exposed surfaces, or other sub-sets of the excavation.

Second Binder

Section 3. Specific Excavation Records

Section 4. Feature Records

Third Binder

Section 5. Mapping and Land-Survey Notes

Reviewing Field Notes

The field notes from an archaeological site represent the equivalent of back-up information storage for one's computer hard drive, but in a way as if the data on the hard drive were permanently and irrevocably destroyed, byte by byte, as the information was backed up. The field notes from a project are one of three sets of permanent records, the other two being the photographs from the site and the artifacts recovered. Even then, the artifacts become virtually useless unless the field notes are sound.

Field notes are crucial for all phases of the compliance process, of course, but they are most critical for the Phase III data recovery project. This is because, unlike the Phase I or Phase II, the site undergoing mitigation through data recovery will cease to exist. True, sites identified during Phase I and Phase II may well also cease to exist, but in those cases where mitigation was not required, there are known to exist comparable repositories of the information that the site contained. There is a bit of leeway for errors in record keeping.

This is not true for Phase III, and therefore requires that the field notes be kept to the highest standard possible, and that they be continually checked to make sure that that quality is there, and is there at the level of detail needed.

The basic chain-of-command for field notes on a project goes like this:

*   the people excavating a given area and producing the original notes;

*   the field supervisor or crew chief under whom those field technicians work; and then

*   the project manager.

The field technicians must assemble the best notes relative to the time available that they can. Most firms will assist in this by setting out excavation and feature forms, which save the field technician the headache of repeatedly writing out the same things while also serving as a reminder for what needs to be recorded.

The field supervisor is expected to review those specific notes, and to make sure that the essential information is present, and that the notes themselves are legible, readable, and otherwise neat. If the core information is not present, then the field technician needs to be told what to put in and why (this happens most often when field laborers move from one region of the country to another). If the notes are messy, then the field technician must be required to copy those notes over neatly, *and on his or her own time before the start of the next field day.* Field supervisors should review each set of notes each day. Remember, this is a situation where the data on the hard disk are destroyed as backed-up; daily review of field notes is essential.

Records kept by or under the supervision of the field supervisor need to be reviewed by the project manager. For primary records, which are generated in situations where the project is very large and the field supervisor is essentially a deputy project manger with a field assignment, the project manager needs to review the overall field notes only periodically (frequently at first to confirm that all are in agreement with the needs of the project, then occasionally thereafter to make sure that nothing has slipped through). In situations where the project is so small that the excavation notes can be reviewed by the project manager while the field supervisor serves more for crew management, the project manager must review those on a daily basis. Again, if work needs to be redone, it must be redone.[a]

For those in supervisory roles, be they crew chiefs or project managers, there should never be a hesitation to call those under supervision to task for the quality of the field notes. This obviously is done within the managerial sense outlined in the discussion "Management" above. However, the standards *must* be set high, and they *must be uncompromising.* If the field notes fail, the project fails. Professionals immediately recognize the importance of this, and view correction as the important help needed that improves both the project and their own professional skills.

---

a. Daily review of notes actually is not micro-management. Rather, it reflects the intense and irreversible nature of the archaeological data-recovery process. It should be thought of and projected more as a second set of eyes looking out after the quality of the work, and definitely *not* an attempt to catch someone making a mistake. Data recovery records are absolutely so critical that no one can afford to have a recordation method error last over a day.

Section 6. Photo Log

Section 7. Bag Inventory

Section 8. Soil, Matrix, and Flotation Sample Inventory

For very large projects where there are a number of sites or site-like areas, then each site will maintain a notebook or series of notebooks like that just outlined, which is maintained by the senior supervisor on the particular site or sub-area within the site. To all of this is added the equivalent of the first binder, which would be maintained by the overall project director. The project director also will add the overall plan for the project along with the overall schedule, while each of the subsidiary project notebooks would have plans and schedules specific to their responsibilities. And instead of the overall notebook keeping a running narrative on excavation areas within site, it keeps a running commentary on the overall excavation activity at each site or major sub-area. Review procedures are adjusted in these situations, where the project director

On Physically Keeping Field Notes

Field notes, especially those for Phase III data recovery, are permanent records that will be archived. This requires that they be physically recorded in the field in such a way that they will survive extremely long-term storage, storage in increments of centuries. For those who have worked with field notes from the middle nineteenth century, or historic records from the eighteenth (or earlier), a sense of this scale already is present, as is an appreciation for the vagaries and limitations of those earlier notes. Archaeologists work and think and store information on a temporal scale that works as if it is done in increments of 50 years.

Field notes need to be kept on paper that will not deteriorate (usually, 100 percent cotton/rag, which also is acid-free and will last). Inking needs to be basic carbon. Recording should be done in pencil with HB lead (never ballpoint pen), with a typewriter with a carbon-impregnated ribbon, or with a computer-and-printer where the record is printed out in equally permanent ink and placed in the notebook each day.

Where it is possible, typed field notes should be kept. This reflects two things: The early twenty-first century, where penmanship has disappeared (and, in any case, penmanship styles change over the centuries); and the speed and ease that typing out information allows information to be recorded. Typed field notes may indeed be possible at the unit/excavation area level using a lap-top computer with local printer. It is critical to *never, ever* store primary field notes on computer disk without also generating a curatable printed record of those notes. That is, where a lap-top computer is used to record an excavation level, just as soon as those notes are written out, the record MUST be printed out. *Under absolutely no circumstances should any primary field notes be stored only as computer files; no excavation step should be started where the record of the previous step exists only as information stored on computer file.* Field notes must be stored as physical hard copies.[a]

While lap-tops are common and now reasonably accessible, they are not necessarily affordable at this time for general issue, although printers are. Further, the initial reaction of equipping crew with lap-tops but maintaining one printer places the entire excavation at the mercy of the vagaries of that printer, *since no further work should be started in any excavation until a permanent paper record of the previous step physically exists.*

Many project managers will cart a standard manual (sometimes even electric) typewriter into the field. (Typewriters of any kind, manual or electric, are increasingly hard to locate. They may be found in Salvation Army, Goodwill, and St. Vincent de Paul stores, although they are there to allow those who cannot afford a computer system access at least to an affordable printer, and therefore should be purchased with the moral sensitivity that that implies. They also are available through stores like the "Vermont Country Store" in Weston, Vermont.) Equipped with a standard cloth ribbon (still available in all drugstores, package/mail-room centers, and office supply stores), these generate legible field notes in carbon that are, when typed on suitable paper, curatable. For most people now, composing at the keyboard is quicker, easier, and less of an effort than writing things out long-hand. Keypad-generated field notes probably are the better option. And, for a manual typewriter, access to electricity rarely is an issue.

Figure 7.5. *Assortment of manual typewriters. Manual typewriters have been used in harsh field conditions for over a century. They are ideally suited for field recordation because of their robust construction. Left to right: Corona portable used by 330th U.S. Infantry in the front-line trenches in France during World War I; Remington portable from the 1920s used in the field during World War II; Royal portable from the 1950s used for archaeological field notes in the 1980s and 1990s; Smith Corona portable from the 1960s used for archaeological field notes in Middle America in the 1970s and 1980s.*

---

a. This also allows for checking quality. Several years ago, a university-based cultural resources program attempted a three-dimensional piece-plot of an archaeological deposit using a total station. A total station will record the information in a way that can be downloaded to a computer, which in turn can generate a map. Piece-plotting with a total station would have given the x-y-z coordinates for each mapped object in the site, and as one might imagine, supplied incredible recordation of the site overall. The only problem: No one coded for the vertical or elevation variable in the total station. All of the vertical provenience was lost. This was not caught until after the project was over: No one had taken the time or effort to generate a hard-copy map, each day, of where artifacts within the deposit were located. Thus, no one caught the error until well after the project was over.

will go through the area supervisor's notes on a regular -- usually daily -- basis, but leave the details of monitoring the specific area/room/architectural notes to the subordinate supervisors.

7.4.3.　Closing Field Operations

Phase III projects represent something different than the previous Phase I survey and Phase II testing projects. Phase I and Phase II work really is diagnostic and evaluative work; the idea is to get a sense of what is present then, if appropriate, recommend additional work. Closure of the field aspect of the project usually is little more than regular backfilling of shovel tests, or filling in test units or trenches from which the plowzone was mechanically removed. In essence, the land normally is restored to its previous condition, and often enough for a Phase III project in built-up areas, a landscaper will be retained by the firm to make sure that that is the case.

The Phase III data recovery project presents different issues on closing field operations. These include:

* physically closing the excavations;

* returning rented equipment;

* finding storage for the additional equipment first purchased for this particular project;

* cleaning, repairing, and maintaining field equipment;

* cleaning the site or disassembling the site architecture; and

* demobilizing the project-hires while reassigning permanent employees who served as field staff.

Physically closing the excavations will vary by two factors: the nature of the data recovery and the needs of the land-alteration project that caused the project to be undertaken. Many people envision a data recovery exercise being prompted by pending large-scale construction and land disturbance. This *is* often the case. However, situations where there is a change of ownership from Federal to private, or in situations where the site is located in the area of potential adverse effects well beyond the actual physical alteration of the landscape, this may not be an issue.

There are three options:

* complete closure of the excavation and restoration of the land to its original condition;

* partial closure and restoration of the land; or

* no closure, with the original construction project making use of the archaeological excavations for their own excavation needs.

The option chosen will depend upon the project and will have been anticipated in the Phase III SOW.

Returning rented equipment is straightforward. Finding space for additional equipment purchased for the Phase III project is more difficult, but is solvable.

Perhaps most important to the long-term functioning of the firm is equipment repair and maintenance. As a good friend of ours constantly notes, tools represent investments and therefore maintenance and attention devoted to their good condition represent wise business practices.

With closure of the field aspect of the Phase III project, the crew chief/field supervisor should be delegated the responsibility of making sure that all field equipment is in prime condition and repair. All equipment should be kept in top condition in the field: Shovels cleaned each day, always kept sharpened, and kept free of rust; tools in the tool box also should be clean and free of rust (as a tip for anyone assessing quality of a field operation: Look in the tool box for a wire brush; quality professional field operations will have a wire brush in the tool box, along with the mill-bastard files, the brush serving to clean the filings from the teeth of the file); and those independently minded letters with the photo menu board should be in order.

The site architecture will also need to be disassembled. Large projects can result in an abundance of mud-caked plywood, two-by-fours, pile lumber, and a tremendous amount of bric-a-brac that was assembled to execute the field portion of the data recovery project. At times, this results in an enormous pile of *stuff*. A good data recovery plan will have anticipated this and made provision either for storage or disposal. The decision of what to do will depend upon the firm, its ability to store material, the cost of such storage, and the likelihood that the material will be used again. The rule-of-thumb is to always try to store what has been acquired for the project, but to also prepare a detailed and descriptive list of what has been stored, and to structure the storage area in a way that such materials can be identified. Equipment is a library of tools for executing tasks; set things up so that the range of tools available is known for those who will need to plan for them, and are accessible for those who need to draw from them.

The last step in closing the field portions of the Phase III data recovery project involves reassignment of personnel. This is a managerial responsibility. For project-hires, it is proper to advise them about other projects, either those within the firm or those known to be starting under other firms. All sound managers -- and all wise businesses -- will try to set things up to place project-hires. This helps the project-hire, but also creates a legitimate sense of the concern and care that the firm has in looking after employees. Thus, when the need for project-hires comes up again, the firm has an established reputation for looking after its own. Further, when the need comes during the Phase II or Phase III project for which the temporary field technician was hired to demand the utmost effort under trying conditions, that person will be even more willing to put in the extra effort. After all, the firm has a reputation of looking after the needs of those under its care, even project-hires.

For permanent employees, the end of the field aspect of the project will require reassignment. This again is a managerial issue, and involves shunting people from the field project to another assignment, be it the start-up or field needs of another project, or the laboratory and report preparation of the ongoing Phase III project. Reassignment is done both to address the needs of individual projects as well as to address the overall needs of the firm. Professional courtesy dictates that this must be done in consultation with the project manager, who should be given first choice from the field personnel in post-field staffing relative to his or her project needs and budget.

7.5. Post-Field

At the end of the field portion of the Phase III data recovery, there are four tasks that need to be addressed:

(1) dealing with the field equipment;

(2) dealing with field personnel;

(3) dealing with the records and notes generated by the project; and

(4) doing the analyses and the draft report.

The issues of equipment and personnel reassignment have been treated in section 7.4.2.2. These are demobilization issues that reflect on the infrastructural and logistical commitments of the firm or division, and have to do with continued operational integrity.

The third and fourth have to do with the archaeology, both in itself and as part of the compliance process. More specifically, the archaeological site recovered during Phase III survives only as the field records and the associated artifacts, and those artifacts have little meaning in the absence of the field records.

The final goal of the Phase III project is to produce a detailed written analysis of the archaeological site that meets compliance needs as set forth in the SOW, and prepare the artifacts and site/analysis records for permanent curation.

As with the Phase II project, the following tasks will need to be done as soon as possible after returning

Unemployment

Unemployment is a central issue for the project-hire. The project for which a person was hired represents temporary employment. When the project ends and the person is no longer employed, that person is no longer employed because of a lack of work. They may be eligible for unemployment. All professional archaeologists, by virtue of the basics of their academic training, are alerted to this issue, which is experienced by nearly every project-hire and one out of every two academic archaeologists in their careers.

Unemployment funds are paid for by the particular firm, which in effect is paying the equivalent of an insurance premium to the state to cover for situations where personnel are laid off. The project-hire will be, in effect, laid off unless he or she has been beguiled into some kind of subcontracting, limited duration contract (different issue and beyond the scope of this text). Being laid off makes the person eligible for unemployment compensation, *subject to the rules and governance of the state.* Each state differs, and the project-hire contemplating this as an option must contact the state's Department of Labor or equivalent agency and learn what restrictions apply.

For the firm, this is another one of the standing issues about the approach-avoidance nature of project-hires. When a Phase III project – or any project requiring project-hires – is planned, then the potential of unemployment claims being filed has to be considered. For the project-hire – really, for anyone who is employed – it is important to explore the requirements and restrictions of unemployment compensation within their residence state.

from the field to expedite production of the draft final report by its scheduled date:

*   The artifacts, flotation samples, and matrix samples will go to the lab with the bag inventories, and general cleaning, cataloguing, processing, and analyses will begin (see Chapter 8);

*   samples for any specialized analyses will need to be shipped to the subcontracting specialist just as soon as the laboratory staff has processed the materials (including dating and similar samples);

*   draft figures for the report will be prepared then submitted to the graphics department;

*   remaining film or other images will be processed;

*   a site map will be prepared if needed, and that too will be submitted to the graphics department; and

*   the writing of the report will be started (see Chapter 9).

On larger projects, it often is best to have seen to it that all except the last three tasks were underway long before field work itself ended, with the possible exception of the submission of samples for dates. It is quite possible to start processing flotation samples or to start cleaning and cataloguing artifacts before work on the site ends. Doing this, though, is a matter of scheduling that is under the jurisdiction of the laboratory director; the project manager is only responsible for saying what needs to be done by what date, and how much in the way of person-hours is available to get those tasks done.

7.5.1. Collections Processing

Phase III data recovery projects return from the field with three general categories of physical data:

(1) artifacts;

(2) fill or matrix samples intended for additional processing; and

(3) field records.

Coordination of the first two, which represent the collection from the site, are the responsibility of the laboratory director. The project manager is responsible for the third.

Processing of artifacts requires first comparison of the standing bag inventory from the field records with the artifact bags returned from the field. Although it is not supposed to happen, we have yet to be a part of a Phase III project where at least one bag or inventoried artifact was not accounted for. Such eventually shows up, but results in the laboratory personnel and project manager (and the field supervisor, now caught up in the hectic agitation) literally turning the office upside down trying to locate whatever was missing. Just as was noted in Chapter 5 about the inevitable artifact bag placed in a field technician's pocket and forgotten, such also can and does happen in Phase II and Phase III projects.

Having accounted for all of the items listed on the bag inventory from the field, the laboratory director will begin the processing of the artifacts. This will involve the cleaning (when and where appropriate), cataloguing, labeling, and re-bagging. This is discussed both in the method-and-theory literature and in Chapter 8. The reader is directed to those sources.

The processing of flotation and matrix samples will depend upon their nature and upon requirements in the SOW. In most instances, such samples consist of flotation samples and whole-matrix samples. Flotation samples may be from features or from general excavation-level fill where they are some previously set

percent of the pre-screened fill; matrix samples tend to be fixed-volume samples removed in their entirety either from a fixed place in the excavation floor as field work continues, or as a column from a unit or block wall after excavation of that section is done.

Flotation samples from features tend to be floated by the firm and separated into light and heavy fractions. After that processing, the fractions may be analyzed in-house, or sent to subcontracted specialists for detailed study.

Matrix samples usually are recovered to assist in understanding the physical properties of the deposit. These may be sent in their unprocessed entirety to a subcontracted specialist for detailed analysis, or they may be curated and not processed at all. This will depend upon what was requested in the SOW. It is not as common for the firm to process these.

7.5.2. Analysis and Report Production

Phase III reports are expected to be comprehensive site monographs, and the SOW and budget will have allowed for this. Indeed, the kinds of analyses and research issues they address will have been stipulated in the data recovery plan and in the SOW derived from that plan. Occasionally additional work is possible or somehow can be squeezed in within the budget limits; many project managers will check and re-check the status of their analysis budget to see what more can be done to make the report itself just all that more thorough. Remember, the better the *draft* final report, the more likelihood there will be of a favorable agency and SHPO/THPO review, and the less of the budget allocated to producing the *final* final report will have to be used.

The Phase III report is a thorough analysis of the portion of an archaeological site examined. It is *not always* an exhaustive analysis. The purpose of the Phase III report is to make sure that some form of complete, professional-level analysis of the deposit has been done and written up. This expectation is very much in reaction to the failure of many sites excavated under the auspices of the WPA to be duly reported, even in an abridged way.

While the analyses and report correspond to what would be produced by an academic research unit, they differ in that the Phase III analyses and report must address any and all issues raised in the SOW and in the corresponding data recovery plan. Further, while the Phase III analyses and report are meant to be the last statement needed for the site -- by the time the report is completed and the artifacts processed, the existence of the part of the site destroyed is to be *redundant*; it must be remembered that the notes and report can always be reviewed in the future, with the artifacts further analyzed. And it is quite likely that in

50 or 100 years this will be a common academic research practice.

The allocation of analysis tasks will be essentially the same as that for a Phase II report, and was given in sections 7.3.3. and 7.3.4. above. Usually the project manager or the laboratory director will do most of the basic specialized artifact analyses, and usually one of the two will do the statistical tests. More so than even the Phase II testing report, the Phase III report requires that all comparative statements be supported with the appropriate statistical test.

The general structure of the Phase III report is outlined in Chapter 9. Again, it really is no different in its basic organization than any other standard compliance report.

Report production tasks are essentially the same as they were for Phase II, and also were given in sections 7.3.3. and 7.3.4. above. The project manager will do most of the writing, and will coordinate the written analyses of others, especially the laboratory director, the staff historian or prehistorian, and any specialists retained for particular analyses.

It is well to repeat what has been said about the Phase I and Phase II project here: With the Phase III project out of the field, it is not at all unusual for all people with assigned tasks involving that project to be working on other projects as well. This will include the project manager. In this, the Phase III project differs greatly from the research situation found in an academic setting. For the extra-academic archaeologist, everyone has to be working on or reviewing several different projects at the same time. For the private-sector archaeologist, this is required to keep cash coming into the firm. For the public-sector archaeologist, this is to stay abreast of the permitting and compliance process.

7.6.   Closing the Project

The end of the Phase III project represents the end of the compliance process as it bears upon the archaeological site. How projects wind down and end is pretty much the same, regardless of the type of site or scale of the project. The sequence will be:

*   submission of the draft final report to the agency and to the SHPO/THPO for review;

*   after a set review period, the SHPO/THPO and the agency will return comments on the draft report, including any recommended changes;

*   a cover letter responding to those recommended changes will be drafted, and where appropriate the requested changes will be made in the report;

Other Deliverables: Progress Reports, Management Letters/Summaries

Large and/or long-running projects will require production of short status reports, called variously "progress reports," "management letters," and "management summaries." These will be specified in the SOW as deliverables, and for long-running projects it is not unusual that incremental payments – often monthly *in response to a bill sent by the firm* – will be based upon receipt of these. Such deliverables are found in large Phase II and nearly all Phase III projects.

Progress reports and management letters serve as periodic status reports, submitted to the Lead agency either at calendric intervals (say, monthly) or at the conclusion of given "project milestones." ("Project milestones" refers to specified stages in the performance of the project.) These summarize the nature of the work to-date, outlining what has been done and what has been discovered thus far. Sometimes these letter reports are short; more often, they run to 5,000 - 8,000 words. Their purpose is to keep the Lead agency and/or client apprised of the work being done and its progress. With receipt, funds may be released to the firm in proportion to the work accomplished thus far.

For projects requiring management letters or progress reports, that requirement will continue through the analysis stage as well, with short letters summarizing work to-date being submitted up until the time that the draft final report is delivered for review. Again, for projects like this, partial payment will be contingent upon receipt of such status summaries.

Management summaries are written at the end of the field work but before the analyses and report production begin. Management summaries summarize the field work, what has or has not been accomplished, and how that seems to relate to the issues at hand. For Phase II testing, these can alert the agency to what the final recommendation might be (based upon evidence to-date). For the Phase III data recovery, they tend more to describe what the site seems to have produced, and what the major findings will be. Management summaries can be large: We have prepared summaries that ran over 10,000 words.

The management summary will be re-worked and serve as a long abstract that appears at the start of the project report. That also will be called a "management summary."

*   a final report will then be produced and duplicated to the number of copies requested in the SOW, plus additional copies for the office and report authors;

*   usually the copies of the final report will be delivered to whoever issued the SOW, along with a copy to the SHPO/THPO; then

* the field notes will be purged of propriety records, the residue will be copied for in-house records, then the original field records -- notes, photographs, negatives, slides, and maps -- will be physically turned over to an appropriate curatorial facility along with the artifacts, other physical remains from the site, and a copy of the final report.

At that point, called "turn-over," most of the archaeology staff will end its involvement with the project and with the site. For the firm, with "turn-over" completed, a final bill will be submitted to the client for the outstanding balance of the project award. When final payment is received, the firm will then calculate the balance of the per diem payment due to those who worked in the field. Those calculations will be done by the CFO or business office along with the project manager. The firm will then generate the per diem cheques and distribute them.

For the office, the project will survive as the final report and as the total project notebooks.

8: Laboratory Structure, Processing, Analysis

8.1. Purpose and Objectives

Two somewhat overlapping tasks are required at the end of the field portion of a compliance project: processing and analysis of the recovered material, and preparation of the project report. The first is of concern here; the second is discussed in Chapter 9.

The processing and analysis steps in a compliance project are similar to those steps in any standard archaeological research project. With a couple qualifications unique to the compliance needs of the project, the purposes of those steps are generally the same, too:

*   to identify, record, label, and prepare for curation artifacts and other materials recovered from the archaeological site, in accord with **36 CFR Part 79** (see also proposed **36 CFR 66** [42 FR 5374-5479]) and the Secretary of the Interior's Guidelines [48 FR 44716-44742];

*   to provide data for answering questions about the site *relative to* the needs of the compliance project at its particular phase of investigation; and

*   to make a start -- sometimes a substantial start -- into the analysis and interpretation of the assemblage so that future researchers can make use of the analysis as is or continue that analysis.

Processing and analysis activities represent data management, storage, and partial to nearly complete data reduction (see Secretary of the Interior's Guidelines [48 FR 44716-44742). There will be three products from this step:

*   labeled, catalogued, and curated material remains from the archaeological site;

*   analysis notes and similar records; and

*   a collection inventory.

Processing and analysis seeks to reduce and condense the physical remains as much as possible to "paper" records, be they actually on paper or temporarily held in a computer file. It will be those analysis records, rather than the artifacts themselves, that will be manipulated and referred to by the project manager and others when they produce the project report.

The idea of the processing and analysis step is to leave the collection in such a state that future workers can come into the assemblage and, armed with the field records and analysis notes, resume the research from the point where the professional has left off. Remember, the site probably will be severely compromised, if not lost entirely, and that archaeological sites are non-renewable resources.

8.2. Basic Laboratory Structure

Processing and analysis of the material from the field requires some kind of laboratory facility. That facility serves three functions:

*   collection processing, which includes conservation/ stabilization, cleaning, cataloguing, and labeling;

*   analysis; and

*   short-term storage until turn-over.

In some firms, the archaeology laboratory space also serves for the storage both of field equipment and of field and laboratory notes. This use depends entirely upon space configuration of the office.

Collections processing refers to the initial mechanics involved in organizing the collection that has come in from the field. This is the step where the artifact bags are compared to the bag inventory list; then material is removed from the bags or other containers, cleaned (if appropriate) or stabilized, classified by type of object, labeled, then recorded by label designation and classification. For matrix samples, it will be at this point that the flotation samples will be reduced relative to the specifications in the SOW. All of this work usually will be done within the archaeology laboratory space proper or, for initial reduction of flotation samples, someplace suited to the needs of that processing step.

Analysis will vary by the needs of the project, which will include the goals of the particular level of work (Phase I, Phase II, Phase III), requirements set forth in the SOW, and budget and time constraints. The purpose of the analysis for Phase I survey and Phase II testing is to provide specific answers to compliance-related questions (see Chapters 5, 6), particularly the cultural-historical affiliation of the deposit as well as its *significance* (**36 CFR 60.4**) relative to the eligibility of the site for listing on the National Register of Historic Places.

Analysis activities associated with compliance archaeology take place in three places. The first is within the laboratory proper, where collection preparation, basic cataloguing, and general mensuration will be done. The second place often will be the project manager's office, particularly on Phase II and Phase III projects where there is an issue of typological assessment of diagnostic artifacts ("diagnostic artifacts" refer to artifacts that are capable of establishing a set time and/or cultural association for a deposit). A surprising amount of analysis takes place on the project manager's desk. The third place will be with the subcontracted specialist.

Short-term storage is the third basic use of laboratory space. The laboratory becomes a holding station until such time as the project is completed and the collections, along with the field records and analysis notes, are turned over to an appropriate curatorial facility. This means that there not only must be adequate space, but that that space must be suitable, in terms of climate control, fire-suppression capabilities, and pest-management, for such curation, however temporary.

Archaeology laboratory facilities involve four things:

*   the physical plant and equipment;

*   the physical arrangement or configuration;

*   budgeting; and

*   internal and external administration.

The archaeology laboratory in corporate settings differs substantially from those found in university and museum settings. In the university setting, say, the archaeology laboratory often serves both for analysis and instruction, and will be located in one of the several buildings that form the academic village. It will have reasonably open access, meaning that the space will be accessible without first having to pass through other offices, or a receptionist or security station. Further, the space will frequently serve for long-term curation; for many public universities, that space *is* one of the state's permanent curatorial facilities.

In a corporate setting, the archaeology laboratory is part of a more extensive physical plant. In some situations, as with a stand-alone archaeology firm, the firm itself will be housed in a single structure, and the archaeology laboratory will make up part of the space of that structure. In other situations, such as an engineering/architecture firm, the archaeology laboratory will be located somewhere amidst the general offices of the overall corporation.

8.2.1. Physical Plant and Equipment Needs

Any archaeology laboratory facility, including the corporate laboratory, is composed of three elements:

* space;

* furnishings; and

* equipment.

Ideally, 1,500 square feet are needed in any setting, private-sector or academic, for a basic archaeology laboratory and its associated roles in equipment and short-term collections storage. However, the amount of space actually needed or available in a corporate setting varies by several factors, including the size of the firm, how it organizes then delegates basic laboratory chores, and how it pays for space. In private practice, approximately 40 percent of that space will be dedicated to analysis proper; another 35 percent, to storage of collections; and the remaining 25 percent, to equipment, maintenance, cleaning, and the like.

One factor regulating space allocation in the private sector is that most firms end up having to pay for their space. A number of firms rent office space, and rental of office space is computed by the square foot. Reducing the amount of space required reduces overhead costs, which can allow the firm to reduce total costs and therefore bidding rates, thus increasing its competitive advantage.

In a corporate setting, analysis itself is a two-step process, with the laboratory technicians doing the basic measurements or counts after the collection has been processed, and the laboratory manager, project manager, and sometimes a senior field supervisor doing more detailed analyses. That second step in the analysis means that the project manager's office will double as analysis space.[1]

Regardless of how *much* space is devoted to the laboratory, that space must have a fire-detection/suppression system, be climate controlled, and have regular pest management [see also **36 CFR 79.9 (b)(3), (6)**]. Since most work is close-eye work, the area must be well lit by windows, fluorescent lights, or preferably both. Lighting should be at least 1.5 watts for every square foot of laboratory floor space. The laboratory should have hot-and-cold running water with a discharge rate of at least 5 liters per minute to facilitate whatever washing and rinsing is done, and a large sink (on the order of 60 x 40 cm,

Figure 8.1. Interior of a typical corporate laboratory. In the corner on the left is the general reference library along with project files. The laboratory has drafting chairs with casters, as well as a number of dissecting microscopes used in preliminary artifact identification. On top of the book shelves near the center of the photograph is an old Macintosh computer. The firm uses this to access project files that no longer can be read given changes in technology and software. (Photo courtesy of Paul Brockington and Brockington and Associates, Inc.)

and 30 cm deep) with a good silt-trap system, flanked with counter space and adjacent to drying racks.[2]

The furnishings necessary in a corporate laboratory and its auxiliary space differ from those in an university or museum setting. The following will be included (see also Neumann, Bates, and Sanford 1998):

* tables for artifact processing and preliminary analyses; although a surface space of around 215 ft^2 would be ideal, it is sufficient to allow 45 ft^2 in table space per project manager on staff, along with 40 - 50 ft^2 for every full-time person or fraction thereof in the laboratory proper;

* a number of drafting stools or chairs equivalent to the common number of personnel that might be brought in to work in the lab on days when field work is not done; it is best is the chairs or stools have casters;

* the functional equivalent of a standard wall-mounted laboratory cabinet system, with drawers, counter space, and preferably glass-fronted doors, for the storage of miscellaneous equipment, supplies, project field notes/laboratory notes

---

1. We have done entire Phase III data recovery analyses, including cataloguing and labeling of the artifacts, of large (approximately 50,000 artifacts [500 kg]) collections in office space of 150 ft^2. It *is* possible. We do not recommend it as a standard practice.

2. These issues go back to the "Comments on Management" in Chapter 7 section 7.3.4. about providing a good working environment for one's people. With respect to lighting: The lighting should be sufficient for "fine" or "extra fine" assembly tasks, 500 and 1,000 foot-candles, respectively, according to the *Illuminating Engineering Society Handbook*, 5th edition, IES, New York, 1972.

(labeled on their spines for ready access, hence the remarks on this in Chapter 7 section 7.4.2.2.), and commonly used reference books;

* a refrigerator, 15 ft³ or larger with at least 20 percent of that as frost-free freezer space (top or bottom is good for large volumes of individually bulky items; side-by-side freezers are useful for storage of sediment cores), for storage of film, project negatives until turn-over, the occasional organic material recovered, staff lunches, and other critical time-sensitive items;

* the equivalent of 80 linear feet of drying rack, along with window-screen-bottom frames similar to Phase I survey screens, located next to the sink where the artifacts are washed and used for the drying of processed collections;

* a sink or utility wash tub with flanking counter space;

* between 150 - 380 ft² of shelving for collections holding, consisting of enameled metal shelf systems or hybrid systems of metal and wood (no firm wants to serve as a repository, the idea being to get rid of the collections just as soon as possible relative to project time frames; however, materials do accumulate; it probably would be best if the shelving were covered with heavy clear plastic in case the fire-suppression system goes off);

* one wrap-around or receptionist-style office station with chair and computer, which serves as the main station for the laboratory supervisor should the firm be large enough to have a full-time laboratory manager (sometimes the laboratory manager has an office that opens directly onto the laboratory, which serves the same purpose);

* four-drawer file cabinets dedicated to the laboratory proper; and

* map cabinets or map-tube holders (cabinets are better, since the maps can lay flat).[3]

The analytical equipment required in a corporate archaeology laboratory is aimed more at the initial and basic processing of assemblages and rarely at highly detailed research and certainly not instruction. Understanding what is needed, as set out in Table 8.1,

requires some sense of how archaeological materials move through a corporate facility and what is required in the analysis of each.

Archaeology firms or divisions are involved with any number of projects simultaneously. This means that several different collections may be moving through a laboratory at the same time. Usually, of every 20 or so projects that a firm secures, 15 will be Phase I exercises, three or four will be Phase II exercises, and one or two will be Phase III data recovery operations. The issues are keeping track of collections belonging to different projects and making sure that the appropriate level of analysis is performed.

The equipment in a private-sector laboratory falls into four categories:

* cleaning, processing, stabilizing, and conserving;

* viewing, sorting, and identifying;

* measuring; and

* cataloguing and recording.

These categories reflect the basic sequence of steps that a collection goes through within the facility.

Artifacts returned from the field often are cleaned, either by brushing in some way or by soaking in a deflocculating solution such as sodium hexametaphosphate or equivalent. It is because of the need for cleaning and drying that the sink and the drying racks are needed.

If flotation was required by the SOW, the soil samples will need to be processed. This will be done separate from the artifact processing, with the resultant flotation samples separately bagged and labeled. Some firms maintain in-house capabilities for analyzing botanical materials from a flotation sample -- the so-called "light fraction." Most, however, do not. If the SOW demands analysis of the flotation sample and not just the reduction of the soil to its constitution weight fractions, then those materials often will be sent to a subcontractor for analysis. Something similar may hold for the "heavy fraction" as well, although it is more likely that the laboratory staff -- again if this is expected by the SOW -- will go through the heavy fraction first for non-faunal materials.

Generally, though, flotation sample processing is not an issue. Either the level of field examination did not call for collection of such samples, or the project was not budgeted for the processing of samples collected (more common than one might think, which results in space-consuming soil samples that the laboratory supervisor often is eager to get rid of just as soon as possible).

---

3. There will be at least three kinds of maps stored. The first will be USGS topographic maps. Most firms maintain an extensive and up-to-date collection of the USGS maps for the areas in which they work. The second set of maps stored will be various project blue-line renderings supplied by clients. The third set of maps will be duplicates of various site maps, the originals of course having been turned over with other field records at the end of the project.

Table 8.1. Basic Equipment for a Corporate Archaeology Laboratory (after Neumann, Bates, and Sanford 1998:347)

Item	#	Comment
Cleaning, Processing, Stabilizing, Conserving		
▸ plastic buckets (3 l)	50	Needed if deflocculating solutions are used to clean artifacts.
▸ large 2-mm strainers	2	Needed if deflocculating solutions are used to clean artifacts.
▸ flotation system	-	
▸ electrolysis system	-	
Viewing, Sorting, Identifying		
▸ hardness set	1	
▸ folding arm magnifying lamp (fluorescent)	-	One per anticipated work station.
▸ dissecting scope w/ boom stand & photo attch	1	One dissecting microscope with photographic capabilities always is needed.
▸ basic dissecting microscope	-	Additional dissecting microscopes may be needed for principal investigators.
Measuring		
▸ balance (x 0.1g)	1	A second balance may be a good idea in a corporate setting with large numbers of Phase II and Phase III projects.
▸ balance (x 0.01g)	1	Can be justified only if the firm has in-house capacity to do ethnobotanical analyses.
▸ micrometers (metric)	10	
▸ pairs of protractors	6	These serve for measuring edge angles on lithic tools.
▸ Munsell soil color book	1	Primarily used in the field.
▸ pH meter (garden)	1	Also used in the field.
Cataloguing and Recording		
▸ cameras	2	Needed for microscope photographs.
▸ wide-angle lens	1	Not needed if there is a separate graphics department.
▸ close-up lens/attachments	1	Not needed if there is a separate graphics department.
▸ photo stand	1	Not needed if there is a separate graphics department.
▸ computer, monitor	-	One computer system, dedicated specifically to laboratory management, is needed.
▸ back-up system	-	Same number of back-up systems as computer systems.
▸ printer	1	Dot-matrix or laser printers are preferable to ink-jet printers for curatorial reasons, since the print from an ink-jet print runs in high humidity; laser printers are preferable because of speed.
▸ data management software	-	
Maintenance and Safety		
▸ hand tools (hammers, pliers, screwdrivers)	-	Also used in the field.
▸ first-aid kit	1	

Some materials recovered will require stabilization or conservation. Such items would include fragile and perishable organic materials, and some corroded metal artifacts. If some sort of action needs to be taken, the field supervisor or project manager will inform the laboratory manager *before returning from the field with the materials* so that the necessary arrangements can be made to deal with the item of concern. Some firms maintain limited in-house capabilities for artifact stabilization and conservation; this varies by the region and nature of the firm.

With materials processed, artifacts are sorted then (1) discarded, (2) discarded with some kind of measurement first (usually this involves weighing fire-cracked rock), or (3) retained and placed into general artifact categories usually based on material from which they are made and their original function (see box "Discard Protocols" below). Materials are labeled following protocols indicated in the SOW and following SHPO/THPO and/or agency requirements or preferences, placed in labeled plastic bags with labels of spun-bonded polyethylene paper or acid-free paper put inside, then placed back into Hollinger™ boxes or their equivalents.

Adhesive polyethylene label sleeves with acid-free paper inserts identifying the box contents will be attached to the boxes (direct labeling of boxes no longer is recommended).

For Phase I work, nearly all analyses are done by eye or with a magnifier lamp; even given the common presence of microliths on prehistoric sites in the eastern United States, it is not part of laboratory procedure to use a dissecting microscope in hopes of identifying items whose functional classification is based upon microscopic features. Weights generally are not taken, nor are any other measurements -- short of counting or associated with some kind of diagnostic exercise -- made. Phase I after all is concerned with seeing if anything is present, what that "anything" might be in cultural-historical terms, and whether or not there is a possibility that that "anything" retains depositional integrity. The issues involve the structure of the deposit and what that deposit might represent; the issues do not involve the fine nuances of the deposit that one would get through further analyses. Thus, most measurements at this stage would be a waste of time: The artifacts and field notes will be curated; if someone determines in the future that measurements *are* important, then they can go and do that work. The artifacts, field and laboratory notes, and associated locational information are and will remain at the curatorial facility readily available.

For most Phase II and all Phase III analyses, the use of a dissecting microscope, as well as more extensive weighing and dimensional measuring, are expected. Basic measurements -- dimensions, weight, edge angles, and so on -- are then recorded, often along

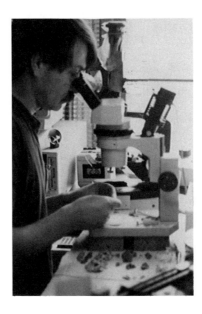

Figure 8.2. Certainly for Phase II and Phase III analyses, all prehistoric flakes should be examined under a dissecting microscope. It is not unusual to find that upwards of 15 percent of flakes classified as "unmodified" from prehistoric archaeological sites in the eastern United States are in fact heavily used microliths. Further, lithic raw material assignation generally assumes use of magnification comparable to a dissecting scope. (Photo courtesy Pocket Park - Wentworth Analytical Facility.)

with additional details and analyses associated with a standard archaeological report, such as ceramic temper characteristics, stone flake morphology, high-magnification use-wear, and so on.

Much of the more specialized analytical work either is subcontracted -- high-magnification work or paleoethnobotanical work, for example -- or performed by the principal investigator or project manager -- formal ceramic analyses being a case in point. In the interests of keeping time devoted to the task down, work of a more detailed nature may actually be done at the project manager's desk, allowing the results to be entered directly into the same computer file where the draft report is being assembled. This avoids the wasted effort of taking measurements, writing them out in the laboratory, trotting down the hall with the forms clutched in one's hands, then entering that information into the computer.

Many firms maintain analytical flexibility in terms of space and equipment by assembling "virtual" laboratories for the duration of a project, or arranging a series of "virtual laboratories" that can be accessed given different kinds of projects. Thus, many firms will have preferred or retained vendors who provide specialized lithic analyses, geoarchaeological analyses, pedological analyses, statistical analyses, and so on. That collection of specialists represents a virtual

Additional Analytical Capabilities

The equipment needed to do additional and more detailed analyses, beyond what is generally required for most projects, will be present only if it is cost-effective. This is an important consideration for those entering private practice to understand. There are three conditions under which it may be advisable to maintain specialized analytical equipment:

* The equipment allows the firm to market specialized analyses;

* the equipment can be used in a way that the quality of the project report is significantly increased; or

* the equipment can be used by other people in the company.

Examples of the first case would be maintaining brightfield/dark field metallurgical microscopes for high-magnification use-wear analyses, or thin-sectioning equipment along with the necessary microscopes needed for obsidian hydration measurements. Such analyses are associated with Phase III projects, and while a wonderful addition to the research, still are not very common. In such a situation, though, it may be possible to market such analytical capabilities to a wider audience, in effect increasing the size of the hinterland feeding into the specialized capabilities.

Examples of the second case, where the quality of the work is improved, would be the purchase of sophisticated statistical programs or the maintenance of dissecting microscopes with camera attachments. Both cases represent investments that increase the capacity of the firm to do more detailed and professional work on Phase II and Phase III projects, such that agency review questions may be anticipated. Anything that anticipates then answers agency questions will shorten the amount of time taken during the review process. This in turn will result in fewer changes being needed for the final report; indeed, draft reports often are then accepted as the final reports (thus securing with only incidental extra labor the 2.5 - 5.0 percent of the project award normally set aside in the budget to deal with review agency comments and report revisions).

Further, the firm will be seen as dependable by the SHPO/THPO and agency reviewers, as well as by the client. This has two future benefits. First, the SHPO/THPO will be inclined to listen with greater attention to the firm when inevitable professional differences-of-opinion arise, which will be of benefit to the firm, the client, and the cultural resource. Second, that reputation for dependability and quality will be noted by the client. Since the client is part of a social network, a benefit of good words being spoken about the quality and sensitivity of one's firm helps in getting additional business (either unsolicited or, in a competitive bid situation, a telling factor that will be known to the reviewers or the private-sector client but not mentioned in the qualifications statement, that results in the firm being selected).

An example of the third case, where the purchased equipment can be used by others in the firm, would be soil texture analysis apparatus or fine-resolution analytical balances. In engineering/environmental firms, there is a standing need for such analytical capabilities, such that that kind of equipment can be shared among and kept in use by different divisions. In large firms especially, it is important to couch arguments for specialized analytical equipment in terms of its benefit to other divisions and the firm overall, and not just the cultural resources division.

The first and last, the ultimate argument for any additional equipment, above and beyond what would be expected in a basic archaeology laboratory, has to do with its cost-effectiveness. That is, does it make sense for the firm to purchase this equipment? Will it pay for itself? If so, then in what ways will it, and when will that investment – that purchase cost – be recouped? It must be remembered that, in acquiring specialized equipment, the firm in effect is being committed to having an employee who knows how to make maximum use of that equipment. Since the standard rule-of-thumb is that the addition of each new permanent, middle-level employee will cost around $150,000 (1995 dollars) in start-up costs, equipment, office furnishings, benefits, salary, and so forth, it often makes much better sense just to subcontract such specialized work. This actually is the more common corporate strategy nationally, which is why there is a wealth of subcontracting specialists in any number of fields. For division managers, this must be the basic consideration. For those arguing for purchasing such equipment, such a purchase must be couched in terms of how the investment costs will be recouped, especially where it would mean that the firm is suddenly committed to the expertise of one employee.

We learned about archaeology from that ... The Closed Door

The idea of a facility being out of sight and suffering as a result sounds a bit rhetorically poetic, but actually is not. All Anthropology students are aware of the basic Primate trait of "out-of-sight = out-of-mind," which is responsible not just for chimps turning their backs on another member of the group in pain, but for closets and attics being filled with unorganized clutter. This is a very real political issue not only on university campuses, but in the corporate world as well.

We were involved with the branch office of an engineering/ environmental firm a number of years ago. The branch office provided both NEPA and NHPA compliance, and maintained offices in rented space. We were asked to assess the relationship of the cultural resources division to the overall operation of the firm.

The situation was striking. The cultural resources division was based on archaeological compliance (only the additions of a historian and architectural historian would have broadened market share). Indeed, the engineering/environmental divisions had grown around the Section 106 compliance projects, and actually now were generating the greater amount of revenues for the branch office.

The management personnel, all with environmental science or biological science degrees, were sound professionals: They had a good sense of how to manage a professional office, and where there were short-comings, would listen with a humbling intensity. Good firm, and it was an honor to work with them.

The cultural resources division had developed a bunker attitude, which had been exacerbated when the original cultural resources manager accepted a position elsewhere and left the firm. Its offices were located in the building in such a way that the members were separate from the rest of the firm. Indeed, after entering the office building, it was easy to wander about through the offices and speak with people. Not so for the cultural resources people there. Instead, they

kept the door to their area SHUT, and one was reminded of children defending their bedrooms with closed doors and "Keep OUT!" signs. Very unprofessional.

As a result of this self-sequestering, the rest of the firm viewed the cultural resources division – which had and still contributed a substantial amount of the revenues to the overall office – as wayward and difficult, almost not worth the effort to keep ... although after saying that, they would calm down and say in effect that there was an enormous problem, and what ideas do you guys have (then, as always, that intense listening).

They clearly needed a full-time cultural resources manager who could re-integrate the division into the larger business and re-establish an air of professionalism. Given that, we recommended a number of things. The first and obvious: opening the door that separated the cultural resources people from the rest of the building. The laboratory space was a nightmarish jumble of shelves and boxes, the walls painted a mind-numbing drab and dark color. Paint the walls white, we advised (they ultimately hired a new cultural resources manager who did just that and addressed many of the other things mentioned below).

To the cultural resources people, we advised them that rubber-band fights probably were not contributing to a sense of professional competence in a multi-million-dollar firm, and that it would not be a good idea to continue this (great annoyance at that, since they felt this was their right because they worked so hard; most eventually took positions at other firms). We also advised them to get out and wander the halls: "How many of you can name the other people working in this office?" we asked at a group meeting. The number of people in the firm's office was 12 non-archaeologists and five archaeologists. No one could name their other 12 colleagues, with the added challenge of why that should matter anyway. The idea of intra-office collegiality, and how all would benefit from it, had not occurred to them.

There are many lessons here. The first is the basic out-of-sight/out-of-mind

issue: Closed doors mean that the person or division will be forgotten and kept out of the chain-of-command (indeed, the last we heard, that particular firm had reached a point where the cultural resources branch had been drawn into and administratively devoured by a larger unit managed by an environmental scientist who had no first-hand knowledge of cultural resources, and actually who was 10 years younger and one graduate degree lower than the people supervised in the cultural resources division). The second is to make sure that the physical space presents a professional, positive environment for the people working in it: The dark, drab walls and the clutter of that office arrangement will forever be stuck in our minds. Considering that the rest of the offices *were* bright and airy, the contrast for anyone entering into the dreariness of the cultural resources area must have reinforced the view that this bunch really was not interested in the kind of team concept central to any environmental firm.[a]

_____

a. This perception of not being part of the corporate team was compounded by appearance. Most firms, regardless of the kind of business done, have some kind of understood if not explicit dress code. For stand-alone archaeology firms, this is comparatively informal and often reflects how the principals of the firm dressed when they started the concern. Professional archaeology is comparatively young, and many such stand-alone firms are still run by their founders.

For larger firms in which cultural resources exists as one of several divisions, there often is a bit more formality in dress. The exact nature depends upon region of the country and nature of the clientele. Such firms are older and more established, with founding members long since retired and current upper management being senior engineers or architects. The situation here was similar: an older firm in which cultural resources existed as a division.

The issue of appearance was creating enormous problems for the archaeologists, and they were entirely unaware of this. Except for the cultural resources division, the rest of the firm dressed in the self-assured professional way that we have come to call "field professional," this particular lot consisting of field botanists, zoologists, and environmental scientists. Attire generally was calf-length skirts in beige or grey with cotton blouses for women; golf or button-

Further, the rented building resulted in the cultural resources division and its laboratory being located on the second floor, accessible only by stairs. Considering that the building itself was in poor repair, we suggested that the branch office think about relocating to a building that would have some kind of place where field vehicles could be easily loaded or unloaded. (It turned out that they *had* been considering relocating.)

The third point: space. The cultural resources branch was cluttered in large measure because it did not have space adequate for basic professional needs. Although it had a large number of Phase II and Phase III projects draining into the facility, the space available was insufficient even for a Phase I project. It not only was dark, it was cluttered because there was no place to dump the excess material. Space was insufficient.[b]

Part of the reason that the space was insufficient was because of that overall attempt by the archaeologists to remain separate and aloof from the rest of the firm. Amazingly, while the cultural resources division started as the first and largest part of the branch office, it soon was out-voted and over-run by other corporate interests as that office expanded and other services were added. This was due entirely to a lack of understanding of space allocation and corporate operations.

And that lack of understanding existed because the cultural resources people – archaeologists – had used up whatever good will and "office political capital" in an isolationist, unprofessional attitude that reflected a substantial nescience of the extra-academic world. No one else in the larger company would take them seriously, which was further compounded by how they dressed (their fault) and the cluttered air of their work space (not entirely their fault). And, as near as we could tell – despite the quality of the archaeological work they did (which was just fine, by the way) – for good reason.

---

down Oxford shirts (long-sleeve) with cotton trousers and sport coats for mid-management males; and collar and tie for upper-management males, or silk scarf with jacket for upper-management females. A comfortable, professional air to an office made up of people who would rather have been in the field (and in most cases who had their field boots stashed in the office).

The male archaeologists all dressed in blue jeans and, for reasons that perplexed us, nearly everyone, male or female, chose shades of dingy brown for the remainder of their attire: the males preferring brown-and-navy plaid shirts; the females, ankle-length, no-waist, relaxed-fit, brown-and-navy floral dresses. With one notable exception, there were no sport coats or equivalent to be seen, even though they had plenty of notice of our visit. (And do not forget the shoes: Why ever were the archaeologists wearing *soiled* jogging shoes while the entire remainder of the firm wore leather loafers or sensible flats – except the upper-management males, who had laced wing-tips?)

Physical presentation of self expresses not only one's sense of the importance and professionalism of one's own field, but also the respect one feels for those with whom one interacts, be they clients or other workers. This is a basic aspect of human communication – parasemantics and display -- taught in introductory Anthropology classes.

Perhaps within a different firm, one made up only of archaeologists, such dress by the cultural resources division would have been acceptable. But in this particular case, where corporate and local office culture – and decision making – was governed by senior environmental professionals, it was a serious mistake.

The cultural resources division was stating, parasemantically, that it did not want to be considered a part of the larger firm and further, given the style of dress adopted, wanted to be considered the equivalent of undergraduates or graduate students. And the rest of the firm was, unconsciously, reacting to and then treating the cultural resources people in just that way. Added to the closed door and refusal to mingle with others in the office, the archaeologists had created a dismal working environment.

b. So, too, was laboratory equipment. The entire office building had only one 10-power dissecting microscope. We suggested that the archaeology lab itself have two, as well as a triple-beam balance. The branch manager said initially that everyone could share the lone dissecting microscope, and we had to explain why such dedicated equipment constituted minimum professional standards. We were put into this position because the cultural resources division itself had lost the professional respect of the others in the firm and, as result, was being ignored. The unprofessional dress and rubber-band fights merely confirmed the firm's impression that the cultural resources people did not have a professional outlook and were not team players.

physical plant as well as a virtual laboratory and can be mixed and matched in a modular fashion to accomplish the needs of the given firm relative to the work required.

8.2.2. Configuration

Archaeologists are products of academic environments. Archaeology laboratories in those environments are stand-alone facilities within the larger, balkanized academic community.

Unlike the academic archaeology laboratory, the corporate archaeology laboratory is an integral part of a larger organization. The private-sector archaeology laboratory really is a lot like a laboratory in a clinic, both in terms of its place in the organization and its location within a physical plant: Physically, it will be located in back of the reception areas and positioned to allow access from offices. The laboratory is part of a larger whole, and is an essential part of the overall operation. Universities and even doctoral Anthropology programs often can survive without an archaeology laboratory; a private-sector archaeology firm usually cannot.

The corporate laboratory needs to be accessible to field vehicles so that field equipment and collections can be loaded and unloaded. This generally requires that the archaeology laboratory be located on the ground floor and that there be some kind of drive or alley that allows the laboratory to be reached by a field vehicle. The loading area for most firms will also correspond to where field equipment is stored and maintained, and where project staging -- assembling of the equipment needed for the project field work -- is done. (It is not unusual for this area to have the stationary tubs used for artifact cleaning.) These parts of the corporate office space tend to be located "around the back" of the physical plant. This space, where people come in from the field, will be reached by a traffic pattern that keeps muddy boots out of the more formal parts of the office.

The laboratory serves to reduce the physical remains brought into the firm to paper-based data that can be manipulated. Because of this and the lack of need for immediate instructional access, it matters less in a corporate setting just how close project manager offices are to the laboratory. The project manager's office serves many functions, and analysis is only one; it also will serve as a space to entertain clients or subcontractors. This means that it needs to reflect parasemantically the level of quality that the firm devotes to its work. How one dresses communicates not only how one expects to be treated, but also the respect that a person has for the people being treated. This holds for office space, which is why the front of an archaeology firm's office space is more formal and definitely cleaner than the back.

Figure 8.3a. More often than not, the typical archaeology firm is located in an office park. (Photo courtesy of Paul Brockington and Brockington and Associates, Inc.)

Figure 8.3b. It is critical that the archaeology laboratory be accessible to field vehicles. Office parks are designed for this. By the way, the "garage door" is the right-hand opening. The equal-sized area to the left is the tinted glass for the firm's laboratory. (Photo courtesy of Paul Brockington and Brockington and Associates, Inc.)

8.2.3. Budgeting

The private-sector archaeology laboratory is a support facility as well as project node or intersection. All field projects will be involved with the laboratory in some way; all recovered materials will pass through the laboratory and at some point be under the jurisdiction of the laboratory manager. It may be a support facility, but it is a support facility in that the rest of the firm depends heavily upon its performance.

The archaeology laboratory rarely generates revenues on its own, and, aside from labor, seldom has included within the project budget any budget items of its own. Instead, the laboratory has an overall laboratory budget that is supported through the indirect cost revenues generated by all of the projects.

Use of Space and Generic Layout of a Private-Sector Archaeology Office

Archaeology firms or divisions usually will be located either within their own office space, such as in a stand-alone structure, or with other offices in an office park; sometimes they will be intermingled with other offices in the larger building of a firm.

Office space for most firms is arranged in similar ways. Offices, and especially offices associated with field sciences, tend to have a "front" and a "back." The front consists of receptionist space and offices. This is a formal area, akin to the way most houses in the United States are set out. The back areas are where loading docks, equipment storage, and of course the archaeology laboratory are located. People returning from the field will come in from this direction. This then becomes a less formal area, and again corresponds to how space is set out in an American household, with its mud room or kitchen area, even the laundry room on occasion, sometimes coming immediately off of a garage.

In situations where the firm is located in a two- or three-storey structure, the arrangement will still be like this, although the upper floors will be dedicated to project manager offices: The ground floor still will have the laboratory space, and the back parts of the building will tend to be less formal and public than the front.

Traffic flow through the office will reflect the reality of archaeological field work. Many firms have a policy limiting people who have just come in from the field from going into the more formal areas. Some of the concern is for the damage that muddy boots can do to the carpet, but just as much of the concern is for maintaining an air of professionalism.

The laboratory area may or may not be immediately accessible to all in the firm. Some offices will have a laboratory area off of which will be different offices. In many ways, that arrangement results in the laboratory space being a kind of commons area as well, which has the advantage of giving project managers immediate access to analysis space but the disadvantage of the laboratory manager and technicians being distracted by non-essential traffic flow. Some offices have the laboratory as a stem space attached to one side of the overall office, often as a room off of a corridor or hall.

Situations where the archaeology division is part of a larger corporation seems, in our experience, to result in organizational problems. Those problems come from three basic aspects of the archaeology itself:

* the need for a substantial amount of laboratory space,

* the need for that space to be immediately accessible to field vehicles, and

* the realities that the people needing access to that laboratory and equipment storage space often arrive back from the field dirty.

Corporations do not want to have grungy field people wandering through the carpeted and chrome-steel cleanliness of the office building. Businesses are stratified, class societies; people who work with their hands, wear jeans, and are covered with dirt have lower social class and command less deference than people who work with paper, wear wool, and are clean.

Corporations also do not want to spend any more than necessary in renting office space. As a result, the laboratory space will be limited in size, and/or it will be located well away from the offices used by the archaeologists.

We know of one instance where the project managers were located on the fifth floor of the firm's multi-storey office building, but the laboratory facility was located about a mile away in what originally had been retail space within a small strip mall. This separation obviously created logistical problems for the archaeologists, and seriously constrained the opportunities for the archaeologists to interact with and be viewed as part of the larger corporation. However, that separation reflected in a backwards way how necessary certain space arrangements are for private-sector archaeology. Again, there was formal business space, and there was the informal analysis space. There was the "front" and the "back," the presentable and the not presentable.

Laboratory costs fall into three basic sets:

* supplies;

* permanent equipment and furniture; and

* replacement and facilities maintenance.

Supplies refer to expendable items that are used up over the course of time (Table 8.2.). To budget for these, the laboratory manager needs must track the use of those supplies.

Equipment and furniture present a different budgetary issue. These are equivalent to -- and sometimes are -- capital investments that are expected to last for a certain amount of time. Purchases are made only if the item in question has been damaged beyond repair, or if the equipment can contribute to expanded business opportunities.

This leads into the third and most often overlooked laboratory budget item: maintenance and replacement. Most items, be they furniture, field tools, or laboratory equipment, have use-lives. The use-life of those objects is known to the industry that manufactures the product, and the length of that use-

Table 8.2.   Basic Annual Laboratory Supplies (after Neumann, Bates, and Sanford 1998:Table 2)

- brushes and toothbrushes
- sodium [hexa]metaphosphate
- dilute hydrochloric acid
- hydrogen peroxide
- miscellaneous laboratory glassware
- computer disks
- microscope light bulbs
- archival-grade paper (100 percent rag)
- archival-grade paper (spunbonded polyethylene)
- archival-grade (≥ 4 mil) plastic bags (ziploc)
- archival-grade (≥ 4 mil) plastic bags (twist-tied)
- archival-grade packing materials
- Hollinger boxes
- adhesive polyethylene plastic label holders for boxes
- indelible markers (medium point)
- indelible markers (fine point)
- India ink (black)
- India ink (white)
- pen nibs
- camera film
- analysis forms
- archival-grade slide and negative holders
- binders (always D-ring)
- clear acrylic "nail polish"
- brown paper (rolls)
- medicine vials (not meant as primary storage but to be placed in labeled bags)
- miscellaneous office supplies

life informs warranty information. This becomes an issue for the archaeology laboratory not only because of the analytical equipment present, but also because most archaeology firms or divisions tacitly assign a quartermaster role to the laboratory facility. Further, funding for maintenance, repair, or replacement often will come out of a laboratory budget that is funded mostly through indirect cost revenues and not directly through project budget lines.

Some repair and maintenance situations are obvious: The refrigerator in the laboratory will have a use-life of 15 years; the bulb for the dissecting microscope illuminator will last about a year of constant use, and will cost around $25 to replace, although the microscope itself may last for 50 years.

Some repair and maintenance situations are not obvious: It is generally recommended that office walls -- including the laboratory -- be repainted every five to seven years, and that carpeting in commercial settings be replaced every 10 years. If the firm owns its own physical plant, then these and similar contingency planning budget items need to be worked into the laboratory and overall facility budgets (which can be a substantial investment: Flat, built-up roofs cost around $3.50 per square foot and last only 10 years; a 10-ton HVAC compressor alone will cost around

$6,700 and also will last an average of 10 years; see also Neumann 1995). If the firm rents its space, then upkeep like painting and carpet-replacement need to be worked into the lease agreement.

The basic guide we have used in facilities planning and maintenance is to allow 10 years for the average use-life of the laboratory equipment, and 20 years for the average use-life of the furniture. The tables will probably last much longer, but the chairs will give out much sooner. A good laboratory planning budget will include a set-aside, adjusted for inflation, equivalent to 10 percent of the original cost of the laboratory equipment to cover future repair or replacement, and around five percent of the original cost of the furniture, again for repair or replacement. It is normal for businesses to allow a certain percentage depreciation value to cover for equipment or furniture repair or replacement, but in our experience those numbers usually are off by a factor of three (see also Neumann, Bates, and Sanford 1998).

8.2.4.   Management and Administrative Issues

8.2.4.1.   Management and Internal Scheduling

The archaeology laboratory often is supervised by a laboratory manager who may have a small permanent staff of laboratory technicians, supplemented by field technicians who are between field assignments.

The laboratory provides services that are shared among members of the firm. There often are several projects of differing levels of analysis and corresponding deadlines all being handled at the same time. It is the laboratory manager's responsibility to coordinate not just those tasks, but to do so relative to the amount of time allocated under the project's overall budget. In theory, the laboratory manager has jurisdiction over that portion of the budget that concerns laboratory tasks proper; however, the project manager will be held accountable for that budget being followed, and therefore will hold the laboratory manager accountable.

Many laboratory managers in larger firms coordinate the multiple demands made on the lab by setting out project time lines on a white-board. This allows the processing and analysis needs of different projects to be anticipated and, where several projects must be handled at the same time, some sense of how to schedule laboratory staff and resources. This coordination of different tasks is similar to being a short-order cook, sufficiently so that some laboratory managers request that project managers give them a memo or work order form that indicates

*   how much labor is budgeted for the laboratory portion of the project,

*   how that labor breaks out by pay grade,

*   what level of analyses is desired, what curatorial protocol is to be followed, and

*   when the work must be completed to keep the project itself on schedule.

The laboratory manager is then responsible for making sure that the necessary work is done in a timely manner.

8.2.4.2. Corporate Administrative Issues

Anthropologists generally and archaeologists specifically rarely have the participant-observer, native perspective on the internal functioning of a corporation that would prepare them to deal with the kind of cultural dynamics that exist outside of an academic setting. This really is true for most traditional arts and sciences fields, even those like Chemistry where most graduates long have worked in industry research settings (see for example Travis 1994; Gibbons 1994). The reverse also is true, which is where problems can exist for someone entering the corporate world from a lifetime in the academic world: Extra-academic people really know precious little about what Anthropology needs. While the field is one of the highest paid in an university setting,[4] the command of respect that might suggest in the academic world does not carry over into the private sector.

This is a round-about way of saying that those things that an archaeologist would consider to be self-evidently important in field work or analysis are not self-evident to those who actually run the firm of which the archaeologist is a part. The practical effects, though, are that replacement and upgrades of equipment are often difficult to achieve, and can only be done by the archaeologist justifying the purchase or outlay on business principles. Since the archaeologist just out of college seldom has learned how to communicate in the language of the person who actually controls the resources in a business environment, the result as often as not is failure and an extraordinary sense of undirected frustration. There are still major firms with archaeology divisions, for example, that still do not have a basic dissecting microscope in the laboratory, the argument being that the expense would be too great.

Stand-alone archaeology firms normally have little trouble with equipping a laboratory, if for no other reason than that the principals are themselves archaeologists who also are fortunate enough to understand extra-academic culture.   The real difficulties emerge in situations where archaeology is a division within a larger firm, almost always an engineering firm.   Unless that division has been blessed with archaeologists capable of explaining what is done and why in terms understandable -- and in terms that mean that everyone else who benefits from the payroll funded through the firm understands -- the archaeology arm of the overall operation will, eventually, dwindle and fade.

It is for these reasons that it is advisable for all archaeologists, and especially those seeking or anticipating being laboratory managers, to take one or two business administration courses. The importance rests not only with the information and training given by such a course, but also with learning the language of a new culture into which one will move and live (see also Appendix B).

8.3.   Processing

The processing of the collection from the archaeological site is meant to prepare it both for analysis and for curation.

8.3.1. Verification with Field Inventory

The first step in processing the collection involves comparing the material brought in from the field with the appropriate bag or field specimen inventory. This is a basic organizing, bookkeeping activity meant to make sure that all items from the field are accounted for.

Once that bag inventory has been matched to what has been returned from the field, the laboratory manager can decide if the same numbering system is to be retained or a new one introduced.

8.3.2. Artifacts

8.3.2.1. Cleaning, Stabilization, Conservation

There are three sets of guidelines for cleaning, stabilization, and conservation:

*   the overall professional standards of the discipline;

*   the guidelines of the SHPO/THPO or agency; and

*   the guidelines set forth in the SOW.

---

4. See *The Chronicle of Higher Education*, 2 September 1996, p.A26. Of the 29 fields listed, Anthropology ranked ninth, but that includes accounting, business, computer science, engineering, and health-related fields. With those non-liberal arts/sciences removed, Anthropology ranked just behind Chemistry and Physics as the highest-paid faculty discipline. Indeed, university anthropologists on average make 10 percent more than university sociologists. (This is also true in the Federal workplace.) And that of course is as it should be.

Hopefully these will all be in agreement. This is not always the case, and disparities need to be handled on a case-by-case basis with direct communication among the SHPO/THPO, client or agency issuing the SOW, laboratory manager, and project manager.

In the vast majority of cases, the non-metallic inorganic artifacts will be washed either by brushing under tap water or by soaking in a deflocculating solution. Those artifacts will then be set to one side to dry before processing continues.

Metallic artifacts may be left alone, dry-brushed, or stabilized. Some firms maintain small electrolysis systems to help in conserving iron artifacts. More extensive or intricate situations may call for subcontracting a conservator. This holds for organic remains as well, especially basketry, textiles, and waterlogged wood.

Figure 8.4. Small electrolysis system used to stabilize iron artifacts. Such systems, which provide a great deal of conservatory range to the corporate laboratory, are comparatively inexpensive to set up. (Photo courtesy of Paul Brockington and Brockington and Associates, Inc.)

There is an enormous literature on handling and conserving material remains. The appropriate professional standards are given in various laboratory (e.g., Joukowsky 1980; Sutton and Arkush 1998), field (e.g., Hester, Shafer, and Feder 1997), and method-and-theory texts, as well as in the myriad of conservation texts and articles (e.g., Singley 1981, Sease 1987). Some states have very specific guidelines for all aspects of processing, including cleaning, labeling, and storage. North Carolina for example has detailed curatorial information posted and readily accessible from its Web site (http://www.arch.dcr.state.nc.us/curation.htm). It is the responsibility of the laboratory manager to be familiar with the specific guidelines and to know what each situation requires.

On Cleaning Artifacts

Whether or not artifacts are cleaned, and how they are cleaned, depends upon the guidelines of the SHPO/THPO as set forth in the SOW. Usually, artifacts still are washed under running water with gentle brushing, then set to one side to dry. However, some SOW request that a percentage of prehistoric applications-industry tools (for example, utilized flakes or projectile points) or unflaked stone tools (for example, palette stones or metates) *not* be washed. This restriction is meant to permit future residue or phytolith analyses of the objects. (However, those who do use-wear analysis, like high-magnification and handling-wear analyses, need to have those same objects washed clean.)

Artifacts can be cleaned either by dry brushing, by brushing under running water, or by soaking in a deflocculating solution. The first requires only a brush and is reasonably safe for nearly all artifacts. The second requires a sink where the clearance between the spigot, the bottom of the wash tub, and the leading edge of that tub all allow for easy access. Such washing is not safe for insufficiently fired ceramics, for water-sensitive materials, and of course for most artifacts where residues or adhering debris, like phytoliths, are themselves objects of study.

The third option, soaking in a deflocculating solution like sodium hexametaphosphate, requires sufficient clearance between bottom of the tub, the spigot, and the edge of the sink, as well as sufficient water flow to adequately flush off silt along with enough table or counter space to place the containers in which artifacts from different proveniences will soak. As with the second option of washing under tap water, the option of soaking in a deflocculant excludes water-damageable items along with clay objects that are not baked (such a soaking exercise would be a slaking test). However, compared to the second option, it requires less labor time and is more cost effective.

The protocols of the SHPO/THPO as presented in the SOW hold precedence. If there is confusion or a clear problem with recommended procedure, then the SHPO/THPO, the issuer of the SOW, and the professional archaeologist and/or laboratory manager need to sort matters out.

See also:

Neumann, Thomas W., and Robert M. Sanford. 1998. Cleaning artifacts with Calgon™ (sodium [hexa]metaphosphate). *American Antiquity* 63:157-160.

8.3.2.2. Cataloguing

With the artifacts cleaned (or not), the next step in processing will be cataloguing the collection. Cataloguing will involve three things:

(1) identification or classification of the artifact or material remain;

(2) assignment of some sort of catalogue or accession number; and

(3) preparation of a written record or inventory that cross-lists the number and kinds of artifacts with where they were found on the site and their catalogue number.

While the collection from the site will be cleaned all at once, cataloguing and the next step, labeling, will be done one provenience at a time. The written record will be maintained as a computer file with hard copy masters. A copy of that inventory generally will be placed as an appendix in the project report.

Cataloguing basically is separating the artifacts into meaningful groups, usually based on material then function. It is at this point that decisions will be made about what the artifacts actually represent. The resolution of the cataloguing depends upon the resolution of the artifact analysis, and that in turn depends upon if the project is a Phase I survey, Phase II testing, or Phase III data recovery.

Cataloguing of the assemblage is an exercise in analytical interpretation, since cataloguing classifies the material remains from the archaeological site. It is also a decision-making process. The cataloguing usually will be done either by laboratory technicians or by the laboratory manager. From that point, the nature of the items will be entered into a computerized record or artifact inventory, and as often as not it will be that inventory that is handed to the project manager when he or she sets about to write up the results of the project.

Because of the separation of the project manager from much of the initial laboratory processing and cataloguing, the project manager becomes dependent upon the analytical expertise and consequent decisions of those in the laboratory. It is at this point that the compliance process is most vulnerable to error, since the project manager and the laboratory manager each will be required to depend upon laboratory technicians and their judgments about what actually is being looked at.

Unfortunately, the only way that a person becomes adept at identifying artifacts is by handling a large number of objects. All of the preparation afforded by a sound university background still will leave gaps, simply because the volume and variety of artifacts that pass through most private-sector laboratories are usually greater than that experienced in most university programs. There really is no other way to learn than by looking at then identifying a lot of artifacts. This means that, for new or comparatively inexperienced laboratory technicians, there is a period of learning when mistakes will occur. Since those mistakes are inevitable, the idea is to devise a process that minimizes those mistakes or misidentifications.

To handle this situation and the inherent dangers, many firms have a four-step approach:

* ready and visible access to basic classificatory schemes, such as projectile point charts, wall-mounted displays, and extensive collections of reference books;

* augmenting the process with magnifiers and dissecting microscopes;

Discard Protocols

Not everything recovered and brought back from the field will be retained. Some items need only to be counted and/or weighed, and that will constitute their entire meaning for the purposes of the analysis. After that, those items will be discarded. What is discarded depends upon the nature of the project, SHPO/THPO and SOW requirements, and the concerns of the project manager.

For example, many Federal SOW require that ALL artifacts recovered in the field be retained, regardless of their age, size, or abundance. Thus, we once did a Phase I survey over a historic site and located an over-the-hill midden. The shovel test unit struck sheet metal. At first we thought it was a can but, on enlarging the shovel test, started to think, no, it's an old 1950s bread box, with its white enamel paint and red floral pattern. But it continued to grow: It turned out to be a kitchen table top, which was dutifully recovered.

In another case, mentioned in Chapter 6, we encountered enormous quantities of broken window glass. In that case, the agency suspended its artifact retention policy and the bulk of the glass was discarded on site. (Although it would have made no difference in this case, current Federal regulations allow unaccessioned artifacts to be discarded.)

In many areas of the country, fire-cracked rock will be counted, weighed, then discarded. For some projects, though, it may be important to first track the kind of stone involved. In areas of the country with huge volumes of prehistoric pottery, sometimes any body sherd smaller than a certain size will simply be weighed then discarded.

All projects and firms will have a discard policy. It is important to know not only what that policy is, but what it is meant to accomplish relative to the needs of the project.

*   supplemental training, including some sense of what should be present in proportion to other artifacts in the collection; and

*   a protocol for who makes the decisions regarding identification of diagnostic or potentially diagnostic artifacts.

In our experience, the greatest problems have occurred in Phase II and Phase III projects involving prehistoric assemblages and the misclassification of utilized flakes versus unmodified flakes, and recognition of unflaked stone tools versus unused cobbles and fire-cracked rock. Even though historic assemblages often have much greater internal variability and represent a much more complex artifact array, especially in terms of the ceramics and container glass, for some reason there usually is less of a problem in basic cataloguing. This very likely may be due to the familiarity of the artifacts as artifacts.

Because of the dependence on the results from the laboratory technicians, both the project manager and the laboratory manager must attempt to anticipate where errors may occur and prepare the laboratory technicians accordingly. That is, the technical staff needs to be sensitized to the subtleties of the particular assemblage. This is particularly important for Phase II and Phase III analyses, where much more detailed work is needed.

8.3.2.3. Labeling and Preparation for Curation

Labeling refers to writing or placing a permanent label on the artifact that links the object to site and provenience. Labeling and cataloguing are done usually one provenience (e.g., test unit-level, shovel test unit-level) at a time. It is with this step in processing that the artifacts will be placed in the containers where they are meant to be stored in perpetuity. Artifact labeling and storage procedures usually are taught as part of university field and laboratory courses, and are discussed in method-and-theory and field textbooks. Specific protocols will be given by the SHPO for each state.

Federal curatorial guidelines are given in **36 CFR Part 79**. Labeling and preparing a collection for curation will follow two sets of guidelines:

*   professional standards; and

*   review agency/curatorial facility requirements.

There are three factors involved in this stage of processing the collection:

(1) the physical procedure for labeling the object;

(2) the labeling system; and

(3) the storage system.

The physical procedure for labeling the artifact often is spelled out by the SHPO/THPO or the curatorial facility, and may or may not be specified in the SOW. The idea is to have a label permanently affixed to the object. Historically, this involved writing directly on the object in black or white India ink a catalogue or accession number. Over the years this has not been changed, only refined: Many SHPOs require that the inked label be sealed over with the acrylic equivalent of the clear nail polish popular well into the 1980s.[5]

White-out no longer is used on dark or irregular objects simply because it eventually will flake off after the object is handled too much. Instead, white India ink, a coat of the acrylic "nail polish" on which the label will be written, or both will be used instead.

What is labeled? Of what does that label consist? This is dictated by the SHPO/THPO and/or the curatorial facility, and therefore varies. In many situations, the SHPO/THPO will require that each diagnostic artifact and a certain percentage of the non-diagnostic artifacts be labeled with the site number and provenience (unit and level) of the artifact. Thus, when we did the Hobo Hill site in northern Virginia, Fairfax County required that each artifact be labeled in the following way

44FX1517
N4E3
L.2

where "N4E3" stood for the excavation unit and the "L.2" stood for the excavation level. Such information would be sufficient to place all artifacts in their relative positions, even if the field records and analysis notes were lost.[6] There was no additional number classifying

---

5. Actual nail polish, shellac, and other clear sealers are not archivally stable and generally are prohibited from use.

6. After harping in Chapter 6 section 6.3.2.3., especially footnote 5, on the need to provide all four unit corner numbers, it should be explained why just *one* stake number was used. The main reason in cases like this is having adequate space to write on the artifact; the entire label generally will not fit. In any event, regardless of *which* stake coordinate was used, the same stake would have been used for each unit. Thus, while it might not be known some day which stake was involved, it still would be possible to arrange all of the units the correct distance from each other on a map. That is what was sought. By the way, the same reasoning holds for using a level number instead of depth: There is nothing inherent in the labeling system to say if the levels were

Figure 8.5. Labeled artifact. The labeling system used here has the advantage of identifying the site, unit area, and relative level from whence the artifact came.

Figure 8.6. Labeled 4-mil ziploc artifact bags, as well as labeled bag insert.

the object, it being realized that what the object was, classificatorily, was inherent in the object and did not need a number to cross-list it with a paper record.

Other firms -- and ourselves on sites in other areas -- have used a system where the unit number was given, along with the depth and a catalogue number for the type or artifact. In some labeling systems, this gets to be byzantine -- we know, because we have been responsible for some incredibly obtuse labeling systems. One system, not ours amazingly, actually supplied an artifact catalogue identification number based upon the ordinal sequence that the artifact enjoyed in a hierarchical scheme, unique to the company concerned, that ranged from ceramics (first rim decorated, then rim undecorated, then body sherd) to lithics (first projectile point, then biface, then...). *No one* short of an experienced cryptographer could possibly have deciphered such a system without the artifact inventory.

If one has discretion to act, we think it best to use the system that Fairfax County uses. One could lose the field records and the analysis notes and still be able to put the essentials of the site back together. Thus, the core information of the site will last just as long as the labels on the artifacts last, a comforting thought. The less dependent upon supplemental records the artifact labeling system is for reconstructing artifact provenience, the better that labeling system is.

Generally all diagnostic artifacts will be labeled. In smaller collections, all larger general artifacts will be labeled as well. Often, though, only a previously set percentage of the undiagnostic artifacts will be labeled. For example, maybe one out of every 10 pieces of the retained plate glass fragments will have a label written on them, or perhaps one out of every 10 unmodified flakes from a prehistoric site. The SHPO/THPO and the SOW usually will have protocols.

With the artifacts labeled, the next step in the process is to place the labeled artifacts into some sort of container. That "container" usually is a 4-mil or greater polyethylene storage bag. Sometimes it is a ziploc bag; sometimes it is a bag closed by a twist tie. This reflects SHPO or THPO protocol: Pennsylvania, for example, argues that ziploc bags can spring open and disgorge their contents, and therefore twist-ties are a better method; North Carolina argues that twist-ties deteriorate and that ziploc bags certainly are more secure and dependably reusable. Federal curation standards currently require ziploc bags.

Regardless of the bag or container used, it is just as important that a site and provenience label be placed *inside* of the bag. This information is usually arranged on that label in the following manner:

site number   bag number

unit number (all coordinates here)

feature number if appropriate

soil horizon

depth in centimeters below surface

---

in 5-, 10, or 20-cm increments (it was 5 cm, actually). However, the number would always allow the artifacts to be placed in their relative spatial relationships.

The information will be done in basic carbon ink on a slip of spunbonded polyethylene paper, which will be put within the bag. Hand-lettered labels in India ink will do; so will dot-matrix generated labels with a standard carbon ribbon (no longer available except for those of us who refuse to upgrade their computer systems). If more than one bag is associated with a provenience, then it will be noted on the label as "n-th of n" bags or something similar (for example, if there were seven artifact bags from the unit-level, then the bags would be numbered arbitrarily one through seven such that one of the bags would have written on it "2 of 7," "2 of 7 bags," or sometimes "2/7").

The idea of the archivally stable label within the bag is to make sure that, if the exterior bag label is rubbed off, some record of bag contents will still be present. This will be *in addition to* the labeled artifacts within the bag. This is redundancy and actually is intended to last for as long as the collection itself will last.

As with the label inside of the bag, the label on the outside of the bag will have the information arranged in the following style (see also Figure 6.2.):

site number   bag number

unit number (all coordinates again)

feature number if applicable

soil horizon

depth in centimeters below surface

Again, the labeling will be done with an indelible marker. Indelible marker ink, as one would suspect given the name and how the product is advertised, will come off under gentle, mechanical abrasion -- that is, the rubbing associated with normal handling. This is why it is called "indelible." Again, the existence of multiple bags would be indicated in the labeling, if this was the case.

Once the artifacts are labeled and placed in the labeled bags -- with labels placed within the bags -- the bags themselves need to be put into some kind of archivally stable container. All of this, we hope it has been noticed, is a response to the curatorial disasters, mentioned in Chapter 1, that attended WPA archaeology: The paper bags of unlabeled and unprocessed artifacts breaking and spilling in a chaotic cascade of artifacts, rendering the archaeological work not one of data recovery but of make-work pillage, so contrary to what everyone had hoped for.

Generally, most collections will be placed in the 1.1 x 1.3 x 0.8 ft acid-free cardboard boxes manufactured by Hollinger; Federal projects and collections require acid-free boxes for storage. Some SHPOs/THPOs and many SOWs will stipulate using such acid-free boxes to curate collections, as well as to hold the field

Superseal® Food Storage Containers

Shortly after establishing the doctoral-level archaeology program and associated laboratory at Syracuse University in 1979, we initiated a policy whereby archaeological materials in their polyethylene bags were stored in plastic food storage containers. Supplied by Eagle Affiliates/APL Corporation of Brooklyn, New York, these Superseal® food storage containers were of archivally stable polypropylene, and came in a range of sizes ideally suited for storing unit-level proveniences of the bagged artifacts. They had the further advantage of being re-sealable and of a size that made them manageable and stackable.

Several years later, other programs, notably the University of Arkansas, adopted the same policy of using generic plastic food storage containers to store archaeological materials. (We know this was an instance of independent – albeit delayed – invention, but sometimes we flatter ourselves in thinking we set a trend.)

records and analysis notes received by the curatorial facility during turn-over. Adhesive polyethylene label holders with acid-free paper inserts identifying the box contents will be affixed to the boxes.

8.3.2.4. Data Bases and Related Management

Most laboratory processing will load the artifact inventory into a data management program. For the needs of the project, the data management program needs to do three things:

* generate an artifact inventory;

* be able to sort that inventory; and

* be able to do statistical analyses of that inventory.

The current industry preference is the latest avatar of Dbase, which has hierarchical, alphanumeric sort capabilities. Most data management is descriptive information management: numbers, types, overall weights. Most data management programs are awkward for handling specific numbers in quantitative ways. For example, Dbase was never meant to provide a numerical taxonomy based upon single-lineage Euclidian distances, yet such an analysis is used to sort out projectile point types.

Analyses based upon dimensional metrics requires different program capabilities, and as a result project managers -- and some laboratory managers -- will load the metrics of the individual artifacts into a spreadsheet or statistics program, Paradox or Excel (or less often, Lotus) for the former, Minitab by preference or even MathCad for the latter. Such programs have the ability to do sophisticated analyses, either in their own right (some spread sheet programs and Minitab) or can be programmed to do specific and sophisticated analyses (most spreadsheet programs). All have the capacity to do sorts and to generate simple graphs.

8.3.3. Matrix Samples

Matrix samples generally consist of flotation samples and constant-volume samples. Flotation samples are taken from features and from the fill of given excavation levels (preferably from the screened backfill, which has been randomized and which presents a sample with a known upper limit on particle size). The amount and source of flotation sample retained, usually given in liters, will be stipulated in the SOW.

Flotation samples are meant to recover a sample of materials that otherwise would be missed by dry-screening. These include items smaller than 0.35 inch (0.898 cm) in length (the maximum linear dimension that can drop cleanly through a 1/4-inch [0.635 cm] screen), as well as materials that cannot be discerned during dry screening, such as carbonized plant remains.

Matrix samples are retained in part for the materials that would be obtained through flotation, but in part of the information that they can provide about the physical structure of the deposit. These are *not* meant to be reduced by most archaeology firms; instead, they will be taken either to be stored in perpetuity for future pedological or sedimentological analyses, or to be sent to the geomorphologist retained by the firm to work out characteristics of the deposit.

8.3.3.1. Reduction

Reduction of flotation samples usually involves a froth flotation system. These are adequately described in the method-and-theory, field methods, and laboratory methods literature, and are available through archaeological equipment suppliers. Most archaeology firms have a froth flotation unit.

Reduction of the flotation sample is little more than running the flotation sample volume through the flotation system. This will produce two sample sets: A so-called "light fraction," which consists of organics such as roots and root-hairs as well as charcoal; and a so-called "heavy fraction," which consists of sands, gravels, micro-debitage, fish scales, burnt and unburnt bone fragments, and everything else that did not float to the surface.

The initial processing in this fashion constitutes "reduction." The archaeology firm is taking away all of the presumably inconsequential parts of the matrix

-- the inorganic particles that are smaller than the 2-mm or so diameter that would be retained by the flotation processes. The resultant organics will often be a waded mess that *must* be allowed to dry or mold will form. The inorganic sludge also needs to dry, not just to avoid the mold but also to reduce weight.

The actual running of a flotation system requires that the firm have a place where the sediment can be safely discarded. This may be the storm sewer system (provided municipal engineers feel that the system can accommodate the sediment load), the firm's vehicle maintenance shed, or even an open and unused field. Otherwise, the operation of the flotation system will be required to capture then properly dispose of the sediment produced by processing the samples.

8.3.3.2. Sorting

After the flotation samples are reduced and dried, they may be catalogued and stored as-is, sorted and examined in-house, or sent to a specialist for sorting and analysis. All of this depends first upon stipulations in the SOW, followed by the capabilities of the firm and who has been retained to provided specialized services.

Most firms lack the in-house expertise to sort through the light fraction of a flotation sample. However, most firms actually *do* have the in-house expertise to do a preliminary sort through the heavy fraction. Whether or not this is done is entirely dependent upon the SOW and therefore the project budget: Dried, the sample will kept indefinitely, and the amount of time required to sort a flotation sample is very great.

8.3.3.3. Labeling and Preparation for Curation

As with the artifacts and other material remains, unprocessed flotation and matrix samples need to be stored. Leaving aside the space and weight problems that such samples might present, the most critical issue is having those samples placed in containers that will be strong enough to withstand the weight and durable enough not to be compromised by damp.

Generally, unprocessed flotation and matrix samples should be stored in heavy-duty spunbonded polypropylene or canvas sample bags. Both types will be used in the field for collecting the sample. Canvas bags are better suited for situations where the flotation sample will be processed in the near future, since after the sample is emptied out the bags can be cleaned and re-used. Bags of spunbonded polypropylene are better suited for long-term storage, since they will not deteriorate and fail over time like canvas bags will. Both types of sample bags are readily available from geological and engineering equipment suppliers.

Because of the weight and the volume involved, unprocessed flotation samples can be extremely troublesome to manage, be it in the field or in the laboratory. Further, such flotation samples have the ability to accumulate at rates far greater than the firm's ability to process the samples. This has always been the case, ever since Struever introduced the method in 1968. Every field archaeologist we know has his or her own horror stories regarding unprocessed flotation samples, and we may as well mention ours.

We once worked as field laborers on a project in the Midwest, not long after water flotation was introduced. This was back in the days when the process consisted of a round, galvanized-steel wash tub, about two feet across and a foot deep, with a pair of handles on either side. The bottom would be removed, and in its place would be window screen reinforced with quarter-inch hardware cloth, brazened into place. One would go and stand out in the shallows of a stream, river, or lake, one person holding the tub and swishing it about, while a companion poured the flotation sample in then, using a tea-strainer, skimmed off whatever floated to the surface, and flipped the floating debris into a plastic sandwich bag. When the sample was reduced, the heavy fraction at the bottom, on that window-screen, would be transferred to another plastic sandwich bag. It worked, and on hot summer days was a pleasant exercise, messing about in the water.

The project we were a part of required taking a 10 percent sample of fill from each excavation unit. Those units were 10 feet on a side, and were being taken down in 0.5 ft increments. A 10 percent sample, then, was a large

sample both in terms of weight (about 380 kg per unit-level) and in terms of volume (about 280 liters per unit-level, the fill having doubled in volume by being screened first). There were eight units like that, each eventually taken down to about two-feet below the surface.

How to store the flotation samples until processing? The solution chosen was double-lined paper grocery bags. Each bag was filled with about a foot of soil: About 16.6 liters or 22.5 kg each, all told. Each level of each unit, then, was producing something like 17 paper grocery bags worth of flotation sample that needed processing; the entire project generating almost 550 such bags.

At that time, early in the history of water flotation, no one really had a sense of how much of a flotation sample was needed, nor did anyone really have a sense of just how long it would take to process 12,160 kg of fill by holding a screen-bottomed metal wash tub and swishing it about in a stream. In any case, the units and levels were dutifully dug, field forms filled out, bags filled with the requisite amount of soil, and all 17 bags from each level of each unit were stored ... on site in an abandoned tobacco barn. On the earthen floor of that barn. In the summer. In a bottomland setting.

Confronted with the growing ranks of filled paper bags, multiplying in the barn like dragon's teeth, as well as a project that had a week left to run, the field director shifted from doing flotation occasionally in the afternoons to a daily, day-long attempt to reduce that enormous (and still increasing) sample. It may actually have been possible to do, had the project had more than one flotation tub to work with. In any case, the field director must have felt more and more like Mickey Mouse in "The Sorcerer's

Apprentice," a feeling that probably was not helped by a field crew that kept whistling or humming the Dukas melody as they carried yet more bags into the barn for storage.

It finally reached the point where it was clear that all of the samples were not going to get processed, and the field director decided to start loading the samples into the institution's field truck to be taken back to the laboratory. And it was then that the real problems began.

From early in the project, the bags had been carried into the barn and set down, with each new set being placed in the ever expanding ranks in front of the older samples. By the time that the heroic attempt was made to subdue the samples, it was really the most recent of those samples that were being placed in the wheelbarrow and carted a furlong over floodplain terrace to the stream, because the crew was drawing bags from the front of the standing ranks of bags. The other bags, the first samples collected, had stood shadowed, in lurking silence, on the dirt floor of the barn for weeks and weeks.

What happened next was predictable. Because of the damp earth, the damp and humid air of a Midwest bottomland in the summer, and the dampness in the fill itself, the bottoms of nearly every one of the bags remaining in the barn had all but dissolved into a moldy sodden mass. The bags could not be shifted without bursting and the fill pouring out. As a result, most of the samples were lost.

That incident taught us two things. The first was to keep on top of processing tasks in a project. But mainly it taught us to make sure that strong and damp-resistant containers were used to store flotation samples.

Labeling of the bags is more of an issue than for artifacts because the sample itself can contribute to the destruction of the label. Labeling is done in two ways: On the outside of the bag by physically affixing a label to the bag, and on the inside of the bag. The exterior label will be secured to the bag: Often, tags of stiff paper with a reinforced grommet for securing with wire or string serves the needs for the exterior of the

bag. (Writing directly on the bag of course can be done, but if there is any intention of re-using the bags, this is not as good an option as a tag.)

On the interior of the bag, a label on a piece of spunbonded polyethylene paper will be sealed inside of a small plastic bag, which will then be sealed inside of a second plastic bag. The label itself will be made out in indelible ink. The concern with interior labels is that the high humidity of most flotation samples otherwise causes the paper to turn back into pulp.

The labels themselves will be similar to those used for artifacts: Site number, bag or sample number, unit coordinates, depth below surface. Again, if there are several bags from a given provenience, then the bag label should include something along the lines of "2 of 7," "2 of 7 bags," or "2/7," all indicating that other portions of the sample exist, as well as the size of that sample.

8.4.   Levels of Analysis

There are two steps in the analysis of any archaeological assemblage. The first involves the documentation and recordation of information regarding the artifacts and other material remains from the site. This is work done in a laboratory setting, be it the institution's facility or that of a specialist. The second step in analysis involves manipulating the recorded information. That work uses the records generated in the laboratory and manipulates those data, and will be done as part of the writing of the report.

For the professional archaeologist, the level of detail for each step depends upon the nature of the compliance project. Overall levels of analysis relative to the nature of the compliance exercise have been discussed in Chapters 5, 6, and 7. These are addressed as well in the Secretary of the Interior's Standards and Guidelines [48 FR 44721 - 44723, 44734 - 44736], the Advisory Council for Historic Preservation's *Manual of Mitigative Measures*, and proposed 36 CFR Part 66 [42 FR 53774 - 5479].

8.4.1.   Levels of Analysis: Laboratory Recordation

For Phase I survey projects, the laboratory analyses are meant to provide sufficient information on the archaeological assemblage to allow its cultural-historic placement, number of components (horizontal, or vertical within the testing depth used), and basic site function. Generally, then, artifact analyses rarely involve anything more extensive than the identification, classification, and counting or weighing classificatory sets. For example, dimensional metrics normally will not be taken on projectile points, since all that is needed at this stage is an idea of what kind of projectile point it is. This will be true for historic artifacts as well: What kind of ceramics, say, are present? What kind of glass and when was such glass first available?

In most instances, it is hoped that an approximate age or cultural-historical affiliation can be assigned to the deposit through *type dating*. *Type dating* is nothing more than using diagnostic, typable artifacts that have

been associated with given periods and archaeological deposits, and projecting that established cultural-temporal association to the site under consideration. For prehistoric sites, the most common artifacts used for type dating are projectile points and ceramics. For historic sites there is a much wider range of suitable artifacts since manufacturing dates or availability dates are known. Glass, ceramics, nail types, barbwire types, and even plastics can help secure the estimated age range for a deposit.[7] It is also possible to estimate the age of a deposit by measuring pipe-stem bore diameters for kaolin trade pipes; as mentioned in Chapter 7 section 7.3.1., there are regression equations that link the bore diameters to the approximate year in which the trade pipe was made.[8]

Usually the only actual measuring that will take place for a Phase I analysis will be in the measurement of pipe-stem bore diameters or similar exercises, as with bullet calibers. In any case, excepting those instances, nearly all that is needed in the way of analysis is the precise *classification* of the artifacts.

The artifact data from most Phase I surveys will be plotted on a project map to give some sense of site bounds as well as artifact density within those bounds. Counts or weights become useful in constructing iso-frequency maps that will assist in the design of the Phase II testing program. If the site is clearly not eligible for listing on the National Register, and the SHPO/THPO and agency concur in this assessment, then there will be no need for further artifact analyses. Any additional work can then be done by the academic community, should future changes in the field warrant re-examination of such collections.

There are, of course, exceptions to this: Sites that seem to satisfy the criteria for listing on the National Register, even after only a Phase I survey, may benefit from more detailed analyses, such as plotting lithic raw material distribution by weight over the site, or tracking the size or average weight of building plaster. Even in situations like this, though, such increased analytical work would be better done as part of a Phase II testing regime. Often, because of that

---

7.   The replacement of machine-cut nails by wire nails for construction in the eastern United States follows a rough linear regression from their initial manufacture in quantity for general construction around 1870, to 50 percent of all nails used in 1890. The ratio of machine-cut to wire nails has been used to approximate the age of deposits: Neumann, Thomas W. 1989. *A Phase I Archeological Investigation of Catoctin Furnace (18 FR 29), Cunningham Falls State Park, Frederick County, Maryland*. State of Maryland/Office of Engineering and Construction/Department of General Services, Baltimore, pp.54, 56.

8.   All of the regression equations we have seen are linear (e.g., Binford 1961; Heighton and Degan 1971; Thomas 1976), even though when graphed over the full range of manufacture the change in diameters is a very elongated S-shape. However, for the periods most working with historic deposits are concerned, the change is sufficiently linear not to make much real difference.

Resources for Identification

The ability to recognize and correctly identify material remains is central to archaeological laboratory analysis. Even when the university or college training environment does provide an archaeology laboratory or historic materials analysis course, this will be only an introduction compared to the volume and variety that will be faced in private practice. The way that all archaeologists learn to identify material remains is by identifying material remains: That is, by being faced with collections and working out just what it is that is being looked at.

Where is this information? How is it found? Most of the identifications will be based upon published information and will be available as books. That literature consists of

*   books of museum collections;

*   auction catalogues;

*   specialist collectors or antiques books;

*   historic handbooks, manuals, and catalogues;

*   geology field and laboratory guides; and

*   academic typological classifications.

Project managers and laboratory managers will each have a personal professional library that has a range of such references, depending upon their own expertise as well as the responsibilities that they have within the firm.

The laboratory itself will also have a set of basic references meant to assist laboratory technicians in artifact classification and identification. In our experience, most university courses do not come right out and say that there are books of projectile point types or of historic bottle types; the existence of such references is learned informally by talking with instructors or more advanced students.

Summary classifications of prehistoric artifacts exist in a series of state-level and regional typology guides; these usually are restricted to projectile point types and to ceramic types. Such compilations will present the name, age, distribution, and physical characteristics or diagnostic features of the items in question. Those involving projectile points tend to be much more common and better worked out (e.g., Cambron and Hulse 1964; Ritchie 1971; Justice 1987; Hranicky 1994; Hranicky and Painter 1993). Ceramic typologies often are parts of site monographs that themselves are out of print (e.g., Wauchope 1966; Kinsey 1972), although statewide compilations exist (e.g., Ritchie and MacNeish 1949; Prufer 1968; Anfinson ed. 1979; Williams

and Thompson 1999), most of which are also out of print. In both situations, the typologies tend to be regionally sensitive, so much so that SHPO and enabling agency reviewers often disapprove of reference to identical types found outside of their area of jurisdiction.

Typologies for historic artifacts exist as well-illustrated books that focus on particular artifact sets: Medicine bottles (e.g., Fike 1987) or bottles in general (e.g., Toulouse 1971), redware (e.g., Ketchum 1991a), stoneware (e.g., Ketchum 1991b), and even bricks (e.g., Gurke 1987). They also exist as specialized compilations of features, such as makers' marks used on pottery (e.g., Kovel and Kovel 1986; DeBolt 1988). There are a huge number of such publications, just as many as there are types or classes of historic artifacts. Some are compiled by university researchers; many more are compiled by antiques dealers and collectors. They are written and illustrated specifically to assist others in identifying the items of concern. These books usually are *not* regionally restrictive in the same way as prehistoric typologies are, because historic artifacts were products of nation-states that had global distributions. We do not expect to find Chance Phase Onondaga pottery in the Georgia Piedmont; it is restricted to central New York. However, it is not at all surprising to find British gun flints in both states.

The most often overlooked general reference constantly used in a laboratory setting is one for rocks and minerals (e.g., Kraus et al. 1936; Deer et al. 1966; Mason 1978; Chesterman 1979; Cvancara 1985; Lapidus 1987), although occasionally there are state-level references for types and sources of prehistoric lithic raw materials (e.g., Goad 1979; Fogelman 1983). This lack of sensitivity to basic lithic identification is compounded because many universities no longer teach basic rock and mineral identification courses, so few archaeologists have formal training in the identification of hand specimens.

Anfinson, Scott F., editor. 1979. *A Handbook of Minnesota Prehistoric Ceramics*. Occasional Publications in Minnesota Anthropology No. 5. Minnesota Historical Society, Ft. Snelling.

Cambron, James W., and David C. Hulse. 1964. *Handbook of Alabama Archaeology, Part I: Point Types*. University of Alabama Press, University.

Chesterman, Charles W. 1979. *The Audubon Society Field Guide to North American Rocks and Minerals*. Knopf, New York.

Cvancara, Alan M. 1985. *A Field Manual for the Amateur Geologist*. Prentice Hall, New York.

DeBolt, C. Gerald. 1988. *The Dictionary of American Pottery Marks: Whiteware and Porcelain (The First Book of Its Kind in Over Eighty Years)*. Charles E. Tuttle Company, Rutland. [See title and publication date of Kovel and Kovel 1986].

Deer, W.A., R.A. Howie, and J. Zussman. 1966. *An Introduction to the Rock-Forming Minerals*. Longman Group, London.

Fike, Richard E. 1987. *The Bottle Book: A Comprehensive Guide to Historic, Embossed Medicine Bottles*. Gibbs M. Smith, Inc., Salt Lake City.

Fogelman, Gary L. 1983. *Lithics Book*. The Pennsylvania Artifact Series No. 34. Fogelman Publishing Co., Turbotville.

Goad, Susan I. 1979. *Chert Resources in Georgia: Archaeological and Geological Perspectives*. Wallace Reservoir Project Contributions No. 3. University of Georgia Laboratory of Archaeology Series Report Number 21.

Gurke, Karl. 1987. *Bricks and Brickmaking: A Handbook for Historical Archaeology*. University of Idaho Press, Moscow.

Hranicky, Wm Jack. 1994. *Middle Atlantic Projectile Point Typology and Nomenclature*. Archeological Society of Virginia Special Publication No. 33.

Hranicky, Wm Jack, and Floyd Painter. 1993. *A Guide to the Identification of Virginia Projectile Points*. Archeological Society of Virginia Special Publication No. 17.

Justice, Noel D. 1987. *Stone Age Spear and Arrow Points of the Midcontinental and Eastern United States*. Indiana University Press, Bloomington.

Ketchum, William C., Jr. 1991a. *American Redware*. Henry Holt and Company, New York.

Ketchum, William C., Jr. 1991b. *American Stoneware*. Henry Holt and Company, New York.

Kinsey, W. Fred. 1972. *Archeology in the Upper Delaware Valley: A Study of the Cultural Chronology of the Tocks Island Reservoir*. Anthropological Series No. 2. The Pennsylvania Historical and Museum Commission, Harrisburg.

Kovel, Ralph and Terry Kovel. 1986. *Kovels' New Dictionary of Marks: Pottery and Porcelain 1850 to the Present*. Crown Publishers, New York.

Kraus, Edward H., Walter F. Hunt, and Lewis S. Ramsdell. 1936. *Mineralogy: An Introduction to the Study of Minerals and Crystals*. Third edition. McGraw-Hill, New York.

Lapidus, Dorothy F. 1987. *Dictionary of Geology and Geophysics*. Facts on File, New York.

Mason, Roger. 1978. *Petrology of the Metamorphic Rocks*. George Allen & Unwin, Ltd., London.

Prufer, Olaf H. 1968. *Ohio Hopewell Ceramics: An analysis of the Extant Collections*. University of Michigan Museum of Anthropology Anthropological Papers No. 33.

Ritchie, William A. 1971. *A Typology and Nomenclature for New York Projectile Points*. New York State Museum Bulletin Number 384.

Ritchie, William A., and Richard S. MacNeish. 1949. The pre-Iroquoian pottery of New York state. *American Antiquity* 15:97-124.

Toulouse, Julian Harrison. 1971. *Bottle Makers and Their Marks*. Thomas Nelson, Inc., New York.

Wauchope, Robert W. 1966. *Archaeological Survey of Northern Georgia with a Test of Some Cultural Hypotheses*. Society for American Archaeology Memoir 21.

Williams, Mark, and Victor Thompson. 1999. A guide to Georgia Indian pottery types. *Early Georgia* 27 (1):1-167.

realization, the Phase II testing will be added on by the client or agency, at the recommendation of the SHPO/THPO, to the original Phase I survey project, resulting in a combined Phase I/Phase II investigation of the site.

Phase II testing exercises require more detailed analyses for all aspects of the project, and this applies to the laboratory aspects as well. A Phase II project is a formal investigation of an archaeological site, albeit a comparatively small formal investigation. Thus, there is a professional obligation to perform at least a basic archaeological analysis on the assemblage from the site.

There are also the questions that a Phase II testing exercise is meant to answer:

*   What is the archaeological structure of the site?

*   In what ways was the site used?

*   Is there information contained within the site that is unique relative to what is known for the period, culture, or type of site represented?

Being able to address these questions requires not only the classification or recognition of the artifacts in the assemblage, it often also requires closer examination and measurement of those artifacts. As a result, the laboratory aspect of the Phase II analysis will require both the identification of diagnostic artifacts and the measuring or otherwise detailed descriptions of other parts of the collection.

The level of analysis expected for most Phase II projects is of the kind where a person, using a dissecting microscope, triple-beam balance, micrometers, and angle-measuring devices can secure

36 CFR Part 79: Curation of Federally-Owned and Administered Archeological Collections

All curatorial facilities housing Federal collections are required to abide by **36 CFR Part 79**. While the facility may not be under the direct jurisdiction of the Federal government, the collections held by that facility are the property of the Federal government and constitute a public trust. The facility, then, is required to comply with **36 CFR Part 79** guidelines.

36 CFR Part 79 applies to all archaeological collections that were generated not only as a by-product of NHPA Section 106, but also those generated under the authority of the Antiquities Act of 1935, the Reservoir Salvage Act, and the Archeological Resources Protection Act [**36 CFR 79.3 (a)**; see also Chapters 1, 2].

The regulations set and maintain curatorial standards not by specifying what exactly to do, but by specifying the standards of those charged with doing and maintaining the curation, and specifying the requirements for funding and facilities management for the place where the collections are held.

Thus, the collections are to be placed in a repository with adequate long-term curatorial capabilities [**36 CFR 79.5**]. That curation is to be according to [current] professional museum and archival practices [**36 CFR 79.4 (b)**], and managed by a qualified museum professional [**36 CFR 79.4 (h)**], defined as a person who meets the OPM "Position Classification Standards for Positions under the General Schedule Classification System." ""Professional" is defined as holding the appropriate graduate degree in museum science along with having three years of professional experience at the equivalent of a GS-11 or higher.[a]

By setting requirements in this fashion, the curatorial facility is quite likely to have very high archival standards, simply because the person in charge of setting and enforcing those standards will have had several years of advanced professional experience doing exactly that.

The museum profession has detailed requirements for collections management and curation. The Federal regulations are structured to in effect access and implement those requirements. Indeed, the default phrase in **36 CFR Part 79** is equivalent to "current museum and archival standards." But it is in the areas of facility management, and Federal oversight and inspections, that **36 CFR Part 79** becomes specific in its own right.

36 CFR 79.9 provides a detailed list of the criteria a facility must satisfy to qualify as a repository for Federally generated archaeological collections. These criteria, to be verified by a Federal official, include:

*   maintaining a long-term cataloguing and conservation system based on professional museum and archival practices [**36 CFR 79.9 (a)**];

*   maintaining complete records regarding the collection, including everything having to do with the archaeological investigation as well as the holding of the collection itself [**36 CFR 79.9 (b)(1)**];

*   making sure that there is space dedicated solely to the curation and study of those archaeological collections and associated records, and that the space is not also used for other, non-curatorial purposes [**36 CFR 79.9 (b)(2)**];

*   housing the collections in space that meets local building, safety, and health codes, has a fire detection *and suppression* system, has an intrusion detection and deterrent system, has an emergency management plan, has a special collections arrangement with appropriate

---

a. An approximate academic conversion based upon education, experience, and pay grade would have a GS-11 equivalent to an assistant professor in an AAUP I institution, to an associate professor in an AAUP IIa or IIb institution, and to a full professor in an AAUP III and some IIb institutions.

all of the information necessary to the analysis. Specialized analyses, such as paleoethnobotanical analysis of flotation samples, high-magnification use-wear analyses, or residue analyses, normally are not expected nor budgeted. The only exception is securing radiometric dates, which often is mentioned in the SOW and allowed for in the project budget; this will occur, though, usually only in situations where it is suspected that Phase III data recovery will be required.

Most Phase II analyses are capable of standing on their own as finished archaeological investigations; these are the collections that actually might prove the most productive in the distant future for additional analysis, simply because so much already will have been established about the collection and therefore the site, yet so much more specialized analysis could be done.

Phase III data recovery analyses are comprehensive analyses limited only by the SOW and the budget. The laboratory aspect will vary by the kind of site, nature of assemblage, and the resources available to do the work. It is with Phase III analyses that subcontracted specialists become involved in the investigation: It is here that the flotation samples will be processed and analyzed; here that high-magnification use-wear analyses will be done. Phase III analyses really are examples of the analyses that the method-and-theory text books and their associated courses are directed at.

As mentioned in Chapter 7, while the Phase III laboratory analysis is thorough, it will not be exhaustive. While most Phase III data recovery projects are extremely large and sophisticated, there usually is a budget and time limit that would prevent every possible research avenue being explored. Even

---

security for valuable and fragile items, has limited access, and is inspected by an appropriate Federal official periodically to make sure that these standards are followed [**36 CFR 79.9 (b)(3)**];

* requiring that the facility is under the supervision of a qualified museum professional as defined above [**36 CFR 79.9 (b)(4)**];

* storing the collections in a way that protects them from deterioration and preserves the original data for future analyses [**36 CFR 79.9 (b)(5)**];

* storing all of the field and analysis records, including a copy of the final report in a manner that protects them from fire and theft [**36 CFR 79.9 (b)(6)**];

* periodically inspecting all collections to make sure that they are not subject to deterioration [**36 CFR 79.9 (b)(7)**];

* conducting periodic collection inventories to make sure that everything that is supposed to be present actually is [**36 CFR 79.9 (b)(8)**]; and

* providing legitimate access to the collections [**36 CFR 79.9 (b)(9)**].

Not only must those physical plant and collections management conditions be in place, it is also required that the Federal agency conduct period inspections to make sure that those criteria are being followed [**36 CFR 79.11**].[b]

What stands out about the criteria set forth in **36 CFR 79** – the expectations for professional-level collections management, appropriate facilities, and outside reviewers of compliance – is how much it reflects the basic reasons for the Section 106 Process. That Process is meant to give society the right of first refusal on the material remains that may be of interest and use to it, and the stipulations for collections curation reinforce that importance. It is useful to remember that **36 CFR Part 79** was produced because the proposed **36 CFR 66** was considered to be too vague regarding curation [cf. **42 FR 5374 - 5479**]. However, the inspiration of that proposed set of regulations can be seen in **36 CFR Part 79**, especially given the following passage:

*it is important that the data and material resulting from the data recovery programs be maintained as cared for **in the public trust** [proposed **36 CFR Part 66.3 (a)**: **42 FR 5376**, emphasis added; see also Archeology and Historic Preservation; Secretary of the Interior's Guidelines **48 FR 44737** Curation for equivalent wording].*

By the time the archaeological site is being curated because of a compliance project, all that is left of that site *are* the material remains and whatever records were produced regarding its extraction and analysis. It is, indeed, a public trust.

---

b. It is in the area of structure and maintenance of physical plant that many universities and colleges no longer are capable of maintaining professional-level archaeological facilities. The required physical plant and budgetary commitment contrasted, from an administrative perspective, with a major field that accounts for

only a percent or two of the undergraduate enrollment, often results in a placing of such facility maintenance – much less upgrades – on the back burner.

so, the scale of many Phase III projects can be such that the laboratory staff is all but overwhelmed by the volume of material and the needs of the analysis.

8.4.2. Levels of Analysis: Data Manipulation

The laboratory analyses provide a condensation of the artifactual evidence from the site. That information will exist as a series of inventories and tables, some generated by the laboratory staff and the remainder generated by senior archaeologists or specialists, that are handed over to whoever is responsible for writing up the "Results" section of the compliance report. In most cases, that person will be the project manager.

For Phase I and Phase II projects, the data manipulation that occurs while the "Results" section is being written is meant as much to address the compliance needs of the project as it is to make archaeological sense of the site. Data manipulation for Phase I projects generally will involve working up a project map that shows artifact distributions relative to the Phase I testing pattern, and possibly an assessment of vertical frequencies of artifacts.

The primary Phase I questions involve if integrity can be ruled out, cultural-historical affiliation, and horizontal and, with subsurface testing to a lesser extent, vertical distribution of artifacts. Physical integrity of the deposit will have been assessed based upon the presence or absence of intrusive artifacts, as well as upon the presence of absence of site disturbance. Cultural-historical affiliation will have been established through classification of the diagnostic artifacts from the site. The vertical and horizontal distribution of artifacts will be based upon simple graphic displays and tables.

In situations where it is thought that the site had once been plowed but no longer showed visible evidence of an Ap horizon, or in situations where an argument is being made for horizontal patterning (or its lack), it is necessary to document such arguments with the appropriate statistical tests.

The primary Phase II questions will again involve site physical integrity, cultural-historical affiliation, and vertical/horizontal distribution of the artifacts. However, the analysis also will explore in its own right the nature of the artifactual patterning as well as site function and internal site dynamics.

There are two ways in which the artifacts will be used in a Phase II analysis. One has to do with the physical structure of the deposit. The other has to do with the archaeology represented by the deposit.

The physical structure of the deposit involves not only the soils or sediments, it also involves the extent to which the assemblage has or has not moved within the

deposit. This is a constant, recurring issue in open-air sites located in active soils, since soils behave as viscous fluids and artifacts sink in that fluid. Assessing the extent of movement, and if there were earlier occupations now represented amidst the downward spread of artifacts, will require plotting the vertical distribution of artifact classes, then testing those patterns statistically. All of this is being done both to get a sense of the site's integrity in terms of artifact arrangement just as much as to get a sense of what belongs with what.

The archaeology of the site obviously is also an issue. In many respects, the artifactual analyses of a Phase II project are meant to assess the data potential of the deposit; any association with historically important people or events will have been established during background historic research. The issue in terms of the archaeology is what physically is present that makes the site an important information repository. Association as a criterion for Register-eligibility usually requires corresponding physical evidence for the archaeology if the historical documentation has been ambivalent.

Such questions are addressed by considering the archaeological assemblage as a behavioral unit, just as it done in any standard archaeological report. Again, as mentioned in Chapter 6, not only are statistical tests used to support all comparative statements made, but often it becomes useful to do surface-trend analyses, using a correlation coefficient matrix, of artifact relationships over the site.

There are some things that a Phase II analysis will not do: For example, interpretations that would require specialized analysis or significant amounts of detailed analyses. The purpose of the Phase II analysis is to say what the site is, its structure, and what kinds of information it contains. Anything else, such as designation of activity areas based upon high-magnification use-wear analysis of spent microliths, normally would be beyond the intent (and probably budget) of the project.

Phase III data recovery analyses are as sophisticated and thorough as the project budget allows. As was mentioned for the laboratory aspect of the project, the kind of data manipulation expected for a Phase III project is what normally is described in method-and-theory textbooks for the analysis of a site.

8.5.   Turn-Over

The last step involving the archaeology laboratory and the physical remains from the compliance project is *turn-over*. Turn-over is the term used for the handing over of the archaeological collections, field records, analysis records, and a copy of the final report to an appropriate curatorial facility.

8.5.1. Ownership, Curation, Jurisdiction

For Federal undertakings where the Lead agency is also the client, the Federal government owns all that has been produced by the project: the artifacts, the field records (notes, maps, photographs and other images), the analysis notes, and the report. This is generally true at the state and local levels as well, where the state or local government also is the client: The materials produced during the archaeological compliance investigation belong to the particular government concerned.

For Federally-enabled projects undertaken by non-Federal parties, whoever owns the land generally owns the materials, be it the client, the state, the tribe, or the local governing authority. However, ownership varies by jurisdiction and situation.

In both situations, be it a government agency actually serving directly as the client, or the client being enabled by a government agency, the collections are seen to be a public trust that must be responsibly curated to the best standards available at the time. This requires that the collections be properly prepared then stored in a facility that is sufficient to the task of maintaining long-term curation of archaeological collections.

Guidelines for curation at the Federal level are given in **36 CFR Part 79**. Basic curatorial standards at the state and local level usually have been set out by the SHPO or the THPO. Some states, such as North Carolina, will provide a check-list for how collections should be prepared.

The SHPO/THPO will also have a list of suitable curatorial facilities. Those facilities should have been contacted at the time that the project was bid so that storage fees could have been set out in the project budget; most curatorial facilities now levy a one-time per-box or per unit-volume fee. At the time that the project was awarded, a curatorial facility should have been selected then advised of the pending project. If the facility accepts the role of serving as the final curatorial facility for the project, then the professional archaeologist will need to get whatever curatorial guidelines that facility uses so that the collections and records may be correctly prepared. It is generally expected that curation will be done at an in-state facility and preferably at the facility closest to the undertaking.[9]

In most cases, preparation of the collections for curation requires that

* diagnostic artifacts are labeled in a curatorially stable way and in some unambiguous fashion;

* a fraction of small non-diagnostic artifacts be labeled, if the number of those is very large;

* artifacts be placed in 4-mil or greater polyethylene storage bags that are labeled with site number or project name, horizontal and vertical provenience, bag inventory number, and date, with that same information also placed on acid-free paper or preferably spun-bonded polyethylene paper with India ink or pencil inside of the bag (hard-plastic medicine vials should not be used as primary storage; if used, they should be placed inside of 4-mil or greater polyethylene bags);

* packing the artifact bags in a manner that they do not shift, using archival-grade packing materials;

* boxes made of acid-free materials (such as Hollinger boxes), with adhesive polyethylene label holders with acid-free paper label inserts, be used to store artifact collections and site records;

* a complete inventory, including bag inventory numbers relative to provenience and collection contents, be prepared;

* the field records, such as the general field notes, the excavation and feature records, the bag and other field specimen inventories, survey notes, photographs and negatives, and so on, be placed together in a suitable binders, sleeves, folders, or envelopes; and

* a catalogue sheet listing the above items be present.

Professional archaeologists are expected to be familiar with general curatorial standards; laboratory managers particularly are required to understand and employ the latest curation and archival practices. The fundamental rule of thumb regarding curation is that all paper products intimately involved in storage, such as field notes, boxes, packing, and so forth, must be acid-free. This is required of course at the Federal level, and generally Federal curatorial requirements are ahead of state requirements.

The location for curation must conform to the minimum curatorial standards specified by **36 CFR**

9. Many universities no longer are able to meet **36 CFR Part 79** criteria (e.g., Trimble, Michael K., and Thomas B. Meyers. 1991. *Saving the Past from the Future: Archaeological Curation in the St. Louis District.* U.S. Army Corps of Engineers, St. Louis District). There are many historic reasons for this: Archaeological collections have been relegated to building basements, to converted residential structures located on the frontier fringe of the university where it had expanded in the 1960s and 1970s, and/or to warehouses. University administrations rarely consider curation of

archaeological collections important, while the Anthropology department and its archaeology program seldom have the budget or the political strength needed to upgrade or expand facilities, ironic in that Anthropology faculty command some of the highest salaries in an academic setting.

Computer Records

Under absolutely no circumstances should computer files be used as a primary medium of records storage. Always, always provide archivally stable hard copies of computer files. This is for two basic reasons. The first is that information storage on magnetic computer disks begins deteriorating as soon as it is stored. Most magnetic-based disks have information storage half-lives of two years. (CDs, we are told by electrical engineers, have storage half-lives of 10 years.) As a good friend of ours in Federal service remarked: "Paper lasts."

Considering that the 200-year-old documents we have in our libraries are still readable, while several of the five-year-old back-up disks for the computer system are not (not to mention the 15-year-old AppleWorks files or the 25-year-old punch-card FORTRAN files), dependence on electronic storage as the sole or main curation system is unwise. Further, the information stored on paper is much more accessible than any information stored in a medium that can be accessed only through a technological intermediary: Anyone who can read English, even those living with their herds in the remote corners of Kazakstan or Mongolia, can read the hard copies of our compliance reports from 25 years ago; but even the computer mavens at Georgia Tech would have difficulty generating hard copies from the computer records that produced those reports. And that brings up the second reason.

The second reason that computer-based records are inappropriate for curation involves compatibility. The computer industry is driven by planned obsolescence; computer files even 10 years old may require software, or even hardware, that no longer exists. For example, we have duplicate computer files from projects we did 15 years ago: The files were done in AppleWorks on an Apple II, and were stored on 5¼-inch double-density disks. If we did not have hard copies of that information, it would be inaccessible if not lost entirely: How many readers have a disk drive that will read a 5¼-inch disk, let alone an AppleWorks word-processing file? (Actually, like any number of archaeologists who were around when the computer revolution hit, we also consolidated assemblage information on computer punch cards. As a result, we have stacks and STACKS of such cards. We suspect that we are not the only ones in this situation.)

Some firms we work with keep older hardware in house to have access to the computer files from earlier in the firms project history. This is a stop-gap measure; in 30 years, the hardware will not work because the clock battery will fail and not be replaceable.

Technology is meant to be a tool, a servant. It should never become the master.

Part 79 if the materials were generated from a Federally enabled undertaking [**36 CFR 79.3 (a)**: "The regulations in this part [36 CFR Part 79] apply to collections ... that are the result of a prehistoric or historic resource survey, excavation or other study conducted in connection with a Federal action, assistance, license or permit."].

8.5.2. Managerial Responsibilities and Miscellaneous Matters

The project manager will be responsible for determining what in the field records can be purged as corporate privileged information -- budget figures, say, or records of communication -- then gathering the remainder of the field records together.[10] A copy of the records that will be handed over often will be made first, although this is as much a matter of the firm's internal procedures and nature of the site as it is of normal practice.

The project manager will hand over to the laboratory manager whatever records are necessary; the laboratory manager generally is charged with the responsibility of putting those records together with everything else from the site, boxing those materials, then physically delivering what amounts to the archaeological site as it now exists to a curatorial facility. All of this will take place after the final project report has been produced. A copy of that report will be part of the materials handed over to the curatorial facility.

---

10. For Section 106 projects subject to **36 CFR Part 79** mandates, part of the records required at turn over include the SOW, the RFP, the contract, and other administrative information from the project needed for understanding the cultural resources recovered and curated [**36 CFR 79.4 (2)(v)**].

9: Report Preparation and Production

9.1. Purpose and Objectives

The last step in the cultural resources processes is the production of the report. The report on the compliance archaeological investigation serves two purposes:

* explication of the study conducted sufficient for government regulators to afford determinations of significance and of adverse effect; and

* long-term information storage of the archaeological deposit.

The cultural resources process allows society the right of first refusal on the information contained within archaeological sites, structures, buildings, and the like. It does this as part of a planning process. The report satisfies both needs by summarizing the status of the cultural resource while also addressing planning concerns. Thus, the written report supplied as a product of the archaeological compliance process is meant to do two things:

(1) to serve as the documentation required under 36 CFR 800.11 allowing a determination of adverse effect to be made; and

(2) to serve as the summation of the archaeological research required by professional standards.

There are three parts to the archaeological site once the compliance exercise is done:

(1) the artifacts and other material remains;

(2) the field and laboratory records; and

(3) the report.

Federal regulations, particularly 36 CFR Part 79 and the Secretary of the Interior's Standards and Guidelines, list the compliance report as part of the overall archaeological collection. The report is primary, archived information. It is that central, that important. Yet, to be included as part of that collection it must satisfy both statutory requirements and a stringent peer review. Failure results not just in a requirement to do the work again until it is correct, but delays in award payments. And the threat of civil fines. The compliance report produced by professional archaeologists demands a quality of execution, with commensurate penalties for failing to meet such expectations, unknown for traditional academic research and publication.

In terms of the report itself: The report produced must be sufficient in detail and quality such that agency and SHPO/THPO archaeologists can judge for themselves the merits of the conclusions reached by the practicing archaeologist. The archaeologist is serving as the agency's and SHPO's or the THPO's eyes, as it were; the report is actually a statement of what those eyes saw and understood.

Federal Regulations, Standards, and Guidelines on Documentation

The role, nature, and quality of the archaeological compliance report have been set forth in Federal regulations and guidelines. It is important at the outset to understand the roles of the report, what is expected of it, and how it fits into the larger compliance process.

Archaeological Documentation: Kind

36 CFR 800.11 (d) and **(e)** involve what *kind* of documentation is required to allow the consulting parties in the Section 106 Process to make determinations of adverse effect. Those requirements are to provide sufficient documentation in the following areas:

* A description of the undertaking, including photographs, maps, and drawings as necessary [**36 CFR 800.11 (d)(1)** and **36 CFR 800.11 (e)(1)**];

* a description of the historic properties [strict sense of the term; see Chapter 2 section 2.2.3.1.] that may be affected by the undertaking [**36 CFR 800.11 (e)(3)**];

* a description of the efforts made to identify historic properties if there is a finding by the agency of no adverse effect [**36 CFR 800.11 (d)(2)**], as well as an explanation why there will be no adverse effect [**36 CFR 800.11 (d)(3)**]; or a description of the affected properties and their eligibility for listing on the National Register is there is a finding by the agency of adverse effect and what those adverse effects will be [**36 CFR 800.11 (e)(5)**]; and

* a description of the views of the SHPO/THPO and of other consulting parties, as well as a summary of how those views were obtained, if there is a finding of no adverse effect [**36 CFR 800.11 (e)(6)**].

Similar documentation is required where the SHPO/THPO and the Lead agency have not been able to agree or generate a Memorandum of Agreement, and the Advisory Council for Historic Preservation has been asked to comment [**36 CFR 800.6 (b)(1)**].

Archaeological Documentation: Intent and Structure

36 CFR 800 sets out the specific procedures and rules for implementing Section 106, including documentation. The National Park Service Archeology and Historic Preservation;

Secretary of the Interior's Standards and Guidelines [**48 FR 44716-44742**; see also Appendix A] explains how that documentation is intended to be used, and therefore of what it should consist. It also sets forth the standards expected for that documentation and related work, so that it will serve its intended need. This is done by setting the standards for who is allowed to do the documentation.

The Secretary's Standards and Guidelines are an explication of the historic preservation planning process; Section 106 and related sections are meant to be planning instruments. The central part of planning involves developing the necessary plans, identifying historic properties (strict sense), evaluating those properties, registering those properties, then treating those properties. This involves not only archaeology, but also history and the built environment. Part of the planning process, then, requires some form of field work, various kinds of field surveys, sampling, and the like. This is all part of the documentation process, the final product being some form of report or, in the case of historic architecture and engineering, measured drawings, plans, photographs, and similar records.

The investigations done by the practicing archaeologist usually involve four parts of that process: Identification of historic properties, evaluation of historic properties, historical documentation, and of course archaeological documentation. The Secretary of the Interior's Standards and Guidelines sets for specific standards and guidelines for the execution of each of those procedural steps. The standards given here set forth what is expected of the compliance work; the guidelines actually stipulate of what in a general sense that work should consist (see Appendix A).

Phase I survey work and, to a lesser extent, Phase II testing come under the **Secretary of the Interior's Standards for Identification [48 FR 44720 - 44721]**, which are:

* *Standard I. Identification of historic properties is undertaken to the degree required to make decisions;*

* *Standard II. Results of identification activities are integrated into the preservation planning process;* and

* *Standard III. Identification activities include explicit procedures for record-keeping and information distribution.*

Assessing identified properties is addressed by **Secretary of the Interior's Standards for Evaluation [48 FR 44723]**, which are

* *Standard I. Evaluation of the significance of historic properties uses established criteria;*

* *Standard II. Evaluation of significance applies the criteria within historic contexts; and*

* *Standard III. Evaluation results in a list or inventory of significant properties that is consulted in assigning registration and treatment priorities.*

These standards require some form of historic and prehistoric background research to be done, and for those backgrounds in effect to be couched in terms of the state's historic preservation plan (which will have set out the requisite historic contexts).

For the historic research that will be done, certainly as part of the Phase I or Phase III project, **Secretary of the Interior's Standards for Historical Documentation [48 FR 44728-44729]** apply. These are

* *Standard I. Historical documentation follows a research design that responds to needs identified in the planning process;*

* *Standard II. Historical documentation employs an appropriate methodology to obtain the information required by the research design;*

* *Standard III. The results of historical documentation are assessed against the research design and integrated into the planning process; and*

* *Standard IV. The results of historical documentation are reported and made available to the public.*

For archaeological documentation, be it Phase I, Phase II, or Phase III, the **Secretary's Standards for Archeological Documentation** also stresses its planning role:

> [Archeological documentation] is guided by a framework of objectives and methods derived from the planning process, and makes use of previous planning decisions, such as those on evaluation of significance [**48 FR 44734**].

There are four standards:

* *Standard I. Archeological documentation activities follow an explicit statement of objectives and methods that responds to needs identified in the planning process;*

* *Standard II. The methods and techniques of archeological documentation are selected to obtain the information required by the statement of objectives;*

* *Standard III. The results of archeological documentation are assessed against the statement of objectives and integrated into the planning process; and*

* *Standard IV. The results of archeological documentation are reported and made available to the public.*

Archaeological documentation consists of the background, field, and laboratory research. The resultant data and other products of that documentation then are applied to the specified planning needs. Those results are then to be reported.

Part of the guidelines, then, is devoted to *Reporting Results* [**48 FR 44736-44737**], which notes that:

> Archeological documentation concludes with written report(s) including minimally the following topics:
>
> 1. Description of the study area;
>
> 2. Relevant historical documentation/background research;
>
> 3. The research design;
>
> 4. The field studies as actually implemented ...;
>
> 5. All field observations;
>
> 6. Analyses and results, illustrated as appropriate with tables, charts, and graphs;
>
> 7. *Evaluation of the investigation in terms of the goals and objectives of the investigation, including discussion of how well the needs dictated by the planning process were served* [italics added];
>
> 8. *Recommendations for updating the relevant historic contexts and planning goals and priorities,*

and generation of new or revised information needs [italics added];

9. Reference to related on-going or proposed treatment activities ...; and

10. Information on the location of original data in the form of field notes, photographs, and other materials.

The report, the guidelines add, must be made available "to the full range of potential users."

The reason that the archaeology is being done is to assist in the historic preservation planning process. The archaeological documentation becomes the entire sequence of work associated with archaeological research: research design, background work, field work, analysis, report production, and curation of the products of the investigation (records as well as artifacts). To be sufficient, though, the archaeological report not only must be a research document, it also must address planning and preservation concerns. There are, then, additional concerns in a compliance archaeological report that are not of moment to most university and museum archaeologists.

Archaeological Documentation: Standards

Ensuring the quality of the archaeological documentation, including that of the report, is done in two ways. The first is by specifying the level of training, amount of supervised and supervisory experience, and the kind of degrees. These standards are set forth for all involved in the historic preservation process, including archaeologists, both in **36 CFR Part 61** [**36 CFR Part 61 Appendix A (b)**] and again in the Secretary's Standards and Guidelines [**48 FR 44739**]. By specifying minimum training standards, the regulations attempt to guarantee a minimum level of professional work. Included in those training and experiential expectations is the requirement that the practicing professional archaeologist have demonstrated the ability to carry research to completion, which will include producing a final, peer-review quality research document of monograph scale.

The second way that quality is assured is in the report review process as set out in **36 CFR 800**. The archaeological report is to be used as part of the planning process. Its approval depends upon the approval of the enabling agency as well as the SHPO/THPO.

Role of the Report and its Distribution

The archaeological report serves not only as a planning document and as a research compilation, it also serves as a summary storage of the data recovered from the archaeological site. This is reflected not only in the expectation that, after each step in the field evaluation process – here labeled Phase I, Phase II, and Phase III – a written report is required, but that such a report is to be considered a part of the curated collection from the site.

36 CFR Part 79 focuses on curation. It in effect expects to exist a written report on the site from which the archaeological materials. The definition of a *collection* from an archaeological site [**36 CFR 79 (a)(2)**] includes not only the material remains recovered, but also the records of that recovery and interpretation. These records specifically include the manuscripts and reports produced as part of the archaeological investigation [**36 CFR 79 (a)(2)(i)**]. Just as important, **36 CFR Part 79** directs repositories holding Federally generated collections to make that collection available, to qualified individuals, for scientific and education purposes [**36 CFR 79.10**]. Obviously, if part of the collection is the report on the archaeological site, then that report must be made available. This is an extremely round-about way requiring that such documents be available. Such reports are, though, public records and usually do not have restrictions placed on access or distribution.

The Secretary of the Interior's Standards and Guidelines **Guidelines for Identification** *Reporting Identification Results* [**48 FR 44723**], **Guidelines for Historical Documentation** *Reporting Results* [**48 FR 44730**], and **Guidelines for Archeological Documentation** *Reporting Results* [**48 FR 44737**] all require that the results of the investigations be made available to the full range of potential users (although the information provided during the identification needs to consider whether such a release of information would threaten the resource). This is to be done in part by publishing the results in articles or monographs, or by distributing the compliance report to libraries and technical clearinghouses.

For Phase I and Phase II projects especially, the report must provide enough detail to allow another investigator, armed with the field notes, to continue from where the report ends. This means the report must contain details regarding site location, condition, pedology and/or stratigraphy, and field and analytical methods. Maps must be present, and they must be accurate enough to enable another person to locate the previous surface collection areas, test units, shovel tests, or whatever examination was employed.

The report also must be able to stand on its own, independent of any special knowledge of the local archaeology or of the project. This "stand-alone" capability will be essential when, in succeeding decades, the report becomes a primary information source of the archaeological evidence in the project area. In some respects, it may seem to the firm producing the report, and certainly to the regulators reviewing reports from the same firm, that the prehistoric background, say, is nearly the same from one study to the next. There is nothing wrong with this, by itself, so long as care is taken to make sure that the information is updated as circumstances warrant (see section 9.2.2. text box "Remarks on Boilerplate"). There is nothing inherently wrong with information redundancy, when that redundancy involves physically different reports. The report generated as part of professional archaeological practice is, in itself, a primary archival record. In planning for the long-term future, assume always that *that* record and no other will survive.

The report is one of five records that will exist of the cultural resources investigation. The other records are

(1) the project documents, ranging from the SOW (scope of work) to correspondence with the client;

(2) the field notes;

(3) the field photographs; and

(4) the laboratory notes and artifact inventory.[1]

Some review agencies request inclusion of the SOW and the artifact inventory as appendices in the report. In other cases, as mentioned in Chapter 8 section 8.5.2., the SOW will be placed as a separate item within the collection when it is turned over.

However, of all of these, the report produced as a result of the compliance archaeological project arguably provides the most information, since in effect it has consolidated and organized other bits of information into a unified corpus that places the artifacts, other material remains, and therefore the field and analyses records into some kind of unified whole.

From an archaeological perspective, the compliance report is a fundamental source of information. Indeed, it is now impossible to do adequate archaeological research in the United States without reference to the compliance reports for the particular region or cultural-historical tradition. But that is only part of the reason that such a document exists. The primary reason that the compliance report exists is because, as a consequence of the Section 106 Process or its counterpart at the state or local level, it represents a planning document.

9.2. Tasks, Contents, and Report Structure

9.2.1. Tasks

There are three basic pieces -- in terms of task sets -- that go into a compliance report:

* the background information that was assembled on the history, prehistory, environment, and previous investigations of the area;

* the results from the field and laboratory analyses, as well as the consolidation and interpretation of those results; and

* the graphics and other illustrations.

The research and other preparatory work for these will need to have been completed before the report itself is written. Some of these result in finished, or nearly finished, products: The historic background, for example, may be a completely finished narrative; while the field photographs may only require selecting the best copies. Some of these require further work before being done: The line drawings showing the field work relative to the project area, or portraying the features from the site, usually will have to be redrawn before they are suitable for publication in the compliance report.

9.2.1.1. Background

The first broad task set involved in the compliance project involves background information. As mentioned in Chapter 4, there are five broad sets of background that need to be assembled for the compliance report:

* the history of the undertaking;

---

1. A sixth set of records, comprising the company's time sheets, mileage records, and so on, that provide information of time needed to conduct the work and the day-to-day structure of the investigation, rarely are available for inspection, even within a firm. This information is privileged information; professional etiquette limits its distribution. The essentials of any time-motion data base should be present somewhere within the field notes.

* the history of previous cultural resources investigations into the site or the project area;

* the past and present structure of the ecological system, including soils, geology, vegetation, and wildlife/fish;

* the specific as well as regional prehistory; and

* the specific as well as regional history.

To a greater or lesser extent all of these, but especially the last two, need to be couched in terms of the state historic preservation plan. Theoretically, all are supposed to have been completed before the field aspects of the project began, although in our experience that is not always the case.

The history of the undertaking was discussed in Chapter 4 section 4.2.1. This will deal with:

* what is planned and the reason(s) for the undertaking;

* the chronology of the project, both how it has developed through time and what the current schedule is;

* the designers and contractors who are responsible for the undertaking; and

* the nature of planned land alteration.

These and similar topics need to be documented, since the issues involved in evaluating adverse effects include the potential for damage to the cultural resource just as much as they do trying to avoid damage. *However, the cultural resources process was never meant to stop a land-alteration activity*; rather, it was meant to give society an opportunity, if it so desires, to recover information that it should have *before* that information is lost. One driving principle, then, in the historic planning process of which compliance archaeology is a part is what strategy or approach is cost-effective. A brief history of the undertaking will provide the agency archaeologists/historic preservation officers as well as the SHPO or the THPO with a sense of what the basic give-and-take issues are, information needed for Section 106 projects as outlined in **36 CFR 800.11**.

The history of previous investigations was discussed in Chapter 4 section 4.2.2. This work summarizes what is known about possible cultural resources within the area of potential effects. That information consists of:

* interviews of people familiar with the area;

* review of the state site files;

* review of previous research reports filed either with the state site files or with the SHPO/THPO;

* examination of local histories and historical documents; and

* examination of maps of the area.

This information is provided so that the agency archaeologists/historic preservation officers as well as the SHPO/THPO are aware of what already exists or could exist in the area of potential effects (or, conversely, if anything ever *has* been located despite previous attempts). Again, for Section 106 projects, this is requested in **36 CFR 800.11**.

The environmental background was discussed in Chapter 4 section 4.3. This presents the past and present structure of the local physical/ecological setting, and serves three purposes:

* to recount what the ecological system involving the project area was like and how it changed through time, so that any cultural resources -- especially archaeological sites -- may be understood in their context;

* to explain what the ecological world involving the project area is like now, or at least what it should be like, so that questions involving landscape ecology and site integrity have a baseline comparison; and

* to set out the geological or pedological properties that may influence doing archaeology within the project area.

The environmental background serves both to provide a possible world-setting for any cultural resources that might be discovered or are already known to exist within the project area, and to provide a sense of what the physical world there is like now (or at least, what should be there). To this information eventually will be added a description of the project area or site as it currently exists.

Given the first three sets of background information, the prehistoric and historic backgrounds now have meaning. The cultural resources identified within the project area will not just be assessed in their own right, they will be assessed relative to the state historic preservation plan and, therefore, in terms of the eligibility for listing on the National Register. The prehistoric and historic background narratives supply an understanding of the current status of knowledge, particularly in terms of standing research questions. And once more, for Section 106 projects, such cultural contexts are requested in **36 CFR 800.11**.

9.2.1.2. Analysis

The second broad task set that requires completion for the compliance project is the collection and analysis of the data. The data collection as a field exercise has been discussed in Chapters 5, 6, and 7, as have levels of analysis.

There are really three steps in the analysis of an archaeological site, be it at the professional or the academic level. The first involves analyses done in the field, which are recorded in the field notes. The second involves the analyses done on the material remains brought back from the field. This work is done in the laboratory and is recorded in the analysis notes and similar records. The extent of analyses in both the first and second step depend upon if the project is Phase I survey, Phase II testing, or Phase III data recovery.

The third step takes place as the part of the report dealing with the results of those analyses is written. It will be at that stage that the writer -- usually the project manager -- begins to assess the patterning of physical remains over the site, and compare what was found with what is known already about the archaeological culture represented. This step involves (to the extent warranted by the archaeological deposit) both refined use of the existing literature and appropriate use of statistical tests.

When analyses are thought of, they usually will be thought of in terms of understanding the archaeology represented. However, a compliance archaeology project is not only archaeological research in its own right, it also is a planning exercise. The compliance report becomes as much a planning document as it does a stand-alone research monograph. Hence, analysis is also done in terms of the eligibility of the archaeological site for listing on the National Register, as well as in terms of what changes may or may not be needed in the proposed undertaking. This will constitute a "Recommendations" chapter in the report submitted by the practicing archaeologist, and results in a level of professional responsibility well beyond anything normally expected in the traditional archaeological literature.

9.2.1.3. Figures and General Art Work

The third task set involved in setting up the compliance report is preparation and production of figures and other art work. Archaeologists are visually oriented, and professional reports can contain a large number of figures and illustrations. Some types of figures are found in all levels of compliance report; others are special to the needs of the particular report, be it Phase I, Phase II, or Phase III. In situations where there is a separate graphics department, the sooner the figures can be handed over to the staff for final rendering, the better. Like the laboratory, a graphics department represents a service that is shared by the entire firm, and they have scheduling concerns of their own.

Who takes the artifact photographs depends upon the nature of the project and the structure of the firm. In smaller firms, usually the project manager or the laboratory manager will do the artifact photographs. In larger firms, the project manager or laboratory manager may select the artifacts to be photographed, schedule a time with a member of the graphics department, then work with the staff member to get the pictures taken.

Many states have report preparation guidelines that stipulate some of the figures, drawings, or maps that must be included in the report. It is the professional archaeologist's responsibility to have a copy of those guidelines. The following gives some sense of the more common figures used or needed.

General Location of the Project or Undertaking

The first figure normally needed consists of an outline of the state and where, in the state, the project was located. Such figures usually consist of two parts presented as one figure:

* an outline of the state with the county outlined or shown, superimposed over

* a portion of the USGS 7.5. minute topographic map showing more specifically where the project area was.

That locational map serves a couple purposes. It allows the agency and SHPO/THPO reviewers to visualize the setting that is being described. It also helps to locate the project area for future researchers. The compliance report may be an archaeological monograph, and it may be a planning document, but it also is an archival record that gives meaning to collections recovered (or the failure of any collections to be recovered). The physical world changes -- towns are abandoned, houses built -- and the maps within the cultural resources reports document the cultural geographic world at the time the field work was done.

Map or Plans for the Proposed Project

The second figure that will be included in all reports will be a map of the proposed undertaking. This may be compiled by the graphics department, but for most projects -- especially Phase I projects -- this usually consists of a photocopy reduction of the plans submitted by the developer or agency to state or county planners for permitting and review.

Regional Map Showing Locations of Known Cultural Resources

The presence of a map showing structures listed or considered eligible for listing on the National Register, along with previously identified archaeological sites, varies by SHPO/THPO protocol. Some states prefer this to be done, since it gives a sense of what is known in the area; other states do not want such a map made, since it may compromise the privileged information contained in the site files. New York, for example, in the past generally has just given a list of what sites are located within a given distance of the project area, and has been careful about releasing specifics. Both Georgia and Maryland, though, will have reports that not only provide locations, but actual site boundaries presented on the appropriate segment of the USGS 7.5 minute topographic map.

Such a figure, if prepared, usually will be found in Phase I and Phase II reports. The sites and structures will be identified on the figure, which will use the most recent USGS 7.5 minute sheet as its base. Accompanying the figure will be a table listing the sites shown on the figure, along with their cultural-historical affiliation, National Register status, previous investigations and reports, and so on.

Map of State or Regional Physiographic Provinces

Often, a map of the state or region's physiographic provinces will be included in the section of the report treating the environmental background. Some states request such inclusion; others do not. The purpose is again to give a sense of location within a larger physical world.

Historic Maps

The nature and inclusion of historic maps vary by area of the country, by project, and by company. The purpose of including such maps is to document the presence or absence of possible historic archaeological sites. Usually such maps are expected as part of Phase I highway corridor surveys and bridge replacements. Inclusion of such maps for areal project areas is necessary only if structures and other historic features are actually shown to have been present in the project area. Chapter 4 section 4.2.2.5. gives a listing of what kinds of maps may be available.

Historic Photographs

For historic archaeological sites especially, photographs showing previously standing structures or land use are particularly useful and will be reproduced on an as-needed basis.

Tip: Photocopy Reduction of Project Maps

Project maps prepared in response to planning and permitting needs often are 24 x 36 inch blue line renderings. These need to be reduced to fit on the largest sheet of paper normally bound into a compliance report: 11 x 17 inches. With one-inch margins, that requires reduction of the image to 9 x 15 inches (38 percent reduction); with half-inch margins, to an image of 11 x 16 inches (46 percent reduction). There is a trick to doing this.

The idea is to do a series of photo-reduced images from the project map, align them, then paste together a final composite image that is a seamless as possible. Photocopy machines create a distorted image during the reduction process. This means that several images need to be made of different parts of the map. These can then be assembled as a mosaic, which helps make sure that all of the lines of the image will line up.

Just as important, though, before any reduction is started, is to provide, in light pencil somewhere on the original plans, a bar scale for the plans being reduced. Nearly all blue line design drawings will present the scale as a verbal ratio, such as "one inch = 50 feet." Engineers, as a by-product of their sequestering during college, do not think that project maps will ever be used at any other size than the size they are made at. As a result, there almost never is a bar scale included. With an image reduced to 46 percent of the original, a scale that reduced at the same time makes life easier for whoever is doing the final paste-up to produce a new and reasonably accurate bar scale.

Map of the Project Area Showing Field Tests Locations

A figure required of all reports is one showing where within the project area field work was done. For Phase I survey projects, this will present locations of surface collection/examination areas or shovel test transects. For Phase II testing projects, this will present the locations of test units or of controlled surface collection areas. For Phase III data recovery projects, this will show the areas of excavation, and will then be accompanied by a site map. All should also show places where structures once stood, structures now stand, and bounds of sites previously recorded.

For Phase I projects where subsurface testing was done, the map usually will also serve in subsequent figures as a base map showing locations of shovel test units that contained or did not contain artifacts, as well as approximate site boundaries if materials were indeed found. In situations where a large number of artifacts were recovered, the shovel test units become points used for generating an iso-frequency contour map of artifact distribution.

We learned about archaeology from that ... Historic Photographs

The report generated as part of the compliance process will serve as an archival record in its own right. That does not mean that it needs to be dull; anything (within reason) that enhances the human nature of the enterprise will be welcomed. An excellent example of this is the approach taken by Southeastern Archeological Services, Inc., toward the handling of the historic backgrounds and project histories.

Most of the reports we have done have had a minimum of illustrations for the historic background: We have just kind of gone in and provided a verbal summary of events, along with appropriate maps and, for those infamous NYS-DOT reports, an enormous number of photographs showing project corridors. Functional, to be sure, but hardly engaging.

One aspect of the reports produced by Southeastern Archeological Services, Inc., is the use of historic photographs to give a sense of temporal and spatial context to the reports. The report on the Bull Creek Site (9ME1) located maybe four kilometers south of Columbus, Georgia, is an excellent example. The second chapter, "Early Investigations Background to the WPA Excavations," includes not only a verbal description, but a series of photographs from the 1920s and 1930s showing the principals involved (a young Frank Schnell with Margaret Ashley in October of 1928, for example, A.R. Kelly with others in a 1936 photograph) and various images of the land along the Chattahoochee in 1936. Indeed, 39.9 percent of the page area of the 14-page discussion consists of historic illustrations.

The result of the time taken to gather the photographic records, copy them, then work them physically into the final report is a truly wonderful record that is very much in keeping with the original intent of the compliance process. That it also is incredibly engaging is just a natural by-product of such attention not only to detail, but to the detail in keeping with the spirit of the cultural resources process.

Where does one gain access to photographs such as these? In addition to the standard background historic research sources mentioned in Chapter 4, there are two other locations for historic photographs germane to cultural resources projects:

* the National Archives; and

* the National Park Service Historic Photography Collection.

The structure and the quality of the reports produced by Southeastern Archeological Services, Inc., continue to serve, for us, as a model for how to produce first-rate compliance reports.

See

Ledbetter, R. Jerald. 1997. *The Bull Creek Site, 9ME1, Muscogee County, Georgia.* Occasional Papers in Cultural Resource Management #9. Georgia Department of Transportation, Office of Environment/Location, Atlanta.

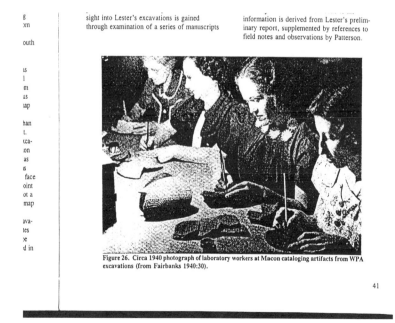

sight into Lester's excavations is gained through examination of a series of manuscripts

information is derived from Lester's preliminary report, supplemented by references to field notes and observations by Patterson.

g
ɔm

outh

ıs
l
m
us
ıap

han
t.
ıca-
ɔn
as
ıs
face
ɔint
ɔt a
map

ıva-
tes
ɔe
d in

Figure 26. Circa 1940 photograph of laboratory workers at Macon cataloging artifacts from WPA excavations (from Fairbanks 1940:30).

41

Figure 9.1. *An image from the 1997 Ledbetter report on 9ME1. It is little details like this that make a report both engaging and instructive. The fascinating thing about this image, too, is that we all are still labeling artifacts in the same way they were labeled in the 1940s.*

For Phase I project maps, it also is important to indicate areas that were not tested, as well as why they were not tested (e.g., slope exceeding SHPO specifications, standing water, fill, paved).

For Phase II and Phase III projects, the corresponding map usually will be the site map. For Phase III projects, this normally is a made-to-order topographic map, the kind expected of any formal, set-piece archaeological investigation.

For Phase II testing projects, a topographic map also usually is expected. However, this map can either be a made-to-order map, or it can make use of the topographic map prepared by the engineering firm or developer for the project area. This depends greatly on the nature of the site, protocols in the state, and the requirements of the SOW.

Unit Profiles and Feature Drawings

Renderings of unit wall profiles occur as line drawings and photographs for Phase II and Phase III reports. For Phase I survey projects, some states require a line drawing or photograph of a typical shovel test profile.

A photograph of each feature (as opposed to posthole stain) identified in the field will be presented in the report. The plan view and profile drawing of the feature, prepared in the field, will be given in the report as well.

Landscape features, like foundations, should be photographed. Again, these will be presented in the report.

Artifacts

For all reports, examples of all diagnostic artifacts should be photographed. Field and laboratory texts provide adequate information on how to produce such photographs, and the reader is referred to those sources.

9.2.2. Contents and Report Structure

The generic report includes the following components, usually in this order:

*   Cover

*   Title page

*   For Department of Defense (DoD) Clients, including COE: DD Form 1473 or equivalent Report Documentation Page (will include an abstract of the report)

*   Table of contents

*   List of tables

*   List of figures

*   Abstract and Management/Executive Summary for reports that result from Federally enabled undertakings; Abstract OR Management/ Executive Summary for most reports that result from non-Federally enabled undertakings;

*   Acknowledgments

*   Chapter 1: Introduction and Statement of Problem

*   Chapter 2: Environmental Background

*   Chapter 3: Prehistoric and Historic Background

*   Chapter 4: Field and Analytical Methods

*   Chapter 5: Results of Investigations

*   Chapter 6: Summary and Recommendations

*   References Cited

*   Appendices (often includes artifact inventories and site forms for new sites)

Cover, Title Page, Contents, Forms

The cover, title page, contents, and completion of any required document forms will be done by the project manager or the principal investigator.

In addition to the title, author(s), firm, client, and date, the cover of the compliance report sometimes requires other information. The cover for many state and Federal reports has a specific format that must be followed. For example, for the Corps of Engineers, the report will have the two-tower castle COE symbol accompanied by a designation: U.S. Army Corps of Engineers, _____ District. Also on the cover will be the contract number as well as a clearance statement, such as "Unclassified. Distribution is Unlimited." Cover page protocols should be specified either in the SOW or the RFP. And it never hurts to ask one's Federal project officer just to make sure.[2]

_____

2. As was mentioned in Chapter 3, all Federal projects have, at the time the RFP is issued, a designated project officer. The project officer is the government's representative charged with making sure that the vendor or contractor carries out the requirements of the SOW and RFP. Funding authorization usually does not go directly through the project officer, but instead through a contracting or awards officer, who acts in part on the approval and recommendation of the project officer, subject to specific contracting and award guidelines. The project officer, in effect,

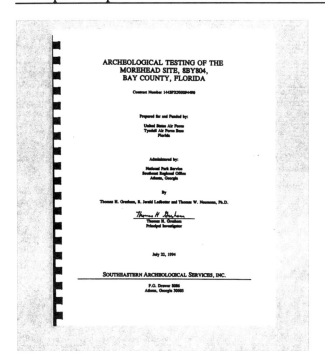

Figure 9.2. Example of a typical compliance report title page. Information includes agency for which the work was done, the contract number, and similar administrative information. Also included will be the signature of the individual who served as principal investigator for the project.

The title page will carry again the title, author(s), firm, client, and date. For government reports, it will have contract numbers. It also will have something else not encountered for academic-generated studies: The signature of the principal investigator.

Different agencies, regions, firms, and SHPOs/THPOs have different ways of titling reports. We have found it useful to present, either as the title or the sub-title, the nature of the project itself, thus:

A Phase II Archeological Investigation of the Johnson's Spring Site (21HU35), Houston County, Minnesota

Where there is a site number, it should be used in the title, as should the county and state.

Some Federal agencies will require that a title page form summarizing the nature of the document also be completed and included.

---

represents the expectations of society for how the project is done; the contracting officer represents the financial interests of society. All whom we have known are zealously conscientious of the responsibility that has been entrusted to them by the country. They are interested in the work being done correctly, which means in the spirit of the statutes and in satisfaction of the SOW. If there are questions or needs for clarification, then do not hesitate to ask the project officer.

Authorship, Principal Investigator

The *principal investigator* is the individual who developed the research design, coordinated the field and laboratory research, performed a substantial part of the analyses, and authored the bulk of the report. That is, the *principal investigator* was the principal investigator. If the project manager directs the field investigation, supervises or performs the analyses, and authors the bulk of the report, and yet is not designated the principal investigator of that report, then there are some problems.

The *author* is the individual who wrote the bulk of the report. Usually the author and the principal investigator are synonymous, and come together as the *project manager* or *project director*.

There are situations where heads of firms or of cultural resource divisions remove the names of the main author and substitute their own. A similar practice occurs where such supervisory personnel add their names to the list of authors simply because of their positions within the firm. Both are done with the justification that, without the existence of the CEO, branch chief, or division head, the project would not exist; a poor argument for the fiscal and organizational integrity of the firm. As discussed in Chapter 6 fn. 5, such acts are unethical. Further, such acts are considered plagiarism: Most Federal agencies are specific in their requirement that the author of the report be listed as the author, and that those listed as authors did, indeed, write – not just edit or supervise the people who authored – a substantial amount of the report.

The table of contents, list of tables, and list of figures all will be assembled by the project manager, who will be the senior author of the report and, under most circumstances, the principal investigator as well.

Abstracts, Management/Executive Summaries

All compliance reports begin with a summary statement of the report contents. This will be given variously as the abstract, preface, management summary, or executive summary, and will be written by the project manager. This summary statement does three things:

* It summarizes the nature of the archaeological investigation performed;

* it summarizes the results of that investigation; and

* it states what the professional archaeologist's recommendations are.

This will be the very first part of the document that is actually read. The review agency and SHPO/THPO archaeologists will go from this summary statement directly to the Recommendations chapter for clarification, and then will start working through the report.[3]

Acknowledgments

All reports will carry an acknowledgments page. This will be assembled if not written entirely by the project manager. The tone is unemotional, straightforward, and courteous, and will state what contributions the individual made to the project. Acknowledgments also follow a general order:

* members of the client firm directly involved with the project;

* project officers and related individuals of the government agency enabling or regulating the project;

* local government officials who may have assisted in making the project work;

* staff and crew who participated in the field work and subsequent analyses;

* specialists and additional authorities who assisted with the research; and

* production staff who assembled and produced the report.

Some SHPO/THPO reporting guidelines request that the compliance report contain a complete listing of all who participated in the field and laboratory aspects of the project, and the nature of their roles. Placing those names in an acknowledgments section often satisfies that request.

Chapter 1: Introduction and Statement of Problem

The opening chapter will be written by the project manager and will follow a basic formula:

* nature of the project, including where and when it was done;

* authorizing code that has initiated the cultural resources process;

* who directed or supervised the work;

* history of the undertaking and reason that the field investigation was needed;

* summary of project impacts;

* research design and objectives; and

* the contents of the report.

The first chapter addresses *Standard I* and to some extent *Standard II* of the **Secretary of the Interior's Standards for Archeological Documentation**, and was discussed in Chapter 4 section 4.2.1. Most of the information for the first chapter will be contained in the SOW and in the firm's bid proposal.

The first chapter also will have at least two figures. The first figure will be a map showing the location of the project area relative to local civil landmarks, along with some inset figure showing where that figure is located in the state. The second figure will be of the project area itself. The first figure will be made to order by the professional archaeologists or the graphics department. The second usually will be a photocopy reduction of the project map.

Chapter 2: Environmental Background

The environmental background may be a stand-alone chapter, or it may be integrated into a larger background or context chapter that includes historic and prehistoric backgrounds. The environmental background may be assembled by the project manager, the field supervisor, or any other member of the staff seen sufficiently capable of providing the information required; in engineering/environmental firms, this may be done by resident ecologists or environmental scientists. The environmental background addresses three concerns:

(1) what the general structure of the ecological system has been over time, so that the past cultures represented by the archaeological remains can be understood in their larger ecological context;

(2) what the structure of the local ecological system over the project area or site is like now relative to what potentially could be present; and

(3) what the expected pedological and geological conditions should be.

The information needed for the environmental background is located in several places, such as paleoecological review articles for the given region, forestry and wildlife regional summaries, and USDA NRCS county soil surveys.

---

3. Actually, like all archaeologists, they probably will flip through the report, find the pictures, and read the captions, before they do anything else.

Occasionally a separate figure may be produced for the chapter on the environmental setting. The figure may show physiographic provinces, forest types, structure of the actual vegetation community, or even an idealized schematic of how physiographic provinces relate to regional topography. In wooded project areas, a useful figure to have prepared and placed in this chapter, particularly for Phase I reports, is one portraying tree demographics as part of an analysis of succession. Such a figure helps in documenting land-use history relative to site integrity.

Chapter 3: Prehistoric and Historic Background

The prehistoric and historic background narratives will be written by the project manager, the project's field supervisor, or other members of the staff able to do this. Many firms have staff historians whose tasks will include preparing the historic background and assembling the information from the state site files.

The prehistoric and historic backgrounds serve two basic purposes:

*   summarizing what is known about existing prehistoric and historic cultural resources within the vicinity of the proposed undertaking; and

*   providing what amounts to a cultural context for understanding any existing or potential cultural resources.

This chapter has four purposes: To identify research questions; to describe where cultural resources will be found; to show command of the area's research; and to show interaction with area's professional social network.

The need for prehistoric and historic backgrounds is addressed often in the Secretary of the Interior's Standards and Guidelines. This work provides a summary status of research to date, which in turn allows the review agencies and the SHPO/THPO to understand how common -- or not -- the particular resource is and what its potential contribution might be. This is even more critical in historic situations where there is a possibility of a historically recorded person or event of consequence known for the area: The archaeological site may gain significance and Register-eligibility by being directly associated.

Details on the contents of and information sources for this chapter were given in Chapter 4 sections 4.4. and 4.5. The prehistoric and the historic backgrounds usually will be subdivisions within the project report chapter devoted to this topic. Often, this portion of the report will be based upon corporate boilerplate, especially those parts treating the prehistory. It becomes the project manager's responsibility to make

sure that the document has been reworded and corrected to address the current project (few things are more disastrous than to have cannibalized text from another project but to have forgotten to delete the previous project specifics, like site number or name; see box "Remarks on Boilerplate Material").

Usually at least one figure and one table will be required for this chapter. The figure would be one showing the locations of known prehistoric and historic sites within a given distance of the undertaking. *However, the presence of such figures depends upon SHPO/THPO protocols, since in some parts of the country this provides too much specific information to collectors.* The table provides a list of the known cultural resources in the vicinity of the project area, as well as a brief listing of what the site represents, when it was investigated, and where the results were published.

Additional figures and tables depend upon the nature of the report. Some may include photographs of standing structures; occasionally reports will have a table or chart showing the cultural-historical sequence for the region.

Chapter 4: Field and Analytical Methods

The field and analytical methods[4] will be written by the project manager, the laboratory manager, and the field supervisor. In situations that involved specialists, either in the field or during the analyses, those individuals should have provided summaries of their methods that the project manager will need to integrate into this section of the report. Most of these methods sections are formulaic and previously written.

The field methods need to address:

*   number of units or transects and how they were positioned over the landscape, or how the surface collection area was prepared and the size of collection areas used;

*   how excavations were done, the depth to which they were taken, and the fill processed;

*   any mapping protocols;

*   any sampling protocols, such as flotation (how much from what contexts, how stored, and was it screened first); and

*   any kind of in-field discard policy.

---

4. The concern here is with *methods*, not *methodology*. "Methods" refers to how things were done; "methodology" refers to how the overall research is organized, designed, and logically structured. The two words do not mean the same thing, even though they often are used as synonyms.

Remarks on Boilerplate Material

As mentioned in Chapter 3, "boilerplate" refers to written material that is used over and over again with only slight modification. It is, indeed, a mainstay of archaeological compliance reports, primarily the prehistoric background and laboratory methods sections of those reports.

The boilerplate used for the prehistoric background, the laboratory methods, and, to a lesser extent, the historic background and environmental setting, represents a sort of Volkswagen Beetle approach to those parts of the report: the seemingly same thing that is modified slightly as information improves or the project changes. Each report should be a stand-alone document, prepared as if no other compliance report for the area will survive. Each must, then, have a prehistoric background that is adequate in and of itself. This drives reviewers crazy, of course, especially after they have read through the same thing 20 or 30 times in a year. Nevertheless, it is necessary.

There is a danger with boilerplate, though: failure to alter it as the circumstances demand. There are two cases here:

* changes in what is now known about the field; and

* failure to remove the references made to whatever project report the text was lifted from for the new report.

Failure to upgrade information is a problem in staying abreast of advances in the discipline. Most of this information will be in the reports curated at the SHPO/THPO or state site files, or will be published as research articles generated by professionals in regional archaeology journal series. While proportionally less in the way of primary data for the United States is produced now by university or museum research, the information that does come from that research tends to provide the critical syntheses that needs must be addressed in any archaeological report. If there is anything out there that has been overlooked, hopefully the agency reviewers or the SHPO/THPO will catch the omission and mention it; the more eyes keeping track of things, the better. The public-sector archaeology people most often are the ones who know what is being done, if for no other reason than that large amounts of the most recent research must cross their desks each month as part of the review process.

The second case, failure to remove references to previous projects, is at best embarrassing. This happens because the person preparing the background document of concern downloads the word-processing file from the last time the particular background was used, alters it as is warranted, then saves it under a new title that eventually gets placed in the draft report. There are at least two sets of eyes that should catch a failure to change things like site name or project area: the person who originally accessed then worked on the document and the project manager. Although this sort of thing happens, it is a bit careless.

The analysis methods need to address:

* how artifacts and other materials from the site were processed, catalogued, labeled, and prepared for curation;

* how individual artifacts were analyzed (Were they weighed and measured? Were they examined using magnifiers or dissecting microscopes?); and

* was the information loaded into a computer file.

The methods chapter also must state where the materials will be curated.

The methods chapter satisfies the stipulations in the Secretary of the Interior's Guidelines for details on how information was obtained, especially in terms of the procedures used to examine and area for potential cultural resources. The field methods section specifically is seen to be critical to the Section 106 Process, since one of the review concerns for determinations of adverse effect is how it is known that archaeological materials were or were not present.

As a note: The figure or site map showing the distribution of collection areas, shovel tests, or excavation units will be presented, not in the "Methods" chapter, but in the following "Results" chapter.

Chapter 5: Results of Investigations

The results of the investigation will be written by the project manager, who will integrate contributions by the laboratory manager and any specialists involved in the project. The graphics department or equivalent will also contribute photographs and line drawings, the latter based on drafts prepared by the field supervisor or the project manager.

The results chapter will vary in structure by the nature of the project: Phase I, Phase II, or Phase III. The contents serve two basic roles:

* analysis and interpretation of the data in terms of the archaeology of the site or project area; and

* application of the information to the basic compliance issues that necessitated the investigation.

The archaeology is used in Phase I and Phase II analyses to support recommendations made to the review agencies. For Phase I, those recommendations essentially are whether or not there are any archaeological sites present that will be adversely affected by the proposed undertaking. For Phase II, those recommendations are whether or not the archaeological site present is eligible for listing on the National Register and will be adversely affected by the proposed undertaking.

The levels of analysis expected for Phase I and Phase II were explained in Chapters 5, 6, and 8, and need not be repeated. The analyses done are to be sufficient to answer the questions implied by the particular stage of the compliance process, as well as to satisfy any professional obligation that having accessed the archaeological materials entails.

For Phase III data recovery, usually the only issue is the analysis of the archaeological materials. Phase III is implemented because the site will be compromised as a by-product of the undertaking; the report then becomes, with the artifacts and the field records, one of three interlinked bodies of information that preserves what has been otherwise lost. The levels of analyses expected were given in Chapters 7 and 8.

The amount of graphics and tables required in the results chapter depends upon both the level of analysis and the circumstances. Common to all reports will be

* the equivalent of a site or project map showing where excavations or surface collections were done;

* the equivalent of a site or project map showing planned impacts relative to the distribution of known or discovered archaeological deposits;

* portrayal of all feature as line drawings and as photographs; and

* photographs of all diagnostic artifacts.

After that, the level of documentation varies by the level of analysis. Phase I reports seldom require any more documentation than the above, although some SHPO/THPO protocols request photographs showing typical shovel test profiles or the condition of the project area at the time field work was done.

Phase II reports often will have photographs showing the appearance of the site at the time that it was investigated as well as tables given the metrics of artifacts or artifact classes. Phase II reports also will have schematic or actual renderings of unit profiles, and often will have photographs of the same. This reflects the concern for the structure of the deposit.

Phase III reports will have a thorough presentation of

field photographs, line drawings, and artifact photographs. There will be a surfeit of tables as well; tables help to condense the essentials of information in an accessible way.

Chapter 6: Summary and Recommendations

The summary and recommendations will be written by the project manager. This reflects the planning nature of the entire compliance process, and while at one level formulaic, at another level is tailored to the specific needs of the undertaking and whatever cultural resources might be present.

For Phase I and Phase II reports, the summary and recommendations chapter summarizes the nature of the project (the report's chapter 1), how the work was done (the report's chapter 3), and what the analyses of the field results were (the report's chapter 5). This usually requires no more than one or two paragraphs.

The recommendations then follow from the summary. Based upon the results of the field investigation (the report's chapter 5), and following from what was revealed during the background research (the report's chapter 4), the professional archaeologist will make recommendations (*never* determinations; see **36 CFR Part 63 - Determinations of Eligibility for Inclusion in the National Register of Historic Places**). These often will be one of the following.

Phase I:

* No materials present and no further work is needed (Agency interpretation: Therefore no possible adverse effects); or

* Materials present, but the disturbed context and/or lack of data potential means that the site does not satisfy criteria for listing on the National Register, and therefore no further work appears warranted (Agency interpretation: Therefore, no adverse effects); or

* Materials present, and there is sufficient evidence to suggest that the site might satisfy criteria for listing on the National Register; either further testing is recommended (Phase II) or some kind of project redesign is needed to avoid the site (Agency interpretation: Therefore there may be adverse effects); or

* Materials present reflecting the previously documented presence of a site listed, or considered eligible for listing on the National Register; either further testing is recommended (Phase II) or some kind of project redesign is needed to avoid the site (Agency interpretation: Therefore there may be adverse effects).

Some Options for Avoiding Adverse Effects

Phase III data recovery is also called mitigation because full-scale excavation is seen to mitigate or offset the adverse effects of the proposed undertaking. Data recovery is always to be viewed as the option of last resort; it is considered itself to be an adverse effect, although one that can offset the adverse effects of the undertaking. If there is a way to avoid having the site or its threatened portion destroyed, then it is preferable to adopt that strategy rather than excavate.

There are many options, but some of the more common involve

* re-designing the project so that it does not damage the site;

* restructuring the use of the property so that the site cannot be damaged;

* trading one portion of the property to the public jurisdiction in exchange for another portion; or

* selling the land.

In some situations, it may be possible to re-design a project so that the site itself is not damaged. This of course depends upon the nature of the project: For instance, bridge footings generally cannot be re-located without re-designing the entire bridge or moving the highway, both being cost-prohibitive. However, a situation where a building foundation will compromise the site might be solved by switching the location of the parking lot and the building, such that the site is paved over and therefore preserved.

The most common way in which a compromise is reached is through re-arranging how the land will be used. This will involve *protective covenants* and *plat notations*, which in effect restrict how the land can be used. These agreements are entered into the deed to the property, and are recorded at the county level in most cases. Such limitations often can reduce the value of the land, and the developer is entitled to take that reduced value as a business loss [see also **36 CFR Part 67 - Historic Preservation Certifications Pursuant to Sec. 48(g) and Sec. 170(h) of the Internal Revenue Code of 1986**]. This is a matter that the developer needs to discuss with his or her accountant and tax attorney.

Another option is for the land containing the cultural resource to be traded to the government or civil authority for an equally suitable parcel. This is a wonderful win-win situation, although it is not often possible.

The equivalent of trading the land is having the land purchased. The Archaeological Conservancy purchases threatened archaeological sites for preservation, as do various state and national historic preservation groups. Usually it is of service to the client for the professional archaeologist to be aware of what options do exist, so again everyone can come out a winner in the Process: The developer and the society writ large that would benefit from continued preservation of the archaeological site. It is also possible at times that the archaeological site is part of a larger environmental setting where it might be saved through purchase by The Nature Conservancy or similar group.

Remember that the whole idea of the Section 106 Process, and its counterparts at the state and local level, is to give enough notice ahead of time so that contingencies can be planned for. This usually does not happen because most engineering, architecture, and business schools do not mention the need to consider cultural resources as part of project design (in contrast, all programs in Urban Planning and Regional Planning *do*). Although the archaeologist, be it as a private practitioner or government regulator, often will be blamed unjustly for what to the developers and designers appear to be unpublicized – and certainly will be unanticipated – requirements, it still remains his or her professional responsibility to come up with ideas for solutions that assist the client while protecting the needs and rights of society.

Phase II:

* Further testing from the Phase I project indicates that the site does not satisfy the criteria needed for listing on the National Register, and no further work appears warranted (Agency interpretation: Therefore there will be no adverse effects); or

* The site does satisfy criteria for listing on the National Register, and either data recovery (Phase III) is recommended to mitigate those adverse effects, or the project needs to be redesigned (Agency interpretation: Therefore there will be adverse effects).

Phase III:

* Usually the only recommendation that will be involved with a Phase III project is under situations where only part of the site was lost because the project was otherwise redesigned. In that situation, the recommendations usually involve protecting in perpetuity those portions of the site left undamaged.

Often, Phase I and Phase II reports treating materials considered potentially eligible for listing on the National Register will provide a figure showing the project area, the extent of the site, and how the area might be or might not be used. This is possible, although much less likely, for Phase III data recovery reports.

References Cited

The list of references cited will be assembled by the project manager from the various contributors. It is helpful for each contributor to provide not only a computer file, but also a separate file or at least section of the document where the full reference is given.

Appendices

The appendices generally include the artifact inventory from the site and, for Phase I surveys, the site forms for any new sites discovered. Additional materials sometimes include the SOW, the RFP, and certain kinds of correspondence and communications. For example, the surveys performed on behalf of the New York State Department of Transportation required summaries of all interviews performed; those were placed in an appendix at the end of the particular report.

The laboratory manager will be responsible for supplying the artifact inventory. The remainder of the material usually will be the responsibility of the project manager or someone delegated by the project manager to assist with these aspects of the report production.

9.3. Production and Assembly of the Draft Report

The mechanics in assembling a report under contract deadlines requires fine choreography. The pieces break down into

* the writing,

* the figure production,

* the table production,

* the text production,

* the duplication and assembly, and

* the delivery.

Although many individuals have the talents and skills to perform all of these steps, the time it would take for one or two people to assemble a report is too great for the needs of the client. Small companies tend to double up assembly tasks; larger firms, or the archaeology branch of an engineering firm will have a graphics department, secretarial pool, production staff, and laboratory staff who, under the coordination of the project manager or principal investigator, will produce the draft final report and the final report.

The first node is the project manager. The project manager will have written a sizeable part of the report, and will be designated the primary author. He or she is responsible for

* gathering together all of the other material that people may have written, including a master list of references cited;

* putting it together into one continuous document;

* preparing many of the tables used in the text;

* integrating all of the figure and table references; and

* compiling the table of contents, list of figures, and list of tables.

At this point, the project manager should have sole charge over the proto-report, which under most circumstances will exist as some kind of word-processing file.

The second node where the pieces come together involves editing, and depends upon the size and structure of the firm. Some firms maintain full-time in-house editors. It is their responsibility to serve as copy editors as well as document editors, checking to make sure that all figures cited indeed are listed, that all references cited indeed are listed, and so on. In other firms, this task may be the responsibility of the division or branch manager, or whoever is the immediate supervisor of the project manager. In any case, it is always wise to have a second person go through the document.

The third node where the pieces of the proto-report come together involves whether or not the document is submitted electronically for review. If it is, then the draft report must be assembled electronically, which means that the figures and tables need to be integrated into the text. Electronic submission also requires a file-server sufficiently large -- and a technical staff that has allowed the file server to stay sufficiently large -- to permit movement of large documents as e-mail attachments, especially at the government reviewer's end (which is increasingly *not* the case) -- to work.

In most cases, submission will be as a hardcopy. This means that the third decision node will require formatting the document. In larger firms, this may be the task of the editor or of a full-time desk-top publishing specialist; in smaller firms, this may be the responsibility of the secretary or even the project manager.

Formatting refers to setting up the document as it is meant to appear in hardcopy form. There is a caution here. Many Federal agencies have a preferred formatting style for the draft report: For example,

Tip: Typefaces and Style of Presentation

In situations where the Lead agency or the SHPO/THPO has specified how the draft and final reports are to look, there is little leeway for how the report should appear. However, in situations where such are not stipulated, then the flexibility afforded by current word-processing programs enable a number of enhancements to be made to the text-rendering of the report.

The first and most fundamental enhancement is typeface: **Use a serif typeface for the body of the report.** This is related to legibility and readability.

Words are read as entire units, generally by looking at the upper half of the word. Serif fonts, such as the AGaramond used for the body of *Practicing Archaeology*, are much less ambiguous over the top half of their letters than are sans-serif letters, where the stroke is uniform in thickness (that is, uniform in "weight of line," of thickness and thinness, over the entire face of the printed letter). Thus, words rendered with serif characters are much easier to read (Tschichold 1962:35-36; McLean 1997:42-44; see also Doak, Doak, and Root 1985; Beaumont 1987; Groff 1990; MS Neumann 1994). Serif characters have variations in the thicknesses of the strokes that further increase legibility. Since the serifs of the letters making up the word also help link the associated letters together, and since words are read as units (and not letter-by-letter), the result is a more legible text compared with sans-serif type faces such as Helvetica.

Serif type faces also lend an air of authority. The way in which information is presented in most research fields is done by using serif typefaces, usually in what is called an Old Face,

roman style. Textbooks are printed that way; journals are printed that way. Using a similar print face then draws a connection between the authority of the formal knowledge of the field and the authority of the compliance report.

By the way, where there are extensive tables of numbers, the recommendation is to use a typeface that also has numbers that will extend above or below the line. This makes distinguishing the numbers easier.

(For aesthetic reasons as well as layout reasons, at times a sans-serif type may be preferred. The rule-of-thumb is to make use of a sans-serif typeface that has variable line thickness within the letter, such as the CG Omega in which the text boxes in *Practicing Archaeology* are done. The variations in stroke thickness, compared to the monoline of pure sans-serif letters, assist in readability. This, though, rarely will be an issue in a compliance report, since text boxes and similar asides will not be present, and since captions will be rendered in the type face used for the body of the document.)

The second enhancement decision involves font size and text layout. Again, it is usually best to chose a font size and layout that duplicates, as close as possible, how formal knowledge in the field is published. This is because the equation will be made in reviewing the document that it, too, has an equal level of authority and expertise (which for a compliance report it most certainly does). These are conditioned responses. Generally, professional publications are produced in 9 - 12-point, and two or three columns. *Science*, for example, is in an 9-point, three-column format; most Anthropology textbooks are in 10-point, two-column formats. Double columns carry

---

double-spaced and single-sided, with page numbers centered at the bottom, and certain margin allowances. Before formatting is done, the SOW and the RFP need to be checked to make sure about how the draft report is supposed to look. If there are *any* questions, just call and ask the agency project officer who has oversight of this particular project.

In some situations, the figures will be stand-alone pages. In other cases, the figures will be scanned into the document and be integrated into the overall text.

With the document now edited and formatted in the manner requested for the draft report, the entire document can be printed.

The second-to-last step is duplicating and physically assembling the draft report. This usually will be the task of the secretarial staff in smaller firms, or the document production staff in larger firms. Some firms will have a copy shop or printer do the copying and binding. Such production requires that a prototype be assembled, unbound, before hand. This will be the master copy from which the duplicates will be made.

The number of draft copies required will be specified in the SOW.

The draft report will then be delivered to the Lead agency and/or to the client. Sometimes a copy of the draft report will go directly to the SHPO/THPO for comment; this depends upon the nature of the project, agency/SHPO/THPO protocols, and actually how well the agency, SHPO/THPO, and professional communities get along. For Federal projects, the draft report generally goes only to the Lead agency for comment, since the professional archaeologist really is serving as the Lead agency's archaeologist.

9.4. The Review Process

The draft report will be submitted by the professional archaeologist ostensibly either to the Federal Lead agency for review, or to the client for review. In reality, it is not unusual for copies of the draft report to go simultaneously to the Lead agency and to the SHPO/THPO, or to the client and the SHPO/THPO or counterpart regulatory authority.[5]

---

5. Archaeology is funny this way. There are protocols and formalities, and a carefully maintained sense of professionalism, yet still everyone recognizes the importance of the resource and their role in its protection that Federal archaeologists and the SHPO/THPO often each will get copies of the draft report. The typical

more sense of authority than do single-column/no-column presentations. Text should always be full-justified. Columns also have the benefit of reducing the number of words per line. Again for readability, it is generally best to limit the number of words per line to 10 - 12.

The third enhancement is overall layout. This requires having a sense of balance between the body of text versus the body of figures or tables as presented. Usually, two-sided printing carries more of a sense of a finished, authoritative product, than does one-sided. As a result, distribution of text bodies and figure/table bodies need to be based on how the entire page-spread will look.

The fourth enhancement is selecting a paper quality that gives a sense of quality while also being cost-effective. It rarely makes sense, for example, to use clay paper/coated paper (in any case, book conservationists have told us that clay paper – glossy paper – is not archivally stable). Usually though, the higher the quality of materials, the more authority the document has.

In summary:

*   Serif typefaces are more readable and project more authority than do sans-serif typefaces;

*   columned text presentation carries more authority than non-column presentations;

*   full-justified text carries more authority (and uses less paper) than unjustified text;

*   figures and tables integrated into the text carry more authority than figures and tables placed on individual pages;

*   two-sided printing carries more authority (and uses less paper) than one-sided; and

*   quality paper carries more authority than low-quality paper.

Beaumont, Michael. 1987. *Type: Design, Color, Character, & Use.* North Light Books, Cincinnati.

Doak, C.C., L.G. Doak, and J.H. Root. 1985. *Teaching Patients with Low Literacy Skills.* Lippincott Co., New York.

Groff, Vern. 1990. *The Power of Color in Design for Desktop Publishing.* Management Information Source Press, Portland OR.

McLean, Ruari. 1997. *The Thames and Hudson Manual of Typography.* Thames and Hudson, London.

Neumann, Mary Spink. 1994. *Developing Effective Educational Print Materials.* Centers for Disease Control and Prevention, Division of STD/HIV Prevention, Training and Education Branch, Atlanta.

Tschichold, Jan. 1962. *Treasury of Alphabets & Lettering* [Translation by Wolf von Eckardt of *Meisterbuch der Schrift*]. Norton, New York.

The review process varies if the project is part of the Section 106 Process or is part of a local or state compliance process.

9.4.1. Section 106 Review

For the Section 106 projects, the Lead agency will have, on staff, archaeologists or a historic preservation specialist. The report will be reviewed, and will be returned to the professional archaeologists will comments. Either those comments must be addressed by the professional archaeologist, or an explanation must be supplied about why they were not incorporated.

procedure is for the agency to review the draft, return it to the professional subcontractor for revision, then send along the revised copy to the SHPO/THPO. This has more to do with common courtesy if not chain-of-command: The agency underwriting/ sponsoring the work should have a chance to see the draft product before an outsider does. And it does happen this way, of course. What is refreshing and human, though, is that this is not always the case, with everyone more concerned about the entire system working as it is meant to work. A self-developed win-win procedure, which may be why so very few agency determinations are challenged by the governing SHPO /THPO and go before the ACHP. The head might say to use Castiglione; but the heart says to follow Thomas Merton.

A second and usually FINAL report will be prepared that meets agency conditions. That report will be passed along to the SHPO/THPO. The SHPO/ THPO has 30 days to comment if the agency argues a finding of no adverse effect. If no comment is received in 30 days, then the SHPO/THPO has accepted the results "without comment," and the agency has satisfied its obligations under Section 106 [see **36 CFR 800.5 (c)**].

If the finding is of an adverse effect, and SHPO/THPO agrees, the situations moves along smoothly with the drafting of an MOA (such a situation, if everyone has been paying attention, means that the site has been deemed eligible for listing on the National Register and will be compromised, and that some sort of mitigative measures are needed). In situations where there is a historic property that will be compromised by a Federally enabled undertaking, the ACHP must be notified. Accompanying that notification must be a copy of the archaeological report -- usually the Phase II report -- along with the MOA (Memorandum of Agreement) [**36 CFR 800.06 (a)(1)**]. The ACHP has 15 days to respond [**36CFR 800.6 (a)(1)(iii)**], whether of not the agency and the SHPO/THPO are in agreement.

What the Physical Product Looks Like and How It Is Made

Archaeological compliance reports are exercises in desk-top publishing. Nearly all firms produce their own reports in house, although many will do the copying and physical assembly in house, then send it to a printer or copy shop for binding.

The vast majority of compliance reports are presented on plain surface 20-lb 8½ x 11-inch paper with at least 90-lb card stock front and back covers. The size and to some degree the paper stock correspond to many documents produced by Federal agencies as well as by the U.S. Government Printing Office. Some SOWs and SHPOs/THPOs will specify the nature and quality of the paper to be used, as well as the stock preference for the covers. Since one copy of the final report will be part of the collection at turn-over, consideration must be given to the archival quality of the paper used for at least that copy of the report.

The physical production of the compliance report consists of the integration of text, images, and tables. In some cases, each of those three sets will be produced on separate pages, and the entire document then collated. This is how almost everyone was producing reports until the widespread availability of image scanners, of word-processing software that easily allowed integration of images, and of desk-top computers with sufficient memory to hold and manipulate scanned images.

In the early 1990s, reports frequently were produced that had the images and tables placed within the flow of the text, but that actually represented an illusion: Those images often were cut then physically pasted onto a master page that then was duplicated. The word-processing software – at the time almost always WordPerfect 5.1 – allowed for setting up figure boxes that provided printed boundaries to frame the

image; scanners were not as available as now and computers commonly found in offices at the time had insufficient memory to handle images anyway. All that was needed was to cut out and mount whatever the image was that fit.

Variations on hand versus electronic pre-assembly of the report depends upon how well-equipped the particular firm is for doing this kind of thing, as well as the demands of the report itself along with any SHPO/THPO or SOW requirements. For example, scanned images probably will be just fine for most cases, but if there is a need for particularly sharp detail, then the images may have to be off-set printed. Some SHPOs/THPOs prefer color photos because of the added detail; many more, though, prohibit the use of color images – despite the increased image quality – because the colors in such images will fade over time.

Another variant involves oversized pages. While most compliance reports will be 8½ x 11 inches, frequently there are images or tables that will not fit on a page that small. Instead, 11 x 17-inch paper will be used, and the page will be folded to allow it to fit within the bounds of the document (the folding consists of placing the side to be bound on the left, folding the right edge up and over and down to be even with that future bound edge, creasing, *then* folding in half that top 8½ x 11 half of the page so that the original paper edge comes back to the right to be even with the first crease). Some firms will do the folding by hand and physically insert the page where it belongs in the yet-to-be-bound document.

Printing in most cases will use a laser printer, and of course photocopying is a form of laser printing. (Indeed, many photocopy machines are now designed to accept print commands directly from the desk-top computer, serving at

Figure 9.3a. *The most common binding system used for compliance reports is comb-binding. This uses a tube-like plastic cylinder, cut with 19 comb-like teeth, to hold together pre-punched pages. Such binding is done using a lever-operated machine that both punches the holes, then assists in spreading the comb binder so that the pages can be put together. Here, the pages are being punched.*

Figure 9.4b. *After the report pages are punched, the plastic binding comb is placed over the teeth on the top of the machine. That plastic comb will need to be spread apart, then held that way so that the comb teeth can be placed through the pages. The same lever used to punch the holes also serves to spread the comb binder apart.*

once as a printer and as a document duplicator.) Ink-jet printers should be avoided in most cases unless the purpose is to produce an unarchived master copy for production purposes, simply because ink-jet inks are water-soluble.

The cover format is often a matter of corporate policy as well as of agency requirements. Some firms design a special cover with some sort of illustration, such as a map of the site, a line drawing of a building, or a suitable photograph. Many more simply provide the standard title information. In any case, the document produced on behalf of Federal clients especially represents the private-sector firm serving as a subcontractor on behalf of the agency, and the document is expected to correspond to agency protocols.

The four most common binding options are, in decreasing order of use:

*   Comb-binding, where a series of 19 rectangular holes are punched along the margin of the page and a tubular plastic "comb," with solid back and 19 plastic "teeth" that slip through the punched holes, is used to hold the document together;

*   a pressed glued system where a card stock cover is wrapped around the pages, the margins impregnated with glue, and the cover and pages pressed together (this is the assembly technique for a paperback or soft-cover books and monographs);

*   a metal or plastic rivet system that places straight metal or plastic posts through round-punched holes in the margins; and

*   infrequently, variants on loose-leaf binders.

Rivet systems are possibly the worst option and are to be avoided. Press-glue binding has tremendous face value but, unless the pages are stitched together as well (and they very seldom will be), vary greatly in durability under use. The use of binders, occasionally requested by some agencies, represents needs special to the agency and how it expects the report to be used.

Plastic comb-binding is by far the most common. It has several advantages: It is inexpensive, accessible to assembly by office staff, and leaves the document capable of modification if needed. Comb-bound volumes also can open and lay flat without assistance, and without placing strain on the bound margins of the pages.

Most firms will have a comb-binding machine, which both punches the holes then allows the comb binder to be spread open and the pages placed over the teeth. Such devices also are widely available for use at print and copy shops.

Most firms will present the comb-bound document with the card-stock cover exposed. Some, though, will place a heavy (0.2 mm) clear-plastic cover over the front and back of the card-stock cover to provide additional protection. This is more a matter of taste and preference; if this option is chosen, it should use plastic sheets that are also 8½ x 11 inches, since this will allow the volume to stand upright on a bookshelf (there are over-sized plastic covers that extend beyond 8½ x 11 inches, resulting in any document set upright resting not on the combined pages of the document but on the plastic sheets).

Figure 9.4c. *This shows the assembling of the punched pages onto the binding comb. The machine holds the binder open, allowing the pages to be dropped into place, much like pages placed in a three-ring binder.*

Figure 9.4d. *With all of the pages placed in the comb, the lever is eased back and the comb closes. The picture here shows again how the teeth of the machine lace through the comb.*

Figure 9.4e. *The final product is a bound document that is robust, durable, and usable. (Photos courtesy Sherri and Joe Thomas, Mail Boxes Etc., Lawrenceville, Georgia)*

For the practicing archaeologist, the final report has been submitted and is now being used by the Lead agency. The firm may be retained to advise the agency; this is fair, and again corresponds to the etymological implications of being a consultant.

9.4.2. Non-Section 106 Review

The review procedure for non-Federal regulations and projects varies by the jurisdiction involved. In our experience, this has meant developing a compliance report for a private-sector or government agency client, which then is presented on behalf of that client either to the SHPO/THPO, or to a state/local government planning commission or equivalent of its historic preservation officer. It is not unusual, for example, to have a formal presentation made by the professional archaeologist before a township planning board. The non-Federal situation is generally both less structured but also more Jeffersonian in the latitude that those charged with reviewing the implications of the archaeologist's results have in treating the results.

9.5. Final Report and Dissemination

For Section 106 projects, the Federal agency generally will return the draft report with a series of requested changes along with a myriad of comments. The practicing archeologist is, after all, the agency's eyes; the archaeologist was hired to do the work because Federal-level funding is such that it is supposed to be more cost-effective to hire outside consultants than to maintain on-staff archaeologists to do the same work.[6]

The practicing archaeologist will address and incorporate, under advisement, the changes suggested by his or her client. With those changes made and accepted, the firm will produce the final report.

The final report may or may not physically look like the draft report. It is always useful to get the agency, SHPO/THPO, or firm for whom the work is being done to allow the draft report to approximate the appearance of the final report. This saves labor and therefore costs, and also from time to time results in the draft report, because everyone found it quite satisfactory, to stand as the final report.

Production of the final report will mean duplication. Most SOWs request a certain number of copies.

These may include an unbound copy so that the SHPO or agency has a master copy available for future production.

Finally, the report is distributed. A core requirement of Federal guidelines is that the compliance report be made available to the interested public (e.g., **Secretary of the Interior's Guidelines for Archeological Documentation**: "Results must be made available to the full range of potential users" [**48 FR 44737**]). How this distribution is done varies by the nature of the agency and its policies, and the nature of the state. Usually, hard copies of the report will be distributed at minimum to

* the client;

* the Lead agency;

* the SHPO/THPO;

* the state site files (if separate from the SHPO);

* the curatorial facility (since a copy of the report is to be part of the collections turned over to that facility); and

* the authors/contributors.

It is usually wise to make sure that principals identified in the Acknowledgments section also each receive copies. This is especially important for civil authorities who were helpful in seeing that the project was done. In some cases, additional copies will be distributed to a mailing list of professional and academic archaeologists within the state, and will be sent as well to the local public and college libraries.

Courtesy Copies

Authors, co-authors, and contributors should each receive a courtesy copy of the final report. If courtesy is not motive enough – and everyone should recognize that ethical behavior is adaptive behavior – then common sense might be. Such exercises in goodwill and professionalism, at a minimal expense (even a 200-page report costs, bound, no more than $10, inclusive of the time needed to run it off and bind it), reaps much more in goodwill.

Some agencies will maintain a publication series that distributes some or all of the studies: The Georgia Department of Transportation, for example, maintains its *Occasional Papers in Cultural Resource Management*. In other cases, the reports are available on demand for the cost of duplication and shipping: New York State Department of Transportation reports done through

---

6. Since the start of the reduction of the Federal work force under the Carter Administration, the GAO and the OPM both have periodically done studies about the cost-effectiveness of maintaining full-time Federal employees to do various tasks, or subcontracting firms from the private-sector to do the same work. For the last quarter-century, the results have indicated that it costs more to subcontract consultants to do the work than it would to do the work in-house, were the staff positions re-established.

Tips: Hearings

Often at the state or local level, the professional archaeologist will need to make a presentation before a planning commission on behalf of the client. The archaeologist, as a specialty witness, should be prepared to inform the public about a subject often shrouded in mystery and misconception. Here are a few tips.

* If using additional witnesses, prepare a list of them in addition to a short summary of yourself. All witness should be identified in terms of their affiliations, qualifications, addresses, and telephone numbers, and availability to answer questions.

* All witnesses should have been to the project location or archaeological site. This is true even for experts on a particular analytical technique such as thermoluminescence who may have been brought in to assist at the hearing. The public (and other decision-makers) appreciate the real-world connection.

* Prepare a written and oral outline of the presentation and testimony. Include the main points to be covered and by whom.

* All potential witnesses and speakers should participate in a dress rehearsal. This is particularly reassuring to the client, plus it lets you see whether or not the team members can communicate effectively and credibly.

* Witnesses and speakers should use references and plans that illuminate main points or help the audience get its bearings.

* Practice the viewing distance for interpreting maps, photos and drawings. Typically, information is presented at too small a scale for effective viewing for an audience member in the back seat. One approach is to make photos of large drawings and illustrations. These can be handed out (and included in the official exhibits in the case of evidentiary hearings).

* Prepare an 8½ x 11-inch copy of your reports and testimony.

* Prepare a single-page fact sheet of critical information about the archaeological aspects of the project. This background information can help the reader interpret your testimony.

* Prepare proposed draft *findings of fact* to help the members of the hearing panel determine if the project meets the applicable regulations.

* Bring extra copies for alternates, staff, clerks, and the audience, including the opposition.

* Visit the hearing room to determine acoustics, behavioral issues, and availability of presentation equipment. Locate a place to stand where the audience and the decision makers will be addressed simultaneously.

the State University of New York Research Foundation have been available that way, as have most Corps of Engineers reports. Many states are now scanning the compliance reports into a master computer file that is accessible through the Internet.

For most states, the SHPO will serve as a de facto if not formal clearinghouse for access to if not distribution of compliance reports. There should be a list of the reports available (hence the importance of providing a title in the report that identifies level as well as location of the archaeological investigation).

For the archaeologist whose research is located within the jurisdiction of the SHPO or the THPO, it is his or her responsibility to check with the SHPO/THPO and be aware of the current holdings. This usually is not a problem for the professional community, since each new project will require someone going in and checking, either directly at the SHPO/THPO or indirectly through references made in the state site files. This may be more of a problem for the academic archaeologist, who usually will need to travel to where those reports are housed if copies are not available through the mail or over the Internet.

Appendix A: Core Federal Regulations and Standards

36 CFR Part 60: National Register of Historic Places

36 CFR Part 800: Protection of Historic Properties

Department of the Interior/National Park Service: Secretary of the Interior's Standards and Guidelines for Archeology and Historic Preservation

PART 60—NATIONAL REGISTER OF HISTORIC PLACES

255

AUTHORITY: National Historic Preservation Act of 1966, as amended, 16 U.S.C. 470 et seq., and E.O. 11593.

SOURCE: 46 FR 56187, Nov. 16, 1981, unless otherwise noted.

§ 60.1 Authorization and expansion of the National Register.

(a) The National Historic Preservation Act of 1966, 80 Stat. 915, 16 U.S.C. 470 et seq., as amended, authorizes the Secretary of the Interior to expand and maintain a National Register of districts, sites, buildings, structures, and objects significant in American history, architecture, archeology, engineering and culture. The regulations herein set forth the procedural requirements for listing properties on the National Register.

(b) Properties are added to the National Register through the following processes.

(1) Those Acts of Congress and Executive orders which create historic areas of the National Park System administered by the National Park Service, all or portions of which may be determined to be of historic significance consistent with the intent of Congress;

(2) Properties declared by the Secretary of the Interior to be of national significance and designated as National Historic Landmarks;

(3) Nominations prepared under approved State Historic Preservation Programs, submitted by the State Historic Preservation Officer and approved by the NPS;

(4) Nominations from any person or local government (only if such property is located in a State with no approved State Historic Preservation Program) approved by the NPS and;

(5) Nominations of Federal properties prepared by Federal agencies, submitted by the Federal Preservation Officer and approved by NPS.

§ 60.2 Effects of listing under Federal law.

The National Register is an authoritative guide to be used by Federal, State, and local governments, private groups and citizens to identify the Nation's cultural resources and to indicate what properties should be considered for protection from destruction or impairment. Listing of private property on the National Register does not prohibit under Federal law or regulation any actions which may otherwise be taken by the property owner with respect to the property.

(a) The National Register was designed to be and is administered as a planning tool. Federal agencies undertaking a project having an effect on a listed or eligible property must provide the Advisory Council on Historic Preservation a reasonable opportunity to comment pursuant to section 106 of the National Historic Preservation Act of 1966, as amended. The Council has adopted procedures concerning, inter alia, their commenting responsibility in 36 CFR part 800. Having complied with this procedural requirement the Federal agency may adopt any course of action it believes is appropriate. While the Advisory Council comments must be taken into account and integrated into the decisionmaking process, program decisions rest with the agency implementing the undertaking.

(b) Listing in the National Register also makes property owners eligible to be considered for Federal grants-in-aid for historic preservation.

(c) If a property is listed in the National Register, certain provisions of the Tax Reform Act of 1976 as amended by the Revenue Act of 1978 and the Tax Treatment Extension Act of 1980 may apply. These provisions encourage the preservation of depreciable historic structures by allowing favorable tax treatments for rehabilitation, and discourage destruction of historic buildings by eliminating certain otherwise available Federal tax provisions both for demolition of historic structures and for new construction on the site of demolished historic buildings. Owners of historic buildings may benefit from the investment tax credit provisions of the Economic Recovery Tax Act of 1981 generally replaces the rehabilitation tax incentives under these laws beginning January 1, 1982 with a 25% investment tax credit for rehabilitations of historic commercial, industrial and residential buildings. This can be combined with a 15-year cost recovery period for the adjusted basis of the historic building. Historic buildings with certified rehabilitations receive additional tax

savings by their exemption from any requirement to reduce the basis of the building by the amount of the credit. The denial of accelerated depreciation for a building built on the site of a demolished historic building is repealed effective January 1, 1982. The Tax Treatment Extension Act of 1980 includes provisions regarding charitable contributions for conservation purposes of partial interests in historically important land areas or structures.

(d) If a property contains surface coal resources and is listed in the National Register, certain provisions of the Surface Mining and Control Act of 1977 require consideration of a property's historic values in the determination on issuance of a surface coal mining permit.

§ 60.3 Definitions.

(a) Building. A building is a structure created to shelter any form of human activity, such as a house, barn, church, hotel, or similar structure. Building may refer to a historically related complex such as a courthouse and jail or a house and barn.

Examples

Molly Brown House (Denver, CO)
Meek Mansion and Carriage House (Hayward, CA)
Huron County Courthouse and Jail (Norwalk, OH)
Fairintosh Plantation (Durham vicinity, NC)

(b) Chief elected local official. Chief elected local official means the mayor, county judge, county executive or otherwise titled chief elected administrative official who is the elected head of the local political jurisdiction in which the property is located.

(c) Determination of eligibility. A determination of eligibility is a decision by the Department of the Interior that a district, site, building, structure or object meets the National Register criteria for evaluation although the property is not formally listed in the National Register. A determination of eligibility does not make the property eligible for such benefits as grants, loans, or tax incentives that have listing on the National Register as a prerequisite.

(d) District. A district is a geographically definable area, urban or rural, possessing a significant concentration, linkage, or continuity of sites, buildings, structures, or objects united by past events or aesthetically by plan or physical development. A district may also comprise individual elements separated geographically but linked by association or history.

Examples

Georgetown Historic District (Washington, DC)
Martin Luther King Historic District (Atlanta, GA)
Durango-Silverton Narrow-Gauge Railroad (right-of-way between Durango and Silverton, CO)

(e) Federal Preservation Officer. The Federal Preservation Officer is the official designated by the head of each Federal agency responsible for coordinating that agency's activities under the National Historic Preservation Act of 1966, as amended, and Executive Order 11593 including nominating properties under that agency's ownership or control to the National Register.

(f) Keeper of the National Register of Historic Places. The Keeper is the individual who has been delegated the authority by NPS to list properties and determine their eligibility for the National Register. The Keeper may further delegate this authority as he or she deems appropriate.

(g) Multiple Resource Format submission. A Multiple Resource Format submission for nominating properties to the National Register is one which includes all or a defined portion of the cultural resources identified in a specified geographical area.

(h) National Park Service (NPS). The National Park Service is the bureau of the Department of Interior to which the Secretary of Interior has delegated the authority and responsibility for administering the National Register program.

(i) National Register Nomination Form. National Register Nomination Form means (1) National Register Nomination Form NPS 10-900, with accompanying continuation sheets (where necessary) Form NPS 10-900a, maps and photographs or (2) for Federal nominations, Form No. 10-306, with continuation sheets (where necessary)

Form No. 10-300A, maps and photographs. Such nomination forms must be "adequately documented" and "technically and professionally correct and sufficient." To meet these requirements the forms and accompanying maps and photographs must be completed in accord with requirements and guidance in the NPS publication, "How to Complete National Register Forms" and other NPS technical publications on this subject. Descriptions and statements of significance must be prepared in accord with standards generally accepted by academic historians, architectural historians and archeologists. The nominating authority certifies that the nomination is adequately documented and technically and professionally correct and sufficient upon nomination.

(j) *Object.* An object is a material thing of functional, aesthetic, cultural, historical or scientific value that may be, by nature or design, movable yet related to a specific setting or environment.

Examples

Delta Queen Steamboat (Cincinnati, OH)
Adams Memorial (Rock Creek Cemetery, Washington, DC)
Sumpter Valley Gold Dredge (Sumpter, OR)

(k) *Owner or owners.* The term owner or owners means those individuals, partnerships, corporations or public agencies holding fee simple title to property. Owner or owners does not include individuals, partnerships, corporations or public agencies holding easements or less than fee interests (including leaseholds) of any nature.

(l) *Site.* A site is the location of a significant event, a prehistoric or historic occupation or activity, or a building or structure, whether standing, ruined, or vanished, where the location itself maintains historical or archeological value regardless of the value of any existing structure.

Examples

Cabin Creek Battlefield (Pensacola vicinity, OK)

Mound Cemetery Mound (Chester vicinity, OH)
Mud Springs Pony Express Station Site (Dalton vicinity, NE)

(m) *State Historic Preservation Officer.* The State Historic Preservation Officer is the person who has been designated by the Governor or chief executive or by State statute in each State to administer the State Historic Preservation Program, including identifying and nominating eligible properties to the National Register and otherwise administering applications for listing historic properties in the National Register.

(n) *State Historic Preservation Program.* The State Historic Preservation Program is the program established by the Secretary of Interior for the purpose of carrying out the provisions of the National Historic Preservation Act of 1966, as amended, and related laws and regulations. Such program shall be approved by the Secretary before the State may nominate properties to the National Register. Any State Historic Preservation Program in effect under prior authority of law before December 12, 1980, shall be treated as an approved program until the Secretary approves a program submitted by the State for purposes of the Amendments or December 12, 1983, unless the Secretary chooses to rescind such approval because of program deficiencies.

(o) *State Review Board.* The State Review Board is a body whose members represent the professional fields of American history, architectural history, historic architecture, prehistoric and historic archeology, and other professional disciplines and may include citizen members. In States with approved State historic preservation programs the State Review Board reviews and approves National Register nominations concerning whether or not they meet the criteria for evaluation prior to their submittal to the NPS.

(p) *Structure.* A structure is a work made up of interdependent and interrelated parts in a definite pattern of organization. Constructed by man, it is often an engineering project large in scale.

Examples

Swanton Covered Railroad Bridge (Swanton vicinity, VT)
Old Point Loma Lighthouse (San Diego, CA)
North Point Water Tower (Milwaukee, WI)
Reber Radio Telescope (Green Bay vicinity, WI)

(q) *Thematic Group Format submission.* A Thematic Group Format submission for nominating properties to the National Register is one which includes a finite group of resources related to one another in a clearly distinguishable way. They may be related to a single historic person, event, or developmental force; of one building type or use, or designed by a single architect; of a single archeological site form, or related to a particular set of archeological research problems.

(r) *To nominate.* To nominate is to propose that a district, site, building, structure, or object be listed in the National Register of Historic Places by preparing a nomination form, with accompanying maps and photographs which adequately document the property and are technically and professionally correct and sufficient.

§60.4 **Criteria for evaluation.**

The criteria applied to evaluate properties (other than areas of the National Park System and National Historic Landmarks) for the National Register are listed below. These criteria are worded in a manner to provide for a wide diversity of resources. The following criteria shall be used in evaluating properties for nomination to the National Register, by NPS in reviewing nominations, and for evaluating National Register eligibility of properties. Guidance in applying the criteria is further discussed in the "How To" publications, Standards & Guidelines sheets and Keeper's opinions of the National Register. Such materials are available upon request.

National Register criteria for evaluation. The quality of significance in American history, architecture, archeology, engineering, and culture is present in districts, sites, buildings, structures, and objects that possess integrity of location, design, setting, materials, workmanship, feeling, and association and

(a) that are associated with events that have made a significant contribution to the broad patterns of our history; or

(b) that are associated with the lives of persons significant in our past; or

(c) that embody the distinctive characteristics of a type, period, or method of construction, or that represent the work of a master, or that possess high artistic values, or that represent a significant and distinguishable entity whose components may lack individual distinction; or

(d) that have yielded, or may be likely to yield, information important in prehistory or history.

Criteria considerations. Ordinarily cemeteries, birthplaces, or graves of historical figures, properties owned by religious institutions or used for religious purposes, structures that have been moved from their original locations, reconstructed historic buildings, properties primarily commemorative in nature, and properties that have achieved significance within the past 50 years shall not be considered eligible for the National Register. However, such properties will qualify if they are integral parts of districts that do meet the criteria of if they fall within the following categories:

(a) A religious property deriving primary significance from architectural or artistic distinction or historical importance; or

(b) A building or structure removed from its original location but which is significant primarily for architectural value, or which is the surviving structure most importantly associated with a historic person or event; or

(c) A birthplace or grave of a historical figure of outstanding importance if there is no appropriate site or building directly associated with his productive life.

(d) A cemetery which derives its primary significance from graves of persons of transcendent importance, from age, from distinctive design features, or from association with historic events; or

(e) A reconstructed building when accurately executed in a suitable environment and presented in a dignified manner as part of a restoration master plan, and when no other building or structure with the same association has survived; or

(f) A property primarily commemorative in intent if design, age, tradition, or symbolic value has invested it with its own exceptional significance; or

(g) A property achieving significance within the past 50 years if it is of exceptional importance.

This exception is described further in NPS "How To" #2, entitled "How to Evaluate and Nominate Potential National Register Properties That Have Achieved Significance Within the Last 50 Years" which is available from the National Register of Historic Places Division, National Park Service, United States Department of the Interior, Washington, D.C. 20240.

§ 60.5

§ 60.5 Nomination forms and information collection.

(a) All nominations to the National Register are to be made on standard National Register forms. These forms are provided upon request to the State Historic Preservation Officer, participating Federal agencies and others by the NPS. For archival reasons, no other forms, photocopied or otherwise, will be accepted.

(b) The information collection requirements contained in this part have been approved by the Office of Management and Budget under 44 U.S.C. 3507 and assigned clearance number *1024–0018*. The information is being collected as part of the nomination of properties to the National Register. This information will be used to evaluate the eligibility of properties for inclusion in the National Register under established criteria. The obligation to respond is required to obtain a benefit.

§ 60.6 Nominations by the State Historic Preservation Officer under approved State Historic Preservation programs.

(a) The State Historic Preservation Officer is responsible for identifying and nominating eligible properties to the National Register. Nomination forms are prepared under the supervision of the State Historic Preservation Officer. The State Historic Preservation Officer establishes statewide priorities for preparation and submittal of nominations for all properties meeting National Register criteria for evaluation within the State. All nominations from the State shall be submitted in accord with the State priorities, which shall be consistent with an approved State historic preservation plan.

(b) The State shall consult with local authorities in the nomination process. The State provides notice of the intent to nominate a property and solicits written comments especially on the significance of the property and whether or not it meets the National Register criteria for evaluation. The State notice also gives owners of private property an opportunity to concur in or object to listing. The notice is carried out as specified in the subsections below.

36 CFR Ch. I (7-1-99 Edition)

(c) As part of the nomination process, each State is required to notify in writing the property owner(s), except as specified in paragraph (d) of this section, of the State's intent to bring the nomination before the State Review Board. The list of owners shall be obtained from either official land records or tax records, whichever is more appropriate, within 90 days prior to the notification of intent to nominate. If in any State the land recordation or tax records is not the most appropriate list from which to obtain owners that State shall notify the Keeper in writing and request approval that an alternative source of owners may be used.

The State is responsible for notifying only those owners whose names appear on the list consulted. Where there is more than one owner on the list, each separate owner shall be notified. The State shall send the written notification at least 30 but not more than 75 days before the State Review Board meeting. Required notices may vary in some details of wording as the States prefer, but the content of notices must be approved by the National Register. The notice shall give the owner(s) at least 30 but not more than 75 days to submit written comments and concur in or object in writing to the nomination of such property. At least 30 but not more than 75 days before the State Review Board meeting, the States are also required to notify by the above mentioned National Register approved notice the applicable chief elected official of the county (or equivalent governmental unit) and municipal political jurisdiction in which the property is located. The National Register nomination shall be on file with the State Historic Preservation Program during the comment period and a copy made available by mail when requested by the public, or made available at a location of reasonable access to all affected property owners, such as a local library courthouse, or other public place, prior to the State Review Board meeting so that written comments regarding the nomination can be prepared.

(d) For a nomination with more than 50 property owners, each State is required to notify in writing at least 30 but not more than 75 days in advance

National Park Service, Interior

of the State Review Board meeting the chief elected local officials of the county (or equivalent governmental unit) and municipal political jurisdiction in which the property or district is located. The State shall provide general notice to property owners concerning the State's intent to nominate. The general notice shall be published at least 30 days but not more than 75 days before the State Review Board meeting and provide an opportunity for the submission of written comments and provide the owners of private property or a majority of such owners for districts an opportunity to concur in or object in writing to the nomination. Such general notice must be published in one or more local newspapers of general circulation in the area of the nomination. The content of the notices shall be approved by the National Register. If such general notice is used to notify the property owners for a nomination containing more than 50 owners, it is suggested that a public information meeting be held in the immediate area prior to the State Review Board meeting. If the State wishes to individually notify all property owners, it may do so, pursuant to procedures specified in subsection 60.6(c), in which case, the State need not publish a general notice.

(e) For Multiple Resource and Thematic Group Format submission, each district, site, building, structure and object included in the submission is treated as a separate nomination for the purpose of notification and to provide owners of private property the opportunity to concur in or object in writing to the nomination in accord with this section.

(f) The commenting period following notifications can be waived only when all property owners and the chief elected local official have advised the State in writing that they agree to the waiver.

(g) Upon notification, any owner or owners of a private property who wish to object shall submit to the State Historic Preservation Officer a notarized statement certifying that the party is the sole or partial owner of the private property, as appropriate, and objects to the listing. In nominations with multiple ownership of a single private

§ 60.6

property or of districts, the property will not be listed if a majority of the owners object to listing. Upon receipt of notarized objections respecting a district or single private property with multiple owners, it is the responsibility of the State Historic Preservation Officer to ascertain whether a majority of owners of private property have objected. If an owner whose name did not appear on the list certifies in a written notarized statement that the party is the sole or partial owner of a nominated private property such owner shall be counted by the State Historic Preservation Officer in determining whether a majority of owners has objected. Each owner of private property in a district has one vote regardless of how many properties or what part of one property that party owns and regardless of whether the property contributes to the significance of the district.

(h) If a property has been submitted to and approved by the State Review Board for inclusion in the National Register prior to the effective date of this section, the State Historic Preservation Officer need not resubmit the property to the State Review Board; but before submitting the nomination to the NPS shall afford owners of private property the opportunity to concur in or object to the property's inclusion in the Register pursuant to applicable notification procedures described above.

(i) [Reserved]

(j) Completed nomination forms or the documentation proposed for submission on the nomination forms and comments concerning the significance of a property and its eligibility for the National Register are submitted to the State Review Board. The State Review Board shall review the nomination forms or documentation proposed for submission on the nomination forms and any comments concerning the property's significance and eligibility for the National Register. The State Review Board shall determine whether or not the property meets the National Register criteria for evaluation and make a recommendation to the State Historic Preservation Officer to approve or disapprove the nomination.

(k) Nominations approved by the State Review Board and comments received are then reviewed by the State Historic Preservation Officer and if he or she finds the nominations to be adequately documented and technically, professionally, and procedurally correct and sufficient and in conformance with National Register criteria for evaluation, the nominations are submitted to the Keeper of the National Register of Historic Places, National Park Service, United States Department of the Interior, Washington, D.C. 20240. All comments received by a State and notarized statements of objection to listing are submitted with a nomination.

(l) If the State Historic Preservation Officer and the State Review Board disagree on whether a property meets the National Register criteria for evaluation, the State Historic Preservation Officer, if he or she chooses, may submit the nomination with his or her opinion concerning whether or not the property meets the criteria for evaluation and the opinion of the State Review Board to the Keeper of the National Register for a final decision on the listing of the property. The opinion of the State Review Board may be the minutes of the Review Board meeting. The State Historic Preservation Officer shall submit such disputed nominations if so requested within 45 days of the State Review Board meeting by the State Review Board or the chief elected local official of the local, county or municipal political subdivision in which the property is located but need not otherwise do so. Such nominations will be substantively reviewed by the Keeper.

(m) The State Historic Preservation Officer shall also submit to the Keeper nominations if so requested under the appeals process in §60.12.

(n) If the owner of a private property or the majority of such owners for a district or single property with multiple owners have objected to the nomination prior to the submittal of a nomination, the State Historic Preservation Officer shall submit the nomination to the Keeper only for a determination of eligibility pursuant to subsection (s) of this section.

(o) The State Historic Preservation Officer signs block 12 of the nomination form if in his or her opinion the property meets the National Register criteria for evaluation. The State Historic Preservation Officer's signature in block 12 certifies that:

(1) All procedural requirements have been met;

(2) The nomination form is adequately documented;

(3) The nomination form is technically and professionally correct and sufficient;

(4) In the opinion of the State Historic Preservation Officer, the property meets the National Register criteria for evaluation.

(p) When a State Historic Preservation Officer submits a nomination form for a property that he or she does not believe meets the National Register criteria for evaluation, the State Historic Preservation Officer signs a continuation sheet Form NPS 10-900a explaining his/her opinions on the eligibility of the property and certifying that:

(1) All procedural requirements have been met;

(2) The nomination form is adequately documented;

(3) The nomination form is technically and professionally correct and sufficient.

(q) Notice will be provided in the FEDERAL REGISTER that the nominated property is being considered for listing in the National Register of Historic Places as specified in §60.13.

(r) Nominations will be included in the National Register within 45 days of receipt by the Keeper or designee unless the Keeper disapproves a nomination, an appeal is filed, or the owner of private property (or the majority of such owners for a district or single property with multiple owners) objects by notarized statements received by the Keeper prior to listing. Nominations which are technically or professionally inadequate will be returned for correction and resubmission. When a property does not appear to meet the National Register criteria for evaluation, the nomination will be returned with an explanation as to why the property does not meet the National Register criteria for evaluation.

(s) If the owner of private property (or the majority of such owners for a district or single property with multiple owners) has objected to the nomination by notarized statement prior to listing, the Keeper shall review the nomination and make a determination of eligibility within 45 days of receipt, unless an appeal is filed. The Keeper shall list such properties determined eligible in the National Register upon receipt of notarized statements from the owner(s) of private property that the owner(s) no longer object to listing.

(t) Any person or organization which supports or opposes the nomination of a property by a State Historic Preservation Officer may petition the Keeper during the nomination process either to accept or reject a nomination. The petitioner must state the grounds of the petition and request in writing that the Keeper substantively review the nomination. Such petitions received by the Keeper prior to the listing of a property in the National Register or a determination of its eligibility where the private owners object to listing will be considered by the Keeper and the nomination will be substantively reviewed.

(u) State Historic Preservation Officers are required to inform the property owners and the chief elected local official when properties are listed in the National Register. In the case of a nomination where there are more than 50 property owners, they may be notified of the entry in the National Register by the same general notice stated in §60.6(d). States which notify all property owners individually of entries in the National Register need not publish a general notice.

(v) In the case of nominations where the owner of private property (or the majority of such owners for a district or single property with multiple owners) has objected and the Keeper has determined the nomination eligible for the National Register, the State Historic Preservation Officer shall notify the appropriate chief elected local official and the owner(s) of such property of this determination. The general notice may be used for properties with more than 50 owners as described in §60.6(d) or the State Historic Preserva-

tion Officer may notify the owners individually.

(w) If subsequent to nomination a State makes major revisions to a nomination or renominates a property rejected by the Keeper, the State Historic Preservation Officer shall notify the affected property owner(s) and the chief elected local official of the revisions or renomination in the same manner as the original notification for the nomination, but need not resubmit the nomination to the State Review Board. Comments received and notarized statements of objection must be forwarded to the Keeper along with the revisions or renomination. The State Historic Preservation Officer also certifies by the resubmittal that the affected property owner(s) and the chief elected local official have been renotified. "Major revisions" as used herein means revisions of boundaries or important substantive revisions to the nomination which could be expected to change the ultimate outcome as to whether or not the property is listed in the National Register by the Keeper.

(x) Notwithstanding any provision hereof to the contrary, the State Historic Preservation Officer in the nomination notification process or otherwise need not make available to any person or entity (except a Federal agency planning a project, the property owner, the chief elected local official of the political jurisdiction in which the property is located, and the local historic preservation commission for certified local governments) specific information relating to the location of properties proposed to be nominated to, or listed in, the National Register if he or she determines that the disclosure of specific information would create a risk of destruction or harm to such properties.

(y) With regard to property under Federal ownership or control, completed nomination forms shall be submitted to the Federal Preservation Officer for review and comment. The Federal Preservation Officer, may approve the nomination and forward it to the Keeper of the National Register of Historic Places, National Park Service,

36 CFR Ch. I (7-1-99 Edition)

§§ 60.7—60.8

United States Department of the Interior, Washington, D.C. 20240.

[46 FR 56187, Nov. 16, 1981, as amended at 48 FR 46308, Oct. 12, 1983]

§§ 60.7—60.8 [Reserved]

§ 60.9 Nominations by Federal agencies.

(a) The National Historic Preservation Act of 1966, as amended, requires that, with the advice of the Secretary and in cooperation with the State Historic Preservation Officer of the State involved, each Federal agency shall establish a program to locate, inventory and nominate to the Secretary all properties under the agency's ownership or control that appear to qualify for inclusion on the National Register. Section 2(a) of Executive Order 11593 provides that Federal agencies shall locate, inventory, and nominate to the Secretary of the Interior all sites, buildings, districts, and objects under their jurisdiction or control that appear to qualify for listing on the National Register of Historic Places. Additional responsibilities of Federal agencies are detailed in the National Historic Preservation Act of 1966, as amended, Executive Order 11593, the National Environmental Policy Act of 1969, the Archeological and Historic Preservation Act of 1974, and procedures developed pursuant to these authorities, and other related legislation.

(b) Nomination forms are prepared under the supervision of the Federal Preservation Officer designated by the head of a Federal agency to fulfill agency responsibilities under the National Historic Preservation Act of 1966, as amended.

(c) Completed nominations are submitted to the appropriate State Historic Preservation Officer for review and comment regarding the adequacy of the nomination, the significance of the property and its eligibility for the National Register. The chief elected local officials of the county (or equivalent governmental unit) and municipal political jurisdiction in which the property is located are notified and given 45 days in which to comment. The State Historic Preservation Officer signs block 12 of the nomination form with his/her recommendation.

(d) After receiving the comments of the State Historic Preservation Officer, and chief elected local official, or if there has been no response within 45 days, the Federal Preservation Officer may approve the nomination and forward it to the Keeper of the National Register of Historic Places, National Park Service, United States Department of the Interior, Washington, D.C. 20240. The Federal Preservation Officer signs block 12 of the nomination form if in his or her opinion the property meets the National Register criteria for evaluation. The Federal Preservation Officer's signature in block 12 certifies that:

(1) All procedural requirements have been met;

(2) The nomination form is adequately documented;

(3) The nomination form is technically and professionally correct and sufficient;

(4) In the opinion of the Federal Preservation Officer, the property meets the National Register criteria for evaluation.

(e) When a Federal Preservation Officer submits a nomination form for a property that he or she does not believe meets the National Register criteria for evaluation, the Federal Preservation Officer signs a continuation sheet Form NPS 10-900a explaining his/her opinions on the eligibility of the property and certifying that:

(1) All procedural requirements have been met;

(2) The nomination form is adequately documented;

(3) The nomination form is technically and professionally correct and sufficient.

(f) The comments of the State Historic Preservation Officer and chief local official, or if there are no comments from the State Historic Preservation Officer an explanation is attached. Concurrent nominations (see § 60.10) cannot be submitted, however, until the nomination has been considered by the State in accord with Sec. 60.6, supra. Comments received by the State concerning concurrent nominations and notarized statements of objection must be submitted with the nomination.

National Park Service, Interior

§ 60.11

(g) Notice will be provided in the FEDERAL REGISTER that the nominated property is being considered for listing in the National Register of Historic Places in accord with § 60.13.

(h) Nominations will be included in the National Register within 45 days of receipt by the Keeper or designee unless the Keeper disapproves such nomination or an appeal is filed. Nominations which are technically or professionally inadequate will be returned for correction and resubmission. When a property does not appear to meet the National Register criteria for evaluation, the nomination will be returned with an explanation as to why the property does not meet the National Register criteria for evaluation.

(i) Any person or organization which supports or opposes the nomination of a property by a Federal Preservation Officer may petition the Keeper during the nomination process either to accept or reject a nomination. The petitioner must state the grounds of the petition and request in writing that the Keeper substantively review the nomination. Such petition received by the Keeper prior to the listing of a property in the National Register or a determination of its eligibility for the private owner(s) object to listing will be considered by the Keeper and the nomination will be substantively reviewed.

§ 60.10 Concurrent State and Federal nominations.

(a) State Historic Preservation Officers and Federal Preservation Officers are encouraged to cooperate in locating, inventorying, evaluating, and nominating all properties possessing historical, architectural, archeological, or cultural value. Federal agencies may nominate properties where a portion of the property is not under Federal ownership or control.

(b) When a portion of the area included in a Federal nomination is not located on land under the ownership or control of the Federal agency, but is an integral part of the cultural resource, the completed nomination form shall be sent to the State Historic Preservation Officer for notification to property owners, to give owners of private property an opportunity to concur in or object to the nomination, to solicit written comments and for submission to the State Review Board pursuant to the procedures in §60.6.

(c) If the State Historic Preservation Officer and the State Review Board agree that the nomination meets the National Register criteria for evaluation, the nomination is signed by the State Historic Preservation Officer and returned to the Federal agency initiating the nomination. If the State Historic Preservation Officer and the State Review Board disagree, the nomination shall be returned to the Federal agency with the opinions of the State Historic Preservation Officer and the State Review Board concerning the adequacy of the nomination and whether or not the property meets the criteria for evaluation. The opinion of the State Review Board may be the minutes of the State Review Board meeting. The State Historic Preservation Officer's signed opinion and comments shall confirm to the Federal agency that the State nomination procedures have been fulfilled including notification requirements. Any comments received by the State shall be included with the letter as shall any notarized statements objecting to the listing of private property.

(d) If the owner of any privately owned property, (or a majority of the owners of such properties within a district or single property with multiple owners) objects to such inclusion by notarized statement(s) the Federal Historic Preservation Officer shall submit the nomination to the Keeper for review and a determination of eligibility. Comments, opinions, and notarized statements of objection shall be submitted with the nomination.

(e) The State Historic Preservation Officer shall notify the non-Federal owners when a concurrent nomination is listed or determined eligible for the National Register as required in §60.6.

§ 60.11 Requests for nominations.

(a) The State Historic Preservation Officer or Federal Preservation Officer as appropriate shall respond in writing within 60 days to any person or organization submitting a completed National Park Service nomination form or requesting consideration for any previously prepared nomination form on record with the State or Federal agency. The response shall provide a technical opinion concerning whether or not the property is adequately documented and appears to meet the National Register criteria for evaluation in §60.4. If the nomination form is determined to be inadequately documented, the nominating authority shall provide the applicant with an explanation of the reasons for that determination.

(b) If the nomination form does not appear to be adequately documented, upon receiving notification, it shall be the responsibility of the applicant to provide necessary additional documentation.

(c) If the nomination form appears to be adequately documented and if the property appears to meet the National Register criteria for evaluation, the State Historic Preservation Officer shall comply with the notification requirements in §60.6 and schedule the property for presentation at the earliest possible State Review Board meeting. Scheduling shall be consistent with the State's established priorities for processing nominations. If the nomination form is adequately documented, but the property does not appear to meet National Register criteria for evaluation, the State Historic Preservation Officer need not process the nomination, unless so requested by the Keeper pursuant to §60.12.

(d) The State Historic Preservation Officer's response shall advise the applicant of the property's position in accord with the State's priorities for processing nominations and of the approximate date the applicant can expect its consideration by the State Review Board. The State Historic Preservation Officer shall also provide notice to the applicant of the time and place of the Review Board meeting at least 30 but not more than 75 days before the meeting, as well as complying with the notification requirements in §60.6.

(e) Upon action on a nomination by the State Review Board, the State Historic Preservation Officer shall, within 90 days, submit the nomination to the National Park Service, or, if the State Historic Preservation Officer does not consider the property eligible for the National Register, so advise the applicant within 45 days.

(f) If the applicant substantially revises a nomination form as a result of comments by the State or Federal agency, it may be treated by the State Historic Preservation Officer or Federal Preservation Officer as a new submittal and reprocessed in accord with the requirements in this section.

(g) The Federal Preservation Officer shall request the comments of the State Historic Preservation Officer and notify the applicant in writing within 90 days of receipt of an adequately documented nomination form as to whether the Federal agency will nominate the property. The Federal Preservation Officer shall submit an adequately documented nomination to the National Park Service unless in his or her opinion the property is not eligible for the National Register.

[48 FR 46308, Oct. 12, 1983]

§ 60.12   Nomination appeals.

(a) Any person or local government may appeal to the Keeper the failure or refusal of a nominating authority to nominate a property that the person or local government considers to meet the National Register criteria for evaluation upon decision of a nominating authority to not nominate a property for any reason when requested pursuant to §60.11, or upon failure of a State Historic Preservation Officer to nominate a property recommended by the State Review Board. (This action differs from the procedure for appeals during the review of a nomination by the National Park Service where an individual or organization may "petition the Keeper" during the nomination process," as specified in §§60.6(t) and 60.9(i). Upon receipt of such petition the normal 45-day review period will be extended for 30 days beyond the date of the petition to allow the petitioner to provide additional documentation for review.)

(b) Such appeal shall include a copy of the nomination form and documentation previously submitted to the State Historic Preservation Officer or

Federal Preservation Officer, an explanation of why the applicant is submitting the appeal in accord with this section and shall include pertinent correspondence from the State Historic Preservation Officer or Federal Preservation Officer.

(c) The Keeper will respond to the appellant and the State Historic Preservation Officer or Federal Preservation Officer with a written explanation either denying or sustaining the appeal within 45 days of receipt. If the appeal is sustained, the Keeper will:

(1) Request the State Historic Preservation Officer or Federal Preservation Officer to submit the nomination to the Keeper within 15 days if the nomination has completed the procedural requirements for nomination as described in §§ 60.6 or 60.9 except that concurrence of the State Review Board, State Historic Preservation Officer or Federal Preservation Officer is not required; or

(2) If the nomination has not completed these procedural requirements, request the State Historic Preservation Officer or Federal Preservation Officer to promptly process the nomination pursuant to §§ 60.6 or 60.9 and submit the nomination to the Keeper without delay.

(d) State Historic Preservation Officers and Federal Preservation Officers shall process and submit such nominations if so requested by the Keeper pursuant to this section. The Secretary reserves the right to list properties in the National Register or determine properties eligible for such listing on his own motion when necessary to assist in the preservation of historic resources and after notifying the owner and appropriate parties and allowing for a 30-day comment period.

(e) No person shall be considered to have exhausted administrative remedies with respect to failure to nominate a property to the National Register until he or she has complied with procedures set forth in this section. The decision of the Keeper is the final administrative action on such appeals.

[48 FR 46308, Oct. 12, 1983]

§ 60.13   Publication in the Federal Register and other NPS notification.

(a) When a nomination is received, NPS will publish notice in the FEDERAL REGISTER that the property is being considered for listing in the National Register. A 15-day commenting period from date of publication will be provided. When necessary to assist in the preservation of historic properties this 15-day period may be shortened or waived.

(b) NPS shall notify the appropriate State Historic Preservation Officer, Federal Preservation Officer, person or local government when there is no approved State preservation program of the listing of the property in the National Register and will publish notice of the listing in the FEDERAL REGISTER.

(c) In nominations where the owner of any privately owned property (or a majority of the owners of such property within a district or single property with multiple owners) has objected and the Keeper has determined the nomination eligible for the National Register, NPS shall notify the State Historic Preservation Officer (for Federal or concurrent nominations), the person or local government where there is no approved State Historic Preservation Program and the Advisory Council on Historic Preservation. NPS will publish notice of the determination of eligibility in the FEDERAL REGISTER.

§ 60.14   Changes and revisions to properties listed in the National Register.

(a) Boundary changes. (1) A boundary alteration shall be considered as a new property nomination. All forms, criteria and procedures used in nominating a property to the National Register must be used. In the case of boundary enlargements only those owners in the newly nominated as yet unlisted area need be notified and will be counted in determining whether a majority of private owners object to listing. In the case of a diminution of a boundary, owners shall be notified as specified in §60.15 concerning removing properties from the National Register. A professionally justified recommendation by the State Historic Preservation

Officer, Federal Preservation Officer, or person or local government where there is no approved State Historic Preservation Program shall be presented to NPS. During this process, the property is not taken off the National Register. If the Keeper or his or her designee finds the recommendation in accordance with the National Register criteria for evaluation, the change will be accepted. If the boundary change is not accepted, the old boundaries will remain. Boundary revisions may be appealed as provided for in §§60.12 and 60.15.

(2) Four justifications exist for altering a boundary: Professional error in the initial nomination, loss of historic integrity, recognition of additional significance, additional research documenting that a larger or smaller area should be listed. No enlargement of a boundary should be recommended unless the additional area possesses previously unrecognized significance or American history, architecture, archeology, engineering or culture. No diminution of a boundary should be recommended unless the properties being removed do not meet the National Register criteria for evaluation. Any proposal to alter a boundary has to be documented in detail including photographing the historic resources falling between the existing boundary and the other proposed boundary.

(b) *Relocating properties listed in the National Register.* (1) Properties listed in the National Register should be moved only when there is no feasible alternative for preservation. When a property is moved, every effort should be made to reestablish its historic orientation, immediate setting, and general environment.

(2) If it is proposed that a property listed in the National Register be moved and the State Historic Preservation Officer, Federal Preservation Officer having Federal ownership or control or person or local government where there is no approved

State Historic Preservation Program, shall submit documentation to NPS prior to the move. The documentation shall discuss:

(i) The reasons for the move;

(ii) The effect on the property's historical integrity;

(iii) The new setting and general environment of the proposed site, including evidence that the proposed site does not possess historical or archeological significance that would be adversely affected by the intrusion of the property; and

(iv) Photographs showing the proposed location.

(3) Any such proposal with respect to the new location shall follow the required notification procedures, shall be approved by the State Review Board if it is a State nomination and shall continue to follow normal review procedures. The Keeper shall also follow the required notification procedures for nominations. The Keeper shall respond to a properly documented request within 45 days of receipt from the State Historic Preservation Officer or Federal Preservation Officer, or within 90 days of receipt from a person or local government where there is no approved State Historic Preservation Program, concerning whether or not the move is approved. Once the property is moved, the State Historic Preservation Officer, Federal Preservation Officer, or person or local government where there is no approved State Historic Preservation Program shall submit to the Keeper for review:

(i) A letter notifying him or her of the date the property was moved;

(ii) Photographs of the property on its new site; and

(iii) Revised maps, including a U.S.G.S. map,

(iv) Acreage, and

(v) Verbal boundary description.

The Keeper shall respond to a properly documented submittal within 45 days of receipt with the final decision on whether the property will remain in the National Register. If the Keeper approves the move, the property will remain in the National Register during and after the move unless the integrity of the property is in some unforeseen manner destroyed. If the Keeper does not approve the move, the property

will be automatically deleted from the National Register when moved. In cases of properties removed from the National Register, if the State, Federal agency, or person or local government where there is no approved State Historic Preservation Program has neglected to obtain prior approval for the move or has evidence that previously unrecognized significance exists, or has accrued, the State, Federal agency, person or local government may resubmit a nomination for the property.

(4) In the event that a property is moved, deletion from the National Register will be automatic unless the above procedures are followed prior to the move. If the property has already been moved, it is the responsibility of the State, Federal agency or person or local government which nominated the property to notify the National Park Service. Assuming that the State, Federal agency or person or local government wishes to have the structure reentered in the National Register, it must be nominated again on new forms which should discuss:

(i) The reasons for the move;

(ii) The effect on the property's historical integrity, and

(iii) The new setting and general environment, including evidence that the new site does not possess historical or archeological significance that would be adversely affected by intrusion of the property.

In addition, new photographs, acreage, verbal boundary description and a U.S.G.S. map showing the structure at its new location must be sent along with the revised nomination. Any such nomination submitted by a State must be approved by the State Review Board.

(5) Properties moved in a manner consistent with the comments of the Advisory Council on Historic Preservation, in accord with its procedures (36 CFR part 800), are granted as exception to §60.12(b). Moving of properties in accord with the Advisory Council's procedures should be dealt with individually in each memorandum of agreement. In such cases, the State Historic Preservation Officer or the Federal Preservation Officer, for properties under Federal ownership or control, shall notify the Keeper of the new location after

the move including new documentation as described above.

§60.15 **Removing properties from the National Register.**

(a) Grounds for removing properties from the National Register are as follows:

(1) The property has ceased to meet the criteria for listing in the National Register because the qualities which caused it to be originally listed have been lost or destroyed, or such qualities were lost subsequent to nomination and prior to listing;

(2) Additional information shows that the property does not meet the National Register criteria for evaluation;

(3) Error in professional judgement as to whether the property meets the criteria for evaluation; or

(4) Prejudicial procedural error in the nomination or listing process. Properties removed from the National Register for procedural error shall be reconsidered for listing by the Keeper after correction of the error or errors by the State Historic Preservation Officer, Federal Preservation Officer, person or local government which originally nominated the property, or by the Keeper, as appropriate. The procedures set forth for nominations shall be followed in such reconsiderations. Any property or district removed from the National Register for procedural deficiencies in the nomination and/or listing process shall automatically be considered eligible for inclusion in the National Register without further action and will be published as such in the FEDERAL REGISTER.

(b) Properties listed in the National Register prior to December 13, 1980, may only be removed from the National Register on the grounds established in paragraph (a)(1) of this section.

(c) Any person or organization may petition in writing for removal of a property from the National Register by setting forth the reasons the property should be removed on the grounds established in paragraph (a) of this section. With respect to nominations determined eligible for the National Register because the owners of private property object to listing, anyone may petition for reconsideration of whether or not the property meets the criteria for evaluation using these procedures. Petitions for removal are submitted to the Keeper by the State Historic Preservation Officer for State nominations, the Federal Preservation Officer for Federal nominations, and directly to the Keeper from persons or local governments where there is no approved State Historic Preservation Program.

(d) Petitions submitted by persons or local governments where there is no approved State Historic Preservation Program shall include a list of the owner(s). In such cases the Keeper shall notify the affected owner(s) and the chief elected local official and give them an opportunity to comment. For approved State programs, the State Historic Preservation Officer shall notify the affected owner(s) and chief elected local official and give them an opportunity to comment prior to submitting a petition for removal. The Federal Preservation Officer shall notify and obtain the comments of the appropriate State Historic Preservation Officer prior to forwarding an appeal to NPS. All comments and opinions shall be submitted with the petition.

(e) The State Historic Preservation Officer or Federal Preservation Officer shall respond in writing within 45 days of receipt to petitions for removal of property from the National Register. The response shall advise the petitioner of the State Historic Preservation Officer's or Federal Preservation Officer's views on the petition.

(f) A petitioner desiring to pursue his removal request must notify the State Historic Preservation Officer or the Federal Preservation Officer in writing within 45 days of receipt of the written views on the petition.

(g) The State Historic Preservation Officer may elect to have a property considered for removal according to the State's nomination procedures unless the petition is on procedural grounds and shall schedule it for consideration by the State Review Board as quickly as all notification requirements can be completed following procedures outlined in §60.6, or the State Historic Preservation Officer may elect to forward the petition for removal to

the Keeper with his or her comments without State Review Board consideration.

(h) Within 15 days after receipt of the petitioner's notification of intent to pursue his removal request, the State Historic Preservation Officer shall notify the petitioner in writing either that the State Review Board will consider the petition on a specified date or that the petition will be forwarded to the Keeper after notification requirements have been completed. The State Historic Preservation Officer shall forward the petitions to the Keeper for review within 15 days after notification requirements or Review Board consideration, if applicable, have been completed.

(i) Within 15 days after receipt of the petitioner notification of intent to pursue his petition, the Federal Preservation Officer shall forward the petition with his or her comments and those of the State Historic Preservation Officer to the Keeper.

(j) The Keeper shall respond to a petition for removal within 45 days of receipt, except where the Keeper must notify the owners and the chief elected local official. In such cases the Keeper shall respond within 90 days of receipt. The Keeper shall notify the petitioner and the applicable State Historic Preservation Officer, Federal Preservation Officer, or person or local government where there is no approved State Historic Preservation Program, of his decision. The State Historic Preservation Officer or Federal Preservation Officer transmitting the petition shall notify the petitioner, the owner(s), and the chief elected local official in writing of the decision. The Keeper will provide such notice for petitions from persons or local governments where there is no approved State Historic Preservation Program. The general notice may be used for properties with more than 50 owners. If the general notice is used it shall be published in one or more newspapers with general circulation in the area of the nomination.

(k) The Keeper may remove a property from the National Register on his own motion on the grounds established in paragraph (a) of this section, except for those properties listed in the National Register prior to December 13,

1980, which may only be removed from the National Register on the grounds established in paragraph (a)(1) of this section. In such cases, the Keeper will notify the nominating authority, the affected owner(s) and the applicable chief elected local official and provide them an opportunity to comment. Upon removal, the Keeper will notify the nominating authority of the basis for the removal. The State Historic Preservation Officer, Federal Preservation Officer, or person or local government which nominated the property shall notify the owner(s) and the chief elected local official of the removal.

(l) No person shall be considered to have exhausted administrative remedies with respect to removal of a property from the National Register until the Keeper has denied a petition for removal pursuant to this section.

PART 800—PROTECTION OF HISTORIC PROPERTIES

Subpart A—Purposes and Participants

Sec.
800.1 Purposes.
800.2 Participants in the section 106 process.

Subpart B—The Section 106 Process

800.3 Initiation of the section 106 process.
800.4 Identification of historic properties.
800.5 Assessment of adverse effects.
800.6 Resolution of adverse effects.
800.7 Failure to resolve adverse effects.
800.8 Coordination with the National Environmental Policy Act.
800.9 Council review of section 106 compliance.
800.10 Special requirements for protecting National Historic Landmarks.
800.11 Documentation standards.
800.12 Emergency situations.
800.13 Post-review discoveries.

Subpart C—Program Alternatives

800.14 Federal agency program alternatives.
800.15 Tribal, State and Local Program Alternatives. [Reserved]
800.16 Definitions.
APPENDIX A—CRITERIA FOR COUNCIL INVOLVEMENT IN REVIEWING INDIVIDUAL SECTION 106 CASES

AUTHORITY: 16 U.S.C. 470s.

SOURCE: 64 FR 27071, May 18, 1999, unless otherwise noted.

Subpart A—Purposes and Participants

§ 800.1 Purposes.

(a) *Purposes of the section 106 process.* Section 106 of the National Historic Preservation Act requires Federal agencies to take into account the effects of their undertakings on historic properties and afford the Council a reasonable opportunity to comment on such undertakings. The procedures in this part define how Federal agencies meet these statutory responsibilities. The section 106 process seeks to accommodate historic preservation concerns with the needs of Federal undertakings through consultation among the Agency Official and other parties with an interest in the effects of the undertaking on historic properties, commencing at the early stages of project planning. The goal of consultation is to

identify historic properties potentially affected by the undertaking, assess its effects and seek ways to avoid, minimize or mitigate any adverse effects on historic properties.

(b) *Relation to other provisions of the Act.* Section 106 is related to other provisions of the Act designed to further the national policy of historic preservation. References to those provisions are included in this part of identify circumstances where they may affect actions taken to meet section 106 requirements. Such provisions may have their own implementing regulations or guidelines and are not intended to be implemented by the procedures in this part except insofar as they relate to the section 106 process. Guidelines, policies and procedures issued by other agencies, including the Secretary, have been cited in this part for ease of access and are not incorporated by reference.

(c) *Timing.* The Agency Official must complete the section 106 process "prior to the approval of the expenditure of any Federal funds on the undertaking or prior to the issuance of any license." This does not prohibit Agency Official from conducting or authorizing nondestructive project planning activities before completing compliance with Section 106, provided that such actions do not restrict the subsequent consideration of alternatives to avoid, minimize or mitigate the undertaking's adverse effects on historic properties. The Agency Official shall ensure that the section 106 process is initiated early in the undertaking's planning, so that a broad range of alternatives may be considered during the planning process for the undertaking.

§ 800.2 Participants in section 106 process.

(a) *Agency Official.* It is the statutory obligation of the Federal agency to fulfill the requirements of section 106 and to ensure that an Agency Official with jurisdiction over an undertaking takes legal and financial responsibility for section 106 compliance in accordance with subpart B of this part. The Agency Official has approval authority for the undertaking and can commit the

Federal agency to take appropriate action for a specific undertaking as a result of section 106 compliance. For the purposes of subpart C of this part, the Agency Official has the authority to commit the Federal agency to any obligation it may assume in the implementation of a program alternative. The Agency Official may be a State, local, or tribal government official who has been delegated legal responsibility for compliance with section 106 in accordance with Federal law.

(1) *Professional standards.* Section 112(a)(1)(A) of the Act requires each Federal agency responsible for the protection of historic resources, including archeological resources, to ensure that all actions taken by employees or contractors of the agency shall meet professional standards under regulations developed by the Secretary.

(2) *Lead Federal agency.* If more than one Federal agency is involved in an undertaking, some or all the agencies may designate a lead Federal agency, which shall identify the appropriate official to serve as the Agency Official who shall act on their behalf, fulfilling their collective responsibilities under section 106. Those Federal agencies that do not designate a lead Federal agency remain individually responsible for their compliance with this part.

(3) *Use of contractors.* Consistent with applicable conflict of interest laws, the Agency Official may use the services of applicants, consultants, or designees to prepare information, analyses and recommendations under this part. The Agency Official remains legally responsible for all required findings and determinations. If a document or study is prepared by a non-Federal party, the Agency Official is responsible for ensuring that its content meets applicable standards and guidelines.

(4) *Consultation.* The Agency Official shall involve the consulting parties described in §800.2(c) in findings and determinations made during the section 106 process. The Agency Official should plan consultations appropriate to the scale of the undertaking and the scope of Federal involvement and coordinated with other requirements of other statutes, as applicable, such as the National Environmental Policy Act, the Native American Graves Protection

and Repatriation Act, the American Indian Religious Freedom Act, the Archeological Resources Protection Act and agency-specific legislation. The Council encourages the Agency Official to use to the extent possible existing agency procedures and mechanisms to fulfill the consultation requirements of this part.

(b) *Council.* The Council issues regulations to implement section 106, provides guidance and advice on the application of the procedures in this part, and generally oversees the operation of the section 106 process. The Council also consults with and comments to Agency Officials on individual undertakings and programs that affect historic properties.

(1) *Council entry into the section 106 process.* When the Council determines that its involvement is necessary to ensure that the purposes of section 106 and the Act are met, the Council may enter the section 106 process. Criteria guiding Council decisions to enter the section 106 process are found in appendix A to this part. The Council will document that the criteria have been met and notify the parties to the section 106 process as required by this part.

(2) *Council assistance.* Participants in the section 106 process may seek advice, guidance and assistance from the Council on the application of this part to specific undertakings, including the resolution of disagreements, whether or not the Council is formally involved in the review of the undertaking. If questions arise regarding the conduct of the section 106 process, participants are encouraged to obtain the Council's advice on completing the process.

(c) *Consulting parties.* The following parties have consultative roles in the section 106 process.

(1) *State Historic Preservation Officer.* (i) The State Historic Preservation Officer (SHPO) reflects the interests of the State and its citizens in the preservation of their cultural heritage. In accordance with section 101(b)(3) of the Act, the SHPO advises and assists Federal agencies in carrying out their section 106 responsibilities.

(ii) If an Indian tribe has assumed the functions of the SHPO in the section 106 process for undertakings on tribal

lands, the SHPO shall participate as a consulting party if the undertaking takes place on tribal lands but affects historic properties off tribal lands, if requested in accordance with §800.3(c)(1), or if the Indian tribe agrees to include the SHPO pursuant to §800.3(f)(3).

(2) *Tribal Historic Preservation Officer.* (i) The Tribal Historic Preservation Officer (THPO) appointed or designated in accordance with the Act is the official representative of an Indian tribe for the purposes of section 106. If an Indian tribe has assumed the responsibilities of the SHPO for section 106 on tribal lands under section 101(d)(2) of the Act, the Agency Official shall consult with the THPO in lieu of the SHPO regarding undertakings occurring on or affecting historic properties on tribal lands.

(ii) If an Indian tribe has not assumed the responsibilities of the SHPO for section 106 on tribal lands under section 101(d)(2) of the Act, the Agency Official shall consult with a representative designated by such Indian tribe in addition to the SHPO regarding undertakings occurring on or affecting historic properties on its tribal lands. For the purposes of subpart B of this part, such tribal representative shall be included in the term "THPO."

(3) *Indian tribes and Native Hawaiian organizations.* Section 101(d)(6)(B) of the Act requires the Agency Official to consult with any Indian tribe or Native Hawaiian organization that attaches religious and cultural significance to historic properties that may be affected by an undertaking. Such Indian tribe or Native Hawaiian organization shall be a consulting party.

(i) The Agency Official shall ensure that consultation in the section 106 process provides the Indian tribe or Native Hawaiian organization a reasonable opportunity to identify its concerns about historic properties, advise on the identification and evaluation of historic properties, including those of traditional religious and cultural importance, articulate its views on the undertaking's effects on such properties, and participate in the resolution of adverse effects. It is the responsibility of the Agency Official to make a reasonable and good faith effort to

identify Indian tribes and Native Hawaiian organizations that shall be consulted in the section 106 process. Consultation should commence early in the planning process, in order to identify and discuss relevant preservation issues and resolve concerns about the confidentiality of information on historic properties.

(ii) The Federal government has a unique legal relationship with Indian tribes set forth in the Constitution of the United States, treaties, statutes, and court decisions. Consultation with Indian tribes should be conducted in a sensitive manner respectful of tribal sovereignty. Nothing in this part is intended to alter, amend, repeal, interpret or modify tribal sovereignty, any treaty rights, or other rights of an Indian tribe, or to preempt, modify or limit the exercise of any such rights.

(iii) Consultation with an Indian tribe must recognize the government-to-government relationship between the Federal government and Indian tribes. The Agency Official shall consult with representatives designated or identified by the tribal government or the governing body of a Native Hawaiian organization. Consultation with Indian tribes and Native Hawaiian organizations should be conducted in a manner sensitive to the concerns and needs of the Indian tribe or Native Hawaiian organization.

(iv) When Indian tribes and Native Hawaiian organizations attach religious and cultural significance to historic properties off tribal lands, section 101(d)(6)(B) of the Act requires Federal agencies to consult with such Indian tribes and Native Hawaiian organizations in the section 106 process. Federal agencies should be aware that frequently historic properties of religious and cultural significance are located on ancestral, aboriginal or ceded lands of Indian tribes and Native Hawaiian organizations and should consider them when complying with the procedures in this part.

(v) An Indian tribe or a Native Hawaiian organization may enter into an agreement with an Agency Official that specifies how they will carry out responsibilities under this part, including concerns over the confidentiality of information. An agreement may cover

§800.3

all aspects of tribal participation in the section 106 process, provided that no modification may be made in the roles of other parties to the section 106 process without their consent. An agreement may grant the Indian tribe or Native Hawaiian organization additional rights to participate or concur in agency decisions in the section 106 process beyond those specified in subpart B of this part. The Agency Official shall provide a copy of any such agreement to the Council and the appropriate SHPOs.

(vi) An Indian tribe that has not assumed the responsibilities of the SHPO for section 106 on tribal lands under section 101(d)(2) of the Act may notify the Agency Official in writing that it is waiving its rights under §800.6(c)(1) to execute a Memorandum of Agreement.

(4) *Representatives of local governments.* A representative of a local government with jurisdiction over the area in which the effects of an undertaking may occur is entitled to participate as a consulting party. Under other provisions of Federal law, the local government may be authorized to act as the Agency Official for purposes of section 106.

(5) *Applicants for Federal assistance, permits, licenses and other approvals.* An applicant for Federal assistance or for a Federal permit, license or other approval is entitled to participate as a consulting party as defined in this part. The Agency Official may authorize an applicant to initiate consultation with the SHPO/THPO and others, but remains legally responsible for all findings and determinations charged to the Agency Official. The Agency Official shall notify the SHPO/THPO and other consulting parties when an applicant is so authorized.

(6) *Additional consulting parties.* Certain individuals and organizations with a demonstrated interest in the undertaking may participate as consulting parties due to the nature of their legal or economic relation to the undertaking or affected properties, or their concern with the undertaking's effects on historic properties.

(d) *The public*—(1) *Nature of involvement.* The views of the public are essential to informed Federal decisionmaking. The Agency Official shall seek and consider the views of the public in a manner that reflects the nature and complexity of the undertaking and its effects on historic properties, the likely interest of the public in the effects on historic properties, confidentiality concerns of private individuals and businesses, and the relationship of the Federal involvement to the undertaking.

(2) *Providing notice and information.* The Agency Official must, except where appropriate to protect confidentiality concerns of affected parties, provide the public with information about an undertaking and its effects on historic properties and seek public comment and input. Members of the public may also provide views on their own initiative for the Agency Official to consider in decisionmaking.

(3) *Use of agency procedures.* The Agency Official may use the agency's procedures for public involvement under the National Environmental Policy Act or other program requirements in lieu of public involvement requirements in subpart B of this part, if they provide adequate opportunities for public involvement consistent with this subpart.

Subpart B—The Section 106 Process

§800.3 Initiation of the section 106 process.

(a) *Establish undertaking.* The Agency Official shall determine whether the proposed Federal action is an undertaking as defined in §800.16(y) and, if so, whether it is a type of activity that has the potential to cause effects on historic properties.

(1) *No potential to cause effects.* If the undertaking does not have the potential to cause effects on historic properties, the Agency Official has no further obligations under section 106 or this part.

(2) *Program alternatives.* If the review of the undertaking is governed by a Federal agency program alternative established under §800.14 or a Programmatic Agreement in existence before the effective date of these regulations, the Agency Official shall follow the program alternative.

§800.3

(b) *Coordinate with other reviews.* The Agency Official should coordinate the steps of the section 106 process, as appropriate, with the overall planning schedule for the undertaking and with any reviews required under other authorities such as the National Environmental Policy Act, the Native American Graves Protection and Repatriation Act, the American Indian Religious Freedom Act, the Archaeological Resources Protection Act and agency-specific legislation, such as section 4(f) of the Department of Transportation Act. Where consistent with the procedures in this subpart, the Agency Official may use information developed for other reviews under Federal, State or tribal law to meet the requirements of section 106.

(c) *Identify the appropriate SHPO and/or THPO.* As part of its initial planning, the Agency Official shall determine the appropriate SHPO or SHPOs to be involved in the section 106 process. The Agency Official shall also determine whether the undertaking may occur on or affect historic properties on any tribal lands and, if so, whether a THPO has assumed the duties of the SHPO. The Agency Official shall then initiate consultation with the appropriate Officer or Officers.

(1) *Tribal assumption of SHPO responsibilities.* Where an Indian tribe has assumed the section 106 responsibilities of the SHPO on tribal lands pursuant to section 101(d)(2) of the Act, consultation for undertakings occurring on tribal land or for effects on tribal land is with the THPO for the Indian tribe in lieu of the SHPO. Section 101(d)(2)(D)(iii) of the Act authorizes owners of properties on tribal lands which are neither owned by a member of the tribe nor held in trust by the Secretary for the benefit of the tribe to request the SHPO to participate in the section 106 process in addition to the THPO.

(2) *Undertakings involving more than one State.* If more than one State is involved in an undertaking, the involved SHPOs may agree to designate a lead SHPO to act on their behalf in the section 106 process, including taking actions that would conclude the section 106 process under this subpart.

(3) *Conducting consultation.* The Agency Official should consult with the SHPO/THPO in a manner appropriate to the agency planning process for the undertaking and to the nature of the undertaking and its effects on historic properties.

(4) *Failure of the SHPO/THPO to respond.* If the SHPO/THPO fails to respond within 30 days of receipt of a request for review of a finding or determination, the Agency Official may either proceed to the next step in the process based on the finding or determination or consult with the Council in lieu of the SHPO/THPO. If the SHPO/THPO re-enters the section 106 process, the Agency Official shall continue the consultation without being required to reconsider previous findings or determinations.

(d) *Consultation on tribal lands.* Where the Indian tribe has not assumed the responsibilities of the SHPO on tribal lands, consultation with the Indian tribe regarding undertakings occurring on such tribe's lands or effects on such tribal lands shall be in addition to and on the same basis as consultation with the SHPO. If the SHPO has withdrawn from the process, the Agency Official may complete the section 106 process with the Indian tribe and the Council, as appropriate. An Indian tribe may enter into an agreement with a SHPO or SHPOs specifying the SHPO's participation in the section 106 process for undertakings occurring on or affecting historic properties on tribal lands.

(e) *Plan to involve the public.* In consultation with the SHPO/THPO, the Agency Official shall plan for involving the public in the section 106 process. The Agency Official shall identify the appropriate points for seeking public input and for notifying the public of proposed actions, consistent with §800.2(d).

(f) *Identify other consulting parties.* In consultation with the SHPO/THPO, the Agency Official shall identify any other parties entitled to be consulting parties and invite them to participate as such in the section 106 process. The Agency Official may invite others to participate as consulting parties as the section 106 process moves forward.

§ 800.4

(1) *Involving local governments and applicants.* The Agency Official shall invite any local governments or applicants that are entitled to be consulting parties under § 800.2(c).

(2) *Involving Indian tribes and Native Hawaiian organizations.* The Agency Official shall make a reasonable and good faith effort to identify any Indian tribes or Native Hawaiian organizations that might attach religious and cultural significance to historic properties in the area of potential effects and invite them to be consulting parties. Such Indian tribe or Native Hawaiian organization that requests in writing to be a consulting party shall be one.

(3) *Requests to be consulting parties.* The Agency Official shall consider all written requests of individuals and organizations to participate as consulting parties and, in consultation with the SHPO/THPO and any Indian tribe upon whose tribal lands an undertaking occurs or affects historic properties, determine which should be consulting parties.

(g) *Expediting consultation.* A consultation by the Agency Official with the SHPO/THPO and other consulting parties may address multiple steps in §§ 800.3–800.6 where the Agency Official and the SHPO/THPO agree it is appropriate as long as the consulting parties and the public have an adequate opportunity to express their views as provided in § 800.2(d).

§ 800.4 Identification of historic properties.

(a) *Determine scope of identification efforts.* The Agency Official shall consult with the SHPO/THPO to:

(1) Determine and document the area of potential effects, as defined in § 800.16(d);

(2) Review existing information on historic properties within the area of potential effects, including any data concerning possible historic properties not yet identified;

(3) Seek information, as appropriate, from consulting parties, and other individuals and organizations likely to have knowledge of, or concerns with, historic properties in the area, and identify issues relating to the under-

taking's potential effects on historic properties; and

(4) Gather information from any Indian tribe or Native Hawaiian organization identified pursuant to § 800.3(f) to assist in identifying properties, including those located off tribal lands, which may be of religious and cultural significance to them and may be eligible for the National Register, recognizing that an Indian tribe or native Hawaiian organization may be reluctant to divulge specific information regarding the location, nature, and activities associated with such sites. The Agency Official should address concerns raised about confidentiality pursuant to § 800.11(c).

(b) *Identify historic properties.* Based on the information gathered under § 800.4(a), and in consultation with the SHPO/THPO and any Indian tribe or native Hawaiian organization that might attach religious and cultural significance to properties within the area of potential effects, the Agency Official shall take the steps necessary to identify historic properties within the area of potential effects.

(1) *Level of effort.* The Agency Official shall make a reasonable and good faith effort to carry out appropriate identification efforts, which may include background research, consultation, oral history interviews, sample field investigation, and field survey. The Agency Official shall take into account past planning, research and studies, the magnitude and nature of the undertaking and the degree of Federal involvement, the nature and extent of potential effects on historic properties, and the likely nature and location of historic properties within the area of potential effects. The Secretary's Standards and Guidelines for Identification provide guidance on this subject. The Agency Official should also consider other applicable professional, State, tribal and local laws, standards and guidelines. The Agency Official shall take into account any confidentiality concerns raised by Indian tribes or Native Hawaiian organizations during the identification process.

(2) *Phased identification and evaluation.* Where alternatives under consideration consist of corridors or large

land areas, or where access to properties is restricted, the Agency Official may use a phased process to conduct identification and evaluation efforts. The Agency Official may also defer final identification and evaluation of historic properties if it is specifically provided for in a Memorandum of Agreement executed pursuant to § 800.6, a Programmatic Agreement executed pursuant to § 800.14(b), or the documents used by an Agency Official to comply with the National Environmental Policy Act pursuant to § 800.8. The process should establish the likely presence of historic properties within the area of potential effects for each alternative or inaccessible area through background research, consultation and an appropriate level of field investigation, taking into account the number of alternatives under consideration, the magnitude of the undertaking and its likely effects, and the views of the SHPO/THPO and any other consulting parties. As specific aspects or locations of an alternative are refined or access is gained, the Agency Official shall proceed with the identification and evaluation of historic properties in accordance with §§ 800.4(b)(1) and (c).

(c) *Evaluate historic significance*—(1) *Apply National Register Criteria.* In consultation with the SHPO/THPO and any Indian tribe or Native Hawaiian organization that attaches religious and cultural significance to identified properties and guided by the Secretary's Standards and Guidelines for Evaluation, the Agency Official shall apply the National Register Criteria (36 CFR part 63) to properties identified within the area of potential effects that have not been previously evaluated for National Register eligibility. The passage of time, changing perceptions of significance, or incomplete prior evaluations may require the Agency Official to reevaluate properties previously determined eligible or ineligible. The Agency Official shall acknowledge that Indian tribes and Native Hawaiian organizations possess special expertise in assessing the eligibility of historic properties that may possess religious and cultural significance to them.

(2) *Determine whether a property is eligible.* If the Agency Official determines any of the National Register Criteria are met and the SHPO/THPO agrees, the property shall be considered eligible for the National Register for section 106 purposes. If the Agency Official determines the criteria are not met and the SHPO/THPO agrees, the property shall be considered not eligible. If the Agency Official and the SHPO/THPO do not agree, or if the Council or the Secretary so request, the Agency Official shall obtain a determination of eligibility from the Secretary pursuant to 36 CFR part 63. If an Indian tribe or Native Hawaiian organization that attaches religious and cultural significance to a property off tribal lands does not agree, it may ask the Council to request the Agency Official to obtain a determination of eligibility.

(d) *Results of identification and evaluation*—(1) *No historic properties affected.* If the Agency Official finds that either there are no historic properties present or there are historic properties present but the undertaking will have no effect upon them as defined in § 800.16(i), the Agency Official shall provide documentation of this finding as set forth in § 800.11(d) to the SHPO/THPO. The Agency Official shall notify all consulting parties, including Indian tribes and Native Hawaiian organizations, and make the documentation available for public inspection prior to approving the undertaking. If the SHPO/THPO, or the Council if it has entered the section 106 process, does not object within 30 days of receipt of an adequately documented finding, the Agency Official's responsibilities under section 106 are fulfilled.

(2) *Historic properties affected.* If the Agency Official finds that there are historic properties which may be affected by the undertaking or the SHPO/THPO or the Council objects to the Agency Official's finding under § 800.4(d)(1), the Agency Official shall notify all consulting parties, including Indian tribes or Native Hawaiian organizations, invite their views on the effects and assess adverse effects, if any, in accordance with § 800.5.

§800.5 Assessment of adverse effects.

(a) *Apply criteria of adverse effect.* In consultation with the SHPO/THPO and any Indian tribe or Native Hawaiian organization that attaches religious and cultural significance to identified historic properties, the Agency Official shall apply the criteria of adverse effect to historic properties within the area of potential effects. The Agency Official shall consider any views concerning such effects which have been provided by consulting parties and the public.

(1) *Criteria of adverse effect.* An adverse effect is found when an undertaking may alter, directly or indirectly, any of the characteristics of a historic property that qualify the property for inclusion in the National Register in a manner that would diminish the integrity of the property's location, design, setting, materials, workmanship, feeling, or association. Consideration shall be given to all qualifying characteristics of a historic property, including those that may have been identified subsequent to the original evaluation of the property's eligibility for the National Register. Adverse effects may include reasonably foreseeable effects caused by the undertaking that may occur later in time, be farther removed in distance or be cumulative.

(2) *Examples of adverse effects.* Adverse effects on historic properties include, but are not limited to:

(i) Physical destruction of or damage to all or part of the property;

(ii) Alteration of a property, including restoration, rehabilitation, repair, maintenance, stabilization, hazardous material remediation and provision of handicapped access, that is not consistent with the Secretary's Standards for the Treatment of Historic Properties (36 CFR part 68) and applicable guidelines;

(iii) Removal of the property from its historic location;

(iv) Change of the character of the property's use or of physical features within the property's setting that contribute to its historic significance;

(v) Introduction of visual, atmospheric or audible elements that diminish the integrity of the property's significant historic features;

(vi) Neglect of a property which causes its deterioration, except where such neglect and deterioration are recognized qualities of a property of religious and cultural significance to an Indian tribe or Native Hawaiian organization; and

(vii) Transfer, lease, or sale of property out of Federal ownership or control without adequate and legally enforceable restrictions or conditions to ensure long-term preservation of the property's historic significance.

(3) *Phased application of criteria.* Where alternatives under consideration consist of corridors or large land areas, or where access to properties is restricted, the Agency Official may use a phased process in applying the criteria of adverse effect consistent with phased identification and evaluation efforts conducted pursuant to §800.4(b)(2).

(b) *Finding of no adverse effect.* The Agency Official, in consultation with the SHPO/THPO, may propose a finding of no adverse effect when the undertaking's effects do not meet the criteria of §800.5(a)(1) or the undertaking is modified or conditions are imposed, such as the subsequent review of plans for rehabilitation by the SHPO/THPO to ensure consistency with the Secretary's Standards for the Treatment of Historic Properties (36 CFR part 68) and applicable guidelines, to avoid adverse effects.

(c) *Consulting party review.* If the Agency Official proposes a finding of no adverse effect, the Agency Official shall notify all consulting parties of the finding and provide them with the documentation specified in §800.11(e). The SHPO/THPO shall have 30 days from receipt to review the finding.

(1) *Agreement with finding.* Unless the Council is reviewing the finding pursuant to §800.5(c)(3), the Agency Official may proceed if the SHPO/THPO agrees with the finding. The Agency Official shall carry out the undertaking in accordance with §800.5(d)(1). Failure of the SHPO/THPO to respond within 30 days from receipt of the finding shall be considered agreement of the SHPO/THPO with the finding.

(2) *Disagreement with finding.* (i) If the SHPO/THPO or any consulting party

disagrees within the 30-day review period, it shall specify the reasons for disagreeing with the finding. The Agency Official shall either consult with the party to resolve the disagreement, or request the Council to review the finding pursuant to §800.5(c)(3).

(ii) The Agency Official should seek the concurrence of any Indian tribe or Native Hawaiian organization that has made known to the Agency Official that it attaches religious and cultural significance to a historic property subject to the finding. If such Indian tribe or Native Hawaiian organization disagrees with the finding, it may within the 30-day review period specify the reasons for disagreeing with the finding and request the Council to review the finding pursuant to §800.5(c)(3).

(iii) If the Council on its own initiative so requests within the 30-day review period, the Agency Official shall submit the finding, along with the documentation specified in §800.11(e), for review pursuant to §800.5(c)(3). A Council decision to make such a request shall be guided by the criteria in appendix A to this part.

(3) *Council review of findings.* When a finding is submitted to the Council pursuant to §800.5(c)(2), the Agency Official shall include the documentation specified in §800.11(e). The Council shall review the finding and notify the Agency Official of its determination as to whether the adverse effect criteria have been correctly applied within 15 days of receiving the documented finding from the Agency Official. The Council shall specify the basis for its determination. The Agency Official shall proceed in accordance with the Council's determination. If the Council does not respond within 15 days of the receipt of the finding, the Agency Official may assume concurrence with the Agency Official's findings and proceed accordingly.

(d) *Results of assessment*—(1) *No adverse effect.* The Agency Official shall maintain a record of the finding and provide information on the finding to the public on request, consistent with the confidentiality provisions of §800.11(c). Implementation of the undertaking in accordance with the finding as documented fulfills the Agency Official's responsibilities under section 106 and this part. If the Agency Official will not conduct the undertaking as proposed in the finding, the Agency Official shall reopen consultation under §800.5(a).

(2) *Adverse effect.* If an adverse effect is found, the Agency Official shall consult further to resolve the adverse effect pursuant to §800.6.

§800.6 Resolution of adverse effects.

(a) *Continue consultation.* The Agency Official shall consult with the SHPO/THPO and other consulting parties, including Indian tribes and Native Hawaiian organizations, to develop and evaluate alternatives or modifications to the undertaking that could avoid, minimize or mitigate adverse effects on historic properties.

(1) *Notify the Council and determine Council participation.* The Agency Official shall notify the Council of the adverse effect finding by providing the documentation specified in §800.11(e).

(i) The notice shall invite the Council to participate in the consultation when:

(A) The Agency Official wants the Council to participate;

(B) The undertaking has an adverse effect upon a National Historic Landmark; or

(C) A Programmatic Agreement under §800.14(b) will be prepared;

(ii) The SHPO/THPO, an Indian tribe or Native Hawaiian organization, or any other consulting party may at any time independently request the Council to participate in the consultation.

(iii) The Council shall advise the Agency Official and all consulting parties whether it will participate within 15 days of receipt of notice or other request. Prior to entering the process, the Council shall provide written notice to the Agency Official and the consulting parties that its decision to participate meets the criteria set forth in appendix A to this part. The Council shall also advise the head of the agency of its decision to enter the process. Consultation with Council participation is conducted in accordance with §800.6(b)(2). (iv) If the Council does not join the consultation, the Agency Official shall proceed with consultation in accordance with §800.6(b)(1).

§ 800.6

(2) *Involve consulting parties.* In addition to the consulting parties identified under §800.3(f), the Agency Official, the SHPO/THPO and the Council, if participating, may agree to invite other individuals or organizations to become consulting parties. The Agency Official shall invite any individual or organization that will assume a specific role or responsibility in a Memorandum of Agreement to participate as a consulting party.

(3) *Provide documentation.* The Agency Official shall provide to all consulting parties the documentation specified in §800.11(e), subject to the confidentiality provisions of §800.11(c), and such other documentation as may be developed during the consultation to resolve adverse effects.

(4) *Involve the public.* The Agency Official shall make information available to the public, including the documentation specified in §800.11(e), subject to the confidentiality provisions of §800.11(c). The Agency Official shall provide an opportunity for members of the public to express their views on resolving adverse effects of the undertaking. The Agency Official should use appropriate mechanisms, taking into account the magnitude of the undertaking and the nature of its effects upon historic properties, the likely effects on historic properties, and the relationship of the Federal involvement to the undertaking to ensure that the public's views are considered in the consultation. The Agency Official should also consider the extent of notice and information concerning historic preservation issues afforded the public at earlier steps in the Section 106 process to determine the appropriate level of public involvement when resolving adverse effects so that the standards of §800.2(d) are met.

(5) *Restrictions on disclosure of information.* Section 304 of the Act and other authorities may limit the disclosure of information under §§800.6(a)(3) and (4). If an Indian tribe or Native Hawaiian organization objects to the disclosure of information or if the Agency Official believes that there are other reasons to withhold information, the Agency Official shall comply with §800.11(c) regarding the disclosure of such information.

(b) *Resolve adverse effects*—(1) *Resolution without the Council.* (i) The Agency Official shall consult with the SHPO/THPO and other consulting parties to seek ways to avoid, minimize or mitigate the adverse effects.

(ii) The Agency Official may use standard treatments established by the Council under §800.14(d) as a basis for a Memorandum of Agreement.

(iii) If the Council decides to join the consultation, the Agency Official shall follow §800.6(b)(2).

(iv) If the Agency Official and the SHPO/THPO agree on how the adverse effects will be resolved, they shall execute a Memorandum of Agreement. The Agency Official must submit a copy of the executed Memorandum of Agreement, along with the documentation specified in §800.11(f), to the Council prior to approving the undertaking in order to meet the requirements of section 106 and this subpart.

(v) If the Agency Official, and the SHPO/THPO fail to agree on the terms of a Memorandum of Agreement, the Agency Official shall request the Council to join the consultation and provide the Council with the documentation set forth in §800.11(g). If the Council decides to join the consultation, the Agency Official shall proceed in accordance with §800.6(b)(2). If the Council decides not to join the consultation, the Council will notify the agency and proceed to comment in accordance with §800.7(c).

(2) *Resolution with Council participation.* If the Council decides to participate in the consultation, the Agency Official shall consult with the SHPO/THPO, the Council, and other consulting parties, including Indian tribes and Native Hawaiian organizations under §800.2(c)(3), to seek ways to avoid, minimize or mitigate the adverse effects. If the Agency Official, the SHPO/THPO, and the Council agree on how the adverse effects will be resolved, they shall execute a Memorandum of Agreement.

(c) *Memorandum of Agreement.* A Memorandum of Agreement executed and implemented pursuant to this section evidences the Agency Official's compliance with section 106 and this part and shall govern the undertaking and all of its parts. A Memorandum of

Agreement executed pursuant to §800.6(b)(1) that is filed with the Council shall be considered to be an agreement with the Council for the purposes of Section 110(1) of the Act. The Agency Official shall ensure that the undertaking is carried out in accordance with the Memorandum of Agreement.

(1) *Signatories.* The signatories have sole authority to execute, amend or terminate the agreement in accordance with this subpart.

(i) The Agency Official and the SHPO/THPO are the signatories to a Memorandum of Agreement executed pursuant to §800.6(b)(1).

(ii) The Agency Official, the SHPO/THPO, and the Council are the signatories to a Memorandum of Agreement executed pursuant to §800.6(b)(2).

(iii) The Agency Official and the Council are signatories to a Memorandum of Agreement executed pursuant to §800.7(a)(2).

(2) *Invited signatories.* (i) The Agency Official may invite an Indian tribe or Native Hawaiian organization that attaches religious and cultural significance to historic properties located off tribal lands to be a signatory to a Memorandum of Agreement concerning such properties.

(ii) The signatories should invite any party that assumes a responsibility under a Memorandum of Agreement to be a signatory.

(iii) The refusal of any party invited to become a signatory to a Memorandum of Agreement pursuant to §800.6(c)(2)(i) or (ii) does not invalidate the Memorandum of Agreement.

(3) *Concurrence by others.* The Agency Official may invite all consulting parties to concur in the Memorandum of Agreement. The signatories may agree to invite others to concur. The refusal of any party invited to concur in the Memorandum of Agreement does not invalidate the Memorandum of Agreement.

(4) *Reports on implementation.* Where the signatories agree it is appropriate, a Memorandum of Agreement shall include a provision for monitoring and reporting on its implementation.

(5) *Duration.* A Memorandum of Agreement shall include provisions for termination and for reconsideration of

§ 800.7

terms if the undertaking has not been implemented within a specified time.

(6) *Discoveries.* Where the signatories agree it is appropriate, a Memorandum of Agreement shall include provisions to deal with the subsequent discovery or identification of additional historic properties affected by the undertaking.

(7) *Amendments.* The signatories to a Memorandum of Agreement may amend it. If the Council was not a signatory to the original agreement and the signatories execute an amended agreement, the Agency Official shall file it with the Council.

(8) *Termination.* If any signatory determines that the terms of a Memorandum of Agreement cannot be carried out, the signatories shall consult to seek amendment of the agreement. If the agreement is not amended, any signatory may terminate it. The Agency Official shall either execute a Memorandum of Agreement with signatories under §800.6(c)(1) or request the comments of the council under §800.7(a).

(9) *Copies.* The Agency Official shall provide each consulting party with a copy of any Memorandum of Agreement executed pursuant to this subpart.

§ 800.7 **Failure to resolve adverse effects.**

(a) *Termination of consultation.* After consulting to resolve adverse effects pursuant to §800.6(b)(2), the Agency Official the SHPO/THPO, or the Council may determine that further consultation will not be productive and terminate consultation. Any party that terminates consultation shall notify the other consulting parties and provide them the reasons for terminating in writing.

(1) If the Agency Official terminates consultation, the head of the agency or an Assistant Secretary or other officer with major department-wide or agency-wide responsibilities shall request that the Council comment pursuant to §800.7(c) and shall notify all consulting parties of the request.

(2) If the SHPO terminates consultation, the Agency Official and the Council may execute a Memorandum of Agreement without the SHPO's involvement.

(3) If a THPO terminates consultation regarding an undertaking occurring on or affecting historic properties on its tribal lands, the Council shall comment pursuant to §800.7(c).

(4) If the Council terminates consultation with the agency's Federal Agency Official, the Council shall notify the agency's Federal Preservation Officer and all consulting parties of the termination and comment under §800.7(c). The Council may consult with the agency's Federal Preservation Officer prior to terminating consultation to seek to resolve issues concerning the undertaking and its effects on historic properties.

(b) *Comments without termination.* The Council may determine that it is appropriate to provide additional advisory comments upon an undertaking for which a Memorandum of Agreement will be executed. The Council shall provide them to the Agency Official when it executes the Memorandum of Agreement.

(c) *Comments by the Council*—(1) *Preparation.* The Council shall provide an opportunity for the Agency Official, all consulting parties, and the public to provide their views within the time frame for developing its comments. Upon request of the Council, the Agency Official shall provide additional existing information concerning the undertaking and assist the Council in arranging an onsite inspection and an opportunity for public participation.

(2) *Timing.* The Council shall transmit its comments within 45 days of receipt of a request under §§800.7(a) (1) or (3) or §800.8(c)(3), or termination by the Council under §800.6(b)(1)(v) or §800.7(a)(4), unless otherwise agreed to by the Agency Official.

(3) *Transmittal.* The Council shall provide its comments to the head of the agency requesting comment with copies to the Agency Official, the agency's Federal Preservation Officer, all consulting parties, and others as appropriate.

(4) *Response to Council comment.* The head of the agency shall take into account the Council's comments in reaching a final decision on the undertaking. Section 110(l) of the Act directs that the head of the agency shall document this decision and may not delegate his or her responsibilities pursuant to section 106. Documenting the agency head's decision shall include:

(i) Preparing a summary of the decision that contains the rationale for the decision and evidence of consideration of the Council's comments and providing it to the Council prior to approval of the undertaking;

(ii) Providing a copy of the summary to all consulting parties; and

(iii) Notifying the public and making the record available for public inspection.

§800.8 Coordination with the National Environmental Policy Act.

(a) *General principles*—(1) *Early coordination.* Federal agencies are encouraged to coordinate compliance with section 106 and the procedures in this part with any steps taken to meet the requirements of the National Environmental Policy Act (NEPA). Agencies should consider their Section 106 responsibilities as early as possible in the NEPA process, and plan their public participation, analysis, and review in such a way that they can meet the purposes and requirements of both statutes in a timely and efficient manner. The determination of whether an undertaking is a "major Federal action significantly affecting the quality of the human environment," and therefore requires preparation of an Environmental Impact Statement (EIS) under NEPA, should include consideration of the undertaking's likely effects on historic properties. A finding of adverse effect on a historic property does not necessarily require an EIS under NEPA.

(2) *Consulting party rules.* SHPO/THPOs, Indian tribes and Native Hawaiian organizations, other consulting parties, and organizations and individuals who may be concerned with the possible effects of an agency action on historic properties should be prepared to consult with agencies early in the NEPA process, when the purpose of and need for the proposed action as well as the widest possible range of alternatives are under consideration.

(3) *Inclusion of historic preservation issues.* Agency Officials should ensure that preparation of an Environmental Assessment (EA) and Finding of No Significant Impact (FONSI) and an EIS

and Record of Decision (ROD) includes appropriate scoping, identification of historic properties, assessment of effects upon them, and consultation leading to resolution of any adverse effects.

(b) *Actions categorically excluded under NEPA.* If a project, activity or program is categorically excluded from NEPA review under an agency's NEPA procedures, the Agency Official shall determine if it still qualifies as an undertaking requiring review under section 106 pursuant to §800.3(a). If so, the Agency Official shall proceed with Section 106 review in accordance with the procedures in this subpart.

(c) *Use of the NEPA process for section 106 purposes.* An Agency Official may use the process and documentation required for the preparation of an EA/FONSI or an EIS/ROD to comply with section 106 in lieu of the procedures set forth in §§800.3 through 800.6 if the Agency Official has notified in advance the SHPO/THPO and the Council that it intends to do so and the following standards are met.

(1) *Standards for developing environmental documents to comply with section 106.* During preparation of the EA or Draft EIS (DEIS) the Agency Official shall:

(i) Identify consulting parties either pursuant to §800.3(f) or through NEPA scoping process with results consistent with §800.3(f);

(ii) Identify historic properties and assess the effects of the undertaking on such properties in a manner consistent with the standards and criteria of §§800.4 through 800.5, provided that the scope and timing of these steps may be phased to reflect the Agency Official's consideration of project alternatives in the NEPA process and the effort is commensurate with the assessment of other environmental factors;

(iii) Consult regarding the effects of the undertaking on historic properties with the SHPO/THPO, Indian tribes and Native Hawaiian organizations that might attach religious and cultural significance to affected historic properties, other consulting parties, and the Council, where appropriate, during NEPA scoping, environmental analysis, and the preparation of NEPA documents;

(iv) Involve the public in accordance with the agency's published NEPA procedures; and

(v) Develop in consultation with identified consulting parties alternatives and proposed measures that might avoid, minimize or mitigate any adverse effects of the undertaking on historic properties and describe them in the EA or DEIS.

(2) *Review of environmental documents.*

(i) The Agency Official shall submit the EA, DEIS or EIS to the SHPO/THPO, Indian tribes and Native Hawaiian organizations that might attach religious and cultural significance to affected historic properties, and other consulting parties prior to or when making the document available for public comment. If the document being prepared is a DEIS or EIS, the Agency Official shall also submit it to the Council.

(ii) Prior to or within the time allowed for public comment on the document, a SHPO/THPO, an Indian tribe or Native Hawaiian organization, another consulting party or the Council may object to the Agency Official that preparation of the EA, DEIS or EIS has not met the standards set forth in §800.8(c)(1) or that the substantive resolution of the effects on historic properties proposed in an EA, DEIS or EIS is inadequate. If the Agency Official receives such an objection, the Agency Official shall refer the matter to the Council.

(3) *Resolution of objections.* Within 30 days of the Agency Official's referral of an objection under §800.8(c)(2)(ii), the Council shall notify the Agency Official either that it agrees with the objection, in which case consultation in accordance with §800.6(b)(2) or seek Council comments in accordance with §800.7(a), or that it disagrees with the objection, in which case the Agency Official shall continue its compliance with this section. Failure of the Council to respond within the 30 day period shall be considered disagreement with the objection.

(4) *Approval of the undertaking.* If the Agency Official has found during the preparation of the EA, DEIS or EIS that the effects of the undertaking on historic properties are adverse, the

§800.9

Agency Official shall specify in the FONSI or the ROD the proposed measures to avoid, minimize or mitigate such effects and ensure that the approval of the undertaking is conditioned accordingly. The Agency Official's responsibilities under Section 106 and the procedures in this subpart shall then be satisfied when either the proposed measures have been adopted through a binding commitment or the agency, the applicant or other entities, as appropriate, or the Council has commented and received the response to such comments under §800.7. Where the NEPA process results in a FONSI, the Agency Official must adopt such a binding commitment through a Memorandum of Agreement drafted in compliance with §800.6(c). Where the NEPA process results in an EIS, the binding commitment does not have to be in the form of a Memorandum of Agreement drafted in compliance with §800.6(c).

(5) *Modification of the undertaking.* If the undertaking is modified after approval of the FONSI or the ROD in a manner that changes the undertaking or alters its effects on historic properties, or if the Agency Official fails to ensure that the measures to avoid, minimize or mitigate adverse effects (as specified in either the FONSI or the ROD, or in the binding commitment adopted pursuant to §800.8(c)(4)) are carried out, the Agency official shall notify the Council and all consulting parties that supplemental environmental documents will be prepared in compliance with NEPA or that the procedures in §§800.3 through 800.6 will be followed as necessary.

§800.9 Council review of Section 106 compliance.

(a) *Assessment of Agency Official compliance for individual undertakings.* The Council may provide to the Agency Official its advisory opinion regarding the substance of any finding, determination or decision or regarding the adequacy of the Agency Official's compliance with the procedures under this part. The Council may provide such advice at any time at the request of any individual, agency or organization or on its own initiative. The Agency Official shall consider the views of the

Council in reaching a decision on the matter in question.

(b) *Agency foreclosure of the Council's opportunity to comment.* Where an Agency Official has failed to complete the requirements of section 106 in accordance with the procedures in this part prior to the approval of an undertaking, the Council's opportunity to comment may be foreclosed. The Council may review a case to determine whether a foreclosure has occurred. The Council shall notify the Agency Official and allow 30 days for the Agency Official to provide information as to whether foreclosure has occurred. If the Council determines foreclosure has occurred, the Council shall transmit the determination to the Agency Official and the head of the agency. The Council shall also make the determination available to the public and any parties known to be interested in the undertaking and its effects upon historic properties.

(c) *Intentional adverse effects by applicants*—(1) *Agency responsibility.* Section 110(k) of the Act prohibits a Federal agency from granting a loan, loan guarantee, permit, license or other assistance to an applicant who, with intent to avoid the requirements of section 106, has intentionally significantly adversely affected a historic property to which the grant would relate, or having legal power to prevent it, has allowed such significant adverse effect to occur, unless the agency, after consultation with the Council, determines that circumstances justify granting such assistance despite the adverse effect created or permitted by the applicant. Guidance issued by the Secretary pursuant to section 110 of the Act governs its implementation.

(2) *Consultation with the Council.* When an Agency Official determines, based on the actions of an applicant, that section 110(k) is applicable and that circumstances may justify granting the assistance, the Agency Official shall notify the Council and provide documentation specifying the circumstances under which the adverse effects to the historic property occurred and the degree of damage to the integrity of the property. This documentation shall include any views obtained

---

§800.10

from the applicant, SHPO/THPO, an Indian tribe if the undertaking occurs on or affects historic properties on tribal lands, and other parties known to be interested in the undertaking.

(i) Within thirty days of receiving the Agency Official's notification, unless otherwise agreed to by the Agency Official, the Council shall provide the Agency Official with its opinion as to whether circumstances justify granting assistance to the applicant and any possible mitigation of the adverse effects.

(ii) The Agency Official shall consider the Council's opinion in making a decision on whether to grant assistance to the applicant, and shall notify the Council, the SHPO/THPO, and other parties known to be interested in the undertaking prior to granting the assistance.

(3) *Compliance with Section 106.* If an Agency Official, after consulting with the Council, determines to grant assistance, the Agency Official shall comply with §§800.3–800.6 to take into account the effects of the undertaking on any historic properties.

(d) *Evaluation of Section 106 operations.* The Council may evaluate the operation of the Section 106 process by periodic reviews of how participants have fulfilled their legal responsibilities and how effectively the outcomes reached advance the purposes of the Act.

(1) *Information from participants.* Section 203 of the Act authorizes the Council to obtain information from Federal agencies necessary to conduct evaluation of the Section 106 process. The Council may request available information and documentation from other participants in the Section 106 process.

(2) *Improving the operation of Section 106.* Based upon any evaluation of the section 106 process, the Council may make recommendations to participants, the heads of Federal agencies, and the Secretary of actions to improve the efficiency and effectiveness of the process. Where the Council determines that an Agency Official or a

SHPO/THPO has failed to properly carry out the responsibilities assigned under the procedures in this part, the Council may participate in individual case reviews in a manner and for a period that it determines is necessary to improve performance or correct deficiencies. If the Council finds a pattern of failure by a Federal agency in carrying out its responsibilities under section 106, the Council may review the policies and programs of the agency related to historic preservation pursuant to section 202(a)(6) of the Act and recommend methods to improve the effectiveness, coordination, and consistency of those policies and programs with section 106.

§800.10 Special requirements for protecting National Historic Landmarks.

(a) *Statutory requirement.* Section 110(f) of the Act requires that the Agency Official, to the maximum extent possible undertake such planning and actions as may be necessary to minimize harm to any National Historic Landmark that may be directly and adversely affected by an undertaking. When commenting on such undertaking, the Council shall use the process set forth in §§800.6 through 800.7 and give special consideration to protecting National Historic Landmarks as specified in this section.

(b) *Resolution of adverse effects.* The Agency Official shall request the Council to participate in any consultation to resolve adverse effects on National Historic Landmarks conducted under §800.6.

(c) *Involvement of the Secretary.* The Agency Official shall notify the Secretary of any consultation involving a National Historic Landmark and invite the Secretary to participate in the consultation where there may be an adverse effect. The Council may request a report from the Secretary under section 213 of the Act to assist in the consultation.

(d) *Report of outcome.* When the Council participates in consultation involving this section, it shall report the outcome of the section 106 process, providing its written comments or any Memoranda of Agreement to which it is a signatory, to the Secretary and the

§ 800.11

head of the agency responsible for the undertaking.

§ 800.11 Documentation standards.

(a) *Adequacy of documentation.* The Agency Official shall ensure that a determination, finding, or agreement under the procedures in this subpart is supported by sufficient documentation to enable any reviewing parties to understand its basis. When an Agency Official is conducting phased identification or evaluation under this subpart, the documentation standards regarding description of historic properties may be applied flexibly. If the Council, or the SHPO/THPO when the Council is not involved, determines the applicable documentation standards are not met, the Council or the SHPO/THPO, as appropriate, shall notify the Agency Official and specify the information needed to meet the standard. At the request of the Agency Official or any of the consulting parties, the Council shall review any disputes over whether documentation standards are met and provide its views to the Agency Official and the consulting parties.

(b) *Format.* The Agency Official may use documentation prepared to comply with other laws to fulfill the requirements of the procedures in this subpart, if that documentation meets the standards of this section.

(c) *Confidentiality*—(1) *Authority to withhold information.* Section 304 of the Act provides that the head of a Federal agency or other public official receiving grant assistance pursuant to the Act, after consultation with the Secretary, shall withhold from public disclosure information about the location, character, or ownership of a historic property when disclosure may cause a significant invasion of privacy; risk harm to the historic property; or impede the use of a traditional religious site by practitioners. When the head of a Federal agency or other public official has determined that information should be withheld from the public pursuant to the criteria above, the Secretary, in consultation with such Federal agency head or official, shall determine who may have access to the information for the purpose of carrying out the Act.

(2) *Consultation with the Council.* When the information in question has been developed in the course of an agency's compliance with this part, the Secretary shall consult with the Council in reaching determinations on the withholding and release of information. The Federal agency shall provide the Council with available information, including views of Indian tribes and Native Hawaiian organizations, related to the confidentiality concern. The Council shall advise the Secretary and the Federal agency within 30 days of receipt of adequate documentation.

(3) *Other authorities affecting confidentiality.* Other Federal laws and program requirements may limit public access to information concerning an undertaking and its effects on historic properties. Where applicable, those authorities shall govern public access to information developed in the Section 106 process and may authorize the Agency Official to protect the privacy of non-governmental applicants.

(d) *Finding of no historic properties affected.* Documentation shall include:

(1) A description of the undertaking, specifying the Federal involvement, and its area of potential effects, including photographs, maps, drawings, as necessary;

(2) A description of the steps taken to identify historic properties, including, as appropriate, efforts to seek information pursuant to § 800.4(b); and

(3) The basis for determining that no historic properties are present or affected.

(e) *Finding of no adverse effect or adverse effect.* Documentation shall include:

(1) A description of the undertaking, specifying the Federal involvement, and its area of potential effects, including photographs, maps, and drawings, as necessary;

(2) A description of the steps taken to identify historic properties;

(3) A description of the affected historic properties, including information on the characteristics that qualify them for the National Register;

(4) A description of the undertaking's effects on historic properties;

(5) An explanation of why the criteria of adverse effect were found applicable

or inapplicable, including any conditions or future actions to avoid, minimize or mitigate adverse effects; and

(6) Copies or summaries of any views provided by consulting parties and the public.

(f) *Memorandum of Agreement.* When a Memorandum of Agreement is filed with the Council, the documentation shall include any substantive revisions or additions to the documentation provided the Council pursuant to § 800.6(a)(1), an evaluation of any measures considered to avoid or minimize the undertaking's adverse effects and a summary of the views of consulting parties and the public.

(g) *Requests for comment without a Memorandum of Agreement.* Documentation shall include:

(1) A description and evaluation of any alternatives or mitigation measures that the Agency Official proposes to resolve the undertaking's adverse effects;

(2) A description of any reasonable alternatives or mitigation measures that were considered but not chosen, and the reasons for their rejection;

(3) Copies or summaries of any views submitted to the Agency Official concerning the adverse effects of the undertaking on historic properties and alternatives to reduce or avoid those effects; and

(4) Any substantive revisions or additions to the documentation provided the Council pursuant to § 800.6(a)(1).

§ 800.12 Emergency situations.

(a) *Agency procedures.* The Agency Official, in consultation with the appropriate SHPOs/THPOs, affected Indian tribes and Native Hawaiian organizations, and the Council, is encouraged to develop procedures for taking historic properties into account during operations which respond to a disaster or emergency declared by the President, a tribal government or the governor of a State or which respond to other immediate threats to life or property. If approved by the Council, the procedures shall govern the agency's historic preservation responsibilities during any disaster or emergency in lieu of §§ 800.3 through 800.6.

(b) *Alternatives to agency procedures.* In the event an Agency Official pro-

§ 800.12

poses an emergency undertaking as an essential and immediate response to a disaster or emergency declared by the President, a tribal government or the governor of a State or another immediate threat to life or property, and the agency has not developed procedures pursuant to § 800.12(a), the Agency Official may comply with section 106 by:

(1) Following a Programmatic Agreement developed pursuant to § 800.14(b) that contains specific provisions for dealing with historic properties in emergency situations; or

(2) Notifying the Council, the appropriate SHPO/THPO and any Indian tribe or Native Hawaiian organization that may attach religious and cultural significance to historic properties likely to be affected prior to the undertaking and affording them an opportunity to comment within seven days of notification. If the Agency Official determines that circumstances do not permit seven days for comment, the Agency Official shall notify the Council, the SHPO/THPO and the Indian tribe or Native Hawaiian organization and invite any comments within the time available.

(c) *Local governments responsible for section 106 compliance.* When a local government official serves as the Agency Official for section 106 compliance, § 800.12 (a) and (b) also apply to an imminent threat to public health or safety as a result of a natural disaster or emergency declared by a local government's chief executive officer or legislative body, provided that if the Council or SHPO/THPO objects to the proposed action within seven days, the Agency Official shall comply with §§ 800.3 through 800.6.

(d) *Applicability.* This section applies only to undertakings that will be implemented within 30 days after the disaster or emergency has been formally declared by the appropriate authority. An agency may request an extension of the period of applicability from the Council prior to the expiration of the 30 days. Immediate rescue and salvage operations conducted to preserve life or property are exempt from the provisions of section 106 and this part.

§800.13

§800.13 Post-review discoveries.

(a) *Planning for subsequent discoveries*—(1) *Using a Programmatic Agreement.* An Agency Official may develop a Programmatic Agreement pursuant to §800.14(b) to govern the actions to be taken when historic properties are discovered during the implementation of an undertaking.

(2) *Using agreement documents.* When the Agency Official's identification efforts in accordance with §800.4 indicate that historic properties are likely to be discovered during implementation of an undertaking and no Programmatic Agreement has been developed pursuant to §800.13(a)(1), the Agency Official shall include in any finding of no adverse effect or Memorandum of Agreement a process to resolve any adverse effects upon such properties. Actions in conformance with the process satisfy the Agency Official's responsibilities under section 106 and this part.

(b) *Discoveries without prior planning.* If historic properties are discovered or unanticipated effects on historic properties found after the Agency Official has completed the section 106 process without establishing a process under §800.13(a), the Agency Official shall make reasonable efforts to avoid, minimize or mitigate adverse effects to such properties and:

(1) If the Agency Official has not approved the undertaking or if construction on an approved undertaking has not commenced, consult to resolve adverse effects pursuant to §800.6; or

(2) If the Agency Official, the SHPO/THPO and any Indian tribe or Native Hawaiian organization that might attach religious and cultural significance to the affected property agree that such property is of value solely for its scientific, prehistoric, historic or archaeological data, the Agency Official may comply with the Archaeological and Historic Preservation Act instead of the procedures in this part and provide the Council, the SHPO/THPO, and the Indian tribe or Native Hawaiian organization a report on the actions within a reasonable time after they are completed; or

(3) If the Agency Official has approved the undertaking and construction has commenced, determine actions that the Agency Official can take

to resolve adverse effects, and notify the SHPO/THPO, any Indian tribe or Native Hawaiian organization that might attach religious and cultural significance to the affected property, and the Council within 48 hours of the discovery. The notification shall describe the actions proposed by the Agency Official to resolve the adverse effects. The SHPO/THPO, the Indian tribe or Native Hawaiian organization and the Council shall respond within 48 hours of the notification and the Agency Official shall take into account their recommendations and carry out appropriate actions. The Agency Official shall provide the SHPO/THPO, the Indian tribe or Native Hawaiian organization and the Council a report of the actions when they are completed.

(c) *Eligibility of properties.* The Agency Official, in consultation with the SHPO/THPO, may assume a newly-discovered property to be eligible for the National Register for purposes of Section 106. The Agency Official shall specify the National Register Criteria used to assume the property's eligibility so that information can be used in the resolution of adverse effects.

(d) *Discoveries on tribal lands.* If historic properties are discovered on tribal lands, or there are unanticipated effects on historic properties found on tribal lands, after the Agency Official has completed the section 106 process without establishing a process under §800.13(a) and construction has commenced, the Agency Official shall comply with applicable tribal regulations and procedures and obtain the concurrence of the Indian tribe on the proposed action.

Subpart C—Program Alternatives

§800.14 Federal agency program alternatives.

(a) *Alternate procedures.* An Agency Official may develop procedures to implement section 106 and substitute them for all or part of subpart B of this part if they are consistent with the Council's regulations pursuant to section 110(a)(2)(E) of the Act.

(1) *Development of procedures.* The Agency Official shall consult with the Council, the National Conference of State Historic Preservation Officers or

Advisory Council on Historic Preservation

individual SHPO/THPOs, as appropriate, and Indian tribes and Native Hawaiian organizations, as specified in §800.14(f), in the development of alternate procedures, publish notice of the availability of proposed alternate procedures in the FEDERAL REGISTER and take other appropriate steps to seek public input during the development of alternate procedures.

(2) *Council review.* The Agency Official shall submit the proposed alternate procedures to the Council for a 60-day review period. If the Council finds the procedures to be consistent with this part, it shall notify the Agency Official and the Agency Official may adopt them as final alternate procedures.

(3) *Notice.* The Agency Official shall notify the parties with which it has consulted and publish notice of final alternate procedures in the FEDERAL REGISTER.

(4) *Legal effect.* Alternate procedures adopted pursuant to this subpart substitute for the Council's regulations for the purposes of the agency's compliance with section 106, except that where an Indian tribe has entered into an agreement with the Council to substitute tribal historic preservation regulations for the Council's regulations under section 101(d)(5) of the Act, the agency shall follow those regulations regarding undertakings on tribal lands. Prior to the Council entering into such agreements, the Council will provide federal agencies notice and opportunity to comment on the proposed substitute tribal regulations.

(b) *Programmatic Agreements.* The Council and the Agency Official may negotiate a Programmatic Agreement to govern the implementation of a particular program or the resolution of adverse effects from certain complex project situations or multiple undertakings.

(1) *Use of Programmatic Agreements.* A Programmatic Agreement may be used:

(i) When effects on historic properties are similar and repetitive or are multi-State or regional in scope;

(ii) When effects on historic properties cannot be fully determined prior to approval of an undertaking;

§800.14

(iii) When nonfederal parties are delegated major decisionmaking responsibilities;

(iv) Where routine management activities are undertaken at Federal installations, facilities, or other land-management units; or

(v) Where other circumstances warrant a departure from the normal section 106 process.

(2) *Developing Programmatic Agreements for agency programs*—(i) *Consultation.* The consultation shall involve, as appropriate, SHPO/THPOs, the National Conference of State Historic Preservation Officers (NCSHPO), Indian tribes and Native Hawaiian organizations, other Federal agencies, and members of the public. If the Programmatic Agreement has the potential to affect historic properties on tribal lands or historic properties of religious and cultural significance to an Indian tribe or Native Hawaiian organization, the Agency Official shall also follow §800.14(f).

(ii) *Public Participation.* The Agency Official shall arrange for public participation appropriate to the subject matter and the scope of the program and in accordance with subpart A of this part. The Agency Official shall consider the nature of the program and its likely effects on historic properties and take steps to involve the individuals, organizations and entities likely to be interested.

(iii) *Effect.* The Programmatic Agreement shall take effect when executed by the Council, the Agency Official and the appropriate SHPOs/THPOs when the Programmatic Agreement concerns a specific region or the President of NCSHPO when NCSHPO has participated in the consultation. A Programmatic Agreement shall take effect on tribal lands only when the THPO, Indian tribe or a designated representative of the tribe is a signatory to the agreement. Compliance with the procedures established by an approved Programmatic Agreement satisfies the agency's section 106 responsibilities for all individual undertakings of the program covered by the agreement until it expires or is terminated by the agency, the President of NCSHPO when a signatory, or the Council. Termination by an individual SHPO/THPO shall only terminate the application of a regional Programmatic Agreement within the jurisdiction of the SHPO/THPO. If a THPO assumes the responsibilities of a SHPO pursuant to section 101(d)(2) of the Act and the SHPO is signatory to the Programmatic Agreement, the THPO assumes the role of a signatory, including the right to terminate a regional Programmatic Agreement on lands under the jurisdiction of the tribe.

(iv) *Notice.* The Agency Official shall notify the parties with which it has consulted that a Programmatic Agreement has been executed under this subsection, provide appropriate public notice before it takes effect, and make any internal agency procedures implementing the agreement readily available to the Council, SHPO/THPOs, and the public.

(v) *Terms not carried out or termination.* If the Council determines that the terms of a Programmatic Agreement are not being carried out, or if such an agreement is terminated, the Agency Official shall comply with subpart B of this part with regard to individual undertakings of the program covered by the agreement.

(3) *Developing Programmatic Agreements for complex or multiple undertakings.* Consultation to develop a Programmatic Agreement for dealing with the potential adverse effects of complex projects or multiple undertakings shall follow §800.6. If consultation pertains to an activity involving multiple undertakings and the parties fail to reach agreement, then the Agency Official shall comply with the provisions of subpart B of this part for each individual undertaking.

(c) *Exempted categories*—(1) *Criteria for establishing.* An Agency Official may propose a program or category of agency undertakings that may be exempted from review under the provisions of subpart B of this part, if the program or category meets the following criteria:

(i) The actions within the program or category would otherwise qualify as "undertakings" as defined in §800.16;

(ii) The potential effects of the undertakings within the program or category upon historic properties are foreseeable and likely to be minimal or not adverse; and

(iii) Exemption of the program or category is consistent with the purpose of the Act.

(2) *Public participation.* The Agency Official shall arrange for public participation appropriate to the subject matter and the scope of the exemption and in accordance with subpart A of this part. The Agency Official shall consider the nature of the exemption and its likely effects on historic properties and take steps to involve individuals, organizations and entities likely to be interested.

(3) *Consultation with SHPOs/THPOs.* The Agency Official shall notify and consider the views of the SHPOs/THPOs on the exemption.

(4) *Consultation with Indian tribes and Native Hawaiian organizations.* If the exempted program or category of undertakings has the potential to affect historic properties of religious and cultural significance to an Indian tribe or Native Hawaiian organization, the Council shall follow the requirements for the Agency Official set forth in §800.14(f).

(5) *Council review of proposed exemptions.* The Council shall review a request for an exemption that is supported by documentation describing the program or category for which the exemption is sought, demonstrating that the criteria of §800.14(c)(1) have been met, describing the methods used to seek the views of the public, and summarizing any views submitted by the public. Unless it requests further information, the Council shall approve or reject the proposed exemption within 30 days of receipt. The decision shall be based on the consistency of the exemption with the purposes of the Act, taking into consideration the magnitude of the exempted undertaking or program and the likelihood of impairment of historic properties in accordance with section 214 of the Act.

(6) *Legal consequences.* Any undertaking that falls within an approved exempted program or category shall require no further review pursuant to subpart B of this part, unless the Agency Official or the Council determines that there are circumstances under which the normally excluded undertaking should be reviewed under subpart B of this part.

(7) *Termination.* The Council may terminate an exemption at the request of the Agency Official or when the Council determines that the exemption no longer meets the criteria of §800.14(c)(1). The Council shall notify the Agency Official 30 days before termination becomes effective.

(8) *Notice.* The Agency Official shall publish notice of any approved exemption in the FEDERAL REGISTER.

(d) *Standard treatments*—(1) *Establishment.* The Council, on its own initiative or at the request of another party, may establish standard methods for the treatment of a category of historic properties, a category of undertakings, or a category or effects on historic properties to assist Federal agencies in satisfying the requirements of subpart B of this part. The Council shall publish notice of standard treatments in the FEDERAL REGISTER.

(2) *Public participation.* The Council shall arrange for public participation appropriate to the subject matter and the scope of the standard treatment and consistent with subpart A of this part. The Council shall consider the nature of the standard treatment and its likely effects on historic properties and the individuals, organizations and entities likely to be interests. Where an Agency Official has proposed a standard treatment, the Council may request the Agency Official to arrange for public involvement.

(3) *Consultation with SHPOs/THPOs.* The Council shall notify and consider the views of SHPOs/THPOs on the proposed standard treatment.

(4) *Consultation with Indian tribes and Native Hawaiian organizations.* If the proposed standard treatment has the potential to affect historic properties on tribal lands or historic properties of religious and cultural significance to an Indian tribe or Native Hawaiian organization, the Council shall follow the requirements for the Agency Official set forth in §800.14(f).

(5) *Termination.* The Council may terminate a standard treatment by publication of notice in the FEDERAL REGISTER 30 days before the termination takes effect.

(e) *Program comments.* An Agency Official may request the Council to comment on a category of undertakings in lieu of conducting individual reviews under §§800.4 through 800.6. The Council may provide program comments at its own initiative.

(1) *Agency request.* The Agency Official shall identify the category of undertakings, specify the likely effects on historic properties, specify the steps the Agency Official will take to ensure that the effects are taken into account, identify the time period for which the comment is requested and summarize any views submitted by the public.

(2) *Public participation.* The Agency Official shall arrange for public participation appropriate to the subject matter and the scope of the category and in accordance with the standard in subpart A of this part. The Agency Official shall consider the nature of the undertakings and their likely effects on historic properties and the individuals, organizations and entities likely to be interested.

(3) *Consultation with SHPOs/THPOs.* The Council shall notify and consider the views of SHPOs/THPOs on the proposed program comment.

(4) *Consultation with Indian tribes and Native Hawaiian organizations.* If the program comment has the potential to affect historic properties on tribal lands or historic properties of religious and cultural significance to an Indian tribe or Native Hawaiian organization, the Council shall follow the requirements for the Agency Official set forth in §800.14(f).

(5) *Council action.* Unless the Council requests additional documentation, notifies the Agency Official that it will decline to comment, or obtains the consent of the Agency Official to extend the period for providing comment, the Council shall comment within 45 days of the request.

(i) If the Council declines to comment, the Agency Official shall take into account the comments of the Council in carrying out the undertakings within the category and publish notice in the FEDERAL REGISTER of the Council's comments and steps the agency will take to ensure that effects to historic properties are taken into account.

(ii) If the Council declines to comment, the Agency Official shall continue to comply with the requirements in

§ 800.15

of §§ 800.3 through 800.6 for the individual undertakings.

(6) *Withdrawal of comment.* If the Council determines that the consideration of historic properties is not being carried out in a manner consistent with the program comment, the Council may withdraw the comment and the Agency Official shall comply with the requirements of §§ 800.3 through 800.6 for the individual undertakings.

(f) *Consultation with Indian tribes and Native Hawaiian organizations when developing program alternatives.* Whenever an Agency Official proposes a program alternative pursuant to § 800.14 (a)–(e), the Agency Official shall ensure that development of the program alternative includes appropriate government-to-government consultation with affected Indian tribes and consultation with affected Native Hawaiian organizations.

(1) *Identifying affected Indian tribes and Native Hawaiian organizations.* If any undertaking covered by a proposed program alternative has the potential to affect historic properties of religious and cultural significance to an Indian tribe or a Native Hawaiian organization which are located off tribal lands, the Agency Official shall identify those Indian tribes and Native Hawaiian organizations that might attach religious and cultural significance to such properties and consult with them.

(2) *Results of consultation.* The Agency Official shall provide summaries of the views, along with copies of any written comments, provided by affected Indian tribes and Native Hawaiian organizations to the Council as part of the documentation for the proposed program alternative. The Agency Official and the Council shall take those views into account in reaching a final decision on the proposed program alternative.

36 CFR Ch. VIII (7-1-99 Edition)

§ 800.15 Tribal, State, and Local Program Alternatives. [Reserved]

§ 800.16 Definitions.

(a) *Act* means the National Historic Preservation Act of 1966, as amended, 16 U.S.C. 470–470w–6.

(b) *Agency* means agency as defined in 5 U.S.C. 551.

(c) *Approval of the expenditure of funds* means any final agency decision authorizing or permitting the expenditure of Federal funds or financial assistance on an undertaking, including any agency decision that may be subject to an administrative appeal.

(d) *Area of potential effects* means the geographic area or areas within which an undertaking may directly or indirectly cause changes in the character or use of historic properties, if any such properties exist. The area of potential effects is influenced by the scale and nature of an undertaking and may be different for different kinds of effects cause by the undertaking.

(e) *Comment* means the findings and recommendations of the Council formally provided in writing to the head of a Federal agency under section 106.

(f) *Consultation* means the process of seeking, discussing, and considering the views of other participants, and, where feasible, seeking agreement with them regarding matters arising in the section 106 process. The Secretary's, "Standards and Guidelines for Federal Agency Preservation Programs pursuant to the National Historic Preservation Act" provide further guidance on consultation.

(g) *Council* means the Advisory Council on Historic Preservation or a Council member or employee designated to act for the Council.

(h) *Day or days* means calendar days.

(i) *Effect* means alteration to the characteristics of a historic property qualifying it for inclusion in or eligibility for the National Register.

(j) *Foreclosure* means an action taken by an Agency Official that effectively precludes the Council from providing comments which the Agency Official

Advisory Council on Historic Preservation

can meaningfully consider prior to the approval of the undertaking.

(k) *Head of the agency* means the chief official of the Federal agency responsible for all aspects of the agency's actions. If a State, local or tribal government has assumed or has been delegated responsibility for section 106 compliance, the head of that unit of government shall be considered the head of the agency.

(l) *Historic property* means any prehistoric or historic district, site, building, structure, or object included in, or eligible for inclusion in, the National Register of Historic Places maintained by the Secretary of the Interior. This term includes artifacts, records, and remains that are related to and located within such properties. The term includes properties of traditional religious and cultural importance to an Indian tribe or Native Hawaiian organization and that meet the National Register criteria. The term *eligible for inclusion in the National Register* includes both properties formally determined as such in accordance with regulations of the Secretary of the Interior and all other properties that meet the National Register criteria.

(m) *Indian tribe* means an Indian tribe, band, nation, or other organized group or community, including a Native village, Regional Corporation or Village Corporation, as those terms are defined in section 3 of the Alaska Native Claims Settlement Act (43 U.S.C. 1602), which is recognized as eligible for the special programs and services provided by the United States to Indians because of their status as Indians.

(n) *Local government* means a city, county, parish, township, municipality, borough, or other general purpose political subdivision of a State.

(o) *Memorandum of Agreement* means the document that records the terms and conditions agreed upon to resolve the adverse effects of an undertaking upon historic properties.

(p) *National Historic Landmark* means a historic property that the Secretary of the Interior has designated a National Historic Landmark.

(q) *National Register* means the National Register of Historic Places maintained by the Secretary of the Interior.

§ 800.16

(r) *National Register Criteria* means the criteria established by the Secretary of the Interior for use in evaluating the eligibility of properties for the National Register (36 CFR part 60).

(s) *Native Hawaiian organization* means any organization which serves and represents the interests of Native Hawaiians; has as a primary and stated purpose the provision of services to Native Hawaiians; and has demonstrated expertise in aspects of historic preservation that are significant to Native Hawaiians. *Native Hawaiian* means any individual who is a descendant of the aboriginal people who, prior to 1778, occupied and exercised sovereignty in the area that now constitutes the State of Hawaii.

(t) *Programmatic Agreement* means a document that records the terms and conditions agreed upon to resolve the potential adverse effects of a Federal agency program, complex undertaking or other situations in accordance with § 800.14(b).

(u) *Secretary* means the Secretary of the Interior acting through the Director of the National Park Service except where otherwise specified.

(v) *State Historic Preservation Officer (SHPO)* means the official appointed or designated pursuant to section 101(b)(1) of the Act to administer the State historic preservation program or a representative designated to act for the State Historic Preservation Officer.

(w) *Tribal Historic Preservation Officer (THPO)* means the tribal official appointed by the tribe's chief governing authority or designated by a tribal ordinance or preservation program who has assumed the responsibilities of the SHPO for purposes of section 106 compliance on tribal lands in accordance with section 101(d)(2) of the Act. For the purposes of subpart B of this part, the term also includes the designated representative of an Indian tribe that has not formally assumed the SHPO's responsibilities when an undertaking occurs on or affects historic properties on the tribal lands of the Indian tribe. (See § 800.2(c)(2)).

(x) *Tribal lands* means all lands within the exterior boundaries of any Indian reservation and all dependent Indian communities.

(y) *Undertaking* means a project, activity, or program funded in whole or in part under the direct or indirect jurisdiction of a Federal agency, including those carried out by or on behalf of a Federal agency; those carried out with Federal financial assistance; those requiring a Federal permit, license or approval; and those subject to state or local regulation administered pursuant to a delegation or approval by a Federal agency.

APPENDIX A TO PART 800—CRITERIA FOR COUNCIL INVOLVEMENT IN REVIEWING INDIVIDUAL SECTION 106 CASES

Introduction. This appendix sets forth the criteria that will be used by the Council to determine whether to enter an individual section 106 review that it normally would not be involved in.

General Policy. The Council may choose to exercise its authorities under the section 106 regulations to participate in an individual project pursuant to the following criteria. However, the Council will not always elect to participate even though one or more of the criteria may be met.

Specific Criteria. The Council is likely to enter the section 106 process at the steps specified in the revised regulations when an undertaking:

(1) *Has substantial impacts on important historic properties.* This may include adverse effects on properties that possess a national level of significance or on properties that are of unusual or noteworthy importance or are a rare property type; or adverse effects to large numbers of historic properties, such as impacts to multiple properties within a historic district.

(2) *Presents important questions of policy or interpretation.* This may include questions about how the Council's regulations are being applied or interpreted, including possible foreclosure or anticipatory demolition situations; situations where the outcome will set a precedent affecting Council policies or program goals; or the development of programmatic agreements that alter the way the section 106 process is applied to a group or type of undertakings.

(3) *Has the potential for presenting procedural problems.* This may include cases with substantial public controversy that is related to historic preservation issues; with disputes among or about consulting parties which the Council's involvement could help resolve; that are involved or likely to be involved in litigation on the basis of section 106; or carried out by a Federal agency, in a State or locality, or on tribal lands where the Council has previously identified problems with sec-

tion 106 compliance pursuant to Section 800.9(d)(2).

(4) *Presents issues of concern to Indian tribes or Native Hawaiian organizations.* This may include cases where there have been concerns raised about the identification of, evaluation of or assessment of effects on historic properties to which an Indian tribe or Native Hawaiian organization attaches religious and cultural significance; where an Indian tribe or Native Hawaiian organization has requested Council involvement to assist in the resolution of adverse effects; or where there are questions relating to policy, interpretation or precedent under section 106 or its relation to other authorities, such as the Native American Graves Protection and Repatriation Act.

44716　Federal Register / Vol. 48, No. 190 / Thursday, September 29, 1983 / Notices

DEPARTMENT OF THE INTERIOR

National Park Service

Archeology and Historic Preservation; Secretary of the Interior's Standards and Guidelines

AGENCY: National Park Service, Interior.

ACTION: Notice.

SUMMARY: This notice sets forth the Secretary of the Interior's Standards and Guidelines for Archeology and Historic Preservation. These standards and guidelines are not regulatory and do not set or interpret agency policy. They are intended to provide technical advice about archeological and historic preservation activities and methods.

DATE: These Standards and Guidelines are effective on September 29, 1983.

FOR FURTHER INFORMATION CONTACT: Lawrence E. Aten, Chief, Interagency Resources Division, National Park Service, United States Department of the Interior, Washington, D.C. 20240 (202–343–9500). A Directory of Technical Information listing other sources of supporting information is available from the National Park Service.

SUPPLEMENTARY INFORMATION: The Standards and Guidelines are prepared under the authority of Sections 101(f), (g), and (h), and Section 110 of the National Historic Preservation Act of 1966, as amended. State Historic Preservation Officers; Federal Preservation Officers including those of the Department of Agriculture, the Department of Defense, Smithsonian Institution and General Services Administration; the Advisory Council on Historic Preservation; the National Trust for Historic Preservation; and other interested parties were consulted during the development of the Standards and Guidelines; additional consultation with these agencies will occur as the Standards and Guidelines are tested during their first year of use.

Purpose

The proposed Standards and the philosophy on which they are based result from nearly twenty years of intensive preservation activities at the Federal, State, and local levels.

The purposes of the Standards are:
To organize the information gathered about preservation activities.
To describe results to be achieved by Federal agencies, States, and others when planning for the identification, evaluation, registration and treatment of historic properties.
To integrate the diverse efforts of many entities performing historic preservation into a systematic effort to preserve our nation's cultural heritage.

Uses of the Standards

The following groups or individuals are encouraged to use these Standards:
Federal agency personnel responsible for cultural resource management pursuant to Section 110 of the National Historic Preservation Act, as amended, in areas under Federal jurisdiction. A separate series of guidelines advising Federal agencies on their specific historic preservation activities under Section 110 is in preparation.
State Historic Preservation Offices responsible under the National Historic Preservation Act, as amended, for making decisions about the preservation of historic properties in their States in accordance with appropriate regulations and the Historic Preservation Fund Grants Management Manual. The State Historic Preservation Offices serve as the focal point for preservation planning and act as a central state-wide repository of collected information.
Local governments wishing to establish a comprehensive approach to the identification, evaluation, registration and treatment of historic properties within their jurisdictions.
Other individuals and organizations needing basic technical standards and guidelines for historic preservation activities.

Organization

This material is organized in three sections: Standards; Guidelines; and recommended technical sources, cited at the end of each set of guidelines. Users of this document are expected to consult the recommended technical sources to obtain guidance in specific cases.

Review of the Standards and Guidelines

The Secretary of the Interior's Standards for Rehabilitation have recently undergone extensive review and their guidelines are made current after 5 years of field use. Users and other interested parties are encouraged to submit written comments on the utility of these Standards and Guidelines except for the Rehabilitation Standards mentioned above. This edition will be thoroughly reviewed by the National Park Service (including consultation with Federal and State agencies), after the end of its first full year of use and any necessary modifications will be made. Subsequent reviews are anticipated as needed. Comments should be sent to Chief, Interagency Resources Division, National Park Service, United States Department of the Interior, Washington, D.C. 20240.

Contents

Standards for Preservation Planning
Guidelines for Preservation Planning
Standards for Identification
Guidelines for Identification
Standards for Evaluation
Guidelines for Evaluation
Standards for Registration
Guidelines for Registration
Standards for Historical Documentation
Guidelines for Historical Documentation
Standards for Architectural and Engineering Documentation
Guidelines for Architectural and Engineering Documentation
Standards for Archeological Documentation
Guidelines for Archeological Documentation
Standards for Historic Preservation Projects
Professional Qualifications Standards
Preservation Terminology

Secretary of the Interior's Standards for Preservation Planning

Preservation planning is a process that organizes preservation activities (identification, evaluation, registration and treatment of historic properties) in a logical sequence. The Standards for Planning discuss the relationship among these activities while the remaining activity standards consider how each activity should be carried out. The Professional Qualifications Standards discuss the education and experience required to carry out various activities.

The Standards for Planning outline a process that determines when an area should be examined for historic properties, whether an identified property is significant, and how a significant property should be treated.

Preservation planning is based on the following principles:
—Important historic properties cannot be replaced if they are destroyed. Preservation planning provides for conservative use of these properties, preserving them in place and avoiding harm when possible and altering or destroying properties only when necessary.
—If planning for the preservation of historic properties is to have positive effects, it must begin before the identification of all significant properties has been completed. To make responsible decisions about historic properties, existing information must be used to the maximum extent and new information must be acquired as needed.
—Preservation planning includes public participation. The planning process should provide a forum for open discussion of preservation issues. Public involvement is most meaningful when it is used to assist in defining values of properties and preservation planning issues, rather than when it is limited to review of decisions already made. Early

---

44717　Federal Register / Vol. 48, No. 190 / Thursday, September 29, 1983 / Notices

and continuing public participation is essential to the broad acceptance of preservation planning decisions.

Preservation planning can occur at several levels or scales: in a project area; in a community; in a State as a whole; or in the scattered or contiguous landholdings of a Federal agency. Depending on the scale, the planning process will involve different segments of the public and professional communities and the resulting plans will vary in detail. For example, a State preservation plan will likely have more general recommendations than a plan for a project area or a community. The planning process described in these Standards is flexible enough to be used at all levels while providing a common structure which promotes coordination and minimize duplication of effort. The Guidelines for Preservation Planning contain additional information about how to integrate various levels of planning.

Standard I. Preservation Planning Establishes Historic Contexts

Decisions about the identification, evaluation, registration and treatment of historic properties are most reliably made when the relationship of individual properties to other similar properties is understood. Information about historic properties representing aspects of history, architecture, archeology, engineering and culture must be collected and organized to define these relationships. This organizational framework is called a "historic context." The historic context organizes information based on a cultural theme and its geographical and chronological limits. Contexts describe the significant broad patterns of development in an area that may be represented by historic properties. The development of historic contexts is the foundation for decisions about identification, evaluation, registration and treatment of historic properties.

Standard II. Preservation Planning Uses Historic Contexts To Develop Goals and Priorities For the Identification, Evaluation, Registration and Treatment of Historic Properties

A series of preservation goals is systematically developed for each historic context to ensure that the range of properties representing the important aspects of each historic context is identified, evaluated and treated. Then priorities are set for all goals identified for each historic context. The goals with assigned priorities established for each historic context are integrated to produce a comprehensive and consistent set of goals and priorities for all historic contexts in the geographical area of a planning effort.

The goals for each historic context may change as new information becomes available. The overall set of goals and priorities are then altered in response to the changes in the goals and priorities for the individual historic contexts.

Activities undertaken to meet the goals must be designed to deliver a useable product within a reasonable period of time. The scope of the activity must be defined so the work can be completed with available budgeted program resources.

Standard III. The Results of Preservation Planning Are Made Available for Integration Into Broader Planning Processes

Preservation of historic properties is one element of larger planning processes. Planning results, including goals and priorities, information about historic properties, and any planning documents, must be transmitted in a useable form to those responsible for other planning activities. Federally mandated historic preservation planning is most successfully integrated into project management planning at an early stage. Elsewhere, this integration is achieved by making the results of preservation planning available to other governmental planning bodies and to private interests whose activities affect historic properties.

Secretary of the Interior's Guidelines for Preservation Planning

Introduction

These Guidelines link the Standards for Preservation Planning with more specific guidance and technical information. They describe one approach to meeting the Standards for Preservation Planning. Agencies, organizations or individuals proposing to approach planning differently may wish to review their approaches with the National Park Service.

The Guidelines are organized as follows:

Managing the Planning Process
Developing Historic Contexts
Developing Goals for a Historic Context
Integrating Individual Historic Contexts—Creating the Preservation Plan
Coordinating with Management Frameworks
Recommended Sources of Technical Information

Managing the Planning Process

The preservation planning process must include an explicit approach to implementation, a provision for review and revision of all elements, and a mechanism for resolving conflicts within the overall set of preservation goals and between this set of goals and other land use planning goals. It is recommended that the process and its products be described in public documents.

Implementing the Process

The planning process is a continuous cycle. To establish and maintain such a process, however, the process must be divided into manageable segments that can be performed within a defined period, such as a fiscal year or budget cycle. One means of achieving this is to define a period of time during which all the preliminary steps in the planning process will be completed. These preliminary steps would include setting a schedule for subsequent activities.

Review and Revision

Planning is a dynamic process. It is expected that the content of the historic contexts described in Standard I and the goals and priorities described in Standard II will be altered based on new information obtained as planning proceeds. The incorporation of this information is essential to improve the content of the plan and to keep it up-to-date and useful. New information must be reviewed regularly and systematically, and the plan revised accordingly.

Public Participation

The success of the preservation planning process depends on how well it solicits and integrates the views of various groups. The planning process is directed first toward resolving conflicts in goals for historic preservation, and second toward resolving conflicts between historic preservation goals and other land-use planning goals. Public participation is integral to this approach and includes at least the following actions:

1. Involving historians, architectural historians, archeologists, historical architects, folklorists and persons from related discipline to define, review and revise the historic contexts, goals and priorities;

2. Involving interested individuals, organizations and communities in the planning area in identifying the kinds of historic properties that may exist and suitable protective measures;

3. Involving prospective users of the preservation plan in defining issues, goals and priorities;

4. Providing for coordination with other planning efforts at local, state, regional and national levels, as appropriate; and

Appendix A: Core Federal Regulations and Standards A-25

44718 Federal Register / Vol. 48, No. 190 / Thursday, September 29, 1983 / Notices

5. Creating mechanisms for identifying and resolving conflicts about historic preservation issues.

The development of historic contexts, for example, should be based on the professional input of all disciplines involved in preservation and not be limited to a single discipline. For prehistoric archeology, for example, data from fields such as geology, geomorphology and geography may also be needed. The individuals and organizations to be involved will depend, in part, on those present or interested in the planning area.

Documents Resulting from the Planning Process

In most cases, the planning process produces documents that explain how the process works and that discuss the historic contexts and related goals and priorities. While the process can operate in the absence of these documents, planning documents are important because they are the most effective means of communicating the process and its recommendations to others. Planning documents also record decisions about historic properties.

As various parts of the planning process are reviewed and revised to reflect current information, related documents must also be updated. Planning documents should be created in a form that can be easily revised. It is also recommended that the format, language and organization of any documents or other materials (visual aids, etc.) containing preservation planning information meet the needs of prospective users.

Developing Historic Contexts

General Approach

Available information about historic properties must be divided into manageable units before it can be useful for planning purposes. Major decisions about identifying, evaluating, registering and treating historic properties are most reliably made in the context of other related properties. A historic context is an organizational format that groups information about related historic properties, based on a theme, geographic limits and chronological period. A single historic context describes one or more aspects of the historic development of an area, considering history, architecture, archeology, engineering and culture; and identifies the significant patterns that individual historic properties represent, for example, Coal Mining in Northeastern Pennsylvania between 1860 and 1930. A set of historic contexts is a comprehensive summary of all aspects of the history of the area.

The historic context is the cornerstone of the planning process. The goal of preservation planning is to identify, evaluate, register and treat the full range of properties representing each historic context, rather than only one or two types of properties. Identification activities are organized to ensure that research and survey activities include properties representing all aspects of the historic context. Evaluation uses the historic context as the framework within which to apply the criteria for evalution to specific properties or property types. Decisions about treatment of properties are made with the goal of treating the range of properties in the context. The use of historic contexts in organizing major preservation activities ensures that those activities result in the preservation of the wide variety of properties that represent our history, rather than only a small, biased sample of properties.

Historic contexts, as theoretical constructs, are linked to actual historic properties through the concept of property type. Property types permit the development of plans for identification, evaluation and treatment even in the absence of complete knowledge of individual properties. Like the historic context, property types are artifical constructs which may be revised as necessary.

Historic contexts can be developed at a variety of scales appropriate for local, State and regional planning. Given the probability of historic contexts overlapping in an area, it is important to coordinate the development and use of contexts at all levels. Generally, the State Historic Preservation Office possesses the most complete body of information about historic properties and, in practice, is in the best position to perform this function.

The development of historic contexts generally results in documents that describe the prehistoric processes or patterns that define the context. Each of the contexts selected should be developed to the point of identifying important property types to be useful in later preservation decision-making. The amount of detail included in these summaries will vary depending on the level (local, state, regional, or national) at which the contexts are developed and on their intended uses. For most planning purposes, a synopsis of the written description of the historic context is sufficient.

Creating a Historic Context

Generally, historic contexts should not be constructed so broadly as to include all property types under a single historic context or so narrowly as to contain only one property type per historic context. The following procedures should be followed in creating a historic context.

1. Identify the concept, time period and geographical limits for the historic context

Existing information, concepts, theories, models and descriptions should be used as the basis for defining historic contexts. Biases in primary and secondary sources should be identified and accounted for when existing information is used in defining historic contexts.

The identification and description of historic contexts should incorporate contributions from all disciplines involved in historic preservation. The chronological period and geographical area of each historic context should be defined after the conceptual basis is established. However, there may be exceptions, especially in defining prehistoric contexts where drainage systems or physiographic regions often are outlined first. The geographical boundaries for historic contexts should not be based upon contemporary political, project or other contemporary boundaries if those boundaries do not coincide with historical boundaries. For example, boundaries for prehistoric contexts will have little relationship to contemporary city, county or state boundaries.

2. Assemble the existing information about the historic context

a. *Collecting information:* Several kinds of information are needed to construct a preservation plan. Information about the history of the area encompassed by the historic context must be collected, including any information about historic properties that have already been identified. Existing survey or inventory entries are an important source of information about historic properties. Other sources may include literature on prehistory, history, architecture and the environment; social and environmental impact assessments; county and State land use plans; architectural and folklife studies and oral histories; ethnographic research; State historic inventories and registers; technical reports prepared for Section 106 or other assessments of historic properties; and direct consultation with individuals and organized groups.

In addition, organizations and groups that may have important roles in defining historic contexts and values should be identified. In most cases a range of knowlegeable professionals drawn from the preservation, planning and academic communities will be available to assist in defining contexts and in identifying sources of information. In other cases, however, development of historic contexts may occur in areas whose history or prehistory has not been extensively studied. In these situations, broad general historic contexts should be initially identified using available literature and expertise, with the expectation that the contexts will be revised and subdivided in the future as primary source research and field survey are conducted. It is also important to identify such sources of information as existing planning data, which is needed to establish goals for identification, evaluation, and treatment, and to identify factors that will affect attainment of those goals.

The same approach for obtaining information is not necessarily desirable for all historic contexts. Information should not be gathered without first considering its relative importance to the historic context, the cost and time involved, and the expertise required to obtain it. In many cases, for example, published sources may be used in writing initial definitions of historic contexts; archival research or field work may be needed for subsequent activities.

b. *Assessing information:* All information should be reviewed to identify bias in historic perspective, methodological approach, or area of coverage. For example, field surveys for archeological sites may have ignored historic archelolgical sites, or county land use plans may have emphasized only development goals.

3. Synthesize information

The information collection and analysis results in a written narrative of the historic context. This narrative provides a detailed synthesis of the data that have been collected and analyzed. The narrative covers the history of the area from the chosen perspective and identifies important patterns, events, persons or cultural values. In the process of identifying the important patterns, one should consider:

a. Trends in area settlement and development, if relevant;

b. Aesthetic and artistic values embodied in architecture, construction technology or craftsmanship;

c. Research values or problems relevant to the historic context; social and physical sciences and humanities; and cultural interests of local communities; and

Federal Register / Vol. 48, No. 190 / Thursday, September 29, 1983 / Notices 44719

d. Intangible cultural values of ethnic groups and native American peoples.

4. Define property types

A property type is a grouping of individual properties based on shared physical or associative characteristics. Property types link the ideas incorporated in the theoretical historic context with actual historic properties that illustrate those ideas. Property types defined for each historic context should be directly related to the conceptual basis of the historic context. Property types defined for the historic context "Coal Mining in Northeastern Pennsylvania, 1860–1930" might include coal extraction and processing complexes; railroad and canal transportation systems; commercial districts; mine workers' housing; churches, social clubs and other community facilities reflecting the ethnic origins of workers; and residences and other properties associated with mine owners and other industrialists.

a. *Identify property types:* The narrative should discuss the kinds of properties expected within the geographical limits of the context and group them into those property types most useful in representing important historic trends.

Generally, property types should be defined after the historic context has been defined. Property types in common usage ("Queen Anne houses," "mill buildings," or "stratified sites") should not be adopted without first verifying their relevance to the historic contexts being used.

b. *Characterize the locational patterns of property types:* Generalizations about where particular types of properties are likely to be found can serve as a guide for identification and treatment. Generalizations about the distribution of archeological properties are frequently used. The distribution of other historic properties often can be estimated based on recognizable historical, environmental or cultural factors that determined their location. Locational patterns of property types should be based upon models that have an explicit theoretical or historical basis and can be tested in the field. The model may be the product of historical research and analysis ("Prior to widespread use of steam power, mills were located on rivers and streams able to produce water power" or "plantation houses in the Mississippi Black Belt were located on sandy clay knolls"), or it may result from sampling techniques. Often the results of statistically valid sample surveys can be used to describe the locational patterns of a representative portion of properties belonging to a particular property type. Other surveys can also provide a basis for suggesting locational patterns if a diversity of historic properties was recorded and a variety of environmental zones was inspected. It is likely that the identification of locational patterns will come from a combination of these sources. Expected or predicted locational patterns of property types should be developed with a provision made for their verification.

c. *Characterize the current condition of property types:* The expected condition of property types should be evaluated to assist in the development of identification, evaluation and treatment strategies, and to help define physical integrity thresholds for various property types. The following should be assessed for each property type:

(1) Inherent characteristics of a property type that either contribute to or detract from its physical preservation. For example, a property type commonly constructed of fragile materials is more likely to be deteriorated than a property type constructed of durable materials; structures whose historic function or design limits the potential for alternative uses (water towers) are less likely to be reused than structures whose design allows a wider variety of other uses (commercial buildings or warehouses).

(2) Aspects of the social and natural environment that may affect the preservation or visibility of the property type. For example, community values placed on certain types of properties (churches, historic cemeteries) may result in their maintenance while the need to reuse valuable materials may stimulate the disappearance of properties like abandoned houses and barns.

It may be most efficient to estimate of the condition of property types based on professional knowledge of existing properties and field test these estimates using a small sample of properties representative of each type.

5. Identify information needs

Filling gaps in information is an important element of the preservation plan designed for each historic context. Statements of the information needed should be as specific as possible, focusing on the information needed, the historic context and property types it applies to, and why the information is needed to perform identification, evaluation, or treatment activities.

Developing Goals for a Historic Context

Developing Goals

A goal is a statement of preferred preservation activities, which is generally stated in terms of property types.

The purpose of establishing preservation goals is to set forth a "best case" version of how properties in the historic context should be identified, evaluated, registered and treated. Preservation goals should be oriented toward the greatest possible protection of properties in the historic context and should be based on the principle that properties should be preserved in place if possible, through affirmative treatments like rehabilitation, stabilization or restoration. Generally, goals will be specific to the historic context and will often be phrased in terms of property types. Some of these goals will be related to information needs previously identified for the historic context. Collectively, the goals for a historic context should be a coherent statement of program direction covering all aspects of the context.

For each goal, a statement should be prepared identifying:

1. The goal, including the context and property types to which the goal applies and the geographical area in which they are located;

2. The activities required to achieve the goal;

3. The most appropriate methods or strategies for carrying out the activities;

4. A schedule within which the activities should be completed; and

5. The amount of effort required to accomplish the goal, as well as a way to evaluate progress toward its accomplishment.

Setting priorities for goals

Once goals have been developed they need to be ranked in importance. Ranking involves examining each goal in light of a number of factors.

1. General social, economic, political and environmental conditions and trends affecting (positively and negatively) the identification, evaluation, registration and treatment of property types in the historic context.

Some property types in the historic context may be more directly threatened by deterioration, land development patterns, contemporary use patterns, or public perceptions of their value, and such property types should be given priority consideration.

2. Major cost or technical considerations affecting the identification, evaluation and treatment of property types in the historic context.

The identification or treatment of some property types may be technically possible but the cost prohibitive; or techniques may not currently perfected (for example, the identification of submerged sites or objects, or the evaluation of sites containing material for which dating techniques are still being developed).

3. Identification, evaluation, registration and treatment activities previously carried out for property types in the historic context.

If a number of properties representing one aspect of a historic context have been recorded or preserved, treatment of additional members of that property type may receive lower priority than treatment of a property type for which no examples have yet been recorded or preserved. This approach ensures that the focus of recording or preserving all elements of the historic context is retained, rather than limiting activities to preserving properties representing only some aspects of the context.

The result of considering the goals in light of these concerns will be a list of refined goals ranked in order of priority.

Integrating Individual Contexts—Creating the Preservation Plan

When historic contexts overlap geographically, competing goals and priorities must be integrated for effective preservation planning. The ranking of goals for each historic context must be reconciled to ensure that recommendations for one context do not contradict those for another. This important step results in an overall set of priorities for several historic contexts and a list of the activities to be performed to achieve the ranked goals. When applied to a specific geographical area, this is the preservation plan for that area.

It is expected that in many instances historic contexts will overlap geographically. Overlapping contexts are likely to occur in two combinations—those that were defined at the same scale (i.e., textile development in Smithtown 1850–1910 and Civil War in Smithtown 1855–1870) and those defined at different scales (i.e., Civil War in Smithtown and Civil War in the Shenandoah Valley). The contexts may share the same property types, although the shared property types will probably have different levels of importance, or they may group the same properties into different property types, reflecting either a different scale of analysis or a different historical perspective.

As previously noted, many of the goals that the formulated for a historic context will focus on the property types defined for that context. Thus it is critical that the integration of goals include the explicit consideration of the potential for shared property type membership by individual properties. For example, when the same property types are used by two contexts, reconciling the goals will require weighing the level of importance assigned to each property type. The degree to which integration of historic contexts must involve reconciling property types may be limited by the coordinated development of historic contexts used at various levels.

Integration with Management Frameworks

Preservation goals and priorities are adapted to land units through integration with other planning concerns. This integration must involve the resolution of conflicts that arise when competing resources occupy the same land base. Successful resolution of these conflicts can often be achieved through judicious combination of inventory, evaluation and treatment activities. Since historic properties are irreplaceable, these activities should be heavily weighted to discourage the destruction of significant properties and to be compatible with the primary land use.

Recommended Sources of Technical Information

Resource Protection Planning Process. State and Plans Grants Division, 1980. Washington, D.C. Available from Survey and Planning Branch, Interagency Resources Division, National Park Service, Department of the Interior, Washington, D.C. 20240. Outlines a step-by-step approach to implementing the resource protection planning process.

Resource Protection Planning Process Case Studies. Available from Survey and Planning Branch, Interagency Resources Division, National Park Service, Department of the Interior, Washington, D.C. 20240. Reports prepared by State Historic Preservation Offices and other using the planning process.

Planning Theory. Andreas Faludi, 1980. Oxford: Pergamon Press. Constructs a model of planning using concepts borrowed from general systems theory.

SECRETARY OF THE INTERIOR'S STANDARDS FOR IDENTIFICATION

Identification activities are undertaken to gather information about historic properties in an area. The scope of these activities will depend on: existing knowledge about properties; goals for survey activities developed in the planning process; and current management needs.

Standard I. Identification of Historic Properties Is Undertaken to the Degree Required To Make Decisions

Archival research and survey activities should be designed to gather the information necessary to achieve defined preservation goals. The objectives, chosen methods and techniques, and expected results of the identification activities are specified in a research design. These activities may include archival research and other techniques to develop historic contexts, sampling an area to gain a broad understanding of the kinds of properties it contains, or examining every property in an area as a basis for property specific decisions. Where possible, use of quantitative methods is important because it can produce an estimate, whose reliability may be assessed, of the kinds of historic properties that may be present in the studied area. Identification activities should use a search procedure consistent with the management needs for information and the character of the area to be investigated. Careful selection of methods, techniques and level of detail is necessary so that the gathered information will provide a sound basis for making decisions.

Standard II. Results of Identification Activities are Integrated Into the Preservation Planning Process

Results of identification activities are reviewed for their effects on previous planning data. Archival research or field survey may refine the understanding of one or more historic contexts and may alter the need for additional survey or study of particular property types. Incorporation of the results of these activities into the planning process is necessary to ensure that the planning process is always based on the best available information.

Standard III. Identification Activities Include Explicit Procedures for Record-Keeping and Information Distribution

Information gathered in identification activities is useful in other preservation planning activities only when it is systematically gathered and recorded, and made available to those responsible for preservation planning. The results of identification activities should be reported in a format that summarizes the design and methods of the survey, provides a basis for others to review the results, and states where information on identified properties is maintained. However, sensitive information, like the location of fragile resources, must be safeguarded from general public distribution.

Secretary of the Interior's Guidelines for Identification

Introduction

These Guidelines link the Standards for Identification with more specific guidance and technical information. The Guidelines outline one approach to meet the Standards for Identification. Agencies, organizations and individuals proposing to approach identification differently may wish to review their approaches with the National Park Service.

The Guidelines are organized as follows:

Role of Identification in the Planning Process
Performing Identification
Integrating Identification Results
Reporting Identification Results
Recommended Sources of Technical Information

Role of Identification in the Planning Process

Identification is undertaken for the purpose of locating historic properties and is composed of a number of activities which include, but are not limited to archival research, informant interviews, field survey and analysis. Combinations of these activities may be selected and appropriate levels of effort assigned to produce a flexible series of options. Generally identification activities will have multiple objectives, reflecting complex management needs. Within a comprehensive planning process, identification is normally undertaken to acquire property-specific information needed to refine a particular historic context or to develop any new historic contexts. (See the Guidelines for Preservation Planning for discussion of information gathering to establish plans and to develop historic contexts.) The results of identification activities are then integrated into the planning process so that subsequent activities are based on the most up-to-date information. Identification activities are also undertaken in the absence of a comprehensive planning process, most frequently as part of a specific land-use or development project. Even lacking a formally developed preservation planning process, the benefits of efficent, goal-directed research may be obtained by the development of localized historic contexts, suitable in scale for the project area, as part of the background research which customarily occurs before field survey efforts.

Performing Identification

Research Design

Identification activities are essentially research activities for which a statement of objectives or research design should be prepared before work is performed. Within the framework of a comprehensive planning process, the research design provides a vehicle for integrating the various activities performed during the identification process and for linking those activities directly to the goals and the historic context(s) for which those goals were defined. The research design stipulates the logical integration of historic context(s) and field and laboratory methodology. Although these tasks may be performed individually, they will not contribute to the greatest extent possible in increasing information on the historic context unless they relate to the defined goals and to each other. Additionally, the research design provides a focus for the integration of interdisciplinary information. It ensures that the linkages between specialized activities are real, logical and address the defined research questions. Identification activities should be guided by the research design and the results discussed in those terms. (See Reporting Identification Results)

The research design should include the following:

1. *Objectives* of the identification activities. For example: to characterize the range of historic properties in a region; to identify the number of properties associated with a context; to gather information to determine which properties in an area are significant.

The statement of objectives should refer to current knowledge about the historic contexts or property types, based on background research or assessments of previous research. It should clearly define the physical extent of the area to be investigated and the amount and kinds of information to be gathered about properties in the area.

2. *Methods* to be used to obtain the information. For example: archival research or field survey. Research methods should be clearly and specifically related to research problems.

Archival research or survey methods should be carefully explained so that others using the gathered information can understand how the information was obtained and what its possible limitations or biases are.

The methods should be compatible with the past and present environmental character of the geographical area under study and the kinds of properties most likely to be present in the area.

3. *The expected results* and the reasons for those expections.

Expectations about the kind, number, location, character and condition of historic properties are generally based on a combination of background research, proposed hypotheses, and analogy to the kinds of properties known to exist in areas of similar environment or history.

Archival Research

Archival or background research is generally undertaken prior to any field survey. Where identification is undertaken as part of a comprehensive planning process, background research may have taken place as part of the development of the historic contexts (see the Guidelines for Preservation Planning). In the absence of previously developed historic contexts, archival research should address specific issues and topics. It should not duplicate previous work. Sources should include, but not be limited to, historical maps, atlases, tax records, photographs, ethnographies, folklife documentation, oral histories and other studies, as well as standard historical reference works, as appropriate for the research problem. (See the Guidelines for Historical Documentation for additional discussion.)

Field Survey

The variety of field survey techniques available, in combination with the varying levels of effort that may be assigned, give great flexibility to implementing field surveys. It is important that the selection of field survey techniques and level of effort be responsive to the management needs and preservation goals that direct the survey effort.

Survey techniques may be loosely grouped into two categories, according to their results. First are the techniques that result in the characterization of a region's historic properties. Such techniques might include "windshield" or walk-over surveys, with perhaps a limited use of sub-surface survey. For purposes of these Guidelines, this kind of survey is termed a "reconnaissance." The second category of survey techniques is those that permit the identification and description of specific historic properties in an area; this kind of survey effort is termed "intensive." the terms "reconnaissance" and "intensive" are sometimes defined to mean particular survey techniques, generally with regard to prehistoric sites. The use of the terms here is general and is not intended to redefine the terms as they are used elsewhere.

Reconnaissance survey might be most profitably employed when gathering data to refine a developed historic context—such as checking on the presence or absence of expected property types, to define specific property types or to estimate the distribution of historic properties in an area. The results of regional characterization activities provide a general understanding of the historic properties in a particular area and permit management decisions that consider the sensitivity of the area in terms of historic preservation concerns and the resulting implications for future land use planning. The data should allow the formulation of estimates of the necessity, type and cost of further identification work and the setting of priorities for the individual tasks involved. In most cases, areas surveyed in this way will require resurvey if more complete information is needed about specific properties.

A reconnaissance survey should document:

1. The kinds of properties looked for;
2. The boundaries of the area surveyed;
3. The method of survey, including the extent of survey coverage;
4. The kinds of historic properties present in the surveyed area;
5. Specific properties that were identified, and the categories of information collected; and
6. Places examined that did not contain historic properties.

Intensive survey is most useful when it is necessary to know precisely what historic properties exist in a given area or when information sufficient for later evaluation and treatment decisions is needed on individual historic properties. Intensive survey describes the distribution of properties in an area; determines the number, location, and condition of properties; determines the types of properties actually present within the area; permits classification of individual properties; and records the physical extent of specific properties.

An intensive survey should document:

1. The kinds of properties looked for;
2. The boundaries of the area surveyed;
3. The method of survey, including an estimate of the extent of survey coverage;
4. A record of the precise location of all properties identified; and
5. Information on the appearance, significance, integrity and boundaries of each property sufficient to permit an evaluation of its significance.

Sampling

Reconnaissance or intensive survey methods may be employed according to a sampling procedure to examine less-than-the-total project or planning area.

Sampling can be effective when several locations are being considered for an undertaking or when it is desirable to estimate the cultural resources of an area. In many cases, especially where large land areas are involved, sampling can be done in stages. In this approach, the results of the initial large area survey are used to structure successively smaller, more detailed surveys. This "nesting" approach is an efficient technique since it enables characterization of both large and small areas with reduced effort. As with all investigative techniques, such procedures should be designed to permit an independent assessment of results.

Various types of sample surveys can be conducted, including, but not limited to: random, stratified and systematic. Selection of sample type should be guided by the problem the survey is expected to solve, the nature of the expected properties and the nature of the area to be surveyed.

Sample surveys may provide data to estimate frequencies of properties and types of properties within a specified area at various confidence levels. Selection of confidence levels should be based upon the nature of the problem the sample survey is designed to address.

Predictive modeling is an application of basic sampling techniques that projects or extrapolates the number, classes and frequencies of properties in unsurveyed areas based on those found in surveyed areas. Predictive modeling can be an effective tool during the early stages of planning an undertaking, for targeting field survey and for other management purposes. However, the accuracy of the model must be verified; predictions should be confirmed through field testing and the model redesigned and retested if necessary.

Special survey techniques

Special survey techniques may be needed in certain situations.

Remote sensing techniques may be the most effective way to gather background environmental data, plan more detailed field investigations, discover certain classes of properties, map sites, locate and confirm the presence of predicted sites, and define features within properties. Remote sensing techniques include aerial, subsurface and underwater techniques. Ordinarily the results of remote sensing should be verified through independent field inspection before making any evaluation or statement regarding frequencies or types of properties.

Integrating Identification Results

The results of identification efforts must be integrated into the planning process so that planning decisions are based on the best available information. The new information is first assessed against the objectives of the identification effort to determine whether the gathered information meets the defined identification goals for the historic context(s); then the goals are adjusted accordingly. In addition, the historic context narrative, the definition of property types and the planning goals for evaluation and treatment are all adjusted as necessary to accommodate the new data.

Reporting Identification Results

Reporting of the results of identification activities should begin with the statement of objectives prepared before undertaking the survey. The report should respond to each of the major points documenting:

1. Objectives;
2. Area researched or surveyed;
3. Research design or statement of objectives;
4. Methods used, including the intensity of coverage. If the methods differ from those outlined in the statement of objectives, the reasons should be explained.
5. Results: how the results met the objectives; result analysis, implications and recommendations; where the compiled information is located.

A summary of the survey results should be available for examination and distribution. Identified properties should then be evaluated for possible inclusion in appropriate inventories.

Protection of information about archeological sites or other properties that may be threatened by dissemination of that information is necessary. These may include fragile archeological properties or properties such as religious sites, structures, or objects, whose cultural value would be compromised by public knowledge of the property's location.

Recommended Sources of Technical Information

The Archeological Survey: Methods and Uses. Thomas F. King. Interagency Archeological Services, U.S. Department of the Interior, 1978. Washington, D.C. Available through the Superintendent of Documents, U.S. Government Printing Office, Washington, D.C. 20402. GPO stock number 024–016–00091. Written primarily for the non-archeologist, this publication presents methods and objectives for archeological surveys.

Cultural Resources Evaluation of the Northern Gulf of Mexico Continental Shelf. National Park Service, U.S. Department of the Interior, 1977.

Guidelines for Local Surveys: A Basis for Preservation Planning. Anne Derry, H. Ward Jandl, Carol Shull and Jan Thorman. National Register Division, U.S. Department of the Interior, 1978. Washington, D.C. Available through the Superintendent of Documents, U.S. Government Printing Office, Washington, D.C. 20402. GPO stock number 024–016–0089–7. General guidance about designing and carrying out community surveys.

The Process of Field Research: Final Report on the Blue Ridge Parkway Folklife Project. American Folklife Center, 1981.

Regional Sampling in Archeology. David Hurst Thomas. University of California, Archeological Survey Annual Report, 1968–9, 11:87–100.

Remote Sensing: A Handbook for Archeologists and Cultural Resource Managers. Thomas R. Lyons and Thomas Eugene Avery. Cultural Resource Management Division, National Park Service, U.S. Department of the Interior, 1977.

Remote Sensing and Non-Destructive Archeology. Thomas R. Lyons and James L. Ebert, editors. Remote Sensing Division, Southwest Cultural Resources Center, National Park Service, U.S. Department of the Interior and University of New Mexico, 1978.

Remote Sensing Experiments in Cultural Resource Studies: Non-Destructive Methods of Archeological Exploration, Survey and Analysis. Thomas R. Lyons, assembler. reports of the Chaco Center, Number One. National Park Service, U.S. Department of the Interior and University of New Mexico, 1976.

Sampling in Archeology. James W. Mueller, editor. University of Arizona Press, 1975. Tucson, Arizona.

Scholars as Contractors. William J. Mayer-Oakes and Alice W. Portnoy, editors. Cultural Resource Management Studies. U.S. Department of the Interior, 1979.

Sedimentary Studies of Prehistoric Archeological Sites. Sherwood Gagliano, Charles Pearson, Richard Weinstein, Diana Wiseman, and Christopher McClendon. Division of State Plans and Grants, National Park Service, U.S. Department of the Interior, 1982. Washington, D.C. Available from Coastal Environments Inc., 1260 Main Street, Baton Rouge, Louisiana 70802. Establishes and evaluates a method for employing sedimentological analysis in distinguishing site areas from non-site areas when identifying submerged archeological sites on the continental shelf.

State Survey Forms. Available from Interagency Resource Management Division, National Park Service, Department of the Interior, Washington, D.C. 20240. Characterizes cultural resource survey documentation methods in State Historic Preservation Offices.

Truss Bridge Types: A Guide to Dating and Identifying. Donald C. Jackson and T. Allan Comp. American Association for State and Local History, 1977. Nashville, Tennessee. Technical leaflet #95. Available from AASLH, 708 Berry Road, Nashville, Tennessee 37204. Information about performing surveys of historic bridges and identifying the types of properties encountered.

Secretary of the Interior's Standards for Evaluation

Evaluation is the process of determining whether identified properties meet defined criteria of significance and therefore should be included in an inventory of historic properties determined to meet the criteria. The criteria employed vary depending on the inventory's use in resource management.

Standard I. Evaluation of the Significance of Historic Properties Uses Established Criteria

The evaluation of historic properties employs criteria to determine which properties are significant. Criteria should therefore focus on historical, architectural, archeological, engineering and cultural values, rather than on treatments. A statement of the minimum information necessary to evaluate properties against the criteria should be provided to direct information gathering activities.

Because the National Register of Historic Places is a major focus of preservation activities on the Federal, State and local levels, the National Register criteria have been widely adopted not only as required for Federal purposes, but for State and local inventories as well. The National Historic Landmark criteria and other criteria used for inclusion of properties in State historic site files are other examples of criteria with different management purposes.

Standard II. Evaluation of Significance Applies the Criteria Within Historic Contexts

Properties are evaluated using a historic context that identifies the significant patterns that properties represent and defines expected property types against which individual properties may be compared. Within this comparative framework, the criteria for evaluation take on particular meaning with regard to individual properties.

Standard III. Evaluation Results in A List or Inventory of Significant Properties That Is Consulted In Assigning Registration and Treatment Priorities

The evaluation process and the subsequent development of an inventory of significant properties is an on-going activity. Evaluation of the significance of a property should be completed before registration is considered and before preservation treatments are selected. The inventory entries should contain sufficient information for subsequent activities such as registration or treatment of properties, including an evaluation statement that makes clear the significance of the property within one or more historic contexts.

Standard IV. Evaluation Results Are Made Available to the Public

Evaluation is the basis of registration and treatment decisions. Information about evaluation decisions should be organized and available for use by the general public and by those who take part in decisions about registration and treatment. Use of appropriate computer-assisted data bases should be a part of the information dissemination effort. Sensitive information, however, must be safeguarded from general public distribution.

Secretary of the Interior's Guidelines for Evaluation

Introduction

These Guidelines link the Standards for Evaluation with more specific guidance and technical information. These Guidelines describe one approach to meeting the Standards for Evaluation. Agencies, organizations, or individuals proposing to approach evaluation differently may wish to review their approach with the National Park Service.

The Guidelines are organized as follows:

The Evaluation Process
Criteria
Application of Criteria within a Historic Context
Inventory
Recommended Sources of Technical Information

The Evaluation Process

These Guidelines describe principles for evaluating the significance of one or more historic properties with regard to a given set of criteria.

Groups of related properties should be evaluated at the same time whenever possible; for example, following completion of a theme study or community survey.

Evaluation should not be undertaken using documentation that may be out of date. Prior to proceeding with evaluation the current condition of the property should be determined and previous analyses evaluated in light of any new information.

Evaluation must be performed by persons qualified by education, training and experience in the application of the criteria. Where feasible, evaluation should be performed in consultation with other individuals experienced in applying the relevant criteria in the geographical area under consideration; for example, the State Historic Preservation Officer or local landmarks commission.

Evaluation is completed with a written determination that a property is or is not significant based on provided information. This statement should be part of the record.

Criteria: The purposes of evaluation criteria should be made clear. For example, the criteria may be used "to evaluate properties for inclusion in the county landmarks list," or "to implement the National Register of Historic Places program."

For Federal cultural resource management purposes, criteria used to develop an inventory should be coordinated with the National Register criteria for evaluation as implemented in the approved State comprehensive historic preservation plan.

Content of Criteria: Criteria should be appropriate in scale to the purpose of the evaluation. For example, criteria designed to describe national significance should not be used as the basis for creating a county or State inventory. Criteria should be categorical and not attempt to describe in detail every property likely to qualify. Criteria should outline the disciplines or broad areas of concern (history, archeology, architectural history, engineering and culture, for example) included within the scope of the inventory; explain what kinds of properties, if any, are excluded and the reasons for exclusion; and define how levels of significance are measured, if such levels are incorporated into the criteria. If the criteria are to be used in situations where the National Register criteria are also widely used, it is valuable to include a statement explaining the relationship of the criteria used to the National Register criteria, including how the scope of the inventory differs from that defined by the National Register criteria and how the inventory could be use to identify properties that meet the National Register criteria.

Information Needed to Evaluate Properties: The criteria should be accompanied by a statement defining the minimum information necessary to evaluate properties to insure that this information is collected during identification activities intended to locate specific historic properties. Generally, at least the following will be needed:

1. Adequately developed historic contexts, including identified property types. (See the Guidelines for Preservation Planning for discussion of development of historic contexts.)

2. Sufficient information about the appearance, condition and associative values of the property to be evaluated to:

a. Classify it as to property type;

b. Compare its features or characteristics with those expected for its property type; and

c. Define the physical extent of the property and accurately locate the property.

To facilitate distinguishing between facts and analysis, the information should be divided into categories including identification and description of pertinent historical contexts; description of the property and its significance in the historical context; and analysis of the integrity of the property relative to that needed to represent the context.

Usually documentation need not include such items as a complete title history or biography of every owner of a property, except where that information is important in evaluating its significance. Information on proposed or potential treatments or threats, such as destruction of a property through uncontrollable natural processes, is also not needed for evaluation, unless those effects are likely to occur prior to or during the evaluation, thereby altering the significant characteristic of the property. If archeological testing or structural analysis is needed for evaluation, it should not proceeded beyond the point of providing the information necessary for evaluation and should not unnecessarily affect significant features or values of the property.

When more information is needed: Evaluation cannot be conducted unless all necessary information is available. (See Information Needed to Evaluate Properties.) Any missing information or analysis should be identified (e.g. development of context or information on the property) as well as the specific activities required to obtain the information (archival research, field survey and testing, or laboratory testing). When adequate information is not available, it is important to record that fact so that evaluation will not be undertaken until the information can be obtained. In some cases needed information is not obtainable, for example, where historical records have been destroyed or analytical techniques have not been developed to date materials in archeological sites. If an evaluation must be completed in these cases, it is important to acknowledge what information was not obtainable and how that missing information may affect the reliability of the evaluation.

Application of the Criteria within a Historic Context

The first step in evaluation is considering how the criteria apply to the particular historic context. This is done by reviewing the previously developed narrative for the historic context and determining how the criteria would apply to properties in that context, based on the important patterns, events, persons and cultural values identified. (See the discussion of the historic context narrative in the Guidelines for Preservation Planning.) This step includes identification of which criteria each property type might meet and how integrity is to be evaluated for each property type under each criterion. Specific guidelines for evaluating the eligibility of individual properties should be established. These guidelines should outline and justify the specific physical characteristics or data requirements that an individual property must possess to retain integrity for the particular property type; and define the process by which revisions or additions can be made to the evaluation framework.

Consideration of property type and integrity: After considering how the criteria apply to the particular historic context, the evaluation process for a property generally includes the following steps:

1. A property is classified as to the appropriate historic context(s) and property type(s). If no existing property type is appropriate, a new property type is defined, its values identified, and the specific characteristics or data requirements are outlined and justified as an addition to the historic context. If necessary, a new historic context is defined for which values and property types and their integrity requirements are identified and justified.

2. A comparison is made between the existing information about the property and the integrity characteristics or data required for the property type.

a. If the comparison shows that the property possesses these characteristics, then it is evaluated as significant for that historic context. The evaluation includes a determination that the property retains integrity for its type.

b. If the comparison shows that the property does not meet the minimum requirements, one of several conclusions is reached:

(1) The property is determined not significant because it does not retain the integrity defined for the property type.

(2) The property has characteristics that may make it significant but these differ from those expected for that property type in that context. In this case, the historic context or property types should be reexamined and revised if necessary, based on subsequent research and survey.

The evaluation should state how the particular property meets the integrity requirements for its type. When a property is disqualified for loss of integrity, the evaluation statement should focus on the kinds of integrity expected for the property type, those that are absent for the disqualified property, and the impact of that absence on the property's ability to exemplify architectural, historical or research values within a particular historic context.

The integrity of the property in its current condition, rather than its likely condition after a proposed treatment, should be evaluated. Factors such as structural problems, deterioration, or abandonment should be considered in the evaluation only if they have affected the integrity of the significant features or characteristics of the property.

Inventory

An inventory is a repository of information on specific properties evaluated as significant.

Content: The inventory should include:

1. Summaries of the important historic contexts. These may be in the form of an approved plan or analyses of historic contexts important in the history of the geographical area covered by the inventory.

2. Descriptions of significant property types of these contexts, whether or not any specific properties have been identified.

3. Results of reconnaissance surveys or other identification activities, even if the level of information on specific properties identified as part of those activities is not sufficient to evaluate individual properties.

4. Information on individual properties that was used in evaluation.

Historic contexts are identified by name, with reference to documents describing those contexts, or with a narrative statement about the context(s) where such documents do not exist.

A description of the property. Part of this description may be a photographic record.

A statement that justifies the significance of the property in relation to its context(s). This statement should include an analysis of the integrity of the property.

Boundaries of the property.

A record of when a property was evaluated and included in the inventory, and by whom.

Records on demolished or altered properties and properties evaluated as not significant should be retained, along with full description of areas surveyed, for the planning information these records provide about impacts to properties and about the location and character of non-significant properties to prevent redundant identification work at a later time.

Maintenance: Inventory entries should be maintained so that they accurately represent what is known about historic properties in the area covered by the inventory. This will include new information gained from research and survey about the historic contexts, property types, and previously evaluated properties, as well as information about newly evaluated properties. For individual properties, addition of kinds of significance, change in the boundaries, or loss of significance through demolition or alteration should be recorded.

Uses and Availability: An inventory should be managed so that the information is accessible. Its usefulness depends on the organization of information and on its abilty to incorporate new information. An inventory should be structured so that entries can be retrieved by locality or by historic context.

The availability of the inventory information should be announced or a summary should be distributed. This may be in the form of a list of properties evaluated as significant or a summary of the historic contexts and the kinds of properties in the inventory. Inventories should be avilable to managers, planners, and the general public at local, State, regional, and Federal agency levels.

It is necessary to protect information about archeological sites or other properties whose integrity may be damaged by widespread knowledge of their location. It may also be necessary to protect information on the location of properties such as religious sites, structures, or objects whose cultural value would be compromised by public knowledge of the property's location.

Recommended Sources of Technical Information

How to Apply the National Register Critera. Available through the National Register Branch, Interagency Resources Division, National Park Service, U.S. Department of the Interior, Washington, D.C. 20240. Provides detailed technical information about interpretation of the significance and integrity criteria used by the National Register of Historic Places program.

How To Series. Available through the National Register Branch, Interagency Resources Division, National Park Service, U.S. Department of the Interior, Washington, D.C. 20240. Discusses application of the National Register criteria for evaluation. Titles include:

How To Establish Boundaries for National Register Properties.
How To Evaluate and Nominate Potential National Register Properties That Have Achieved Significance Within the Last 50 Years.
How To Improve Quality of Photos for National Register Nominations.
How To Apply for Certification of Significance Under Section 2124 of the Tax Reform Act of 1976.
How To Apply for Certification of State and Local Statutes and Historic Districts.
How To Quality Historic Properties Under the New Federal Law Affective Easements.

Importance of Small, Surface, and Disturged Sites as Sources of Significant Archeological Data. Valerie Talmage and Olga Chesler. Interagency Archeological Service 1977. Washington, D.C. Available from the National Technical Information Service. NTIS Publication Number PB 270939/AS. Discusses the role of small, surface, and disturbed sites as sources of significant information about a variety of prehistoric activities. These types of sites are frequently ignored in the development of regional archeological research designs.

Secretary of the Interior's Standards For Registration

Registration is the formal recognition of properties evaluated as significant. Preservation benefits provided by various registration programs range from honorific recognition to prohibition of demolition or alteration of included properties. Some registration programs provide recognition and other broad benefits while other programs authorize more specific forms of protection.

Standard I. Registration Is Conducted According To Stated Procedures

Registration of historic properties in the National Register of Historic Places must be done in accordance with the National Register regulations published in the Code of Federal Regulations, 36 CFR 60. Registration for other lists or purposes follow an established process that is understood by the public, particularly by those interests that may be affected by registration.

Standard II. Registration Information Locates, Describes and Justifies the Significance and Physical Integrity of a Historic Property

Registers are used for planning, research and treatment. They must contain adequate information for users to locate a property and understand its significance. Additional information may be appropriate depending on the intended use of the register.

Standard III. Registration Information is Accessible to the Public

Information should be readily available to the public and to government agencies responsible for the preservation of historic properties and for other planning needs.

Secretary of the Interior's Guidelines for Registration

Introduction

These Guidelines link the Standards for Registration with more specific guidance and technical information. They describe one approach to meeting the Standards for Registration. Agencies, organizations, or individuals proposing to approach registration differently may wish to review their approach with the National Park Service.

The Guidelines are organized as follows:

Purpose of Registration Programs
Registration Procedures
Documentation on Registered Properties
Public Availability
Recommended Sources of Technical Information

Purpose of Registration Programs

Registration of historic properties is the formal recognition of properties that have been evaluated as significant according to written criteria. Registration results in an official inventory or list that serves an administrative function. A variety of benefits or forms of protection accure to a registered property, ranging from honorific recognition to prohibition of demolition or alteration.

Some registration programs provide recognition and other broad benefits or entitlements, while other registrations of properties may, in addition, authorize more specific forms of protection. The application of the registration process should be a logical outgrowth of the same planning goals and priorities that guided the identification and evaluation activities. All registration programs should establish priorities for recognition of their authorized range of properties; provide for confidentiality of sensitive information; and establish a means of appealing the registration or non-registration of a property.

Registration Procedures

Explicit procedures are essential because they are the means by which the public can understand and participate in the registration process. Procedures for registration programs should be developed by professionals in the field of historic preservation, in consultation with those who will use or be affected by the program. Prior to taking effect, procedures should be published or circulated for comment at the governmental level at which they will be used. (Procedures for registration of properties in the National Register of Historic Places and the National Historic Landmarks list, for example, are published in the **Federal Register**.)

Any registration program should include:

1. A professional staff to prepare or assess the documentation;
2. A professional review, independent of the nominating source, to provide an impartial evaluation of the documented significance;
3. Adequate notice to property owners, elected officials and the public about proposed registrations and the effects of listing, if any; and
4. A means of public participation.

Professional Review: The registration process should include an independent evaluation of the significance of the property and of the quality and thoroughness of the documentation supporting that significance. Such evaluation ensures that significance is adequately justified and that registration documentation meets the technical requirements of the registration process.

State and local preservation programs, concerned with both public and private properties, generally use a review board, panel or commission. This level of professional review has proven to be effective in assessing the significance of properties considered for registration.

Review boards and other forms of independent review should include professionals in the fields or diciplines included in the criteria; representatives of other fields or disciplines may be desirable to reflect other values or aspects of the register. Key personnel must be qualified by education, training or experience to accomplish their designated duties. (See the Professional Qualifications Standards.)

The scope of the independent review should be clearly stated in the registration procedures and should not include issues outside the scope of the applicable criteria for evaluation and other areas specified in the procedures. Generally, independent reviewers should not be involved in any primary research or analysis related to properties under consideration; this information should be gathered and organized prior to review meetings. Documentation presented to the reviewers should be made available to the public prior to review meetings or public hearings. Registration of properties should not take place until review of documentation has been completed.

Public Notice: Adequate notice allows property owners, officials and other interested parties to comment on proposed registrations prior to action by the independent reviewers. The degree of protection and control provided by a registration program may be a factor in determining what constitutes adequate notice. For example, adequate notice of proposed inclusion in honorific registers may be less complex than that for registration that results in local controls on alteration or demolition of registered properties.

Notice to elected officials and the public is necessary to distribute information about potential registrations of concern to planning and development interests.

Adequate notice to property owners may be accomplished through means ranging from individual notification by mail to publication of a public notice, depending on the nature of the registration program and the number and character of the properties involved.

Public notices and owner notification about proposed registrations should include the dates and times of public meetings and review meetings, the kinds of comments that are appropriate, and how comments will be considered in the evaluation process. The notice should also state where information can be obtained about the registration program, the criteria used to evaluate properties for inclusion, and the significance of specific properties under consideration.

The procedures should include a means of public participation in the form of submission of written comments or a review meeting open to the public or a public hearing.

The procedures should state time periods within which reviews, notices, comments, public hearings, review meetings and appeals will occur. The time periods should be short enough to allow for efficient recognition of historic properties but also allow adequate time for public comment and participation by those affected. Time periods may vary depending on whether activities are carried out at the local, State, or national level. These time schedules should be widely circulated so that the process is widely understood.

Appeal Process: A means of appeal should be included in the registration process to allow for reconsideration of a property's inclusion. Reasons for appeal may range from existence of additional information about the property supporting or refuting its significance to administrative or procedural error. An appeal process should specify to whom an appeal may be made and how the information that is provided will be evaluated. The appeal procedures should also state the time limit, if any, on appealing a decision and on consideration of information and issuance of a decision by the appeal authority.

Documentation on Registered Properties

Documentation requirements should be carefully weighed to provide the information *actually* needed to reach a registration decision and should be made public. It should be made certain that identification and evaluation activities obtain and record the information necessary for registration. Documentation should be prepared in a standardized format and on materials that are archivally stable and easy to store and retrieve.

Location: The precise location of a historic property must be clearly identified.

Street address, town or vicinity, and county should be provided. Properties should also be located on maps; these may be USGS maps, county planning maps, or city base maps or real estate maps. A uniform system of noting location, such as UTM grid points or longitude and latitude, should supplement mapping. It is recommended that each registration process standardize the preferred choice of maps appropriate to the scope of the process.

Description: An accurate description of a property includes a description of both the current and historical physical appearance and condition of the property and notes the relevant property type(s) for the applicable historic context(s). Discussion should include alterations, deterioration, relocation and other changes to the property since its period of significance.

Significance: A statement of significance should explain why a property meets the criteria for inclusion in the register to which it has been nominated.

This statement should contain at least 3 elements:

1. Reference to the relevant historic context(s);
2. Identification of relevant property types within the context and their characteristics; and
3. Justification that the property under consideration has the characteristics required to qualify it.

Relevant historic contexts can be identified through reference to the preservation plan or other documents where the contexts have been previously described or can be provided by a narrative discussion of the context. (The development of contexts and their use in evaluating properties are discussed in the Guidelines for Preservation Planning and the Guidelines for Evaluation.) A significant property type and its characteristics are identified either through reference to the historic context(s) or by a narrative in the documentation that describes historic contexts. Justification of a specific property is made by systematic comparison of its characteristics to those required for the property type.

Boundaries: The delineation and justification of boundaries for a registered property are important for future treatment activities. It is expecially critical when legal restraints or restrictions may result from the registration of properties. Thus, boundaries should correspond as closely as possible to the actual extent and configuration of the property and should be carefully selected to encompass, but not exceed, the extent of the significant resource(s). The selection of boundaries should reflect the significant aspects of the property.

Arbitrary boundaries should not be chosen for ease of description since this can result in the inclusion of unrelated land or in exclusion of a portion of the historic property. Present property lines should not be chosen as property boundaries without careful analysis of whether they are appropriate to the historic property. A single uniform boundary description and acreage should not be applied to a group or class of properties (antebellum plantations, for example) without examination of the actual extent of each property. The selected boundaries should be justified as appropriate to the historic property.

Boundaries should be clearly and precisely described, using a verbal boundary description, legal description, accurate sketch map, or lines drawn on base maps, or a combination of these where needed to specify the limits of the property being registered. When used, maps should show the location of buildings, structures, sites or objects within the boundary.

Updating Information on Registered Properties: A change in the condition of the significant features of a property may require a change in the official registration record. Alteration of a significant architectural feature, for example, could mean that a property is no longer significant for its architectural design.

Additional significance of registered properties may be identified through development of new historic contexts.

Research may reveal that a property is significant in other historic contexts or is significant at a higher level. For example, a property previously recognized as of local significance could be found to be of national significance.

A change in location or condition of a registered property may mean that the property is no longer significant for the reasons for which it was registered and the property should be deleted from the registered list.

Public Availability

Lists of registered properties should be readily available for public use, and information on registered properties should be distributed on a regular basis. Lists of properties registered nationally are distributed through publication in the Federal Register and to Congressional Offices and State Historic Preservation Offices. Comprehensive information should be stored and maintained for public use at designated national, State and local authorities open to the public on a regular basis.

Information should be retrievable by the property name, and location, historic context or property type. The specific location of properties that may be threatened by dissemination of that information must be withheld. These may include fragile archeological properties or properties such as religious sites, structures, or objects whose cultural value would be compromised by public knowledge of the property location.

Recommended Sources of Technical Information

How to Complete National Register Forms. National Register Division, National Park Service, U.S. Deparment of the Interior, 1977. Washington, D.C. Available through the Superintendent of Documents, US Government Printing Office, Washington, D.C. 20402. GPO Stock Number 024-005-00666-4. This publication is the standard reference on the documentation requirements of the National Register of Historic Places program.

How To Series. Available through the National Register Branch, Interagency Resources Division, National Park Service, Department of the Interior 20240. These information sheets contain supplementary information about interpreting the National Register criteria for evaluation and documentation requirements of the National Register registration program. Title include:

How To Establish Boundaries for National Register Properties.
How To Evaluate and Nominate Potential National Register Properties That Have Achieved Significance Within the Last 50 Years.
How To Improve the Quality of Photographs for National Register Nominations.
How To Apply for Certification of Significance Under Section 2124 of the Tax Reform Act of 1976.
How To Apply for Certification of State and Local Statutes and Historic Districts.
How To Qualify Historic Properties Under the New Federal Law Affecting Easements.

Note on Documentation and Treatment of Historic Properties

Documentation and treatment of historic properties includes a variety of techniques to preserve or protect properties, or to document their historic values and information. While documentation activities may be applied to any potentially historic property, generally only those properties that first have been evaluated as significant against specified criteria (such as those of the National Register) are treated. Some commonly applied treatments are preservation in place, rehabilitation, restoration and stabilization; there are other types of treatments also. Documentation and treatment may be applied to the same property; for example, archeological, historical, and architectural documentation may be prepared before a structure is stabilized or before foundations or chimneys or other lost features are reconstructed.

Alternatives for treatment will usually be available, and care should be applied in choosing among them. Preservation in place is generally preferable to moving a property. Over time, the preferred treatment for a property may change; for example, an archeological site intended for preservation in place may begin to erode so that a combination of archeological documentation and stabilization may be required. If a decision is made that a particular property will not be preserved in place, the need for documentation must then be considered.

The three sets of documentation standards (i.e., the Standards for Historical Documentation, Standards for Architectural and Engineering Documentation, and Standards for Archeological Documentation) as well as the Standards for Historic Preservation Projects (Acquisition, Preservation, Stabilization, Protection, Rehabilitation, Restoration, and Reconstruction) describe the techniques of several disciplines to treat historic properties, and to document or preserve information about their historical values. The integration of planning for documentation and treatment with their execution is accomplished in a statement of objectives, or research design. Because both the goals and appropriate methodologies are likely to be interdisciplinary in nature, the relationship among these various activities should be specified in the research design to ensure that the resulting documentation produces a comprehensive record of historic properties in an efficient manner.

Secretary of the Interior's Standards for Historical Documentation

Historical documentation provides important information related to the significance of a property for use by historians, researchers, preservationists, architects, and historical archeologists. Research is used early in planning to gather information needed to identify and evaluate properties. (These activities are discussed in the Standards and Guidelines for Preservation Planning and the Standards and Guidelines for Identification.) Historical documentation is also a treatment that can be applied in several ways to properties previously evaluated as significant; it may be used in conjunction with other treatment activities (as the basis for rehabilitation plans or interpretive programs, for example) or as a final treatment to preserve information in cases of threatened property destruction. These Standards concern the use of research and documentation as a treatment.

Standard I. Historical Documentation Follows a Research Design That Responds to Needs Identified in the Planning Process

Historical documentation is undertaken to make a detailed record of the significance of a property for research and interpretive purposes and for conservation of information in cases of threatened property destruction. Documentation must have defined objectives so that proposed work may be assessed to determine whether the resulting documentation will meet needs identified in the planning process. The research design or statement of objectives is a formal statement of how the needs identified in the plan are to be addressed in a specific documentation project. This is the framework that guides the selection of methods and evaluation of results, and specifies the relationship of the historical documentation efforts to other proposed treatment activities.

Standards II. Historical Documentation Employs an Appropriate Methodology to Obtain the Information Required by The Research Design

Methods and techniques of historical research should be chosen to obtain needed information in the most efficient way. Techniques should be carefully selected and the sources should be recorded so that other researchers can verify or locate information discovered during the research.

Standard III. The Results of Historical Documentation Are Assessed Against the Research Design and Integrated Into the Planning Process

Documentation is one product of research; information gatherd about the usefulness of the research design itself is another. The research results are assessed against the research design to determine how well they meet the objectives of the research. The results are integrated into the body of current knowledge and reviewed for their implications for the planning process. The research design is reviewed to determine how future research designs might be modified based on the activity conducted.

Standard IV. The Results of Historical Documentation Are Reported and Made Available to the Public

Research results must be accessible to prospective users. Results should be communicated to the professional community and the public in reports summarizing the documentation activity and identifying the repository of additional detailed information. The goal of disseminating information must be balanced, however, with the need to protect sensitive information whose disclosure might result in damage to properties.

Secretary of the Interior's Guidelines for Historical Documentation

Introduction

These Guidelines link the Standards for Historical Documentation with more specific guidance and technical information. They describe one approach to meeting the Standards for Historical Documentation. Agencies, organizations or individuals proposing to approach historical documentation differently may wish to review their approaches with the National Park Service.

The Guidelines are organized as follows:

Historical Documentation Objectives
Research Design
Methods
Integrating Results
Reporting Results
Recommended Sources of Technical Information

Documentation Objectives

Documentation is a detailed record, in the form of a report or other written document, of the historical context(s) and significance of a property. Historical research to create documentation uses archival materials, oral history techniques, ethnohistories, prior research contained in secondary sources and other sources to make a detailed record of previously identified values or to investigate particular questions about the established significance of a property or properties. It is an investigative technique that may be employed to document associative, architectural, cultural or informational values of properties. It may be used as a component of structural recording or archeological investigation, to enable interpretation or to mitigate the anticipated loss of a property through conservation of information about its historical, architectural or archeological significance. Documentation generally results in both greater factual knowledge about the specific property and its values, and in better understanding of the property in its historical context. In addition to increasing factual knowledge about a property and its significance in one historical context, documentation may also serve to link the property to or define its importance in other known or yet-to-be defined historic contexts.

Documentation should incorporate, rather than duplicate, the findings of previous research. Research may be undertaken to identify how a particular property fits into the work of an architect or builder; to analyze the historical relationship among several properties; or to document in greater detail the historical contexts of properties. The kinds of questions investigated will generally depend on what is already known or understood and what information is needed. For example, documentation of a bridge whose technological significance is well understood, but whose role in local transportation history is not, would summarize the information on the former topic and focus research on the associative values of the property. The questions that research seeks to answer through deed, map or archival search, oral history and other techniques may also relate to issues addressed in structural documentation or archeological investigation; for example, the reasons for and history of modification of a building to be the subject of architectural or engineering documentation.

Research Design

Historical documentation is guided by a statement of objectives, research design or task directive prepared before research is performed. The research design is a useful statement of how proposed work will enhance existing archival data and permits comparison of the proposed work with the results. The purpose of the research design is to define the proposed scope of the documentation work and to define a set of expectations based on the information available prior to the research. Generally, the research design also ensures that research methods are commensurate with the type, quality and source of expected information.

The research design for a property should identify:

1. Evaluated significance of the property(ies) to be investigated;
2. Historical, architectural, archeological or cultural issues relevant to the evaluated significance of the property;
3. Previous research on those issues and how the proposed work is related to existing knowledge;
4. The amount and kinds of information required to produce reliable historical analyses;
5. Methods to be used to obtain the information;
6. Types of sources to be investigated; types of personnel required;
7. Expected results or findings based on available knowledge about the property and its context; and
8. Relationship of the proposed historical documentation to other proposed treatment activities; for example, recommendations on the use of documentation in interpretive programs or other aspects of treatment such as anticipated architectural, engineering or archeological documentation).

Research Methods

Research methods should be chosen based on the information needs, be capable of replication and be recorded so that another researcher could follow the same research procedure. Sources should be recorded so that other researchers can locate or verify the information discovered during the search.

Use of Sources: The variety of available written and graphic materials and the number of individuals that can serve as sources, including but not limited to personal records, deed and title books, newspapers, plats, maps, atlases, photographs, vital records, censuses, historical narratives, interviews of individuals and secondary source materials, should be considered in developing the research design. Part of the development of the research design is deciding what kinds of source materials are most likely to contain needed information and at what point in the research process that information will be most valuable. For example, often secondary sources are most valuable for gathering background information, while primary sources are more useful to gather or confirm specific facts. The documentation goals may not *require* exhaustive investigation of sources, such as deed records or building permits. Research may be kept cost-effective by making careful decisions about when to use particular sources, thereby limiting the use of time-consuming techniques to when absolutely necessary. Decisions about when to gather information may also affect the quality of information that can be gathered. When dealing with large project areas where loss of many properties is anticipated, it is important to gather information from local archival sources and oral histories before project activities destroy or disperse family or community records and residents.

Analysis of the accuracy and biases of source materials is critical in analyzing the information gathered from these sources. Maps, historical atlases and insurance maps should be assessed like written records for errors, biases and omissions; for example, some map sources may omit structures of a temporary nature or may not fully depict ethnic or minority areas. Likewise, building plans and architectural renderings may not reflect a structure as it was actually built.

Analysis: Analysis should not only focus on the issues defined in the research design, but should also explore major new issues identified during the course of research or analysis. The documentation gathered may raise important issues not previously considered, and further investigation may be important, particularly when contradictory information has been gathered. It is important to examine the implications of these new issues to ensure that they are investigated in a balanced way.

Questions that should be considered in analyzing the information include:

1. Has enough information been gathered to anwser the questions that were posed?

2. Do the answers contradict one another? If so, it may be necessary to search for more evidence. If no additional evidence is available, judgements must be based on the available sources, weighing their biases. Conflicts of source materials should be noted.

In general, the more the researcher knows about the general historical period and setting, and limitations of the source materials under investigation, the better the individual is prepared to evaluate the information found in the documentary sources investigated. Peer review or consultation with other knowledgeable individuals about the information and the tentative conclusions can be an important part of the analysis.

Integrating Results

The results of documentation must be integrated into the planning process so that planning decisions are based on the best available informaiton. The new information is first assessed against the research design to determine whether the gathered information meets the defined objectives of the research. Then the relevant historic contexts, property types, and treatment goals for those contexts are all adjusted, as necessary, based on the historical documentation results.

Reporting Results

Reports should contain:

1. Summaries of the purpose of the documentation, the research design and methods and techniques of investigation.

2. Sources of facts or analyses so that other researchers can locate the information in its original context. Notation of any conflicts in source materials and how the individual performing the documentation interpreted these conflicts.

3. Sources consulted, including those expected to contain useful information and those that contained no information about the property(s).

4. Assessment of the accuracy, biases and historical perspective of all sources. This information and that identified in No. 3 may be provided in an annotated bibliography.

5. Discussion of major analyses and results, including conclusions regarding all major research issues identified in the research design, as well as important issues raised in the course of research. The analysis should be summarized in terms of its impact on interpretating the property's significance and expanding or altering the knowledge about the property and its context.

6. Researchers' interpretation of historical events or trends. These interpretations should be clearly identified.

Primary results should be preserved and made accessible in some manner, although they need not necessarily be contained in the report. At a minimum, the report should reference the location of notes and analyses.

Results of historical documentation should be made available for use in preservation planning and by the general public. Report formats may vary, depending on the audience and the anticipated uses of the documentation, but professionally accepted rules of report writing should be followed. If reports are of a technical nature, the format of the major scientific journal of the pertinent discipline may be the most appropriate format. Peer review of draft reports is one means of ensuring that state-of-the-art technical reports are produced.

Recommended Sources of Technical Information

Folklife and Fieldwork: A Layman's Introduction to Field Techniques. Peter Bartis. American Folklife Center, Washington, D.C., 1979.

Ordinary People and Everyday Life: Perspectives on the New Social History. James B. Gardner and George Rollie Adams, editors. American Association for State and Local History, Nashville, Tennessee. 1983.

The Process of Field Research. Carl Fleischhauer and Charles K. Wolfe. American Folklife Center, Washington, D.C., 1981.

Researching Heritage Buildings. Margaret Carter. Ministry of the Environment, Ottawa, Canada, 1983.

Secretary of the Interior's Standards for Architectural and Engineering Documentation

These standards concern the development of documentation for historic buildings, sites, structures and objects. This documentation, which usually consists of measured drawings, photographs and written data, provides important information on a property's significance for use by scholars, researchers, preservationists, architects, engineers and others interested in preserving and understanding historic properties. Documentation permits accurate repair or reconstruction of parts of a property, records existing conditions for easements, or may preserve information about a property that is to be demolished.

These Standards are intended for use in developing documentation to be included in the Historic American Building Survey (HABS) and the Historic American Engineering Record (HAER) Collections in the Library of Congress. HABS/HAER, in the National Park Service, have defined specific requirements for meeting these Standards for their collections. The HABS/HAER requirements include information important to development of documentation for other purposes such as State or local archives

Standard I. Documentation Shall Adequately Explicate and Illustrate What is Significant or Valuable About the Historic Building, Site, Structure or Object Being Documented.

The historic significance of the building, site, structure or object identified in the evaluation process should be conveyed by the drawings, photographs and other materials that comprise documentation. The historical, architectural, engineering or cultural values of the property together with the purpose of the documentation activity determine the level and methods of documentation. Documentation prepared for submission to the Library of Congress must meet the HABS/HAER Guidelines.

Standard II. Documentation Shall be Prepared Accurately From Reliable Sources With Limitations Clearly Stated to Permit Independent Verification of the Information.

The purpose of documentation is to preserve an accurate record of historic properties that can be used in research and other preservation activities. To serve these purposes, the documentation must include information that permits assessment of its reliability.

Standard III. Documentation Shall be Prepared on Materials That are Readily Reproductible, Durable and in Standard Sizes.

The size and quality of documentation materials are important factors in the preservation of information for future use. Selection of materials should be based on the length of time expected for storage, the anticipated frequency of use and a size convenient for storage.

Standard IV. Documentation Shall be Clearly and Concisely Produced.

In order for documentation to be useful for future research, written materials must be legible and understandable, and graphic materials must contain scale information and location references.

Secretary of the Interior's Guidelines for Architectural and Engineering Documentation

Introduction

These Guidelines link the Standards for Architectural and Engineering Documentation with more specific guidance and technical information. They describe one approach to meeting the Standards for Architectural Engineering Documentation. Agencies, organizations or individuals proposing to approach documentation differently may wish to review their approaches with the National Park Service.

The Guidelines are organized as follows:

Definitions

These definitions are used in conjunction with these Guidelines:

Architectural Data Form—a one page HABS form intended to provide identifying information for accompanying HABS documentation.

Documentation—measured drawings, photographs, histories, inventory cards or other media that depict historic buildings, sites, structures or objects.

Field Photography—photography, other than large-format photography, intended for the purpose of producing documentation, usually 35mm.

Field Records—notes of measurements taken, field photographs and other recorded information intended for the purpose of producing documentation.

Inventory Card—a one page form which includes written data, a sketched site plan and a 35mm contact print dry-mounted on the form. The negative, with a separate contact sheet and index should be included with the inventory card.

Large Format Photographs—photographs taken of historic buildings, sites, structures or objects where the negative is a 4 X 5", 5 X 7" or 8 X 10" size and where the photograph is taken with appropriate means to correct perspective distortion.

Measured Drawings—drawings produced on HABS or HAER formats depicting existing conditions or other relevant features of historic buildings, sites, structures or objects. Measured drawings are usually produced in ink on archivally stable material, such as mylar.

Photocopy—A photograph, with large-format negative, of a photograph or drawing.

Select Existing Drawings—drawings of historic buildings, sites, structures or objects, whether original construction or later alteration drawings that portray or depict the historic value or significance.

Sketch Plan—a floor plan, generally not to exact scale although often drawn from measurements, where the features are shown in proper relation and proportion to one another.

Goal of Documentation

The Historic American Buildings Survey (HABS) and Historic American Engineering Record (HAER) are the national historical architectural and engineering documentation programs of the National Park Service that promote documentation incorporated into the HABS/HAER collections in the Library of Congress. The goal of the collections is to provide architects, engineers, scholars, and interested members of the public with comprehensive documentation of buildings, sites, structures and objects significant in American history and the growth and development of the built environment.

The HABS/HAER Collections: HABS/HAER documentation usually consists of measured drawings, photographs and written data that provide a detailed record which reflects a property's significance. Measured drawings and properly executed photographs act as a form of insurance against fires and natural disasters by permitting the repair and, if necessary, reconstruction of historic structures damaged by such disasters. Documentation is used to provide the basis for enforcing preservation easement. In addition, documentation is often the last means of preservation of a property; when a property is to be demolished, its documentation provides future researchers access to valuable information that otherwise would be lost.

HABE/HAER documentation is developed in a number of ways. First and most usually, the National Park Service employs summer teams of student architects, engineers, historians and architectural historians to develop HABS/HAER documentation under the supervision of National Park Service professionals. Second, the National Park Service produces HABS/HAER documentation, in conjunction with restoration or other preservation treatment, of historic buildings managed by the National Park Service. Third, Federal agencies, pursuant to Section 110(b) of the National Historic Preservation Act, as amended, record those historic properties to be demolished or substantially altered as a result of agency action or assisted action (referred to as mitigation projects). Fourth, individuals and organizations prepare documentation to HABS/HAER standards and donate that documentation to the HABS/HAER collections. For each of these programs different Documentation Levels will be set.

The Standards describe the fundamental principles of HABS/HAER documentation. They are supplemented by other material describing more specific guidelines, such as line weights for drawings, preferred techniques for architectural photography, and formats for written data. This technical information is found in the HABS/HAER Procedures Manual.

These Guidelines include important information about developing documentation for State or local archives. The State Historic Preservation Officer or the State library should be consulted regarding archival requirements if the documentation will become part of their collections. In establishing archives, the important questions of durability and reproducibility should be considered in relation to the purposes of the collection.

Documentation prepared for the purpose of inclusion in the HABS/HAER collections must meet the requirements below. The HABS/HAER office of the National Park Service retains the right to refuse to accept documentation for inclusion in the HABS/HAER collections when that documentation does not meet HABS/HAER requirements, as specified below.

Standard I: Content

1. *Requirement:* Documentation shall adequately explicate and illustrate what is significant or valuable about the historic building, site, structure or object being documented.

2. *Criteria:* Documentation shall meet one of the following documentation levels to be considered adequate for inclusion in the HABS/HAER collections.

a. Documentation Level I;

(1) Drawings: a full set of measured drawings depicting existing or historic conditions.

(2) Photographs: photographs with large-format negatives of exterior and interior views; photocopies with large format negatives of select existing drawings or historic views where available.

(3) Written data: history and description.

b. Documentation Level II;

(1) Drawings: select existing drawings, where available, should be photographed with large-format negatives or photographically reproduced on mylar.

(2) Photographs: photographs with large-format negatives of exterior and interior views, or historic views, where available.

(3) Written data: history and description.

c. Documentation Level III;

(1) Drawings: sketch plan.

(2) Photographs: photographs with large-format negatives of exterior and interior views.

(3) Written data: architectural data form.

d. Documentation Level IV: HABS/HAER inventory card.

3. *Test:* Inspection of the documentation by HABS/HAER staff.

4. *Commentary:* The HABS/HAER office retains the right to refuse to accept any documentation on buildings, site, structures or objects lacking historical significance. Generally, buildings, sites, structures or objects must be listed in, or eligible for listing in the National Register of Historic Places to be considered for inclusion in the HABS/HAER collections.

The kind and amount of documentation should be appropriate to the nature and significance of the buildings, site, structure or object being documented. For example, Documentation Level I would be inappropriate for a building that is a minor element of a historic district, notable only for streetscape context and scale. A full set of measured drawings for such a minor building would be expensive and would add little, if any, information to the HABS/HAER collections. Large format photography (Documentation Level III) would usually be adequate to record the significance of this type of building.

Similarly, the aspect of the property that is being documented should reflect the nature and significance of the building, site, structure or object being documented. For example, measured drawings of Dankmar Adler and Louis Sullivan's Auditorium Building in Chicago should indicate not only facades, floor plans and sections, but also the innovative structural and mechanical systems that were incorporated in that building. Large format photography of Gunston Hall in Fairfax County, Virginia, to take another example, should clearly show William Buckland's hand-carved moldings in the Palladian Room, as well as other views.

HABS/HAER documentation is usually in the form of measured drawings, photographs, and written data. While the criteria in this section have addressed only these media, documentation need not be limited to them. Other media, such as films of industrial processes, can and have been used to document historic buildings, sites, structures or objects. If other media are to be used, the HABS/HAER office should be contacted before recording.

The actual selection of the appropriate documentation level will vary, as discussed above. For mitigation documentation projects, this level will be selected by the National Park Service Regional Office and communicated to the agency responsible for completing the documentation. Generally, Level I documentation is required for nationally significant buildings and structures, defined as National Historic Landmarks and the primary historic units of the National Park Service.

On occasion, factors other than significance will dictate the selection of another level of documentation. For example, if a rehabilitation of a property is planned, the owner may wish to have a full set of as-built drawings, even though the significance may indicate Level II documentation.

HABS Level I measured drawings usually depict existing conditions through the use of a site plan, floor plans, elevations, sections and construction details. HAER Level I measured drawings will frequently depict original conditions where adequate historical material exists, so as to illustrate manufacturing or engineering processes.

Level II documentation differs from Level I by substituting copies of existing drawings, either original or alteration drawings, for recently executed measured drawings. If this is done, the drawings must meet HABS/HAER requirements outlined below. While existing drawings are rarely as suitable as as-built drawings, they are adquate in many cases for documentation purposes. Only when the desirability of having as-built drawings is clear are Level I measured drawings required in addition to existing drawings. If existing drawings are housed in an accessible collection and cared for archivally, their reproduction for HABS/HAER may not be necessary. In other cases, Level I measured drawings are required in the absence of existing drawings.

Level III documentation requires a sketch plan if it helps to explain the structure. The architectural data form should supplement the photographs by explaining what is not readily visible.

Level IV documentation consists of completed HABS/HAER inventory cards. This level of documentation, unlike the other three levels, is rarely considered adequate documentation for the HABS/HAER collections but is undertaken to identify historic resources in a given area prior to additional, more comprehensive documentation.

Standard II: Quality

1. *Requirement:* HABS and HAER documentation shall be prepared accurately from reliable sources with limitations clearly stated to permit independent verification of information.

2. *Criteria:* For all levels of documentation, the following quality standards shall be met:

a. Measured drawings: Measured drawings shall be produced from recorded, accurate measurements. Portions of the building that were not accessible for measurement should not be drawn on the measured drawings, but clearly labeled as not accessible or drawn from available construction drawings and other sources and so identified. No part of the measured drawings shall be produced from hypothesis or non-measurement related activities. Documentation Level I measured drawings shall be accompanied by a set of field notebooks in which the measurements were first recorded. Other drawings, prepared for Documentation Levels II and III, shall include a statement describing where the original drawings are located.

b. Large format photographs: Large format photographs shall clearly depict the appearance of the property and areas of significance of the recorded building, site, structure or object. Each view shall be perspective-corrected and fully captioned.

c. Written history: Written history and description for Documentation Levels I and II shall be based on primary sources to the greatest extent possible. For Levels III and IV, secondary sources may provide adequate information; if not, primary research will be necessary. A frank assessment of the reliability and limitations of sources shall be included. Within the written history, statements shall be footnoted as to their sources, where appropriate. The written data shall include a methodology section specifying name of researcher, date of research, sources searched, and limitations of the project.

3. *Test:* Inspection of the documentation by HABS/HAER staff.

4. *Commentary:* The reliability of the HABS/HAER collections depends on documentation of high quality. Quality is not something that can be easily prescribed or quantified, but it derives from a process in which thoroughness and accuracy play a large part. The principle of independent verification HABS/HAER documentation is critical to the HABS/HAER collections.

Standard III: Materials

1. *Requirement:* HABS and HAER documentation shall be prepared on materials that are readily reproducible for ease of access; durable for long storage; and in standard sizes for ease of handling.

2. *Criteria:* For all levels of documentation, the following material standards shall be met:

a. Measured Drawings:

Readily Reproducible: Ink on translucent material.

Durable: Ink on archivally stable materials.

Standard Sizes: Two sizes: 19 × 24" or 24 × 36".

b. Large Format Photographs:

Readily Reproducible: Prints shall accompany all negatives.

Durable: Photography must be archivally processed and stored. Negatives are required on safety film only. Resin-coated paper is not accepted. Color photography is not acceptable.

Standard Sizes: Three sizes: 4 × 5", 5 × 7", 8 × 10".

c. Written History and Description:

Readily Reproducible: Clean copy for xeroxing.

Durable: Archival bond required.

Standard Sizes: 8½ × 11".

d. Field Records:

Readily Reproducible: Field notebooks may be xeroxed. Photo identification sheet will accompany 35 mm negatives and contact sheets.

Durable: No requirement.

Standard Sizes: Only requirement is that they can be made to fit into a 9½ × 12" archival folding file.

3. *Test:* Inspection of the documentation by HABS/HAER staff.

4. *Commentary:* All HABS/HAER records are intended for reproduction; some 20,000 HABS/HAER records are reproduced each year by the Library of Congress. Although field records are not intended for quality reproduction, it is intended that they be used to supplement the formal documentation. The basic durability performance standard for HABS/HAER records is 500 years. Ink on mylar is believed to meet this standard, while color photography, for example, does not. Field records do not meet this archival standard, but are maintained in the HABS/HAER collections as a courtesty to the collection user.

Standard IV: Presentation

1. *Requirement:* HABS and HAER documentation shall be clearly and concisely produced.

2. *Criteria:* For levels of documentation as indicated below, the following standards for presentation will be used:

a. Measured Drawings: Level I measured drawings will be lettered mechanically (i.e., Leroy or similar) or in a handprinted equivalent style. Adequate dimensions shall be included on all sheets. Level III sketch plans should be neat and orderly.

b. Large format photographs: Level I photographs shall include duplicate photographs that include a scale. Level II and III photographs shall include, at a minimum, at least one photograph with a scale, usually of the principal facade.

c. Written history and description: Data shall be typewritten on bond, following accepted rules of grammar.

3. *Test:* Inspection of the documentation by HABS/HAER staff.

Architectural and Engineering Documentation Prepared for Other Purposes

Where a preservation planning process is in use, architectural and engineering documentation, like other treatment activities, are undertaken to achieve the goals identified by the preservation planning process. Documentation is deliberately selected as a treatment for properties evaluated as significant, and the development of the documentation program for a property follows from the planning objectives. Documentation efforts focus on the significant characteristics of the property, as defined in the previously completed evaluation. The selection of a level of documentation and the documentation techniques (measured drawings, photography, etc.) is based on the significance of the property and the management needs for which the documentation is being performed. For example, the kind and level of documentation required to record a historic property for easement purposes may be less detailed than that required as mitigation prior to destruction of the property. In the former case, essential documentation might be limited to the portions of the property controlled by the easement, for example, exterior facades; while in the latter case, significant interior architectural features and non-visible structural details would also be documented.

The principles and content of the HABS/HAER criteria may be used for guidance in creating documentation requirements for other archives. Levels of documentation and the durability and sizes of documentation may vary depending on the intended use and the repository. Accuracy of documentation should be controlled by assessing the reliability of all sources and making that assessment available in the archival record; by describing the limitations of the information available from research and physical examination of the

Appendix A: Core Federal Regulations and Standards A-33

44734 Federal Register / Vol. 48, No. 190 / Thursday, September 29, 1983 / Notices

property; and by retaining the primary data (field measurements and notebooks) from which the archival record was produced. Usefulness of the documentation products depends on preparing the documentation on durable materials that are able to withstand handling and reproduction, and in sizes that can be stored and reproduced without damage.

Recommended Sources of Technical Information

Recording Historic Buildings. Harley J. McKee. Government Printing Office, 1970. Washington, D.C. Available through the Superintendent of Documents, U.S. Government Printing Office, Washington, D.C. 20402. GPO number 024–005–0235–9.

HABS/HAER Procedures Manual. Historic American Buildings Survey/Historic American Engineering Record, National Park Service, 1980. Washington, D.C.

Photogrammetric Recording of Cultural Resources. Perry E. Borchers. Technical Preservation Services, U.S. Department of the Interior, 1977. Washinton, D.C.

Rectified Photography and Photo Drawings for Historic Preservation. J. Henry Chambers. Technical Preservation Services, U.S. Department of the Interior, 1975. Washington, D.C.

Secretary of the Interior's Standards for Archeological Documentation

Archeological documentation is a series of actions applied to properties of archeological interest. Documentation of such properties may occur at any or all levels of planning, identification, evaluation or treatment. The nature and level of documentation is dictated by each specific set of circumstances. Archeological documentation consists of activities such as archival research, observation and recording of above-ground remains, and observation (directly, through excavation, or indirectly, through remote sensing) of below-ground remains. Archeological documentation is employed for the purpose of gathering information on individual historic properties or groups of properties. It is guided by a framework of objectives and methods derived from the planning process, and makes use of previous planning decisions, such as those on evaluation of significance. Archeological documentation may be undertaken as an aid to various treatment activities, including research, interpretation, reconstruction, stabilization and data recovery when mitigating archeological losses resulting from construction. Care should be taken to assure that documentation efforts do not duplicate previous efforts.

Standard I. Archeological Documentation Activities Follow an Explicit Statement of Objectives and Methods That Responds to Needs Identified in the Planning Process

Archeological research and documentation may be undertaken to fulfill a number of needs, such as overviews and background studies for planning, interpretation or data recovery to mitigate adverse effects. The planning needs are articulated in a statement of objectives to be accomplished by the archeological documentation activities. The statement of objectives guides the selection of methods and techniques of study and provides a comparative framework for evaluating and deciding the relative efficiency of alternatives. Satisfactory documentation involves the use of archeological and historical sources, as well as those of other disciplines. The statement of objectives usually takes the form of a formal and explicit research design which has evolved from the interrelation of planning needs, current knowledge, resource value and logistics.

Standard II. The Methods and Techniques of Archeological Documentation are Selected To Obtain the Information Required by the Statement of Objectives

The methods and techniques chosen for archeological documentation should be the most effective, least destructive, most efficient and economical means of obtaining the needed information. Methods and techniques should be selected so that the results may be verified if necessary. Non-destructive techniques should be used whenever appropriate. The focus on stated objectives should be maintained throughout the process of study and documentation.

Standard III. The Results of Archeological Documentation are Assessed Against the Statement of Objectives and Integrated Into the Planning Process

One product of archeological documentation is the recovered data; another is the information gathered about the usefulness of the statement of objectives itself. The recovered data are assessed against the objectives to determine how they meet the specified planning needs. Information related to archeological site types, distribution and density should be integrated in planning at the level of identification and evaluation. Information and data concerning intra-site structure may be needed for developing mitigation strategies and are appropriately integrated at this level of planning. The results of the data analyses are integrated into the body of current knowledge. The utility of the method of approach and the particular techniques which were used in the investigation (i.e. the research design) should be assessed so that the objectives of future documentation efforts may be modified accordingly.

Standard IV. The Results of Archeological Documentation are Reported and Made Available to the Public

Results must be accessible to a broad range of users including appropriate agencies, the professional community and the general public. Results should be communicated in reports that summarize the objectives, methods, techniques and results of the documentation activity, and identify the repository of the materials and information so that additional detailed information can be obtained, if necessary. The public may also benefit from the knowledge obtained from archeological documentation through pamphlets, brochures, leaflets, displays and exhibits, or by slide, film or multi-media productions. The goal of disseminating information must be balanced, however, with the need to protect sensitive information whose disclosure might result in damage to properties. Curation arrangements sufficient to preserve artifacts, specimens and records generated by the investigation must be provided for to assure the availability of these materials for future use.

Secretary of the Interior's Guidelines for Archeological Documentation

Introduction

These Guidelines link the Standards for Archeological Documentation with more specific guidance and technical information. They describe one approach to meeting the Standards for Documentation. Agencies, organizations or individuals proposing to approach archeological documentation differently may wish to review their approach with the National Park Service.

The Guidelines are organized as follows:

1. Collection of base-line data;

Federal Register / Vol. 48, No. 190 / Thursday, September 29, 1983 / Notices 44735

2. Problem-oriented research directed toward particular data gaps recognized in the historic context(s);
3. Preservation or illustration of significance which has been identified for treatment by the planning process; or
4. Testing of new investigative or conservation techniques, such as the effect of different actions such as forms of site burial (aqueous or non-aqueous).

Many properties having archeological components have associative values as well as research values. Examples include Native American sacred areas and historic sites such as battlefields. Archeological documentation may preserve information or data that are linked to the identified values that a particular property possesses. Depending on the property type and the range of values represented by the property, it may be necessary to recover information that relates to an aspect of the property's significance other than the specified research questions. It is possible that conflicts may arise between the optimal realizations of research goals and other issues such as the recognition/protection of other types of associative values. The research design for the archeological documentation should provide for methods and procedures to resolve such conflicts, and for the close coordination of the archeological research with the appropriate ethnographic, social or technological research.

Archeological Documentation Objectives

The term "archeological documentation" is used here to refer specifically to any operation that is performed using archeological techniques as a means to obtain and record evidence about past human activity that is of importance to documenting history and prehistory in the United States. Historic and prehistoric properties may be important for the data they contain, or because of their association with important persons, events, or processes, or because they represent architectural or artistic values, or for other reasons. Archeological documentation may be an appropriate option for application not only to archeological properties, but to above-ground structures as well, and may be used in collaboration with a wide range of other treatment activities.

If a property contains artifacts, features, and other materials that can be studied using archeological techniques, then archeological documentation may be selected to achieve particular goals of the planning process—such as to address a specified information need, or to illustrate significant associative values. Within the overall goals and priorities established by the planning process, particular methods of investigation are chosen that best suit the types of study to be performed.

Relationship of archeological documentation to other types of documentation or other treatments: Archeological documentation is appropriate for achieving any of various goals, including:

Documentation Plan

Research Design: Archeological documentation can be carried out only after defining explicit goals and a methodology for reaching them. The goals of the documentation effort directly reflect the goals of the preservation plan and the specific needs identified for the relevant historic contexts. In the case of problem oriented archeological research, the plan usually takes the form of a formal research design, and includes, in addition to the items below, explicit statements of the problem to be addressed and the methods or tests to be applied. The purpose of the statement of objectives is to explain the rationale behind the documentation effort; to define the scope of the investigation; to identify the methods, techniques, and procedures to be used; to provide a schedule for the activities; and to permit comparison of the proposed research with the results. The research design for an archeological documentation effort follows the same guidelines as those for identification (see the Guidelines for Identification) but has a more property-specific orientation.

The research design should draw upon the preservation plan to identify:
1. Evaluated significance of the property(ies) to be studied;
2. Research problems or other issues relevant to the significance of the property;
3. Prior research on the topic and property type; and how the proposed documentation objectives are related to previous research and existing knowledge;
4. The amount and kinds of information (data) required to address the documentation objectives and to make reliable statements, including at what point information is redundant and documentation efforts have reached a point of diminishing returns;
5. Methods to be used to find the information; and
6. Relationship of the proposed archeological investigation to anticipated historical or structural documentation, or other treatments.

The primary focus of archeological documentation is on the data classes that are required to address the specified documentation objectives. This may mean that other data classes are deliberately neglected. If so, the reasons for such a decision should be carefully justified in terms of the preservation plan.

Archeological investigations seldom are able to collect and record all possible data. It is essental to determine the point at which further data recovery and documentation fail to improve the usefulness of the archeological information being recovered. One purpose of the research design is to estimate those limits in advance and to suggest at what point information becomes duplicative. Investigation strategies should be selected based on these general principles, considering the following factors:
1. Specific data needs;
2. Time and funds available to secure the data; and
3. Relative cost efficiency of various strategies.

Responsiveness to the concerns of local groups (e.g., Native American groups with ties to specific properties) that was built into survey and evaluation phases of the preservation plan, should be maintained in archeological investigation, since such activity usually involves site disturbance. The research design, in addition to providing for appropriate ethnographic research and consultation, should consider concerns voiced in previous phases. In the absence of previous efforts to coordinate with local or other interested groups, the research design should anticipate the need to initiate appropriate contracts and provide a mechanism for responding to sensitive issues, such as the possible uncovering of human remains or discovery of sacred areas.

The research design facilitates an orderly, goal directed and economical project. However, the research design must be flexible enough to allow for examination of unanticipated but important research opportunities that arise during the investigation.

Documentation Methods

Background Review: Archeological documentation usually is preceded by, or integrated with historical research (i.e. that intensive background information gathering including identification of previous archeological work and inspection of museum collections; gathering relevant data on geology, botany, urban geography and other related disciplines; archival research; informant interviews, or recording of oral tradition, etc.).

Depending on the goals of the archeological documentation, the background historical and archeological research may exceed the level of research accomplished for development of the relevant historic contexts or for identification and evaluation, and focuses on the unique aspects of the property to be treated. This assists in directing the investigation and locates a broader base of information than that contained in the property itself for response to the documentation goals. This activity is particularly important for historic archeological properties where information sources other than the property itself may be critical to preserving the significant aspects of the property. (See the Secretary of the Interior's Standards and Guidelines for Historical Documentation for discussion of associated research activities.)

Field Studies: The implementation of the research design in the field must be flexible enough to accommodate the discovery of new or unexpected data classes or properties, or changing field conditions. A phased approach may be appropriated when dealing with large complex properties or groups of properties, allowing for changes in emphasis or field strategy, or termination of the program, based on analysis of recovered data at the end of each phase. Such an approach permits the confirmation of assumptions concerning property extent, content or organization which had been made based on data gathered from identification and evaluation efforts, or the adjustment of those expectations and resulting changes in procedure. In some cases a phased approach may be necessary to gather sufficient data to calculate the necessary sample size for a statistically valid sample. A phased documentation program may often be most cost-effective, in allowing for early termination of work if the desired objectives cannot be achieved.

Explicit descriptive statements of and justification for field study techniques are important to provide a means of evaluating results. In some cases, especially those employing a sampling strategy in earlier phases (such as identification or evaluation), it is possible to estimate parameters of certain classes of data in a fairly rigorous statistical manner. It is thus desirable to maintain some consistency in choice of sampling designs throughout multiple phases of work at the same property. Consistency with previously employed areal sampling frameworks also improves potential replication in terms of later locating sampled and unsampled areas. It often is desirable to estimate the nature and frequency of data parameters based on existing information or analogy to other similar cases. These estimates may then be tested in field studies.

An important consideration in choosing methods to be used in the field studies should be assuring full, clear, and accurate descriptions of all field operations and observations, including excavation and recording techniques and stratigraphic or inter-site relationships.

To the extent feasible, chosen methodologies and techniques should take into account the possibility that future researchers will need to use the recovered data to address problems not recognized at the time the data were recovered. The field operation may recover data that may not be fully analyzed; this data, as well as the data analyzed, should be recorded and preserved in a way to facilitate future research.

A variety of methodologies may be used. Choices must be explained, including a measure of cost-effectiveness relative to other potential choices. Actual results can then be measured against expectations, and the information applied later in similar cases.

Destructive methods should not be applied to portions or elements of the property if nondestructive methods are practical. If portions or elements of the property being documented are to be preserved in place, the archeological investigation should employ methods that will leave the property as undisturbed as possible. However, in cases where the property will be destroyed by, for example, construction following the investigation, it may be most practical to gather the needed data in the most direct manner, even though that may involve use of destructive techniques.

Logistics in the field, including the deployment of personnel and materials and the execution of sampling strategies, should consider site significant, anticipated location of most important data, cost effectiveness, potential time limitations and possible adverse environmental conditions.

The choice of methods for recording data gathered in the field should be based on the research design. Based on that statement, it is known in advance of field work what kinds of information are needed for analysis; record-keeping techniques should focus on these data. Field records should be maintained in a manner that permits independent interpretation in so far as possible. Record-keeping should be standardized in format and level of detail.

Archeological documentation should be conducted under the supervision of qualified professionals in the disciplines appropriate to the data that are to be recovered. When the general public is directly involved in archeological documentation activities, provision should be made for training and supervision by qualified professionals. (See the Professional Qualifications Standards.)

Analysis: Archeological documentation is not completed with field work; analysis of the collected information is an integral part of the documentation activity, and should be planned for in the research design. Analytical techniques should be selected that are relevant to the objectives of the investigation. Forms of analysis that may be appropriate, depending on the type of data recovered and the objectives of the investigation, include but are not limited to: studying artifact types and distribution; radiometric and other means of age determination; studies of soil stratigraphy; studies of organic matter such as human remains, pollen, animal bones, shells and seeds; study of the composition of soils and study of the natural environment in which the property appears.

Reporting Results

Report Contents: Archeological documentation concludes with written report(s) including minimally the following topics:

1. Description of the study area;
2. Relevant historical documentation/background research;
3. The research design;
4. The field studies as actually implemented, including any deviation from the research design and the reason for the changes;
5. All field observations;
6. Analyses and results, illustrated as appropriate with tables, charts, and graphs;
7. Evaluation of the investigation in terms of the goals and objectives of the investigation, including discussion of how well the needs dictated by the planning process were served;
8. Recommendations for updating the relevant historic contexts and planning goals and priorities, and generation of new or revised information needs;
9. Reference to related on-going or proposed treatment activities, such as structural documentation, stabilization, etc.; and

10. Information on the location of original data in the form of field notes, photographs, and other materials.

Some individual property information, such as specific locational data, may be highly sensitive to disclosure, because of the threat of vandalism. If the objectives of the documentation effort are such that a report containing confidential information such as specific site locations or information on religious practices is necessary, it may be appropriate to prepare a separate report for public distribution. The additional report should summarize that information that is not under restricted access in a format most useful to the expected groups of potential users. Peer review of draft reports is recommended to ensure that state-of-the-art technical reports are produced.

Availability: Results must be made available to the full range of potential users. This can be accomplished through a variety of means including publication of results in monographs and professionals journals and distribution of the report to libraries or technical clearinghouses such as the National Technical Information Service in Springfield, Virginia.

Curation

Archeological specimens and records are part of the documentary record of an archeological site. They must be curated for future use in research, interpretation, preservation, and resource management activities. Curation of important archeological specimens and records should be provided for in the development of any archeological program or project.

Archeological specimens and records that should be curated are those that embody the information important to history and prehistory. They include artifacts and their associated documents, photographs, maps, and field notes; materials of an environmental nature such as bones, shells, soil and sediment samples, wood, seeds, pollen, and their associated records; and the products and associated records of laboratory procedures such as thin sections, and sediment fractions that result from the analysis of archeological data.

Satisfactory curation occurs when:

1. Curation facilities have adequate space, facilities, and professional personnel;
2. Archeological specimens are maintained so that their information values are not lost through deterioration, and records are maintained to a professional archival standard;
3. Curated collections are accessible to qualified researchers within a reasonable time of having been requested; and
4. Collections are available for interpretive purposes, subject to reasonable security precautions.

Recommended Sources of Technical Information

Archeomagnetism: A Handbook for the Archeologist. Jeffrey L. Eighmy. U.S. Department of the Interior, Washington, D.C., 1980.

The Curation and Management of Archeological Collections: A Pilot Study. Cultural Resource Management Series. U.S. Department of the Interior. September 1980.

Human Bones and Archeology. Douglas H. Ubelaker. Interagency Archeological Services, Heritage Conservation and Recreation Service, U.S. Department of the Interior, Washington, D.C., 1980. Available from the Superintendent of Documents, U.S. Government Printing Office, Washington, D.C. 20402

Manual for Museums. Ralph H. Lewis. National Park Service, U.S. Department of the Interior, 1976.

Treatment of Archeological Properties: A Handbook. Advisory Council on Historic Preservation. Washington D.C., 1980.

Secretary of the Interior's Standards for Historic Preservation Projects

General Standards for Historic Preservation Projects

The following general standards apply to all treatments undertaken on historic properties listed in the National Register.

1. Every reasonable effort shall be made to provide a compatible use for a property that requires minimal alteration of the building, structure, or site and its environment, or to use a property for its originally intended purpose.

2. The distinguishing original qualities or character of a building, structure, or site and its environment shall not be destroyed. The removal or alteration of any historic material or distinctive architectural features should be avoided when possible.

3. All buildings, structures, and sites shall be recognized as products of their own time. Alterations which have no historical basis and which seek to create an earlier appearance shall be discouraged.

4. Changes which have taken place in the course of time are evidence of the history and development of a building, structure, or site and its environment. These changes may have acquired significance in their own right, and this significance shall be recognized and respected.

5. Distinctive architectural features or examples of skilled craftsmanship which characterize a building, structure, or site shall be treated with sensitivity.

6. Deteriorated architectural features shall be repaired rather than replaced, wherever possible. In the event replacement is necessary, the new material should match the material being replaced in composition, design, color, texture, and other visual qualities. Repair or replacement of missing architectural features should be based on accurate duplications of features, substantiated by historic, physical, or pictorial evidence rather than on conjectural designs or the availability of different architectural elements from other buildings or structures.

7. The surface cleaning of structures shall be undertaken with the gentlest means possible. Sandblasting and other cleaning methods that will damage the historic building materials shall not be undertaken.

8. Every reasonable effort shall be made to protect and preserve archeological resources affected by, or adjacent to, any acquisition, stabilization, preservation, rehabilitation, restoration, or reconstruction project.

Specific Standards for Historic Preservation Projects

The following specific standards for each treatment are to be used in conjunction with the eight general standards and, in each case, begin with number 9. For example, in evaluating acquisition projects, include the eight general standards plus the four specific standards listed under standards for Acquisition. The specific standards differ from those published for use in Historic Preservation Fund grant-in-aid projects (36 CFR Part 68) in that they discuss more fully the treatment of archeological properties.

Standards for Acquisition

9. Careful consideration shall be given to the type and extent of property rights which are required to assure the preservation of the historic resource. The preservation objectives shall determine the exact property rights to be acquired.

10. Properties shall be acquired in fee simple when absolute ownership is required to insure their preservation.

11. The purchase of less-than-fee-simple interests, such as open space or facade easements, shall undertaken when a limited interest achieves the preservation objective.

12. Every reasonable effort shall be made to acquire sufficient property with the historic resource to protect its historical, archeological, architectural or cultural significance.

Standard for Protection

9. Before applying protective measures which are generally of a temporary nature and imply future historic preservation work, an analysis of the actual or anticipated threats to the property shall be made.

10. Protection shall safeguard the physical condition or environment of a property or archeological site from further deterioration or damage caused by weather or other natural, animal, or human intrusions.

11. If any historic material or architectural features are removed, they shall be properly recorded and, if possible, stored for future study or reuse.

Standards for Stabilization

9. Stabilization shall reestablish the structural stability of a property through the reinforcement of loadbearing members or by arresting deterioration leading to structural failure. Stabilization shall also reestablish weather resistant conditions for a property.

10. Stabilization shall be accomplished in such a manner that it detracts as little as possible from the property's appearance and significance. When reinforcement is required to reestablish structural stability, such work shall be concealed wherever possible so as not to intrude upon or detract from the aesthetic and historical or archeological quality of the property, except where concealment would result in the alteration or destruction of historically or archeologically significant material or spaces. Accurate documentation of stabilization procedures shall be kept and made available for future needs.

11. Stabilization work that will result in ground disturbance shall be preceded by sufficient archeological investigation to determine whether significant subsurface features or artifacts will be affected. Recovery, curation and documentation of archeological features and specimens shall be undertaken in accordance with appropriate professional methods and techniques.

Standards for Preservation

9. Preservation shall maintain the existing form, integrity, and materials of a building, structure, or site. Archeological sites shall be preserved undisturbed whenever feasible and practical. Substantial reconstruction or restoration of lost features generally are not included in a preservation undertaking.

10. Preservation shall include techniques of arresting or retarding the deterioration of a property through a program of ongoing maintenance.

11. Use of destructive techniques, such as archeological excavation, shall be limited to providing sufficient information for research, interpretation and management needs.

Standards for Rehabilitation

9. Contemporary design for alterations and additions to existing properties shall not be discouraged when such alterations and additions do not destroy significant historic, architectural, or cultural material and such design is compatible with the size, scale, color, material, and character of the property, neighborhood, or environment.

10. Wherever possible, new additions or alterations to structures shall be done in such a manner that if such additions or alterations were to be removed in the future, the essential form and integrity of the structure would be unimpaired.

Standards for Restoration

9. Every reasonable effort shall be made to use a property for is originally intended purpose or to provide a compatible use that will require minimum alteration to the property and its environment.

10. Reinforcement required for structural stability or the installation of protective or code required mechanical systems shall be concealed wherever possible so as not to intrude or detract from the property's aesthetic and historical qualities, except where concealment would result in the alteration or destruction of historically significant materials or spaces.

11. Restoration work such as the demolition of non-contributing additions that will result in ground or structural disturbance shall be preceded by sufficient archeological investigation to determine whether significant subsurface or structural features or artifacts will be affected. Recovery, curation and documentation of archeological features and specimens shall be undertaken in accordance with appropriate professional methods and techniques.

Standards for Reconstruction

9. Reconstruction of a part or all of a property shall be undertaken only when such work is essential to reproduce a significant missing feature in a historic district or scene, and when a contemporary design solution is not acceptable. Reconstruction of archeological sites generally is not appropriate.

10. Reconstruction of all or a part of a historic property shall be appropriate when the reconstruction is essential for understanding and interpreting the value of a historic district, or when no other building, structure, object, or landscape feature with the same associative value has survived and sufficient historical or archeological documentation exists to insure an accurate reproduction of the original.

11. The reproduction of missing elements accomplished with new materials shall duplicate the composition, design, color, texture, and other visual qualities of the missing element. Reconstruction of missing architectural or archeological features shall be based upon accurate duplication of original features substantiated by physical or documentary evidence rather than upon conjectural designs or the availability of different architectural features from other buildings.

12. Reconstruction of a building or structure on an original site shall be preceded by a thorough archeological investigation to locate and identify all subsurface features and artifacts. Recovery, curation and documentation of archeological features and specimens shall be undertaken in accordance with professional methods and techniques.

13. Reconstruction shall include measures to preserve any remaining original fabric, including foundations, subsurface, and ancillary elements. The reconstruction of missing elements. The reconstruction of missing elements and features shall be done in such a manner that the essential form and integrity of the original surviving features are unimpaired.

Secretary of the Interior Guidelines for Historic Preservation Projects

The guidelines for the Secretary of the Interior's Standards for Historic Preservation Projects, not included here because of their length, may be obtained separately from the National Park Serivce.

Professional Qualifications Standards

The following requirements are those used by the National Park Service, and have been previously published in the Code of Federal Regulations, 36 CFR Part 61. The qualifications define minimum education and experience required to perform identification, evaluation, registration, and treatment activities. In some cases, additional areas or levels of expertise may be needed, depending on the complexity of the task and the nature of the historic properties involved. In the following definitions, a year of full-time professional experience need not consist of a continuous year of fulltime work but

may be made up of discontinuous periods of full-time or part-time work adding up to the equivalent of a year of full-time experience.

History

The minimum professional qualifications in history are a graduate degree in history or closely related field; or a bachelor's degree in history or closely related field plus one of the following:

1. At least two years of full-time experience in research, writing, teaching, interpretation, or other demonstrable professional activity with an academic institution, historic organization or agency, museum, or other professional institution; or

2. Substantial contribution through research and publication to the body of scholarly knowledge in the field of history.

Archeology

The minimum professional qualifications in archeology are a graduate degree in archeology, anthropology, or closely related field plus:

1. At least one year of full-time professional experience or equivalent specialized training in archeological research, administration or management;

2. At least four months of supervised field and analytic experience in general North American archeology; and

3. Demonstrated ability to carry research to completion.

In addition to these minimum qualifications, a professional in prehistoric archeology shall have at least one year of full-time professional experience at a supervisory level in the study of archeological resources of the prehistoric period. A professional in historic archeology shall have at least one year of full-time professional experience at a supervisory level in the study of archeological resources of the historic period.

Architectural History

The minimum professional qualifications in architectural history are a graduate degree in architectural history, art history, historic preservation, or closely related field, with coursework in American architectural history; or a bachelor's degree in architectural history, art history, historic preservation or closely related field plus one of the following:

1. At least two years of full-time experience in research, writing, or teaching in American architectural history or restoration architecture with an academic institution, historical organization or agency, museum, or other professional institution; or

2. Substantial contribution through research and publication to the body of scholarly knowledge in the field of American architectural history.

Architecture.

The minimum professional qualifications in architecture are a professional degree in architecture plus at least two years of full-time experience in architecture; or a State license to practice architecture.

Historic Architecture

The minimum professional qualifications historic in architecture are a professional degree in architecture or a State license to practice architecture, plus one of the following:

1. At least one year of graduate study in architectural preservation, American architectural history, preservation planning, or closely related field; or

2. At least one year of full-time professional experience on historic preservation projects.

Such graduate study or experience shall include detailed investigations of historic structures, preparation of historic structures research reports, and preparation of plans and specifications for preservation projects.

Preservation Terminology

Acquisition—the act or process of acquiring fee title or interest other than fee title of real property (including acquisition of development rights or remainder interest).

Comprehensive Historic Preservation Planning—the organization into a logical sequence of preservation information pertaining to identification, evaluation, registration and treatment of historic properties, and setting priorities for accomplishing preservation activities.

Historic Context—a unit created for planning purposes that groups information about historic properties based on a shared theme, specific time period and geographical area.

Historic Property—a district, site, building, structure or object significant in American history, architecture, engineering, archeology or culture at the national, State, or local level.

Integrity—the authenticity of a property's historic identity, evidenced by the survival of physical characteristics that existed during the property's historic or prehistoric period.

Intensive Survey—a systematic, detailed examination of an area designed to gather information about historic properties sufficient to evaluate them against predetermined criteria of significance within specific historic contexts.

Inventory—a list of historic properties determined to meet specified criteria of significance.

National Register Criteria—the established criteria for evaluating the eligibility of properties for inclusion in the National Register of Historic Places.

Preservation (treatment)—the act or process of applying measures to sustain the existing form, integrity and material of a building or structure, and the existing form and vegetative cover of a site. It may include initial stabilization work, where necessary, as well as ongoing maintenance of the historic building materials.

Property Type—a grouping of individual properties based on a set of shared physical or associative characteristics.

Protection (treatment)—the act or process of applying measures designed to affect the physical condition of a property by defending or guarding it from deterioration, loss or attack, or to cover or shield the property from danger or injury. In the case of buildings and structures, such treatment is generally of a temporary nature and anticipates future historic preservation treatment; in the case of archeological sites, the protective measure may be temporary or permanent.

Reconnaissance Survey—an examination of all or part of an area accomplished in sufficient detail to make generalizations about the types and distributions of historic properties that may be present.

Reconstruction (treatment)—the act or process of reproducing by new construction the exact form and detail of a vanished building, structure, or object, or any part thereof, as it appeared at a specific period of time.

Rehabilitation (treatment)—the act or process of returning a property to a state of utility through repair or alteration which makes possible an efficient contemporary use while preserving those portions or features of the property which are significant to its historical, architectural and cultural values.

Research design—a statement of proposed identification, documentation, investigation, or other treatment of a historic property that identifies the project's goals, methods and techniques, expected results, and the relationship of the expected results to other proposed activities or treatments.

Restoration—the act or process of accurately recovering the form and details of a property and its setting as it appeared at a particular period of time by means of the removal of later work or by the replacement of missing earlier work.

Sample Survey—survey of a representative sample of lands within a given area in order to generate or test predictions about the types and distributions of historic properties in the entire area.

Stabilization (treatment)—the act or process of applying measures designed to reestablish a weather resistant enclosure and the structural stability of an unsafe or deteriorated property while maintaining the essential form as it exists at present.

Statement of objectives—see Research design.

Dated: September 20, 1983.

Russell E. Dickenson,
Director, National Park Service

[FR Doc. 83-26407 Filed 9-28-83; 8:45 am]

BILLING CODE 4310-70-M

Appendix B: Basic Training

Training in archaeology, especially at the undergraduate level, should be sufficiently broad so that it allows the student access to all areas of archaeology, academic or extra-academic. This training needs to include not only specialty training in Anthropology and archaeology, and in various support fields, but also training in those areas that the student will need to understand in professional life, such as business and environmental law, personnel management, and so on. The ability to adequately provide such training depends upon the university or college having or providing students with access to a training curriculum and the proper facilities or infrastructure.

B.1. Curriculum

There are three basic curricular areas in archaeological instruction:

(1) *classroom training*, which provides concepts and access to things already known, the ability to develop a research topic then explore it, and the skills to express what is known not only in terms of one's discipline, but also in terms understandable to the greater human community;

(2) *field training*, which involves not just the systematic disassembly of an archaeological site, but also logistics, field crew management, budgeting, note-taking, and court house protocols; and

(3) *laboratory training*, which ranges from basic mensuration to collections and data management.

B.1.1. Classroom Training

Training in general archaeology usually takes place at the undergraduate level. The goal is to provide the student with the skills needed for wherever he or she wishes to continue. There are, then, archaeologically specific fields, social science fields, and extra-disciplinary fields that are needed.

B.1.1.1. Archaeology Fields

* *Basic or World Prehistory*: Such courses provide a sense of geographic and temporal context.

* *North American Archaeology*: A general knowledge of North American archaeology is required for professional practice in the United States.

* *Regional Archaeology*: Regional courses can range from continental subdivisions -- Southeastern, Great Basin, Middle Atlantic archaeology -- to global subdivisions -- Mesoamerican or European prehistory. These provide a comparative data set for the student, serving much the same function as different ethnography courses will.

* *Method-and-Theory*: Method-and-theory courses are central to archaeological training. Best delivered with a laboratory section (see below), method-and-theory courses provide the basics of the field's history, the government regulations, the data extraction techniques, and the conceptual procedures needed to access information about technology, environment, social organization, and cosmology for given archaeological cultures. Method-and-theory courses rank equal with analysis and field courses in the training of undergraduates.

Professional Training Requirements

The archaeology curriculum selected by the student needs to provide, as much as is reasonable at the undergraduate level, the training necessary to later work as a professional in historic preservation and cultural resource management positions. The qualifications expected of such individuals are specified by Federal law, which in turn serves as a guide for most state laws (**36 CFR 61 Appendix A, 48 FR 44738-44739**; see also Chapter 2, Section 2.2.4.). These requirements correspond to those originally set forth by the Society for American Archaeology (SAA) and the Society of Professional Archaeologists (SOPA), the latter now replaced by the Registry of Professional Archaeologists (ROPA).

"Professional" means qualified to be principal investigator on a Federally or state-mandated historic preservation project. The minimum professional qualifications for archaeologists and related historic preservation individuals are given in **36CFR 61 Appendix A**. These are given below.

Archaeology:

(1) graduate degree in archaeology, Anthropology, or closely related field;
(2) evidence of research completion (e.g., thesis, research report); and

* *Historical Archaeology*: Most of the archaeology projects done in the United States involve historical archaeology, either as sites or as components. Archaeologists in private practice as well as government regulators of that practice deal most often with historic sites. Students should be familiar with historical archaeology as well as with the analysis of historic assemblages. Such courses may be part of Anthropology curricula, or may be found in History, Art History, Museum, or Classics departments, depending upon the institution.

* *Cultural Resources / Historic Preservation*: Archaeology in the United States is a regulated field dominated by private-sector firms and the Federal and state agencies that oversee their practice. Fewer than one in 20 academic archaeologists have any familiarity with the governing laws; fewer than one in 30 have any full-time experience in government or private-sector settings.[1] Despite this, most of the data needed for academic research are under the control of agencies or private interests regulated by

(3) 16 months of full-time professional experience and/or specialized training in field, laboratory, or management procedures, including

(a) four months full-time supervised field and analytical experience in general North American archaeology; and
(b) 12 months full-time experience/training in a specialty or practice, six months of which must be supervisory.

History:

(1) graduate degree in history of closely related field; or
(2) bachelor's degree in history or closely related field *plus* two years of full-time experience in professional activities within some form of professional institution.

Architectural History:

(1) graduate degree in architectural history, art history, historic preservation, or closely related field; or
(2) bachelor's degree in the above fields *plus* two years full-time experience in professional activities within some form of professional institution.

that extra-academic environment. Since four out of every five archaeologists work in a world regulated by Federal and state codes, and since a large number of planners, architects, historians, and civil engineers also are constrained by those same codes, a course in cultural resources management statutes is essential if the student wishes to practice archaeology.

* *Senior Thesis, Independent Study, Master's Thesis*: A clever twist for undergraduate programs is to provide for undergraduate theses in field-based or laboratory-based archaeological projects. This allows the student to do the entire sequence of archaeology, from research formulation through data collection and analysis to report preparation, once under close supervision. This of course holds for master's theses as well, but is more an issue in student training since many graduate programs offer the student the option of a master's degree with a thesis or without a thesis. A thesis path normally should be the one taken. Federal code requires the professional archaeologist to, sooner or later, perform a data-based independent analysis at the level of a master's thesis anyway, and this affords the perfect opportunity.

---

1. Sanford, Robert M., Thomas W. Neumann, and James F. Palmer. 1989. Developing local cultural resource policy through environmental impact assessments, pp. 107-117 in *Policy through Impact Assessment: Institutionalized Analysis as a Policy Strategy*, edited by Robert V. Bartlett. Greenwood, New York.

Architecture:

(1)   professional degree plus two years full-time professional experience; or
(2)   state license to practice.

Historic Architecture:

(1)   same as architecture plus at least one year in some form of architectural preservation.

Archaeological requirements are clearly rigorous compared to the other four fields, since considerable experience is expected in addition to a graduate degree. A bachelor's degree, even with experience, does not provide professional qualification. Further, the professional archaeologist must have the equivalent of four months (about 693 hours) of full-time, supervised experience in North American archaeology.

The qualifications to work on cultural resources projects vary by the level of government serving as the review agency (Federal, state, or local) or the level of government serving as the lead agency. For example, U.S. Army Corps of Engineers regulations require that field technicians have a BA or BS in anthropological archaeology or Anthropology, a field school, and six months of full-time supervised field and laboratory experience in general North American archaeology. State and local government requirements vary by locale, but usually are less demanding and can permit individuals with field schools but lacking a college degree to work in the field.

The curriculum set forth below would permit students to begin satisfying most Federal agency expectations for a field technician: A field course provides six weeks (240 hours) of supervised field and laboratory training; a method-and-theory course provides another 42 hours of supervised classroom training as well as another 28 hours of supervised laboratory training, depending on the institution, its academic term/contact-hour system, and the presence or absence of a laboratory component for the method-and-theory class. An 10-week full-time internship program can provide for the 383-hour balance. A thesis or equivalent independent project would provide the evidence of research completion.

B.1.1.2. Social Science

Archaeology is a melding of diachronic ethnography and diachronic cultural Geography. Most archaeologists are, of necessity, sound cultural anthropologists. This is because they have to be able to recognize second-hand and from only the patterning of artifacts the human cultural behavior that would have produced an archaeological deposit. The old saw about why failed veterinarians become physicians holds here: The archaeological data base is silent; one does not expect -- or certainly does not hope in the absence of theological training -- the data base to directly express what it represents. An archaeological site is silent; the archaeologists must recognize the patterning that can give the remains in the deposit a voice. A sick cat cannot say much about what is wrong; the vet must work through a broad knowledge of animal physiology to deduce what the probable problem is.

A good archaeologist has a wealth of ethnographic information; further, that information must always be linked from the cosmology of the people through their social organization to the final physical expression that may be encountered in an archaeological site. Archaeologists end up taking lots of sociocultural Anthropology and other social science courses, including many of the following.

*   *Basic Cultural Anthropology and Linguistics*: A basic cultural Anthropology course is required so that any archaeology student has a sense of how human behavior is expressed in material remains. Regardless of if the practice is professional or academic, the idea of archaeology is to understand why it is people have done what they have done, and the strategy that behavior has taken. Cultural Anthropology, which is what archaeologists do, treats this.

*   *Social Anthropology/Kinship*: An advanced social Anthropology course treating kinship and related non-Western social structure is important for the archaeologist to understand possible social-structural options that would produce the artifact/activity patterning found in a given site, or the patterning of different kinds of sites over the region. This holds both for historic and for prehistoric sites.

*   *Introductory Sociology*: An introduction to Sociology provides an archaeologist with two kinds of information: (1) a general understanding of social structure and operation in stratified societies, along with detail about how groups are organized; and (2) a practical understanding about how their own society functions. The first point assists with historical archaeological

interpretations; the second point is important for those with extra-academic careers.

* *Cultural Geography*: Archaeology is very much a diachronic cultural Geography. Anthropology itself emerged in the United States from Geography, not Sociology; there is a great amount of intellectual debt and cross-fertilization between anthropological archaeology and cultural Geography.

* *Regional Ethnography*: A regional ethnography or culture area course provides the student with a data base for making assessments of past cultural behavior.

* *History or Regional History*: A basic regional history course is just as useful as a regional ethnography or culture area course.

* *Demography*: A sound demography class provides the archaeologist with a sense of what demographic structures may have been present in the past. This is extremely useful in considering regional site distribution and past populations.

* *Public Administration*: A strategically useful course for archaeologists is one that examines the structure and mechanics of public administration. Most archaeologists will either serve as public administrators themselves, or they will have to treat with such.

* *Cultural Ecology*: Cultural ecology is the basic theoretical orientation for extra-academic archaeology -- as well as for most extra-academic Anthropology. This approach views human culture as a behavioral adaptation that enables a given human population to survive and reproduce in its ecological setting.

* *Anthropological Theory*: All anthropologists need a basic Anthropology theory class. Part of this is because useful, applicable information is presented in such a course. For archaeologists, the information in theory courses of this kind assists in archaeological interpretations. Such courses also helps in appreciating the approaches taken by synchronic and academic-based colleagues.

B.1.1.3. Extra-Disciplinary

Archaeology is an inter-disciplinary field. It must be. The goal is to figure out what it was that caused people to do what they did in the past. And that often in the absence of written records or verbal accounts. That means that one needs to know what those now-dead people were doing to begin with, and to understand

the world in which they lived.[2] And such knowledge only would get the archaeologist to the point where any ethnographer or sociologist is to start with when they go out of their office door on the way to the field.

Archaeologists need an operating knowledge of the physical sciences, since much involving past technology as well as the post-depositional dynamics of a site are matters of Physics and Chemistry. Matters of site structure, technology, and even agricultural productivity involve Soil Science, Geology, and physical Geography. A knowledge of how ecosystems are structured is critical for understanding the kind of world in which people lived, and the constraints of that world. People had to eat in the past. A knowledge of plants or animals is quite useful, as much as a starting field (archaeologists tend to continue teaching themselves about those aspects of the world that they never had time to study formally in college or graduate school) as a knowledge base. A command of calculus and of statistics is essential: The first allows students the equivalent of an undergraduate's access to the professional literature in Ecology, Soils, Geology, Physics, and the like; the second enables students to design operative research programs then assess the results. A knowledge of logic, obtained either from a logic or a rhetoric course, is invaluable for the framing of questions and the structuring of arguments, be they for reports or proposals.

A solid understanding of the social sciences, particularly Anthropology, is critical. This includes concepts as well as methods. Thus, not only History,

---

2. A fundamental principle in Anthropology is that understanding a culture requires a person to be as much a participant or member of that culture as possible. The best way to do this is to think like a member of the culture, and since people think in and classify reality through their languages, the best way to understand the ins and outs of another culture is to be an active participant while thinking in the native language. Understanding this, by the way, allows a person to understand why Anthropology curricula are structured the way they are.

Archaeologists have tremendous difficulties in learning the languages of then interacting with people who have been dead for a long time and did not have the sense to write their languages down beforehand. The way that archaeologists become participants in a culture and try to see the world as their now-dead informants saw it is threefold: They try to reconstruct as accurately as possible the world in which those people lived, while having a very good idea of what living in such a world would have required (e.g., if you fish, you are going to have to scale and gut the fish); they try to learn as much about how other peoples recorded by ethnographers actually classified reality and functioned in the world; and they try out and attempt to experience, first-hand, as many of the activities that would have been needed by past peoples to be alive. This is probably why archaeologists have more than their fair share of active, constructive imaginations: They must envision entire human behavioral worlds that would have produced the material remains encountered in their and their colleague's archaeological sites. This is definitely why archaeologists are forever messing about with seemingly primitive technologies or hiking in snowshoes through forests in the dead of winter with stop-watches in hand: It gives a first-hand, participant-observer sense of what the demands of the past world would have been.

but the methods of historiography are invaluable. The physical, life, and earth sciences merely provide the archaeologist with a description of the world in which past people lived, a sense of how they themselves made a living and structured their physical world, and how the archaeological deposit may or may not have changed over time. The statistics tells of the patterning of remains. It requires a knowledge of how people organize themselves to then make sense of the archaeological remains recovered, to take them that final step to actually being a revelation about the past culture of a people, a diachronic ethnography.

An assortment of miscellaneous skills also are important. The ability to write with facility is essential, just as much for preparation of reports as for the keeping of meticulous field notes. Since most archaeologists work in or regulate private-sector environments, an understanding of business practices is mandatory. Archaeology is the only social science that regularly requires logistical preparation and crew management; therefore, a personnel management and a general management course are desirable. Such training rarely is provided by Anthropology departments or included in archaeology programs.

There are several appropriate fields that would profit an archaeologist to know in addition to those above: Nutrition, architecture, art history, materials science, civil engineering, land surveying, cartography, drawing, library science. Since courses in composition, literature, foreign languages, and computers are inescapable in any college setting, there is no reason to single them out. Any manner of list of suitable courses could be made; however, the list below reflects the skills we have needed, both in ourselves and in our employees.

Core Curriculum: should include

> Math through fourth-semester calculus (80 percent of academic fields require four semesters of calculus for a bachelor's degree; thus, to have even an undergraduate's capacity to understand their professional literature, the nascent archaeologist must be equipped with the conceptual tools and a knowledge of the language in which those ideas are expressed and demonstrated)
> Basic Statistics
> General Chemistry
> General Physics
> Basic Soil Science
> General Management
> Logic or Rhetoric

Ancillary Courses:

> Field Botany (either herbs or trees, but preferably trees since they are more often better land-use/land-history signatures)
> Zoology (rarely offered now)/Wildlife Ecology
> Basic Ecology
> Basic Physical Geography
> Basic Cultural Geography
> Fluvial Hydrology
> Geology (either Basic Petrology [rarely offered now] or Mineralogy, along with Sedimentology/Fluvial or Glacial Geology)
> Basic Environmental Law (especially an explanation of NEPA)
> Historiography
> Museology
> Personnel Management
> Business Administration/Business Law
> Business Accounting

B.1.2. Field Training

A second part of archaeological training is field training. This may be even more important than the classroom training, at least in the sense of being allowed to work outside of a university setting: A student often is required, as a contract condition for employment, to have had a field course. This often is true for any field technician working on Federally funded projects.

An archaeological site may be considered a three-dimensional information storage matrix; field techniques represent the procedure for accessing that information. In essence, a field course represents one-third of the student's training package.

Field training involves several parts: project management, including logistics, crew management, budgeting, housing, transportation, provisioning, and public relations; site identification; mapping; field note recordation procedures; artifact tracking; informant interviews; court house research; terrain identification; soil science; and of course excavation proper. In field training, many of the courses identified under B.1.1. Classroom Training come into play in an orchestrated fashion. That is, instead of considering Physics one field, Statistics another, Management a third, and Soils a fourth, and composition/creative writing a fifth, the student suddenly must coordinate the application of each and all disciplines for the successful execution of the field part of the research project.

The excavation process itself is not straightforward. At its simplest, it represents refinement of coarse motor skills along with the ability to recognize subtle changes in soil color and texture. In a phrase: How to dig carefully with a shovel and trowel. But archaeology is rarely simple. Field work in urban settings requires moving concrete slabs and coordinating heavy machinery. Deep sites require knowing OSHA regulations for shoring, understanding the efficiency of water pumps, and understanding how to put all of the pieces together when one's crew is working in unstable deposits 4 m below the surface. Industrial sites require extensive historic research along with sound mapping, otherwise crews will be trying to carefully excavate industrial-scale volumes of foundry slag.

Students learn two general things from field courses. The first is the confidence that comes from having experiential familiarity with an archaeological deposit. The second is a collection of field procedure tricks and strategies that cannot be explained -- or at least are not explained -- in textbooks and course lectures.

Students usually take only one field course as undergraduates. Field courses normally are offered during the summer terms, although this depends upon the region. Additional field experience may include special contract work during a given term. Summer field courses depend as much upon enrollment size as upon pedagogical need, which is true of any college course. Some programs have field training courses that focus on site survey -- the locating then initial assessing of sites in a given area. Other programs have focused on one site for a sustained period, such as Solomon Ruins for Eastern New Mexico State, the Thunderbird Site for Catholic University, and St. Mary's City for the College of St. Mary's on Maryland's Western Shore (which is and will remain an ongoing exercise for many years to come). Regardless of focus, though, all field programs are expected to produce students who can be hired to do all aspects of basic archaeological field work, and do so well. Employers are not in the business of training personnel in the basics of the employee's degree field.

B.1.3. Laboratory Training

Classroom training provides the concepts and the strategies needed to work up data. Field courses teach how to recover that data from the archaeological site. Laboratory training, the third piece of the curriculum, teaches how to extract the behavioral information from the materials recovered from that archaeological site.

People tend to think of archaeology as a field science, but this is because the bulk of the fun is messing about in the field. Actually, archaeology is much more of a laboratory science: The bulk of the time spent is in laboratory analysis.

A basic undergraduate curriculum should familiarize the student with the laboratory aspect of archaeology. That aspect includes processing and accessioning collections, performing basic analyses, performing detailed or problem-specific analyses, preparing a summary report of that analysis, curation, and assemblage turn-over to a permanent curatorial facility.

Laboratory courses teach the rudiments of analysis and collections management. All archaeology students need this background. Those who go immediately into private-sector or government staff positions will be expected to work in the lab preparing assemblages for analysis by the principal investigator. Those who continue into graduate school will have the unenviable task of having to do all of the analysis themselves for their master's thesis or doctoral dissertation.

B.1.4. Internships and Cooperative (Co-Curricular) Agreements

There is no better learning experience than to actually do the archaeology under real-world conditions. The value of internships for other fields holds for archaeology as well: providing a full-time, total immersion into the field, allowing the student to hone skills while being enculturated into the professional world of the discipline. Internships with private firms, state and Federal agencies, and museums exist.

Standing cooperative agreements to share courses or facilities, or to work together on a large project as part of a virtual project team also are valuable parts of the education process. Spending a semester on another campus, working with instructors there or taking advantage of facilities not present on the home campus, is to everyone's benefit. While some of the benefit is pedagogical, much involves establishing social networks that benefit the profession just as much as the student.

Large research projects, be they site-specific or regionally based, often will be done as a joint venture with other schools and firms. Again, the students also profit from the professional social network to which they are exposed. Just as with internships, those who continue on in archaeology, be it academic or extra-academic, will draw upon their knowledge of the field's social organization throughout their careers.

B.2. Infrastructure

Archaeology is not just a classroom experience. It includes field training and laboratory analysis. Together with the classroom work, there are three infrastructural requirements for any institution attempting to prepare individuals to do archaeology: Library holdings; field equipment and operations budget; and laboratory equipment, space, and budget In reviewing then selecting places to enroll, students should make sure that proper facilities are present first.

B.2.1. Library

A legitimate undergraduate program requires Research Library Group (RLG) *Conspectus* 2 library holdings in archaeology. If there is an expectation at the institution that faculty promotion or tenure in any way will depend upon original research, then a RLG *Conspectus* 4 archaeological library collection is, by definition, required.

It currently is possible to provide access to a virtual archaeology library through Internet resources, at least as far as some journals go. Some of access goes well beyond what was available before on line resources existed, such as specialized journals that would not be cost-effective to maintain as individual subscriptions. Actually, that kind of on line library is rather neat and offers a lot of possibilities (see Neumann and Sanford 1998b), but there are two cautions when considering using a Web based system as the core for the undergraduate library holdings.

The first caution pertains to how journal volumes can be accessed, both in terms of text and/or graphics, and in terms of back issues. Historically, it has always been possible to get the entirety of most journal series on microfiche or microfilm. It is not always possible to gain access to the complete journal set over the Internet, and at times only text versions of the series will be available. A lot of archaeological research makes use of literature that in other fields would be dismissed as out of date. It is important to be aware of what exists.

The second caution pertains to what is or is not available over the Internet. Journal series, or at least some journal series, often are (although we can think of a couple local and regional journal series, used in compliance work and expected to be cited by review agencies, that are not available). Monograph series and books usually are not. And again as with older numbers in journal series, older monographs and books often retain research value in North American archaeology. These resources often can be obtained only through the use-book market.

B.2.2. Field Equipment and Operations

Field training requires the matériel to actually do the work, along with the operations budget needed to carry it out. In a way, field work may be compared to open-chest surgery: One does not enter into the exercise without having the wherewithal to bring closure to the job. Archaeological ethics along with Federal and state preservation laws prohibit excavating archaeological sites without the capacity to complete the work undertaken, which by the way includes laboratory analysis and report preparation.

Although specific field equipment needs vary by region, the minimum general needs are given in Jourkowsky (1980) and in Hester, Shafer, and Feder (1997).

B.2.3. Laboratory Facilities

Any institution with a field training program requires laboratory analysis. The two -- excavation and lab work -- are co-dependent. If an active field program exists, then it is required by professional ethics and Federal law (and in states like Pennsylvania, state law) that the excavated materials be analyzed and curated. A laboratory element requires laboratory space, analytical equipment, curatorial space, and staff. In some places, staffing is done with work-study students, and this can afford the apprentice archaeologist additional supervised work-place experience. The minimum facilities that need to be present are given in Neumann, Bates, and Sanford (1998; see also Chapter 8 here and **36 CFR Part 79**).

Library Rating System

The Research Library Group (RLG) provides a suitability ranking (*Conspectus* rating) of disciplinary holdings on a scale of 1 - 5:

"1"   suitable for non-major undergraduate work;

"2"   suitable for undergraduate work in the major;

"3"   suitable for graduate work in the field;

"4"   suitable for original faculty and doctoral-level research; and

"5"   original, primary source materials that make the collection itself suitable as a research topic.

References Cited

Advisory Council on Historic Preservation (ACHP)
1991   *Treatment of Archeological Properties: A Handbook.* National Park Service, U.S. Department of the Interior, Washington, D.C.

Ambrose, Stephen E.
1996   *Undaunted Courage: Meriwether Lewis, Thomas Jefferson, and the Opening of the American West.* Simon and Schuster, New York.

American Anthropological Association (AAA)
1977 to 1999   *Guide to Departments.* American Anthropological Association, Washington, D.C.

1978   NSF Funding for Anthropology October 1, 1976, to September 30, 1977. *Anthropology Newsletter* 19(3):9-11.

1980   Anthropology funding in FY '79 tops $22 million. *Anthropology Newsletter* 21(7):1, 5.

1981a   NSF Awards: FY 1980. *Anthropology Newsletter* 22(4):3-4.

1981b   Profile of an anthropologist: Mastering the business of archeology. *Anthropology Newsletter* 22 (9):10.

1983   Profile of an Anthropologist: Archeology, prehistoric ethnology, and the professionalization of a discipline. *Anthropology Newsletter* 24(3):8.

Anderson, T.W.
1984   *Introduction to Statistical Multivariate Analysis.* Second edition. Wiley, New York.

Anfinson, Scott F., editor
1979   *A Handbook of Minnesota Prehistoric Ceramics.* Occasional Publications in Minnesota Anthropology No. 5. Minnesota Historical Society, Ft. Snelling.

Baldridge, Letitia
1993   *Letitia Baldridge's New Complete Guide to Executive Manners.* Rawson Associates/Macmillian Publishing, New York.

Beaumont, Michael
1987   *Type: Design, Color, Character, & Use.* North Light Books, Cincinnati.

Beer, Michael
1980   *Organization Change and Development: A Systems View.* Goodyear Publishing, Santa Monica.

Bender, Susan J., and George S. Smith, editors
2000   *Teaching Archaeology in the Twenty-First Century.* Society for American Archaeology, Washington, D.C.

Binford, Lewis R.
1961   A new method of calculating dates from kaolin pipe stems. *Southeastern Archaeological Conference Newsletter* 9 (1).

1962   Archaeology as Anthropology. *American Antiquity* 28:217-225.

1964   A consideration of archaeological research design. *American Antiquity* 29:425-441.

Bradley, James W.
1979   *The Onondaga Iroquois: 1500 - 1655: A Study of Acculturative Change and Its Consequences.* Ph.D. dissertation, Syracuse University. University Microfilms International, Ann Arbor.

1987   *Evolution of the Onondaga Iroquois: Accommodating Change, 1500 - 1655.* Syracuse University Press, Syracuse.

Bradley, Omar N.
1951   *A Soldier's Story.* Henry Holt and Company, New York.

Brady, Nyle C., and Ray R. Weil
1998   *The Nature and Properties of Soils.* Twelfth edition. Prentice Hall, Upper Saddle River, NY.

Brentlinger, Ann
1992   *Guide to Federal Jobs.* Third edition. Resource Directions, Toledo, OH.

Buck, Polly Stone
    1986   *The Blessed Town: Oxford, Georgia, at the
            Turn of the Century.* Algonquin Books of
            Chapel Hill, Chapel Hill, NC.

Bush, Vannevar
    1945.   *Science: The Endless Frontier.* U.S. Govern-
            ment Printing Office, Washington D.C.

Byerly, Radford, Jr., and Roger A. Pielke, Jr.
    1995   The changing ecology of United States
            science. *Science* 269:1531-1532.

Cambron, James W., and David C. Hulse
    1964   *Handbook of Alabama Archaeology, Part I:
            Point Types.* University of Alabama Press,
            University, AL.

Chesterman, Charles W.
    1979   *The Audubon Society Field Guide to North
            American Rocks and Minerals.* Knopf, New
            York.

Coates, Earl J., and Dean S. Thomas
    1990   *An Introduction to Civil War Small Arms.*
            Thomas Publications, Gettysburg, PA.

College Blue Book, The
    1997   *Volume 3. Degrees Offered by College and
            Subject.* Twenty-sixth edition. Macmillian
            Reference USA/Simon and Schuster Mac-
            millian, New York.

Costanza, Robert
    1980   Embodied energy and economic valuation.
            Science 210:1219-1224.

Cvancara, Alan M.
    1985   *A Field Manual for the Amateur Geologist.*
            Prentice Hall, New York.

Daniel, Glyn
    1962   *The Idea of Prehistory.* Penguin, Baltimore.

DAP/OAGM/OMA/OS/DHHS (Division of Acquisition
Policy/Office of Acquisition and Grants Management/
Office of Management and Acquisition/Office of the Secre-
tary/Department of Health and Human Services)
    1991   *DHHS Project Officers' Contracting Handbook.*
            Department of Health and Human Services,
            Washington, D.C.

Davis, George B., Leslie J. Perry, and Joseph W. Kirkley.
Compiled by Calvin D. Cowles
    1891-1895 *Atlas to Accompany the Official Records of
            the Union and Confederate Armies.*
            Government Printing Office,
            Washington, D.C.

Davis, George B., Leslie J. Perry, and Joseph W. Kirkley.
Compiled by Calvin D. Cowles. Introduction by Richard
Sommers
    1983 [1891-1895] *The Official Military Atlas of the
            Civil War.* Gramercy Books, New
            York.

DeBolt, C. Gerald
    1988   *The Dictionary of American Pottery Marks:
            Whiteware and Porcelain (The First Book of Its
            Kind in Over Eighty Years).* Charles E. Tuttle
            Company, Rutland. [See title and publica-
            tion date of Kovel and Kovel 1986].

Deer, W.A., R.A. Howie, and J. Zussman
    1966   *An Introduction to the Rock-Forming Minerals.*
            Longman Group, London.

Doak, C.C., L.G. Doak, and J.H. Root
    1985   *Teaching Patients with Low Literacy Skills.*
            J.B. Lippincott Co., New York.

Drennan, Robert D
    1987   Sampling to estimate whether in situ features
            are present. Ms. on file at the Cultural
            Resource Management Program, University
            of Pittsburgh.

Dyer, Thomas G.
    1999   *Secret Yankees: The Union Circle in Confeder-
            ate Atlanta.* Johns Hopkins University Press,
            Baltimore.

Espenshade, Edward B., Jr., and Joel L. Morrison
    1980   *Goode's World Atlas.* Fifteenth edition. Rand
            McNally & Co., Chicago.

Fagan, Brian M.
    1997   *In the Beginning.* Ninth edition. Longman,
            New York.

Feder, Kenneth L.
    1997   Chapter 4. Site survey. Pp. 41-68 in *Field
            Methods in Archaeology,* by Thomas R.
            Hester, Harry J. Shafer, and Kenneth L.
            Feder. Seven edition. Mayfield, Mountain
            View.

Fike, Richard E.
   1987   *The Bottle Book: A Comprehensive Guide to Historic, Embossed Medicine Bottles.* Gibbs M. Smith, Inc., Salt Lake City.

Firth, Ian J.W.
   1985   *Cultural Landscape Bibliography.* National Park Service/Southeast Region. U.S. Government Printing Office, Washington, D.C.

Fish, Paul R.
   1980   Federal policy and legislation for archaeological conservation. *Arizona Law Review* 22:681-699.

Fish, Suzanne K., and Stephan A. Kowalewski, editors
   1990   *The Archaeology of Regions: A Case for Full-Coverage Survey.* Smithsonian Institution Press, Washington, D.C.

Fisher, Roger, and Danny Ertel
   1995   *Getting Ready to Negotiate: The Getting to Yes Workbook. A Step-by-Step Guide to Preparing for Any Negotiation.* Penguin Books, New York.

Fisher, Roger, William Ury, and Bruce Patton
   1991   *Getting to Yes: Negotiating Agreement without Giving In.* Second edition. Penguin Books, New York.

Fogelman, Gary L.
   1983   *Lithics Book.* The Pennsylvania Artifact Series No. 34. Fogelman Publishing Co., Turbotville, PA.

Foss, J.E., F.P. Miller, and A.V. Segovia
   1985   *Field Guide to Soil Profile Description and Mapping.* Second edition. Soil Resources International, Moorhead, MN.

Fowler, Don D.
   1982   Cultural resources management. Pp. 1-50 in *Advances in Archaeological Method and Theory,* edited by Michael B. Schiffer. Academic Press, New York.

Fox, Richard A., Jr.
   1988   *Discerning History Through Archaeology: The Custer Battle.* Ph.D. dissertation, Department of Archaeology, University of Calgary.

Fox, Robin
   1996   State of the art/science in Anthropology. Pp. 327-345 in *The Flight from Science and Reason,* edited by Paul R. Gross, Norman Levitt, and Martin W. Lewis. Annals of the New York Academy of Sciences Volume 775. Fox's assessment is thematically identical to that of A.L. Kroeber 1935 History and science in Anthropology. *American Anthropologist* 37:539-569.

Fraser, George MacDonald
   1983   *Flashman & the Redskins.* Plume/Penguin Group, New York.

Freidson, Eliot
   1970   *Profession of Medicine: A Study of the Sociology of Applied Knowledge.* The University of Chicago Press, Chicago.

   1986   *Professional Powers: A Study of the Institutionalization of Formal Knowledge.* University of Chicago Press, Chicago.

Fussell, Paul
   1983   *Class: A Guide through the American Status System.* Summit Books, New York.

Garreau, Joel
   1981   *The Nine Nations of North America.* Houghton Mifflin, Boston.

   1991   *Edge City: Life on the New Frontier.* Doubleday, New York.

Gibbons, Ann
   1994   Making the grade as a scientific manager. *Science* 265:1937-1938.

Goad, Susan I.
   1979   *Chert Resources in Georgia: Archaeological and Geological Perspectives.* Wallace Reservoir Project Contributions No. 3. University of Georgia Laboratory of Archaeology Series Report Number 21.

Goodstein, David
   1996   Conduct and misconduct in science. Pp. 31-38 in *The Flight from Science and Reason,* edited by Paul R. Gross, Norman Levitt, and Martin W. Lewis. Annals of the New York Academy of Sciences Volume 775.

Greene, Mary Wilder
1985 The support of Anthropology at the National Science Foundation. *Anthropology Newsletter* 26 (3):1, 12-13.

Groff, Vern
1990 *The Power of Color in Design for Desktop Publishing.* Management Information Source Press, Portland, OR.

Gross, Paul R., and Norman Levitt
1994 *Higher Superstition: The Academic Left and Its Quarrels with Science.* Johns Hopkins University Press, Baltimore.

Gunn, Mary Kemper
1969 *A Guide to Academic Protocol.* Columbia University Press, New York.

Gurke, Karl
1987 *Bricks and Brickmaking: A Handbook for Historical Archaeology.* University of Idaho Press, Moscow.

Hamburg, Morris
1970 *Statistical Analysis for Decision Making.* Harcourt, Brace, & World, New York.

Hamermesh, Daniel S.
1996 Not so bad: the Annual Report on the Economic Status of the Profession 1995 - 1996. *Academe* (March-April):14-37.

Hay, Conran, James W. Hatch, and J. Sutton
1987 *A Management Plan for Clemson Island Archaeological Resources in the Commonwealth of Pennsylvania.* Pennsylvania Historical and Museum Commission, Bureau of Historic Preservation, Harrisburg, PA.

Heighton, Robert F., and Kathleen Deagan
1971 A new formula for dating kaolin clay pipestems. *The Conference on Historic Archaeological Site Archaeology Papers* 6:220-229.

Hester, Thomas R.
1997 Chapter 5. Methods of excavation. Pp. 69-112 in *Field Methods in Archaeology*, by Thomas R. Hester, Harry J. Shafer, and Kenneth L. Feder. Seven edition. Mayfield, Mountain View, CA.

Hester, Thomas R., Harry J. Shafer, and Kenneth L. Feder, editors.
1997 *Field Methods in Archaeology.* Seven edition. Mayfield, Mountain View, CA.

Hirsh, Sandra Krebs, and Jean M. Kummerow
1990 *Introduction to Type in Organizations.* Second edition. Consulting Psychologist Press, Palo Alto, CA.

Hobbs, Walter C., and G. Lester Anderson
1971 The operation of academic departments. *Management Science* (October 1971):B134-B144.

Holder, Jack J., Jr.
1972 Decision making by consensus. *Business Horizons* (April 1972):47-54.

Hole, Frank, and Robert F. Heizer
1969 *An Introduction to Prehistoric Archeology.* Second edition. Holt, Rinehart, and Winston, New York.

Hopke, William E.
1993 *The Encyclopedia of Careers and Vocational Guidance. Volume 3 Fis- Para.* Ninth edition. Ferguson Publications, Chicago.

1993 *The Encyclopedia of Careers and Vocational Guidance. Volume 4 Park - Z.* Ninth edition. Ferguson Publications, Chicago.

Hosmer, Charles B., Jr.
1981 *Preservation Comes of Age: From Williamsburg to the National Trust, 1926-1949.* Two volumes. National Trust for Historic Preservation in the United States/University Press of Virginia, Charlottesville.

Hothem, Lar
1983 *Arrowheads and Projectile Points: Identification and Values.* Collectors Books, Paducah, KY.

1996 *Indian Axes and Related Stone Artifacts.* Collectors Books, Paducah, KY.

1999a *Indian Artifacts of the Midwest. Volume II.* Collectors Books, Paducah, KY.

1999b *Indian Artifacts of the Midwest. Volume III.* Collectors Books, Paducah, KY.

Hranicky, Wm Jack
1994 *Middle Atlantic Projectile Point Typology and Nomenclature.* Archeological Society of Virginia Special Publication No. 33.

Hranicky, Wm Jack, and Floyd Painter
1993 *A Guide to the Identification of Virginia Projectile Points.* Archeological Society of Virginia Special Publication No. 17.

Illinois Archaeological Survey
1983 *Professional Standards* (Table 5.4 under "Illinois")

Internal Revenue Service (IRS)
1998 *Your Federal Income Tax for Individuals.* Internal Revenue Service Publication 17. U.S. Government Printing Office, Washington, D.C.

1999 *Per Diem Rates.* Internal Revenue Service Publication 1542. U.S. Government Printing Office, Washington, D.C.

International Committee of Medical Journal Editors
1991 Special report: Uniform requirements for manuscripts submitted to biomedical journals. *The New England Journal of Medicine* 324:424-428.

IES
1972 *Illuminating Engineering Society Handbook.* Fifth edition. IES, New York.

Jameson, John H., Jr., John E. Ehrenhard, and Wilfred Husted
1992 *Federal Archeological Contracting: Utilizing the Competitive Procurement Process.* Archeology and Ethnology Program Technical Brief 7. NPA February 1992.

Johnson, Frederick, Emil W. Haury, and James B. Griffin
1945 Report of the Planning Committee. *American Antiquity* 9:142-144.

Jordon, Robert Paul
1986 Ghosts on the Little Bighorn. *National Geographic* 170:786-813.

Jourkowsky, Martha
1980 *A Complete Manual of Field Archaeology: Tools and Techniques of Field Work for Archaeologists.* Prentice-Hall, Englewood Cliffs.

Journal of the American Medical Association (JAMA)
1992 Instructions for authors. *Journal of the American Medical Association* 268:41-42.

Justice, Noel D.
1987 *Stone Age Spear and Arrow Points of the Midcontinental and Eastern United States.* Indiana University Press, Bloomington.

Kanefield, Adina W.
1996 *Federal Historic Preservation Case Law, 1966-1996: Thirty Years of the National Historic Preservation Act.* A Special Report Funded in Part by the United States Army Environmental Center/Advisory Council on Historic Preservation, U.S. Government Printing Office, Washington, D.C.

Kavanagh, Maureen
1982 *Archeological Resources of the Monocacy River Region.* Maryland Geological Survey Division of Archaeology File Report No. 164.

Kay, Charles E.
1994 Aboriginal overkill: The role of Native Americans in structuring western ecosystems. *Human Nature* 5:359-398.

1996 Ecosystems then and now: A historical-ecological approach to ecosystem management. Pp. 79-87 in *Proceedings of the Fourth Prairie Conservation and Endangered Species Workshop*, edited by W.D. Wilms and J.F. Dormaar. Provincial Museum of Alberta Natural Historic Occasional Papers 23.

1997 Aboriginal overkill and the biogeography of moose in western North America. *Alces* 33:141-164.

Keeley, Lawrence H.
1980 *Experimental Determination of Stone Tool Uses: A Microwear Analysis.* University of Chicago Press, Chicago.

Keirsey, David, and Marilyn Bates
1984 *Please Understand Me.* Fourth edition. Prometheus Nemesis, Del Mar.

Kelso, William M., and Rachel Most, editors
1990 *Earth Patterns: Essays in Landscape Archaeology.* University Press of Virginia, Charlottesville.

Ketchum, William C., Jr.
1991a *American Redware.* Henry Holt and Company, New York.

1991b *American Stoneware.* Henry Holt and Company, New York.

King, Thomas F.
  1998 *Cultural Resource Laws and Practice: An Introductory Guide.* AltaMira Press, Walnut Creek, CA.

  2000a *Federal Planning and Historical Places: The Section 106 Process.* AltaMira Press, Walnut Creek, CA.

  2000b What should be the "cultural resources" element of an EIA? *Environmental Impact Assessment Review* 20:5-30.

Kinsey, W. Fred
  1972 *Archeology in the Upper Delaware Valley: A Study of the Cultural Chronology of the Tocks Island Reservoir.* Anthropological Series No. 2. The Pennsylvania Historical and Museum Commission, Harrisburg, PA.

Kovel, Ralph and Terry Kovel
  1986 *Kovels' New Dictionary of Marks: Pottery and Porcelain 1850 to the Present.* Crown Publishers, New York.

Kraus, Edward H., Walter F. Hunt, and Lewis S. Ramsdell
  1936 *Mineralogy: An Introduction to the Study of Minerals and Crystals.* Third edition. McGraw-Hill, New York.

Kroeger, Otto, and Janet M. Thuesen
  1992 *Type Talk at Work.* Dell Trade, New York.

Kummerow, Jean M., Nancy J. Barger, and Linda K. Kirby
  1997 *Work Types.* Warner Books, New York.

Laabs, Jennifer J.
  1999 Corporate anthropologists. Pp. 141-147 in *Applying Anthropology*, edited by Aaron Podolefsky and Peter Brown. Fifth edition. Mayfield, Mountain View.

Lapidus, Dorothy F.
  1987 *Dictionary of Geology and Geophysics.* Facts on File, New York.

Ledbetter, R. Jerald
  1992 *Archeological Investigations of the Vulcan Tract, Bartow County, Georgia.* Southeastern Archeological Services, Inc., Athens, for Vulcan Materials Co., Inc., Georgia.

  1997 *The Bull Creek Site, 9ME1, Muscogee County, Georgia.* Occasional Papers in Cultural Resource Management #9. Georgia Department of Transportation, Office of Environment/Location, Atlanta.

Lederman, Leon M.
  1991 *Science: The End of the Frontier?* American Association for the Advancement of Science, Washington, D.C.

Lehmer, Donald J.
  1971 *Introduction to Middle Missouri Archeology.* Anthropological Papers 1. National Park Service. U.S. Department of Interior, Government Printing Office, Washington.

Lundberg, George D., and Annette Flanagin
  1989 New requirements for authors: Signed statements of authorship responsibility and financial disclosure. *Journal of the American Medical Association* 262:2003-2004.

Management Concepts Incorporated
  1991 *Department of Health and Human Services Basic Project Officer.* Prepared by Management Concepts Incorporated, Vienna VA, on behalf of the Department of Health and Human Services.

Manchester, William
  1978 *American Caesar: Douglas MacArthur 1880 - 1964.* Little, Brown, and Company, Boston.

Mason, Roger
  1978 *Petrology of the Metamorphic Rocks.* George Allen & Unwin, Ltd., London.

McLean, Ruari
  1997 *The Thames and Hudson Manual of Typography.* Thames and Hudson, London.

Miles, Raymond E., Charles C. Snow, Alan D. Meyer, and Henry J. Coleman, Jr.
  1983 Organizational strategy, structure, and process. Pp. 375-390 in *Decision Making: An Organizational Behavior Approach*, edited by Johannes M. Pennings. Marcus Wiener Publishing, New York.

Minderhout, David J.
  1986 Research and Commentary: Introductory tests and social sciences stereotypes. *Anthropology Newsletter* 27(3):20, 14-15.

Miner, John B.
1985 *Introduction to Management.* Charles E. Merrill Publishing, Columbus, OH.

Mintzberg, Henry
1971 Managerial work: analysis from observation. *Management Science* (October 1971):B97-B110.

Molloy, John T.
1988 *New Dress For Success.* Warner Books, New York.

1996 *New Women's Dress for Success.* Warner Books, New York.

Myers, Isabel Briggs
1993 *Introduction to Type.* Fifth edition. Consulting Psychologists Press, Palo Alto, CA.

Myers, Isabel Briggs, and Mary H. McCaulley
1985 *Manual: A Guide to the Development and Use of the Myers-Briggs Type Indicator.* Consulting Psychologists Press, Palo Alto, CA.

Nanda, Serena, and Richard L. Warms
1998 *Cultural Anthropology.* Sixth edition. West/Wadsworth, Belmont, CA.

Narramore, Kevin
1994 *Personality on the Job.* Servant Publications, Ann Arbor.

National Park Service
1995 *How to Apply the National Register Criteria.* National Register Bulletin 15. National Park Service, Washington, D.C. (http://www.cr.nps.gov/nr/bulletins/nr15_8.html)

Neumann, Mary Spink
1994 *Developing Effective Educational Print Materials.* Centers for Disease Control and Prevention, Division of STD/HIV Prevention, Training and Education Branch, Atlanta.

Neumann, Thomas W.
1978 A model for the vertical distribution of flotation-size particles. *Plains Anthropologist* 23:85-101.

1988 *Phase II Investigations at 36Ti31 and 36Ti47, Tioga County, Pennsylvania.* U.S. Army Corps of Engineers, Baltimore District.

1989a *Phase I Intensive Archeological Investigation of Catoctin Furnace (18 FR 29), Cunningham Falls State Park, Frederick County, Maryland.* State of Maryland/Office of Engineering and Construction/Department of General Services, Baltimore.

1989b *Phase II Intensive Survey, Historic and Prehistoric Archeological Investigations at Lock Haven, Clinton County, Pennsylvania.* Three volumes. U.S. Army Corps of Engineers, Baltimore.

1992 The physiographic variables associated with prehistoric site location in the upper Potomac River Basin, West Virginia. *Archaeology of Eastern North America* 20:81-124.

1993 Soil dynamics and the sinking of artifacts: Procedures for identifying components in non-stratified sites. *Journal of Middle Atlantic Archaeology* 9:94-108.

1995 (with the Task Force for Building Maintenance) *Setting Up a Maintenance Planning Budget for Your Parish: Scheduling and Budgeting for Maintenance, Repair, and Replacement of Archdiocesan Facilities and Equipment.* Archdiocese of Atlanta, Atlanta.

1996 *Phase III Intensive Analysis of Site 44FX1517 (Hobo Hill): An Early Archaic - Late Archaic Resource Extraction Site.* Prepared for the Fairfax County Heritage Resources Branch, Falls Church, Virginia.

1998 Early Holocene climatic warming and the energetics of culture change: The ecology of Early - Middle Archaic transitions in Georgia and South Carolina. *Journal of Middle Atlantic Archaeology* 14:65-93.

Neumann, Thomas W., Brian D. Bates, and Robert M. Sanford
1998 Chapter 15: Setting up the basic archaeology laboratory. Pp.343-358 in *Archaeological Laboratory Methods: An Introduction*, edited by Mark Q. Sutton and Brooke S. Arkush. Second edition. Kendall/Hunt Publishing, Dubuque, IA.

Neumann, Thomas W., William C. Johnson, Jennifer Cohen, and Neal H. Lopinot
  1990   *Archeological Data Recovery from Prehistoric Site 36Fa363, Grays Landing Lock and Dam.* U.S. Army Corps of Engineers, Pittsburgh District.

Neumann, Thomas W., and Christopher R. Polglase
  1992   The microlithic compound tool industry in the Middle Atlantic region. *Journal of Middle Atlantic Archaeology* 8:41-56.

Neumann, Thomas W., and Robert M. Sanford
  1985a   *A Cultural Resource Assessment of the Proposed Onondaga Senior Center.* Prepared by Neumann & Sanford Cultural Resource Assessments for the Syracuse-Onondaga County Planning Agency, Syracuse.

  1985b   *Test Excavations at the OSC Site: Phase II Cultural Resource Assessment.* Prepared by Neumann & Sanford Cultural Resource Assessments for the Syracuse-Onondaga County Planning Agency, Syracuse.

  1986   *A Cultural Resources Survey: PIN 3045.29 Route 104, Mexico, New York.* SUNYC-Potsdam Public Archaeology Report 6 (5).

  1987   The use of vegetation successional stages in cultural resource assessments. *American Archaeology* 6:119-127.

  1987   *The Weston Site: Phase III Cultural Resource Mitigation of the Southeast Area.* Prepared by Neumann & Sanford Cultural Resource Assessments, Syracuse, New York, on behalf of Goodfellow Construction, Inc., Jamesville, New York.

  1998a   Cleaning artifacts with Calgon (sodium [hexa]metaphosphate). *American Antiquity* 63:157-160.

  1998b   The role of information technology in the practice of archaeology. *Information Technology* 8 (3):4-12.

Neumann, Thomas W., Robert M. Sanford, and James F. Palmer
  1992   Managing archaeological cultural resources as environmental resources: An aid for local governments. *The Environmental Professional* 14:117-125.

Neumann, Thomas W., Robert M. Sanford, and Richard L. Warms
  1993   Using vegetation successional stages to reconstruct landscape history for cultural resource assessments in south-central Texas. On file, Wentworth Analytical Facility, Lilburn, Georgia.

Neumann, Thomas W., and Martha R. Williams
  1990   *A Phase I Archeological Investigation of the Novak Property, Anne Arundel County, Maryland.* Prepared by R. Christopher Goodwin & Associates, Inc., for Brown & Brown Builders, Ltd., Crofton.

  1991   *Phase I Archeological Survey of the 230-KV Transmission Line Corridor and Proposed Access Road Corridor, Clover Generating Plant, Halifax County, Virginia.* Prepared by R. Christopher Goodwin & Associates, Inc., for Old Dominion Electric Cooperative, Glen Allen, Virginia.

Newcomer, M.H., and L.H. Keeley
  1979   Testing a method of microwear analysis with experimental flint tools. Pp. 195-205 in *Lithic Use-Wear Analysis*, edited by Brian Hayden. Academic Press, New York.

New York Archaeological Council
  1994   *Standards for Cultural Resource Investigations and the Curation of Archaeological Collections in New York State.* Albany.

New York Times
  1991   Transco settles claims in Alabama. *New York Times* 31 May 1991:D4.

Noël Hume, Audrey
  1974   *Archaeology and the Colonial Gardener.* Colonial Williamsburg Archaeological Series No. 7. The Colonial Williamsburg Foundation, Williamsburg.

Noël Hume, Ivor
  1974   *Digging for Carter's Grove.* Colonial Williamsburg Archaeological Series No. 8. The Colonial Williamsburg Foundation, Williamsburg.

Odell, George H., and Frank Cowan
  1987   Estimating tillage effects on artifact distribution. *American Antiquity* 52:456-484.

Office of Personnel Management (OPM)
1998   *Federal Civilian Workforce Statistics. Occupations of Federal White-Collar and Blue-Collar Workers as of September 30, 1997*, U.S. Office of Personnel Management, Washington, D.C.

Olson, Gerald W.
1976   *Criteria for Making and Interpreting a Soil Profile Description: A Compilation of the Official USDA Procedure and Nomenclature for Describing Soils.* Kansas Geological Survey Bulletin 212. University of Kansas Publications, Lawrence.

Overstreet, Robert M
1996   *The Overstreet Indian Arrowheads Identification and Price Guide.* Fifth edition. Avon Books, New York.

Paludan, Ann
1998   *Chronicle of the Chinese Emperors: The Reign-by-Reign Record of the Rulers of Imperial China.* Thames and Hudson, London.

Parker, Patricia L., and Thomas F. King
1995   *Guidelines for Evaluating and Documenting Traditional Cultural Properties.* National Register Bulletin. National Park Service, Washington, D.C.

Patterson, Thomas C.
1995   *Toward a Social History of Archaeology in the United States.* Harcourt Brace College Publishers, Fort Worth.

Poirier, David
1987   *The Environmental Review Primer for Connecticut's Archaeological Resources.* Connecticut Historical Commission.

Prufer, Olaf H.
1968   *Ohio Hopewell Ceramics: An Analysis of the Extant Collections.* University of Michigan Museum of Anthropology Anthropological Papers No. 33.

Renfrew, Colin, and Paul Bahn
1991   *Archaeology: Theories, Methods, and Practice.* Thames and Hudson, London.

Rice, T.D., and L.T. Alexander
1938   The physical nature of soil. Pp. 887-896 in *Soils and Men. Yearbook of Agriculture, 1938*, edited by the Committee on Soils. USDA, Government Printing Office, Washington, D.C.

Ritchie, William A.
1971   *A Typology and Nomenclature for New York Projectile Points.* New York State Museum Bulletin Number 384.

Ritchie, William A., and Richard S. MacNeish
1949   The pre-Iroquoian pottery of New York state. *American Antiquity* 15:97-124.

Rogers, Lori M.
1991   FERC hears gas industry concerns, announces Transco settlement. *Public Utilities Fortnightly* 1 July 1991:36-37.

Rosenberg, Ronald H.
1981   Archeological resource preservation: The role of state and local government. *Utah Law Review* 4:727-802.

Rouse, Irving
1972   *Introduction to Prehistory: A Systematic Approach.* McGraw-Hill, New York. Don't look at this, even if you can find it, to learn how to dig; it is assumed that you will have taken the effort to learn this elsewhere. Rather, study this to learn how to *think* in diachronic anthropological terms.

Russell, Emily W.B.
1997   *People and the Land Through Time: Linking Ecology and History.* Yale University Press, New Haven.

Sanford, Robert M.
1984   *Archaeological Resources Preservation Reference Guide with Emphasis on New York State.* Vance Publ. Public Administration Series: Bibliography P-1370. Vance Bibliographies, Monticello, Illinois.

Sanford, Robert M., and Thomas W. Neumann
1987   The urban tree as cultural artifact. *Northeastern Environmental Science* 6:46-52.

Sanford, Robert M., Thomas W. Neumann, and James F. Palmer
1989   Developing local cultural resource policy through environmental impact assessments. Pp. 107-118 in *Policy Through Impact Assessment: Institutionalized Analysis as a Policy Strategy*, edited by Robert V. Bartlett. Contributions in Political Science, Number 235. Greenwood Press, New York

Sanford, Robert M., Thomas W. Neumann, and Gary F. Salmon
1997   Reading the landscape: Archaeological inference of historic land use in Vermont forests. *Journal of Vermont Archaeology* 23:15-23.

Sanford, Robert M., Don Huffer, Nina Huffer, Tom Neumann, Giovanna Peebles, Mary Butera, Ginger Anderson, and Dave Lacy
1994   *Stonewalls & Cellarholes: A Guide for Land-owners on Historic Features and Landscapes in Vermont's Forests.* Department of Forest, Parks, and Recreation, Waterbury.

Sassaman, Kenneth E.
2001   Archeology Division -- AD Executive Committee minutes. *Anthropology News* 42 (2):40-41.

Schuldenrein, Joseph, and Jeffrey H. Altschul
2000   Archaeological education and private sector employment. Pp. 59-64 in *Teaching Archaeology in the Twenty-First Century*, edited by Susan J. Bender, and George S. Smith. Society for American Archaeology, Washington, D.C.

Scovill, Douglas H., Garland J. Gordon, and Keith M. Anderson
1977   Guidelines for the preparation of statements of environmental impact on archaeological resources. Pp. 43-62 in *Conservation Archaeology*, edited by M.B. Shiffer and G.J. Gumerman. Academic Press, New York

Sease, Catherine
1987   *A Conservation Manual for the Field Archaeologist.* Archaeological Research Tools Volume 4, Institute of Archaeology, University of California, Los Angeles.

Shannon, Claude E.
1951   Predication and entropy of printed English. *Bell System Technical Journal* 30:50-64.

Sharer, Robert J., and Wendy Ashmore
1993   *Archaeology: Discovering Our Past.* Second edition. Mayfield, Mountain View, CA.

Shay, C. Thomas
1971   *The Itasca Bison Kill Site: An Ecological Analysis.* Minnesota Historical Society, St. Paul.

Singley, Katherine R.
1981   Caring for artifacts after excavation: Some advice for archaeologists. *Historical Archaeology* 15:35-48.

Smith, Philip M., and Barbara Boyle Torrey
1996   The future of the behavioral and social sciences. *Science* 271:611-612.

Society for American Archaeology (SAA)
1995   *1995 Membership Directory.* Society for American Archaeology, Washington, D.C.

Soil Survey Staff
1951   *Soil Survey Manual.* USDA Handbook No. 18. U.S. Government Printing Office, Washington, D.C.

1975   *Soil Taxonomy.* USDA Handbook No. 436. U.S. Government Printing Office, Washington, D.C.

1981   Chapter 4 from the unedited text of *Soil Survey Manual.* Soil Conservation Service, U.S. Government Printing Office, Washington, D.C.

South, Stanley
1977   *Methods and Theory in Historical Archeology.* Academic Press, New York.

Squier, E.G., and E.H. Davis
1848   *Ancient Monuments of the Mississippi Valley.* Smithsonian Contributions to Knowledge, Volume 1.

Steward, Julian H.
1942   The direct historical approach to archaeology. *American Antiquity* 7:337-343.

Sutton, Mark Q., and Brooke S. Arkush, editors.
1998   *Archaeological Laboratory Methods.* Second edition. Kendall/Hunt Publishing, Dubuque.

Tannenbaum, Robert, and Warren H. Schmidt
1973   How to chose a leadership pattern. *Harvard Business Review* (May-June 1973):162-180

Thomas, Cyrus
  1894   *Twelfth Annual Report of the Bureau of Ethnology 1890-'91.* Smithsonian Institution, Washington, D.C.

Thomas, David Hurst
  1976   *Figuring Anthropology: First Principles of Probability and Statistics.* Holt, Rinehart, and Winston, New York. One of the best introductory statistics books ever produced, and a dandy presentation of anthropological information as well.

Thomas, Dean S.
  1985   *Cannons: An Introduction to Civil War Artillery.* Thomas Publications, Gettysburg.

Thomas, Keith
  1983   *Man and the Natural World: Changing Attitudes in England 1500 - 1800.* Oxford University Press, Oxford.

Tieger, Paul D., and Barbara Barron-Tieger
  1992   *Do What You Are.* Little, Brown and Company, New York.

Toulouse, Julian Harrison
  1971   *Bottle Makers and Their Marks.* Thomas Nelson, Inc., New York.

Travis, John
  1994   Science's "Fourth Estate": Signing up for contract research and development. *Science* 265:1915-1916.

Tribus, Myron, and E.C. McIrvine
  1971   Energy and information. *Scientific American* 225 (2):179-188.

Trimble, Michael K., and Thomas B. Meyers
  1991   *Saving the Past from the Future: Archaeological Curation in the St. Louis District.* U.S. Army Corps of Engineers, St. Louis District.

Tschichold, Jan
  1962   *Treasury of Alphabets & Lettering* [Translation by Wolf von Eckardt of *Meisterbuch der Schrift*]. Norton, New York.

Tuchman, Barbara W.
  1978   *A Distant Mirror: The Calamitous 14th Century.* Knopf, New York.

Tuck, James A.
  1969   *Iroquois Cultural Development in Central New York.* Ph.D. dissertation, Syracuse University. University Microfilms International, Ann Arbor.

  1971   *Onondaga Iroquois Prehistory: A Study in Settlement Archaeology.* Syracuse University Press, Syracuse.

U.S. Army Corps of Engineers
  1996   *Safety and Health Requirements Manual.* EM-385-1-1. U.S. Government Printing Office, Washington, D.C.

U.S. Council on Environmental Quality
  1978   Regulations for implementing procedural provisions of NEPA. *Federal Register* 43: 55978-56007.

United States Government
  1992   *Policy and Supporting Positions.* Committee on Governmental Affairs, United States Senate, 102d Congress, 2d Session. Government Printing Office, Washington, D.C.

Ury, William
  1993   *Getting Past No: Negotiating Your Way from Confrontation to Cooperation.* Penguin Books, New York.

Ward, Geoffrey C., and Ken Burns
  1994   *Baseball: An Illustrated History.* Knopf, New York.

Watts, May Theilgaard
  1975   *Reading the Landscape of America.* Revised and expanded edition. Collier, New York.

Wauchope, Robert
  1966   *Archaeological Survey of Northern Georgia, with a Test of Some Cultural Hypotheses.* Society for American Archaeology Memoir 21.

Weichman, Michael S.
  1986   *Guidelines for Contract Cultural Resource Survey Reports and Professional Qualifications.* Missouri Department of Natural Resources.

Weiss, Gerald.
  1977   Rhetoric in Campa narrative. *Journal of Latin American Lore* 3:169-182.

Wessels, Tom
1997   *Reading the Forested Landscape: A Natural History of New England.* Countryman Press, Woodstock, VT.

Westmeyer, Paul
1985   *A History of American Higher Education.* Charles C. Thomas, Publisher, Springfield, IL.

Wheat, Joe Ben
1972   *The Olsen-Chubbuck Site: A Paleo-Indian Bison Kill.* Memoirs of the Society for American Archaeology Number 26.

Wheeler, Mortimer
1954   *Archaeology from the Earth.* Penguin, Baltimore.

Willey, Gordon R., and Philip Phillips
1958   *Method and Theory in American Archaeology.* University of Chicago Press, Chicago.

Willey, Gordon R., and Jeremy A. Sabloff
1993   *A History of American Archaeology.* Third edition. Freeman, New York.

Williams, Mark, and Victor Thompson
1999   A guide to Georgia Indian pottery types. *Early Georgia* 27 (1):1-167.

Yamin, Rebecca, and Karen Bescherer Metheny, editors
1996   *Landscape Archaeology: Reading and Interpreting the American Historical Landscape.* University of Tennessee Press, Knoxville.

Yerkes, Richard W., and P. Nick Kardulias
1993   Recent developments in the analysis of lithic artifacts. *Journal of Archaeological Research* 1:89-119.

Zaleznik, Abraham
1983   Managers and leaders: Are they different? Pp. 162-179 in *Harvard Business Review -- On Human Relations,* edited by the Harvard Business Review. Harper and Row, New York.

Zeder, Melinda A.
1997   *The American Archaeologist: A Profile.* AltaMira Press, Walnut Creek, CA.

Index

H

HABS/HAER (Historic American Buildings Survey/Historic Architecture and Engineering Recordation), 41, 46, 202
Hamburg, Morris, 166
Hamermesh, Daniel S., 4
hard hats (indicators of social status), 213
hard hats (safety equipment), 123, 189
Hatch, James W., 107
Haury, Emil W., 9, 14
Hay, Conran, 107
Hawai'i, 53, 125, 126
    basic Phase I requirements, 126
    native organizations, 29, 37, 38, 40
hearings, 45, 115, 209, 294
Heighton, Robert F., 265
Heizer, Robert F., 20
Hester, Thomas R., 139, 143, 258, B-7
high-magnification use-wear analyses, 171, 197, 229, 251, 269, 270
hiring (see also "staffing"), 25, 26, 77, 111, 118, 120, 159, 172, 201, 215, 217, 223
    differences between academic-sector and private-sector, 77
    job announcements, 25, 26
    Phase I staffing, 111, 118, 120
    Phase II staffing, 159, 172
    Phase III staffing, 201, 215, 217, 223
Hirsh, Sandra Krebs, 80
historian, 1, 22, 23, 67, 73, 80, 82, 91, 92-97, 106-109, 117, 243, 285, B-2
    community, as information sources, 91, 92
    Myers-Briggs Type, 80
    project role, 92-97, 106-109, 117, 243, 285
    staff, 67, 73, 82
    where employed, 1, 22, 23, B-2
historic artifacts, 98, 130, 154-156, 265, 266
historic background narrative, 87, 106, 108, 109
historic maps, 95, 101, 103, 280
historic photographs, 280, 281
Historic Property (as technical term; see also "Property, historic"), 7, 29, 30, 33, 34, 40, 45, 291
Historic Sites Act of 1935, 8, 9, 15-17
history, 5-21, 87-93, 96-100, 102-107, 111, 117, 118, 120, 130, 131-139, 153, 156, 157, 159, 161, 177-179, 187, 196, 197, 201, 204-211, 221, 224-227, 229, 274, 277, 278, 284, 285
    land-use, 131-139, 161, 177-179, 197
    part of Phase I research, 111, 117, 118, 120, 130, 131-139, 153, 156, 157
    part of Phase II research, 159, 161, 162, 177, 178, 187, 196, 197
    part of Phase III research, 201, 204-211, 221, 224-227, 229
    part of report, 274, 277, 278, 284, 285
    preparing for project background, 87-93, 96-100, 102-107
    professional archaeology in United States, 5-21
history of the project area, 87, 88, 91, 93, 97, 137, 146, 153, 161
history of the undertaking, 87-91, 277, 278, 284
history of site investigations, 201, 206
Hobbs, Walter C., 230
Hobo Hill Site (44FX1517), 97, 229, 260
Holder Jack J., Jr., 80

Hole, Frank, 19, 20
Hollinger boxes (trademarked name for acid-free curation storage box), 256, 262, 271
Hopke, William E., 1, 23
Hosmer Charles B., Jr., 7, 14, 22, 46
Hothem, Lar, 98, 99
Housing and Community Development Act, 17, 50
housing (billeting for crew), 111, 121, 122, 159, 173, 201, 223
Howie, R.A., 266
Hranicky, Wm Jack, 266
Hunt, Walter F., 266
Huron (Indian tribe), 210
Hustead, Wilfred, 63

I

Idaho, 125, 126, 141, 266
    basic Phase I requirements, 126
IFB (Invitation for Bid), 59, 61
Illinois, 24, 126, 140
    basic Phase I requirements, 126
Illustrator, 73
inclement weather, dealing with in field, 182, 186
income taxes and per diem, 121-122
Independence Hall, 7
Indiana, 24, 53, 126, 208, 266
    basic Phase I requirements, 126
informants (see also "interviews"), 135, 157, 165, B-4
Information Theory, 163, 170
integrity, 33-36, 41, 44-46, 87, 97, 98, 102, 111-113, 124, 125, 131-138, 153-156, 159-163, 177-179, 196-199, 206, 207, 225, 228, 250, 270, 278, 285
    assessing for archaeological sites, 41, 87, 97, 98, 102, 112, 124, 125, 131-138, 153-156, 160-163, 177-179, 196-199, 206, 207, 225, 228, 250, 270
    criteria for cultural resources, 33-36
    features and, 15
    Register-eligibility and, 33-36, 44-46, 112, 125, 159-161, 278, 285
intensive survey (see instead "Phase I")
Internal Revenue Service (IRS), 32, 93, 121, 122, 173
International Committee of Medical Journal Editors, 172
interviews (see also "informants"), 76, 87, 91-93, 96, 97, 114, 150, 157, 191, 278, 289, B-5
invitation for bid (IFB), 59, 61
Iowa, 97, 127, 140, 141
    basic Phase I requirements, 127
Ireland, 6, 108
Iroquois kinship system, NAGPRA and, 52
iso-frequency artifact contour map, 161
Israel, 6

J

Jameson, John H., Jr. 63
Japan, 6, 36
Jefferson, Thomas, 6
jobs, locating archaeology (See also "Positions"), 23, 25, 174

N

S

T

About the Authors

THOMAS W. NEUMANN has been directing Section 106 projects since 1975. Neumann grew up in Ft. Thomas, Kentucky. He graduated from the University of Kentucky, with a major in Anthropology and with minors in Physics, Forestry, and English Literature. He received his M.A. and Ph.D. in Anthropology from the University of Minnesota.

Neumann established, then directed for many years, the doctoral program in archaeology at Syracuse University, served as a research associate for the State University of New York Research Foundation, and since 1985 has worked as a corporate archaeologist and research administrator, serving variously as senior partner or senior scientist for national cultural resources firms. Between 1982 and 1984, he was Director of the Center for Archaeological Research and Education, Inc., a non-profit community-education and historic-preservation organization in Minnesota. He has taught at the University of Minnesota, Syracuse University, the University of Georgia Honors Program, and Emory University. He currently manages the Diachronics Division at the Pocket Park - Wentworth Analytical Facility in Georgia.

Although Neumann's personal research centers on human-wildlife interactions and human ecology, cultural landscapes, lithic assemblage analysis, and professional archaeology, he particularly enjoys the variety and challenges that attend private-sector research. He has directed over 70 field/laboratory projects on prehistoric and historic archaeological sites in the eastern and midwestern United States. He is the author or co-author of around 80 books and cultural-resource monographs, 40 chapters and research articles, and 30 major conference papers.

Neumann has served as an external grants reviewer for the National Endowment for the Humanities and for the National Science Foundation, and as a member of the Board of Directors of the Georgia Council of Professional Archaeologists. Among various historic preservation awards, he was co-recipient of the Honor Award from the National Trust for Historic Preservation (1992) for his work on the Third Haven Meeting House in Easton, Maryland. He is listed in *Who's Who in America* as well as in *Who's Who in Science and Engineering*. He has received a number of awards for outstanding teaching from student organizations, most recently as visiting faculty at Emory University.

Right: Neumann and Sanford on the Glenfield - Lowville NYS-DOT Project. Timber-framed structure in background was still owned and occupied by descendants of the same family that had come out from Connecticut and built it in the 1780s.

ROBERT M. SANFORD began directing Section 106 projects in 1984. Sanford is a native of Potsdam, New York. After service in the Navy, he received his B.A. from State University of New York College at Potsdam, majoring in Anthropology after completing two years of study in civil and environmental engineering . He earned his M.S. and Ph.D. in Environmental Science from the SUNY College of Environmental Science and Forestry.

Sanford served for several years as a research associate for the State University of New York Research Foundation and later as a partner and corporate archaeologist in New York cultural resources firms. Between 1988 and 1996, he served as one of Vermont's nine District Environmental Board Coordinators, administering Vermont's Act 250 land-development regulations. During that same period, Sanford taught Anthropology, environmental science, and environmental policy as adjunct faculty at the Community College of Vermont, Johnson State College, and Antioch New England Graduate School. He currently is a faculty member in the University of Southern Maine's Environmental Science and Policy Program, a position he has held since 1996.

Sanford's research interests focus on cultural resources policy, particularly in the area of treating archaeological resources as non-renewable environmental resources. He has been instrumental in formulating cultural resources policy in New England, as well as in devising practical ways to operationalize that policy. His articles treating archaeology, environmental policy, and landscape analysis have appeared in *The Environmental Professional, Land Use Policy, Journal of Vermont Archaeology, American Archaeology,* and *American Antiquity.*